CIVILIZATION
IN THE WEST

Volume 1

PENGUIN ACADEMICS

CIVILIZATION IN THE WEST

Volume 1

MARK KISHLANSKY
Harvard University

PATRICK GEARY
University of California, Los Angeles

PATRICIA O'BRIEN
University of California, Los Angeles

Longman

Boston Columbus Indianapolis New York San Francisco Upper Saddle River
Amsterdam Cape Town Dubai London Madrid Milan Munich Paris Montreal Toronto
Delhi Mexico City Sao Paulo Sydney Hong Kong Seoul Singapore Taipei Tokyo

Editorial Director: Leah Jewell
Acquisitions Editor: Charles Cavaliere
Editorial Assistant: Lauren Aylward
Director of Marketing: Brandy Dawson
Senior Marketing Manager: Maureen Prado Roberts
Marketing Assistant: Marissa O'Brien
Senior Managing Editor: Ann Marie McCarthy
Project Manager: Debra Wechsler
Senior Operations Supervisor: Nick Sklitsis
Operations Specialist: Christina Amato
Senior Art Director: Jayne Conte
Art Director: Mirella Signoretto
Text and Cover Designer: Karen Salzbach
Manager, Rights and Permissions: Zina Arabia
Manager, Visual Research: Beth Brenzel

Manager, Cover Visual Research & Permissions: Karen Sanatar
Image Permission Coordinator: Nancy Seise
Cover Art: "Musicians and Dancers". Fragment of a wall painting from the Tomb of Nebamun, Thebes. 1350 B.C. H: 24" (61 cm). Art Resource/The British Museum Great Court Ltd.
Media Director: Brian Hyland
Lead Media Project Manager: Sarah Kinney
Supplements Editor: Emsal Hasan
Full-Service Project Management: Elm Street Publishing Services
Printer/Binder: R. R. Donnelley/Harrisonburg
Cover Printer: R. R. Donnelley/Harrisonburg
Text Font: 9.75/13 NexusMix-Regular

Credits and acknowledgments borrowed from other sources and reproduced, with permission, in this textbook appear on page C-1.

Library of Congress Cataloging-in-Publication Data

Kishlansky, Mark A.
    Civilization in the West: Volume 1 / Mark Kishlansky, Patrick Geary, Patricia O'Brien.
        p. cm.—(Penguin academics)
    Includes bibliographical references and index.
    ISBN 978-0-205-66473-3 (single volume edition)
    1. Civilization, Western—Textbooks.   2. Europe—Civilization—Textbooks.   I. Geary, Patrick J.
II. O'Brien, Patricia.   III. Title.
    CB245.K546 2010
    909'.09821—dc22

                                                        2009034110

10 9 8 7 6 5 4 3 2 1

Longman
is an imprint of

PEARSON

www.pearsonhighered.com

ISBN 13: 978-0-205-66472-6
ISBN 10:   0-205-66472-5

brief contents

contents

INTRODUCTION The Idea of Western Civilization 1

CHAPTER 1 The First Civilizations 4

Before Civilization 4

The Dominance of Culture 5 ▪ Social Organization, Agriculture, and Religion 6

Mesopotamia: Between the Two Rivers 8

The Ramparts of Uruk 8 ▪ Tools: Technology and Writing 10 ▪ Gods and Mortals in Mesopotamia 11 ▪ Sargon and Mesopotamian Expansion 13 ▪ Hammurabi and the Old Babylonian Empire 14

The Gift of the Nile 16

Tending the Cattle of God 16 ▪ Democratization of the Afterlife 19 ▪ The Egyptian Empire 20 ▪ Religious and Royal Consolidation Under Akhenaten 21

Between Two Worlds 22

The Hebrew Alternative 23 ▪ A King Like All the Nations 24 ▪ Exile 26

Nineveh and Babylon 26

The Assyrian Empire 27 ▪ The New Babylonian Empire 28

CHAPTER 2 Early Greece, 2500–500 B.C.E. 31

Greece in the Bronze Age to 700 B.C.E. 31

Islands of Peace 32 ▪ Mainland of War 34 ▪ The Dark Age 34

maps

chronologies, genealogies, and figures

When we set out to write *Civilization in the West*, we tried to write, first of all, a book that students would *want* to read. Throughout many years of planning, writing, revising, rewriting, and numerous meetings together, this was our constant overriding concern. Would the text work across the variety of Western civilization courses, with the different levels and formats that make up this fundamental course? We also solicited the reactions of scores of reviewers to this single question: "Would students *want* to read these chapters?" Whenever we received a resounding "No!" we began again—not just rewriting, but rethinking how to present material that might be complex in argument or detail or that might simply seem too remote to engage the contemporary student. Though all three of us were putting in long hours in front of computers, we quickly learned that we were engaged in a teaching rather than a writing exercise. And though the work was demanding, it was not unrewarding. We enjoyed writing this book, and we wanted students to enjoy reading it. We have been gratified to learn that our book successfully accomplished our objectives. It stimulated student interest and motivated students to want to learn about European history. *Civilization in the West* was successful beyond our expectations.

The text was so well received, in fact, that we decided to publish this alternative, brief version: *Civilization in the West, Penguin Academics*. In an era of rapidly changing educational materials, alternative formats and models should be available. We believe that students and general readers alike will enjoy a conveniently sized book that offers them a coherent, well-told story. In this edition of the brief text, we have enlarged and added detail to many of the maps so that they are easier to see and use. We have also added a new feature, "Map Discovery," that teaches students how to think critically about maps.

Approach

The approach used in *Civilization in the West, Penguin Academics*, upholds and confirms a number of decisions made early in the writing of *Civilization in the West*. First, this brief, alternative version is, like the full-length text, a mainstream text in which most of our energies have been focused on developing a solid, readable narrative of Western civilization that integrates coverage of women and minorities into the discussion. We highlight personalities while identifying trends. We spotlight social history, both in sections of chapters and in separate chapters, while maintaining a firm grip on political developments.

Neither *Civilization in the West, Penguin Academics* nor *Civilization in the West* is meant to be an encyclopedia of Western civilization. Information is not included in a chapter unless it fits within the themes of that chapter. In both the full-length and brief versions of this text, we are committed to integrating the history of ordinary men and women into our narrative. We believe that isolated sections placed at the end of chapters that deal with the experiences of women or minority groups in a particular era profoundly distort historical experience. We call this technique "caboosing," and whenever we found ourselves segregating women or families or the masses, we stepped back and asked how we might recast our treatment of historical events to account for a diversity of actors. How did ordinary men, women, and children affect the course of world historical events? How did world historical events affect the fabric of daily life for men, women, and children from all walks of life? We also tried to rethink critical historical problems of civilization as gendered phenomena.

We take the same approach to the coverage of central and eastern Europe that we did to women and minorities. Even before the epochal events of the late 1980s and early 1990s that returned this region to the forefront of international attention, we realized that many textbooks treated the Slavic world as marginal to the history of Western civilization. Therefore, we worked to integrate more of the history of eastern Europe into our text than is found in most others and to do so in a way that presented these regions, their cultures, and their institutions as integral rather than peripheral to Western civilization.

Features

In *Civilization in the West, Penguin Academics*, we wanted to present features that would have the most immediate and positive impact on our readers and fulfill our goal of involving students in learning.

"Discovering Western Civilization Online" encourages students to explore the study of Western civilization beyond the confines of a textbook. These end-of-chapter Website resources link students to enriching documents, images, and cultural sites. They have been updated for this edition.

Changes in the New Edition

In *Civilization in the West, Penguin Academics*, we have made several changes to the book's content and coverage:

Revised and Improved Map Program

When teachers of Western civilization courses are surveyed, no single area of need is cited more often than that of geographical knowledge. Most students simply have no mental image of Europe, no familiarity with those geophysical features that are a fundamental part of the geopolitical realities of Western history. We realized that maps, carefully planned and skillfully executed, would be an important component of our text. In this edition, we have revised the entire map program, improving the look of the maps and increasing the sizes of many of them for easier readability. The great number of maps throughout the text, the specially designed "Map Discovery" feature, and the ancillary programs of map transparencies and workbook exercises combine to provide the strongest possible program for teaching historical geography.

Map Discovery

"Map Discovery," which appears two to three times per chapter, offers specially designed maps with supporting caption information and questions designed to engage students in analyzing the map data and making larger connections to chapter discussions. We have found that focusing students' attention on the details of a map and asking them to consider why that information is important is an effective way to strengthen critical thinking skills, as well as to expand geographical knowledge.

acknowledgments

We want to thank the many conscientious historians who gave generously of their time and knowledge to review our manuscript. We would like to thank the reviewers of the previous editions of *Civilization in the West*, as well as those of the current edition. Their valuable critiques and suggestions have contributed greatly to the final product. We are grateful to the following:

Daniel F. Callahan, *University of Delaware*; Michael Clinton, *Gwynedd-Mercy College*; Bob Cole, *Utah State University*; Gary P. Cox, *Gordon College*; Peter L. de Rosa, *Bridgewater State College*; Frank Lee Earley, *Arapahoe Community College*; Steven Fanning, *University of Illinois at Chicago*; Patrick Foley, *Tarrant County College*; Charlotte M. Gradie, *Sacred Heart University*; Richard Grossman, *Northeastern Illinois University*; David Halamy, *Cypress College*; Gary J. Johnson, *University of Southern Maine*; Cynthia Jones, *University of Missouri at Kansas City*; John Kemp, *Truckee Meadows Community College*; Janilyn Kocher, *Richland Community College*; Lisa M. Lane, *MiraCosta College*; Oscar Lansen, *University of North Carolina at Charlotte*; Michael R. Lynn, *Agnes Scott College*; Mark S. Malaszczyk, *St. John's University*; John M. McCulloh, *Kansas State University*; David B. Mock, *Tallahassee Community College*; Don Mohr, Emeritus, *University of Alaska, Anchorage*; Martha G. Newman, *University of Texas at Austin*; Lisa Pace-Hardy, *Jefferson Davis Community College*; Marlette Rebhorn, *Austin Community College*; Steven G. Reinhardt, *University of Texas at Arlington*; Kimberly Reiter, *Stetson University*; Robert Rockwell, *Mt. San Jacinto College*; Maryloy Ruud, *University of West Florida*; Jose M. Sanchez, *St. Louis University*; Erwin Sicher, *Southwestern Adventist College*; Ruth Suyama, *Los Angeles Mission College*; David Tengwall, *Anne Arundel Community College*; Janet M. C. Walmsley, *George Mason University*; John E. Weakland, *Ball State University*, and Rick Whisonant, *York Technical College*.

Our special thanks go to our colleagues at Marquette University for their long-standing support, valuable comments, and assistance on this edition's design: Lance Grahn, Lezlie Knox, Timothy G. McMahon, and Alan P. Singer.

We also acknowledge the assistance of the many reviewers of *Civilization in the West* whose comments have been invaluable in the development of *Civilization in the West, Penguin Academics*:

Joseph Aieta, III, *Lasell College*; Ken Albala, *University of the Pacific*; Patricia Ali, *Morris College*; Gerald D. Anderson, *North Dakota State University*; Jean K. Berger, *University of Wisconsin, Fox Valley*; Susan Carrafiello, *Wright State University*; Andrew Donson, *University of Massachusetts, Amherst*; Frederick Dotolo, *St. John Fisher College*; Janusz Duzinkiewicz, *Purdue University*; Brian Elsesser, *St. Louis University*;

Bryan Ganaway, *University of Illinois*; David Graf, *University of Miami*; Benjamin Hett, *Hunter College*; Mark M. Hull, *St. Louis University*; Barbara Klemm, *Broward Community College*; Lawrence Langer, *University of Connecticut*; Elise Moentmann, *University of Portland*; Alisa Plant, *Tulane University*; Salvador Rivera, *State University of New York*; Thomas Robisheaux, *Duke University*; Ilicia Sprey, *Saint Joseph's College*; George S. Vascik, *Miami University, Hamilton*; Vance Youmans, *Spokane Falls Community College*; Achilles Aavraamides, *Iowa State University*; Meredith L. Adams, *Southwest Missouri State University*; Arthur H. Auten, *University of Hartford*; Suzanne Balch-Lindsay, *Eastern New Mexico University*; Sharon Bannister, *University of Findlay*; John W. Barker, *University of Wisconsin*; Patrick Bass, *Mount Union College*; William H. Beik, *Northern Illinois University*; Patrice Berger, *University of Nebraska*; Lenard R. Berlanstein, *University of Virginia*; Raymond Birn, *University of Oregon*; Donna Bohanan, *Auburn University*; Werner Braatz, *University of Wisconsin, Oshkosh*; Thomas A. Brady, Jr., *University of Oregon*; Anthony M. Brescia, *Nassau Community College*; Elaine G. Breslaw, *Morgan State University*; Ronald S. Brockway, *Regis University*; April Brooks, *South Dakota State University*; Daniel Patrick Brown, *Moorpark College*; Ronald A. Brown, *Charles County Community College*; Blaine T. Browne, *Broward Community College*; Kathleen S. Carter, *High Point University*; Robert Carver, *University of Missouri, Rolla*; Edward J. Champlin, *Princeton University*; Stephanie Evans Christelow, *Western Washington University*; Sister Dorita Clifford, BVM, *University of San Francisco*; Gary B. Cohen, *University of Oklahoma*; Jan M. Copes, *Cleveland State University*; John J. Contreni, *Purdue University*; Tim Crain, *University of Wisconsin, Stout*; Norman Delaney, *Del Mar College*; Samuel E. Dicks, *Emporia State University*; Frederick Dumin, *Washington State University*; Laird Easton, *California State University, Chico*; Dianne E. Farrell, *Moorhead State University*; Margot C. Finn, *Emory University*; Allan W. Fletcher, *Boise State University*; Luci Fortunato De Lisle, *Bridgewater State College*; Elizabeth L. Furdell, *University of North Florida*; Thomas W. Gallant, *University of Florida*; Frank Garosi, *California State University, Sacramento*; Lorne E. Glaim, *Pacific Union College*; Joseph J. Godson, *Hudson Valley Community College*; Sue Helder Goliber, *Mount St. Mary's College*; Manuel G. Gonzales, *Diablo Valley College*; Louis Haas, *Duquesne University*; Eric Haines, *Bellevue Community College*; Paul Halliday, *University of Virginia*; Margaretta S. Handke, *Mankato State University*; David A. Harnett, *University of San Francisco*; Paul B. Harvey, Jr., *Pennsylvania State University*; Neil Heyman, *San Diego State University*; Daniel W. Hollis, *Jacksonville State University*; Kenneth G. Holum, *University of Maryland*; Patricia Howe, *University of St. Thomas*; David Hudson, *California State University, Fresno*; Charles Ingrao, *Purdue University*; George F. Jewsbury, *Oklahoma State University*; Donald G. Jones, *University of Central Arkansas*; William R. Jones, *University of New Hampshire*; Richard W. Kaeuper, *University of Rochester*; David Kaiser, *Carnegie-Mellon University*; Jeff Kaufmann, *Muscatine Community College*; Carolyn Kay, *Trent University*; William R. Keylor, *Boston University*; Joseph Kicklighter, *Auburn University*; Charles L. Killinger, III, *Valencia*

Community College; Alan M. Kirshner, *Ohlone College*; Charlene Kiser, *Milligan College*; Alexandra Korros, *Xavier University*; Cynthia Kosso, *Northern Arizona University*; Lara Kriegel, *Florida International University*; Lisa M. Lane, *MiraCosta College*; David C. Large, *Montana State University*; Catherine Lawrence, *Messiah College*; Bryan LeBeau, *Creighton University*; Robert B. Luehrs, *Fort Hays State University*; Donna J. Maier, *University of Northern Iowa*; Margaret Malamud, *New Mexico State University*; Roberta T. Manning, *Boston College*; Lyle McAlister, *University of Florida*; Therese M. McBride, *College of the Holy Cross*; David K. McQuilkin, *Bridgewater College*; Victor V. Minasian, *College of Marin*; David B. Mock, *Tallahassee Community College*; Robert Moeller, *University of California, Irvine*; R. Scott Moore, *University of Dayton*; Ann E. Moyer, *University of Pennsylvania*; Pierce C. Mullen, *Montana State University*; John A. Nichols, *Slippery Rock University*; Thomas F. X. Noble, *University of Virginia*; J. Ronald Oakley, *Davidson County Community College*; Bruce K. O'Brien, *Mary Washington College*; Dennis H. O'Brien, *West Virginia University*; Maura O'Connor, *University of Cincinnati*; Richard A. Oehling, *Assumption College*; James H. Overfield, *University of Vermont*; Catherine Patterson, *University of Houston*; Sue Patrick, *University of Wisconsin, Barron County*; Peter C. Piccillo, *Rhode Island College*; Peter O'M. Pierson, *Santa Clara University*; Theophilus Prousis, *University of North Florida*; Marlette Rebhorn, *Austin Community College*; Jack B. Ridley, *University of Missouri, Rolla*; Constance M. Rousseau, *Providence College*; Thomas J. Runyan, *Cleveland State University*; John P. Ryan, *Kansas City Community College*; Geraldine Ryder, *Ocean County College*; Joanne Schneider, *Rhode Island College*; Steven Schroeder, *Indiana University of Pennsylvania*; Steven C. Seyer, *Lehigh County Community College*; Lixin Shao, *University of Minnesota, Duluth*; George H. Shriver, *Georgia Southern University*; Ellen J. Skinner, *Pace University*; Bonnie Smith, *University of Rochester*; Patrick Smith, *Broward Community College*; James Smither, *Grand Valley State University*; Sherill Spaar, *East Central University*; Charles R. Sullivan, *University of Dallas*; Peter N. Stearns, *Carnegie-Mellon University*; Saulius Suziedelis, *Millersville University*; Darryl B. Sycher, *Columbus State Community College*; Roger Tate, *Somerset Community College*; Janet A. Thompson, *Tallahassee Community College*; Anne-Marie Thornton, *Bilkent University*; Donna L. Van Raaphorst, *Cuyahoga Community College*; James Vanstone, *John Abbot College*; Steven Vincent, *North Carolina State University*; Richard A. Voeltz, *Cameron University*; Faith Wallis, *McGill University*; Sydney Watts, *University of Richmond*; Eric Weissman, *Golden West College*; Christine White, *Pennsylvania State University*; William Harry Zee, *Gloucester County College*.

Each author also received invaluable assistance and encouragement from many colleagues, friends, and family members over the years of research, reflection, writing, and revising that went into the making of this text:

Mark Kishlansky thanks Ann Adams, Robert Bartlett, Ray Birn, David Buisseret, Ted Cook, Frank Conaway, Constantine Fasolt, James Hankins, Katherine Haskins, Richard Hellie, Matthew Kishlansky, Donna Marder, Mary Beth Rose, Victor Stater,

Jeanne Thiel, and the staffs of the Joseph Regenstein Library, the Newberry Library, and the Widener and Lamont Libraries at Harvard.

Patrick Geary thanks Mary, Catherine, and Anne Geary for their patience, support, and encouragement. He also thanks Anne Picard, Dale Schofield, Hans Hummer, and Richard Mowrer for their able assistance throughout the project.

Patricia O'Brien thanks Christopher Reed for his loving support; Tristan Reed for his intellectual engagement; and Erin and Devin Reed for "keeping me in touch with the contemporary world."

MARK KISHLANSKY
PATRICK GEARY
PATRICIA O'BRIEN

ancillary instructional materials

The ancillary instructional materials that accompany *Civilization in the West, Penguin Academics* are designed to reinforce and enliven the richness of the past and inspire students with the excitement of studying the history of Western civilization.

Primary Source: Documents in Western Civilization DVD.   This DVD-ROM offers a rich collection of textual and visual—many never before available to a wide audience—and serves as an indispensable tool for working with sources. Extensively developed with the guidance of historians and teachers, Primary Source: Documents in Western Civilization includes over 800 sources in Western civilization history—from cave art, to text documents, to satellite images of Earth from space. All sources are accompanied by headnotes and focus questions and are searchable by topic, region, or theme. In addition, a built-in tutorial guides students through the process of working with documents. The DVD can be bundled with *Civilization in the West, Penguin Academics*, at no charge. Please contact your Pearson Arts and Sciences representative for ordering information. (ISBN 0-13-134407-2)

An abridged two-volume print version of Primary Source: Documents in Western Civilization is also available:

> *Primary Sources in Western Civilization, Volume 1: To 1700, 2/e (ISBN 0-13-175583-8)*
> *Primary Sources in Western Civilization, Volume 2: Since 1400, 2/e (ISBN 0-13-175584-6)*

Please contact your Pearson Arts and Sciences representative for ordering information.

Lives and Legacies: Biographies in Western Civilization, Second Edition.   Extensively revised, *Lives and Legacies* includes brief, focused biographies of 60 individuals whose lives provide insight into the key developments of Western civilization. Each biography includes an introduction, prereading questions, and suggestions for additional reading. (Volume 1: ISBN 0-205-64915-7); (Volume 2: ISBN 0-205-64914-9)

 Titles from the renowned **Penguin Classics** series can be bundled with *Civilization in the West, Penguin Academics*, for a nominal charge. Please contact your Pearson Arts and Sciences sales representative for details.

 The Prentice Hall Atlas of Western Civilization, Second Edition. (ISBN 0-13-604246-5) Produced in collaboration with Dorling Kindersley, the leader in cartographic publishing, the updated second edition of *The*

Prentice Hall Atlas of Western Civilization applies the most innovative cartographic techniques to present Western civilization in all of its complexity and diversity. Copies of the atlas can be bundled with *Civilization in the West, Penguin Academics*, for a nominal charge. Contact your Pearson Arts and Sciences sales representative for details.

A Guide to Your History Course: What Every Student Needs to Know. (ISBN 0-13-185087-3) Written by Vincent A. Clark, this concise, spiral-bound guidebook orients students to the issues and problems they will face in the history classroom. Available at a discount when bundled with *Civilization in the West, Penguin Academics*.

A Short Guide to Writing about History, Seventh Edition. (ISBN 0-205-67370-8) Written by Richard Marius, late of Harvard University, and Melvin E. Page, Eastern Tennessee State University, this engaging and practical text helps students get beyond merely compiling dates and facts. Covering both brief essays and the documented resource paper, the text explores the writing and researching processes, identifies different modes of historical writing, including argument, and concludes with guidelines for improving style.

Library of World Biography Series   Series Editor Peter N. Stearns. Concise and incisive, each interpretive biography in the Library of World Biography Series focuses on a person whose actions and ideas either significantly influenced world events or whose life reflects important themes and developments in world history. Contract your local Pearson representative for details.

mysearchlab Pearson's MySearchLab™ is the easiest way for students to start a research assignment or paper. Complete with extensive help on the research process and four databases of credible and reliable source material, MySearchLab™ helps students quickly and efficiently make the most of their research time. (www.mysearchlab.com)

about the authors

MARK KISHLANSKY is Frank B. Baird, Jr., Professor of English and European History and has served as the Associate Dean of the Faculty at Harvard University. He was educated at the State University of New York at Stony Brook, where he first studied history, and at Brown University, where he received his Ph.D. in 1977. For 16 years, he taught at the University of Chicago and was a member of the staff that taught Western Civilization. Currently, he lectures on the History of Western Civilization at Harvard. Professor Kishlansky is a specialist on seventeenth-century English political history and has written, among other works, *A Monarchy Transformed*; *The Rise of the New Model Army*; and *Parliamentary Selection: Social and Political Choice in Early Modern England*. From 1984 to 1991, he was editor of the *Journal of British Studies* and is presently the general editor of *History Compass*, the first online history journal. He is also the general editor for Pearson Custom Publishing's source and interpretations databases, which provide custom book supplements for Western Civilization courses.

PATRICK GEARY holds a Ph.D. in Medieval Studies from Yale University and has broad experience in interdisciplinary approaches to European history and civilization. He has served as President of the Medieval Academy of America, as the director of the Medieval Institute at the University of Notre Dame, as well as director for the Center for Medieval and Renaissance Studies at the University of California, Los Angeles, where he is currently Distinguished Professor of History. He has also held positions at the University of Florida and Princeton University and has taught at the École des Hautes Études en Sciences Sociales in Paris, the Central European University in Budapest, and the University of Vienna. His many publications include *Readings in Medieval History*; *Before France and Germany: The Creation and Transformation of the Merovingian World*; *Phantoms of Remembrance: Memory and Oblivion at the End of the First Millennium*; *The Myth of Nations: The Medieval Origins of Europe*; and *Women at the Beginning: Origin Myths from the Amazons to the Virgin Mary*.

PATRICIA O'BRIEN is a specialist in modern French cultural and social history and received her Ph.D. from Columbia University. She has held appointments at Yale University, the University of California–Irvine, the University of California–Riverside, the École des Hautes Études en Sciences Sociales in Paris, and the University of California–Los Angeles. Between 1995 and 1999, Professor O'Brien worked to foster collaborative interdisciplinary research in the humanities as director of the University of California Humanities Research Institute. Since 2004, she has served as Executive Dean of the College of Letters and Science at UCLA. Professor O'Brien has published widely on the history of French crime and punishment, cultural theory, urban history, and gender issues. Representative publications include *The Promise of Punishment: Prisons in Nineteenth-Century France*; "The Kleptomania Diagnosis: Bourgeois Women and Theft in Late Nineteenth-Century France" in *Expanding the Past: A Reader in Social History*; and "Michel Foucault's History of Culture" in *The New Cultural History*, edited by Lynn Hunt. Professor O'Brien's commitment to this textbook grew out of her own teaching experiences in large, introductory Western civilization courses. She has benefited from the contributions of her students and fellow instructors in her approach to the study of Western civilization in the modern period.

CIVILIZATION IN THE WEST

Volume I

The Idea of Western Civilization

THE WEST IS AN IDEA. IT IS NOT VISIBLE FROM SPACE. AN ASTRONAUT viewing the blue-and-white terrestrial sphere can make out the forms of Africa, bounded by the Atlantic, the Indian Ocean, the Red Sea, and the Mediterranean. Australia, the Americas, and even Antarctica are distinct patches of blue-green in the darker waters that surround them. But nothing comparable separates Asia from Europe, East from West. Viewed from 100 miles up, the West itself is invisible. Although astronauts can see the great Eurasian landmass curving around the Northern Hemisphere, the Ural Mountains—the theoretical boundary between East and West— appear faint from space. Certainly they are less impressive than the towering Himalayas, the Alps, or even the Caucasus. People, not geology, determined that the Urals should be the arbitrary boundary between Europe and Asia.

Even this determination took centuries. Originally, Europe was a name that referred only to central Greece. Gradually, Greeks extended it to include the whole Greek mainland and then the landmass to the north. Later, Roman explorers and soldiers carried Europe north and west to its modern boundaries. Asia too grew with time. Initially, Asia was only that small portion of what is today Turkey inland from the Aegean Sea. Gradually, as Greek explorers came to know of lands farther east, north, and south, they expanded their understanding of Asia to include everything east of the Don River to the north and of the Red Sea to the south.

Western civilization is as much an idea as the West itself. Under the right conditions, astronauts can see the Great Wall of China snaking its way from the edge of the Himalayas to the Yellow Sea. No comparable physical legacy of the West is so massive that its details can be discerned from space. Nor are Western achievements

1

rooted forever in one corner of the world. What we call Western civilization belongs to no particular place. Its location has changed since the origins of civilization; that is, the cultural and social traditions characteristic of the *civitas*, or city. "Western" cities appeared first outside the "West," in the Tigris and Euphrates river basins in present-day Iraq and Iran, a region that we today call the Middle East. These areas have never lost their urban traditions, but in time, other cities in North Africa, Greece, and Italy adapted and expanded this heritage.

Until the sixteenth century C.E., the western end of the Eurasian landmass was the crucible in which disparate cultural and intellectual traditions of the Near East, the Mediterranean, and northern and western Europe were smelted into a new and powerful alloy. Then "the West" expanded by establishing colonies overseas and by giving rise to the "settler societies" of the Americas, Australia and New Zealand, and South Africa.

Western technology for harnessing nature, Western forms of economic and political organization, Western styles of art and music are—for good or ill—dominant influences in world civilization. Japan is a leading power in the Western traditions of capitalist commerce and technology. China, the most populous country in the world, adheres to Marxist socialist principles—a European political tradition. Millions of people in Africa, Asia, and the Americas follow the religions of Islam and Christianity, both of which developed from Judaism in the cradle of Western civilization.

Many of today's most pressing problems are also part of the legacy of the Western tradition. The remnants of European colonialism have left deep hostilities throughout the world. The integration of developing nations into the world economy keeps much of humanity in a seemingly hopeless cycle of poverty as the wealth of poor countries goes to pay interest on loans from Europe and America. Hatred of Western civilization is a central, ideological tenet that inspired terrorist attacks on symbols of American economic and military strength on September 11, 2001, and that continues to fuel anti-Western terrorism around the world. The West itself faces a crisis. Impoverished citizens of former colonies flock to Europe and North America seeking a better life but instead often find poverty, hostility, and racism. Finally, the advances of Western civilization endanger our very existence. Technology pollutes the world's air, water, and soil, and nuclear weapons threaten the destruction of all civilization. Yet these are the same advances that allow us to lengthen life expectancy, harness the forces of nature, and conquer disease. It is the same technology that allows us to view our world from outer space.

How did we get here? In this book we attempt to answer that question. The history of Western civilization is not simply the triumphal story of progress, the creation of a better world. Even in areas in which we can see development, such as technology, communications, and social complexity, change is not always for the better. However, it would be equally inaccurate to view Western civilization as a progressive decline from a mythical golden age of the human race. The roughly 300 generations since the origins of civilization have bequeathed a rich and contradictory legacy to the present. Inherited political and social institutions, cultural forms, and religious and philosophical traditions form the framework within which the future must be created. The past does not determine the future, but it is the raw material from which the future will be made. To use this legacy properly, we must first understand it, not because the past is the key to the future, but because understanding yesterday frees us to create tomorrow.

The First Civilizations

Before Civilization

The first humanlike creatures whose remains have been discovered date from as long as five million years ago. These creatures, neither fully ape nor human, survived for over four million years.

Varieties of the modern species of humans, *Homo sapiens* ("thinking human"), appeared well over 100,000 years ago and spread across the Eurasian landmass and Africa. The earliest *Homo sapiens* in Europe, the *Neanderthal*, differed little from us today. They spread throughout much of Africa, Europe, and Asia during the last great ice age. To survive in the harsh tundra landscape, they developed a cultural system that enabled them to modify their environment. Customs such as the burial of their dead with food offerings indicate that Neanderthals may have developed a belief in an afterlife. DNA studies suggest that Neanderthals are not directly related to modern humans. Their subspecies appears to have been a dead end.

No one knows why or how the Neanderthals were replaced by our subspecies, *Homo sapiens sapiens* ("thinking thinking human"), around 40,000 years ago. Whatever the reason and whatever the process—extinction, evolution, or extermination—this last arrival on the human scene was universally successful. All humans today belong to this same subspecies. Differences in skin color, type of hair, and build are minor variations on the same theme. The identification of races, while selectively based on some of these physical variations, is, like civilization itself, a fact not of biology but of culture.

Early *Homo sapiens sapiens* lived in small kin groups of 20 or 30, following game and seeking shelter in tents, lean-tos, and caves. People of the **Paleolithic era** or Old Stone Age (ca. 600,000–10,000 B.C.E.) worked together for hunting and defense and apparently formed emotional bonds that were based on more than sex or economic necessity.

Chronology

BEFORE CIVILIZATION

ca. 100,000 B.C.E.	*Homo sapiens*
ca. 40,000 B.C.E.	*Homo sapiens sapiens*
ca. 35,000–10,000 B.C.E.	Late Paleolithic era (Old Stone Age)
ca. 8000–6500 B.C.E.	Neolithic era (New Stone Age)
ca. 3500 B.C.E.	Civilization begins

The Dominance of Culture

During the upper or late Paleolithic era (ca. 35,000–10,000 B.C.E.), **culture**, meaning everything about humans that is not inherited biologically, was increasingly determinant in human life. Paleolithic people were not on an endless and all-consuming quest to provide for the necessities of life. They spent less time on such things than we do today. Therefore, they were able to find time to develop speech, religion, and artistic expression. Wall paintings, small clay and stone figurines of female figures (which may reflect concerns about fertility), and finely decorated stone and bone tools indicate not just artistic ability but also abstract and symbolic thought.

The end of the glacial era marked the beginning of the Mesolithic, or Middle Stone Age (ca. 10,000–8000 B.C.E.). This period occurred at different times in different places as the climate grew milder, vast expanses of glaciers melted, and sea levels rose. Mesolithic peoples began the gradual domestication of plants and animals and sometimes formed settled communities. They developed the bow and arrow and pottery, and they made use of small flints (microliths) and fishhooks.

Paintings: A Cultural Record. An amazing continuous record of the civilizing of the West is found in the arid wastes of Africa's Sahara Desert. At Tassili-n-Ajjer in modern Algeria, succeeding generations of inhabitants left over 4,000 paintings on cliff and cave walls that date from about 6000 B.C.E. until the time of Jesus. Like a pictorial time line, these paintings show the gradual transformations of human culture.

The earliest cave paintings were produced by people who, like the inhabitants of Europe and the Near East, lived by hunting game and gathering edible plants, nuts, and fruit.

Sedentarization. Sometime around 5000 B.C.E., the artists at Tassili-n-Ajjer began to include images of domesticated cattle and harnesslike equipment in their paintings. Such depictions give evidence of the arrival in North Africa of two of the most profound transformations in human history: sedentarization, that is, the adoption of a fixed dwelling place, and the agricultural revolution. These fundamental changes in human culture began independently around the world and continued for roughly 5,000 years. They appeared first around 10,000 B.C.E. in the Near East, then elsewhere in Asia around 8000 B.C.E. By 5000 B.C.E., the domestication of plants and animals was under way in Africa and what is today Mexico.

Around 10,000 B.C.E., many hunter-gatherers living along the coastal plains of what is today Syria and Israel and in the valleys and the hill country near the Zagros Mountains between modern Iran and Iraq began to develop specialized strategies that led, by accident, to a transformation in human culture. Rather than constantly traveling in search of food, people living near the Mediterranean coast stayed put and exploited the various seasonal sources of food, fish, wild grains, fruits, and game. Such a sedentary existence was easier on the very young and the very old, and consequently infant mortality dropped and life expectancy rose.

Social Organization, Agriculture, and Religion

No one really knows why settlement led to agriculture. As population growth put pressure on the local food supply, gathering activities demanded more formal coordination and organization and led to the development of political leadership. In any case, people no longer simply looked for favored species of plants and animals where they occurred naturally. Now they introduced these species into other locations and favored them at the expense of plant and animal species that were not deemed useful. Agriculture had begun.

Control of Nature. The ability to domesticate goats, sheep, pigs, and cattle and to cultivate barley, wheat, and vegetables changed human communities from passive harvesters of nature to active partners with it. These peoples of the **Neolithic era**, or New Stone Age (ca. 8000–6500 B.C.E.), organized sizable villages. Jericho, which

In this cave painting in northern Africa, animal magic evokes help from the spirit world in ensuring the prosperity of the cattle herd. A similar ceremony is still performed by members of the Fulani tribes in the Sahel, on the southern fringe of the Sahara.

had been settled before the agricultural revolution, grew into a fortified town complete with ditch, stone walls, and towers and sheltered perhaps 2,000 inhabitants. Çatal Hüyük in southern Turkey may have been even larger.

The really revolutionary aspect of agriculture was not simply that it ensured settled communities a food supply. The true innovation was that agriculture was portable. For the first time, rather than looking for a place that provided them with the necessities of life, humans could carry with them what they needed to make a site inhabitable. This portability also meant the rapid spread of agriculture throughout the region.

Religion. Agricultural societies brought changes in the form and organization of formal religious cults. In larger communities the bonds of kinship that had united small hunter-gatherer bands were being supplemented by religious organization, which helped to control and regulate social behavior. The nature of this religion is a matter of speculation. Images of a female deity, interpreted as a guardian of animals, suggest the religious importance of women and fertility.

Mesopotamia: Between the Two Rivers

Need drove the inhabitants of Mesopotamia—a name that means "between the rivers"—to create a civilization; nature itself offered little for human comfort or prosperity. The upland regions of the north receive most of the rainfall, but the soil is thin and poor. In the south the soil is fertile, but rainfall is almost nonexistent. There, the twin rivers provide life-giving water but also bring destructive floods that usually arrive at harvest time. Therefore, agriculture is impossible without irrigation. But irrigation systems, if not properly maintained, deposit harsh alkaline chemicals on the soil, gradually reducing its fertility. In addition, Mesopotamia's only natural resource is clay. It has no metals, no workable stone, no valuable minerals of use to ancient people. These very obstacles pressed the people to cooperative, innovative, and organized measures for survival. Survival in the region required planning and the mobilization of labor, which was possible only through centralization.

Until around 3500 B.C.E., the inhabitants of the lower Tigris and Euphrates lived in scattered villages and small towns. Then the population of the region, which was known as Sumer, began to increase rapidly. Small settlements became increasingly common; then towns such as Eridu and Uruk in what is now Iraq began to grow rapidly. These towns developed in part because of the need to concentrate and organize population in order to carry on the extensive irrigation systems necessary to support Mesopotamian agriculture. These towns soon spread their control out to the surrounding cultivated areas, incorporating the smaller towns and villages of the region. They also fortified themselves against the hostile intentions of their neighbors.

As population growth increased pressure on the region's food supply, cities supplemented their resources by raiding their more prosperous neighbors. Victims sought protection within the ramparts of the settlements that had grown up around religious centers. As a result, the populations of the towns rose along with their towering temples, largely at the expense of the countryside. Between about 3500 and 3000 B.C.E., the population of Uruk quadrupled, from 10,000 to 40,000. Other Mesopotamian cities, notably Umma, Eridu, Lagash, and Ur, developed along the same general lines as they concentrated water supplies within their districts with artificial canals and dikes. At the same time, the number of smaller towns and villages in the vicinity decreased rapidly. The city had become the dominant force in the organization of economy and society, and the growth of the Sumerian cities established a precedent that would continue throughout history.

The Ramparts of Uruk

Cities did more than simply concentrate population. Within the walls of the city, men and women developed new technologies and new social and political structures. They created cultural traditions such as writing and literature. The pride of the first city dwellers is captured in a passage from the *Epic of Gilgamesh*, the earliest known great heroic poem, which was composed sometime before 2000 B.C.E. In the poem, the hero Gilgamesh boasts of the mighty walls he had built to encircle his city, Uruk:

> Go up and walk on the ramparts of Uruk
> Inspect the base terrace, examine the brickwork:
> Is not its brickwork of burnt brick?
> Did not the Seven Sages lay its foundations?

Gilgamesh was justifiably proud of his city. In his day (ca. 2700 B.C.E.), these walls were marvels of military engineering; even now their ruins remain a tribute to his age. Archaeologists have uncovered the remains of the ramparts of Uruk, which stretched over five miles and were protected by some 900 semicircular tow-

MAP DISCOVERY

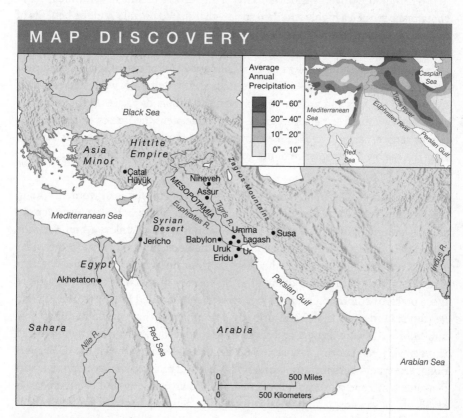

Average Annual Precipitation

- 40"– 60"
- 20"– 40"
- 10"– 20"
- 0"– 10"

0   500 Miles
0   500 Kilometers

THE ANCIENT WORLD

Notice the locations of the earliest civilizations. What geographical similarities can you see between the Nile Valley and the valleys of the Tigris and Euphrates rivers that might have encouraged the appearance of complex civilizations? How dependent on rainfall were the agricultures that supported these civilizations? What problems do river valleys pose to settlement that civilization might solve?

ers. These massive protective walls enclosed about two square miles of houses, palaces, workshops, and temples. Uruk may with reason be called the first true city in the history of Western civilization.

Urban Life. Within Uruk's walls the peculiar circumstances of urban life changed the traditional social structure of Mesopotamia. In Neolithic times, social and economic differences within society had been minimal. Urban immigration increased the power, wealth, and status of two groups. In the first group were the religious authorities who were responsible for the temples. The second consisted of the emerging military and administrative elites, such as Gilgamesh, who were responsible for the construction and protection of the cities. These two groups probably encouraged much of the migration to the cities.

Whether they lived inside the city or on the farmland it controlled, Mesopotamians formed a highly stratified society that shared unequally in the benefits of civilization. Slaves, who did most of the unskilled labor within the city, were the primary victims of civilization. Most were prisoners of war, but some were people forced by debt to sell themselves or their children. Most of the remaining rural people were peasants who were little more than slaves. Better off were soldiers, merchants, and workers and artisans who served the temple or palace. At the next level were land-owning free persons. Above all of these were the priests responsible for temple services and the rulers. Rulers included the *ensi*, or city ruler, and the *lugal*, or king, the earthly representative of the gods. Kings were powerful and feared.

Women's Status. Urban life also redefined the role and status of women, who in the Neolithic period had enjoyed roughly the same roles and status as men. In cities, women tended to exercise private authority over children and servants within the household, while men controlled the household and dealt in the wider world. This change in roles resulted in part from the economic basis of the first civilization. Southern Mesopotamia has no sources of metal or stone. To acquire these precious commodities, trade networks were extended into Syria, the Arabian Peninsula, and even India. The primary commodities that Mesopotamians produced for trade were textiles, and these were produced largely by women captured in wars with neighboring city-states. Some historians suggest that the disproportionate numbers of low-status women in Mesopotamian cities affected the status of women in general. Although women could own property and even appear as heads of households, by roughly 1500 B.C.E. the pattern of patriarchal households predominated. Throughout Western history, while individual women might at times exercise great power, they did so largely in the private sphere.

Tools: Technology and Writing

Changes in society brought changes in technology. The need to feed, clothe, protect, and govern growing urban populations led to major technological and conceptual discoveries. Canals and systems of dikes partially harnessed water supplies. Farmers began to work their fields with improved plows and to haul their produce to town, first on sleds and ultimately on carts. These land-transport devices, along with sailing ships, made it possible not only to produce greater agricultural surplus but also to move this surplus to distant markets. Artisans used a refined potter's wheel to produce ceramic vessels of great beauty. Government officials and private individuals began to use cylinder seals, small stone cylinders engraved with a pattern, to mark ownership. Metalworkers fashioned gold and silver into valuable items of adornment and prestige. They also began to cast bronze, an alloy of copper and tin, which came into use for tools and weapons about 3000 B.C.E.

Pictograms. Perhaps the greatest invention of early cities was writing. As early as 7000 B.C.E., small clay or stone tokens with distinctive shapes or markings were being used to keep track of animals, goods, and fruits in inventories and bartering. By 3500 B.C.E., government and temple administrators were using simplified drawings— today termed **pictograms**—that were derived from these tokens to assist them in keeping records of their transactions.

Cuneiform. In time, these pictograms developed into a true system of writing called **cuneiform** (from the Latin *cuneus*, "wedge") after the wedge shape of the characters. Finally, scribes took a radical step. Rather than simply using pictograms to indicate single objects, they began to use cuneiform characters to represent concepts. Ultimately, pictograms came to represent sounds divorced from any particular meaning.

The implications of the development of cuneiform writing were revolutionary. Since symbols were liberated from meaning, they could be used to record any language. Writing soon allowed those who had mastered it to achieve greater centralization and control of government, to communicate over enormous distances, to preserve and transmit information, and to express religious and cultural beliefs. Writing reinforced memory, consolidating and expanding the achievements of the first civilization and transmitting them to the future.

Gods and Mortals in Mesopotamia

A world of many cities, Mesopotamia was also a world of many gods, and Mesopotamian cities bore the imprint of the cult of their gods.

Mesopotamian Divinities. The gods were like the people who worshipped them. They lived in a replica of human society, and each god had a particular responsibility. Every object and element from the sky to the brick or the plow had its own active god. The gods had the physical appearance and personalities of humans as well as human virtues and vices. Greater gods such as Nanna and Ufu were the protectors of Ur and Sippar. Others, such as Inanna, or Ishtar, the goddess of love, fertility, and wars, and her husband Dumuzi, were worshiped throughout Mesopotamia. Finally, at the top of the pantheon were the gods of the sky, the air, and the rivers.

Temples and Rituals. Mesopotamians believed that the role of mortals was to serve the gods and to feed them through sacrifice. By around 2500 B.C.E., although military lords and kings had gained political power, the temples still controlled a major portion of economic resources. They owned vast estates where peasants cultivated crops and tended flocks to support the priests, scribes, artisans, laborers, farmers, teamsters, smiths, and weavers who operated these complex religious centers. A **ziggurat,** or tiered tower, dedicated to the god stood near many temples.

Although Mesopotamians looked to hundreds of personal divinities for assistance, they did not attempt to establish personal relationships with their great gods. However, since they assumed that the gods lived in a structured world that operated rationally, they believed that mortals could deal with the gods and enlist their aid by following the right rituals. Rites centered on the worship of idols.

Through the proper rituals a person could buy the god's protection and favor. Still, mortal life was harsh, and the gods offered little solace in coping with the great issues of human existence. This attitude is powerfully presented in the *Epic of Gilgamesh,* which, while not an accurate picture of Mesopotamian religion, does convey much of the values of this civilization. In this popular legend, Gilgamesh, king of Uruk, civilizes the wild man Enkidu, who was sent by the gods to temper

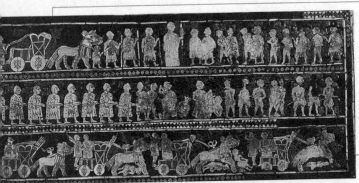

The Standard of Ur, made of shells, lapis lazuli, and limestone, was found at Ur. In the top panel, known as *War,* soldiers and horse-drawn chariots return victorious from battle. In the lower panel *Peace,* the king celebrates the victory, captives are paraded before him, and the conquered people bring him tribute.

the king's harshness. Gilgamesh and Enkidu become friends and undertake a series of adventures. However, even their great feats cannot overcome death. Enkidu displeases the gods and dies. Gilgamesh then sets out to find the magic plant of eternal life with which to return his friend from the somber underworld. On his journey he meets Ut-napishtim, the Mesopotamian Noah, who recounts the story of the Great Flood and tells Gilgamesh where to find the plant. Gilgamesh follows Ut-napishtim's advice and is successful but loses the plant on his journey home. The message is that only the gods are immortal, and the human afterlife is at best a shadowy and mournful existence.

Sargon and Mesopotamian Expansion

The temple was one center of the city; the palace was the other. As representative of the city's god, the king was the ruler and highest judge. He was responsible for the construction and maintenance of religious buildings and the complex system of canals that maintained the precarious balance between swamp and arid steppe. Finally, he commanded the army, defending his community against its neighbors and leading his forces against rival cities.

Competition and War. The cultural and economic developments of early Mesopotamia occurred within the context of almost constant warfare. From around 3000 B.C.E. until 2300 B.C.E. the rulers of Ur, Lagash, Uruk, and Umma fought among themselves for control of Sumer, their name for the southern region of Mesopotamia. The population was a mixture of Sumerians and Semites, peoples who spoke Semitic languages related to modern Arabic or Hebrew, all jealously protective of their cities and gods and eager to extend their domination over their weaker neighbors.

The Akkadian Empire. The extraordinary developments in this small corner of the Middle East might have remained isolated phenomena were it not for Sargon (ca. 2334–2279 B.C.E.), king of Akkad and the most important figure in Mesopotamian history. During his long reign of 55 years, Sargon built on the conquests and confederacies of the past to unite, transform, and expand Mesopotamian civilization. In his youth he was the cupbearer to the king of Kish, another Sumerian city. Sargon overthrew his master and conquered Uruk, Ur, Lagash, and Umma. Then, he extended his military operations east across the Tigris, west along the Euphrates, and north into modern Syria, thus creating the first great multiethnic empire state in the West.

The Akkadian state—so named by contemporary historians for Sargon's capital at Akkad—consisted of a vast and heterogeneous collection of city-states and territories. Sargon attempted to rule it by transforming the traditions of royal government. Rather than eradicating the traditions of conquered cities, he allowed them to maintain their own institutions but replaced many of their autonomous ruling aristocracies with his own functionaries. He was thus the first in a long tradition of Near Eastern rulers who sought to unite his disparate conquests into a true state.

Sargon did more than just conquer cities. Although a Semite, he spread the achievements of Sumerian civilization throughout his vast state.

The Akkadian state proved as ephemeral as Sargon's accomplishments were lasting. All Mesopotamian states tended to undergo a cycle of rising rapidly under a gifted military commander and then beginning to crumble under the internal stresses of dynastic disputes and regional assertions of autonomy. Thus weakened, they could then be conquered by other expanding states. First Ur, under its Sumerian king and first law codifier, Shulgi (2094–2047 B.C.E.), and then Amoritic Babylonia, under its great ruler, Hammurabi (1792–1750 B.C.E.), assumed dominance in the land between the rivers. From about 2000 B.C.E. on, the political and economic centers of Mesopotamia were in Babylonia and in Assyria, the region to the north at the foot of the Zagros Mountains.

Hammurabi and the Old Babylonian Empire

In the tradition of Sargon, Hammurabi expanded his state through arms and diplomacy. He expanded his power south as far as Uruk and north to Assyria. In the tradition of Shulgi, he promulgated an important body of law, known as the Code of Hammurabi.

Law and Society. As the favored agent of the gods, the king had responsibility for regulating all aspects of Babylonian life. Therefore, Hammurabi's code offers a view of many aspects of Babylonian life, though always from the perspective of the royal law. The code lists offenses and prescribes penalties, which vary according to the social status of the victim and the perpetrator. Hammurabi's code thus creates a picture of a prosperous society composed of three legally defined social strata: a well-to-do elite, the mass of the population, and slaves. Each group had its own rights and obligations in proportion to its status.

Much of the code sought to protect women and children from arbitrary and unfair treatment. Husbands ruled their households but did not have unlimited authority over their wives. Women could initiate their own court cases, practice various trades, and even hold public positions. The wife's father gave her a dowry over which she had full control. Some elite women personally controlled great wealth.

The Code of Hammurabi was less a royal attempt to restructure Babylonian society than an effort to reorganize, consolidate, and preserve previous laws in order to maintain the established social and economic order.

Mathematics. Law was not the only area in which the Old Babylonian kingdom began an important tradition. To handle the economics of business and government administration, Babylonians developed the most sophisticated mathematical system known before the fifteenth century C.E. Although Babylonian mathematicians were not interested primarily in theoretical problems and were seldom given to abstraction, their technical proficiency indicates the advanced level of sophistication with which Hammurabi's contemporaries could tackle the problems of living in a complex society.

For all its achievements, Hammurabi's state was no more successful than those of his predecessors at defending itself against internal conflicts or external enemies. Despite his efforts, the traditional organization that he inherited from his Sumerian and Akkadian predecessors could not ensure orderly administration of a far-flung collection of cities. Hammurabi's son lost over half of his father's kingdom to internal revolts. Weakened by internal dissension, the kingdom fell to a new and potent force in Western history: the Hittites.

Chronology

BETWEEN THE TWO RIVERS

ca. 3500 B.C.E.	Pictograms appear
ca. 3000–2316 B.C.E.	War for control of Sumer
ca. 2700 B.C.E.	Gilgamesh
ca. 2334–2279 B.C.E.	Sargon
1792–1750 B.C.E.	Hammurabi
ca. 1600 B.C.E.	Hittites destroy Old Babylonian state
ca. 1286 B.C.E.	Battle of Kadesh

The Hittite Empire. The Hittite state emerged in Anatolia in the shadow of Mesopotamian civilization. The Hittite court reflected Mesopotamian influence in its art and religion and in its adaptation and use of cuneiform script. Unlike the Sumerians, the Semitic nomads, the Akkadians, and the Babylonians, the Hittites were an Indo-European people. Their language was part of the linguistic family that includes most modern European languages as well as Persian, Greek, Latin, and Sanskrit. From their capital of Hattushash (modern Bogazköy in Turkey), they established a centralized state based on agriculture and trade in the metals mined from the ore-rich mountains of Anatolia and exported to Mesopotamia. The Hittites were among the earliest people to succeed in smelting iron.

Perfecting the light horse-drawn war chariot, the Hittites expanded into northern Mesopotamia and along the Syrian coast. They were able to destroy the Babylonian state around 1600 B.C.E. The Hittite Empire was the chief political and cultural force in western Asia from about 1400 to 1200 B.C.E. Its gradual expansion south along the coast was checked at the battle of Kadesh about 1286 B.C.E., when Hittite forces encountered the army of an even greater and more ancient power: the Egypt of Ramses II.

The Gift of the Nile

Like that of the Tigris and Euphrates valleys, the rich soil of the Nile Valley can support a dense population. There, however, the similarities end. Unlike the Mesopotamian floodplain, the Nile floodplain required little effort to make the land productive. Each year, the river flooded at exactly the right time to irrigate crops and to deposit a layer of rich, fertile silt. Egypt knew only two environments: the fertile Nile Valley and the vast wastes of the Sahara Desert surrounding it. This inhospitable and largely uninhabitable region limited Egypt's contact with outside influences. Thus while trade, communication, and violent conquest characterized Mesopotamian civilization, Egypt knew self-sufficiency, an inward focus in culture and society, and stability. In its art, political structure, society, and religion, the Egyptian universe was static. Nothing was ever expected to change.

The earliest sedentary communities in the Nile Valley appeared on the western margin of the Nile Delta around 4000 B.C.E. Farther south, in Upper Egypt, similar communities developed somewhat later but achieved an earlier political unity and a higher level of culture. By around 3200 B.C.E., Upper Egypt was in contact with Mesopotamia and had apparently borrowed something of that region's artistic and architectural traditions. During the same period, Upper Egypt developed a pictographic script.

These cultural achievements coincided with the political centralization of Upper Egypt under a series of kings. Probably around 3150 B.C.E., King Narmer or one of his predecessors in Upper Egypt expanded control over the fragmented south, uniting Upper and Lower Egypt and establishing a capital at Memphis on the border between these two regions. For over 2,500 years, the Nile Valley, from the first cataract to the Mediterranean, enjoyed the most stable civilization the Western world has ever known.

Tending the Cattle of God

Historians divide the vast sweep of Egyptian history into 31 dynasties, regrouped in turn into four periods of political centralization: pre- and early dynastic Egypt (ca. 3150–2770 B.C.E.), the Old Kingdom (ca. 2770–2200 B.C.E.), the Middle Kingdom (ca. 2050–1786 B.C.E.), and the New Kingdom (ca. 1560–1087 B.C.E.). The time gaps between kingdoms were periods of disruption and political confusion termed intermediate periods. While minor changes in social, political, and cultural life certainly occurred during these centuries, the changes were less significant than the astonishing stability and continuity of the civilization that developed along the banks of the Nile.

God-Kings. Divine kingship was the cornerstone of Egyptian life. Initially, the king was the incarnation of Horus, a sky and falcon god. Later, the king was identified with the sun-god Ra (subsequently known as Amen-Re, the great god), as well as with Osiris, the god of the dead. As divine incarnation, the king was obliged

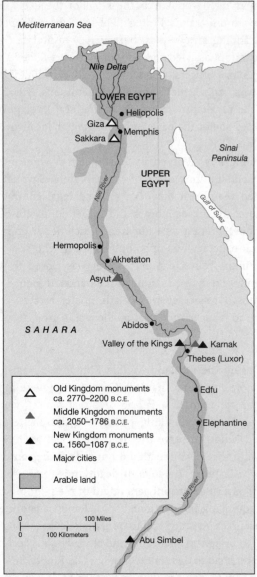

ANCIENT EGYPT. The thin strip of rich land bordering the Nile saw
the development of an extraordinary civilization that endured
for more than 2,000 years.

above all to care for his people. It was he who ensured the annual flooding of the
Nile, which brought water to the parched land. His commands preserved **maat**, the
ideal state of the universe and society, a condition of harmony and justice. In
the poetry of the Old Kingdom, the king was the divine herdsman; the people were
the cattle of god.

Unlike the rulers in Mesopotamia, the kings of the Old Kingdom were not warriors but divine administrators. Protected by the Sahara, Egypt had few external enemies and no standing army. A vast bureaucracy of literate court officials and provincial administrators assisted the god-king. They wielded wide authority as religious leaders, judicial officers, and, when necessary, military leaders. A host of subordinate overseers, scribes, metalworkers, stonemasons, artisans, and tax collectors rounded out the royal administration. At the local level, governors administered provinces called *nomes*, the basic units of Egyptian local government.

Gender and Bureaucracy. Women of ancient Egypt were more independent and involved in public life than those of Mesopotamia. Egyptian women owned property, conducted their own business, entered legal contracts, and brought lawsuits. They shared in the economic and professional life of the country at every level except one: Women were apparently excluded from formal education. The professional bureaucracy was open only to those who could read and write. As a result, the primary route to public power was closed to women, and the bureaucratic machinery remained firmly in the hands of men.

The role of this bureaucracy was to administer estates, collect taxes, and channel revenues and labor toward vast public works projects, which focused on the king.

The Pyramids. During the Old and Middle Kingdoms, great pyramid temple-tomb complexes more imposing than the Great House were built for the kings who ruled from the splendor of a Per-ao or "great house," from which comes the Hebrew term for the Egyptian king, pharaoh. Within the temples, priests and servants performed rituals to serve the dead kings just as they had served the kings when they were alive. Even death did not disrupt the continuity that was so vital to Egyptian civilization. The cults of dead kings reinforced the monarchy, since veneration of past rulers meant veneration of the reigning king's ancestors.

Building and equipping the pyramids focused and transformed Egypt's material and human resources. Artisans had to be trained, engineering and transportation problems had to be solved, quarrying and stoneworking techniques had to be perfected, and laborers had to be recruited. In the Old Kingdom, whose population has been estimated at perhaps 1.5 million, more than 70,000 workers at a time were employed in building these great temple-tombs. The pyramids were constructed by peasants working when the Nile was in flood and they could not till the soil. Although actual construction was seasonal, the work was unending. No sooner was one complex completed than the next was begun.

Feeding the masses of laborers absorbed most of the country's agricultural surplus. Equipping the temples and pyramids provided a constant demand for the highest-quality luxury goods, since royal tombs and temples were furnished as luxuriously as palaces. Thus the construction and maintenance of these vast complexes focused the organization and production of Egypt's economy and government.

Democratization of the Afterlife

In the Old Kingdom, future life was available through the king. The graves of thousands of his attendants and servants surrounded his temple. All the wealth, labor, and expertise of the kingdom thus flowed into these temples, reinforcing the position of the king. Like the tip of a pyramid, the king was the summit, supported by all of society.

Decline of Royal Power. Gradually, however, the absolute power of the king declined. The increasing demands for consumption by the court and the cults forced agricultural expansion into areas where returns were poor, thus decreasing the flow of wealth. As bureaucrats increased their efforts to supply the voracious needs of living and dead kings and their attendants, they neglected the maintenance of the economic system that supplied those needs. The royal government was not protecting society; the "cattle of god" were not being well tended. Finally, tax-exempt religious foundations, established to ensure the perpetual cult of the dead, received donations of vast amounts of property, and their power came to rival the king's. This removed an ever greater amount of the country's wealth from the control of the king and his agents. Thus the wealth and power of the Egyptian kings declined at roughly the time that Sargon was expanding his Akkadian state in Mesopotamia. By around 2200 B.C.E., Egyptian royal authority collapsed entirely, leaving political and religious power in the hands of provincial governors.

The Middle Kingdom. After almost 200 years of fragmentation, the governors of Thebes in Upper Egypt reestablished centralized royal traditions, but with a difference. Kings continued to build vast temples, but they did not resume the tremendous investments in pyramid complexes on the scale of the Old Kingdom. The bureaucracy was opened to all men, even sons of peasants, who could master the complex pictographic writing. Private temple-tombs proliferated and with them new pious foundations. These promised eternal care by which anyone with sufficient wealth could enjoy a comfortable afterlife.

The memory of the Old Kingdom's shortcomings introduced a new ethical perspective that was expressed in the literature written by the elite. For the first time, the elite voiced the concern that justice might not always be served and that the innocent might suffer at the hands of royal agents.

The Hyksos. The greater access to power and privilege in the Middle Kingdom benefited foreigners as well as Egyptians. Assimilated Semites rose to important administrative positions. By around 1600 B.C.E., when the Hittite armies were destroying the state of Hammurabi's successors, large bands of Semites had settled in the eastern Delta, setting the stage for the first foreign conquest of Egypt. A series of kings referred to by Egyptian sources as "rulers of foreign lands," or Hyksos, overran the country and ruled the Nile Valley as far south as

Memphis. These foreigners adopted the traditions of Egyptian kingship and continued the tradition of divine rule.

The Hyksos kings introduced their military technology and organization into Egypt. In particular, they brought with them the light horse-drawn war chariot. This mobile fighting platform transformed Egyptian military tactics. These innovations remained even after the Hyksos were expelled by Ahmose I (1552–1527 B.C.E.), the Theban founder of the Eighteenth Dynasty, with whose reign the New Kingdom began.

The Egyptian Empire

Ahmose did not stop with the liberation of Egypt. He forged an empire. He and his successors used their newfound military might to extend the frontiers of Egypt south up the Nile beyond the fourth cataract and well into Nubia. To the east they absorbed the caravan routes to the Red Sea, from which they were able to send ships to Punt (probably modern Somalia), the source of the myrrh and frankincense that were needed for funeral and religious rituals. Most important was the Egyptian expansion into Canaan. Here Egyptian chariots crushed their foes as kings pressed on as far as the Euphrates. Thutmose I (1506–1494 B.C.E.) proclaimed, "I have made the boundaries of Egypt as far as that which the sun encircles."

This painted limestone head of Hatshepsut was originally from a statue depicting the pharaoh as the god Osiris. Hatshepsut was one of at least four women who ruled as pharaoh and her representations may have been influenced by those of her predecessors. Other statues show her in typically female dress, but as her reign progressed representations of her emphasized her role as pharaoh wearing the nemes or striped headcloth, the uraeus or cobra head, the kilt or shendyt, and the traditional false beard. This is especially true in these Osirian statues, that emphasize her assimilation with the god.

In spite of the efforts of Thutmose and his successors, the Egyptian Empire was never as grand as its kings proclaimed. Many of the northern expeditions were raids rather than conquests. Still, the expanded political frontiers meant increased trade and unprecedented interaction with the rest of the ancient world.

Religious and Royal Consolidation Under Akhenaten

Religion was both the heart of royal power and its only limiting force. Although the king was the embodiment of the religious tradition he was also bound by that tradition as it was interpreted by an ancient and powerful system of priesthoods, pious foundations, and cults. The intimate relationship between royal absolutism and religious cult culminated in the reign of Amenhotep IV (1364–1347 B.C.E.), the most controversial and enigmatic ruler of the New Kingdom, who challenged the very basis of royal religious control. In a calculated break with over a thousand years of Egyptian religious custom, Amenhotep attempted to abolish the cult of Amen-Re along with all of the other traditional gods, their priesthoods, and their festivals. In their place he promoted a new divinity, the sun-disk god Aten. Amenhotep moved his capital from Thebes to a new temple city, Akhetaton, near modern Tel al-'Amarna, and changed his own name to Akhenaten ("It pleases Aten").

Akhenaten has been called the first monotheist, a reformer who sought to revitalize a religion that had decayed into superstition and magic. Yet his monotheism was not complete. The god Aten shared divine status with Akhenaten himself. Akhenaten attacked other cults, especially that of Amen-Re, to consolidate royal power and to replace the old priesthoods with his own family members and supporters.

A New Aesthetic. In attempting to reestablish royal divinity, Akhenaten temporarily transformed the aesthetics of Egyptian court life. Traditional archaic language gave way to the everyday speech of the fourteenth century B.C.E. Wall paintings and statues showed people in the clothing that they actually wore rather than in stylized parade dress. This new naturalism rendered the king at once more human and more divine. It differentiated him from the long line of preceding kings, emphasizing his uniqueness and his royal power.

The strength of royal power was so great that during his reign, Akhenaten could command acceptance of his radical break with Egyptian tradition. However, his ambitious plan did not long survive his death. His innovations annoyed the Egyptian elite, while his abolition of established festivals alienated the masses. His son-in-law, Tutankhamen (1347–1337 B.C.E.), the son of Akhenaten's predecessor, was a child when he became king upon Akhenaten's death. Under the influence of his court advisers, probably inherited from his father's reign, he restored the ancient religious traditions and abandoned the new capital of Akhetaton for his father's palace at Thebes.

The Hittites. Return to the old ways meant return to the old problems. Powerful pious foundations controlled fully 10 percent of the population. Dynastic continuity ended after Tutankhamen, and a new military dynasty seized the throne. These internal problems provided an opportunity for the growing Hittite state in Asia Minor to expand south at the expense of Egypt. Ramses II (1289–1224 B.C.E.) checked the Hittite expansion at the battle of Kadesh, but the battle was actually a draw. Eventually, Ramses and the Hittite king Hattusilis III signed a peace treaty whose terms included nonaggression and mutual defense.

The mutual standoff at Kadesh did not long precede the disintegration of both Egypt and the Hittite state. Within a century, states large and small along the Mediterranean coast from Anatolia to the Delta and from the Aegean Sea in the west to the Zagros Mountains in the east collapsed or were destroyed in what seems to have been a general crisis of the civilized world. The various raiders, sometimes erroneously called the "Sea Peoples," who struck Egypt, Syria, the Hittite state, and elsewhere, were not the primary cause of the crisis. It was rather internal political, economic, and social strains within both Egypt and the Hittite state that provided the opportunity for various groups—including Anatolians, Greeks, Israelites, and others—to raid the ancient centers of civilization. In the ensuing confusion, the small Semitic kingdoms of Syria and Canaan developed a precarious independence in the shadow of the great powers.

Chronology

THE GIFT OF THE NILE

ca. 3150–2770 B.C.E.	Predynastic and early dynastic Egypt
ca. 2770–2200 B.C.E.	Old Kingdom
ca. 2600 B.C.E.	Pyramid of Khufu
ca. 2050–1786 B.C.E.	Middle Kingdom
ca. 1560–1087 B.C.E.	New Kingdom
1552–1527 B.C.E.	Ahmose I
1506–1494 B.C.E.	Thutmose I
1494–1490 B.C.E.	Thutmose II
1490–1468 B.C.E.	Hatshepsut
1364–1347 B.C.E.	Amenhotep IV (Akhenaten)
1347–1337 B.C.E.	Tutankhamen
1289–1224 B.C.E.	Ramses II

Between Two Worlds

City-based civilization was an endangered species throughout antiquity. Just beyond the well-tilled fields of Mesopotamia and the fertile delta of the Nile lay the world of the Semitic tribes of seminomadic shepherds and traders. Of course, not all Semites were nonurban. Many had formed part of the heterogeneous population of the Sumerian world. But the majority of Semitic peoples continued to live a life that was radically different from that of the people of the floodplain civilizations. From these, one small group, the Hebrews, emerged to establish a religious and cultural tradition that was unique in antiquity.

The Hebrew Alternative

Sometime after 2000 B.C.E., small Semitic bands under the leadership of patriarchal chieftains spread into what is today Syria, Lebanon, Israel, and Palestine. These bands crisscrossed the Fertile Crescent, searching for pasture for their flocks. Semitic Aramaeans and Chaldeans brought with them not only their flocks and families, but Mesopotamian culture as well.

Mesopotamian Origins. Hebrew history records such Mesopotamian traditions as the story of the flood (Genesis 6–10), legal traditions strongly reminiscent of those of Hammurabi, and the worship of the gods on high places. Stories such as that of the Tower of Babel (Genesis 11) and the garden of Eden (Genesis 2–4) likewise have a Mesopotamian flavor, but with a difference. For these wandering shepherds, urban culture was a curse. In the Hebrew Bible (the Christian Old Testament) the first city was built by Cain, the first murderer. The Tower of Babel, probably a ziggurat, was a symbol not of human achievement but of human pride.

At least some of these wandering Aramaeans, among them the biblical patriarch Abraham, rejected the gods of Mesopotamia. Religion among these nomadic groups focused on the specific divinity of the clan. In the case of Abraham, this was the god El. Abraham and his successors were not monotheists. They did not deny the existence of other gods. They simply believed that they had a personal pact with their own god.

In its social organization and cultural traditions, Abraham's clan was no different from its neighbors. These independent clans were ruled by a senior male. Women, whether wives, concubines, or slaves, were treated as distinctly inferior, virtually as property.

Egypt and Exodus. Some of Abraham's descendants must have joined the steady migration from Canaan into Egypt that took place during the Middle Kingdom and the Hyksos period. Although they were initially well treated, after the expulsion of the Hyksos in the sixteenth century B.C.E., many of the Semitic settlers in Egypt were reduced to slavery. Around the thirteenth century B.C.E., a small band of Semitic slaves numbering fewer than 1,000 left Egypt for Sinai and Canaan under the leadership of Moses. The memory of this departure, known as the Exodus, became the formative experience of the descendants of those who had taken part and those who later joined them. Moses, a Semite who carried an Egyptian name and who, according to tradition, had been raised in the royal court, was the founder of the Israelite people.

During the years that they spent wandering in the desert and then slowly conquering Canaan, the Israelites forged a new identity and a new faith. From the

A relief on a basalt obelisk (ca. 830 B.C.E.) depicts Jehu, a king of Israel, making obeisance to the Assyrian monarch Shalmaneser III. This is the oldest identified portrait of an Israelite.

Midianites of the Sinai Peninsula, they adopted the god Yahweh as their own. Although composed of various Semitic and even Egyptian groups, the Israelites adopted the oral traditions of the clan of Abraham and identified his god, El, with Yahweh. They interpreted their extraordinary escape from Egypt as evidence of a covenant with this god, a treaty similar to those concluded between the Hittite kings and their dependents. Yahweh was to be the Israelites' exclusive god; they were to make no alliances with any others. They were to preserve peace among themselves, and they were obligated to serve Yahweh with arms. This covenant was embodied in the law of Moses. Inspired by their new identity and their new religion, the Israelites swept into Canaan. Taking advantage of the vacuum of power left by the Hittite-Egyptian standoff following the battle of Kadesh, they destroyed or captured the cities of the region. In some cases, the local population welcomed the Israelites and their religion. In other places, the indigenous people were slaughtered down to the last man, woman, and child.

A King Like All the Nations

During its first centuries, Israel was a loosely organized confederation of tribes whose only focal point was the religious shrine at Shiloh. This shrine, in contrast with the temples of other ancient peoples, housed no idols, only a chest, known as the Ark of the Covenant, which contained the law of Moses and mementos of the Exodus. In times of danger, temporary leaders would lead united tribal armies. The power of these leaders, who were called judges in the Hebrew Bible, rested solely on their personal leadership qualities. This charisma indicated that the spirit of Yahweh was with the leader. Yahweh alone was the ruler of the people.

By the eleventh century B.C.E., this disorganized political tradition placed the Israelites at a disadvantage in fighting their neighbors. The Philistines, who dominated the Canaanite seacoast and had expanded inland, posed the greatest threat. By 1050 B.C.E., the Philistines had defeated the Israelites, captured the Ark of the Covenant, and occupied most of their territory. To consolidate their forces, the Israelite religious leaders reluctantly established a kingdom. Its first king was Saul, and its second was David.

David (ca. 1000–962 B.C.E.) and his son and successor, Solomon (ca. 961–922 B.C.E.), brought the kingdom of Israel to its peak of power, prestige, and territorial expansion. David defeated and expelled the Philistines, subdued Israel's other enemies, and created a united state that included all of Canaan from the desert to the sea. He established Jerusalem as the political and religious capital. Solomon went still further, building a magnificent temple complex to house the Ark of the Covenant and to serve as Israel's national shrine. David and Solomon restructured Israel from a tribal to a monarchical society. The old tribal structure remained only as a religious tradition.

The cost of this transformation was high. The kingdom under David and especially under Solomon grew more tyrannical as it grew more powerful. Solomon behaved like any other king of his time. He contracted marriage alliances with neighboring princes and allowed his wives to practice their own cults. He demanded extraordinary taxes and services from his people to pay for his lavish building projects. When he was unable to pay his Phoenician creditors for supplies and workers, he deported Israelites to work as slaves in Phoenician mines.

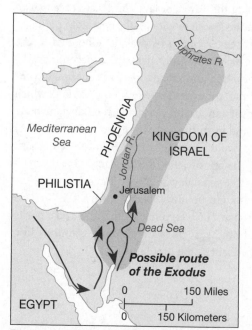

THE KINGDOMS OF ISRAEL AND JUDAH. From its greatest extent under Solomon, the Kingdom of Israel split into rival northern and southern kingdoms and then progressively lost ground against Assyria and Babylon.

Exile

Not surprisingly, the united kingdom did not survive Solomon's death. The northern region broke off to become the Kingdom of Israel with its capital in Shechem. The south, the Kingdom of Judah, continued the tradition of David from his capital of Jerusalem. These small, weak kingdoms did not long maintain their independence. Beginning in the ninth century B.C.E., a new Mesopotamian power, the Assyrians, began a campaign of conquest and unprecedented brutality throughout the Near East. In 722 B.C.E., the Assyrians destroyed the Kingdom of Israel and deported thousands of its people to upper Mesopotamia. In 586 B.C.E., the Kingdom of Judah was conquered by Assyria's destroyers, the New Babylonian Empire under King Nebuchadnezzar II (604–562 B.C.E.). The temple of Solomon was destroyed, Jerusalem was burned, and Judah's elite were deported to Babylon.

The Babylonian captivity ended some 50 years later when the Persians, who had conquered Babylonia, allowed the people of Judah to return to their homeland. Those who returned did so with a new understanding of themselves and their covenant with Yahweh, who was now seen as not just one god among many but as the one universal God. This new understanding was central to the development of Judaism.

The fundamental figures in this transformation were Ezra and Nehemiah (fifth and fourth centuries B.C.E.), who were particularly concerned with keeping Judaism uncontaminated by other religious and cultural influences. They condemned those who had remained in Judaea and who had intermarried with foreigners during the exile. Only the exiles who had remained faithful to Yahweh and who had avoided foreign marriages could be the true interpreters of the **Torah**, or law. This ideal of separatism and national purity came to characterize the Jewish religion in the post-exilic period.

Among its leaders were the Pharisees, a group of zealous adherents to the Torah, who produced a body of oral law termed the **Mishnah**, or second law, by which the law of Moses was to be interpreted and safeguarded. In subsequent centuries this oral law, along with its interpretation, developed into the Talmud, which did not assume its final form until almost a thousand years after the Babylonian exile. Pharisees believed in resurrection and in spirits such as angels and devils. They also believed that a messiah, or savior, would arise as a new David to reestablish Israel's political independence. Among the priestly elite, the hope for a Davidic messiah was seen as more universal: A priestly messiah would arise and bring about the kingdom of glory. Some Jews actively sought political liberation from the Persians and their successors. Others were more intent on preserving ritual and social purity until the coming of the messiah. Still others, such as the Essenes, withdrew into isolated communities to await the fulfillment of the prophecies.

Nineveh and Babylon

The Assyrian state that destroyed Israel accomplished what no other power had ever achieved. It tied together the floodplain civilizations of Mesopotamia and Egypt. But the Assyrian state was not just larger than the nation-states that had preceded it; it differed in nature as well as in size. The nation-states of Akkadia, Babylonia, the Hittites, and even the Egyptian Empire were essentially diverse collections of city-states. The Assyrian Empire was an integrated state in which conquered regions were reorganized and remade along the model of the central government. By the middle of the seventh century B.C.E., the Assyrian Empire stretched from the headwaters of the Tigris and Euphrates rivers to the Persian Gulf, along the coast from Syria to beyond the Nile Delta, and up the Nile to Thebes.

The Assyrian Empire

The Assyrian plain north of Babylonia had long been the site of a small Mesopotamian state. Early expansion soon gave rise to internal revolt and external threats. However, revolt paved the way for the ascension of Tiglath-pileser III (746–727 B.C.E.), the greatest empire builder of Mesopotamia since Sargon. In the sense that the Assyrians not only conquered but created an administrative system by which to rule, theirs was the first true empire, and as such, it served as a model for Persia, Macedonia, and Rome.

From his palace at Nineveh, Tiglath-pileser combined all of the traditional elements of Mesopotamian statecraft with a new religious ideology and social system to create the framework for a lasting multiethnic imperial system. The heart of Tiglath-pileser's program was the most modern army the world had ever seen. In place of traditional armies of peasants and slaves supplied by great aristocrats, he raised professional armies from the conquered lands of the empire and placed them under the command of Assyrian generals. The Assyrian army was also the first to make massive use of iron weapons, which were superior to the bronze swords and shields of their enemies.

In addition to the professional army, Tiglath-pileser created the most developed military-religious ideology of any ancient people. Kings had long been agents of the gods, but Ashur, the god of the Assyrians, had but one command: Enlarge the empire! Thus warfare was the mission and duty of all.

Tiglath-pileser restructured his empire, both at home in Assyria and abroad, so that revolts of the sort that had nearly destroyed it would be less likely. Within Assyria he increased the number of administrative districts, thus decreasing the strength of each, which reduced the likelihood of successful rebellions launched by dissatisfied governors. Outside Assyria proper, the king liquidated traditional leaders whenever possible and appointed Assyrian governors or at least assigned loyal overseers to protect his interests. To shatter regional identities, which could lead to separatist movements, Tiglath-pileser deported and resettled conquered peoples on a massive scale. Finally, in the tradition of his Assyrian predecessors, Tiglath-pileser and his successors maintained control of conquered peoples through a policy of unprecedented cruelty and brutality. One ruler, for example, boasted of once having flayed an enemy's chiefs and used their skins to cover a great pillar that he erected at their city gate and on which he impaled his victims.

The New Babylonian Empire

Ironically, while the imperial military and administrative system created by the Assyrians became in time the blueprint for future empires, its very ferocity led to its downfall. The hatred inspired by such brutality led to the destruction of the Assyrian Empire at the hands of a coalition of its subjects. In what is today Iran, Indo-European tribes coalesced around the Median dynasty. Egypt shook off its Assyrian lords under the leadership of the pharaoh Psamtik I (664–610 B.C.E.). In Babylon, which had always proven difficult for the Assyrians to control, a new Aramaean dynasty began to oppose Assyrian rule. In 612 B.C.E., the Medes and Babylonians joined forces to attack and destroy Nineveh.

However, the lessons that the Assyrians taught the world were not forgotten by the Babylonians, who modeled their imperial system on that of their predecessors. Administration of the New Babylonian Empire, which extended roughly over the length of the Tigris and extended west into Syria and Canaan, owed much to Assyrian tradition. The Code of Hammurabi once more formed the fundamental basis for justice. Babylonian kings restored and enriched temples to the Babylonian gods, and temple lands, administered by priests appointed by the king, played an important role in Babylonian economy and culture. Babylonian priests, using the mathematical methods developed during the Old Kingdom, made important advances in mathematical astronomy. Under King Nebuchadnezzar II, the city of Babylon reached its zenith, covering some 500 acres and containing a population of over 100,000, more than twice the population of Uruk at its height. The city walls, later counted among the seven wonders of the world by the Greeks, were so wide that two chariots could ride abreast on them. Yet this magnificent fortification was never tested. In 539 B.C.E., a Persian army under King Cyrus II (ca. 585–ca. 529 B.C.E.), who had ousted the Median dynasty in 550 B.C.E., slipped into the city through the Euphrates riverbed at low water and took the city by surprise.

BETWEEN TWO WORLDS

ca. 1050 B.C.E.	Philistines defeat the Israelites
ca. 1000–961 B.C.E.	David, king of Israel
ca. 961–922 B.C.E.	Solomon, king of Israel
722 B.C.E.	Assyrians destroy kingdom of Israel
604–562 B.C.E.	Nebuchadnezzar II
586 B.C.E.	Nebuchadnezzar II conquers kingdom of Judah

SUMMARY

Before Civilization   Evolving from earlier humanlike creatures, *Homo sapiens sapiens* emerged around 40,000 years ago. Early *Homo sapiens sapiens* lived in small kin groups of 20 or 30 hunter-gatherers. During the upper or late Paleolithic era (ca. 35,000–10,000 B.C.E.), culture was increasingly determinant in human life. Around 10,000 B.C.E., two profound transformations began: sedentarization and the agricultural revolution. These twin revolutions brought with them dramatic developments in social and political organization, settlement patterns, religion, and the relationship between humans and nature.

Mesopotamia: Between the Two Rivers   The harsh conditions of Mesopotamia drove its inhabitants to create civilization. Early Mesopotamian civilization was city-oriented and dominated by religious, military, and administrative elites. Cities were centers of Mesopotamian religion. The power of Mesopotamian civilization was multiplied many times over by technological innovation, particularly the invention of writing. Sargon's Akkadian state was the first great multiethnic empire in the West, spreading Sumerian civilization as it expanded. The collapse of the Akkadian state made room for new powers to rise. Hammurabi followed in the tradition of Sargon and Shulgi, expanding the Babylonian state and creating a codified body of law.

The Gift of the Nile   Conditions in the Nile Valley helped create an extraordinarily stable civilization in Egypt. Historians divide Egyptian history into four periods of political centralization: pre- and early dynastic Egypt (ca. 3150–2770 B.C.E.), the Old Kingdom (ca. 2770–2200 B.C.E.), the Middle Kingdom (ca. 2050–1786 B.C.E.), and the New Kingdom (ca. 1560–1087 B.C.E.). Egyptian kings were seen as gods whose primary responsibility was the care of their people. The transition from the Old Kingdom to the Middle Kingdom was marked by increased power for elites at the expense of the king. Weakness in the Middle Kingdom allowed for domination by the Hyksos which, in turn, gave way to the New Kingdom, a period of expansion and empire building. Competition between the Egyptian and Hittite empires for regional dominance ended in a draw and the signing of a peace treaty.

Between Two Worlds   Hebrew society and culture were rooted in Mesopotamian traditions. The early Hebrews did not deny the existence of other gods, but believed that they had a special covenant with their god. Led by Moses, the founder of the Israelite people, the Israelites forged a new identity and faith out of their experience of the exodus from Egypt. The conquest of Canaan and pressure from regional rivals led to the establishment of the Kingdom of Israel. After King Solomon's death, the kingdom split into the kingdom of Israel and the kingdom of Judah. These two kingdoms quickly succumbed to the domination of more powerful neighbors. The kingdom of Judah was destroyed and its elites were sent into exile in Babylon. The experience of exile proved to be another transforming moment in the history of Judaism.

Nineveh and Babylon   The Assyrian state tied together the floodplain civilizations of Mesopotamia and Egypt. It differed dramatically from its predecessors in that it was an integrated state in which conquered regions were reorganized and remade along the model of the central government. Assyrian power rested on a professional military, the governing of conquered territories by Assyrian officials, the deportation and resettlement of conquered peoples, and the use of terror. The hatred the Assyrians inspired led to the creation of a Mede and Babylonian coalition that destroyed the Assyrian Empire. The fall of the Assyrians was followed by the rise of the New Babylonian Empire which, in turn, fell to a new power, the Persians.

QUESTIONS FOR REVIEW

1. What cultural developments allowed people to secure food, organize society, and overcome hostile environments before the rise of the first cities?
2. How did urbanization, the invention of writing, and political centralization first develop in the resource-poor area between the Tigris and Euphrates rivers?
3. How did the differing geographic conditions of Mesopotamia and Egypt shape the development of civilization in each?
4. What was the Hebrew people's covenant with Yahweh, and how did this help make a society quite different from the societies around it?
5. What political, religious, and military innovations made the Assyrian Empire more vast and powerful than any previously seen?

Early Greece, 2500–500 B.C.E.

Greece in the Bronze Age to 700 B.C.E.

Unlike the rich floodplains of Mesopotamia and Egypt, Greece is a stark world of mountains and sea. The rugged terrain of Greece, only 10 percent of which is flat, and the scores of islands that dot the Aegean and Ionian seas favor the development of small, self-contained agricultural societies. The Greek climate is uncertain, constantly threatening Greek farmers with failure. Rainfall varies enormously from year to year, and arid summers alternate with cool, wet winters. Wheat, barley, and beans were the staples of Greek life. Greek farmers struggled to produce the Mediterranean triad of grains, olives, and wine, which first began to dominate agriculture around 3000 B.C.E. Constant fluctuations in climate and weather from region to region helped to break down the geographical isolation by forcing insular communities to build contacts with a wider world in order to survive.

Islands of Peace

Since the late nineteenth century, archaeologists have discerned three fairly distinct late Bronze Age cultures—the Cycladic, the Minoan, and the Mycenaean—that flourished in the Mediterranean before the end of the twelfth century B.C.E.

The Cyclades. The first culture appeared on the Cyclades, the rugged islands strewn across the bottom of the Aegean from the Greek mainland to the coast of Asia Minor. As early as 2500 B.C.E., artisans in small settlements on the islands of Naxos and Melos developed a high level of metallurgical and artistic skill. Cycladic society was not concentrated into towns, nor, apparently, was it particularly warlike. Many of the largest Cycladic settlements were unfortified. Cycladic religion, to judge from fragments of large clay statues of female figures found in a temple on the island of Ceos, focused on female deities, perhaps fertility goddesses.

This early Bronze Age society slowly faded, but not before influencing its neighbors, especially Crete, the large Mediterranean island to the south. There, beginning around 2500 B.C.E., a sophisticated centralized civilization developed that was termed Minoan after the legendary King Minos of Crete.

Minoan Crete. Minoan civilization developed on the island of Crete. Crete's location between the civilizations of the Fertile Crescent, Egypt, and the barbarian worlds of the north and west made the island a natural point of exchange and amalgamation of cultures. Still, during the Golden Age of Crete, roughly between 2000 and 1550 B.C.E., the island developed its unique traditions.

Great palace complexes were constructed at Knossos, Phaistos, Hagia Triada, and elsewhere on the island. Palace bureaucrats, using a unique form of syllabic writing known as Linear A, controlled agricultural production and distribution as well as the work of skilled artisans in their surrounding areas.

Chronology

GREECE IN THE BRONZE AGE

ca. 2500 B.C.E.	Beginning of Minoan civilization in Crete
ca. 2000–1500 B.C.E.	Golden Age of Crete
ca. 1600 B.C.E.	Beginning of Mycenaean civilization in Greece
ca. 1450 B.C.E.	Cretan cities, except Knossos, destroyed
ca. 1375 B.C.E.	Knossos destroyed
ca. 1200–700 B.C.E.	Greek Dark Age
ca. 1200 B.C.E.	Mycenaean sites in Greece destroyed; Knossos destroyed again
ca. 1100–1000 B.C.E.	Writing disappears from Greece

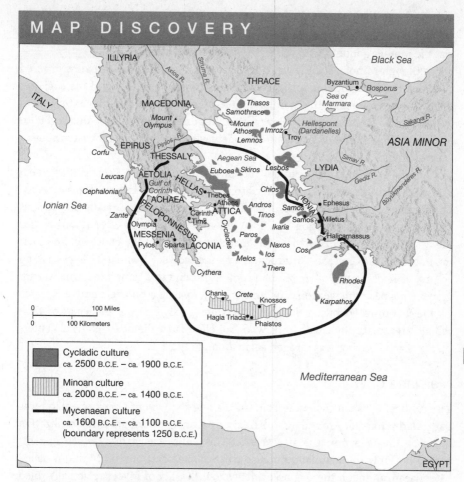

GREECE IN THE BRONZE AGE

What geographical characteristics distinguished Cycladic, Minoan, and Mycenaean civilizations? Given its location, what older civilizations might have exerted a major influence on the civilization of Crete?

Cretan Society and Religion. Like other ancient civilizations, Minoan Crete was strongly stratified. The vast peasantry paid a heavy tribute in olive oil and other produce. Tribute or taxes flowed to local and regional palaces and ultimately to Knossos, which stood at the pinnacle of a four-tiered network uniting the island. To some extent, the palace elites redistributed this wealth back down the system through their patterns of consumption.

Though the system may have been exploitive, it was not militaristic. None of the palaces or towns of Crete was fortified. Nor was the cult of the ruler particularly emphasized. A key to this unique social tone may be Cretan religion and, with it, the unusually high status of women. Although male gods received veneration, Cretans particularly worshipped female deities. Chief among the female deities was the mother goddess, who was the source of good and evil.

Although Minoan society was not clearly matriarchal, it nevertheless differed considerably from the floodplain civilizations of the Near East and the societies that were developing on the mainland. At least until the fourteenth century B.C.E., both men and women seem to have played important roles in religious and public life and together built a structured society without the need for vast armies or warrior kings.

Around 1450 B.C.E., a wave of destruction engulfed all of the Cretan cities except Knossos, which was finally annihilated around 1375 B.C.E. The causes of this catastrophe continue to inspire historical debate. Some argue that a natural disaster such as an earthquake or the eruption of a powerful volcano on Thera was responsible for the destruction. More likely, given the martial traditions of the continent and their total absence on Crete, the destruction was the work of mainland Greeks taking control of Knossos and other Minoan centers. Around this same time, true warrior graves equipped with weapons and armor begin to appear on Crete and at Knossos for the first time. Following this violent conquest, only Knossos and Phaistos were rebuilt, presumably by Greek lords who had eliminated the other political centers on the island. Knossos was ravaged again around 1200 B.C.E.

Mainland of War

The contrast between the vulnerable islands and the violent Greek mainland was particularly marked. Around 1600 B.C.E., a new and powerful warrior civilization arose on the Peloponnesus at Mycenae. This entire civilization, which encompassed not only the mainland but also parts of the coast of Asia Minor, is called **Mycenaean**, although there is no evidence that the city of Mycenae actually ruled all of Greece.

The Mycenaeans quickly adopted artisanal and architectural techniques from neighboring cultures, especially from the Hittites and from Crete, and incorporated these techniques into a distinctive tradition of their own. Unlike the open Cretan palaces and towns, Mycenaean palaces were strongly walled fortresses. From these palaces, Mycenaean kings and their staffs controlled the collection of taxes and tribute as well as the production of bronze and woolen cloth and governed maritime trade. Palace administrators adopted the Linear A script of Crete, transforming it to write their own language, a Greek dialect, in a writing known as **Linear B**, which appears to have been used almost exclusively for record keeping in palaces.

The Dark Age

Mycenaean domination did not last for long. Around 1200 B.C.E., many of the mainland and island fortresses and cities were sacked and totally destroyed. In some areas, such as Pylos, the population fell to roughly 10 percent of what it had

Female divinity from Knossos, ca. 1600 B.C.E. This extraordinary statuette, which has recently been judged by some scholars as a modern fake or at least a composite of modern and ancient parts, draws on traditions that link snakes as symbols of the underworld and sources of wisdom, as well as birds of prey such as that balanced on the head of this divinity. The place of such divinities in Minoan civilization, if it is indeed from Knossos, is uncertain.

been previously. Centralized government, literacy, urban life—civilization itself—disappeared from Greece for over 400 years.

No single invasion or natural disaster destroyed Mycenaean Greece. It self-destructed. Its disintegration was part of the widespread crisis affecting the eastern Mediterranean in the twelfth century B.C.E. The pyramid of Mycenaean lordship, built by small military elites commanding maritime commercial networks, was always threatened with collapse. Overpopulation, the fragility of the agrarian base, the risks of overspecialization in cash crops such as grain in Messenia and sheep raising in Crete, and rivalry among states—all made Mycenaean culture vulnerable. The disintegration of the Hittite Empire and the near-collapse of the Egyptian Empire disrupted Mediterranean commerce, exacerbating hostilities among Greek states.

As internal warfare raged, the delicate structures of elite lordship disappeared in the mutual sackings and destructions of the palace fortresses. With the collapse of the administrative and political system on which Mycenaean civilization was built, the tiny elite that had ruled it vanished as well. From roughly

1200 until 800 B.C.E., the Aegean world entered what is generally termed the Dark Age, a confused period about which little is known, during which Greece returned to a more primitive level of culture and society.

A New Material Culture. In the wake of the Mycenaean collapse, bands of northerners moved slowly into the Peloponnesus while other Greeks migrated out from the mainland to the islands and the coast of Asia Minor. As these tribal groups merged with the indigenous populations, they gave certain regions distinctive dialectic and cultural characteristics. Thus, the Dorians settled in much of the Peloponnesus, Crete, and southwest Asia Minor. Ionians made Attica, Euboea, and the Aegean islands their home; a mixed group called Aeolians began to migrate to central and northwest Asia Minor. As a result, from the eleventh century B.C.E., both shores of the Aegean became part of a Greek-speaking world. Still later, Greeks established colonies in what is today southern Ukraine, Italy, North Africa, Spain, and France. Throughout its history, Greece was less a geographical than a cultural designation.

Everywhere in this world, between roughly 1100 and 1000 B.C.E., architecture and urban traditions declined, and writing disappeared along with the elites for whose exclusive benefit these achievements had served. The Greece of this Dark Age was much poorer, more rural, and more simply organized. It was also a society of ironworkers. Iron began to replace bronze as the most common metal for ornaments, tools, and weapons. At first this was a simple necessity. The collapse of long-distance trade deprived Greeks of access to tin and copper, the essential ingredients of bronze. Gradually, however, the quality of iron tools and weapons began to improve as smiths learned to work hot iron into a primitive steel.

What little is known of this period must be gleaned from archaeology and from the *Iliad* and the *Odyssey*, Homer's two great epic poems that were written down around 750 B.C.E., near the end of the Dark Age. The archaeological record is bleak. Pictorial representation of humans and animals almost disappears. Luxury goods and most imports are gone from tombs. Pottery made at the beginning of the Dark Age shows little innovation, crudely imitating forms of Mycenaean production.

Gradually, beginning in the eleventh century B.C.E., things began to change a bit. New geometric forms of decoration began to appear on pottery. New types of iron pins, weapons, and decorations appeared that owed little or nothing to the Mycenaean tradition. Cultural changes accompanied these material changes. Around the middle of the eleventh century B.C.E., Greeks in some locations stopped burying their dead and began to practice cremation. Whatever the meaning of these changes, they signaled something new on the shores of the Aegean.

The Evidence of Homer. The two epic poems—the *Iliad* and the *Odyssey*—hint at this something new. Traditionally ascribed to Homer, these epics were actually the work of oral bards or performers who composed as they chanted. Although the Homeric poems explicitly harken back to the Mycenaean Age, much of the description of life, society, and culture actually reflects Dark Age

A golden funeral mask (ca.1500 B.C.E.) found in the royal tombs of Mycenae. The mask is one of four masks excavated along with engraved swords and daggers as well as other weapons and, silver and gold drinking cups and horns, at Mycenae by Heinrich Schliemann in the nineteenth century. The artistry shows the influence of Minoan art in Mycenae. Although these objects are at least three centuries older than the period to which the Trojan War is attributed, Schliemann sought to publicize his work by claiming that this was likeness of Agamemnon, the king of Mycenae in the Homeric epics.

conditions. Thus Homer's heroes were petty kings, chieftains, and nobles, whose positions rested on their wealth, measured in land and flocks, on personal prowess, on networks of kin and allies, and on military followings. The Homeric hero Odysseus is typical of these Dark Age chieftains. In the *Iliad* and the *Odyssey* he is king of Ithaca, a small island on the west coast of Greece. He retained command of his men only as long as he could lead them to victory in the raids against their neighbors.

When present, the king was judge, gift giver, lawgiver, and commander. Absent, no legal or governmental institutions preserved his authority. Instead, the nobility, lesser warriors who were constantly at odds with the king, sought to take his place. In the *Odyssey*, only their mutual rivalry saves Odysseus's wife, Penelope, from being forced to marry one of these haughty aristocrats who were eager to replace the king. Odysseus's son Telemachus summoned the assembly of the people to listen to his complaints against the noble suitors of his mother. Thus the people were not entirely excluded from public life; but this does not mean that they were particularly effective. The assembly listened to both sides and did nothing. Still, a time was coming when changes in society would give hitherto unimagined power to the silent farmers and herdsmen of the Dark Age.

From the Bronze Age civilizations, speakers of Greek had inherited distant memories of an original, highly organized urban civilization grafted onto the rural, aristocratic warrior society of the Dark Ages. Most important, this common dimly recollected past gave all Greek-speaking inhabitants of the Mediterranean world common myths, values, and identity.

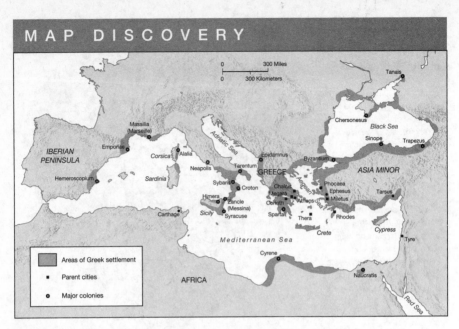

MAP DISCOVERY

GREEK CITIES AND COLONIES OF THE ARCHAIC AGE

Where are the areas of Greek settlement and major colonies in the Archaic Age? What does the location of Greek settlements tell us about the relationship between Greek culture and geography? What regions of Europe and the Near East lacked Greek colonies? Why?

Archaic Greece, 700–500 B.C.E.

Between roughly 800 and 500 B.C.E., extraordinary changes took place in the Greek world. The descendants of the farmers and herdsmen of Homer's Dark Age brought about a revolution in political organization, artistic traditions, intellectual values, and social structures. In a burst of creativity forged in conflict and competition, they invented politics, abstract thought, and the individual. Greeks of the Archaic Age (ca. 700–500 B.C.E.) set the agenda for the rest of Western history.

The first sign of radical change in Greece was a major increase in population in the eighth century B.C.E. The consequences were enormous. First, population increase meant more villages and towns, greater communication among them, and thus the more rapid circulation of ideas and skills. Second, the rising population placed impossible demands on the agricultural system of much of Greece. Third, it led to greater division of labor and, with an increasingly diverse population, to fundamental changes in political systems. The old structure of loosely organized tribes and chieftains became inadequate to deal with the more complex nature of the new society.

The multiplicity of political and social forms developing in the Archaic Age set the framework within which the first flowering of Greek culture developed.

Economic and political transformations laid the basis for intellectual advance by creating a broad class with the prosperity to enjoy sufficient leisure for thought and creative activity. Finally, maritime relations brought people and ideas from around the Greek world together, cross-fertilizing artists and intellectuals in a way never before seen in the West.

Ethnos and Polis

In general, two forms of political organization developed in response to the population explosion of the eighth century B.C.E. On the mainland and in much of the western Peloponnesus, people continued to live in large territorial units called *ethne* (sing. *ethnos*). In each **ethnos**, people lived in villages and small towns scattered across a wide region. Common customs and a common religion focusing on a central religious sanctuary united them. The ethnos was governed by an elite, or **oligarchy** (meaning "rule by the few"), made up of major landowners who met from time to time in one or another town within the region. This form of government, which had its roots in the Dark Ages, continued to exist throughout the classical period.

A much more innovative form of political organization, which developed on the shores of the Aegean and on the islands, was the **polis** (pl. *poleis*), or city-state. Initially, *polis* meant simply "citadel." Villages clustered around these fortifications, which were both protective structures and cult centers for specific deities. These high, fortified sites—*acropolis* means "high citadel"—were sacred to specific gods. In addition to protection, the polis offered a marketplace, or *agora*, where farmers and artisans could trade and conduct business. The rapid population growth of the eighth century B.C.E. led to the fusion of these villages and the formation of real towns. Each town was independent, each was ruled by a monarchy or an oligarchy, and each controlled the surrounding region, the inhabitants of which were on an equal footing with the townspeople. At times of political or military crisis, the rulers might summon an assembly of the free males of the community to the agora to participate in or to witness the decision-making process. In the following centuries these city-states became the center for that most dramatic Greek experiment in government: democracy.

Technology of Writing and Warfare

The general model of the polis may have been borrowed from the eastern Mediterranean Phoenicians, the merchant society that was responsible for much of the contact Greeks of the eighth century B.C.E. had with the surrounding world. The Phoenicians were certainly the source of an equally important innovation that appeared in Greece at the same time: the reintroduction of writing. Sometime in the eighth century B.C.E., Greeks adopted the Phoenician writing system. But unlike the abandoned Mycenaean script, the purpose of the new writing system was not primarily central administrative record keeping. From the start, this writing system was intended for private, personal use and was available to virtually anyone.

Within the polis, political power was not the monopoly of the aristocracy. The gradual expansion of the politically active population resulted largely from the demands of warfare. In the Dark Age, warfare had been dominated by heavily armed, mounted aristocrats who engaged their equals in single combat. In the Archaic Age, such individual combat between aristocratic warriors gave way to battles that were decided by the use of well-disciplined ranks of infantrymen called *phalange* (sing. **phalanx**). Although few Greeks could afford costly weapons, armor, and horses, between 25 and 40 percent of the landowners could provide the shields, lances, and bronze armor needed by the infantrymen, or **hoplites**.

The democratization of war led gradually to the democratization of political life. Those who brought victory in the phalanx were unwilling to accept total domination by the aristocracy in the agora. The rapid growth of the urban population, the increasing impoverishment of the rural peasantry, and the rise of a new class of wealthy merchant commoners were all challenges that traditional forms of government failed to meet. Everywhere, traditional aristocratic rule was being undermined, and cities searched for ways to resolve this social conflict. No one solution emerged, and one of the outstanding achievements of archaic Greece was the almost limitless variety of political forms elaborated in its city-states.

Colonists and Tyrants

Colonization and tyranny were two intertwined results of the political and social turmoil of the seventh century B.C.E. Population growth, changes in economy, and opposition to aristocratic power led Greeks to seek change externally through emigration and internally through political restructuring.

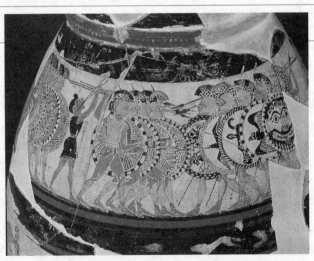

A Corinthian vase showing hoplites marching into battle.

Late in the eleventh century B.C.E., Greeks had begun to migrate to new homes on the islands and along the coast of Asia Minor, in search of commercial advantages or a better life.

Beginning around 750 B.C.E., a new form of colonization began in the western Mediterranean. The impetus for this expansion was not primarily trade, but rather the need to reduce population pressure at home. The colonists were not always volunteers. At Thera, for example, young men were chosen by lot to colonize Cyrene. The penalty for refusing to participate was death and confiscation of property. Usually, colonists were only single males, the most volatile portion of the community. Colonies were thus a safety valve to release the pressures of population growth and political friction. Although colonies remained attached culturally to their mother cities, they were politically independent. The men who settled them were warriors as well as farmers or traders and carved out their new cities at the expense of the local population.

Colonization relieved some of the population pressure on Greek communities, but it did not solve the problem of political conflict. As opposition to entrenched aristocracies grew, new leaders opposed to aristocratic rule seized power. These rulers were known as **tyrants**, a term that originally meant the same as king. In the course of the later sixth century B.C.E., "tyrant" came to designate those who had achieved supreme power without benefit of official position. Often, this rise to power came through popularity with hoplite armies.

However, the term tyrant did not carry the negative connotation associated with it today. Tyrants weakened the power of entrenched aristocratic groups, promoted the prosperity of their supporters by protecting farmers and encouraging trade, undertook public works projects, founded colonies, and entered into marriage alliances with rulers of other cities, which provided some external peace. Although they stood outside the traditional organs of government, tyrants were frequently content to govern through them, leaving magistracies and offices intact but ensuring that through elections these offices were filled with the tyrant's supporters. Thus at Corinth, Mytilene, Athens, and elsewhere, tyrants preserved and even strengthened constitutional structures as a hedge against the return to power of aristocratic factions.

The great weakness of tyrannies was that they depended for their success on the individual qualities of the ruler. Tyrants tended to pass their powers on to their sons, and as tyrannies became hereditary, cities came to resent incompetent or excessively cruel successors. As popular tyranny gave way to harsh and arbitrary rule, opposition brought on civil war and the deposition or abdication of the tyrant. Gradually, "tyranny" acquired the meaning it bears today, and new forms of government emerged.

Gender and Power

Military, political, and cultural life in the city-states became more democratic, but this democratization did not extend to women. Greek attitudes toward gender roles and sexuality were rigid. Except in a few cities and in certain religious cults, women played no public role in the life of the community. They remained firmly under male control throughout their lives, passing from the authority of their fathers to that of their husbands. For the most part, friendship existed only between members of the same sex, and this friendship was often intensely sexual. Bisexuality was the norm in Greek society, although neither Greek homosexuality nor heterosexuality was the same as in modern society. Rather, they coexisted and formed parts of a sexuality of domination by those considered superior in age, rank, or sex over others. Mature men took young boys as their lovers, helped to educate them, and inspired them by word and deed to grow into ideal warriors and citizens.

Those women who were in public life were mostly slaves, frequently prostitutes. Many female slaves were acquired by collecting and raising female infants who had been abandoned. Greek society did not condemn or even question abandonment of infants, prostitution, or sexual exploitation of women and slave boys. These practices formed part of the complex and varied social systems of the developing city-states.

Gods and Mortals

Greeks and their gods enjoyed an ambivalent, almost irreverent relationship. On the one hand, Greeks made regular offerings to the gods, pleaded with them for help, and gave them thanks for assistance. On the other, the gods were thoroughly human, sharing in an exaggerated manner not only human strengths and virtues but also weaknesses and vices.

Greeks offered sacrifices to the gods on altars, which were raised everywhere—in homes, in fields, in sacred groves. No group had the sort of monopoly on the cult of the gods that Mesopotamian and Egyptian priests enjoyed. Unlike the temples of other societies, Greek temples were houses of the gods, not centers of ritual. These temples reflected the wealth and patriotism of the city. They stood as monuments to the human community rather than to the divine.

On special occasions, festivals were celebrated at sanctuaries, honoring the gods of the city with processions, athletic contests, and feasts. Some of these celebrations drew participants from all of the Greek world. The two greatest pan-Hellenic (meaning "all Greek," from *Hellas*, the Greek word for Greece) sanctuaries were Olympia and Delphi. Because both were remote from centers of political power, they were insulated from interstate rivalry and provided neutral ground on which hostile neighbors could meet in peace.

Beginning in 776 B.C.E., every four years, wars and conflicts were temporarily suspended while athletes from the whole Greek world met at Olympia to participate in contests in honor of Zeus. Olympic victors were treated as national heroes.

Delphi, the site of the shrine of Apollo, god of music, archery, medicine, and prophecy, was the second pan-Hellenic cult center. Delphi's fame lay in its oracle, or spokeswoman, for the god Apollo. From the eighth century B.C.E., before undertaking any important decision such as establishing a colony, beginning a war, or even contracting a marriage, individuals and representatives of distant cities traveled to Delphi to ask Apollo's advice or to seek purification from the guilt attached to shedding the blood of others and reconciliation with their fellow citizens.

Though gods were petitioned, placated, and pampered, they were not privileged or protected. Unlike the awe-inspiring gods of the Mesopotamians and Egyptians, the traditional Greek gods, inherited from the Dark Age, were represented in ways that showed them as all too human, vicious, and frequently ridiculous. The Greek gods were immortal, superhuman in strength, and able to interfere in human affairs. But in all things they reflected the values and weaknesses of the Greek mortals, who could bargain with them, placate them, and even trick them.

Religious cults were not under the exclusive control of any priesthood or political group. Therefore there were no official versions of stories of gods and goddesses. No one group or sacred site enjoyed a monopoly on access to the gods. Like literacy and government, the gods belonged to all.

Myth and Reason

The glue holding together the individual and frequently hostile Greek poleis and the ethne scattered throughout the Mediterranean was their common stock of myths. Stories of gods and heroes, told and retold, were fashioned into *mythoi* (myths, literally, "formulated speech"), which explained and described the world both as it was and as it should be. Myths were told about every city, shrine, river, mountain, and island. Myths explained the origins of cities, festivals, the world itself. Such stories were more than simply fanciful explanations of how things came to be. Myths sanctioned and supported the authority of social, political, and religious traditions and provided a means of reasoning about the world.

Chronology

ARCHAIC GREECE

ca. 780–720 B.C.E.	Population increase in Greece
776 B.C.E.	First Olympic Games held
ca. 750–700 B.C.E.	Greeks develop writing system based on Phoenician model; Greeks begin colonizing western Mediterranean
ca. 700–500 B.C.E.	Archaic Age of Greece
ca. 700 B.C.E.	First stone temples appear in Greece
ca. 650 B.C.E.	Cypselus breaks rule of Bacchiads in Corinth; rules city as tyrant
594 B.C.E.	Solon elected chief archon of Athens; institutes social and political reforms
586 B.C.E.	Death of Periander ends tyrants' rule in Corinth
499 B.C.E.	Ionian cities revolt

Art and the Individual

Archaic Greeks borrowed from everywhere and transformed all that they borrowed. Just as they adopted and adapted the Phoenician alphabet and Mesopotamian science, they took Near Eastern and Egyptian painting and sculpture and made them their own. During the Dark Age, the Mycenaean traditions of art had entirely disappeared. Pottery showed only geometric decorations; sculpture was unknown. Gradually, from the ninth century B.C.E., stylized human and animal figures, lions, griffins, and other strange beasts began to appear within the tightly composed geometric patterns. By the eighth century B.C.E., such exotic subjects had given way to the Greek passion for human images taken from their own myths and legends. As the popularity of these mythic and heroic scenes increased, so too did the artists' technical competence. Greek artists competed with one another to overcome technical problems of perspective and foreshortening. From the sixth century B.C.E., many of the finest examples were signed. Such masterpieces celebrated not only the heroes of the past but also the artist as individual and as the interpreter of culture no less original than the poet.

Greek sculpture underwent a similar dramatic development. The earliest and most common subject of archaic sculpture was the standing male nude, or **kouros** figure, which was in wide demand as a grave monument, dedication to a

The Calf-Bearer was commissioned for the temple of Athena ca. 570 B.C.E., which was destroyed by the Persians in 480 B.C.E. when they captured Athens and burned the Acropolis. This archaic statue clearly shows its affinity to the archaic kouros, particularly in the way that the figure steps forward in a tradition that has its origins in Egyptian sculpture. However here one sees a slight adjustment of the weight to the left leg, suggesting genuine movement, as well as the position of the arms and the animal's legs, all suggesting a move toward a more naturalistic depiction of the human and animal forms.

god, or even a cult statue of male deity. In Egypt, Greeks of the seventh century B.C.E. had seen colossal statues and had learned to work stone. The rigidly formulaic position of the kouros followed Egyptian tradition and left little room for creativity. Thus sculptors sought to give their statues originality and individuality, not as representations of individuals, but as the creations of the individual sculptor. To this end, they experimented with increasingly natural molding of limbs and body and began signing their works. Thus, as in vase painting, Greek sculpture reflected the importance of the individual, not in its subject matter, but in its creator.

The real challenges in sculpture came in the portrayal of narrative in decorations on monuments, primarily temples. Unlike kouroi, which were usually private commissions intended to adorn the tombs of aristocrats, these public buildings were constructed as expressions of civic pride and were accessible to everyone. Here the creativity and dynamism of Greek cities could be paralleled in stone. Figures such as the Calf-Bearer (ca. 590 B.C.E.) from the Athenian acropolis are daring in the complexity of composition and the delicacy of execution. (See photo on p. 44.) These are statues that tell stories. In the Calf-Bearer, a master farmer carries a calf to be sacrificed to Athena. The two gentle heads and the cross formed by the farmer's hands and the calf's legs are individual traits without precedent in ancient art. Although formally intended for religious purposes, these figures serve not only the gods and the aristocratic elite, but the whole community.

A Tale of Three Cities

The political, social, and cultural transformations that occurred in the Archaic Age took different forms across the Greek world. No community or city-state was typical of Greece. The best way to understand the diversity of Archaic Greece is to examine three very different cities that by the end of the sixth century B.C.E. had become leading centers of Greek civilization. Corinth, Sparta, and Athens present something of the spectrum of political, cultural, and social models of the Hellenic world.

Wealthy Corinth

Corinth owed its prosperity to its privileged site, dominating both a rich coastal plain and the narrow isthmus connecting the Peloponnesus to the mainland. In the eighth century B.C.E., as Greeks turned their attention to the west, Corinthians led the way. Corinthian trade led to colonization, and settlers from Corinth founded Syracuse and other cities in Sicily and Italy, which served as markets for Corinthian products. Even more important to Corinthian prosperity was its role in the transport of other cities' products from east to west. By carrying goods across the isthmus and loading them onto other ships, merchants could avoid the long, dangerous passage around the Peloponnesus.

Social Tensions. The precise details of early Corinthian government are uncertain. Still, it appears that in Corinth, as in many other cities, a tyranny replaced a ruling clan, and in time this tyranny ended with an oligarchic government. Until the middle of the seventh century B.C.E., Corinth and its wealth were ruled in typical Dark Age fashion by an aristocratic clan known as the Bacchiads. Corinth began its rise under this aristocratic rule, and individual Bacchiads led colonizing expeditions to Italy and Sicily. However, the increasing pressures of population growth, rapidly expanding wealth, and dramatic changes in the economy produced social tensions that the traditional aristocratic rulers were unable to handle. As in cities throughout the Greek world, these tensions led to the creation of a new order.

The early history of Corinth is obscure, but apparently around 650 B.C.E. a revolution led by a dissident Bacchiad named Cypselus (ca. 657–627 B.C.E.) and supported by non-Bacchiad aristocrats and other Corinthians broke the Bacchiads' grip on the city. The revolution led to the establishment of Cypselus as tyrant. Cypselus and his son Periander (ca. 627–586 B.C.E.) seem to have been generally popular with most Corinthians.

Corinth Under Its Tyrants. In Corinth, as in many other cities, the tyrants restructured taxes, relying primarily on customs duties, which were less of a burden on the peasantry. Around 600 B.C.E., Periander began construction of a causeway across the isthmus on which ships could be hauled from the Aegean to the western Mediterranean. This causeway eventually became a major source of Corinth's wealth. Periander attacked conspicuous consumption on the part of the aristocracy. He introduced laws against idleness and put thousands of Corinthians to work in extensive building programs. He erected temples and sent colonists to Italy. Under his leadership, the Corinthian fleet developed into the most powerful naval force in the Adriatic and Aegean seas. Under its tyrants, Corinth led the Greek world in the production of black figure pottery, which spread throughout the Mediterranean.

The tyrants also laid the foundation for broader political participation. Cypselus divided the population into eight tribes, based not on traditional ethnic divisions, but on arbitrary groupings by region. All of Corinth was divided into three large regions. The population of each region was distributed among each of the eight tribes. This assignment prevented the emergence of political factions based on regional disputes. Ten representatives from each tribe formed a council of 80 men. Under the tyrants this council was largely advisory and provided a connection between the autocratic rulers and the citizens.

In Corinth, as elsewhere, the strength or weakness of tyranny rested on the abilities and personality of individual tyrants. Cypselus had been a beloved liberator. His son Periander, in spite of his accomplishments, was remembered for his cruelty and violence. Shortly after Periander's death in 586 B.C.E., a revolt killed his successor, and tyranny in Corinth ended.

Oligarchy. The new government continued the tribal and council system established by Cypselus. From the sixth century B.C.E. until its conquest by Macedonia in 338 B.C.E., Corinth was ruled by an oligarchy. Although an assembly of the *demos,* or adult males, met occasionally, actual government was in the hands of eight deliberators, or *probouloi,* and nine other men from each tribe who together formed the council of eighty. The oligarchs who made up the council avoided the kind of exclusive and arbitrary tendencies that had destroyed both the Bacchiads and the tyrants. They were remarkably successful in maintaining popular support among the citizens and provided a reliable and effective government.

Martial Sparta

At the beginning of the eighth century B.C.E., the Peloponnesus around Sparta and Laconia faced circumstances similar to those of Corinth and other Greek communities. Population growth, increasing disparity between rich and poor, and an expanding economy created powerful tensions. The Spartan solution was a rigid two-tiered social structure. By the end of the Archaic Age, a small, homogeneous class of warriors called *homoioi* ("those alike"), or equals, ruled a vast population of state serfs, or *helots.* The two classes lived in mutual fear and mistrust. Spartans controlled the helots through terror and ritual murder. The helots in turn were in the philosopher Aristotle's words, "an enemy constantly waiting for the disasters of the Spartans."

Messenia. War was the center of Spartan life, and war lay at the origin of the Spartans' extraordinary social and political organization. In the eighth century B.C.E., the Spartans conquered the fertile region of Messenia and compelled the vanquished Messenians to turn over one-half of their harvests. The spoils were not divided equally but went to increase the wealth of the aristocracy, thus creating resentment among the less privileged. Early in the seventh century B.C.E., the Spartans attempted a similar campaign to take the plain of Thyreatis from the city of Argos. This time they were not so fortunate; they were defeated, and resentment of the ordinary warriors toward their aristocratic leaders flared into open conflict. The Messenians seized on this time as a moment to revolt, and for a time, Sparta was forced to fight at home and abroad for its very existence. In many cities, such crises gave rise to tyrants. In Sparta, the crisis led to radical political and social reforms that transformed the polis into a unique military system.

Reforms of Lycurgus. The Spartans attributed these reforms to the legendary lawgiver Lycurgus (seventh century B.C.E.). Whether or not Lycurgus ever existed and was responsible for all of the reforms, they saved the city and ended its internal tensions at the expense of abandoning the mainstream of Greek development. Traditionally, Greeks had placed personal honor above communal concerns. During the crisis of the second Messenian war, Spartans of all social ranks were urged to look not to individual interest but to **eunomia**, good order and obedience to the laws, which alone could unite Spartans and bring victory. United, the Spartans crushed the Messenians. In return for obedience, poor citizens received equality before the law and benefited from a land distribution that relieved their poverty. Conquered land, especially that in Messenia, was divided and distributed to Spartan warriors. However, the Spartan warriors were not expected to work the land themselves. Instead, the state reduced the defeated Messenians to the status of helots and assigned them to individual Spartans. While this system did not erase all economic inequalities among the Spartans (aristocrats continued to hold more land than others), it did decrease some of the disparity. It also provided a minimum source of wealth for all Spartan citizens and allowed them to devote themselves to full-time military service.

This land reform was coupled with a political reform that incorporated elements of monarchy, oligarchy, and democracy. The state was governed by two hereditary kings, probably representing different groups that had formed the Spartan polis earlier, and a council of elders, the *gerousia*. In peacetime, the authority of the two royal families was limited to familial and religious affairs. In war, they commanded the army and held the power of life and death.

In theory at least, the central institution of Spartan government was the gerousia, which was composed of 30 men at least 60 years of age and included the two kings. The gerousia directed all political activity, especially foreign affairs, and served as high court. Members were elected for life by the assembly, or *apella*, which was composed of all equals over the age of 30 and approved decisions of the gerousia. However, this approval, made by acclamation, could easily be manipulated, as could the course of debate within the gerousia itself. Wealth, cunning, and patronage were more important than its formal structures in the direction of the Spartan state.

Actual administration was in the hands of five magistrates, termed *ephors*, whose powers were extremely broad. They presided over joint sessions of the gerousia and apella. They held supreme authority over the kings during wartime, acted as judges for noncitizens, and controlled the *krypteia*, or secret police. The krypteia were a band of youths who practiced state terrorism as part of their rite of passage to the status of equal. On the orders of the ephors, the krypteia assassinated, intrigued, and arrested powerful people and terrorized helots. Service in this corps was considered a necessary part of a youth's education.

Social Control. The key to the success of Sparta's political reform was an even more radical social reform that placed everyone under the direct supervision and service of the state from birth until death. Although admiring aristocratic visitors often exaggerated their accounts of Spartan life, the main outlines are clear enough.

Eunomia was the sole guiding principle, and service to the state came before family, social class, and every other duty or occupation.

Spartan equals were made, not born. True, only a man born of free Spartan parents could hope to become an equal, but birth alone was no guarantee of admission to this select body, or even of the right to live. Public officials examined infants and decided whether they were sufficiently strong to be allowed to live or should be exposed on a hillside to die. From birth until age seven, a boy lived with his mother; he then entered the state education system, or *agoge*, living in barracks with his contemporaries and enduring 13 years of rigorous military training. At age 12, training with swords and spears became more intense, as did the rigors of the lifestyle.

Much of the actual education of the youths was entrusted to older, accomplished warriors, who selected boys as their homosexual lovers. The lover served as tutor and role model, and in time the two became a fighting team. At age 20, Spartan youths were enrolled in the krypteia. Each was sent out into the countryside with nothing but a cloak and a knife, forbidden to return until he had killed a helot.

If a youth survived the rigors of his training until age 30, he could at last be incorporated into the rank of equals, provided that he could pass the last obstacle. He had to be able to furnish a sufficient amount of food from his own lands for the communal dining group to which he would be assigned. This food might come from inherited property or, if he had proved himself an outstanding warrior, from the state. Those who passed this final qualification became full members of the assembly, but they continued to live with the other warriors. Men could marry at age 20, but family life in the usual sense was nonexistent. A man could not live with his wife until age 30 because he was bound to the barracks.

Although their training was not as rigorous as that of males, Spartan women were given an education and allowed a sphere of activity unknown elsewhere in Greece. Girls, like boys, were trained in athletic competition and, like boys, competed naked in wrestling, footraces, and spear throwing. This training was based not on a belief in the equality of the sexes but simply on the desire to improve the physical stamina and childbearing abilities of Spartan women. Women were able to own land and to participate widely in business and agricultural affairs; since men were entirely involved in military pursuits, women were expected to look after economic and household affairs.

Few Lacedaemonians (as Spartans were also called) ever became equals. Not only were there far more helots than Spartans, but many free citizens of their local communities in the region, termed *perioikoi*, or peripherals, were not allowed into the agoge. Others were unable to endure the harsh life, and still others lacked the property qualifications to supply their share of the communal meals. For all the trappings of egalitarianism, equality in Sparta was the privilege of a tiny minority.

The total dedication to military life was reinforced by a deliberate rejection of other activities. From the time of the second Messenian war, Sparta withdrew from the mainstream of Greek civilization. Equals could not engage in crafts, trade, or any other forms of economic activity. Because Sparta banned silver and gold coinage, it could not participate in the growing commercial network of the Greek world. The role of Sparta in the economic, architectural, and cultural life of Greece was negligible after the seventh century B.C.E. Militarily, Sparta cast a long shadow across the Peloponnesus and beyond, but the number of equals was always too small to allow Sparta both to create a vast empire and to maintain control over the helots at home. Instead, Sparta created a network of alliances and nonaggression pacts with oligarchic neighbors. In time, this network came to be known as the Peloponnesian League.

Democratic Athens

Athens did not enjoy the advantages of a strategic site such as that of Corinth, nor was it surrounded by rich plains like Sparta. However, what Homer called the "goodly citadel of Athens" was one of the few Mycenaean cities to have escaped destruction at the start of the Dark Age. Gradually, Athens united the whole surrounding region of Attica into a single polis, by far the largest in the Greek world. Well into the seventh century B.C.E., Athens followed the general pattern of the polis seen in Corinth and Sparta. Like other Dark Age communities, Athens was ruled by aristocratic clans, particularly the Alcmaeonids. Only the members of these clans could participate in the *areopagus*, or council, which they entered after serving a year as one of the nine *archons*, or magistrates, elected yearly. Until the seventh century B.C.E., Athens escaped the social pressures brought on by population growth and economic prosperity that led to civil strife, colonialism, and tyranny elsewhere. This was due largely to its relative abundance of arable land and its commercial prosperity based on the export of grain.

Social Tensions. By the late seventh century B.C.E., however, Athens began to suffer from the same class conflict that had shaken other cities. Sometime around 630 B.C.E., an aristocrat named Cylon attempted to seize power as tyrant. His attempt failed, but when he was murdered by one of the Alcmaeonids, popular revulsion drove the Alcmaeonids from the city. A decade of strife ensued as aristocratic clans, wealthy merchants, and farmers fought for control of the city. Violence between groups and families threatened to tear the community apart.

Reforms of Solon. In 621 B.C.E., the Athenians granted a judge, Draco, extraordinary powers to revise and systematize traditional laws concerning vengeance and homicide. His restructuring of procedures for limiting vengeance and preventing bloodshed was harsh enough to add the term "draconian" to Western legal vocabulary. Still, these measures did nothing to solve the central problems of political control. Finally, in 594 B.C.E., an Athenian merchant who was respected by both aristocrats and commoners was elected chief archon and charged with reforming the city's government. Solon (ca. 630–ca. 560 B.C.E.) based his reform on the ideal of eunomia, as had the Spartans, but he followed a very different path to secure good order.

In Sparta, Lycurgus had begun with a radical redistribution of land. In Athens, Solon began with the less extreme measure of eliminating debt bondage. Athenians who had been forced into slavery or into sharecropping because of their debts were restored to freedom. A law forbade mortgaging free men and women as security for debts. Athenians might be poor, but they would be free. This free peasantry formed the basis of Athenian society throughout its history.

Solon also reorganized the rest of the social hierarchy and broke the aristocracy's exclusive control of the areopagus by dividing the society into four classes based on wealth rather than birth and opening the archonship to the top two classes. He further weakened the areopagus by establishing a council of 400 members drawn from all four classes, to which citizens could appeal decisions of the magistrates.

Solon's efforts to resolve Athens's social tensions did not entirely succeed. His laws were more humane than those of Draco, but Solon himself did not consider his new constitution perfect, only practical. Resistance from the still powerful aristocracy prompted some Athenians to urge Solon to assume the powers of a tyrant to force through his reforms. He refused, but after his death, Peisistratus (d. 527 B.C.E.), an aristocrat who was strongly supported by the peasants against his own class, hired a mercenary force to seize control of the city. After two abortive attempts, Peisistratus ruled as tyrant from 545 B.C.E. until his death.

Athenian Tyranny. Peisistratus and later his son Hippias (d. 490 B.C.E.), who succeeded him until 510 B.C.E., ruled through Solon's constitution but took care to ensure that the archons who were elected each year were their agents. Thus they strengthened the constitution even while they further weakened the aristocracy.

Peisistratus and Hippias drew their support from the *demos,* or people at large, rather than from an aristocratic faction. They claimed divine justification for their rule and made a great show of devotion to the Athenian gods. Peisistratus promoted annual festivals and, in so doing, began the great tradition of Athenian literature. The tyrants also directed a series of popular nationalistic public works programs that beautified the city, increased national pride, and provided work for the poor. They rebuilt the temple of Athena on the acropolis, for which the statue of the Calf-Bearer was commissioned. These internal measures were accompanied

An Athenian silver coin called a *tetradrachm,* dating from the fifth century B.C.E. The owl is the symbol of the goddess Athena. As Athenian wealth and power developed, its coinage became one of the most widely used currencies in the Mediterranean for exchange, even in cities hostile to Athens and the Delian League.

by support for commerce and export, particularly of grain. Soon, Athens was challenging Corinth as the leading commercial power and was trading in grain as far away as the Black Sea.

Peisistratus was firm. His son Hippias was harsh. Still, even Hippias enjoyed the support of the majority of the citizens of both popular and aristocratic factions. Only after the assassination of his younger brother did Hippias become sufficiently oppressive to drive his opponents into exile. Some of these exiles obtained the assistance of Sparta and returned to overthrow Hippias in 510 B.C.E. Hippias's defeat ended the tyrants' rule in Athens and won for Sparta an undeserved reputation as the opponent of all tyranny.

Athenian Democracy. Following the expulsion of Hippias, some aristocrats attempted to return to the "good old days" of aristocratic rule. However, Athenians had been accustomed to Solon's constitution for more than 80 years and were unwilling to give it up. Moreover, the tyrants had created a fierce sense of nationalistic pride among all ranks of Athenians, and few were willing to turn over government to the hands of only a few. When the aristocrats made their bid to recover power, their primary opponent, Cleisthenes (ca. 570–ca. 507 B.C.E.), a descendant of the Alcmaeonids, made the demos his faction and pushed through a final constitutional reform that became the basis for Athenian **democracy**.

The essence of Cleisthenes' reform lay in his reorganization of the major political units by which members of the council were selected. Previously, each citizen had belonged to one of four tribes, which were further broken down into 12 brotherhoods, or *phratries,* which were administrative and religious units. In a manner similar to that of Cypselus in Corinth, Cleisthenes reshuffled these phratries into 30 territorial units comprising urban, inland, or coastal regions. These 30 units in turn were grouped into 10 tribes, each consisting of one unit from each of the urban, inland, and coastal regions. The tribes elected the members of the council, military commanders, jurors, and magistrates. As in Corinth, this reorganization destroyed the traditional kin-based social and political pattern and integrated people of differing social, economic, and regional backgrounds. Aristocrats, merchants, and poor farmers had to work together to find common ground for political action, both regionally and nationally. With this new integrated democracy and its strong sense of nationalism, Athens emerged from the Archaic Age as the leading city of the Hellenic world.

The Coming of Persia and the End of the Archaic Age

By the end of the sixth century B.C.E., the products of Greek experimentation were evident throughout the Mediterranean. Still, these achievements were the product of small, independent, and relatively weak communities on the fringe of the civilized world.

In the second half of the sixth century B.C.E., all this changed. The Persian Empire, under its dynamic king Cyrus II, began a process of conquest and expansion west into Asia Minor, absorbing the kingdom of Lydia and conquering Ionia on the coast of Asia Minor. The Persians placed tyrants loyal to Cyrus to rule over these Greek communities, and for a few decades these centers of Greek culture and thought accepted foreign control. In 499 B.C.E., the passion for democracy, which had swept much of mainland Greece, reached Ionia. Cities such as Miletus, Ephesus, Chios, and Samos revolted, expelled their Persian-appointed tyrants, established democracies, and sent ambassadors to the mainland to seek assistance. Eretria and Athens, two mainland cities with Ionian roots, responded, sending ships and men to aid the Ionian rebels. Athenian interests were more than simple solidarity with their Ionian cousins. Athens depended on grain from the Black Sea region and believed its direct interests to lie with the area. The success of the revolt was short lived. The puny Greek cities were dealing with the largest empire the West had yet known. By 500 B.C.E., the Persian Empire included Asia Minor, Mesopotamia, Palestine, and Egypt, uniting all peoples from the Caucasus to the Sudan.

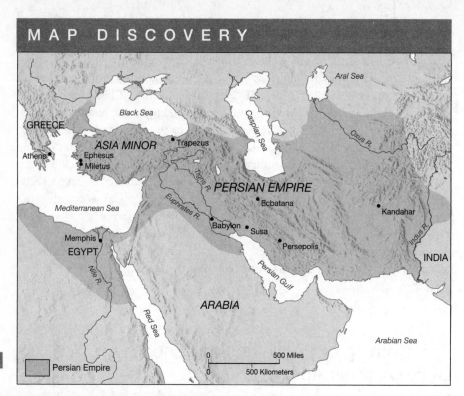

THE PERSIAN EMPIRE, CA. 500 B.C.E.

Examine the extent of the Persian Empire. Which ancient civilizations that you
have studied so far were incorporated into the Persian Empire? What effects on
cultural and economic exchange can you imagine to have resulted from this
territorial conquest?

The giant Persian Empire responded slowly, but with force, to the Greek
revolt. King Darius I (522–486 B.C.E.) gathered a vast international force from
throughout his empire and set about recapturing the rebellious cities. The war
lasted five years and ended in a Persian victory. By 494 B.C.E., the Persians had
retaken the cities of the coast and nearby islands. In the cities that were deemed
most responsible for the revolt, the population was herded together, the boys
were castrated and made into royal eunuchs, the girls were sent to Darius's
court, the remainder of the population was sold into slavery, and the towns were
burned to the ground. Once the rebels had been disposed of, Darius set out to
punish their supporters on the mainland, Eretria and Athens. With the same
meticulous planning and deliberate pace, the Persian king turned his vast
armies toward the Greek mainland.

SUMMARY

Greece in the Bronze Age to 800 B.C.E. The challenges of Greek geography and climate favored the development of small, self-contained agricultural societies. The two most important late Bronze Age cultures in Greece were the Minoan and the Mycenaean. Minoan Crete was a strongly stratified civilization centered on great palace complexes. The society was not militaristic, a fact that may have contributed to its downfall. In contrast, warriors were at the heart of Mycenaean civilization. Between 1600 B.C.E. and 1200 B.C.E., the Mycenaeans dominated Greece. Their demise was followed by the Greek Dark Age, a period of violence and instability.

Archaic Greece, 800–500 B.C.E. Between roughly 800 and 500 B.C.E., the Greeks carried out a revolution in political organization, artistic traditions, intellectual values, and social structures. A dramatic rise in population was key to these changes. Two new forms of political organization developed: the ethnos and the polis. Ethne were large territorial units with scattered populations ruled by an oligarchy. Poleis were independent city-states that controlled their surrounding regions. Colonization and tyranny were two intertwined results of political and social turmoil in the seventh century B.C.E. Public life was the almost exclusive preserve of men. Greek gods had all the virtues and vices of human beings. Greek religion was not monopolized by any particular social group. Greek art celebrated the originality of the individual artist.

A Tale of Three Cities Corinth, Sparta, and Athens present the spectrum of political, cultural, and social models of the Hellenic world. Corinth's was built on trade and colonization. At its height, Corinth was governed by an oligarchy that was remarkably successful in maintaining popular support among the citizens and provided a reliable and effective government. In Sparta, social and economic tensions gave rise to a military government. The individual was subservient to the state and all aspects of life were subject to rigid social control. As was the case with many other Greek city-states, aristocratic rule in Athens gave way to series of tyrants. In Athens, however, tyranny was not replaced by oligarchy, as it was in Corinth, but by democracy.

The Coming of Persia and the End of the Archaic Age In the second half of the sixth century B.C.E., the Persian Empire, under Cyrus II, began a process of conquest and expansion west into Asia Minor, conquering the Greek communities along the Ionian coast. In 499 B.C.E. a number of these communities revolted, prompting Eretria and Athens to come to their aid. The Persians crushed the Greek revolt and retook the coastal cities. This accomplished, they turned to the task of punishing the rebels' supporters on the Greek mainland.

QUESTIONS FOR REVIEW

1. What social and geographic factors shaped Greek culture in the age of the *Iliad* and the *Odyssey?*
2. What social forces spurred colonization, and what impact did colonization have on Archaic Greek civilization?
3. What do the gods, myths, and art of the Greek people reveal about their lives?
4. How did the Corinthian, Spartan, and Athenian cultures differ, and why did these city-states evolve in such different directions?

Classical and Hellenistic Greece, 500–100 B.C.E.

War and Politics in the Fifth Century B.C.E.

The vast Persian army moving west in 490 B.C.E. threatened the fruits of three centuries of Greek political, social, and cultural experimentation. The shared ideal of freedom within community and the common bond of language and culture seemed no basis on which to build an effective resistance to the great Persian Empire. Moreover, Darius I was not marching against the Greeks as such. Few Greek states other than Athens had supported the Ionians against their Persian conquerors. Many Greeks saw the Persians as potential allies or even rulers who were preferable to their more powerful Greek neighbors and to rivals within their own states. Particular interest, rather than patriotism or love of freedom, determined which cities opposed the Persian march. In the end, only Eretria, a badly divided Athens, and the small town of Plataea were prepared to refuse the Persian king's demand for gifts of earth and water, the traditional symbols of submission.

The Persian Wars

Initially, the Persian campaign followed the pattern established in Ionia. In the autumn of 490 B.C.E., Darius quickly destroyed the city of Eretria and carried off its population in captivity. The victorious Persian forces then landed at the Bay of Marathon. The total Athenian force was no more than half that of its enemies, but the Greeks were better armed and commanded the hills facing the Marathon plain on which the Persian troops had massed. The Athenians also benefited from the leadership of Miltiades (ca. 544–489 B.C.E.), an experienced soldier who had served Darius and who knew the Persian's strengths and weaknesses. For more than a week, the two armies faced each other in a battle of nerves. When the battle was finally joined, it was all over in a few hours. Six thousand Persians lay dead, while fewer than 200 Athenians were buried in the heroes' grave that still marks the Marathon plain.

The almost miraculous victory at Marathon had three enormous consequences for Athens and for Greece in general. First, it established the superiority of the hoplite phalanx as the finest infantry formation in the Mediterranean world. Second, Greeks expanded this belief in military superiority to a faith in the general superiority of Greeks over the "barbarians" (those who spoke other languages). Finally, by proving the value of the citizen army, the victory of the Athenians solidified and enhanced the democratic reforms of Cleisthenes.

Common citizens were determined that the victory won by the hoplite phalanx at Marathon should not be lost to an aristocratic faction at home. To guard against this danger, the Athenian assembly began to practice **ostracism**, a ten-year exile without loss of property, which was imposed on those who threatened to undermine the constitution of Cleisthenes. At the same time, Athenians also began to select their chief officers not simply by direct election but by lot. This practice prevented any individual from rising to power by creating a powerful faction. Themistocles (ca. 528–426 B.C.E.), the son of a noble father and a non-Greek mother, took the lead in using the tools of ostracism and selection by lot to hold the aristocratic factions at bay.

Thermopylae and Salamis

Occupied by problems elsewhere in their vast empire and by the unexpected death of Darius I in 486 B.C.E., the Persians paid little attention to Greece for six years. After Darius's death, his son Xerxes (486–465 B.C.E.) began to amass foodstuffs, weapons, and armies for a land assault on his Greek enemies. Though some Greek states more or less willingly allied themselves with the Persians, the others met in Sparta in 481 B.C.E. to plan resistance. The allies agreed that the Spartans would take command of the combined land and sea forces.

Although larger than those mustered by Athens against Darius, the Greek forces were puny compared with Xerxes' infantry and 1,000 light and highly maneuverable Ionian and Phoenician ships. The Spartan commanders sought a strategic point at which the numerical superiority of the Persian forces would be neutralized. The choice fell on the narrow pass of Thermopylae and the adjacent Euboean strait.

At Thermopylae, the Greeks held firm for days against wave after wave of assaulting troops. Finally, Greek allies of the Persians showed them a narrow mountain track by which they were able to attack the Greek position from the rear. Seeing that all was lost, the Spartan king Leonidas (490–480 B.C.E.) sent most of his allies home, leaving him and his 300 Spartan equals to face certain death.

While the Persian troops were blocked at Thermopylae, their fleet was being battered by fierce storms in the Euboean straits and harassed by the heavier

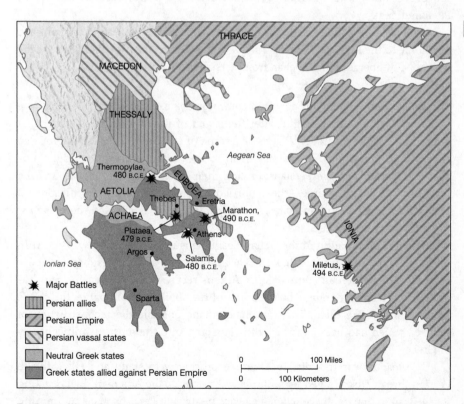

THE PERSIAN WARS. Greeks fought on both sides in the Persian Wars, while many others remained neutral.

Greek ships. Here, the Greeks learned that in close quarters they could stand up to Xerxes' Phoenician navy. This lesson proved vital a short time later. While the Persian army burned Athens and occupied Attica, Themistocles lured Xerxes' fleet into the narrow strait between Salamis and the mainland. There, the slower Greek vessels bottled up the larger and vastly more numerous enemy ships and cut them to pieces.

After Salamis, Xerxes lost his appetite for fighting Greeks. Without his fleet he could not supply a vast army far from home in hostile territory. Leaving a force to do what damage it could, he led the bulk of his army back to Persia. Soon the Athenians were taking the offensive, liberating the Ionian cities of Asia Minor and, in the process, laying the foundations of an Athenian empire that was every bit as threatening to their neighbors as that of Xerxes.

The Athenian Empire

Sparta, not Athens, should have emerged as the leader of the Greek world after 479 B.C.E. However, the constant threat of a helot revolt and the desire of the members of Sparta's Peloponnesian League to go their separate ways left Sparta too preoccupied with internal problems to fill the power vacuum left by the Persian defeat.

Athens, on the other hand, was only too ready to take the lead in bringing the war home to the Persians. With Sparta out of the picture, the Athenian fleet was the best hope of liberating the Aegean from Persians and pirates.

The Delian League. Athens accepted control in 478 B.C.E. of what historians have come to call the **Delian League**, after the island of Delos, a religious center that housed the league's treasury. Athens and some of the states with navies provided ships; others contributed annual payments to the league. Initially, the league pursued the war against the Persians, driving them back along the Aegean and the Black seas. At the same time, Athens hurriedly rebuilt its defensive fortifications, a move that Sparta and other states correctly interpreted as directed more against them than against the Persians.

Athens's domination of the Delian League ensured its prosperity. Attica, with its fragile agriculture, depended on Black Sea wheat, and the league kept these regions under Athenian control. Since Athens received not only cash "contributions" from league members but also half of the spoils taken in battle, the state's public coffers were filled. The new riches made possible the reconstruction of the city, which had been burned by the Persians, into the most magnificent city of Greece.

The league was too vital to Athenian prosperity to stand and fall with the Persian threat. Discouraged by a number of setbacks, the Athenian Callias, acting for the league, apparently concluded a peace treaty with Persia in 449 B.C.E., making the alliance no longer necessary. For a brief moment it appeared that the Delian

League might disband. But it was too late. The league had become an empire, and Athens's allies were its subjects.

Athenian Imperialism. The Athenian Empire was an economic, judicial, religious, and political union that was held together by military might. Athens controlled the flow of grain through the Hellespont to the Aegean, ensuring its own supply and heavily taxing cargoes to other cities. Athens controlled the law courts of member cities and used them to repress anti-Athenian groups. Rich and poor Athenian citizens alike acquired territory throughout the empire. Control over this empire depended on the Athenian fleet to enforce cooperation. Athenian garrisons were established in each city, and "democratic" puppet governments ruled according to the wishes of the garrison commanders. Revolt, resignation from the league, or refusal to pay the annual tribute resulted in brutal suppression. Persian tyranny had hardly been worse than Athenian imperialism.

Private and Public Life in Athens

During the second half of the fifth century B.C.E., Athens was a vital, crowded capital that drew merchants, artisans, and laborers from throughout the Greek world. At its height, the total population of Athens and surrounding Attica numbered perhaps 350,000, although probably fewer than 60,000 were citizens—adult males qualified to own land and participate in Athenian politics. Over one-quarter of the total population were slaves.

Greek slaves were not distinguished by race, ethnicity, or physical appearance. Slaves were as much the property of their owners as land, houses, cattle, and sheep were. Many masters treated their slaves well, but they were under no obligation to do so, and beatings, sexual exploitation, tattooing, starvation, and shackling were all too common.

Metics. Roughly half of Athens's free population were foreigners—*metoikoi*, or **metics**. The number of metics increased after the middle of the fifth century B.C.E.—both because of the flood of foreigners into the empire's capital and because Athenian citizenship was restricted to persons with two parents who were of citizen families. Metics could not own land in Attica, nor could they participate directly in politics. They were required to have a citizen protector and to pay a small annual tax. Otherwise, they were free to engage in every form of activity.

Women. More than half of those born into citizen families were entirely excluded from public life. These were the women who controlled and directed the vital sphere of the Athenian home, but who were considered citizens only for purposes of marriage, transfer of property, and procreation. From birth to death, every

On this fifth-century B.C.E. Athenian vase women are depicted making preparations for a wedding. Vases depicting wedding preparations and wedding scenes were a valued part of a woman's possessions, recalling the day that she passed from the authority of her father to that of her husband. Athenian red-figure pottery, in which the figure itself is outlined in paint but after firing remains unpainted, unlike the relief lines and the background, was extremely popular throughout the Mediterranean and beyond.

female citizen lived under the protection of a male guardian, either a close relative such as a father or brother, or a husband or son. Women spent almost their entire lives in the inner recesses of the home.

An honorable Athenian woman stayed at home and managed her husband's household. Only the poorest citizens sent their wives and daughters to work in the marketplace or the fields. For women, even the most casual contact with other men without permission was strictly forbidden.

Freedom in Community. The male citizens of fifth-century B.C.E. Athens were free to an extent previously unknown in the world. But Athenian freedom was freedom *in* community, not freedom *from* community. The essence of their freedom lay in their participation in public life, especially self-government, which was their passion. This participation was always within a complex network of familial, social, and religious connections and obligations. Each person belonged to a number of groups: a deme, a tribe, a family, various religious associations, and occupational groups. Each of these communities placed different and even contradictory demands on its members. The impossibility of satisfying all of these demands, of responding to the special interests of each, forced citizens to make hard choices, to set priorities, and to balance conflicting obligations. This process of selection was the essence of Athenian freedom, a freedom that, unlike that of the modern world, was based not on individualism but on a multitude of collectivities. The sum of these overlapping groupings was Athenian society, in which friends and opponents alike were united.

Unity did not imply equality. Even in fifth-century B.C.E. Athens, not all Athenians were socially or economically equal. The aristocracy was still strong, and most of the popular leaders of the century came from the ranks of old wealth and influence. Still, sovereignty lay not with these aristocrats but with the demos—the people.

In theory, the adult male citizens of Athens were its sovereigns. Since the time of Solon, they had formed the **ekklesia**, or assembly. They also made up the large juries, always composed of several hundred citizens, who decided legal cases less on law than on the political merits of the case and the quality of the orators who pleaded for each side. Such large bodies were too unwieldy to deal with the daily tasks of government. Therefore, control of these tasks fell to the council, or *boule*, composed of 500 members selected by lot by the tribes; the magistrates, who were also chosen by lot; and ten military commanders or generals, the only major office-holders who were elected rather than chosen at random.

Demagogues. Paradoxically, the resolute determination of Athenian democrats to prevent individuals from acquiring too much power helped to create a series of extraconstitutional power brokers. Since most offices were filled by lot and turned over frequently, real political leadership came not from officeholders but from generals and from popular leaders. These so-called demagogues, while at times holding high office, exercised their power through their speaking skills, informal networks, and knowledge of how to get things done. Governing an empire demanded skill, energy, and experience, but Athenian democracy was formally run by amateurs. Small wonder that the city's public life was dominated by these popular leaders.

Pericles and Athens

For 30 years, one individual dominated Athenian public life: the general Pericles (ca. 495–429 B.C.E.), a great orator and successful military commander who led Athens during the decades of its greatest glory. Athens's system of radical democracy reached its zenith under his leadership, even while Athens's imperial program drew it into a long and fatal war against Sparta, the only state powerful enough to resist it.

Pericles never ruled Athens. As a general he could only carry out the orders of the ekklesia and the boule, and as a citizen he could only attempt to persuade his fellows. Still, he was largely responsible for the extension of Athenian democracy to all free citizens. Under his influence, Athens abolished the last property requirements for officeholding. He convinced the state to pay those who served on juries, thus making it possible for even the poorest citizens to participate in this important part of Athenian government. But he was also responsible for a restriction of citizenship to those whose mothers and fathers had both been Athenians. Such a law would have denied citizenship to many of the most illustrious Athenians of the sixth century B.C.E., including his own ancestors. The law also prevented citizens of Athens's subject states from developing a real stake in the fate of the empire.

Pericles believed that the Athenian Empire had to be preserved at all costs. This policy ultimately drew Athens into deadly conflict with Sparta. The first clash between the two rival powers came around 460 B.C.E. at Megara, which lay between the Peloponnesus and Attica. The Athenians emerged victorious, checking Sparta and absorbing Megara, Aegina, and Boeotia. However, in 446 B.C.E. Megara and Boeotia rebelled, and Sparta invaded the disputed region. Unable to face this new threat at home after the disastrous loss abroad, in 445 B.C.E. the Athenians, under the leadership of Pericles, concluded a peace treaty with Sparta whereby Athens abandoned all of its continental possessions. The treaty was meant to last for 30 years, but it held for only 14.

The two great powers were eager to preserve the peace, but the whole Greek world was a tinderbox ready to burst into flame. The spark came from an unexpected direction. In 435 B.C.E., Corinth and its colony Corcyra on the Adriatic Sea came to blows, and Corcyra sought the assistance of Athens. The Athenians agreed to a defensive alliance with Corcyra and assisted it in defeating its enemy. This assistance infuriated Corinth, an ally of Sparta, and in 432 B.C.E., the Corinthians convinced the Spartans that Athens's imperial ambitions were insatiable. The next year, Sparta invaded Attica, and the Peloponnesian War, which would destroy both great powers, had begun.

The Peloponnesian War

The Peloponnesian War was actually a series of wars and rebellions. Athens and Sparta waged two devastating ten-year wars, from 431 B.C.E. to 421 B.C.E. and then again from 414 B.C.E. to 404 B.C.E. At the same time, cities in each alliance took advantage of the wars to revolt against the great powers, eliciting terrible vengeance from both Athens and Sparta. Within many of the Greek city-states, oligarchs and democrats waged bloody civil wars for control of their governments. Moreover, between 415 and 413 B.C.E., Athens attempted to expand its empire in Sicily, an attempt that ended in disaster. Before it was over, the Peloponnesian War had become an international war, with Persia entering the fray on the side of Sparta. In the end, there were no real victors, only victims.

The Archidamian War. The first phase of the war, called the Archidamian War after the Spartan king Archidamus (431–427 B.C.E.), was indecisive. Sparta pillaged

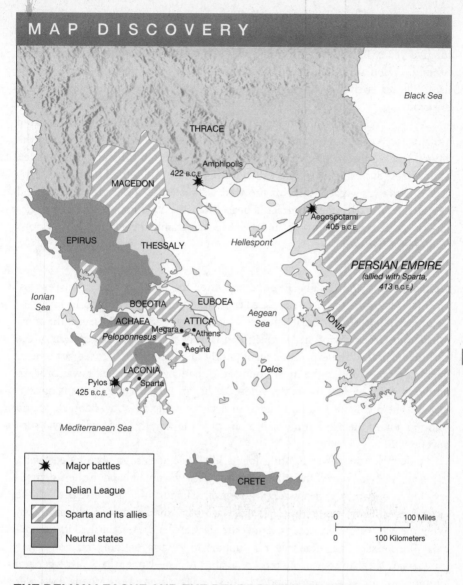

THE DELIAN LEAGUE AND THE PELOPONNESIAN WAR

When Athens turned the Delian League into its own empire, the resulting war pitted the Attica city-state against the combined forces of Sparta and Persia. Examine the extent of the Delian League, Sparta and its allies, and the neutral states. Why would Sparta and its allies feel threatened strategically and economically by the Delian League? Why was an alliance with Persia a vital part of Spartan strategy? What threats faced those states that remained neutral?

Attica but could not breach the great wall or starve Athens. In 430 B.C.E., the Spartans received unexpected help in the form of plague, which ravaged Athens for five years. By the time it ended in 426 B.C.E., as much as one-third of the Athenian population had died, including Pericles. Still Athens held out, establishing bases encircling the Peloponnesus and urging Spartan helots and allies to revolt.

At Pylos in 425 B.C.E., the Athenian generals Cleon and Demosthenes captured a major force of Spartan equals. The Spartans offset this defeat by capturing the city of Amphipolis on the northern Aegean. The defeated Athenian commander, Thucydides (d. ca. 401 B.C.E.), was exiled for his failure and retired to Spartan territory to write his great history of the war. Exhausted by a decade of death and destruction, the two sides contracted peace in 421 B.C.E. Although Athens was victorious in that its empire was intact, the peace changed nothing, and tensions festered for five years.

Alcibiades and the Sicilian Expedition. After the peace of 421 B.C.E., Pericles' kinsman Alcibiades (ca. 450–404 B.C.E.) came to dominate the demos. In 415 B.C.E., he urged Athens to expand its empire westward by attacking Syracuse, the most prosperous Greek city of Sicily, which had largely escaped the devastation of the Archidamian War. The expedition went poorly, and Alcibiades, accused at home of having profaned one of the most important Athenian religious cults, was ordered home. Instead, he fled to Sparta, where he began to assist the Spartans against Athens. The Sicilian expedition ended in disaster. Athens lost over 200 ships and 50,000 men. At the same time, Sparta resumed the war, this time with naval support provided by Persia.

Suddenly, Athens was fighting for its life. Alcibiades soon abandoned Sparta for Persia and convinced the Athenians that if they would abandon their democracy for an oligarchy, Persia would withdraw its support of Sparta. In 411 B.C.E., the desperate Athenian assembly established a brutal, antidemocratic oligarchy, but when the war continued, Athens, amid bitter factionalism, reestablished its democracy. The Persian king renewed his support for Sparta, sending his son Cyrus (ca. 424–401 B.C.E.) to coordinate the war against Athens. Under the Spartan general Lysander (d. 395 B.C.E.), Sparta and its allies finally closed in on Athens. Lysander captured the Athenian fleet in the Hellespont, destroyed it, and severed Athens's vital grain supply. Within months, Athens was entirely cut off from the outside world and starving. In 404 B.C.E., Sparta accepted Athens's unconditional surrender. Athens's fortifications came down, its empire vanished, and its fleet, except for a mere 12 ships, dissolved.

The Peloponnesian War showed not only the limitations of Athenian democracy but the potential brutality of oligarchy as well. More ominously, it demonstrated the catastrophic effects of disunity and rivalry among Greek cities of the Mediterranean.

Athenian Culture in the Hellenic Age

Most of what we today call Greek is actually Athenian. Throughout the Hellenic age (the fifth and early fourth centuries B.C.E., as distinct from the Hellenistic period of roughly the later fourth through second centuries B.C.E.), the turbulent issues of democracy and oligarchy, war and peace, hard choices and conflicting obligations found expression in Athenian culture even as the glory of the Athenian Empire was manifested in art and architecture.

The Examined Life

A primary characteristic of Athenian culture was its critical and rational nature. Secure in their identity and protected by the openness of their radical democracy, Athenians began to examine the past and present and to question the foundations of traditional values. From this climate of inquiry emerged the traditions of moral philosophy and its cousin, history.

The Ionian interest in natural philosophy, the explanation of the universe in rational terms, continued throughout the fifth century B.C.E. But philosophers began also to turn their attention to the human world, in particular to the powers and limitations of the individual's mind and the individual's relationship with society.

The Sophists. In the political world of fifth-century B.C.E. Athens, rhetoric, the art of persuasion, was particularly important because it was the key to political influence. Teachers called **sophists** ("wise people") traveled throughout Greece, offering to provide an advanced education for a fee. Although the sophistic tradition later gained a negative reputation, teachers such as Gorgias (ca. 485–ca. 380 B.C.E.) and Protagoras (ca. 490–421 B.C.E.) trained young men not only in the art of rhetoric but also in logic.

Socrates. The teacher Socrates (ca. 470–399 B.C.E.) was considered by many of his contemporaries as but one more sophist, but he himself reacted against what he saw as the amoral and superficial nature of sophistic education. He was interested in the search for moral self-enlightenment. Socrates' method infuriated his contemporaries. He would approach individuals who had reputations for wisdom or skill and then, through a series of disarmingly simple questions, force them to defend their beliefs. The inevitable result was that in their own words the outstanding sophists, politicians, and poets of the day demonstrated the inadequacy of the foundations of their beliefs.

Since Socrates refused to commit any of his teaching to writing, we know of him only from the conflicting reports of his former students and opponents. One thing is certain, however: While demanding that every aspect of life be investigated, Socrates never doubted the moral legitimacy of the Athenian state.

This bust of Socrates, a Roman copy of a Greek original, portrays him with the traditional beard of a philosopher. Also portrayed is his lack of physical beauty. In Plato's dialogue *Theaetetus*, Plato even playfully boasts of his looks, saying that his flared nostrils improved his sense of smell and his bulging eyes helped his vision, while his discussion partner suggests that Socrates's outsized lips were perhaps better for kissing and his large mouth helped him eat. The point of such characterizations was that this physically ugly man had the most beautiful mind.

Condemned to death in 399 B.C.E. on the trumped-up charges of corrupting the morals of the Athenian youth and introducing strange gods, he declined the opportunity to escape into exile. Rather than reject Athens and its laws, he drank the fatal potion of hemlock given him by the executioner.

Understanding the Past

The philosophical interest in human choices and social constraints found echo in the historical writing of the age. In particular, two writers established the spectrum of how to understand the past.

Herodotus. Herodotus (ca. 484–420 B.C.E.), the first historian, was one of the many foreigners who found in Athens the intellectual climate and audience he needed to write an account of the Persian wars of the preceding generation. His book of inquiries, or *historia,* into the origins and events of the conflict between Greeks and Persians is the first true history.

As Herodotus explained in his introduction, his purpose in writing was first to preserve the memory of the past by recording the achievements of both Greeks and eastern non-Greeks and second to show how the two came into conflict. It was this concern to explain, to go beyond mere storytelling, that earned Herodotus the designation "father of history."

Thucydides. The story of the Peloponnesian War was recorded by a different sort of historian, one who focused more narrowly on the Greek world and on political power. Thucydides had been an Athenian general and a major actor in the first part of the Peloponnesian War until his exile in 425 B.C.E. He began his account at the very outbreak of the conflict, thus writing a contemporary record of the war rather than a history of it.

For Thucydides, the central subject was human society in action. He viewed the Greek states as acting out of rational self-interest. His favorite device for showing the development of such policies was the political set speech in which two opposing leaders attempt to persuade their fellow citizens on the proper course of action.

Still, morality is always just below the surface of Thucydides' narrative. Even as he unflinchingly chronicles the collapse of morality and social order in the face of political expediency, he recognizes that this process will destroy his beloved Athens. In the later, unfinished chapters (Thucydides died shortly after Athens's final defeat), the Peloponnesian War takes on the characteristics of a tragedy. Here Thucydides, the ultimate political historian, shows the deep influence of the dominant literary tradition of his day: Greek drama.

Athenian Drama

Since the time of its introduction by Peisistratus in the middle of the sixth century B.C.E., drama had become popular, not only in Athens but throughout the Greek world. Plays formed part of the annual feast of Dionysus and dealt with mythic subject matter largely taken from the *Iliad* and the *Odyssey*. Three types of plays honored the Dionysian festival. Tragedies dealt with great men who failed because of flaws in their natures. Comedies were more directly topical and political. They parodied real Athenians, often by name, and amused even while making serious points in defense of democracy. Somewhere between tragedies and comedies, satyr plays remained closest to the Dionysian cult. In them, lecherous drunken satyrs, mythical half-man, half-goat creatures, interact with gods and men as they roam in search of Dionysus.

Aeschylus. Only a handful of the hundreds of Greek plays written in the fifth century B.C.E. survive. The first of the great Athenian tragedians whose plays we know is Aeschylus (525–456 B.C.E.). His one surviving trilogy, the *Oresteia*, traces the fate of the family of Agamemnon, the Greek commander at Troy. The three plays of the trilogy explore the chain of violent acts, vengeance, and conflicting obligations that ultimately must be settled by rational yet divinely sanctioned law.

Sophocles. Aeschylus's younger contemporary Sophocles (496–406 B.C.E.), the most successful of the fifth century B.C.E. tragedians, sought in his mature plays to express human character. He shows how humans make decisions and carry them out, constrained by their pasts, their weaknesses, and their vices, but free nonetheless. Sophocles' message is endurance, acceptance of human responsibility and, at the same time, of the ways of the gods, who overrule people's plans.

Euripides. Compared with Aeschylus and Sophocles, Euripides (485–406 B.C.E.) was far more original and daring in his subject matter and treatment of human emotions. His female characters were often wronged and seldom accepted their lot. His plays abound in plot twists and unexpected, violent outbursts. Passion, not reason, rules Euripides' world. His characters are less reconciled to their fates and less ready to accept the traditional gods.

Greek Comedy. Neither passion nor reason but politics rules the world of Greek comedy. Rather than the timelessness of the human condition, Athenian comic playwrights focused their biting satire on the political and social issues of the moment. Particularly, the comic genius Aristophanes (ca. 450–ca. 388 B.C.E.) used wit, imagination, vulgarity, and great poetic sensitivity to attack everything that offended him in his city. In his plays, he mocks and ridicules statesmen, philosophers, rival playwrights, and even the gods. Yet Aristophanes was a deeply patriotic Athenian, dedicated to the democratic system and to the cause of peace. Through the sharp satire and absurd plots of his plays, Aristophanes communicates his sympathy for ordinary people, who must match wits with the charlatans and pompous frauds who attempt to dominate Athens's public life.

Art and the Human Image

The humanity in Greek drama found its parallel in art. In sculpture, we see development toward balance and realism contained within an ideal of human form. The finest bronzes and marbles of the fifth century B.C.E. show freestanding figures whose natural vigor and force, even when they are engaged in strenuous exertion, are balanced by the placidity of their faces and their lack of emotion. The tradition established by the Athenian sculptor Phidias (ca. 500–ca. 430 B.C.E.) sought a naturalism in the portrayal of the human figure, which remained ideal rather than individual.

The greatest sculptural program of the fifth century B.C.E. was that produced for the Athenian acropolis. The reconstruction of the acropolis, which had been destroyed by the Persians, was the culmination of Athenian art. The result was the greatest complex of buildings in the ancient world.

The intellectual and artistic accomplishments of Athens were as enduring as its empire proved ephemeral. Writers and artists alike focused their creative energies on human existence, seeking a proper proportion, order, and meaning, a blend of the practical and ideal, which Athens's political leaders lacked.

From City-States to Macedonian Empire, 404–323 B.C.E.

The Peloponnesian War touched every aspect of Greek life. The war brought changes to the social and political structures of Greece by creating an enduring bitterness between the elites and the populace and a distrust of both democracy and traditional oligarchy. The mutual exhaustion of Athens and Sparta left a vacuum of power in the Aegean. Finally, the war raised fundamental questions about the nature of politics and society throughout the Greek world.

Politics After the Peloponnesian War

Over the decades-long struggle, the conduct of war and the nature of politics had changed, bringing new problems for victor and vanquished alike.

Spartan Imperialism. Victory left Sparta no more capable of assuming leadership in 404 B.C.E. than it had been in 478 B.C.E. Years of war had reduced the population of equals to fewer than 3,000. The Spartans proved to be extremely unpopular imperialists.

The brutality of Spartan rule sparked opposition throughout the Greek world, shattering the fragile peace created by Athens's defeat. For over 70 years, the Greek world boiled in constant warfare. Mutual distrust, fear of any city that seemed about to establish a position of clear superiority, and the machinations of the Persian Empire to keep Greeks fighting each other produced a constantly shifting series of alliances.

Thebes. Persia turned against its former ally when, in 401 B.C.E., Sparta supported an unsuccessful attempt by Cyrus to unseat his brother Artaxerxes II. Soon the unlikely and unstable alliance of Athens, Corinth, Argos, Thebes, and Euboea, financed by Persia, entered a series of vicious wars against Sparta. The first round ended in Spartan victory, due to the shifting role of Persia, whose primary interest was the continued disunity of the Greeks. By 377 B.C.E., however, Athens had reorganized its league and, with Thebes as an ally, was able to break Spartan sea power. The decline of Sparta left a power vacuum that was soon filled by Thebes.

Theban hegemony was short-lived. Before long, the same process of greed, envy, and distrust that had devastated the other Greek powers destroyed Thebes. By the 330s B.C.E., all of the Greek states had proven themselves incapable of creating stable political units larger than their immediate polis.

Philosophy and the Polis

The failure of Greek political forms, oligarchy and democracy alike, profoundly affected Athenian philosophers. Plato (ca. 428–347 B.C.E.), an aristocratic student of Socrates, grew up during the Peloponnesian War and had witnessed the collapse of the empire, the brutality of the Thirty Tyrants, the execution of Socrates, and the revival of the democracy and its imperialistic ambitions. From these experiences he developed a hatred for Athenian democracy and a profound distrust of ordinary people's ability to tell right from wrong.

Platonic Forms. Plato argued that true knowledge is impossible as long as it focuses on the constantly changing, imperfect world of everyday experience. Human beings can have real knowledge only of that which is eternal, perfect, and beyond the experience of the senses, the realm of what Plato called the **Forms**. Plato believed that when one judged individuals or actions to be true or good or beautiful, one did so not because those individuals or actions were truly virtuous, but because one recognized that they participated in some way in the Idea or Form of truth or goodness or beauty.

According to Plato, the evils of the world, in particular the vices and failures of government and society, result from ignorance of the truth. Most people live as though chained in a cave in which all they can see are the shadows cast by a fire on the walls. In their ignorance they mistake these flickering, imperfect images for reality. Their proper ruler must be a philosopher, one who is not deceived by the shadows. The philosopher's task is to break their chains and turn them toward the source of the light so that they can see the world as it really is.

Aristotelian Empiricism. Plato's idealist view (in the sense of the Ideas or Forms) of knowledge dominated much of ancient philosophy. However, his greatest student, Aristotle (384–322 B.C.E.), rejected this view in favor of **empiricism**, a philosophy rooted in observation of the natural world. Systematic investigation and explanation characterize Aristotle's vast work, and his interests ranged from biology to statecraft to the most abstract philosophy. In each field he employed essentially the same method. He observed as many individual examples of the topic as possible and from these specific observations extracted general theories.

In human affairs, Aristotle recommended moderation. Unlike Plato, he did not regard any particular form of government as ideal. Rather, he concluded that the type of government ultimately mattered less than the balance between narrow oligarchy and radical democracy. Moderation was the key to stability and justice. Yet, during the very years that Aristotle was teaching, the vacuum created by the failure of the Greek city-states was being filled by the growing Macedonian monarchy that finally ended a century of Greek warfare and, with it, the independence of the Greek city-states.

The Rise of Macedon

The polis had never been the only form of the Greek state. Alongside the city-states of Athens, Corinth, Syracuse, and Sparta were more decentralized ethne ruled by traditional hereditary chieftains and monarchs. Macedonia, in the northeast of the mainland, was one such ethnos. Macedonia had long served as a buffer between the barbarians to the north and the Greek mainland, and its tough farmers and pastoralists were geared to constant warfare. As Athens, Sparta, and Thebes fought each other to mutual exhaustion, Macedonia under King Philip II (359–336 B.C.E.) moved into the resulting power vacuum.

A Roman copy of a Greek statue of Aristotle. Already in his own lifetime at least one portrait of Aristotle was in existence and his student Alexander the Great commissioned others of him. Ancient authors described him as thin with short hair and a mocking expression on his face. In the Roman world, statues and busts of Aristotle were very popular in gardens, whether or not the owners had actually read the philosopher, which probably accounts for the survival of this and other similar statues.

After some early military successes against northern barbarians, Philip, a skillful politician and outstanding military strategist, turned his attention to the south and relentlessly swallowed up one Greek state after another. In 338 B.C.E., Philip achieved a final victory at Chaeronea and established a new league, the League of Corinth. However, unlike all those that had preceded it, this league was no confederation of sovereign states. It was an empire ruled by a king and supported by wealthy citizens whose cooperation Philip rewarded well. This new model of government, a monarchy drawing its support from a wealthy elite, became a fixture of the Mediterranean world for over 2,000 years.

No sooner had Philip subdued Greece than he announced a campaign against Persia. Before he could begin, however, he was cut down by an assassin's knife, leaving his 20-year-old son, Alexander (336–323 B.C.E.), to lead the expedition. Within 13 years, Alexander had conquered the world.

The Empire of Alexander the Great

In 334 B.C.E., the first year of his campaign, Alexander captured the Greek cities of Asia Minor. Then he continued east. Two months later, he defeated the Persian king Darius III at Issus and then headed south toward the Mediterranean coast and Egypt. After his victories there, he turned again to the north and entered Mesopotamia. At Gaugamela in 331 B.C.E., he defeated Darius a second, decisive time. Shortly afterward, Darius was murdered by the remnants of his followers.

Alexander captured the Persian capital of Persepolis with its vast treasure and became the undisputed ruler of the vast empire.

The conquest of Persia was not enough. Alexander pushed on, intending to conquer the whole world. His armies marched eastward, subduing the rebellious Asian provinces of Bactria and Sogdiana. He negotiated the Khyber Pass from what is now Afghanistan into the Punjab, crossed the Indus River, and defeated the local Indian king. Everywhere he went, he reorganized or founded cities, entrusting them to loyal Macedonians and other Greeks and settling them with veterans of his campaigns, and then pushed on toward the unknown. On the banks of the Hyphasis River in what is now Pakistan, his Macedonian warriors finally halted. Worn out by years of bloody conquest and exhausting travel, they refused to go further. Furious but impotent, Alexander led his troops back to Persepolis in 324 B.C.E.

Binding Together an Empire

Alexander is remembered as a greater conqueror than ruler, but his plans for his reign, had he lived to complete them, might have won him equal fame. He recognized that only by merging local and Greek peoples and traditions could he forge a lasting empire. Whether his program of cultural and social amalgamation could have succeeded is a moot point. In 323 B.C.E., less than two years after his return from India, he died at Babylon at the age of 32.

MAP DISCOVERY

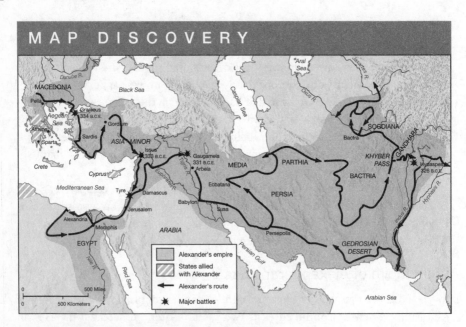

THE EMPIRE OF ALEXANDER THE GREAT

Compare the empire of Alexander with the map of the ancient world (p. 9). How do you account for the specific areas Alexander chose to conquer? Based on information presented in this chapter, what lasting effects remained in this region?

The empire did not outlive the emperor. Vicious fighting soon broke out among his generals and his kin. The various units of the empire broke apart into separate kingdoms and autonomous cities in which each ruler attempted to continue the political and cultural tradition of Alexander in a smaller sphere. By 275 B.C.E., three large kingdoms dominated Alexander's former domain. The most stable was Egypt, which Ptolemy I (323–285 B.C.E.), one of Alexander's closest followers, acquired on Alexander's death and which he and his descendants ruled until Cleopatra VII (51–30 B.C.E.) was defeated by the Roman Octavian in 31 B.C.E. In the east, the Macedonian general Seleucus (246–226 B.C.E.) captured Babylon in 312 B.C.E., and he and his descendants ruled a vast kingdom reaching from what is today western Turkey to Afghanistan. However, whittled away over time by its neighbors, the Seleucid kingdom gradually shrank to a small region of northern Syria before it fell to Rome in 64 B.C.E. After 50 years of conflict, Antigonus Gonatas (276–239 B.C.E.), the grandson of another of Alexander's commanders, secured Macedon and Greece. His Antigonid successors ruled the kingdom until it fell to the Romans in 168 B.C.E.

Alexander's conquests brought Greek traditions of urban organization to a wide area, replacing indigenous ruling elites with Hellenized dynasties. But Alexander's successors never integrated this Greek culture and the more ancient indigenous cultures of their subjects. This failure proved fatal for the Hellenistic kingdoms.

Chronology

CLASSICAL GREECE

525–456 B.C.E.	Aeschylus
ca. 500–ca. 430 B.C.E.	Phidias
496–406 B.C.E.	Sophocles
490 B.C.E.	Battle of Marathon
485–406 B.C.E.	Euripides
ca. 484–ca. 420 B.C.E.	Herodotus
480 B.C.E.	Battles of Thermopylae and Salamis
478 B.C.E	Athens assumes control of Delian League
ca. 470–399 B.C.E.	Socrates
ca. 460–430 B.C.E.	Pericles dominates Athens
ca. 450–ca. 388 B.C.E.	Aristophanes
431–421; 414–404 B.C.E.	Peloponnesian War
ca. 428–347 B.C.E.	Plato
384–322 B.C.E.	Aristotle
384–322 B.C.E.	Demosthenes
338 B.C.E.	Philip of Macedon defeats Athens
336–323 B.C.E.	Reign of Alexander the Great

The Hellenistic World

Although vastly different in geography, language, and custom, the Hellenistic king-doms (so called to distinguish them from the Hellenic civilization of the fifth and early fourth centuries B.C.E.) shared two common traditions. First, great portions of the Hellenistic world, from Asia Minor to Bactria and south to Egypt, had been united at various times by the Assyrian and Persian empires. During these periods they had absorbed much of Mesopotamian civilization, in particular the adminis-trative traditions begun by the Assyrian Tiglath-pileser. Therefore, the Hellenistic kings ruled kingdoms that were already accustomed to centralized government.

Hellenistic monarchs remained Greek and lavished their attentions on the newly created Greek cities, which absorbed vast amounts of the kingdom's wealth. Nonetheless, these cities and their particular form of Greek culture were the second unifying factor in the Hellenistic world. In the tradition of Alexander himself, the Ptolemys, Seleucids, and Antigonids cultivated Greek urban culture and recruited Greeks for their most important positions of responsibility. The new Greek cities became the centers of political control, economic consumption, and cultural diffu-sion throughout the Hellenistic world.

Urban Life and Culture

The Hellenistic kingdoms lived in a perpetual state of warfare with one another. Kings needed Greek soldiers, merchants, and administrators and competed with their rivals in offering Greeks all the comforts of home. These Greeks were drawn from throughout the Greek-speaking world, and in time a universal Greek dialect, *koine*, became the common language of culture and business. Hellenistic cities were Greek in physical organization, constitution, and language.

For all their Greek culture, Hellenistic cities differed fundamentally from Greek cities and colonies of the past. Not only were they far larger than any earlier Greek cities, they were never politically sovereign. The regional kings maintained firm control over the cities, even while working to attract Greeks from the main-land and the islands to them.

At the same time, Hellenistic cities were much less closed than were the tradi-tional poleis of the Hellenic world. In the new cities of the east, Greeks from all over were welcomed as soldiers and administrators regardless of their city of ori-gin. By the second century B.C.E., Greeks no longer identified themselves by their city of origin but as "Hellenes," that is, Greeks. Native elites could also become Greeks by adopting Greek language and culture.

Women in Public Life

The great social and geographical mobility that was possible in the new cities extended to women as well as men. No longer important simply as transmitters of citizenship, women began to assume a greater role in the family, in the economy,

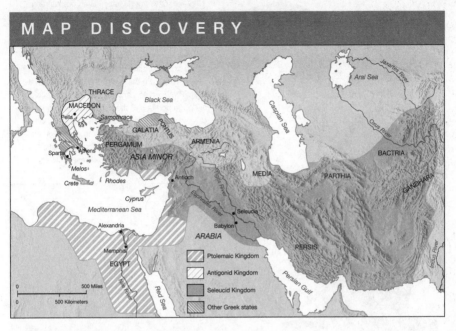

MAP DISCOVERY

THE HELLENISTIC KINGDOMS

Consider the locations of the Hellenistic kingdoms carved out of Alexander's empire by his generals. From what you have read in previous chapters, which indigenous cultures do you think might have most influenced the Ptolemaic and Seleucid Kingdoms? Where would you expect to find Greek culture most important?

and in public life. Marriage contracts, particularly in Ptolemaic Egypt, emphasized the theoretical equality of husband and wife. Since women could control their own property, many engaged in business, and some became wealthy and influential.

Just as monarchs competed with one another in creating Greek cities, they vied in making their cities centers of Greek culture. Socially ambitious and newly wealthy citizens supported poets, philosophers, and artists and endowed gymnasia and libraries.

Alexandria

The most vibrant center of this rich complex of social change and culture was Alexandria in Egypt. Alexander the Great had founded it after having himself crowned pharaoh in the ancient capital of Memphis in 331 B.C.E. After Alexander's death, Ptolemy I made it not only his political and commercial center but the cultural center for Greek art, science, and scholarship for the whole world. In time, the library at Alexandria housed half a million book-rolls, including all of the great classics of Greek literature.

The *Nike,* or Winged Victory, is an outstanding example of third century Hellenistic sculpture. It was found in fragments on the island of Samothrace in the Aegean Sea in 1863 and originally formed part of the Samothrace temple complex. The statue depicted the goddess descending from the sky to the victorious naval fleet. The head and arms were never discovered although portions of the right hand have been discovered. The depiction of movement and the dynamic and naturalistic draping of the figure's torso make it one of the greatest Hellenistic works to have survived to the present. The statue is now in the Louvre in Paris.

Hellenistic Literature

Hellenistic writers developed new forms of literature, including the romance, which often recounted imaginary adventures of Alexander the Great, and the pastoral poem, which the Sicilian Theocritus (ca. 310–250 B.C.E.) developed out of popular shepherd songs. The Athenian playwright Menander's (342–292 B.C.E.) gift was for comedy, but it was a new type of comedy quite removed from the politically biting and often vulgar humor of Aristophanes. Menander wrote with great poetic skill and artistry some 100 wildly complicated, good-natured plays. More than any other ancient poet or playwright, he drew a sympathetic image of ordinary men and women.

Architecture and Art

Political rivalry also encouraged architectural and artistic rivalry, as kings competed for the most magnificent Hellenistic cities.

Freestanding statues and magnificent murals and mosaics adorned the public squares, temples, and private homes of Hellenistic cities. While artists continued the traditions of the Hellenic age, they displayed more freedom in portraying tension and restlessness as well as individuality in the human form.

Hellenistic Philosophy

Philosophy, too, flourished in the Hellenistic world, but in directions different from those initiated by Plato and Aristotle, who both were deeply committed to political involvement in the free polis. The new philosophies appealed to the rootless Greeks of the Hellenistic east, who were no longer tied by bonds of religion or patriotism to any community.

Cynics. The Cynic tradition was established by Antisthenes (ca. 445–ca. 365 B.C.E.), a pupil of Socrates, and Diogenes of Sinope (d. ca. 320 B.C.E.). The **Cynics** taught that excessive attachment to the things of this world was the source of evil and unhappiness and that an individual achieved freedom by renouncing material things, society, and pleasures. The Cynics believed that the more one had, the more one was vulnerable to the whims of fortune.

Epicureans. Like the Cynics, the **Epicureans** sought freedom, but from pain rather than from the conventions of ordinary life. Epicurus (341–270 B.C.E.) and his disciples have often been attacked for their emphasis on pleasure. But, for the Epicureans, the real goal was to reduce desires to those that were simple and attainable. Therefore, Epicureans urged retirement from politics, retreat from public competition, and concentration instead on friendship and private enjoyment. For Epicurus, reason properly applied illuminated how best to pursue pleasure.

Stoics. **Stoics** also followed nature, but rather than leading them to retire from public life, it led them to greater participation in it. Stoics believed that just as the universe is a system in which stars and planets move according to fixed laws, so too was human society ordered and unified. As the founder of Stoicism, Zeno (ca. 335–ca. 263 B.C.E.), expressed it, "All men should regard themselves as members of one city and people, having one life and order." According to the Stoics, every person had a role in the divinely ordered universe, and all roles were of equal value. True happiness consisted in freely accepting one's role, whatever it was, while unhappiness and evil resulted from attempting to reject one's place in the divine plan.

Mathematics and Science

Particularly for mathematics, astronomy, and engineering, the Hellenistic period was a golden age. Ptolemaic Egypt became the center of mathematical studies. Euclid (ca. 300 B.C.E.), whose *Elements* was the fundamental textbook of geometry until the twentieth century, worked there, as did his student Apollonius of Perga (ca. 262–ca. 190 B.C.E.), whose work on conic sections is one of the greatest monuments of geometry. Both Apollonius and his teacher were as influential for their method as for their conclusions. Their treatises follow rigorous logical proofs of mathematical theorems, which established the form of mathematical reasoning to the present day. Archimedes of Syracuse (ca. 287–212 B.C.E.) corresponded with the Egyptian mathematicians and made additional contributions to geometry, such as the calculation of the approximate value of pi, as well as to mechanics, arithmetic, and engineering.

Mathematical Astronomy. Many mathematicians, such as Archimedes and Apollonius, were also mathematical astronomers, and the application of their mathematical skills to the exact data collected by earlier Babylonian and Egyptian empirical astronomers greatly increased the understanding of the heavens and the earth. Archimedes devised a means of measuring the diameter of the sun, and Eratosthenes of Cyrene (ca. 276–194 B.C.E.) calculated the circumference of the earth to within 200 miles.

Medicine. Like astronomy, Hellenistic medicine combined theory and observation. In Alexandria, Herophilus of Chalcedon (ca. 270 B.C.E.) and Erasistratus of Ceos (ca. 260 B.C.E.) conducted important studies in human anatomy. Through his studies, Herophilus recognized the brain as the center of the nervous system and was able to distinguish accurately between motor and sensory nerves. He also produced the first accurate descriptions of such organs as the eye, brain, liver, and salivary glands.

Cultural Resistance. For all of their vitality, the Hellenistic cities remained parasites on the local societies. No real efforts were made to merge the two and to develop a new civilization. Some ambitious members of the indigenous elites tried to adopt the customs of the Greeks; others plotted insurrection.

In time, the Hellenistic kingdoms' inability to bridge the gap between Greek and indigenous populations proved fatal. In the east, the non-Greek kingdom of Parthia replaced the Seleucids in much of the old Persian Empire. In the west, continuing hostility between kingdoms and within kingdoms prepared the way for their progressive absorption by the new power to the west: Rome.

SUMMARY

War and Politics in the Fifth Century B.C.E.   Greek victories over the Persians had important consequences for the Greeks in general, and the Athenians in particular. Athens moved further toward democracy, at the same time as it built an empire. The Athenian Empire was an economic, judicial, religious, and political union that was held together by military might. Only male citizens were full participants in Athenian democracy. Slaves, metics, and women were excluded. Pericles was the most successful of the Athenian demagogues. The Peloponnesian War pitted Athens against Sparta, with Sparta emerging as the eventual victor.

Athenian Culture in the Hellenic Age   A primary characteristic of Athenian culture was its critical and rational nature. The tensions, conflicts, and choices that shaped Athenian politics and society were reflected in art, philosophy, history, and drama. Writers and artists alike focused their creative energies on human existence, seeking proper proportion, order, and meaning.

From City-States to Macedonian Empire, 404–323 B.C.E.   The mutual exhaustion of Athens and Sparta after the Peloponnesian War left a vacuum of power in the Aegean. The war raised fundamental questions about the nature of politics and society throughout the Greek world. Plato's philosophy was one response to the post-war world. Macedonia under King Philip II (359–336 B.C.E.) took advantage of the weakness of Athens, Sparta, and Thebes. Philip's son, Alexander (336–323 B.C.E.), led a campaign against Persia that ended with the conquest of a vast empire. After Alexander's death, his empire broke into a number of kingdoms.

The Hellenistic World   The Hellenistic kingdoms were shaped by both Mesopotamian and Greek civilization. Greeks played a key part in Hellenistic urban life, but Hellenistic cities were very different than Greek poleis. Women experienced greater social and geographical mobility. Writers developed new literary forms. Philosophers turned inward to answer questions about the relationships among the individual, society, and the natural world. Greek cities made little effort to truly merge with local societies.

QUESTIONS FOR REVIEW

1. Why did Athens become Greece's greatest power in the wake of the Persian wars?
2. What social concerns and cultural accomplishments were expressed in Greek philosophy, drama, and art?
3. What does the Peloponnesian War reveal about weaknesses and divisions in Greek culture?
4. What factors explain Alexander the Great's success in expanding his empire?
5. What changes did Greek culture experience as it was carried eastward with the creation of the Hellenistic kingdoms?

Early Rome and the Roman Republic, 800–146 B.C.E.

The Western Mediterranean to 509 B.C.E.

Civilization came late to the western Mediterranean, carried in the ships of Greeks and Phoenicians. While the great floodplain civilizations of Mesopotamia and Egypt and the Greek communities of the eastern Mediterranean were developing sophisticated systems of urban life and political organization, western Europe and Africa knew only the scattered villages of simple farmers and pastoralists. The West was rich in metals, however, and an indigenous Bronze Age culture developed slowly between 1500 and 1000 B.C.E., spreading widely north of the Alps and south into Italy and Spain.

Sometime around the year 1000 B.C.E., a new, distinctive iron-using civilization first appeared in northern Italy. No one knows whether these **Villanovans**, so called for a major archaeological discovery of this civilization at Villanova near Bologna, were new arrivals in Italy or simply the descendants of previous inhabitants. However, around this same time, small groups of people did begin to infiltrate Italy from the east and the north, occupying the mountainous terrain of the Apennines and pushing the indigenous society westward. These new arrivals shared no common organization or identity, but all spoke related Indo-European languages that we call *Italic*, including Latin. These newcomers were warriors. By 800 B.C.E. they were in firm control of the mountainous region of central Italy and threatened the coastal societies of the west and south.

Carthage: The Merchants of Baal

Also around 800 B.C.E., Phoenicians arrived in the West from the regions of Tyre, Sidon, and Byblos. They established a series of bases along the route to and from Spain on the coast and on the islands of Corsica, Sicily, Ibiza, and Motya in the Mediterranean and at Utica and Carthage on the coast of North Africa. Gradually Carthage established itself as the center of an expanding Phoenician presence in the western Mediterranean.

The city was perfectly situated to profit from both the land and the sea. Its excellent double harbor made it an ideal port where ships could lie at rest, protected from storms as well as from enemies by a narrow 70-foot entrance to the sea that could be closed with iron chains. The city was equally protected on land, situated on a narrow isthmus and surrounded by massive walls. As long as Carthage controlled the sea, its commercial center was secure from any enemies.

By the middle of the sixth century B.C.E., Carthage was the center of a real empire. But in contrast with the Athenian Empire of the following century, Carthage was much more successful at integrating other cities and peoples into its mercenary military and thus sharing the burden of warfare. This multiethnic empire endured for three centuries, proving far more stable than any of those created by the Greeks.

Although superficially similar to many Greek cities, the Punic (from *Puni* or *Poeni*, the Roman name for the Carthaginians) state differed profoundly in the relationship between citizen and state. Ordinary citizens had little involvement and, apparently, little interest in government, and officials consistently came from among the wealthy and powerful merchant aristocracy. According to Aristotle, however, the aristocracy treated the rest of the population generously, sharing with it the profits of its commercial and imperial wealth. Thus the class pressures that created the Greek tyrants never emerged in Carthage.

Stable, prosperous, and devout, Carthage was the master of the western Mediterranean. But its dominion was not undisputed. From the sixth century B.C.E., the Punic Empire felt the pressure of ambitious Greek cities that were eager to gain a share of the West's riches.

MAP DISCOVERY

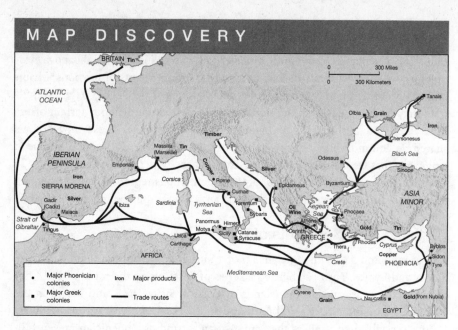

GREEK AND PHOENICIAN COLONIES AND TRADE

Note the location of the major Phoenician and Greek colonies and the extent of the trade routes to and from these colonies. Where, if at all, did Greek and Phoenician colonies come into close proximity and competition? Did the two systems compete for the same trade goods?

The Western Greeks

The Greek arrival in the west was the result of a much more complex process than the trading policy of the Phoenicians. As we saw in Chapter 2, toward the end of the Dark Age, commerce, overpopulation, and civic tension sent Greek colonists out in all directions. In the eighth century B.C.E., Crete, Rhodes, Corinth, Argos, Chalcis, Eretria, and Naxos all established colonies in Sicily and southern Italy.

In the seventh century B.C.E., Syracuse became the greatest city of Sicily and one of the most prosperous cities of the Greek world. Greek colonies spread slowly up the boot of Italy, known as Greater Greece, in pursuit of trade and arable land. By the last quarter of the seventh century B.C.E., the autonomous Greek colonies began to encroach on the Carthaginian empire's sphere of influence.

Both commercial rivalry and open warfare characterized the relationship between Greeks and Phoenicians in the western Mediterranean. In the course of the sixth century B.C.E., Greeks in Sicily attempted to expel the Phoenicians from the island. In the fifth century B.C.E., Syracuse, under its tyrant Gelon (ca. 540–478 B.C.E.), threatened both Punic and Greek cities on the island. In an attempt to defend its colonies, in 480 B.C.E. Carthage launched an enormous force to support Gelon's Greek enemies. The attack took place, probably not coincidentally, at the same moment that Xerxes invaded Greece. At the battle of Himera—fought, we are told, on the same day as the battle of Salamis—the Syracusans soundly defeated the Carthaginians.

Gelon's victory at Himera ushered in a period of prosperity and cultural achievement in Sicily. This prosperity continued after the elimination of the tyranny in midcentury, and in 415 B.C.E., Syracuse was able to withstand Athens's attempt at conquest. (See Chapter 3, p. 65.)

A far more serious threat appeared in 410 B.C.E., when a new Carthaginian army arrived in Sicily seeking revenge. The Carthaginians rapidly captured and destroyed Himera, extending the boundaries of Punic Sicily. This invasion initiated a century of inconclusive conflict between Syracuse and Carthage.

Early on in their struggle with the Sicilian Greeks, the Carthaginians found allies in the third major civilization of the West. These were the Etruscans, who in the seventh century B.C.E. dominated the western part of central Italy, known as Etruria.

Italy's First Civilization

Etruscan civilization was the first great civilization to emerge in Italy. The **Etruscans** have long been regarded as a people whose origins, language, and customs are shrouded in mystery. However, in recent years, while some DNA evidence suggests affinities with Asia Minor, archaeologists have demonstrated that Etruscan culture developed in western Italy out of indigenous tradition long present in Italy. This tradition shares much with Eastern civilizations, such as the importance of underworld gods, fertility cults, and the high status of women.

Etruscan civilization coalesced slowly in Etruria over the course of the seventh century B.C.E. from diverse groups sharing a similar cultural and linguistic tradition. In the mid-sixth century B.C.E., in the face of Greek pressure from the south, 12 of these groups united in a religious and military confederation. Over the next 100 years, the confederation expanded north into the Po Valley and south to Campania. Cities, each initially ruled by a king, were the centers of Etruscan civilization, and everywhere the Etruscans spread, they either improved on existing towns or founded new ones. The Etruscan confederation remained loose and never developed into a centralized empire. Etruscan kings assumed power in conquered towns, but between the sixth and fifth centuries B.C.E., Etruscan kingship gave way to oligarchic governments, much as Greek monarchies had a bit earlier. In the place of kings, aristocratic assemblies selected magistrates, often paired together or combined into "colleges" to prevent individuals from seizing power. These republican institutions provided the foundation for later Roman republican government.

An Archaic Society. The remnants of an ancient civilization, the Etruscans retained throughout their history social and cultural traditions that had long since vanished elsewhere in the Mediterranean. Society was divided sharply into two classes, lords and servants. The lords' wealth was based on the rich agricultural regions of Etruria where grain grew in abundance and on the equally rich deposits of copper and iron. The vast majority of the population were actual slaves, working the lands and mines of the aristocracy.

The aristocrats were aggressive and imaginative landowners. They developed hydraulic systems for draining marshes, produced a wine that was famous throughout the Mediterranean, and put their slaves to work in mines and in smelting. Still, they were largely absentee landlords, spending much of their time in the towns that characterized Etruscan civilization. These cities, with their massive walls, enclosed populations of as many as 20,000.

The most striking aspect of Etruscan life to Greek contemporaries and to later Romans was the elevated status of Etruscan women. As in the much earlier Minoan civilization, women played an active, public role in society. Unlike honorable Greek women, Etruscan women took part in banquets, attended and even occasionally presided over dances, concerts, and sporting events, and were active in political life. Greeks such as Aristotle regarded the public behavior of Etruscan women as lewd. When a king died, his successor had to be designated and consecrated by the Etruscan queen to establish his legitimacy. To later Romans, this practice was shocking.

Etruscan Dominance. While the Etruscans were consolidating their hegemony in western Italy, they were at the same time establishing their maritime power. From the seventh to the fifth centuries B.C.E., Etruscans controlled the Italian coast of the Tyrrhenian Sea as well as Sardinia. Attempts to extend farther south into Greek southern Italy and toward the Greek colonies on the modern French coast brought the Etruscans and the Greeks into inevitable conflict.

Common hostility toward the Greeks as well as complementary economic interests soon brought the Etruscans into alliances with Carthage. Toward the end of the sixth century B.C.E., Etruscan cities including Rome signed a series of pacts with Carthage that created military alliances against the Phocaeans and Syracuse. Etruscan fleets were victorious over the Phocaeans, driving them from Corsica, but they were no match for Syracuse. In 474 B.C.E., shortly after the battle of Himera, the Syracusan fleet destroyed that of the Etruscans off Cumae.

Cumae marked the beginning of Etruscan decline. Through the fifth century B.C.E., Etruscan cities lost control of the sea to the Greeks. Around the same time, Celts from north of the Alps invaded and conquered the Po Valley. And to the south, Etruscans saw their inland territories progressively slipping into the hands of their former subjects, the Romans, who had begun to acquire the commercial, political, and military expertise that would drive their long rise to dominance.

On the Etruscan sarcophagus of Larthia Scianti, a matron reclines as at a banquet. Etruscan scarcophagi, usually made of terracotta, frequently depicted the dead, often husband and wife, together reclining on a couch. Much of our knowledge of the first Italian civilization comes from the elaborate paintings and statuary found in Etruscan cemeteries. Nothing is know of Larthia Scianti, however women in Etruscan society exercised a more public and political role than did the Roman matrons who followed them.

From City to Empire, 509–146 B.C.E.

What manner of people were these Romans who, from obscure origins, came to rule an empire? Their own answer would have been simple: They were farmers and soldiers, simple people accustomed to simple, straightforward actions. Throughout their long history, Romans liked to refer to the clear-cut models provided by their semilegendary predecessors. These were myths, but they were important myths to Romans, who preferred concrete models to abstract principles.

Later Romans liked to imagine the history of their city as one predestined by the gods for greatness. Some liked to trace the origins of Rome to Romulus and Remus, twin sons of the war god Mars and a Latin princess. Other Romans, having absorbed the Homeric traditions of Greece, taught that the founder of Rome was Aeneas, son of the goddess of love, Aphrodite, and the Trojan Anchises, who had wandered west after the fall of Troy. All agreed that Rome had been ruled by kings, who underwent a steady decline in ability and morals until the last, Tarquin the Proud, was expelled by outraged Latins. These legends tell much about the attitudes and values of later Romans. They tell nothing about the actual origins of the city or its rise to greatness.

Latin Rome

Civilization in Italy meant Etruria to the north and Greater Greece to the south. In between lay Latium, a marshy region punctuated by hills on which a sparse population could find protection from disease and enemies.

The Alban Hills south of the Tiber were a center of Latin population. Sometime in the eighth century B.C.E., roughly 40 Latin villages formed a loose confederation, the Alban League, for military and religious purposes. Not long afterward, in the face of an expanding Etruscan confederation from the north and Sabine penetration from the east, the Albans established a village on the steep Palatine hill to the north. This Alban village, called Roma Quadrata, was soon joined by other Latin and Sabine settlements on nearby hills. By the end of the eighth century B.C.E., seven Latin villages along the route from the Tiber to Alba had formed a league for mutual defense and shared religious cults.

Early Roman society was composed of households; clans, or *gentes;* and village councils, or *curiae* (sing. *curia*). The male head of each household, the **paterfamilias**, had the power of life and death over its members and was responsible for the proper worship of the spirits of the family's ancestors, on whom continued prosperity depended.

Male members of village families formed councils, which were essentially religious organizations but also provided a forum for public discussion. These curiae tended to be dominated by gentes, but all males could participate, including those who belonged to the *plebians* or **plebs**, that is, families that were not organized into gentes. Later, the leaders of the gentes called themselves **patricians** ("descendants of fathers") and claimed superiority to the plebs, or common people.

Important plebeian and patrician families increased their power through a system of clientage, which remained a fundamental aspect of social and political organization throughout Roman history. Clients were free men who depended on the protection of a more powerful individual or family and who owed various services, including political support, in return for this protection.

Villages themselves grouped together for military and voting purposes into ethnic *tribus,* or tribes, each composed of a number of curiae. Each curia supplied a contingent of infantry, and each tribe cooperated to supply a unit of horsemen to the Roman army.

Assemblies of all members of the curiae expressed approval of major decisions, especially declaration of war and the selection of new kings, and thus played a real if limited political role. More powerful although less formal was the role of the Senate (assembly of elders), which was composed of heads of families. The Senate's power derived from the individual importance of its members and from its role in selecting a candidate for king, who was then presented to the assembly of the curiae for approval.

Kings served as religious leaders, the primary means of communication between gods and humans. Through the early Latin period, royal power remained fundamentally religious and limited by the Senate, curiae, gentes, and families.

The seven villages that made up primitive Rome developed independently of their Etruscan and Greek neighbors. This independent course of development changed in the middle of the seventh century B.C.E., when the Etruscans overwhelmed Latium and absorbed it into their civilization. Under its Etruscan kings, Rome first entered civilization.

Etruscan Rome

The Etruscans introduced in Latium, especially in Rome, their political, religious, and economic traditions. Etruscan city organization partially replaced Latin tribal structures. Etruscan kings and magistrates ruled Latin towns, increasing the power of traditional Latin kingship. The kings not only were religious leaders, but also led the army, served as judges, and held supreme political power. As Latium became an integral part of the Etruscan world, the Tiber became an important commercial route. For the first time, Rome began to enter the wider orbit of Mediterranean civilization.

Urban Growth. As Rome's importance grew, so did its size. Etruscan engineers drained the marshes into a great canal flowing to the Tiber, thus opening the lowlands between the hills to settlement. This in turn allowed them to create and pave the Forum. The Etruscans constructed a series of vast fortifications encircling the town. Under Etruscan influence, the fortified Capitoline hill, which served much like a Greek acropolis, became the cult center with the erection of the temple to Jupiter, the supreme god; Juno, his consort; and Minerva, an Etruscan goddess of craftwork who was similar to Athena. In its architecture, religion, commerce, and culture, Latin Rome was deeply indebted to its Etruscan conquerors.

As important as the physical and cultural changes brought by the Etruscans was their reorganization of the society. As in Greece, this restructuring was tied to changes in the military. Weakening the traditional Latin social units, the king divided Roman society into two groups: property owners and others. Landowners who were wealthy enough to provide armed military service were organized into five classes and ranked according to the quality of their arms and hence their wealth. Each class was further divided into military units called *centuries*. Members of these centuries constituted the centuriate assembly, which replaced the older curial assemblies for such vital decisions as the election of magistrates and the declaration of war.

The constitution and operation of this centuriate assembly ensured control by the most conservative forces within the society. Small centuries of wealthy well-armed cavalrymen and fully armed warriors outnumbered the more modestly equipped but more numerous centuries. Likewise, men over the age of 47, although in a minority, controlled over half the centuries in each class. Since votes were counted not by individuals but by centuries, this ensured within the assembly the domination of the rich over the poor, the older over the younger. The remainder of the society was the *infra classem* (literally "under class"), who owned no property and were thus excluded from military and political activity.

With this military and political reorganization came a reconstruction of the tribal system. Servius Tullius abolished the old tribal organization in favor of geographically organized tribes into which newcomers could easily be incorporated. Henceforth, while the family remained powerful, involvement in public life was based on property and geography.

Class Divisions. While the old tribal units and curiae declined, divisions between the patricians and the plebeians grew more distinct. During the monarchy, the patricians came to compose an upper stratum of wealthy nobles. Although partially protected by the kings, the plebeians, whether rich or poor, were pressed into a second-class status and denied access to political power.

The transformations brought about by the Etruscan kings became an enduring part of Rome. The Etruscans themselves did not. Around the traditionally reported date of 509 B.C.E. the Roman patricians expelled the last Etruscan king, Tarquin the Proud, and established a republic.

Rome and Italy

Just as in Rome, monarchy was giving way to oligarchic republics across Etruria in the sixth century B.C.E. Rome was hardly exceptional. However, the establishment of the Roman republic coincided roughly with the beginning of the Etruscan decline, allowing Rome to assert itself and to develop its Latin and Etruscan traditions in unique ways.

The Early Republic. The patrician oligarchy had engineered the end of the monarchy, and patricians dominated the offices and institutions of the new republic at the expense of the plebs, who, in losing the king, lost their only defender. Governmental institutions of the early republic developed within this context of patrician supremacy.

Characteristic of republican institutions was that at every level, power was shared by two or more equals who were elected for fixed terms. Replacing the king were the two *consuls*, each elected by the assembly for a one-year term. Initially, only the consuls held the **imperium**, the supreme power to command, to execute the law, and to impose the death penalty. Only in moments of grave crisis might a consul, with the approval of the Senate, name a single **dictator** with extraordinary absolute power for a very brief period, never more than six months. In time, other magistracies developed to perform specialized functions. *Praetors,* who in time also exercised the imperium, administered justice and defended the city in the absence of the consuls. *Quaestors* controlled finances. *Censors* assigned individuals their places in society, determined the amount of their taxes, filled vacancies in the Senate, and negotiated contracts for public construction projects. A variety of military commanders directed wars against neighboring cities and peoples under the imperium of the consuls. In all their actions these officeholders consulted with each other and with the Senate, which was composed of roughly 300 powerful former magistrates. The centuriate assembly functioned as the legislative organ of the state, but it continued to be dominated by the oldest and wealthiest members of society.

Patricians, Plebs, and Public Law. During the early republic, wealthy patricians, aided by their clients, monopolized the Senate and the magistracies. Patricians also controlled the priesthoods, positions which they held for life. With political and religious power came economic power. The poorer plebs in particular found themselves sinking into debt to wealthy patricians, losing their property, and with it the basis for military service and political participation.

The plebs began to organize in response to patrician control. On several occasions in the first half of the fifth century B.C.E., the whole plebeian order withdrew a short distance from the city, refusing to return or to serve in the military until conflicts with the patricians were resolved. In time, the plebs created their own assembly, the Council of the Plebs, which enacted laws that were binding on all plebeians. This council founded its own temples and elected magistrates called *tribunes*, whose persons were declared sacred to the gods. This conflict between the plebeians and the patricians, known as the Struggle of Orders, threatened to tear Roman society apart just as pressure from hostile neighbors placed Rome on the defensive.

Political Expansion. Roman preeminence in Latium had ended with the expulsion of the last king. The Etruscan town of Veii just north of the Tiber began periodic attacks against Rome. To the south, the Volscians had begun to expand northward into the Litis and Trerus valleys. This military pressure from the outside forced the patricians to seek a compromise with the plebeians. One of the first victories won by the plebs around 450 B.C.E. was the codification of basic Roman law, the Law of the Twelve Tables, which recognized the basic rights of all free citizens. The new law was posted publicly so that all could have access to it. Around the same time, the state began to absorb the plebeian political and religious organizations intact. Gradually, priesthoods, magistracies, and thus the Senate were opened to plebeians. In 287 B.C.E., as the result of a final secession of the plebs, the decisions of the plebeian assembly became binding on all citizens, patrician and plebeian alike.

Bitter differences at home did not prevent patricians and plebs from presenting a united front against their enemies abroad. By the beginning of the fourth century B.C.E., the united patrician-plebeian state was expanding its rule both northward and southward. Roman legions, commanded by patricians but formed of the whole spectrum of property-owning Romans, reestablished Roman preeminence in Latium and then began a series of wars that brought most of Italy under Roman control. In 396 B.C.E., Roman forces captured and destroyed Veii and shortly afterward conquered the rest of southern Etruria. In the south, Roman and Latin forces turned back the Volscians. By 295 B.C.E., Rome had secured its rule as far north as the Po Valley. In the south, Roman infantry and persistence proved the equal of professional Greek armies. Rome won a war of attrition against a series of Hellenistic commanders. By 265 B.C.E., Rome had absorbed the Hellenistic cities of the south.

Roman conquest benefited patrician and plebeian alike. While the patricians acquired wealth and power, the plebeians received a prize of equal value: land. After the capture of Veii, for example, the poor of Rome received shares of the conquered land. Since landowning was a prerequisite for military service, this distribution created still more peasant soldiers for further expeditions. Still, while the constant supply of new land did much to diffuse the tensions between orders, it did not actually resolve them. Into the late third century B.C.E., debt and landlessness remained major problems, creating tensions in Roman society. Probably not more than half of the citizen population owned land by 200 B.C.E.

Incorporating the Conquered. The Roman manner of treating conquered populations, radically different from anything seen before, also contributed to Rome's success. In war, no one could match the Roman legions for ruthless, thorough destruction. Yet no conquerors had ever shown themselves so generous in victory. After Rome crushed the Latin revolt of 338 B.C.E., virtually all of the Latins were incorporated into the Roman citizenry. Later colonies founded outside of Latium were given the same status as Latin cities. Other, more distant conquered peoples were considered allies and were required to provide troops but no tribute to Rome. In time, they too might become citizens.

The implications of these measures were revolutionary. By extending citizenship to conquered neighbors and by offering the future possibility to allies, Rome tied their fate to its own. Rather than potentially subversive subjects, conquered populations became strong supporters. Thus, in contrast to the Hellenistic cities of the east, where Greeks jealously guarded their status from the indigenous population, Rome's colonies acted as magnets, drawing local populations into the Roman cultural and political orbit. Finally, in all of its wars of conquest, Rome claimed a moral mandate. Romans went to great lengths to demonstrate that theirs were just wars, basing their claims on alleged acts of aggression by their enemies, on the appeal to Rome by its allies, and, increasingly, by presenting themselves as the preservers and defenders of Greek traditions of freedom. Both these political and propagandistic measures proved successful. Between 265 and 91 B.C.E. few serious revolts shook the peace and security of Italy south of the Po.

By 264 B.C.E., all of Italy was united under Roman hegemony. Roman expansion finally brought Rome into conflict with the great Mediterranean power of the west: Carthage.

Rome and the Mediterranean

Since its earliest days, Rome had allied itself with Carthage against the Greek cities of Italy. The zones of interest of the two cities had been quite separate. However, once Rome had conquered the Greek cities to the south, it became enmeshed in the affairs of neighboring Sicily, a region with well-established Carthaginian interests. There, in 265 B.C.E., a group of Italian mercenary pirates in Messina, threatened by Syracuse, requested Roman assistance. The Senate refused, but the plebeian assembly, eager for booty, exercised its newly won right to legislate for the republic and accepted. Shortly afterward, the Romans invaded Sicily, and Syracuse turned to its old enemy, Carthage, for assistance. The First Punic War had begun.

The First Punic War. This war, which lasted from 265 to 241 B.C.E., was a costly, brutal, and drawn-out affair that Rome won by dint of persistence and methodical calculation rather than strategic brilliance. Rome invaded and concluded an alliance with Syracuse in 263 B.C.E. The Romans won impressive initial victories but still could not deliver a knockout blow in either Sicily or North Africa for over 20 years. Finally, in 241 B.C.E., Rome forced the Carthaginian commander, Hamilcar Barca (ca. 270–229 B.C.E.), to surrender simply because the Romans could afford to build one more fleet than he. Carthage paid a huge indemnity and abandoned Sicily. Syracuse and Messina became allies of Rome. In a break with tradition, Rome obligated the rest of Sicily to pay a true tribute in the form of a tithe (one-tenth) of their crops. Shortly after that, Rome helped itself to Sardinia as well, from which it again demanded tribute, not simply troops. Rome had established an empire.

During the next two decades, Roman legions defeated the Ligurians on the northwest coast, the Celtic Gauls south of the Alps, and the Illyrians along the Adriatic coast. At the same time, Carthage fought a bitter battle against its own mercenary armies, which it had been unable to pay off after its defeat. Carthage then began the systematic creation of an empire in Spain. Trade between Carthage and Rome reached the highest level in history, but trade did not create friendship—only a wary peace. On both sides, powerful leaders saw the treaty of 241 B.C.E. as just a pause in a fight to the death.

Securing Western Hegemony. After the death of Hamilcar, Carthaginian successes in Spain, led by Hamilcar's son-in-law Hasdrubal (d. 221 B.C.E.) and his son Hannibal (247–183 B.C.E.), finally provoked Rome to war in 218 B.C.E. As soon as this Second Punic War had begun, Hannibal began an epic march north out of Spain, along the Mediterranean coast, and across the Alps. In spite of great hardships he was able to transport over 23,000 troops and approximately 18 war elephants into the plains of northern Italy.

Hannibal's brilliant generalship brought victory after victory to the Carthaginian forces. In the first engagement, on the Trebia River in the Po Valley, the Romans lost 20,000 men, two-thirds of their army. Carthaginian success encouraged the Gauls to join the fight against the Romans. Initially, Italian, Etruscan, and Greek allies remained loyal, but after Rome's catastrophic defeats at Lake Trasimene in Etruria in 217 B.C.E. and especially at Cannae in 216 B.C.E., a number of Italian colonies and allies, namely the cities of Capua and Syracuse, went over to the enemy. In the east, Philip V of Macedon (238–179 B.C.E.) made a treaty with Carthage in the hope of taking Illyria (today the coast of Croatia) from a defeated Rome.

MAP DISCOVERY

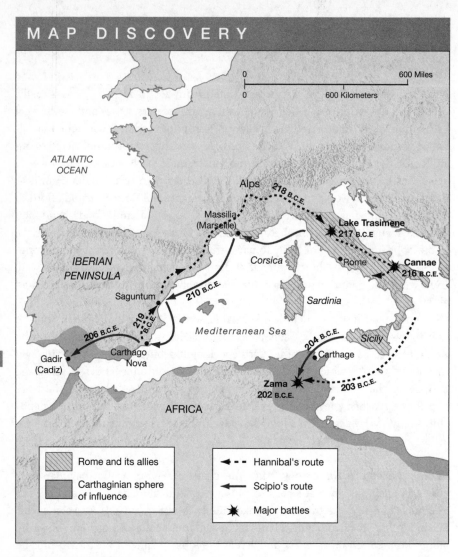

THE PUNIC WARS

What accidents of geography and political expansion made war between Rome and Carthage almost inevitable? What advantages might Hannibal have seen in taking the route he did to attack Rome? What were the long-term effects of Hannibal's route for the inhabitants of the Iberian Peninsula and Gaul? What parts of Carthage's African Empire might have been most attractive to Roman conquerors?

Three things, however, saved the Roman state. First, while some important allies and colonies defected, the majority held firm. Rome's traditions of sharing the fruits of victory with its allies, extending the rights of Roman citizenship, and protecting central and southern Italy against its enemies proved stronger than the appeals of Hannibal. Although he was victorious time and again, without local support Hannibal could not hold the terrain and cities he won.

The second reason for Rome's survival was the tremendous social solidarity that all classes and factions of its population showed during these desperate years. In spite of the internal tensions between patricians and plebeians, their ultimate dedication to Rome never faltered. Much of this loyalty was due to the Roman system of strong family and patronage ties. Kinsmen and clients answered the call of their patriarchs and patrons to bounce back repeatedly from defeat. Roman farmer-soldiers stood firm.

The third reason for Rome's ultimate success was Publius Cornelius Scipio (236–184 B.C.E.), also known as Scipio the Elder, a commander who was able to force Hannibal from Italy. Scipio, who earned the title Africanus for his victory, accomplished this not by attacking Hannibal directly, but by taking the war home to the enemy, first in Spain and then in Africa. In 210 B.C.E., Scipio arrived in Spain and rapidly captured the city of Cartagena (New Carthage). Within four years he destroyed Punic power in Spain. Riding the crest of popular enthusiasm at home, he raised a new army and in 204 B.C.E. sailed for Africa. His victories there drew Hannibal home, where at Zama in 202 B.C.E. the Roman commander destroyed the Carthaginian army. Zama put an end to both the Second Punic War and Carthaginian political power. Saddled with a huge indemnity and forced to abandon all of its territories and colonies to Rome, Carthage was reduced to a small portion of the North African coast. It had, in effect, become a Roman subject.

The Final Destruction. Still, this humiliating defeat was not enough for Rome. While some Roman senators favored allowing Carthage to survive as a means of keeping the Roman plebs under senatorial control, others demanded destruction. Chief among them was the censor Marcus Porcius Cato, known as Cato the Elder (234–149 B.C.E.), who ended every speech with "Carthage must be destroyed." Ultimately, trumped-up reasons were found to renew the war in 149 B.C.E. In contrast to the desperate, hard-fought campaigns of the Second Punic War, the Third was an unevenly matched slaughter. In 146 B.C.E., Scipio Aemilianus (184–129 B.C.E.), or Scipio the Younger, the adopted grandson of Scipio the Elder, overwhelmed Carthage and sold its few survivors into slavery. As a symbolic act of final destruction, he then had the site razed, plowed, and cursed. Carthage's fertile hinterland became the property of wealthy Roman senators.

Expansion into the Hellenistic East. In the same year that Carthage was destroyed, Roman armies destroyed Corinth, a second great center of Mediterranean commerce. This victory marked the culmination of Roman imperialist expansion eastward into the Greek and Hellenistic world, which had begun with the conquest of Illyria. This expansion was not simply the result of Roman imperialist ambitions. The Hellenistic states, in their constant warring and bickering, had drawn Rome into their conflicts against their neighbors. Greek states asked the Roman Senate to arbitrate their disputes. Pergamum requested military assistance against Macedonia. Appealing to Rome's claims as "liberator," cities pressed the Senate to preserve their freedom in the face of aggressive expansion by their more powerful neighbors.

Roman intentions may not have been conquest, but Roman intervention upset the balance of power in the Hellenistic world. The price of Roman arbitration, intervention, and protection was loss of independence. Gradually, the Roman shadow fell over the eastern Mediterranean.

The treaty that Philip V of Macedon concluded with Carthage during the Second Punic War provided an initial excuse for war, one that was seized on more eagerly by the plebeian assembly than by the Senate. Shortly after its victory at Zama, Rome provoked Philip to war and then easily defeated him in 197 B.C.E., proclaiming the freedom of the Greek cities and withdrawing from Greece. In 189 B.C.E., the Seleucid Antiochus III (223–187 B.C.E.) of Syria suffered the same fate, and Rome declared the Greek cities in Asia Minor that he had controlled free. The Greeks venerated the Roman commander, Titus Quinctius Flamininus (228–174 B.C.E.), as a god—the first Roman to be accorded this eastern honor.

In reality, the control of the freed cities lay in the hands of local oligarchs who were favorable to Rome. In 179 B.C.E., Philip's son Perseus (179–168 B.C.E.) attempted to stir up democratic opposition to Rome within the cities. This time, Rome responded more forcefully. The Macedonian kingdom was divided into four republics governed by their own senates and magistrates selected from among the local aristocrats. In Epirus, 70 cities were destroyed, and 150,000 people were sold into slavery.

The final episode of Rome's expansionist drama unfolded during the Third Punic War. When Rome resumed its war with Carthage in 149 B.C.E., several Greek cities attempted once more to assert their autonomy from the hated oligarchies established by Rome. Retribution was swift. Roman legions crushed the rebel forces, and, as an example to all, Corinth was razed and its population was enslaved.

In the west, in northern Italy, Spain, and Africa, Roman conquest had been direct and complete. Tribal structures had been replaced by Roman provinces governed by former magistrates or proconsuls. In the east, Rome preferred to work through the existing political hierarchies. Still, Rome cultivated its image as protector of Greek liberties against the Macedonian and Seleucid monarchies and preferred indirect control to annexation. Its power was no less real for being indirect.

By 146 B.C.E., the Roman republic controlled the whole rim of the Mediterranean from Rhodes in the east across Greece, Dalmatia, Italy, southern Gaul, Spain, and North Africa. Even Syria and Egypt, although nominally independent, had to bow before Roman will. Through perseverance and determination, Rome had risen from obscurity to become the greatest power the West had ever known. The republic had endured great adversity. It would not survive prosperity.

THE ROMAN REPUBLIC

509 B.C.E.	Expulsion of last Etruscan king; beginning of Roman Republic
ca. 450 B.C.E.	Law of the Twelve Tables
396 B.C.E.	Rome conquers southern Etruria
295 B.C.E.	Rome extends rule north to Po Valley
265–241 B.C.E.	First Punic War
264 B.C.E.	All of Italy under Roman control
218–202 B.C.E.	Second Punic War
149–146 B.C.E.	Third Punic War; Carthage is destroyed

Republican Civilization

Territorial conquest, the influx of unprecedented riches, and exposure to sophisticated Hellenistic civilization ultimately overwhelmed earlier Roman civilization. This civilization had been created by stubborn farmers and soldiers who valued authority, simplicity, and piety above all else. This unique culture was the source of strength that led Rome to greatness, but its limitations prevented the republic from resolving its internal social tensions and the external problems caused by the burden of empire.

One of a series of Roman mosaics illustrating tasks appropriate to the months of the year. Here two laborers are using an olive press with a horizontal screw for the December olive pressing.

Farmers and Soldiers

The ideal Roman farmer was not the great estate owner of the Greek world, but the smallholder, the dirt farmer of central Italy. Typical farm families, with holdings of perhaps as little as 10 acres, raised grain, beans, and hogs for their own consumption. In addition, they cultivated vineyards and olive groves for cash crops. But the most important crop of Roman farms was citizens. "From farmers come the bravest men and the sturdiest soldiers," wrote Cato the Elder. Nor was the ideal Roman soldier the gallant cavalryman but rather the solid foot soldier. Cavalry—composed of wealthy citizens who made up the elite **equestrian** order—and especially allies provided reconnaissance and protected Roman flanks. The main fighting force, however, was the infantry. Sometime in the early republic the Greek phalanx was transformed into the Roman legion, a flexible unit composed of 30 companies of 120 men each, armed with javelins and short swords.

These solid, methodical troops, the backbone of the republican armies that conquered the Mediterranean, were among the victims of that conquest. The pressures of constant international warfare were destroying the farmer-soldiers whom the traditionalists loved to praise. When the Roman sphere of interest had been confined to central Italy, farmers could do their planting in spring, serve in the army during the summer months, and return home to care for their farms in time for harvest. When Rome's wars became international expeditions lasting for years, many soldiers, unable to work their lands while doing military service, had to mortgage their farms in order to support their families. When they returned, they often found that during their prolonged absences they had lost their farms to wealthy aristocratic moneylenders. While aristocrats amassed vast landed estates worked by imported slaves, ordinary Romans and Italians lacked even a family farm capable of supporting themselves and their families. Without land they and their sons were excluded from further military service and sank into the growing mass of desperately poor, disfranchised citizens.

The Roman Family

In Roman tradition, the paterfamilias was the master of the family—which in theory included his wife, children, and slaves—over whom he exercised the power of life and death. This authority lasted as long as he lived. Only at his death did his sons, even if they were long grown and married, achieve legal and financial independence. The family was the basic unit of society, of the state.

Although not kept in seclusion as in Greece, Roman women theoretically never exercised independent power in this male-dominated world. Before marriage, a Roman girl was subject to the authority of her father. When she married, her father traditionally transferred legal guardianship to her husband, thus severing her bonds to paternal family. A husband could divorce his wife at will, returning her and her dowry to her father. However, wives did exercise real though informal authority within the family. Part of this authority came from their role in the moral education of their children and the direction of the household. Part also came from their control over their dowries.

Paternal authority over children was absolute. Not all children born into a marriage became members of the family. The Law of the Twelve Tables allowed defective children to be killed for the good of the family. Newborn infants were laid on the ground before the father, who decided whether the child should be raised. If there were too many mouths to feed or the child was simply unwanted, the father could command that the infant be killed or abandoned. Abandoned children might be adopted by childless couples.

Nor were all sons born into Roman families. Romans made use of adoption for many purposes. Families without heirs could adopt children. Powerful political and military figures might adopt promising young men as their political heirs. These adopted sons held the same legal rights as the father's natural offspring and thus were integral members of his family.

Slaves, too, were members of the family. On the one hand, slaves were property without personal rights. On the other, they might live and work alongside the free members of the family, worship the family gods, and enjoy the protection and endure the authority of the paterfamilias.

Social Effects of Expansion

In the wake of imperial conquests, the Roman family and its environment began to change in ways that were disturbing to many of the oligarchy. Some women, perhaps in imitation of their more liberated Hellenistic sisters, began to take a more active role in public life. One example is Cornelia, a daughter of Scipio Africanus. After her husband's death in 154 B.C.E., she refused to remarry, devoting herself instead to raising her children, administering their inheritance, and directing their political careers.

Some married women, too, escaped the authority of their husbands. Fewer and fewer fathers transferred authority over their daughters to their husbands. Instead, daughters remained under their father's authority as long as he lived. This meant that on the father's death, they became independent persons, able to manage their own affairs without their husbands' consent or interference. Although some historians believe that sentimental bonds of affection may have increased between many husbands and wives and parents and children as legal bonds loosened, it also meant that the wife's relationship to her children was weakened. Roman mothers had never been legally related to their children. Wives and mothers were not fully part of their husbands' families. Their brother's families, not their own children, were their natural heirs. Just as adoption created political bonds, marriage to daughters sealed alliances between men. However, when these alliances fell apart or more advantageous ones presented themselves, fathers could force their daughters to divorce their husbands and to marry someone else. Divorce became increasingly common in the second century B.C.E. More and more, wives were temporary visitors in their husbands' homes.

Roman Religion

Romans worshipped many gods, the more the better. Every aspect of daily life and work was the responsibility of individual powers, or *numina*. Every man had his *genius* or personal *numen*, just as every woman had her *juno*. Each family had its household powers, the *lares familiares*, whose proper worship was the responsibility of the paterfamilias. These family spirits exercised a binding power, a *religio*, on the Romans, and the pious Roman householder recognized these claims and undertook the *officia*, or duties, to which the spirits were entitled. These basic attitudes of religion, piety, and office lay at the heart of Roman reverence for order and authority. They extended to other traditional Roman and Latin gods such as Jupiter, the supreme god; Juno, his wife; Mars, the god of war; and the two-faced Janus, spirit of gates and new beginnings.

Outside the household, worship of the gods and the reading of the future in the entrails of sacrificed animals, the flight of birds, or changes in weather were the responsibilities of colleges of priests. Roman priests did not, as did those in the Near East, form a special caste but rather were important members of the elite who held priesthoods in addition to other public offices. Religion was less a matter of personal relationship with the gods than a public, civic activity that bound society together. State-supported cults with their colleges of priests, Etruscan- and Greek-style temples, and elaborate ceremonies were integral parts of the Roman state and society. The world of the gods reflected that of mortals. As the Roman mortal world expanded, so did the divine. Romans were quick to identify foreign gods with their own. Thus Zeus became Jupiter, Hera became Juno, and Aphrodite became Venus.

Still, the elasticity of Roman religion could stretch just so far. With the empire came not only the cults of Zeus, Apollo, and Aphrodite to Rome but that of Dionysus as well. Unlike the formal public cults of the other Greek deities, which were firmly in the control of authorities, that of Dionysus was largely outside state control. Women, in the tradition of the maenads, controlled much of the ecstatic and overtly sexual rituals associated with the god. Following the Second Punic War, the cult of Dionysus, known in Latin as Bacchus, spread rapidly in Italy. At its secret rites, or *Bacchanalia*, men and women were rumored to engage in every kind of sexual act.

In 186 B.C.E., the Senate decreed the cult of Bacchus a conspiracy and ordered an inquiry. The consul Spurius Postumius Albinus, acting on the false testimony of a former prostitute, began a brutal persecution. Rituals were banned, priests and adherents were arrested, and rewards were offered to informants, who provided lurid and fanciful accounts of what had taken place at the Bacchanalia. Hundreds of people were imprisoned, and greater numbers were executed. The Senate ordered all shrines to Bacchus destroyed and Bacchanalia banned throughout Italy. Perhaps more than any other episode, the suppression of the Bacchic cult showed the oligarchy's fear of the changes sweeping Roman civilization.

Republican Letters

As Rome absorbed foreign gods, it also absorbed foreign letters. From the Etruscans the Romans adopted and adapted the alphabet, the one in which most Western languages are written to this day. However, before the third century B.C.E., apart from extravagant funerary eulogies carefully preserved within families, Romans had no apparent interest in writing or literature as such. The birth of Latin letters began with Rome's exposure to Greek civilization.

Greek Historians of Rome. Early in the third century B.C.E., Greek authors had begun to pay attention to expanding Rome. The first serious Greek historian to focus on this new Western power was Timaeus (ca. 356–ca. 260 B.C.E.), who spent most of his productive life in Athens. There he wrote a history of Rome up to the Pyrrhic war, interviewing Roman and Greek witnesses to gain an understanding of this Italian city that had defeated a Hellenistic army. Polybius (ca. 200–ca. 118 B.C.E.), the greatest of the Greek historians to record Rome's rise to power, wrote a history that is both the culmination of the traditions of Greek historiography and its transformation, since it centers on the rise of a non-Greek power to rule "almost the whole inhabited world."

The Origins of Latin Literature. At the same time that Greeks began to take Rome seriously, Romans themselves became interested in Greece, in particular in the international Hellenistic culture of the eastern Mediterranean. The earliest Latin literary works were clearly adaptations if not translations of Hellenistic genres and texts. Already in 240 B.C.E., plays in the Greek tradition were said to have been performed in Rome. The earliest extant literary works, ironically for the sober image of the Roman farmer-soldier, are the plays of Plautus (ca. 254–184 B.C.E.) and Terence (186–159 B.C.E.), lightly adapted translations of Hellenistic comedies.

The Crisis of Roman Virtue

Rome's rise to world power within less than a century profoundly affected every aspect of republican life. Magistrates operating far from senatorial control in conquered provinces exercised power and found opportunities for enrichment never before seen. Successful commanders, honored and even deified by Eastern cities, felt the temptation to ignore the strict requirements of senatorial accountability. Provincial commanders enriched themselves through extortion, collusion with dishonest government contractors and tax collectors, and wholesale bribe-taking. Ordinary citizens, aware of such abuses, felt increasingly threatened by the wealthy and powerful.

In the second century B.C.E., Romans found themselves in a dilemma as the old and the new exerted equal pressures. These tensions led to almost a century of bitter civil strife and ultimately to the disintegration of the republic. The complex interaction of these tensions can best be seen in the life of one man, Marcus Porcius Cato.

Cato the Elder is often presented as the preserver of the old traditions, in contrast to Scipio Aemilianus, destroyer of Carthage and proponent of Hellenism in the Roman world. But if the division between old and new, between Cato and Scipio, had been so clear-cut, the dilemma of republican Rome would not have been so great. As it was, Cato reflected in himself this contradictory clash of values. Like the two-faced god Janus, whom he invoked in all his undertakings, Cato was the stern censor, the guardian and proponent of traditional Roman virtue, as well as the new Roman of shrewd business acumen, influence, and power unimaginable to the simple farmers he professed to admire.

Cato was born in the Latin town of Tusculum in 234 B.C.E. and grew to maturity on a family estate in Sabine territory. He came of age just at the start of the Second Punic War and distinguished himself in campaigns against Hannibal in Italy and Syracuse in Sicily. In between campaigns he became even more famous for his eloquence in pleading legal cases. His talents and energy brought him to the attention of powerful members of the senatorial aristocracy, under whose patronage he came to Rome. There he began to rise through the offices of military tribune, quaestor, and ultimately consul and censor.

This first-generation senator became the spokesman for the traditional values of Rome, for severity and simplicity, for honesty and frugality in private and public life. Cato ridiculed Greek philosophy and education, and he glorified his own simple farm life, the care he took in the management of his estates and of his extended *familia*, and his working in his fields side by side with his slaves.

Actually, Cato, as much as anyone else, was deeply involved in the rapid changes brought about by the empire. He may have worked along with his slaves, but as soon as they grew old, he sold them to the state to avoid having to support them, something no conscientious paterfamilias would ever have done. Although he led the battle to prevent senators from participating in commerce, he was perhaps the first of that body to diversify his holdings and investments. Although he avoided conspicuous

A memorial sculpture of Cato the Elder and his wife. Cato defended the ancient Roman traditions even as he himself was deeply influenced by the changes sweeping Rome. His married life was but one example of this: his treatment of his wives differed little from that of his slaves. After the death of his first wife, Licinia, he used a slave for sexual pleasure until his married son showed his disapproval. Cato immediately asked one of his clients, a former secretary for his daughter, Salonia, whom he promptly married. The sculpture represents him with Salonia.

consumption himself, as consul and censor he was responsible for many of the sumptuous building projects in Rome through which ordinary Romans first experienced the luxuries of the Hellenistic world. While scorning Greek culture, he worked bits of Greek authors even into his attacks on Greek civilization.

Cato was neither duplicitous nor hypocritical. He was simply typical. Many senators agreed with him that the old values were slipping away and, with them, the foundation of the republic. Many feared that personal ambition was undermining the power of the oligarchy. Yet these same people could not resist exploiting the changed circumstances for their own benefit.

SUMMARY

The Western Mediterranean to 509 B.C.E.   Civilization came to the western Mediterranean through Greek and Phoenician expansion. The Phoenicians established bases on the route to and from Spain, including a base at Carthage on the coast of North Africa. By the middle of the sixth century B.C.E., Carthage was the center of a stable and prosperous empire. In the eighth and seventh centuries B.C.E., the Greeks colonized Sicily and parts of Italy. Greek expansion led to conflict with Carthage. The Etruscans laid the foundations of Roman society and government.

From City to Empire, 509–146 B.C.E.   Early Roman society was composed of households headed by a paterfamilias. Over time, Roman society divided into plebians and patricians. Roman political institutions evolved from family and village networks. Etruscan and Latin traditions merged in Rome. Around 509 B.C.E., Roman patricians expelled the last Etruscan king and established a republic, an event that led to greater concentration of power in the hands of the patricians. Roman expansion contributed to social tension. In this context, the plebeians won a series of political victories. The Romans were remarkably successful at incorporating conquered peoples into their society. The Punic Wars with Carthage marked a turning point in the history of the Republic. By 146 B.C.E., the Roman republic controlled the whole rim of the Mediterranean.

Republican Civilization   The Roman ideal was the small farmer. Such people were the backbone of the Roman army. Ironically, Roman military success and expansion concentrated land and wealth in the hands of elites, at the expense of small farmers. The Roman family was centered on the almost unlimited power of the male head of the household, the paterfamilias. Roman expansion created perceived threats to traditional familial order. The Romans worshiped many gods. Religion was less a matter of personal relationship with the gods than a public, civic activity that bound society together. The birth of Latin letters began with Rome's exposure to Greek civilization.

The Crisis of Roman Virtue   Rome's rise to world power within less than a century profoundly affected every aspect of republican life. The life of Marcus Porcius Cato epitomizes the tension between tradition and change in the late Republic. Like many others of his generation, Cato feared change at the same time as he exploited it for his own benefit.

QUESTIONS FOR REVIEW

1. Why might the Greeks have been surprised by certain characteristics of Carthaginian and Etruscan society?
2. What social, political, and military practices made possible the expansion of Rome from a collection of villages into a power that ultimately destroyed Carthage in the Punic Wars?
3. How were family and household life organized in the domus of the Roman Republic?
4. Why were Romans like Cato the Elder concerned by the changes that accompanied the expansion of Roman international power?

Imperial Rome, 146 B.C.E.–192 C.E.

The Price of Empire, 146–121 B.C.E.

Roman victory defeated the republic. The creation of a Mediterranean empire brought in its wake a century of revolutionary change before new and stable social, cultural, and political forms were achieved in the Roman world.

Winners and Losers

Rome had emerged victorious in the Punic and Macedonian wars, but the real winners were the members of the oligarchy, the **optimates** (the "best"), as they called themselves, whose wealth and power had grown beyond all imagining. These optimates included roughly 300 senators and magistrates, most of whom had inherited wealth, political connections, and long-established clientages. Since military command and government of the empire were entrusted to magistrates who were answerable only to the Senate of which they were members, the empire was essentially their private domain.

But new circumstances created new opportunities for many others. Italian merchants, slave traders, entrepreneurs, and bankers, many of lowly origin, poured into the cities of the East in the wake of the Roman legions. These newly enriched Romans constituted a second elite and formed themselves into a separate order, that of the *equites,* or equestrians, who were distinguished by their wealth and honorific military service on horseback but were connected with the old military elite. Since the Senate did not create a government bureaucracy to administer the empire, equestrian tax, farmers became essential to provincial government. Companies of these *publicans,* or tax collectors, purchased the right to collect rents on public land, tribute, and customs duties from provincials. Whatever they collected beyond the amount contracted for by Roman officials was theirs to keep.

The losers in the wars included the vanquished who were sold into slavery by the tens of thousands; the provincials who bore the Roman yoke; the Italian allies who had done so much for the Romans; and even the citizen farmers, small shopkeepers, and free artisans of the republic. All four groups suffered from the effects of empire, and over the next century, all resorted to violence against the optimates.

Roman slaves sifting grain. Roman victories in the Punic and Macedonian wars brought a huge influx of slaves from the conquered lands. Slaves were pressed into service on the estates and plantations of wealthy landowners.

Slave Revolts. The slaves revolted first. Thousands of them, captured in battle or taken after victory, flooded the Italian and Sicilian estates of the wealthy. Estimates vary, but in the first century B.C.E. the slave population of Italy was probably around two million, fully one-third of the total population. This vastly expanded slave world overwhelmed the traditional role of slaves within the Roman familia. Rural slaves on absentee estates enjoyed none of the protections afforded traditional Roman servants. Cato sold off his slaves when they reached old age; others simply worked them to death. Many slaves, born free citizens of Hellenistic states, found such treatment unbearable. Slaves rose up against their masters in Sicily in 135 B.C.E. and again a generation later and in southern Italy between 104 and 101 B.C.E. The most serious slave revolt occurred in Italy between 74 and 71 B.C.E. Gladiators—professional slave fighters trained for Roman amusement—revolted in Capua. Under the competent leadership of the Thracian gladiator Spartacus, over 100,000 slaves took up arms against Rome. Ultimately, eight legions, more troops than had met Hannibal at Zama, were needed to put down the revolt.

Provincial Revolts. Revolts profoundly disturbed the Roman state, all the more because it was not just slaves who revolted. In many cases, poor free peasants and disgruntled provincials rose up against Rome. The most significant provincial revolt was that of Aristonicus, the illegitimate half-brother of Attalus III (ca. 138–133 B.C.E.) of Pergamum, a Roman client state. Attalus had left his kingdom to Rome at his death. In an attempt to assert his right to the kingdom, Aristonicus armed slaves and peasants and attacked the Roman garrisons. The hellenized cities of Asia Minor remained loyal to Rome, but this provincial uprising, the first of many over the centuries, lasted more than three years, from 133 to 130 B.C.E.

Revolts by slaves and provincials were disturbing enough. Revolts by Rome's Italian allies were much more serious. After the Second Punic War, these allies, on whose loyalty Rome had depended for survival, found themselves badly treated and exploited. Government officials used state power to undermine the position of the Italian elites. At the same time, Roman aristocrats used their economic power to drive the Italic peasants from their land, replacing them with slaves. A serious revolt took place between 91 and 89 B.C.E. after the Senate blocked an attempt to extend citizenship to the allies. During this so-called Social War (from *socii*, the Latin word for allies), almost all the Italian allies rose against Rome. These revolts differed from those in the provinces in that the Italian elites as well as the masses aligned themselves against the Roman oligarchy. Even some ordinary Roman citizens joined the rebel forces against the powerful elite.

Optimates and Populares

The despair that could lead ordinary Roman citizens to armed rebellion grew from the social and economic consequences of conquests. While aristocrats amassed vast landed estates worked by cheap slaves, ordinary Romans often lacked even a family farm capable of supporting them and their families. Many found their way to Rome, where they swelled the ranks of the unemployed, crowded into shoddily constructed tenements, and lived off the public subsidies.

In the face of the oligarchy's unwillingness to deal with the problem, the tribune Tiberius Gracchus (ca. 163–133 B.C.E.) in 133 B.C.E. attempted to introduce a land-reform program that would return citizens to agriculture. Gracchus was the first of the **populares**, political leaders appealing to the masses.

Tiberius Gracchus. During the previous century, great amounts of public land had illegally come into private hands. With the support of reform-minded aristocrats and commoners, Gracchus proposed a law that would limit the amount of public land an individual could hold to about 312 acres. He also proposed a commission to distribute to landless peasants the land recovered by the state as a result of the law. Because many senators who illegally held vast amounts of public land strongly opposed the measure, it faced certain failure in the Senate. Gracchus therefore took it to the plebeian assembly, where it was assured support from the rural poor. The law passed, but Gracchus's maneuvering lost him many of his aristocratic supporters, who feared that a popular democracy led by a demagogue was replacing the senatorial oligarchy.

Also in 133 B.C.E., Gracchus introduced another bill that called for the royal treasury of the kingdom of Pergamum, bequeathed to Rome by Attalus III, to be used to help citizens receiving land to purchase livestock and equipment. These laws, which challenged the Senate's traditional control over finance and foreign affairs, angered the conservative elite; but as long as Gracchus held office, he was protected from any sort of attack by the traditional immunity accorded to tribunes. It was no secret, however, that the Senate planned to prosecute him as soon as his one-year term expired. To escape this fate, he appealed to the assembly to reelect him for an unprecedented second consecutive term. To his opponents this appeal smacked of an attempt to make himself sole ruler, a democratic tyrant on the Greek model. A group of senators and their clients, led by one of Gracchus's own cousins, broke into the assembly meeting at which the election was to take place and murdered the tribune and 300 of his supporters.

Gaius Gracchus. The optimates in the Senate could eliminate Tiberius Gracchus, but they could not so easily eliminate the movement he had led. In 123 B.C.E., his younger brother, Gaius Sempronius Gracchus (153–121 B.C.E.), became tribune. During his two one-year terms he initiated an even broader and more radical reform program. Tiberius had been concerned only about poor citizens. Gaius attempted to broaden the citizenry and to shift the balance of power away from the Senate.

In the short run, Gaius's program was a failure. In 121 B.C.E., he was not reelected for a third term and thus lost the immunity of the tribunate. Recalling his brother's fate, he armed his supporters. Once more the Senate acted, ordering the consul to take whatever measures he deemed necessary. Gaius and some 3,000 of his supporters died.

The deaths of Tiberius and Gaius Gracchus marked a new beginning in Roman politics. Not since the end of the monarchy had a political conflict been decided with personal violence. The whole episode provided a model for future attempts at reform. Reformers would look not to the Senate or the aristocracy but to the people, from whom they would draw their political power. The experience of the Gracchi also provided a model for repression of other reform programs: violence.

The End of the Republic

With the Gracchi dead and the core of their reforms dismantled, the Senate appeared victorious against all challengers. In reality, Rome had solved neither the problem of internal conflict between rich and poor nor that of how to govern its enormous empire. The apparent calm ended when revolts in Africa and Italy exposed the fragility of the Senate's control and ushered in an ever-increasing spiral of violence and civil war.

The Crisis of Government

In 112 B.C.E., the Senate declared war against Jugurtha (ca. 160–104 B.C.E.), a North African client state king, who, in his war against a rival, had killed some Roman merchants in the Numidian city of Cirta. The war dragged on for five years amid accusations of corruption, incompetence, and treason. Finally, in 107 B.C.E., the people elected as consul Gaius Marius (157–86 B.C.E.), a "new man" who had risen through the tribunate, and entrusted to him the conduct of the war. To raise an army, Marius ignored property qualifications and enlisted many impoverished Romans, arming them at public expense. Although recruiting of landless citizens had probably taken place before, no one had done it in such an overt and massive manner. Marius quickly defeated Jugurtha in 106 B.C.E.

In the following year, Celtic and Germanic barbarians crossed the Alps into Italy. Although technically disqualified from further terms, Marius was elected consul five times between 104 and 100 B.C.E. to meet the threat. During this period he continued to recruit soldiers from among the poor and, on his own authority, extended citizenship to allies. To his impoverished soldiers, Marius promised land, but after his victory in 101 B.C.E., the Senate refused to give farms to veterans. As a result, Marius's armies naturally shifted their allegiance away from the Roman state and to their popular commander. Soon this pattern of loyalty became the norm. Politicians forged close bonds with the soldiers of their armies. Individual commanders, not the state or the Senate, ensured that their recruits received their pay, shared in the spoils of victory, and obtained land on their retirement. In turn, the soldiers became fanatically devoted to their commanders. Republican armies had become personal armies, potent tools in the hands of ambitious politicians.

The Civil Wars. The outbreak of the Social War in 91 B.C.E. marked the first use of these armies in civil war. Both Marius and the consul Lucius Cornelius Sulla (138–78 B.C.E.) raised armies to fight the Italians, who were pacified only after Roman citizenship was extended to all Italians in 89 B.C.E. The next year, Mithridates VI (120–63 B.C.E.), the king of Pontus, took advantage of the Roman preoccupation in Italy to invade the province of Asia. As soon as the Italian threat receded, Sulla, as the representative of the optimates, raised an army to fight Mithridates. Marius, as leader of the populares who favored reform, attempted to have Sulla relieved of command. Sulla marched on Rome, initiating a bloody civil war. In the course of this war, Rome was occupied three times, once by Marius and twice by Sulla. Each commander ordered mass executions of his opponents and confiscated their property, which he then distributed to his supporters.

Ultimately, Sulla emerged victorious and ruled as dictator from 82 to 79 B.C.E., using this time to shore up senatorial power. In 79 B.C.E., his reforms in place, Sulla stepped down to allow a return to oligarchic republican rule. Although his changes bought a decade of peace, they did not solve the fundamental problems dividing optimates and populares. If anything, his rule had proved that the only real political option was a dictatorship by a powerful individual with his own army.

Republican Crisis. Marcus Tullius Cicero (106–43 B.C.E.) reflected the strengths and weaknesses of the republican tradition in the first century B.C.E. Like Cato in an earlier age, he was a "new man," the son of a wealthy equestrian who provided his children with the best possible education both in Rome and in Athens and Rhodes. After returning to Rome, Cicero quickly earned a reputation for his skills as a courtroom orator.

Cicero identified firmly with the elite, hoping that the republic could be saved through the harmonious cooperation of the equestrian and senatorial orders. In 63 B.C.E., Cicero was elected consul, the first "new man" to hold the office in over 30 years. The real threat to the existence of the republic was posed by the ambitions of powerful military commanders: Pompey (106–48 B.C.E.), Crassus (ca. 115–53 B.C.E.), and Julius Caesar (100–44 B.C.E.).

Pompey and Crassus, both protégés of Sulla, rose rapidly and unconstitutionally through a series of special proconsular commands by judicious use of fraud, violence, and corruption. Pompey first won public acclaim by commanding a victorious army in Africa and Spain. On his return to Rome in 70 B.C.E., he united with Crassus, who had won popularity for suppressing the Spartacus rebellion. Together, they worked to dismantle the Sullan constitution to the benefit of the populares. In return, Pompey received an extraordinary command over all of the coasts of the Mediterranean, in theory to suppress piracy but actually to give him control over all of the provinces of the empire. When, in 66 B.C.E., King Mithridates of Pontus again attacked Greece,

Pompey assumed command of the provinces of Asia. His army not only destroyed Mithridates but continued on and conquered Armenia, Syria, and Palestine.

While Pompey was extending the frontiers of the empire to the Euphrates, Crassus, whose wealth was legendary, was consolidating his power. He allied himself with Julius Caesar, a young, well-connected orator from one of Rome's most ancient patrician families, who nevertheless promoted the cause of the populares. The Senate feared the ambitious and ruthless Crassus. It was to block the election of Crassus's candidate Catiline (Lucius Sergius Catilina, ca. 108–62 B.C.E.) to the consulate in 63 B.C.E. that the Senate elected Cicero instead. Catiline soon joined a conspiracy of Sullan veterans and populares, but Cicero quickly uncovered and suppressed the conspiracy and ordered Catiline's execution.

The First Triumvirate. When Pompey returned from Asia in triumph in 62 B.C.E., he expected to find Italy convulsed with the Catiline revolt and in need of a military savior in the tradition of Sulla. Instead, thanks to Cicero's quick action, all was in order. Although he never forgave Cicero for stealing his glory, Pompey disbanded his army and returned to private life, asking only that the Senate approve his organization of the territories he had conquered and grant land to his veterans. The Senate refused. In response, Pompey formed an uneasy alliance with Crassus and Caesar. This alliance was known as the **First Triumvirate**, from the Latin for "three men." Caesar was elected consul in 59 B.C.E. and the following year received command of the province of Cisalpine Gaul in northern Italy.

Pompey and Crassus may have thought that this command would remove the ambitious young man from the political spotlight. Instead, Caesar used his province as a staging ground for the conquest of a vast area of western Europe to the mouth of the Rhine. In 53 B.C.E., Crassus died leading an army in Syria, leaving Pompey and the popular young Caesar to dispute supreme power. As word of Caesar's military successes increased his popularity at Rome, it also increased Pompey's suspicion of his younger associate. Finally, in 49 B.C.E., Pompey's supporters in the Senate relieved Caesar of his command and ordered him to return to Italy.

Return he did, but not as commanded. Rather than leave his army, as ordered, on the far side of the Rubicon River, which marked the boundary between his province of Cisalpine Gaul and Italy, Caesar marched on Rome at the head of his legions. This meant civil war, a vicious bloodletting that convulsed the whole Mediterranean world. In 48 B.C.E., Caesar defeated Pompey in northern Greece. Pompey was assassinated shortly afterward in Egypt. Still, the wars went on between Pompey's supporters and Caesar until 45 B.C.E., when, with all his enemies defeated, Caesar returned to Rome.

The Second Triumvirate. In Rome, unlike Sulla, Caesar showed his opponents clemency as he sought to heal the wounds of war and to undertake an unprecedented series of reforms.

Still, Caesar made no pretense of returning Rome to republican government. In early 44 B.C.E., although serving that year as consul together with his general

MAP DISCOVERY

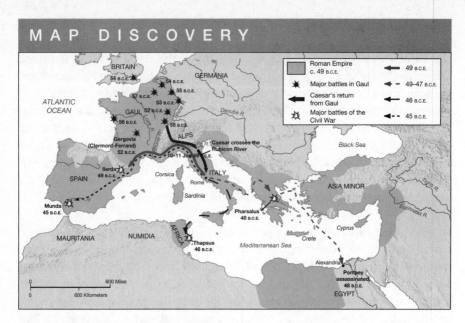

THE CAREER OF JULIUS CAESAR

Examine the extent of the Roman Empire in ca. 49 B.C.E. and the movement of Julius Caesar's military campaigns. How vital was Gaul to the Roman Empire before Caesar's campaigns? Based on the locations of Caesar's campaigns during the civil war, what can you assume about the center of power of his enemies? What geographical considerations might have led Pompey to seek an alliance with Egypt's Cleopatra?

Mark Antony (ca. 81–30 B.C.E.), Caesar had himself declared perpetual dictator. This move was too much for some 60 die-hard republican senators. On 15 March, a group led by two enemies whom Caesar had pardoned, Cassius Longinus and Marcus Junius Brutus, assassinated him as he entered the Senate chamber.

Cicero rejoiced when he heard of the assassination, clear evidence of his political naïveté. The republic was dead long before Caesar died, and the assassination simply returned Rome to civil war, a war that destroyed Cicero himself. Antony, Marcus Lepidus (d. 12 B.C.E.), another of Caesar's generals, and Caesar's grandnephew and adopted son Octavian (63 B.C.E.–14 C.E.), who took the name of his great uncle, soon formed the **Second Triumvirate** to destroy Caesar's enemies. After a bloody purge of senatorial and equestrian opponents, including Cicero, Antony and Octavian set out after Cassius and Brutus, who had fled into Macedonia. At Philippi in 42 B.C.E., Octavian and Antony defeated the armies of the two assassins (or, as they called themselves, liberators), who preferred suicide to capture.

After the defeat of the last republicans at Philippi, the members of the Second Triumvirate began to look suspiciously at one another. Antony took command of the east, protecting the provinces of Asia Minor and the Levant from the Parthians and bleeding them dry in the process. Lepidus received Africa, and Octavian was left to deal with the problems of Italy and the west.

Initially, Octavian had cut a weak and unimposing figure. He was only 18 when he was named adopted son and heir in Caesar's will. Still, he had the magic of Caesar's name with which to inspire the army, he had a visceral instinct for politics and publicity, and he combined these with an absolute determination to succeed at all costs. Aided by more competent and experienced commanders, notably Marcus Agrippa (ca. 63–12 B.C.E.) and Gaius Maecenas (ca. 70–8 B.C.E.), he began to consolidate his power at the expense of his two colleagues. Lepidus was forced out of his position and allowed to retire in obscurity, retaining only the honorific title of pontifex maximus.

Antony, to meet his ever-growing demand for cash, became dependent on the Ptolemaic ruler of Egypt, the clever and competent Cleopatra. For her part, Cleopatra manipulated Antony in order to maintain the integrity and independence of her kingdom. Octavian seized the opportunity to portray Antony as a traitor to Rome, a weakling controlled by an Oriental woman who planned to move the capital of the empire to Alexandria. Antony's supporters replied with propaganda of their own, pointing to Octavian's humble parentage and his lack of military ability. The final break came in 32 B.C.E. Antony, for all his military might, could not attack Italy as long as the despised Cleopatra was with him. Nor could he abandon her without losing her financial support. Instead, he tried to lure Octavian to a showdown in Greece. His plan misfired. Agrippa forced him into a naval battle off Actium in 31 B.C.E. in which Antony was soundly defeated. He and his Egyptian queen committed suicide, and Octavian ruled supreme in the Roman Empire.

A Life Worth Leading

Mere survival was a difficult and elusive goal through the last decades of the republic. Still, some members of the elite sought more. They tried to make sense of the turmoil around them and formulate a philosophy of life and a model of personal conduct. By now, the members of Rome's elite were in full command of Greek literature and philosophy, which they studied and adapted to their needs, creating a distinctive Latin cultural tradition. The most prominent figure in the late republic is Cicero, who combined his active life as lawyer and politician with an abiding devotion to Stoic philosophy. In the Stoics' belief in divine providence, morality, and duty to one's allotted role in the universe, Cicero found a rational basis for his deeply committed public life. For Cicero, humans and gods were bound together in a world governed not simply by might but by justice. The universe, while perhaps not fully intelligible, was nonetheless rational, and reason had to be the basis for society and its laws.

These same concerns for virtue are evident in the writings of the great historians of the late republic, Sallust (86–ca. 34 B.C.E.) and Livy (59 B.C.E.–17 C.E.). For Sallust, as well as for his younger contemporary, Livy, the chaos of civil war was the direct result of moral corruption and decline that followed the successes of the empire. For Sallust, the moral failing was largely that of the Senate and its members, who trampled the plebs in their quest for power and personal glory. Livy, who was much more conservative, condemned plebeian demagogues as well as power-hungry senators.

A different kind of morality dominated the work of Lucretius (ca. 100–55 B.C.E.), the greatest poet of the late republic. Just as Cicero had molded Stoicism into a Roman civic philosophy, Lucretius presented Epicurean materialist philosophy as a Roman alternative to the hunger for power, wealth, and glory. In his great poem *On the Nature of Things*, Lucretius presented the Epicurean's thoroughly physical understanding of the universe. He wrote that "a rational, proportional enjoyment of life is all that matters. Sorrow and anxiety come from but an ignorant emotionalism."

Emotion was precisely the goal of another poetic tradition of the late republic, that of the *neoteric* or new-style poets, especially Catullus (ca. 84–ca. 54 B.C.E.). Avoiding politics and moralistic philosophy, these poets created short, striking lyric poems that, although inspired by Hellenistic poetry, combine polished craftsmanship with a direct realism that is without precedent. One of the most striking differences between such Latin poetry and its Greek antecedents is the reality and individuality of the persons and relationships expressed.

The same interest in the individual affected the way artists of the late republic borrowed from Greek art. Hellenistic artists concentrated on the ideal, but Romans cherished the individual. The result was portraiture that caught the personality of the individual's face, even while portraying him or her as one of a type.

Chronology

THE END OF THE REPUBLIC

135–81 B.C.E.	Revolts against the republic
133–121 B.C.E.	Gracchi reform programs
107 B.C.E.	Gaius Marius elected consul
91–82 B.C.E.	Social War and Civil War (Marius vs. Sulla)
82–79 B.C.E.	Sulla rules as dictator
79–27 B.C.E.	Era of civil wars
63 B.C.E.	Cicero elected consul; First Triumvirate (Pompey, Crassus, Caesar)
59 B.C.E.	Caesar elected consul
45 B.C.E.	Caesar defeats Pompey's forces
44 B.C.E.	Caesar is assassinated; Second Triumvirate (Mark Antony, Lepidus, Octavian)
42 B.C.E.	Octavian and Mark Antony defeat Cassius and Brutus at Philippi
31 B.C.E.	Octavian defeats Mark Antony and Cleopatra at Actium
27 B.C.E.	Octavian is declared Augustus

The Augustan Age and the *Pax Romana*

It took Octavian two years after his victory at Actium in 31 B.C.E. to eliminate remaining pockets of resistance and to work out a system to reconcile his rule with Roman constitutional traditions while not surrendering any of his power. That power rested on three factors: his immense wealth, which he used to secure support; his vast following among the surviving elites as well as among the populares; and his total command of the army. It also rested on the exhaustion of the Roman people, who were eager, after decades of civil strife, to return to peace and stability. Remembering the fate of Julius Caesar, however, Octavian had no intention of rekindling opposition by establishing an overt monarchy. Instead, in 27 B.C.E. he returned the republic from his own charge to the Senate and the people of Rome. In turn the Senate decreed him the title of Augustus, meaning "exalted."

This meant that Augustus, as Octavian was now called, continued to rule no less strongly than before, but he did so not through any autocratic office or title—he preferred to be called simply the "first citizen," or **princeps**—but by preserving the form of the traditional Roman magistracies. For four years he rested his authority on consecutive terms as consul, and after 23 B.C.E. he held a life position as tribune. The Senate granted him proconsular command of the provinces of Gaul, Spain, Syria, and Egypt, the major sources of imperial wealth and the locations of more than three-quarters of the Roman army. Later, the Senate declared his *imperium*, or command, of these "imperial" provinces superior to that of any governors of other provinces.

The Senate's formalities deceived no one. Augustus's power was absolute. However, by choosing not to exercise it in an absolutist manner, he forged a new constitutional system that worked well for himself and his successors. By the end of his reign, few living persons could remember the days of the republic, and fewer still mourned its passing. Under Augustus and his successors the empire enjoyed two centuries of stability and peace, the **Pax Romana**, or "Roman Peace."

The Empire Renewed

Cicero had sought in vain a concord of the orders, a settlement of the social and political frictions of the empire through the voluntary efforts of a public-minded oligarchy. What could not happen voluntarily, Augustus imposed from above, reforming the Roman state, society, and culture.

The Senate. Key to Augustus's program of renewal was the Senate, which he made, if not a partner, then a useful subordinate in his reform. He gradually reduced the number of senators, which had grown to over 1,000, back down to 600. At the same time, he made membership hereditary, although he continued to appoint individuals of personal integrity, ability, and wealth to the body.

Augustus also shared with the Senate the governance of the empire, although again not on an equal footing. The Senate remained a creature of the emperor, seldom asserting itself even when asked to do so by Augustus or his successors and competing within its own ranks to see who could be first to do the emperor's bidding.

The Equites. Augustus undertook an even more fundamental reform of the equites, the wealthy businessmen, bankers, and tax collectors who had vied with the senatorial aristocracy since the reforms of Tiberius Gracchus. After Actium, many equites found themselves proscribed—sentenced to death or banishment—and had their property confiscated. Augustus began to rebuild their ranks by enrolling a new generation of successful merchants and speculators who became the foundation of his administration. The equestrian order was open at both ends. Freedmen and soldiers who acquired sufficient wealth moved into the order, and the most successful and accomplished equestrians were promoted into the Senate.

The Army. The land crisis had provoked much of the unrest in the late republic, and after Actium, Augustus had to satisfy the needs of the loyal soldiers of his 60 legions. Drawing on his immense wealth, acquired largely from the estates of his proscripted enemies, he pensioned off 32 legions, sending them to colonies that he purchased for them throughout the empire. The remaining 28 legions became a permanent professional army stationed in imperial provinces. Augustus established a small elite unit, the praetorian guard, in and around Rome as his personal military force. Initially, the praetorians protected the emperors; in later reigns, they would make them.

These measures created a permanent solution to the problem of the citizen-soldier of the later republic. Veteran colonies—all built as model Roman towns with their central forum, baths, temples, arenas, and theaters as well as their outlying villas and farms—helped to romanize the far provinces of the empire. These colonies, unlike the independent colonies of Greece in an earlier age, remained an integral part of the Roman state. Thus romanization and political integration went hand in hand, uniting through peaceful means an empire that had first been acquired by arms. Likewise, ambitious provincials, through service as auxiliaries and later as citizens, acquired a stake in the destiny of Rome.

Not every citizen, of course, could find prosperity in military service and a comfortable retirement. The problems of urban poverty in Rome continued to grow. By the time of Augustus, the capital city had reached a population of perhaps 600,000 people. The emperors, their power as tribunes making them protectors of the poor, provided over 150,000 resident citizens with a basic dole of wheat brought from Egypt. The emperors also built aqueducts to provide water to the city. In addition, they constructed vast public recreation centers.

These included both the sumptuous baths, which were combination bathing facilities, health clubs, and brothels, and arenas such as the Colosseum, where 50,000 spectators could watch gladiatorial displays, and the Circus Maximus, where a quarter of the city's population could gather at once to watch chariot races. Such mass gatherings replaced the plebeian assemblies of the republic as the occasions on which the populace could express its will. Few emperors were foolish enough to ignore the wishes that the crowd roared out in the Circus.

Divine Augustus. Augustus's renewal of Rome rested on a religious reform. He restored numerous temples and revived ancient Roman cults. He established a series of public religious festivals, reformed priesthoods, and encouraged citizens to participate in the traditional cults of Rome. His goals in all these religious reforms were twofold. After decades of public authority controlled by violence and naked aggression, he was determined to restore the traditions of Roman piety, morality, sacred order, and faith in relationship between the gods and Roman destiny. An equally important goal was Augustus's promotion of his own cult. His adoptive father, Julius Caesar, had been deified after his death,

This idealized marble portrait statue of the emperor Augustus addressing his army was found in the villa of Livia, wife of Augustus, at Prima Porta in Rome. The carvings on his breastplate recall the moment in 20 B.C. when Augustus was able to recover the military standards lost to the Parthians by Mark Anthony and Crassius. Since Augustus accomplished this through diplomacy rather than war, the event commemorates the establishment of the Pax Augusta.

and Augustus benefited from this association with a divine ancestor. His own genius, or guiding spirit, received special devotion in temples throughout the west dedicated to "Rome and Augustus." In the east, he was worshiped as a living god. In this manner, the emperor became identical with the state, and the state religion was closely akin to emperor worship. After his death, Augustus and virtually all of the emperors after him were worshiped as official deities in Rome itself.

Closely related to his fostering of traditional cults was Augustus's attempt to restore traditional Roman virtues, especially within the family. Like the reformers of the late republic, he believed that the declining power of the paterfamilias was at the root of much that was wrong with Rome. To reverse the trend and to restore the declining population of free Italians, Augustus encouraged marriage, procreation, and the firm control of husbands over wives.

Poetry and Patronage. Augustus actively patronized those writers who shared his conservative religious and ethical values and who might be expected to glorify the princeps, and he used his power to censor and silence writers whom he considered immoral. Chief among the favored were the poets Virgil (70–19 B.C.E.) and Horace (65–8 B.C.E.). Through their poetry in praise of the emperor, these poets conferred immortality on Augustus.

The finest of the poets who felt the heavy hand of Augustus's disfavor was Ovid (43 B.C.E.–17 C.E.), the great Latin poet of erotic love. In *Art of Love* and *Amores* he cheerfully preached the art of seduction and adultery. He delighted in poking irreverent fun at everything from the sanctity of Roman marriage to the serious business of warfare. By 8 C.E., Augustus had had enough. He exiled the witty poet to Tomis, a miserable frontier post on the Black Sea.

Augustus's Successors

The problem of succession occupied Augustus throughout much of his long reign and was never satisfactorily solved. Since the princeps was not a specific office, but a combination of offices and honors held together by military might and religious aura, formal dynastic succession was impossible. Instead, Augustus attempted to select a blood relative as successor, include him in his reign, and have him voted the various offices and dignities that constituted his own position.

Unfortunately, Augustus outlived all of his first choices. Augustus's final choice, his stepson Tiberius (14–37 C.E.), proved to be a gloomy and unpopular successor but nevertheless was a competent ruler under whom the machinery of the empire functioned smoothly. The continued orderly functioning of the empire even under the subsequent members of Augustus's family—the mad Gaius, also known as Caligula (37–41), the bookish but competent Claudius (41–54), and initially under Nero (54–68)—is a tribute to the soundness of Augustus's constitutional

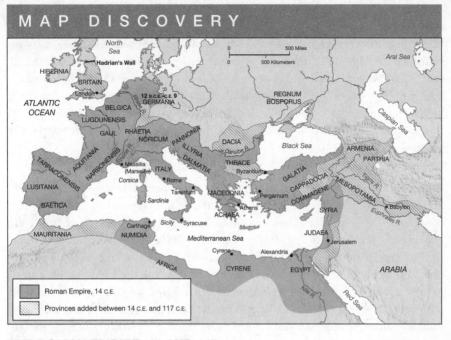

THE ROMAN EMPIRE, 14 AND 117 C.E.

Examine the extent of the Roman Empire in 14 C.E. and in 117 C.E. What civilizations and empires that you previously have studied were incorporated into the Roman Empire by 14 C.E.? By 117 C.E.? Which regions had never before been part of ancient civilizations? What natural geographical features defined the boundaries of the empire in the west, north, south, and east?

changes and the vested interest that the descendants of Augustus's military and aristocratic supporters had in them.

Nero was more than even they could bear, however. Profligate, vicious, and paranoid, Nero divided his time between murdering his relatives and associates—including his mother, his aunt, his wife, his tutors, and eventually his most capable generals—and squandering his vast wealth on mad attempts to gain recognition as a great poet, actor, singer, and athlete. Finally, in 68 C.E., the exasperated commanders in Gaul, Spain, and Africa revolted. Once more, war swept the empire. Nero slit his own throat, and in the next year, the "Year of the Four Emperors," four men in quick succession won the office, only to lose their lives just as quickly. Finally, in 70 C.E., Vespasian (69–79 C.E.), the son of a "new man," who had risen through the ranks to the command in Egypt, secured the principate and restored order.

The emperors of the Flavian dynasty, Vespasian and his sons and successors Titus (79–81) and Domitian (81–96), were stern and unpretentious provincials who restored the authority and dignity of their office, although they also did away with most of the trappings of republican legitimacy that Augustus and his immediate successors had used. They solidified the administrative system, returned the legions to their fairly permanent posts, and opened the highest reaches of power to provincial elites as never before. After the Flavian emperors, the Antonines (96–193)—especially Trajan (98–117), Hadrian (117–138), and Antoninus Pius (138–161)—ruled for what has been termed "the period in the history of the world during which the human race was most happy and prosperous."

Breaking the Peace. Not all was peaceful in this period, however. Trajan initiated a new and final expansion of the imperial frontiers. Between 101 and 106 he conquered Dacia (modern Romania). He resumed war with the Parthians, conquering the provinces of Armenia and Mesopotamia by 116. During the second century the Palestinian Jews revolted in 115–117 and again in 132–135. The emperor Hadrian put down this second revolt and expelled the surviving Jews from Judaea. Along both the eastern and western frontiers, legions had to contend with sporadic border incidents. Within the borders, however, a system of Roman military camps, towns, and rural states constituted a remarkably heterogeneous and prosperous civilization.

Chronology

THE ROMAN EMPIRE

Julio-Claudian Period, 27 B.C.E.–68 C.E.	Augustus (27 B.C.E.–14 C.E.)
	Tiberius (14–37 C.E.)
	Caligula (37–41)
	Claudius (41–54)
	Nero (54–68)
Year of the Four Emperors, 69 C.E.	
Flavian Period, 69–96	Vespasian (69–79)
	Titus (79–81)
	Domitian (81–96)
Antonine Period, 96–192	Trajan (98–117)
	Hadrian (117–138)
	Antoninus Pius (138–161)
	Marcus Aurelius (161–180)
	Commodus (180–192)

Administering the Empire. The imperial government of this vast empire was as oppressive as it was primitive. Taxes, rents, forced labor service, military levies and requisitions, and outright extortion weighed heavily on its subjects. To a considerable extent, the inhabitants of the empire continued to be governed by the indigenous elites whose cooperation Rome won by giving them broad autonomy. In return for their participation in Roman rule, these elites received Roman citizenship, a prize that carried prestige, legal protection, and the promise of further advancement in the Roman world.

In those imperial provinces that were controlled directly by the emperor, the army was much more in evidence, and the professional legions were the ultimate argument of imperial tax collectors and imperial representatives, or *procurators*. Moreover, as the turmoil of the Year of the Four Emperors amply demonstrated, the military was the ultimate foundation of imperial rule itself. Still, soldiers were as much farmers as fighters. Legions usually remained in the same location for years, and veterans' colonies sprang up around military camps.

Finally, much of the governing of the empire was done by the vast households of the Roman elite, particularly that of the princeps. Freedmen and slaves from the emperor's household often governed vast regions, oversaw imperial estates, and managed imperial factories and mines. The descendants of the old Roman nobility might look down their noses at imperial freedmen, but they obeyed their orders.

The empire worked because it rewarded those who worked with it and left alone those who paid their taxes and kept quiet. As provincials were drawn into the Roman system, they were also drawn into the world of Roman culture. Proper education in Latin and Greek, the ability to hold one's own in philosophical discussion, and the absorption of Roman ways, including styles of dress, recreation, and religious cults, all were essential for ambitious provincials. Thus, in the course of the first century C.E., the disparate portions of the empire competed, not to free themselves from the Roman yoke, but to become Roman themselves.

Religions from the East

The same openness that permitted the spread of Latin letters and Roman baths to distant Gaul and the shores of the Black Sea provided paths of dissemination for other, distinctly un-Roman religious traditions. For many in the empire, the traditional rituals offered to the household gods and the state cults of Jupiter, Mars, and the other official deities were insufficient foci of religious devotion. Many educated members of the elite were actually vaguely monotheistic. Many others in the empire sought personal, emotional bonds with the divine world.

As noted in Chapter 4, in the second century B.C.E. the Roman world had been caught up in the emotional cult of Dionysus, an ecstatic, personal, and liberating religion entirely unlike the official Roman cults. Again in the first century C.E., so-called **mystery cults**—that is, religions promising immediate personal contact with a deity that would bring immortality—spread throughout the empire. The cult of the Egyptian goddess Isis spread throughout the Hellenistic world and to Rome in the republican period. From Persia came the cult of Mithras, the ancient Indo-Iranian god of light and truth, who, as bringer of victory, found special favor with Roman soldiers and merchants eager for success in this life and immortality beyond the grave. Generally, Rome tolerated these alien cults as long as they could be assimilated into, or at least reconciled in some way with, the cult of the Roman gods and the genius of the emperor.

Jewish Resistance

With one religious group this assimilation was impossible. The Jews of Palestine had long refused any accommodation with the polytheistic cults of the Hellenistic kingdoms or with Rome. Roman conquerors and emperors, aware of the problems of their Hellenistic predecessors, went to considerable lengths to avoid antagonizing this small and unusual group of people. When Pompey seized Jerusalem in 63 B.C.E., he was careful not to interfere in Jewish religion and even left Judaea under the control of the Jewish high priest. Later, Judaea was made into a client kingdom under the puppet Herod. Jews were allowed to maintain their monotheistic cult and were excused from making sacrifices to the Roman gods.

Still, the Jewish community remained deeply divided about its relationship with the wider world and with Rome. At one end of the spectrum were the Sadducees, a party composed largely of members of priestly families, who enjoyed considerable influence with their foreign rulers. They were staunch defenders of the ancient Jewish law, or Torah, but not to the exclusion of other later religious and legal traditions.

At the other end of the spectrum were the Hasidim (not to be confused with the modern Hasidic movement), those who rejected all compromise with Hellenistic culture and collaboration with foreign powers. Many expected the arrival of a messiah, a liberator who would destroy the Romans and reestablish the kingdom of David. One party within the Hasidim were the Pharisees, who practiced strict dietary rules and rituals to maintain the separation of Jews and Gentiles (literally, "the peoples," that is, all non-Jews). The Pharisees accepted the writings of the Hebrew prophets along with the Torah and abided by a still larger body of orally transmitted law, the "tradition of the elders."

For all their insistence on purity and separation from other peoples, the Pharisees did not advocate violent revolt against Rome. They preferred to await divine intervention. Another group of Hasidim, the Zealots, were less willing to wait. After 6 C.E., when Judaea, Samaria, and Idumaea were annexed and combined into the province of Judaea and administered by imperial procurators, the Zealots began to organize sporadic armed resistance to Roman rule. As ever, armed resistance was met with violent suppression. Throughout the first century C.E., clashes between Roman troops and Zealot revolutionaries grew more frequent and more widespread.

The Origins of Christianity

The already complex landscape of the Jewish religious world became further complicated by the brief career of Joshua ben Joseph (ca. 6 B.C.E.–30 C.E.), known to history as Jesus of Nazareth and to his followers as Jesus the Messiah or the Christ. Jesus came from Galilee, an area known as a Zealot stronghold. However, while Jesus preached the imminent coming of the kingdom, he did so in an entirely nonpolitical manner. He was, like many popular religious leaders, a miracle worker. When people flocked around him to see his wonders, he preached a message of peace and love of God and neighbor. His teachings were entirely within the Jewish tradition. However, while many contemporary religious leaders announced the imminent coming of the Messiah, Jesus' closest followers, the apostles and disciples, began to think that Jesus himself was the Messiah and expected him to restore the kingdom of Israel.

For roughly three years, Jesus preached in Judaea and Galilee, drawing large, excited crowds. Many of his followers pressed him to lead a revolt against Roman authority and reestablish the kingdom of David, even though he insisted that the kingdom he would establish was not of this world. Other Jews saw his claims as blasphemy and his assertion that he was the king of Jews, even if a heavenly one, as a threat to the status quo. Jesus became more and more a figure of controversy, a catalyst for violence. Ultimately, the Roman procurator, Pontius Pilate, decided that Jesus posed a threat to law and order. Pilate, like other Roman magistrates, had no interest in the internal religious affairs of the Jews. However, he was troubled by anyone who had the potential for causing political disturbances, no matter how unintentional. Pilate ordered Jesus scourged and put to death by crucifixion, a common Roman form of execution for slaves, pirates, thieves, and noncitizen troublemakers.

Spreading the Faith. The cruel death of Jesus ended the popular agitation he had stirred up, but it did not deter his closest followers. They soon announced that three days after his death, he had risen and had appeared to them numerous times during the following few weeks. They took this resurrection as proof of his claims to be the Messiah and confirmation of his promise of eternal life to those who believed in him. Soon a small group of his followers, led by Peter

A Roman tombstone inscribed with some of the earliest examples of Christian symbols. The anchor represents hope, while the fish recall Jesus' words, "I will make you fishers of men."

(d. ca. 64 C.E.), formed another Jewish sect—preaching and praying daily in the temple. New members were initiated into this sect, which soon became known as Christianity—through baptism, a purification rite in which the initiate was submerged briefly in flowing water. They also shared a ritual meal in which bread and wine were distributed to members. Otherwise, they remained entirely within the Jewish religious and cultural tradition, and hellenized Jews and pagans who wanted to join the sect had to observe strict Jewish law and custom.

Christianity spread beyond its origin as a Jewish sect because of the work of one man, Paul of Tarsus (ca. 5–ca. 67 C.E.). Although Paul was an observant Jew, he was part of the wider cosmopolitan world of the empire and from birth enjoyed the privileges of Roman citizenship. He saw Christianity as a separate tradition, completing and perfecting Judaism but intended for the whole world.

Paul set out to spread his message, crisscrossing Asia Minor and Greece and even traveling to Rome. Wherever he went, Paul won converts and established churches, called *ecclesiae*, or assemblies. Paul's teachings, while firmly rooted in the Jewish historical tradition, were radically new. God had created the human race, he taught, in the image of God and destined it for eternal life. However, by the deliberate sin of the first humans, Adam and Eve, humans had lost eternal life and introduced evil and death into the world. Even then, God did not abandon his people but began, through the Jews, to prepare for their eventual redemption. That salvation was accomplished by Jesus, the son of God, through his faith, a free and unmerited gift of God to his elect. Through faith, the Christian ritual of baptism, and participation in the church, men and women could share in the salvation offered by God, Paul said.

How many conversions resulted from Paul's theological message and how many resulted from the miracles he and the other disciples were believed to have worked will never be known, but another factor certainly played a part in the success of conversions. That was the courage Christians showed in the face of persecution.

Even Rome's elasticity and tolerance of new religions could be stretched only so far. The Christians' stubborn refusal to acknowledge the existence of the other gods and to participate in the cult of the genius of the emperor was intolerable. Christianity was an aggressive and successful cult, attracting followers throughout the empire. It was viewed not as religion, but as subversion. Beginning during Nero's reign, Roman officials sporadically rounded up Christians, destroyed their sacred scriptures, and executed those who refused to sacrifice to the imperial genius. But instead of decreasing the cult's appeal, persecution only aided it. For those who believed that death was birth into a new and better life, martyrdom was a reward, not a penalty. The strength of their convictions convinced others of the truth of their religion.

Christian Institutions. As the number of Christians increased in the face of persecution, the organization and teaching of this new faith began to evolve. A hierarchy developed within the various communities that Paul and the other apostles established. The leader of each community was the bishop who was assisted by **presbyters** (priests), deacons, and deaconesses.

Christian teaching focused on the Gospels, accounts of Jesus' life written toward the end of the first century; letters, or Epistles; and narratives and visionary writings by his early disciples and their immediate successors. In their preaching, bishops connected these texts to the tradition of Jewish Scriptures, explaining that the life of Jesus was the completion and fulfillment of the Jewish tradition. Over centuries, certain Gospels and Epistles and one book of revelation came to be regarded as authoritative and, together with the version of Jewish Scripture that was in use in Greek-speaking Jewish communities, constituted the Christian Bible. In the second and third centuries, the Christian message began to be challenged. Even within the Christian community, different groups held different views. Monatists argued that Christians were obligated to fast and abstain from marriage until the second coming. Dualist **Gnostics** interpreted the Christian message as a secret wisdom, or *gnosis*, which, combined with baptism, freed men and women from their fates.

Bishops defended the faith and determined what was correct. By the end of the first century, episcopal (from the Greek word for bishop) authority was understood to derive from the bishops' status as successors of the apostles. Gradually, the exalted position of the bishop and his assistants led to a distinction between the clergy and the laity, the rank and file of Christians. At the same time, women, who had played central roles in Jesus' ministry, were excluded from positions of authority within the clergy. In this process, the Christian community came to resemble closely the Roman patriarchal household, a resemblance that increased the appeal of the new sect to nonbelievers.

The Culture of Antonine Rome

The Romans themselves took little interest in natural science. However, they supported Greek science pursued in the East, particularly in Alexandria, where centuries of Greek mathematics, astronomy, and geography came to fruition in the work of Claudius Ptolemaeus (ca. 85–ca.165 C.E.), usually known as Ptolemy. Ptolemy was a cartographer and geographer, but his greatest work was as a mathematician and astronomer.

Building on the work of Hipparchus, Ptolemy developed a complex model for the universe that could explain the apparent motion of the sun, moon, and planets. Ptolemy's theory, which placed the earth in the center of the universe, remained the accepted model of the solar system for the next 1,400 years.

Romans themselves, however, were more interested in how humans should lead their lives than in how the planets moved. Rome's greatest historian, Cornelius Tacitus (ca. 56–ca. 120), recorded the history of the first century of the empire. His picture of Germanic and British societies served as a warning to Rome against excessive self-confidence and laxity.

Tacitus's contemporaries, Plutarch (ca. 46–after 119) and Suetonius (ca. 69–after 122), were biographers rather than historians. Plutarch, who wrote in Greek, composed *Parallel Lives,* a series of character studies in which he compared an eminent Greek with an eminent Roman. Suetonius also wrote biographies, using anecdotes to portray character.

In the later second century, Romans in general preferred the study and writing of philosophy, particularly Stoicism, over history. The most influential Stoic philosopher of the century was Epictetus (ca. 55–135), a former slave who taught that people could be free by the control of their will and the cultivation of inner peace. Like the early Stoics, Epictetus taught the universal brotherhood of humankind and the identity of nature and divine providence.

The philosophy of Epictetus found its most eager pupil in an emperor. Marcus Aurelius (161–180) reigned during a period when the stresses afflicting the empire were beginning to show in a much more alarming manner. Once more, the Parthians attacked the eastern frontier, while in Britain and Germany, barbarians struck across the borders. In 166, a confederation of barbarians known as the Marcomanni crossed the Danube and raided as far south as northern Italy. A plague, brought west by troops returning from the Parthian front, ravaged the entire empire. Aurelius spent virtually the whole of his reign on the Danubian frontier, repelling the barbarians and shoring up the empire's defenses.

This fifteenth-century Latin translation of Ptolemy's *Almagest* presents his model for the motion of the outer planets, Mars, Jupiter, and Saturn. The complicated cycles and epicycles are necessary to explain the motion of these planets while keeping the Earth at the center of the universe.

Throughout his reign, Aurelius found consolation in the Stoic philosophy of Epictetus. In his soldier's tent at night he composed his *Meditations,* a volume of philosophical musings. Like the slave, the emperor sought freedom from the burden of his office in his will and in the proper understanding of his role in the divine order.

However, his Stoic philosophy did not serve the empire well. For all his emphasis on understanding, Aurelius badly misjudged his son Commodus (180–192), who succeeded him. Commodus, whose chief interest was in being a gladiator, saw himself as the incarnation of Heracles and appeared in public clad as a gladiator and as consul. As Commodus sank into insanity, Rome was once more convulsed by purges and proscriptions. Commodus's assassination in 192 did not end the violence. The *Pax Romana* was over.

SUMMARY

The Price of Empire   The creation of an empire brought a century of revolutionary change before new and stable social, cultural, and political norms were established. The optimates, members of the ruling oligarchy, gained the most from Roman conquest. Slaves and provincials revolted against Roman rule. Reformers such as Tiberius and Gaius Gracchus appealed to the people for political support, prompting a violent backlash from the optimates.

The End of the Republic   Revolts in Africa and Italy exposed the fragility of the Senate's control and ushered in an ever-increasing spiral of violence and civil war. Marius and Sulla battled for control of the military, and thus Rome, setting a pattern for future events. Pompey, Crassus, and Caesar ruled Rome as the First Triumvirate. Competition among the three men ended with Caesar's triumph. Caesar's assassination led to a new round of civil wars, from which Caesar's adopted son Augustus emerged as the undisputed ruler of Rome. Roman writers, artists, and philosophers struggled to find meaning in the turbulent events of their time.

The Augustan Age and the *Pax Romana*   The reign of Augustus saw political, social, military, and religious reform. Under his rule, artists who celebrated the empire and his reign were rewarded with imperial patronage. The continued orderly functioning of the empire under the rule of subsequent members of his family is a tribute to the soundness of Augustus's constitutional changes and the vested interest that the descendants of Augustus's military and aristocratic supporters had in them. The suicide of Nero (54–68) ushered in a period of chaos that was followed by two new dynasties: first the Flavians and then the Antonines.

Religions from the East   In the first century C.E. many Romans were attracted to so-called mystery cults, religions promising personal contact with a deity. The Jews of Palestine had a range of responses to Roman rule. Jesus lived and taught in this complex political and religious context. After his death, Christianity spread beyond its origins as a Jewish sect as the result of the efforts of Paul of Tarsus. Christians developed institutions to meet their religious and social needs. The Christian community came to resemble closely the Roman patriarchal household.

The Culture of Antonine Rome   Greeks living under Roman rule took the lead in the natural sciences. Roman thinkers focused on questions of how humans should live their lives. In the later second century, many Romans, including the emperor Marcus Aurelius, were drawn to Stoicism.

QUESTIONS FOR REVIEW

1. How were rifts in Roman society widened by Rome's expansion into an empire?
2. In what ways were the life and thought of Cicero indicative of an age characterized by civil conflict and the collapse of republican traditions?

3. How was religious reform an important part of Augustus's efforts to restore stability to Roman society?
4. What did the Flavian and Antonine emperors do to keep Rome's vast empire intact and in relative peace?
5. How did Paul of Tarsus transform the teachings of Jesus of Nazareth from an outgrowth of Judaism into a separate spiritual tradition?

The Transformation of the Classical World, 192–500

The Crisis of the Third Century

From the reign of Septimius Severus (193–211) to the time of Diocletian (284–305), both internal and external challenges shook the Roman Empire. The empire survived, but its social, political, and economic structures were radically transformed.

Sheer size was a fundamental problem for the empire. Haphazard expansion in many regions—to the north and west, for instance—overextended the frontiers. The labor and resources needed to maintain this vast territory strained the economic system of the empire.

The economic system itself was part of the reason for this strain on resources. For all of its commercial networks, the economy of the empire remained tied to agriculture. To the aristocrats of the ancient world, agriculture was the only honorable source of wealth. The goal of the successful merchant was to liquidate his commercial assets, buy estates, and rise into the leisured landholding elite. As a result, liquid capital for either investment or taxation was always scarce.

The lack of sophistication seen in commercial and industrial business practice characterized the financial system of the empire as well. Government had always been conducted on the cheap. The tax system of the empire had never been very efficient at tapping into the real wealth of the aristocracy. Each individual city made its own collective assessments. Individuals eager to win the gratitude of their local communities were expected to provide essential services from their own pockets. Even with the vast wealth of the empire at its disposal, the government never developed a system of public debt—that is, a policy of borrowing against future revenues. As a result, the only way to solve short-term cash-flow problems was to debase the coinage by using more copper and less silver. This practice became epidemic in the third century, when the price of a bushel of wheat rose over 200 percent.

The failure of the empire to develop a stable political base complicated its economic problems. In times of emergency, imperial control relied on the personal presence and command of the emperor. As the empire grew, it became impossible for this presence to be felt everywhere. Moreover, the empire never developed either a regular system of imperial succession or an adequate power base. Control of the army, which was the ultimate source of imperial power, was possible only as long as the emperor could lead his armies to victory.

Enrich the Army and Scorn the Rest

Through much of the late second and third centuries, emperors failed dismally to lead their armies to victory. When the emperors selected by the distant Roman Senate failed to win victory, frontline armies unhesitatingly raised their own commanders to the imperial office. These commanders set about restructuring the empire in favor of the army. They opened important administrative posts to soldiers, expanded the army's size, raised military pay, initiated expensive building programs in frontier settlements, and in general introduced authoritarian military discipline throughout society. To finance these costly measures, the new military government confiscated senatorial wealth, introduced new forms of taxation, and increasingly debased the coinage.

The Rise of the Military. With their first rise in real income, soldiers in the provinces could improve their standard of living while in service and buy their way into provincial elites on retirement. Free-spending soldiers and imperial extravagance helped the bleak settlements on the edges of military camps grow into prosperous cities with all the comforts of the older parts of the empire. For the first time, capable soldiers could hope to rise to the highest levels of public power, regardless of their birth.

Economic Disaster. Soon, however, the military control of the empire turned into a nightmare even for the provinces and their armies. Exercising their newly discovered power, armies raised and then destroyed pretender after pretender, offering support to whichever imperial candidate promised them the greatest riches. The army's incessant demands for higher pay led emperors to lower the amount of silver in the coins with which the soldiers were paid, leading to ever-escalating inflation. Such drastic inflation wrecked the economic stability of the empire and spurred the army on to greater and more impossible demands for raises. Emperors who could not meet the demands were killed by their troops.

External Threats. The crisis of the third century did not result only from economic and political instability within the empire. Rome's internal crises coincided with an increase of attacks from outside the empire.

The greatest danger to Rome came from the west. There, along the Rhine, various Germanic tribes known collectively as the Franks and the Alemanni began raiding expeditions into the empire. Along the lower Danube and in southern Ukraine, the Gothic confederation raided the Balkans and harassed Roman shipping on the Black Sea.

This cameo was made to the order of Shapur I after the capture of Valerian during the great battle near Antioch in 260. The symbolic scene has Shapur seizing Valerian simply by grasping his hand.

An Empire on the Defensive

The central administration of the empire simply could not deal effectively with the numerous barbarian attacks. Left on their own, regional provincial commanders at times even headed separatist movements. Provincial aristocrats who despaired of receiving any help from distant Rome often supported these pretenders.

Political and military instability had devastating effects on the lives of ordinary people. Citizenship had been extended to virtually all free inhabitants of the empire in 212, but that right was a formality given simply to enlarge the tax base, since only citizens paid inheritance taxes. Society became sharply divided into the privileged **honestiores**—senators, municipal gentry, and the military—and the increasingly burdened **humiliores**—everyone else. The humiliores suffered the most from the tax increases because, unlike the honestiores, they could neither bribe their way out of them nor intimidate tax collectors with private armies. They were also frequent targets of extortion by the military and of violence perpetrated by bandits.

Slave and peasant bandits, rustlers, and even pirates played an ambivalent role in society. Often they terrorized the countryside, descending from the hills to attack villages or travelers. However, at times they also protected peasants from greedy tax collectors and military commanders. In Gaul and Spain, peasants and local leaders organized armed resistance movements, termed *Bacaudae*, to withstand the exorbitant demands of tax collectors. In the first centuries of the empire, bandits operated primarily in peripheral areas that had been recently and poorly subjugated to Roman rule. In the late second and third centuries they became an increasing problem in Italy itself.

The Barbarian Menace

Compounding the internal violence that threatened to destroy the Roman Empire were the external attacks of the Germanic barbarians. These attacks reflected changes within the Germanic world as profound as those within the empire. Between the second and fifth centuries, the Germanic world was transformed from a mosaic of small, decentralized, agricultural tribes into a number of powerful military tribal confederations capable of challenging Rome itself.

Germanic Society. The Germanic peoples typically inhabited small villages organized into patriarchal households, which were integrated into clans, which in turn composed tribes. For the most part, clans governed themselves and, except in war, tribal leaders had little authority over their followers. In the second century, many tribes had kings, but they were religious rather than political leaders.

Germanic communities lived by farming, but cattle raising and especially warfare carried the highest social prestige. Men measured their status by the number of cattle they owned and by their martial ability. Women took care of agricultural chores and household duties. Like the number of cattle, the number of wives showed a man's social position. Polygyny was common among chiefs.

Warfare defined social groupings, and warriors dominated public life. Only within the clan was fighting inappropriate. But rival clans within the same tribe dealt with one another brutally. Conflict took the form of the feud, and each act of aggression was repaid in kind. If an individual within a clan had a grievance with an individual within another clan, all his kinsmen were obliged to assist him. Thus a single incident could result in a continuous escalation of acts of revenge.

Feuding and Peacemaking. Clans in other tribes were fair game for raiding, looting, and conquering. Individuals, clans, and tribes built their wealth and reputations on warfare. The more successful a tribe was in warfare, the more clans it attracted and the greater its position became in the barbarian world.

The practice of feuding, especially within the tribe, had enormous costs. Families were decimated, and strong warriors who were needed to defend the tribe from outside attack faced constant danger from members of their own tribe. Tribal leaders attempted to reduce hostilities by establishing payments called **wergeld** in place of the blood vengeance demanded in reparation for crimes.

Tribes also attempted to reinforce unity through religious cults involving shared myths of common ancestry and rituals intended to underline group cohesion. When not fighting, Germanic warriors spent much of their time drinking beer together at the table of their war leader. Communal beer drinking was a way of uniting potentially hostile neighbors.

Warrior Bands. In contrast to the familial structure of barbarian society stood another warrior group that cut across kindred and even tribal units. This was the warrior band, called in Latin the *comitatus*. Some young warriors formed personal bonds with particularly able leaders and pledged them absolute loyalty. In return, the leaders were obligated to lead their warriors to victory and to share with them the spoils of war. Successful warrior leaders might draw sufficient numbers of followers and conquer so many other groups that in time the band would become a new tribe.

Roman Influence in the Barbarian World

Intratribal and intertribal violence produced a rough equilibrium of power and wealth as long as small Germanic tribes lived in isolation. The presence of the Roman Empire, felt both directly and indirectly in the barbarian world, upset this equilibrium. Unintentionally, Rome itself helped to transform the Germanic tribes into the major threat to the imperial system.

The Lure of Roman Culture. The attraction of Roman luxury goods and the Romans' efforts to establish friendly Germanic buffer zones along the borders drew even distant tribes into the Roman imperial system. Across the barbarian world, tribal leaders and comitatus leaders sought the prestige that Roman goods brought them. Roman provincial commanders encouraged these leaders to enter into commercial arrangements with the Romans. This outside source of wealth greatly increased economic disparity within Germanic society. In addition, some leaders made treaties with Rome, thus receiving the advantage of Roman support, which other tribal leaders lacked. In return for payments of gold and foodstuffs, chieftains of these "federated" tribes agreed to oppose tribes that were hostile to Rome and to prevent young hotheads of their own tribes from raiding across the frontier. Some chiefs supplied warriors for the Roman army. Others even led their comitatus into Roman service. Such "imperial Germans" moved back and forth between the Roman and barbarian worlds, using each as a foundation for increased power in the other and obscuring the cultural and political differences between the two.

The West Germanic Revolution. The effects of contact between barbarians and Romans reached far and wide throughout the empire and beyond the frontier. Along the Rhine and Danube the result was the so-called West Germanic Revolution. To survive in a time of constant warfare, tribes had to become armies. The armies needed a united and effective leadership. Among most of the western Germanic peoples, the tradition of the older tribal king was abandoned. A new kind of nonroyal chieftain emerged as the war leader of the people and as the representative of the war god Woden. In the later second and third centuries, the turmoil resulted in the formation of new tribes and tribal confederations: the Marcomanni, the Alemanni, and the Franks. By the end of the second century, this internal barbarian transformation spilled over into the empire in the form of the Marcomannian wars and the Saxon, Frankish, and Alemannic incursions into the western provinces.

The Gothic Confederation. Around the same time, along the Oder and Vistula rivers to the north, a group later known as the Goths began their slow consolidation around a royal family. The Goths were unique in that their kings exercised more military authority than was usual for a Germanic tribe.

Between the second and fourth centuries, the bearers of this Gothic royal tradition began to filter to the south and east, ultimately transferring their model of barbarian organization to the area of present-day Kiev in southern Ukraine. This move was not so much a physical migration of thousands of people across Europe as the gradual confederation under Gothic leadership of various Germanic, Scythian, and other peoples living around the Black Sea. By the early third century, this Gothic confederation was strong enough to challenge Roman supremacy in the region. These first Gothic wars in the east were even more devastating than the later wars in the west.

The Empire Restored

By the last decades of the third century, the empire seemed in danger of crumbling under combined internal and external pressure. That it did not was largely due to the efforts of the soldier-emperor Aurelian (270–275), who was able to repulse the barbarians, restore the unity of the empire, and then set about stabilizing the internal imperial structure.

Diocletian, the God-Emperor

Diocletian (284–305), a Dalmatian soldier who had risen through the ranks to become emperor, completed the process of stabilization and reorganization of the imperial system begun by Aurelian. The result was a regime that in some ways increased imperial power and in other ways simply did away with the pretenses that had previously masked the emperor's true position.

No longer was the emperor *princeps*, or "first citizen." Now he was *dominus*, or "lord," the term of respect used by slaves in addressing their masters. He also assumed the title of *Iovius*, or Jupiter, thus claiming divine status, and demanded adoration as a living god. Diocletian recognized that the empire was too large and complex for one man to rule. To solve the problem, he divided the empire into eastern and western parts, each part to be ruled by both an augustus and a junior emperor, or caesar. Diocletian was augustus in the east, supported by his caesar, Galerian. In the west, the rulers were the augustus Maximian and his caesar, Constantius.

The Tetrarchy. In theory, this **tetrarchy**, or rule by four, provided for regular succession. The caesars, who were married to daughters of the augusti, were to succeed them. Although from time to time subsequent emperors would rule alone, Diocletian's innovation proved successful and enduring.

In addition to this constitutional reform, Diocletian enacted or consolidated a series of measures to improve the functioning of the imperial administration. He reorganized and expanded the army, approximately doubled the number of provinces, separated their military and civil administration, and greatly increased the number of bureaucrats to administer them. He attempted to stem runaway inflation by increasing the amount of silver in coins and fixing maximum prices and wages throughout the empire. He restructured the imperial tax system, basing it on payments in goods and produce in order to distribute the burden more equitably among all citizens and to avoid problems of currency debasement.

A Militarized Society. The pillar of Diocletian's success was his victorious military machine. He was effective because, like the barbarian chieftains who had turned their tribes into armies, he militarized society and led this military society to victory. Like Diocletian himself, his soldiers were drawn from provincial marginal regions.

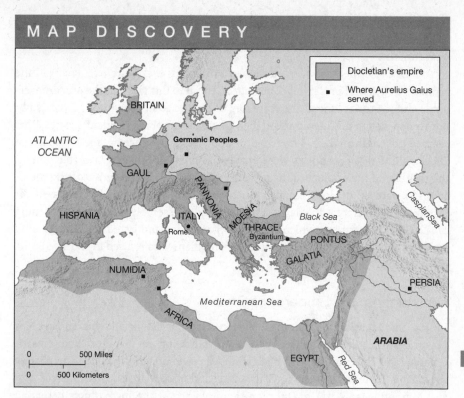

MAP DISCOVERY

Diocletian's empire

■ **Where Aurelius Gaius served**

ATLANTIC OCEAN

BRITAIN

Germanic Peoples

GAUL

PANNONIA

HISPANIA

ITALY

Rome

MOESIA

THRACE

Byzantium

Black Sea

PONTUS

GALATIA

Caspian Sea

NUMIDIA

PERSIA

Mediterranean Sea

AFRICA

ARABIA

EGYPT

Red Sea

0 — 500 Miles

0 — 500 Kilometers

THE EMPIRE UNDER DIOCLETIAN

This map shows the extent of the empire in 305, at the end of Diocletian's reign. Compared with the map on page 119, what portions of the empire had been lost or abandoned during his reign? Why? What geographical challenges did the empire's size pose to the emperor? Note where Aurelius Gaius served. What were the troubles and disturbances that influenced his itinerary?

They showed tremendous devotion to their god-emperor. For Diocletian and his soldiers, the periphery of the empire had become its center; the center was increasingly marginal to the program of the empire.

Fiscal Reform. Some aspects of Diocletian's program, such as the improvement of the civil administration and the military, were successful. Others, such as the reform of silver currency and wage and price controls, were dismal failures. One effect of the fiscal reforms was to bind **coloni**, or hereditary tenant farmers, to their lands, since they were forbidden to leave the villages where they were registered to pay their taxes. In this practice lay the origins of European serfdom. Another effect was the gradual destruction of the local city councils, since their members, the **decurions**, were held personally responsible for the payment of local assessments whether or not they could be collected from the other inhabitants. In time, this led to the dissolution of local civil government.

All of these measures were designed to marshal the entire population in the monumental task of preserving *Romanitas*. Central to this task was the proper reverential attitude toward the divine emperors who directed it. One group seemed stubbornly opposed to this heroic effort: the Christians. In 298, an incident occurred that seemed to confirm their subversive attitude. At a sacrifice in the presence of Diocletian, the Roman priests were unable to obtain the desired favorable omens; they attributed their failure to the presence of Christians, who were crossing themselves to ward off demons. Such blasphemous conduct—it might be compared, for instance, to desecrating the flag at a modern public assembly—led to the launching of the Great Persecution, which formally began in 303 and lasted sporadically until 313. It resulted in the death of hundreds of Christians who refused to sacrifice to the pagan gods.

Constantine, the Emperor of God

In 305, in the midst of the Great Persecution, Diocletian and his co-augustus Maximian took the extraordinary step of abdicating in favor of their caesars, Galerian and Constantius. This abdication was intended to provide for an orderly succession. Instead, the sons of Constantius and Maximian, Constantine (306–337) and Maxentius (306–312), drawing on the prejudice of the increasingly barbarian armies toward hereditary succession, set about wrecking the tetrarchy. In so doing, they plunged the empire once more into civil war as they fought over the western half of the empire.

Victory and Conversion. Victory in the west came to Constantine in 312, when he defeated and killed Maxentius in a battle at the Milvian Bridge outside Rome. Constantine attributed his victory to a vision telling him to paint symbols on the shields of his soldiers. For pagans, this symbol was the solar emblem of the cult of the Unconquered Sun. For Christians, it was the Chi-Rho, formed from the first two letters of the Greek word for Christ. The next year, in Milan, Constantine rescinded the persecution of Christians and granted Christian clergy the same privileges that pagan priests enjoyed. Constantine himself was not baptized until near death, a common practice in antiquity. However, during his reign, Christianity grew from a persecuted minority to the most favored cult in the empire.

Constantinople. Almost as important as Constantine's conversion to Christianity was his decision to establish his capital in Byzantium, a city founded by Greek colonists on the narrow neck of water connecting the Black Sea to the Mediterranean. Later it was known as Constantinople, the city of Constantine. For the next 11 centuries, Constantinople served as the heart of the Roman and then the Byzantine world. From his new city, Constantine began to transform the empire into a Christian state and Christianity into a Roman state religion.

The Triumph of Christianity

While paganism was being disestablished, Christianity was rapidly becoming the established religion. The effects of Constantine's conversion on the empire and on Christianity were enormous. Constantine made large financial contributions to Christian communities to repay them for their losses during persecutions. He erected rich churches on the model of Roman basilicas, or administrative buildings, and converted temples into Christian places of worship. He gave bishops the authority to act as magistrates within the Christian community. Once the particular subjects of persecution, bishops became favored courtiers. Constantine attempted to make himself the de facto head of the Church. Constantine and his successors, with the brief exception of his nephew Julian (r. 361–363), sought to use the cult of the one God to strengthen their control over the empire.

Emperor and Church. After Constantine's death in 337, emperors began restricting paganism. In 341, pagan sacrifice was banned, and by 355 the temples had been closed and the death penalty for sacrificing to pagan gods had been decreed, although not enforced.

Imperial control over Christianity was strong, but not total. One of the most powerful Christian successors to Constantine, Theodosius I (347–395), met his match in Ambrose (339–397), the bishop of Milan. In 390, the emperor, angered by riots in the Greek city of Thessalonica, ordered a general massacre of the population. Ambrose dared to excommunicate, or ban, the emperor from his church in Milan until Theodosius did public penance for that brutal act. Eventually, the emperor acquiesced, acknowledging that even he was subject to the rule of God as interpreted by the bishops.

Conversion. Although imperial support was essential to the spread of Christianity in the fourth century, other factors encouraged conversion as well. Christian miracles, particularly that of exorcism, or the casting out of demons, won many converts.

Over the course of the fourth century, the number of Christians rose from 5 to 30 million. Imperial support, miracles, and preaching could not, by themselves, account for this phenomenal growth. Physical coercion played a large part. The story was told that in one town, on imperial command, all of the local temples were destroyed and "a great number" of leading pagans who refused conversion were tortured to death. The remaining pagan population converted. Conversion—by whatever method—also suited the emperors, who saw a unified cult as an essential means of bolstering their position.

This mosaic found under St. Peter's Basilica in Rome is believed by many to be the earliest representation of Jesus, while others see it as Helios, the sun-god. The catacombs were underground passages near Rome used by the early Christians as cemeteries, for funeral and memorial services, and as places of refuge during times of persecution.

Imperial Christianity

The religion to which Constantine converted had matured institutionally and intellectually since its origins as a reform movement within Judaism. By the late third century, Christian communities existed throughout the empire, each headed by a bishop who was considered divinely guided and answerable only to his flock and to God. In the west, the bishop of Rome, termed the pope, had acquired the position of first among equals. However, the Church as a whole was divided on fundamental questions of belief, and the growing importance of Christianity in the Roman Empire added to the gravity of these divisions.

Divinity, Humanity, and Salvation

Jesus, the savior or Christ, was at the heart of Christian belief, but individual Christian communities interpreted the nature of Christ differently as they attempted to reconcile their faith with the intellectual traditions of late antiquity. Christian Scriptures spoke of the Father, the Son, and the Spirit. Yahweh was generally accepted as the Father and Christ as the Son; the Spirit was understood to be the continuing presence of God sent by Jesus after his resurrection and ascension.

Christology. Generally, Christians saw God as a Trinity, at once one and three. But the relationship among the three was a source of endless debate, particularly for

Greek-speaking Christians attempting to reconcile their faith with the Neoplatonic ideas of successive emanations from God to creation, which were incorporated into the Christian understanding of the Trinity. Was Christ just a man, chosen by God as a divine instrument, or was he God? If he was God, had he simply appeared to be human? These were not trivial or academic questions for Christians, since the possibility of salvation depended on their answers. Throughout the eastern half of the empire, ordinary people were ready to fight not only with words, but even with weapons to defend their positions.

Throughout the so-called **Christological controversies**—which began in the early third century and continued through the fifth—two extremes presented Christ as either entirely human or entirely God, with centrists attempting to hold a middle ground. At one extreme were the Monarchians, who emphasized the oneness of God by arguing that the three represented three activities although God possessed only one substance, and the Gnostics, who argued that Jesus had only appeared to be human but in reality was only divine. At the other extreme were the **Arians**, who explained that Jesus was a man and not divine.

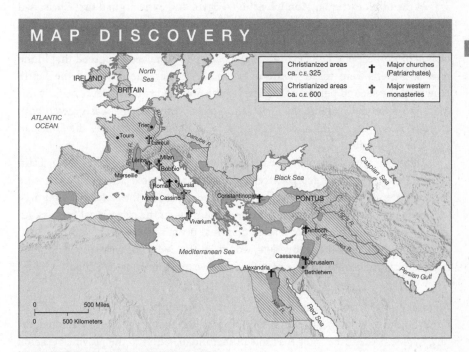

MAP DISCOVERY

THE SPREAD OF CHRISTIANITY

Examine the regions in which Christianity first became established. What is distinctive about the areas Christianized in the first three centuries of Christendom? What major differences can you detect between Christian centers in the eastern and western portions of the Roman Empire? To what extent did Christianity exist outside the empire by 600?

Origen of Alexandria. The first Christian intellectual to undertake a systematic exposition of the Trinity was the great Alexandrine theologian Origen (185–254). In all of his teachings, Origen moved Christian teaching from a literal to a symbolic understanding of Scripture and gave it a sound philosophical foundation by synthesizing the Neoplatonic tradition with Christianity. His trinitarian teachings insisted on the co-eternality of the Son with the Father, but, drawing as he did on Neoplatonic ideas of emanations, he seemed to subordinate the Son to the Father and to make the Spirit a creation of the Son. In the generations following Origen, the controversy continued, particularly between those who taught the equality of the persons of the Trinity and those who, like the Alexandrine theologian Arius (ca. 250–336), insisted that Jesus was not equal to God the Father but was a lesser divinity created by God. By the time of Constantine, the issue of whether or not Jesus was one with God threatened to destroy the unity of Christianity. To settle the controversy, the emperor commanded the bishops of the entire Church to assemble at Nicaea in 325. At the emperor's urging, the council condemned the teachings of Arius and adopted the term *homousion*, "of one being," to describe the equality of the Father and the Son.

At the other extreme, Monophysites in Egypt and Syria argued that Christ had only one nature—the divine. A century after Nicaea, another council was held at Chalcedon in 451 to resolve the issue. Following the recommendation of the bishop of Rome, Pope Leo I (440–461), the bishops at Chalcedon agreed that in the one God there were three divine persons: the Father, the Son, and the Spirit. However, the second person of the Trinity, the Son, had two natures: one fully human, the other fully divine. In Egypt and Palestine the decree was greeted with outrage. Mobs of monks and laity rioted in the streets to oppose the "unclean synod of Chalcedon."

Although a western bishop had provided the formula for Chalcedon, Latin Christians were not as deeply concerned with the Christological debates as were the easterners. For westerners, the great question was less the nature of God than the mechanism of salvation and the role of humans in the salvational process. An attempt to answer this and other key doctrinal questions was provided by a man who, more than any other individual, would set the course of western Christianity and political philosophy for the next thousand years: Augustine of Hippo.

Augustine of Hippo. Augustine (354–430) was born into a well-off North African family in the town of Tagaste. In his *Confessions*, the first psychological autobiography, Augustine describes how his skills in rhetoric took him to the provincial capital of Carthage and then on to Rome and finally Milan, the western imperial residence, where he gained fame as one of the foremost rhetoricians of the empire.

While in Milan, Augustine came into contact with kinds of people he had never encountered in Africa, particularly Neoplatonists and Christians. The most important of these was Ambrose, bishop of Milan. The encounter with a spiritual philosophy and a Christianity that was compatible with it profoundly changed the young professor. After a period of agonized searching, Augustine converted to the new religion. Abandoning his Italian life, he returned to the North African town of Hippo to found a monastery where he could devote himself to reading the Scriptures.

Augustine spent the remainder of his life as bishop of this small provincial town, but his reputation as spokesperson for the Christian tradition spread throughout the empire. As a professor of rhetoric he had become an expert in debate, and much of his episcopal career was spent in refuting opponents within the Church as well as dealing with traditional pagans who blamed the problems of the empire on the new religion.

In responding to these attacks, Augustine elaborated a new Christian understanding of human society and the individual's relationship to God, which dominated Western thought for the next 15 centuries. He rejected elitist attempts to identify the true Church with any earthly community. Likewise, he rejected the claim of pagans that the Roman tradition was the embodiment of true virtue. Instead, he argued that the true members of God's elect necessarily coexisted in the world with sinners. No earthly community, not even the empire or the visible Church, was the true "city of God." Earthly society participated in the true Church, the city of God, through the sacraments and did so quite apart from the individual worthiness of the recipients or even of the ministers of these rites. Belief that the presence of sinners within the Church blocked the plan of salvation or that responsibility for salvation lay with the individual was to deny the omnipotence of God.

According to Augustine, salvation was free, a gift not earned by virtuous lives but freely granted by God to the elect. In this way, Augustine argued for a distinction between the visible Christian empire and the Christian community.

The Call of the Desert

At the same time that intellectuals like Augustine were attempting to explain Christian doctrine, less intellectual but equally determined men and women were searching for a different way of living Christ's message. This was the hermit, monk, or recluse, who taught less by his or her words than by his or her life, a life that was often so unusual that even the most ignorant and worldly citizen of the late empire could recognize in it the power of God. Beneath the apparent eccentricity, however, lay a fundamental principle: the radical rejection of society's values in favor of absolute dedication to God's.

Shortly after the death of Origen in 254, another Egyptian was undertaking a different path to enduring fame. Anthony (ca. 250–355), a well-to-do peasant, heard the same biblical text that later converted Augustine: "Go, sell all you have and give to the poor and follow me." This straightforward peasant did exactly what the text commanded. He disposed of all his goods and left his village for the Egyptian desert. There, for the next 70 years, he sought to follow Christ in a life of constant self-mortification and prayer.

This dropout from civilization deeply touched his fellow Christians, many of whom were disturbed by the abrupt transformation of their religion from persecuted minority to privileged majority. Over the next few centuries, thousands rejected the worldliness of civilization and the easy life of the average Christian to lead a monastic life in the wildernesses of the empire.

Monastic Communities

Monasticism took two forms: communal organization and solitary life. Pachomius (ca. 290–346) and Basil the Great (ca. 329–379) in the east and Benedict of Nursia (ca. 480–547) in the west perfected the communal life. Faced with the impossibility of surviving in a harsh environment without cooperation, Egyptian monks banded together into small monastic towns. As many as 2,000 monks lived in these monasteries. They placed themselves under the control of the abbot, who served as spiritual guide and administrator of the community. These men and women sought spiritual perfection through physical self-mortification and through the subordination of their own wills to that of the abbot. Monks drank no wine, ate no meat, used no oil. They spent their days in prayer and work. During the fourth century, this monastic tradition spread east to Bethlehem, Jerusalem, Caesarea, and Constantinople and west to Rome, Milan, Trier, Marseille, and Tours. In the following centuries, it reached beyond the borders of the empire when Egyptian-style monasticism was introduced into Ireland.

In the Greek-speaking world, the definitive form of the monastic community was provided by Basil the Great. Basil had visited the monasteries of Egypt, Palestine, and Syria before founding his own monastery at Pontus near his family estate at Annesi in present-day Turkey. Although he did not write a specific rule for the governance of his monastery, his collection of commentaries and spiritual advice to his followers outlined a form of monastic life in which a day of agriculture, craft work, and care for the sick and the poor was organized within an ordered progression of liturgical prayer. His emphasis on communal life rather than on heroic acts of individual asceticism provided the model for eastern monasticism from his day to the present.

Unlike Anthony of Egypt, Basil was a brilliant and well-educated intellectual who frequently left his monastery to throw himself into the ecclesiastical politics of the empire. By the end of his life, Basil had become bishop of Caesarea. Eastern monastic communities continued this active involvement in political and secular affairs. Monasteries provided the early religious training for most religious leaders. Monks and abbots often involved themselves wholeheartedly in the politics of the empire.

In the west, Benedict of Nursia was as influential in structuring communal religious life as Basil was in the east. In time, Benedict became abbot of a small community of monks at Monte Cassino, between Rome and Naples. The rule that he drafted for the governance of his community, while drawn largely from earlier monastic rules circulating in Italy, became the definitive statement of western monasticism. Benedict's rule encouraged moderation and flexibility while emphasizing a life of poverty, chastity, and obedience to an elected abbot. Monks were required to perform some physical labor, and the monastery was intended to be a self-sufficient community. However, the real task of the monk was the continuous praise of God. This consisted of gathering at regular intervals through the day and night for communal prayer. Although Benedict lived and died in obscurity, within two and a half centuries his rule became the universal rule for western monasticism.

Western monasteries, too, provided their share of bishops, but unlike those in the east, western monks remained more isolated from population centers and from direct involvement in public affairs. However, western monasteries were not peripheral to western society and religion. Rather, these rustic communities were centers of religious and economic activity as well as education and learning in the largely rural west. They remained under the authority of the local bishops, who were usually drawn from the lay aristocracy of the empire in the west. Also, western monasteries depended on the political and economic support that they received from lay patrons.

Solitaries and Hermits

Although Anthony had begun as a hermit, he and most Egyptian monks eventually settled into communal lives. Elsewhere, particularly in the desert of Syria, the model of the monk remained the individual hermit. The Syrian desert, unlike that of Egypt, was particularly suitable for such an ascetic life. Here, the desert was milder, an individual could find food in wild roots and water in rain pools, and villages were never too far off. Moreover, the life of the wandering hermit was closely connected to traditional seminomadic lifestyles in the Fertile Crescent. But the Christian hermits who appeared across Syria in late antiquity were unlikely to be mistaken for the familiar Bedouin nomads. The Christian hermits were wild men and women who came down from the mountainsides and galvanized the attention of their contemporaries by their lifestyles.

Such people of God, rejecting civilized life in the most overt and radical ways, nevertheless met very real social and cultural needs of the population. Their lack of ties to human society made them the perfect arbitrators in the constant disputes that threatened to disrupt village life. They were individuals of power, whose perceived ability to cast out demons and work miracles made them ideal community patrons at a time when traditional power brokers of the village were being lured away to imperial service or provincial cities. The greatest of these holy people received as visitors not only local peasants but also emperors and empresses, who eagerly sought their advice.

Unlike the eastern monks, the Syrian hermits of the fourth and fifth centuries had few parallels in the west. Hermits did inhabit the caves and forests of Italy and Gaul, and pious women found solitude as recluses even in the center of Rome. But

A gold plaque from a sixth-century Syrian reliquary. The subject is Simeon Stylites on his pillar; the snake represents the vanquished devil. Clients could consult the holy man by climbing up the ladder on the left.

these westerners did not establish themselves either as independent sources of religious power or as political power brokers. Their monasticism remained a personal religious commitment. When one Roman woman was asked why she remained shut up in her cell, she replied, "I am on a journey." When asked where she was going, she answered simply, "To God."

Chronology

IMPERIAL REFORM AND IMPERIAL CHRISTIANITY

284–305	Reign of Diocletian; establishment of the tetrarchy
303–313	Great Persecution of Christians
305	Abdication of Diocletian
306–312	Civil War
312	Victory of Constantine in civil war; Constantine converts to Christianity; establishment of Byzantium as Constantine's capital
325	Council of Nicaea
337	Official restrictions on paganism
341	Pagan sacrifice banned
355	Temples closed and death penalty established for sacrificing to pagan gods
480	Death of Julius Nepos, last legitimate emperor in the west

A Parting of the Ways

Those who remained in "the world" at the end of the fourth century could hardly take so serene a view of life. Christians and pagans might differ in their explanations for the ills that had befallen the empire, but none could deny their severity. The vulnerability of the Constantinian system became clear shortly after 376, when the Huns, a nomadic horse-riding people from central Asia, swept into the Black Sea region and threw the entire barbarian world once more into chaos. The Huns quickly destroyed the Gothic confederation and absorbed many of the peoples who had constituted the Goths. Others sought protection in the empire. The Visigoths, as they came to be known, were the largest of these groups, and their fate illustrated how precarious existence could be for all the inhabitants of the imperial frontier.

Driven from their lands and thus from their food supply, the Visigoths turned to the empire for assistance. But the Roman authorities treated them as brutally as had the Huns, forcing some to sell their children into slavery in return for morsels of dog flesh. In despair, the Visigoths rose up against the Romans, and against all odds, their desperate rebellion succeeded. They annihilated an imperial army at Adrianople in 378, and the emperor Valens himself was killed. His successor, Theodosius (379–395), was forced to allow the Visigoths to settle along the Danube and to be governed by their own leaders even though they lived within the boundaries of the empire.

Theodosius's treaty with the Visigoths set an ominous precedent. Never before had a barbarian people been allowed to settle as a political unit within the empire. Within a few years the Visigoths were again on the move, traveling across the Balkans into Italy under the command of their chieftain Alaric (ca. 370–410). In 410, they captured Rome and sacked it for three days, an event that sent shock waves throughout the entire empire. The symbolic effect of the Visigoths' victory far exceeded the amount of real damage, which was relatively light. Only after Alaric's death did the Visigoths leave Italy, ultimately settling in Spain and southern Gaul with the emperor's approval.

The Barbarization of the West

Rome did not fall. It was transformed. Romans participated in and even encouraged this transformation. Roman accommodation of the Visigoths set the pattern for subsequent settlement of barbarians in the western half of the empire. By this time, barbarians made up the bulk of the imperial army, and commanders were frequently themselves barbarians. However, these barbarian troops had been integrated into existing Roman military structures. In the late fourth and fifth centuries, emperors accepted whole barbarian peoples as integral parts of the Roman army and settled them within the empire.

The Visigoths were not the only powerful barbarian people to challenge the empire. The Vandals, who had entered the empire in 406, crossed over into Africa, the richest region of the western empire, and quickly conquered it. Avowed enemies of the empire, the Vandals used their base in North Africa to raid the European coastline and attack Roman shipping. In 455, they sacked Rome much more thoroughly than had the Goths 45 years earlier.

Another threat appeared in the 430s, when the Huns, formerly Roman allies, invaded the empire under their charismatic leader Attila (ca. 406–453). Although defeated in Gaul by a combined army of barbarians under the command of the Roman general Flavius Aetius in 451, they turned toward Italy and penetrated as far as Rome. There, they were stopped not by the rapidly disintegrating imperial forces but by the bishop of Rome, Pope Leo I, who met Attila before the city's gates. What transpired between the two is not known, but Attila's subsequent withdrawal from Italy vastly increased the prestige of the papacy. Now popes not only were successors of Saint Peter and bishops of the principal city of the west, but were replacing the emperor as protector of the city. The foundation of the political power of the papacy was established.

The confederation of the Huns collapsed after the death of Attila in 453, but imperial power did not revive in Italy. A series of incompetent emperors were pushed aside by barbarian generals who assumed power on the peninsula and sought recognition from Zeno, the emperor in the east. However, after the death in 480 of the last legitimate western emperor, Julius Nepos, Zeno conferred the title of patrician on the Ostrogothic king Theodoric. In 489, Theodoric invaded Italy with imperial blessing and established himself as ruler of Italy.

In Gaul, between the Seine and the Loire, the Roman general Flavius Aetius and, after his death, the general Syagrius continued to represent some imperial presence. But the armies that Aetius and Syagrius commanded consisted entirely of barbarians—particularly Visigoths and Franks—and they represented the interests of local aristocratic factions rather than those of Constantinople. So thoroughly barbarized had these last Roman commanders become in their military command and political control that the barbarians referred to Syagrius as "king of the Romans." Ultimately, in 486, Syagrius was defeated and replaced by the Frank Clovis, son of Syagrius's military commander Childeric, probably with the blessing of the emperor.

Britain met a similar fate. Abandoned by the Roman legions around 407, the Romano-Celtic population in this province concluded a treaty with bands of Saxons and Angles to protect Britain from other barbarian raiders. As had happened elsewhere in the empire, the barbarians came as federated troops and stayed as rulers. Gradually, during the fifth century, Germanic warrior groups conquered much of the island. The Anglo-Saxons pushed the native inhabitants to the west and the north. There, as the Cornish and the Welsh (in Anglo-Saxon, *Welsh* means simply "enemy"), they preserved the Christian religion but largely lost their other Roman traditions.

The New Barbarian Kingdoms

The establishment of barbarian kingdoms within the Roman world meant the end of the western empire as a political entity. However, the emperors in the east and west continued to pretend that all these barbarian peoples, with the exception of the Vandals, were Roman troops commanded by loyal Roman officers who happened to be of barbarian origin. The emperors gave the barbarian kings or war leaders official status within the empire as Roman generals or patricians and occasionally granted them portions of abandoned lands or existing estates. Local Roman elites considered these leaders rude and uncultured barbarians who nevertheless could be made to serve these elites' own interests more easily than better educated imperial bureaucrats.

As a result, the aristocracy of the west, the *maiores*, viewed the decay of the civil government without dismay. This decay was due largely to the poverty of the imperial treasury. In the fifth century, the entire public revenues of the west amounted to little more than the annual incomes of a few wealthy private aristocrats. Managing to escape both taxation and the jurisdiction of public officials, these individuals carved out for themselves vast estates, which they and their families controlled with private armies and which they governed as virtually autonomous lordships. Ordinary freemen, pressed by the remnants of imperial taxation and by barbarians, were forced into accepting the protection and hence control offered by aristocrats, who thereby came to control whole villages and districts.

The primary source of friction between barbarians and provincial elites was religion. Many Goths had converted to Christianity around the time that the Huns had destroyed the Gothic confederation. However, they had chosen the Arian form of Christianity to appease the Arian emperors Constantius and Valens. But the Goths and most other barbarian peoples held to their Arian form of faith long after it had been abandoned in the empire. Therefore, wherever the barbarians settled, they were met with distrust and hostility from the orthodox clergy. In southern Gaul and Italy, this hostility created serious difficulties because during the fifth century bishops had assumed many of the traditional duties and powers held by provincial Roman administrators.

Although during the fifth century the western aristocracy had largely given up on the civil administration, these wealthy landowners increasingly identified with the episcopacy. In Gaul, bishops were regularly selected from members of the greatest Gallo-Roman senatorial families, establishing veritable episcopal dynasties. In Italy and Spain, too, bishops were drawn from the landed aristocracy. These bishops, most of whom were elected after long years of outstanding secular leadership, served as the primary protectors and administrators of their communities, filling the vacuum left by the erosion of other civil offices. They, more than either local civil officials or the Bacaudae, were successful in representing the community before imperial tax collectors or barbarian chieftains.

Thus, in spite of the creation of the barbarian kingdoms, cultural and political leadership at the local level remained firmly in the hands of the aristocracy. Aristocratic bishops, rather than hermits, monopolized the role of mediators of divine power just as their lay brothers, in cooperation with barbarian military leaders, monopolized the role of mediators of secular power.

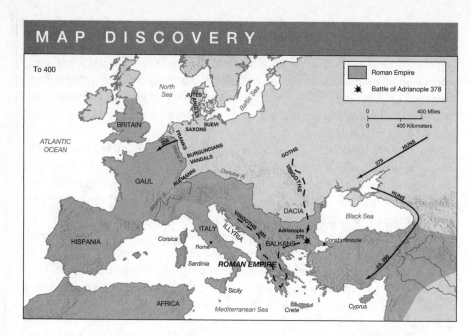

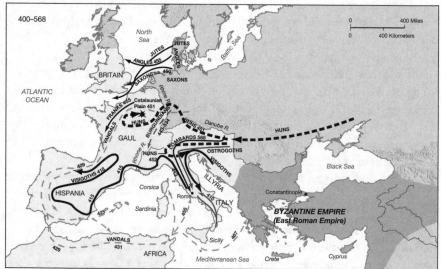

BARBARIAN MIGRATIONS AND INVASIONS

Study these maps of barbarian migrations and invasions. Who were Rome's western neighbors in the fourth century? What effects did the Huns have on barbarian migrations? From these maps, how might you explain the relative stability of the eastern or Byzantine Empire in the sixth century compared with the western?

Barbarian military leaders needed local ties by which to govern the large indigenous populations over whom they ruled. They found cooperation with these aristocrats to be both necessary and advantageous. Thus, while individual landowners might have suffered in the transition from Roman to barbarian rule, for the most part this transition took place with less disturbance of the local social or political scene than was once thought. During the fifth century, the imperial presence simply faded away as barbarian kings came to rule in the name of the emperor. After 480, the emperor resided exclusively in the east. The last western emperors disappeared without serious opposition either from western aristocrats or from their eastern colleagues.

The Hellenization of the East

The eastern half of the empire, in contrast to the west, managed to survive and even to prosper in the fifth and sixth centuries. In the east, beginning in 400, the trends toward militarization and barbarization of the administration were reversed, the strength of the imperial government was reaffirmed, and the vitality and integrity of the empire were restored.

Several reasons account for the contrast between east and west. First, the east had always been more urbanized and civilized than the west. It had an old tradition of civil control that antedated the Roman Empire itself. When the decay of Roman traditions allowed regionalism and tribalism to arise in the west, the same decay brought in the east a return to Hellenistic traditions. Second, the east had never developed the tradition of public poverty and private wealth that was characteristic of the west. In the east, tax revenues continued to support an administrative apparatus, which remained in the hands of civilians rather than barbarian military commanders. Moreover, the local aristocracies in the eastern provinces never achieved the wealth and independence of their western counterparts. Finally, Christian bishops, frequently divided over doctrinal issues, never managed to monopolize either sacred power, which was shared by itinerant holy men and monks, or secular power, which was wielded by imperial agents. Thus, under the firm direction of its emperors, especially Theodosius and later Zeno, the eastern empire not only survived but prepared for a new expansionist phase under the emperor Justinian.

SUMMARY

The Crisis of the Third Century   The crisis of the third century had territorial, economic, political, and military roots. The Roman army became the arbiter of political power. Political and military instability had devastating effects on the lives of ordinary people. Rome faced increasingly serious external threats from Germanic tribes. Rome itself helped transform small and isolated tribes into a major threat to the imperial system.

The Empire Restored   Diocletian carried out a series of military, political, and economic reforms that helped stabilize the empire. The key to Diocletian's success was his militarization of Roman society. Constantine converted to Christianity, established a new capital at Byzantium, and began to transform the empire into a Christian state. Imperial control over Christianity was strong, but not total. Imperial support, Christian miracles, and raw coercion all contributed to the spread of Christianity.

Imperial Christianity   By the late third century, Christian communities existed throughout the empire, each headed by a bishop. The Church as a whole was divided on fundamental questions of belief. In the east, debate centered on the divinity of Christ. In the west, the issue of the role of humans in salvation was paramount. Hermits, monks, and recluses sought escape from the worldly life of the empire. Monasticism took two forms: communal organization and solitary life. Pachomius and Basil the Great in the east and Benedict of Nursia in the west created influential models of the communal life.

A Parting of the Ways   New barbarian threats destabilized the empire. The Visigoths were allowed to settle as a political unit within the empire, setting a dangerous precedent. Rome was transformed by its encounters with barbarians, a transformation that Romans participated in and even encouraged. The establishment of barbarian kingdoms within the Roman world meant the end of the western empire as a political entity. In the west, cultural and political leadership at the local level remained firmly in the hands of the aristocracy. In the east, beginning in 400, the trends toward militarization and barbarization of the administration were reversed, the strength of the imperial government was reaffirmed, and the vitality and integrity of the empire were restored.

QUESTIONS FOR REVIEW

1. How did increasing contact between Roman civilization and the Germanic barbarians transform both?
2. How did Constantine's adoption of Christianity and the movement of his capital to Byzantium contribute to the decline of the western empire?
3. How did different views of the divinity of Christ and the means of salvation divide early Christians?
4. What was the attraction of monasticism, and why did it take so many different forms?
5. What were the differences in politics and culture in the eastern and western portions of the empire by the end of the fifth century C.E.?

CHAPTER 7

The Classical Legacy in the East: Byzantium and Islam

The Byzantines

At the end of the fifth century C.E., the eastern empire of Theodosius and Zeno had escaped the fate that its western counterpart had suffered at the hands of the Germanic peoples. Still, the long-term survival of the eastern empire seemed far from certain.

Little unified the empire of Constantinople. The population of the capital split into two rival political factions, whose violent conflicts often threatened the stability of the government. When these two factions joined forces with the army, they were powerful enough to create or destroy emperors. Beyond Constantinople, the empire's population consisted of the more or less hellenized peoples of Asia

Minor, Armenians, Slavs, Arabs, Syrians, Egyptian Copts, and others. Unlike western Europe, the east was still a world of cities. But the importance of these urban centers began to decline in favor of the rural peasant world.

Finally, the eastern empire was more divided than unified by its Christianity. Rivalry among the great cities of Antioch, Alexandria, Jerusalem, Rome, and Constantinople was expressed in the competition among their bishops, or patriarchs. By the time of Justinian (527–565), emperors were obsessed with maintaining absolute authority and imposing uniformity on their empire.

Justinian and the Creation of the Byzantine State

Although Justinian's goals were essentially conservative, his attempts to return to the past and restore the territory, power, and prestige of the ancient Roman Empire created a new world. With the assistance of his dynamic wife Theodora, his great generals Belisarius and Narses, his brilliant jurist Tribonian, his scientists Anthemius of Tralles and Isidorus of Miletus, and his brutally efficient administrator and tax collector John of Cappadocia, he remade the empire.

Spurred on by Theodora, in 532 Justinian checked the power of the factions by brutally suppressing a riot that left 30,000 dead in the capital city. Belisarius and

A mosaic from the church of San Vitale in Ravenna. The emperor Justinian, along with secular and ecclesiastical officials, is shown bringing an offering to the church. The halo around his head signifies the sacred nature of the imperial office.

Narses recaptured North Africa from the Vandals, Italy from the Ostrogoths, and part of Spain from the Visigoths, restoring for one last moment some of the geographical unity of the empire of Augustus and Constantine. Tribonian revised and organized the existing codes of Roman law into the *Justinian Code,* a great monument of western jurisprudence that remains today the foundation of most of Europe's legal systems. Anthemius and Isidorus combined their knowledge of mathematics, geometry, kinetics, and physics to build the Church of the Holy Wisdom (Hagia Sophia) in Constantinople, one of the largest and most innovative churches ever constructed. Less well appreciated were the achievements of John of Cappadocia, who was able to squeeze the empire's population for the taxes to pay for these conquests, reforms, and building projects.

Ultimately, Justinian's spectacular achievements came at too high a price. He left his successors an empire that had been virtually bankrupted by the costs of his wars and his building projects, was bitterly divided by his attempts to settle religious controversies, and was poorly protected on its eastern border, where the Sassanid Empire was a constant threat. Most of Italy and Spain soon returned to barbarian control. In 602, the Sassanid emperor Chosroes II (d. 628) invaded the empire, capturing Egypt, Palestine, and Syria and threatening Constantinople itself. In a series of desperate campaigns, the emperor Heraclius (610–641) turned back the tide and crushed the Sassanids, but it was too late. A new power, Islam, had emerged in the deserts of Arabia. This new power was to challenge and ultimately absorb both the Sassanids and much of the eastern Roman Empire. As a result, the east became increasingly less Roman and more Greek—or, specifically, more *Byzantine,* a term derived from the original name of Constantinople, Byzantium.

For over 700 years, the Byzantine Empire played a major role in Western history. From the seventh through tenth centuries, when most of Europe was too weak and disorganized to defend itself against the expansion of Islam, the Byzantines stood as the bulwark of Christianity. When organized government had virtually disappeared in the west, the Byzantine Empire provided a model of a centralized bureaucratic state ruled according to principles of Roman law. When, beginning in the fourteenth century, western Europeans began once more to appreciate the heritage of Greek and Roman art and literature, they turned to Constantinople. Perhaps most important, when urban civilization had all but disappeared from the rest of Europe, Greeks and Latins could still look "to The City," *eis ten polin,* or, as the Turks pronounced it, Istanbul.

Emperors and Individuals

The classic age of Byzantine society, roughly from the eighth through the tenth centuries, has been described as "individualism without freedom." Individuals and small family groups stood as isolated units in a society characterized, until the mid-eleventh century, by the direct relationship between an all-powerful emperor and citizens of all ranks.

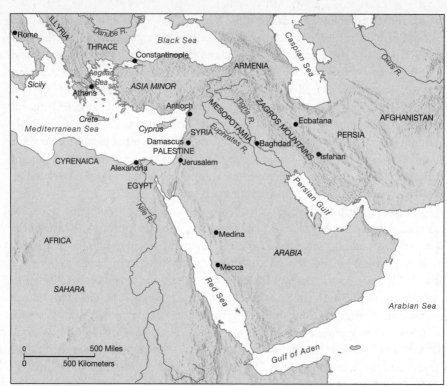

THE EASTERN MEDITERRANEAN. The Arabian Peninsula was peripheral to the Roman and Persian empires until the seventh century when the new Islamic faith suddenly emerged from Arabia to overwhelm its more ancient neighboring empires.

Governing Byzantium. In part, this individualism resulted from the Byzantine form of government. The Byzantine state was, in theory and often in fact, an autocracy. Since the time of Diocletian, all members of society were subjects of the emperor, who alone was the source of law. Although in theory the emperor was elected by the Senate, army, and people of Constantinople, emperors generally selected their own successors and had them crowned in their own lifetimes.

Thus the traditional corporate bodies of the Roman Empire wasted away or became window dressing for the imperial cult. The Senate gradually ceased to play any autonomous role, and its powers were officially abolished in the ninth century.

The factions, which in the sixth century had the power to make or break emperors, met the same fate. From autonomous political groups, they too gradually became no more than participants in imperial ceremonies.

Bureaucracy and Army. Although the emperor was the source of all authority, the actual administration of the empire was carried out by a vast bureaucracy composed of military and civilian officers. The empire was divided into roughly 25 provinces, or *themes*. The soldiers in each theme were also farmers, rather than

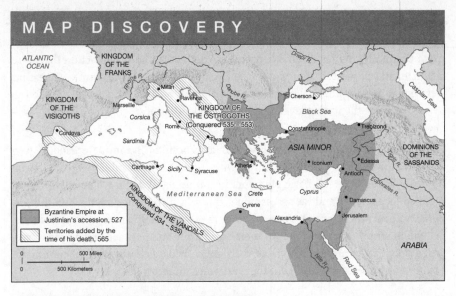

MAP DISCOVERY

BYZANTINE EMPIRE UNDER JUSTINIAN

Examine the boundaries of the Byzantine Empire under Justinian. Why would Justinian have been particularly eager to recover the areas that he reconquered? What problems were posed by the conquest of the Ostrogoths that were not present in the conquest of the Vandals?

full-time warriors. Each soldier received a small farm by which to support himself and his family. When a soldier retired or died, his farm and his military obligation passed to his eldest son. These farmer-soldiers were the backbone of both the imperial military and the economic system. They not only formed a regular, native, locally based army, but they also kept much of Byzantine agriculture in the hands of small free peasants rather than great aristocrats. The themes were governed by military commanders, or **strategoi**, who presided over both civilian and military bureaucrats.

In contrast to the military command of the themes, the central administration, which focused on the emperor and the imperial family, was wholly civil. The most important positions at court were occupied by eunuchs, castrated men who offered a number of advantages to imperial administration. Because they could not have descendants, there was no danger that they would attempt to turn their offices into hereditary positions or that they would plot and scheme on behalf of their children. Moreover, since the sacred nature of the emperor required physical perfection, eunuchs could not aspire to replace their masters on the throne. Finally, although at times their influence with the emperor made them immensely powerful, eunuchs were feared and despised by the general population. Therefore, they had little likelihood of building autonomous power bases outside of imperial favor.

Families and Villages

A godlike emperor and a centralized bureaucracy left little room for the development of the hierarchies of private patronage, lordship, and group action that were characteristic of western Europe. In the Byzantine Empire, aristocrat and peasant were equal in their political powerlessness. Therefore, Byzantine society tended to be organized at the lowest level, that of the nuclear family.

Rural Life. The countryside, which was the backbone of Byzantine prosperity into the eleventh century, was also a world with limited horizontal and vertical social bonds. Villages were the basic elements in the imperial system. The village court handled local affairs and tax assessments, but it in turn dealt directly with the imperial bureaucracy. Most peasants, whether they were landowners, peasant soldiers, or renters, survived on the labor of their own family and perhaps one or two slaves. Large cooperative undertakings, as in Islamic lands, and the use of communal equipment, as became the rule in the west, were unknown.

Urban Life. Constantinople was ideally situated to develop into the greatest commercial center of the west, at its height boasting a population of over one million. Because of Constantinople's strategic location on the Bosporus, that slim ribbon of water uniting the Black and Mediterranean seas, all of the products of the empire and those of the Slavic, Latin, and Islamic worlds, as well as Oriental goods arriving overland from central Asia, had to pass through the city.

The empire's cities were centers for the manufacture of luxury goods that were in demand throughout the Islamic and Christian worlds. Imperial workshops in Constantinople and closely regulated workshops in Corinth and Thebes produced fine silks, brocades, carpets, and other luxury products that were marketed throughout the Mediterranean.

A Foretaste of Heaven

The cultural cement that bound emperor and subjects together was **Orthodox Christianity**. The Islamic capture of Alexandria, Jerusalem, and Antioch had removed the centers of regional religious particularism from the empire. The barbarian domination of Italy had isolated Rome and reduced its influence. These two processes left Constantinople as the only remaining patriarchate in the empire and thus the undisputed center of Orthodox Christianity.

In theory, patriarchs were elected; in reality, emperors appointed them. Patriarchs in turn controlled the various levels of the Church hierarchy. This ecclesiastical structure reflected and reinforced the organization of the state bureaucracy.

The essence of Orthodox religion was the liturgy, or ceremonies, of the Church, which provided, it was said, a foretaste of heaven. Adoration of God and veneration of the emperor went hand in hand as the cornerstone of imperial propaganda.

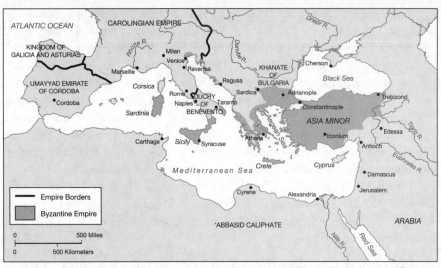

THE BYZANTINE EMPIRE IN 814. By the ninth century, the empire had lost all its territories but Asia Minor, Greece, the boot of Italy, and the islands of Sardinia and Sicily.

Iconoclasm

The one aspect of religious life that was not entirely under imperial control was monasticism. Monasteries were often wealthy and powerful. Moreover, their religious appeal, often based on the possession of miracle-working religious images, or **icons**, posed an independent source of religious authority that was at odds with the imperial centralization of all aspects of Byzantine life.

In this manuscript illustration, an icon is being destroyed while priests try to persuade Leo V to abandon his iconoclast policies.

Beginning with Emperor Leo III, the Isaurian (717–741), the military emperors who had driven back Islam sought to curtail the independence of monastic culture and particularly the cult of icons that was an integral part of it. These emperors and their supporters, termed **iconoclasts** (literally, "breakers of images"), objected to the mediating role of sacred images in worship. Monasteries, with their miracle-working icons, became particular targets of imperial persecution. The defenders of icons—**iconodules**, or image venerators—were imprisoned, tortured, and even executed. Most bishops, the army, and much of the non-European population of the empire supported the iconoclast emperors, but monks, the lesser clergy, and the majority of the populace, particularly women, violently resisted the destruction of their beloved images.

For more than a century, the iconoclast dispute raged. Finally, in 843, the Empress Theodora (842–858), who ruled during the minority of her son, ended the persecution and restored image veneration. Monasteries reopened and regained much of their former wealth and prestige.

The iconoclastic struggle deeply affected Byzantium's relations with the west. The popes considered the iconoclast emperors heretics and looked increasingly to the Frankish Carolingian family for support against them and the Lombards of Italy. In this manner, the Franks first entered Italian politics and began, with papal support, to establish themselves as a rival imperial power in the west.

The Rise of Islam

Arabs lived on the fringes of the Byzantine and Sassanid empires. Trade routes had carried people from the Fertile Crescent and Egypt across northern Arabia for centuries. By the sixth century C.E., Arabic-speaking peoples from the Arabian Peninsula had spread through the Syrian Desert as far north as the Euphrates.

Within both the Byzantine and Sassanid empires the distinction between Arab and non-Arab populations was blurred. Except for the Arabic language and a hazy idea of common Arabic kinship, nothing differentiated Arabs from their neighbors.

This was dramatically changed by an obscure merchant in the Arabian city of Mecca, who embarked on a career that would transform the world. Through faith, Muhammad (ca. 570–632) united the tribes of the Arabian Peninsula and propelled them on an unprecedented mission of conquest. Just as their faith combined elements of traditional Arab worship with Christianity and Judaism, the Arabian conquerors and their subject populations created a vital civilization from a mix of Arabian, Roman, Hellenistic, and Sassanid traditions.

Arabia Before the Prophet

Southern Arabia, with relatively abundant rainfall and fertile soils, was an agricultural region long governed by monarchs. During the fifth century C.E., the kings of the Yemen had extended their influence north over the Bedouin tribes of central Arabia in order to control and protect the caravan trade between north and south. In the late sixth century, however, Ethiopian and then Persian conquerors destroyed the Arabian kingdom of the Yemen and absorbed it into their empires. The result was a power vacuum that left central Arabia and its trade routes across the deserts in confusion.

Bedouin Society. Arabic Bedouins roamed the Arabian peninsula in search of pasturage for their flocks. Theirs was a life of independence, simplicity, and danger.

Although they acknowledged membership in various tribes, the Bedouin's real allegiance was to much narrower circles of lineages and tenting groups. Tribal chieftains, called *sheikhs,* chosen from ruling families, had no coercive power, either to right wrongs or to limit feuds. They served only as arbitrators and executors of tribal consensus.

The individual was unimportant in Bedouin society. Private land ownership was unknown, and flocks and herds were often held in common by kindred. Weapons, ornaments, women, and livestock could be acquired through exchange at the market towns around desert oases. More commonly, these goods and women were taken in raids against other tribes, caravans, and settlements or by exacting payments from weaker neighbors in return for protection.

Some of the Arabs of the more settled south, as well as inhabitants of towns along caravan routes, were Christian or Jewish. As farmers or merchants, these groups were looked down upon by the nomadic Bedouin, most of whom remained pagan. Although they recognized some important gods and even a high god usually called Allah, Bedouin worshiped local tribal deities, who were often thought of as inhabiting a sacred stone or spring.

Harams. Rivalry and feuding among tribes could be set aside at a mutually accepted neutral site, which might grow up around a religious sanctuary, or *haram.* Here, enemies could meet under truce to settle differences under the direction of the holy man or his descendants. Merchant communities sprang up within the safety of these sites, since the sanctuary gave them and their goods protection from their neighbors.

Mecca was just such a sanctuary, around whose sacred black rock, or Ka'bah, a holy man named Qusayy established himself and his tribe, the Quraysh, as its guardians sometime early in the sixth century. During the early seventh century, when increased hostilities between the Byzantine and Sassanid empires severed the direct trading links between the empires, the Quraysh network became the leading commercial organization in northern Arabia. Still, its effectiveness remained tied to the religious importance of Mecca and the Ka'bah. When Muhammad, a descendant of Qusayy, began to preach his monotheistic message, he was seen as a threat to the survival of his tribe and his city.

Muhammad, Prophet of God

A member of a lesser branch of the Quraysh, Muhammad was an orphan raised by relatives. At about age 20, he became the business manager for Khadijah, a wealthy widow whom he later married. This marriage gave him financial security among the middle ranks of Meccan merchants. In his thirties, he began to devote an increasing amount of time to meditation, retiring to the barren, arid mountains outside the city. There, in the month of Ramadan in the year 610, he reported a vision of a man who told him: "O Muhammad! Thou art the Messenger of God."

Preaching Islam. Within a year he began preaching openly. His early teachings stressed the absolute unity of God, the evils of idolatry, and the threat of divine judgment. Further revelations to Muhammad were copied word for word in what came to be the Qur'an, or Koran. These messages offered Arabs a faith founded on a book. In their eyes, this faith was both within the tradition of the Christianity and Judaism of their neighbors and superior to them. The Qur'an was the final revelation and Muhammad the last and greatest prophet.

Muslims believe that Allah's revelation emphasized, above all, his power and transcendence and that the duty of humans is worship. The prayers of Islam, in contrast with those of Christianity and Judaism, are essentially prayers of praise, seldom prayers of petition. Muslims regard the whole Qur'an as the exact and complete revelation of God. It is the complete guide for secular and religious life, the fundamental law of conduct for Islamic society. Muslims are not followers of Muhammad but of the God of Abraham and Jesus, who chose to make the final and complete revelation of his power and his judgment through the Prophet.

Initially, such revelations of divine power and judgment neither greatly bothered nor influenced Mecca's merchant elite. But soon Muhammad began to insist that those who did not accept Allah as the only God were damned, as were those who continued to venerate the sorts of idols on which Mecca's prosperity was founded. With this proclamation, toleration gave way to hostility. Muhammad and his followers were ostracized and even persecuted.

The Hijra. Around 620, some residents of Medina, a smaller trading community populated by rival pagan, Jewish, and Islamic clans and racked by internal political dissension, approached the Prophet and invited him to govern the community in order to end the factional squabbles. Rejected at home, he answered their call. On 24 September 622, Muhammad and one supporter secretly made their way from Mecca to Medina. This short journey of less than 300 miles, known as the **Hijra**, was destined to change the world.

The Triumph of Islam

The Hijra marked the Prophet's shift from preaching to action. He organized his followers from Mecca and Medina into the **Umma**, a community that transcended the old bonds of tribe and clan. He set about turning Medina into a haram like Mecca, with himself as founding holy man and the Umma as his new family. But this was not to be a haram or indeed a family like any other. Muhammad was not merely a sheikh whose authority rested on consensus. He was God's messenger, and his authority was absolute. His goal was to extend this authority far beyond his adopted town of Medina to Mecca and ultimately to the whole Arab world.

First, he gained firm control of Medina at the expense of its Jewish clans. When these clans failed to embrace his teachings, the Prophet expelled them in the name of political and religious unity. Those who were not expelled were executed.

Return to Mecca. In 629, Muhammad and 10,000 warriors marched on Mecca and captured the city in a swift and largely bloodless campaign.

During the three years between Muhammad's triumphant return to Mecca and his death, Islam moved steadily toward becoming the major force in the Arabian Peninsula. The Umma became a sort of supertribe, open to all individuals who would accept Allah and his Prophet. The invitation was extended to women as well as to men.

Women in Early Islam. Islam brought a transformation of the rights of women in Arabian society. This did not mean that they achieved equality with men any more than they did in any premodern civilization, east or west.

Islam did, however, forbid female infanticide, a common practice in pre-Islamic society. Brides, not their fathers or other male relatives, received the dowry from their husbands, thus making marriage more a partnership than a sale. Islamic women acquired inheritance and property rights and had protection against mistreatment in marriage. Although they remained second-class in status, at least women had a status, recognized and protected within the Umma.

An Arabian Faith. The attractions of Islam in this world included both economic prosperity and the opportunity to continue a lifestyle of raiding and warfare in the name of Allah. Muhammad won over the leaders of the Quraysh by making Mecca the sacred city of Islam and by retaining the Ka'bah, cleansed of idols, as the center of Islamic pilgrimage.

Muhammad's message spread to other tribes through diplomatic and, occasionally, military means. The divisive nature of Bedouin society contributed to his success. Frequently, factions within other tribes turned to Muhammad for mediation and support against their rivals. In return for his assistance, petitioners accepted his religious message. Since the Qur'an commanded Muslims to destroy idol worship, conversion provided the occasion for holy wars (**jihads**) of conquest and profitable raids against their still-pagan neighbors. Converts showed their piety by sending part of their spoils as alms to Medina.

The Spread of Islam

Muhammad died in the summer of 632 after a short illness, leaving no successor and no directions concerning the leadership of the Umma. Immediately, his closest and most influential followers selected Abu Bakr (632–634), the fourth convert to Islam, to be **caliph**, or successor of the Prophet. Abu Bakr and, after his death two years later, the caliph 'Umar (634–644) faced formidable obstacles. Within the Umma, tensions between the early Medina followers of the Prophet and the Meccan elite were beginning to surface. A more critical problem was that the tribes that had accepted the Prophet's leadership believed that his death freed them from their treaty obligations.

To prevent the collapse of the Umma, Abu Bakr launched a war of reconversion. Purely by chance, this war developed into wars of conquest that reached far beyond the Arab world. Commanded by Khalid ibn al-Walid (d. 642), the greatest early Islamic general, Muslim forces defeated tribe after tribe and brought them back into the Umma. But long-term survival demanded expansion. Since Muslims were forbidden to raid fellow believers and raids were an integral part of Bedouin life, the only way to keep recently converted Bedouin in line was to lead them on military expeditions against non-Muslims. Under Abu Bakr, Muslim expansion covered all of Arabia. Under 'Umar, Islam conquered Iran, Iraq, Syria, and Egypt.

Muslim expansion was facilitated by protracted fighting between the Byzantine and Sassanid empires as well as internal divisions within the Byzantine world. By 650, the great Sassanid Empire had disappeared, and the Byzantine Empire had lost Egypt, Syria, Mesopotamia, Palestine, portions of Asia Minor, and much of North Africa.

MAP DISCOVERY

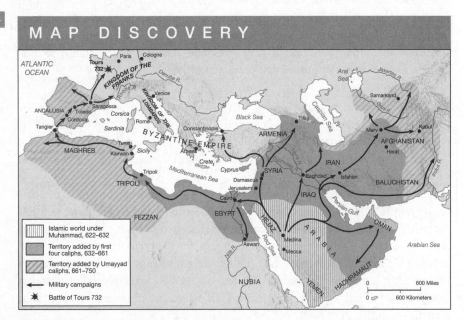

THE SPREAD OF ISLAM

Consider the geographical extent of the Islamic conquest. What trading and cultural networks were united by the spread of Islam? How did the geography of the Islamic world differ from that of its Roman and Sassanid predecessors? What may have prevented Islam's spread through Asia Minor and up the Iberian peninsula?

Authority and Government in Islam

Conquering the world for Islam proved easier than governing it. What had begun as a religious movement within Arabian society had created a vast multinational empire in which Arabs were a tiny minority. Within the first decades following the Prophet's death, two models of governance emerged, models that continue to dominate Islamic politics to the present.

The Umma. The first model was that of pre-Islamic tribal authority. The Umma could be considered a supertribe, governed by leaders whose authority came from their secular power as leaders of the superior military and economic elements within the community. This model appealed particularly to the Quraysh and local tribal leaders who had exercised authority before Muhammad. The second model was that of the authority exercised by the Prophet. In this model, the Umma was more than a supertribe, and its unity and purity had to be preserved by a religiously sanctioned rule exercised by a member of the Prophet's own family. This model was preferred by many of the more recent converts to Islam, especially the poor.

Regardless of their disagreements on the basis of political authority, both groups adopted the administrative systems of their conquered lands. Byzantine and Sassanid bureaucracy and government, only slightly adjusted, became the models for government in the Islamic world until the twentieth century.

Likewise, the Muslims left intact the social structures and economic systems of the empires they conquered. Lands remained in the hands of their previous owners. Only state property or, in the Sassanid Empire, that of the Zoroastrian priesthood became common property of the Muslim community.

The Last Orthodox Caliphs. The division of the spoils of conquest badly divided the Umma and precipitated the first crisis in the caliphate. Under 'Umar, two groups received most of the spoils of the conquests. First were the earliest followers of the Prophet, who received a disproportionate share of revenues. Second were the conquerors themselves, who were often recent converts from tribes on the fringes of Arabia. After 'Umar's death, his successor 'Uthman (d. 656), a member of the powerful Umayya clan of Mecca, attempted to consolidate control over Islam by Quraysh elite. The result was rebellion, both within Arabia and in Egypt. Abandoned at home and abroad, 'Uthman was finally murdered as he sat reading the Qur'an in his home.

In spite of 'Uthman's unpopularity, his murder sent shock waves throughout the Umma. The fate of his successor, Muhammad's beloved son-in-law and nephew 'Ali (656–661), had an even more serious effect on the future of Islam. Although chosen as fourth caliph, 'Ali was immediately charged with complicity in 'Uthman's murder and was strongly opposed by the Umayyad commander of Syria. To protect himself, 'Ali moved the caliphate from Arabia to Iraq, but in 661, 'Ali was murdered by supporters of his Umayyad rivals. Still, the memory of the "last orthodox caliph" remained alive in the Islamic world, especially in Iraq and Iran. Centuries later, a tradition developed in Baghdad that legitimate leadership of Islam could come only from the house of 'Ali. Adherents to this belief developed into a political and religious sect known as Shia Islam. Although frequently persecuted as heretical by the majority of Muslims, **Shiites** remain a potent minority within the Islamic world today.

Umayyad and 'Abbasid Caliphates

The immediate effect of 'Ali's death, however, was the triumph of the old Quraysh and in particular the Umayyads, who established at Damascus in Syria a caliphate that lasted a century. The Umayyads made no attempt to base their rule on spiritual authority. Instead, they ruled as secular leaders, attempting to unite the Islamic Empire through an appeal to Arab unity.

Umayyad Caliphate. The Umayyads extended the Islamic Empire to its farthest reaches. In the north, armies from Syria marched into Anatolia and were stopped only in 677 by the Byzantine fleet before Constantinople itself. In the east, Umayyad armies pressed as far as the Syr Darya River on the edge of the Chinese Tang Empire. In the south and southwest, the general Tariq ibn Ziyad (d. ca. 720) conquered the Mediterranean coast of Africa and in 711 crossed over the strait near the Rock of Gibraltar (the name comes from the Arabic *jabal Tariq*, "Tariq's mountain") and quickly conquered virtually the entire Iberian peninsula.

The Umayyad caliphate's external success in conquering failed to extend to its dealings with the internal tensions of the Umma. The Umayyads could not build a stable empire on the twin foundations of a tiny Arabian elite and a purely secular government taken over from their Byzantine predecessors.

The 'Abbasid Revolution. Growing numbers of devout Muslims—Arabs and non-Arabs alike—were convinced that leadership had to be primarily spiritual and that this spiritual mandate was the exclusive right of the family of the Prophet. Ultimately, a coalition of dissatisfied Persian Muslims and Arabian religious reformers united under the black banners of the descendants of Muhammad's paternal uncle, 'Abbas (566–ca. 653). In 750, this group overthrew the Umayyads everywhere but in Spain and established a new caliphate in favor of the 'Abbasids.

With the fall of the Umayyad caliphate, Arabs lost control of Islam forever. The 'Abbasids attempted to govern the empire according to religious principles. These were found in the Qur'an and in the **sunnah**, or practices established by the Prophet and preserved first orally and then in the **hadith**, or traditions, which were somewhat comparable to the Christian Gospels. This new empire was to be a universal Muslim commonwealth in which Arabs had no privileged position.

The institutional foundations of the new caliphate, however, like those of the Umayyads, remained firmly in the ancient empires they had conquered. The great caliph Mansur (754–775) moved the capital from Damascus to Baghdad, an acknowledgment of the crucial role of Iraqi and Iranian military and economic strength. The 'Abbasids constructed an autocratic imperial system on the model of their Persian predecessors. With firm control of the military, increasingly composed of slave armies known as mamluks, the 'Abbasids governed the Islamic Empire at its zenith.

Division and Revolt. Ultimately, however, the 'Abbasids were no more successful than the Umayyads in maintaining authority over the whole Muslim world. By the tenth century, local military commanders, termed **emirs**, took control of provincial governments in many areas while preserving the fiction that they were appointed by the 'Abbasid caliphs. The majority of Muslims accepted this situation as a necessary compromise. In contrast to the Shiites, who continued to look for a leader from the family of 'Ali, the **Sunnis**, as they came to be known, remain to the present the majority group of Muslims. The Sunnis had no fixed theory of government or succession to the caliphate. Instead, they accepted the events of history in a practical manner, secure in the truth of the hadith: "My umma will never agree upon an error."

In the west, the 'Abbasids could not maintain even a facade of unity. The Shiites launched sporadic revolts and separatist movements. The most successful was that of 'Ubayd Allah the Fatimid (d. 934), who claimed to be the descendant of 'Ali and rightful leader of Islam. By the middle of the eleventh century, the Fatimid caliphate controlled all of North Africa, Sicily, Syria, and western Arabia. In Umayyad Spain, although the Muslim population remained firmly Sunni, the powerful emir 'Abd ar-Rahman III (891–961) in 929 also took the title of caliph, thus making his position religious as well as secular. Everywhere, the political and religious unity of Islam was being torn apart.

The Turks. The arrival in all three caliphates of Muslim peoples who were not yet integrated into the civilization of the Mediterranean world accelerated this disintegration. From the east, Seljuk Turks, long used as slave troops, entered Iraq and in 1055 conquered Baghdad. Within a decade they had conquered Iran, Syria, and Palestine as well. Around the same time, Moroccan Berbers conquered much of North Africa and Spain, while Bedouin raided freely in what are today Libya and Tunisia. These invasions by Muslims from the fringes of the Islamic commonwealth had catastrophic effects on the Islamic world. The Turks, unaccustomed to commerce and to the administrative traditions of the caliphate, divided their empire among their war leaders, displacing traditional landowners and disrupting commerce. The North African Berbers and Bedouin destroyed the agricultural and commercial systems that had survived successive Vandal, Byzantine, and Arabian invasions.

Islamic Civilization

The Islamic conquest of the seventh century brought peace to Iraq and Iran after generations of struggle and set the stage for a major agricultural recovery. In the tradition of their Persian predecessors, the caliphs organized vast irrigation systems, which made Mesopotamia the richest agricultural region west of China.

By uniting the Mediterranean world with Arabia and India, the 'Abbasid Empire created the greatest trade network that had ever been seen. Muslim merchants met in bustling ports on the Persian Gulf and the Red Sea to trade goods from China, India, Africa, and Europe.

The marketplace for ideas was as active as that for merchandise. Within a few generations, descendants of Bedouin established themselves in the great cities of the ancient Near East and absorbed the traditions of Persian, Roman, and Hellenistic civilization. While 'Abassid political unity was falling apart, this new civilization was reaching its first great synthesis.

Science and Faith. Islamic intellectuals synthesized and expanded Greek, Persian, and Indian traditions of astronomy and mathematics and sought to find the proper balance between science and faith. Because of the need to establish hours for prayer, Islamic scholars were particularly interested in practical aspects of astronomy and devices for determining time such as the astrolabe, which allows one to determine the time of day or night as well as to determine the exact time of sunrise and sunset and to solve various astronomical problems.

Abu Ja'far Muhammad ibn Musa Al-Khwarizimi (790–850), known as the father of algebra, developed the solution to quadratic equations and wrote treatises that remained fundamental in the East and the West well into the Renaissance. Muslim intellectuals also introduced the so-called Arabic numerals from India and by the tenth century had perfected the use of decimal fractions.

Medicine was perhaps the area in which Muslims made the greatest contributions in both theory and practice. Charity is fundamental to Islam, and across the Islamic world hospitals were established where the sick could be cared for without

This miniature shows scholars at the Taqf ad Din Observatory in Istanbul. Various scientists are using astrolabes, instruments used to observe and caiculate the position of heavenly bodies, as well as various clocks, an armillary sphere or model of the heavens, and a spherical map, and instruments developed or perfected by generations of Muslim scientists.

cost. Al-Razi (864–930), an Iranian physician who became the head of the hospital in Baghdad, wrote a comprehensive medical encyclopedia that became a standard text, East and West. The Persian physician Ibn Sina (980–1037), known in the West as Avicenna, was the first to recognize the contagious nature of tuberculosis, the value of anesthetics, and the effectiveness of experimenting with new drugs on animals before administering them to humans.

Islamic intellectuals also applied ancient learning to questions of Islamic faith. Legal scholars concerned with the authenticity of hadith used Greek rationalist methods to distinguish genuine from spurious traditions. Religious mystics called Sufis blended Neoplatonic and Muslim traditions to create new forms of religious devotion.

Philosophy. Although Islamic scientists were professional physicians, astronomers, or lawyers, most were also deeply concerned with abstract philosophical questions, particularly those raised by the works of Plato and Aristotle, which had been translated into Arabic. Many sought to reconcile Islam with that philosophical heritage in the same manner that Origen and Augustine had done for Christianity. The Cordoban philosopher Ibn Rushd (1126–1198), called Averroës in the west, taught an authentic Aristotelian philosophy stripped of Neoplatonic mystical trappings. His commentaries on Aristotle were enormously influential even outside the Islamic world. For Christian philosophers of the thirteenth century, Averroës was known simply as "the Commentator."

Christian Invasion. At the same time that Muslim thought and culture were at their most creative, Islam faced invasion from a new and unaccustomed quarter: Constantinople. In the tenth and early eleventh centuries, the Byzantines pressed the local rulers of northern Syria and Iraq in a series of raids, which reached as far as the border of Palestine. At the end of the eleventh century, western Europeans, encouraged and supported by the Byzantines, captured Jerusalem and established a Western-style kingdom in Palestine that survived for over a century. Once more, Constantinople was a power in the Mediterranean world.

The Byzantine Apogee and Decline, 1000–1453

During the tenth and eleventh centuries, Byzantium dominated the Mediterranean world for the last time. Imperial armies under the Macedonian dynasty (867–1059) began to recover some lands that had been lost to Islam during the previous two centuries.

The conquests of the Macedonian dynasty laid the foundation for a short-lived economic prosperity and cultural renaissance. Conquered lands, particularly Anatolia, brought new agricultural wealth. Security of the sea fostered a resurgence of commerce, and customs duties enriched the imperial treasury. New wealth financed the flourishing of Byzantine art and literature.

The Disintegration of the Empire

In all domains, however, the successes of the Macedonian emperors set the stage for serious problems. Rapid military expansion and economic growth allowed new elites to establish themselves as autonomous powers and to position themselves between the imperial administration and the people. The constant demand for troops always exceeded the supply of traditional salaried soldiers. In the eleventh century, emperors began to grant imperial estates to great magnates in return for military service. These grants, termed *pronoia*, often included immunity from imperial taxation and the right to certain administrative activities traditionally carried out by the central government. The practice created in effect a largely independent, landed military aristocracy that stood between the peasantry and the imperial government. This policy weakened the centralized state and reduced its income from taxes.

Internal Conflict. As generals became dissatisfied with the civilian central administration, they began to turn their armies against the emperors, launching over 30 revolts in as many years. To defend itself against both the Muslims without and the generals within, the central government, composed of intellectuals, eunuchs, and urban aristocrats, had to spend vast sums on mercenary armies. These armies, composed largely of Armenians, Germans, and Normans, soon began to plunder the empire they were hired to protect. Further danger came from other, independent Normans who, under their commander Robert Guiscard (ca. 1015–1085), conquered Byzantine Bari and southern Italy and then Muslim Sicily. Soon Guiscard was threatening the empire itself. The hostility between aristocracy and imperial administration largely destroyed the tradition of civilian government.

Under increasing pressure from local magnates on the one hand and desperate imperial tax collectors on the other, villages began to make deals with powerful patrons who would represent them in return for the surrender of their independence. Through the eleventh and twelfth centuries, the Byzantine peasantry passed from the condition of individualism without freedom to that of collectivism without freedom. Through the same process, landlords and patrons acquired the means to exercise a political role, which ended the state's monopoly on public power.

Commercial Threats. At the same time that civil war and external pressure were destroying the provincial administration, Byzantine disdain for commerce was weakening the empire's ability to control its income from customs duties. Initially, the willingness to turn over commerce to Italians and others posed few problems. However, in the tenth and eleventh centuries, merchants of Amalfi, Bari, and then Venice came to dominate Byzantine commerce. Venetian merchant fleets could double as a powerful navy in times of need, and by the eleventh century the Venetians were the permanent military and commercial power in the Mediterranean. When Robert Guiscard and his Normans threatened the empire, the emperors had to turn to the Venetians for protection and were forced to cede them major economic privileges. The Venetians acquired the right to maintain important self-governing communities in major ports throughout the empire and were allowed to pay lower tariffs than the Byzantines paid.

In 1071, the year that Robert Guiscard captured the last Byzantine city in Italy, the empire suffered an even more disastrous defeat in the east. At Manzikert in Anatolia, the emperor Romanus IV (1067–1071) and his unreliable mercenary army fell to the Seljuk Turks, who captured Romanus. The defeat at Manzikert sealed the fate of the empire. Anatolia was lost, and the gradual erosion of the empire in both the west and the east had begun.

The Conquests of Constantinople and Baghdad

At the end of the eleventh century the Comnenian dynasty (1081–1185) briefly halted the political and economic chaos of the empire. Rather than fighting the tendency of the centralized state to devolve into a decentralized aristocratic one, Alexius I Comnenus (1081–1118) tied the aristocracy to his family, thus making it an instrument of imperial government. In the short run the process was successful. Still, by the late twelfth century the empire was a vulnerable second-rate power caught between Latin Europe and Islam.

Initially, the Christian west was a more deadly threat than the Islamic east. In the eleventh century, after more than 500 years of economic and political weakness, western Europe was beginning to reach parity with Byzantium.

Chronology

THE BYZANTINE EMPIRE AND THE RISE OF ISLAM

527–565	Reign of Justinian
610	Muhammad's vision
662	The Hijra, Muhammad's journey from Mecca to Medina
726–787	First phase of iconoclast dispute
732	Muslim advance halted by Franks
750	'Abbasids overthrow Umayyads; take control of Muslim world
802–884	Second phase of iconoclast dispute
843	Empress Theodora ends iconoclast persecution; restores image veneration
867–1059	Macedonian dynasty rules Byzantine Empire; begins recovering lands from Muslims
1054	Schism splits churches of Rome and Constantinople
1071	Robert Guiscard captures Sicily and southern Italy; Battle of Manzikert; Seljuk Turks defeat Byzantines
1099	First Crusade establishes Latin kingdom in Jerusalem
1221	Genghis Khan leads Mongol army into Persia
1453	Constantinople falls to Ottomans

Dangers from the West. The military threat from the west was paralleled by a religious one. In the centuries that Rome had been largely cut off from Constantinople, Western Christianity had developed a number of rituals and beliefs that differed from Orthodox practice. This parting of the ways had already appeared during the iconoclastic controversies of the eighth and ninth centuries. In the eleventh, it was directed by an independent and self-assertive papacy in Rome, which claimed supreme authority throughout Christendom.

Disagreements between the patriarchs of Constantinople and the popes of Rome prevented cooperation between the two Christian worlds and led to further deterioration of relationships between Greeks and Latins. These disagreements came to a head in 1054, when the papal representative, or legate, Cardinal Humbert (ca. 1000–1061) met with the patriarch of Constantinople, Michael Cerularius (ca. 1000–1059), to negotiate ecclesiastical control over southern Italy and Sicily. Humbert was arrogant and demanding, Michael Cerularius haughty and uncompromising. Acting beyond his authority, Humbert excommunicated the patriarch and all his followers. The patriarch responded in kind, excommunicating Humbert and all connected with him. This formal excommunication was lifted in the 1960s, but the split between the churches of Rome and Constantinople continues to the present.

Excommunication was probably the least of the dangers the Byzantines faced from the west. The full fury of the often ignorant, greedy, and violent Western society reached the empire when, after the defeat at Manzikert, the emperor Alexius called on Western Christians for support against the Muslims. To his horror, adventurers of every sort, eager to conquer land and wealth in the name of the cross of Jesus, flooded the empire. Even while recognizing that the crusaders were uncouth and barbarous, the Byzantines had to admit that the Latins were effective. Despite enormous hardships, the First Crusade was able to take advantage of division in the Muslim world to conquer Palestine and establish a Latin kingdom in Jerusalem in 1099.

The Sack of Constantinople. The crusaders' initial victories and the growth of Latin wealth and power created in Constantinople a temporary enthusiasm for western European styles and customs. The Byzantines soon realized, however, that the Latin kingdom posed a threat not only to Islam but to them as well. While crusaders threatened Byzantine territories, Venetian merchants imposed a stranglehold on Byzantine trade. When emperors granted other Italian towns concessions equal to those of the Venetians, they found that they had simply amplified their problems. Anti-Latin sentiment reached the boiling point in 1183. In the riots that broke out in that year, Italians and other westerners in Constantinople were murdered, and their goods were seized. Just 21 years later, in 1204, a wayward crusade, egged on by Venice, turned aside from its planned expedition to Palestine to capture a bigger prize: Constantinople. After pillaging the city for three days, the westerners established one of their own as emperor and installed a Venetian as patriarch.

The Byzantines did manage to hold onto a portion of their empire centering on Nicaea, and before long the Latins fell to bickering among themselves. In 1261, the ruler of Nicaea, Michael Palaeologus (ca. 1224–1282), recaptured Constantinople with the assistance of the Genoese and had himself crowned emperor in the Hagia Sophia. Still, the empire was fatally shattered, its disintegration into autonomous lordships complete. The restored empire consisted of little more than the district around Constantinople, Thessalonica, and the Peloponnesus. Bulgarians and Serbs had expanded far into the Greek mainland. Most of the rich Anatolian regions had been lost to the Turks, and commercial revenues were in the hands of the Genoese allies. The restored empire's survival for almost 200 years was due less to its own prerogative than to the internal problems of the Islamic world.

THE OTTOMAN EMPIRE, CA. 1450. By the mid-fifteenth century the Ottoman Empire had absorbed virtually all of the Byzantine Empire.

Eastern Conquests. The caliphs of Baghdad, like the emperors of Constantinople, succumbed to invaders from the barbarous fringes of their empire. In 1221, the Mongol prince Temujin (ca. 1162–1227), better known to history as Genghis Khan ("Universal Ruler"), led his conquering army into Persia from central Asia. From there, a portion of the Mongols went north, invading Russia in 1237 and dividing it into small principalities ruled by Slavic princes under Mongol control. In 1258, a Mongol army captured Baghdad and executed the last 'Abbasid caliph, ending a 500-year tradition. The Mongol armies then moved westward, shattering the Seljuk principalities in Iraq, Anatolia, and Syria and turning back only before the fierce resistance of the Egyptian Mamluks.

From the ruins of the Seljuk kingdom arose a variety of small Turkish principalities, or emirates. After the collapse of the Mongol Empire, one of these, the Ottoman, began to expand at the expense of both the weakened Byzantine Empire and the Mongol-Seljuk Empire. In the next centuries, the Ottomans expanded east, south, and west. Around 1350, they crossed into the Balkans as Byzantine allies but soon took over the region for themselves. By 1450, the Ottoman stranglehold on Constantinople was complete. The final scene of the conquest, long delayed but inevitable, occurred three years later.

SUMMARY

The Byzantines   In the face of numerous divisive forces, Byzantine emperors were obsessed with maintaining absolute authority and imposing uniformity on their empire. Justinian's achievements came at a high price, and many of his gains were quickly lost. Despite setbacks, the Byzantine Empire played a key role in preserving important elements of ancient civilization for future generations in the west. Although the emperor was the source of all authority, the actual administration of the empire was carried out by a vast bureaucracy composed of military and civilian officers. Villages were the basic elements in the imperial system. Constantinople was a great commercial center and Byzantine cities were centers for the manufacture of luxury goods. The cultural cement that bound emperor and subjects together was Orthodox Christianity. The iconoclast dispute revealed deep fissures within Byzantine society.

The Rise of Islam   Through faith, Muhammad (ca. 570–632) united the tribes of the Arabian Peninsula and propelled them on an unprecedented mission of conquest. In 610 Muhammad had a vision that convinced him he was God's messenger. His early teachings stressed the absolute unity of God, the evils of idolatry, and the threat of divine judgment. Muhammad's preaching upset Mecca's elite and he was forced to move to Medina. In Medina, Muhammad set about creating the Umma, a community that transcended the old bonds of tribe and clan. In 629, Muhammad and his followers captured Mecca and quickly became a major force in the Arabian Peninsula. Muhammad's message spread to other tribes through diplomatic and, occasionally, military means. After Muhammad's death, his successors conquered a vast empire. Conquering the world for Islam proved easier than governing it. The Umayyads attempted to unite the Islamic Empire through an appeal to Arab unity. In 750, the 'Abbasids overthrew the Umayyads everywhere but in Spain, but did not hold on to a unified empire for long. The arrival of the Seljuk Turks accelerated the disintegration of the Islamic Empire. Islamic thinkers made important contributions in science, medicine, mathematics, literature, and philosophy.

The Byzantine Apogee and Decline, 1000–1453   During the tenth and eleventh centuries, Byzantium dominated the Mediterranean world for the last time. The conquests of the Macedonian dynasty laid the foundation for a short-lived economic prosperity and cultural renaissance. The creation of an independent, landed military elite, internal conflicts, and challengers to Constantinople's commercial power all undermined the empire. In 1204 western crusaders pillaged Constantinople. In 1453, the Ottoman Turks conquered Constantinople, ending the Byzantine Empire forever.

QUESTIONS FOR REVIEW

1. In what ways was Byzantine society characterized by individualism without freedom?
2. How and why did Muhammad both break from tribal and clan traditions and build upon them in creating Islam?
3. How did conflicts within Islam after Muhammad's death divide it spiritually but also contribute to Islam's expansion across Africa and Spain?
4. How did the rapid expansion of Byzantium under the Macedonian dynasty contribute to the empire's slow collapse?

The West in the Early Middle Ages, 500–900

The Making of the Barbarian Kingdoms, 500–750

The existence of a united empire had long been but a dream. In the year 500, Emperor Anastasius I (491–518) could delude himself that he ruled the whole empire of Augustus, Diocletian, and Constantine, both east and west. In the west, the governor who ruled Italy had sworn that he "rejoiced to live under Roman law, which we are prepared to defend by arms." The king of the once troublesome Vandals had concluded a marriage alliance with the Italian governor and seemed ready to accept Roman statecraft. Beyond the Alps, a Roman officer called a *patrician* ruled the regions of the upper Rhone, and a consul controlled Gaul. In Aquitaine and Spain, legitimate, recognized officers of the empire ruled both Romans and barbarians. What need was there to speak of the end of the empire in the West?

This imperial unity was more illusionary than real. The Italian governor was the Ostrogothic king Theodoric the Great (493–526), whose Roman title meant less than his Ostrogothic army. The patrician was the Burgundian king Gondebaud (480–516). The Roman officer in Aquitaine and Spain was the Visigothic king Alaric II (485–507), and the Gallic consul was the Frankish king Clovis (482–511). Each of these rulers courted imperial titles and recognition, but none regarded Anastasius as his sovereign.

Italy: From Ostrogoths to Lombards

In the early sixth century, all of the Germanic peoples who were settled within the old Roman Empire acknowledged the Goths as the most successful of the "blond-haired peoples," as the Romans called the barbarians. The Ostrogoths had created an Italian kingdom in which Romans and barbarians lived side by side. The Visigoths ruled Spain and southern Gaul by combining traditions of Roman law and barbarian military might. Yet neither Gothic kingdom endured for more than two centuries.

The Ostrogothic Kingdom. Theodoric the Ostrogoth was the most cultivated, capable, and sophisticated barbarian ruler. He was also the most powerful. Burgundians, Visigoths, and Alemanni looked to him for leadership and protection. Even Clovis, the ambitious Frankish king, usually bowed to his wishes. Theodoric had spent his teenage years as a pampered hostage in Constantinople. There, he had learned to understand and admire Roman ways. Later, after he had conquered Italy

A gold solidus coin bears a portrait of Theodoric. His left hand holds a globe on which stands a personification of victory. The inscription reads "King Theodoric," but the absence of a robe and diadem shows that he was not considered the equal of the emperor.

at the head of his Gothic army, he established a dual government, which respected both the remains of Roman civil administration and Gothic military organization.

Religion as well as government divided Italy's population. The Ostrogoths were Arians; the majority of the Romans were orthodox Christians. Initially, Theodoric made no effort to interfere with the religion of his subjects. This religious toleration attracted into his government outstanding Roman intellectuals and statesmen. Following Theodoric's death in 526, internal conflict over the succession paved the way for a protracted and devastating invasion by the Byzantines, who destroyed not only the Ostrogothic kingdom but also much of what remained of Roman Italy.

Italy was simply too close to Constantinople and too important for the ambitious Emperor Justinian I (527–565) to ignore. Encouraged by his easy victory over the Vandals, he sent an army into Italy, where he anticipated an easy reconquest of the peninsula. Instead, he got almost 20 years of vicious warfare. Not only were the Goths more formidable foes than he had expected, but when Roman tax collectors arrived with the Roman armies, Justinian found that the Italian people did not greet their "liberators" with open arms. In addition, in the midst of the

MAP DISCOVERY

THE BARBARIAN KINGDOMS, CA. 526

Examine the locations of barbarian kingdoms in the sixth century. What strategic geographical advantages did the Ostrogothic kingdom hold that allowed Theodoric the Great to play a dominant role in the West? How did the relative isolation of the kingdom of the Franks aid its future development? Which barbarian kingdoms were in a position to absorb the most Roman traditions? Which the least?

reconquest a new and terrible disease appeared throughout the Mediterranean world. The plague cut down as much as one-third of Europe's population in the next two centuries.

Lombard Conquest. The destruction of Italy by war and disease paved the way for its conquest by the Lombards. In 568, the whole Lombard people left the Carpathian basin to their neighbors, the Avars, and invaded the exhausted and war-torn Italian peninsula. By the end of the sixth century, the Ostrogoths had disappeared, and the Byzantines retained only the heel and toe of the boot of Italy and a narrow strip stretching from Ravenna to Rome. The Byzantine presence in Rome was weak, and by default the popes, especially Gregory the Great (590–604), became the defenders and governors of the city. Gregory organized the resistance to the Lombards, fed the population during famines, and comforted them through the dark years of plague and warfare. A vigorous political as well as spiritual leader, he laid the foundations of the medieval papacy.

The Lombards largely eliminated the Roman tax system under which Italians had long suffered. In the sphere of religion, many of the Lombards initially were Arians, but in the early seventh century the Lombard kings and their followers accepted orthodox Christianity. This conversion paved the way for the unification of the society.

Visigothic Spain: Intolerance and Destruction

Rather than accepting a divided society as did the Ostrogoths or merging into an orthodox Roman culture as did the Lombards, the Visigoths of Gaul and Spain sought to unify the indigenous population of their kingdom through law and religion. Roman law deeply influenced Visigothic law codes and formed an enduring legal heritage to the West. Religious unity was a more difficult goal. The king's repeated attempts to force conversion to Arianism failed and created tension and mistrust. This mistrust proved fatal. In 507, Gallo-Roman aristocrats supported the Frankish king Clovis in his successful conquest of the Visigothic kingdom of Toulouse. Defeat drove the Visigoths deeper into Spain, where they gradually forged a unified kingdom based on Roman administrative tradition and Visigothic kingship.

The long-sought religious unity was finally achieved when King Recared (586–601) and the Gothic aristocracy embraced orthodox Christianity. This conversion further blurred the differences between Visigoths and Roman provincials in the kingdom. It also initiated an unprecedented use of the Church and its ideology to strengthen the monarchy.

Still, the Visigoths continued to distrust anyone who was different, and their suspicion focused especially on the considerable Jewish population, which had lived in Spain since the *Diaspora*, or dispersion, in the first century of the Roman Empire. Almost immediately after Recared's conversion, he and his successors began to enact a series of anti-Jewish measures, culminating in 613 with the command that all Jews accept baptism or leave the kingdom. Although this mandate was never fully carried out, the virulence of the persecution of the Jews grew through the seventh century. At the same time, rivalry within the aristocracy weakened the kingdom and left it vulnerable to attack from without. In 711, Muslims from North Africa invaded and quickly conquered the Visigothic kingdom. While some remnants of the Visigoths held on in small kingdoms in the northwest, most of the population quickly came to terms with their new masters. Jews rejoiced in the religious toleration brought by Islam, and many members of the Christian elite converted to Islam and retained their positions of authority under the new regime.

The Anglo-Saxons: From Pagan Conquerors to Christian Missionaries

The motley collection of Saxons, Angles, Jutes, Frisians, Suebians, and others who came to Britain as federated troops and stayed on as rulers did not coalesce into a united kingdom until almost the eleventh century. Instead, these Germanic warriors carved out small kingdoms for themselves, enslaving the romanized Britons or driving them into Wales. Although independent, these little kingdoms (their number varied from five to as many as eleven at different times) maintained some sort of identity as a group. The king of the dominant kingdom enjoyed some deference from his fellow rulers. Other kings looked to him as first among equals and sought his advice and influence in their dealings with one another. Unlike the Goths, none of these peoples had previously been integrated into the Roman world. Rather than fusing Roman and Germanic traditions, they eradicated the former. Urban life disappeared and, with it, the Roman traditions of administration, taxation, and culture.

In their place developed a world whose central values were honor and glory, whose primary occupation was fighting, and whose economic system was based on plunder and the open-handed distribution of riches. These invaders were not, like the Goths, just a military elite. They also included free farmers who partly replaced and partly absorbed romanized British peasantry, introducing their language, agricultural techniques, social organization, and folkloric traditions to the southeastern part of the island. These ordinary settlers, much more than the kings and aristocrats, were responsible for the gradual transformation of Britain into England, the land of the Angles.

The Anglo-Saxons were pagans, and although Christianity survived, the relationship between conquered and conquerors did not provide a climate conducive to conversion. Christianity came instead from without. The conversion of England resulted from a two-part effort. The first originated in Ireland, the most western society of Europe and the one in which Celtic traditions had survived little changed for over 1,000 years. In the fifth century, merchants and missionaries introduced an eastern monastic form of Christianity to Ireland, which adapted easily to the rural tribal organization of Irish society. Around 565, the Irish monk Columba (521–597) established a monastery on the island of Iona off the coast of Scotland. From there, wandering Irish monks began to convert northern Britain.

The second effort at Christianizing Britain began with Pope Gregory the Great. In 596, he sent the missionary Augustine (known as Augustine of Canterbury to distinguish him from the bishop of Hippo) to attempt to convert the English. Augustine laid the foundations for a hierarchical, bishop-centered church based on the Roman model. In time, the pagan king Ethelbert and much of his southwest kingdom of Kent accepted Christianity, and the pope named Augustine archbishop of Canterbury.

As Irish missionaries spread south from Iona and Roman missionaries moved north from Canterbury, their efforts created in England two opposing forms of orthodox Christianity. One was Roman, episcopal, and hierarchical. The other was Celtic, monastic, and decentralized. The Roman and Celtic churches agreed on basic doctrines. However, each had its own calendar of religious feasts and its own rituals. King Oswy of Northumbria (d. 670) called an episcopal meeting, or **synod**, in 664 at Whitby to settle the issue. After hearing arguments from both sides, Oswy accepted the customs of the Roman Church, thus allying himself and ultimately all of Anglo-Saxon England with the centralized, hierarchical form of Christianity, which could be used to strengthen his monarchy.

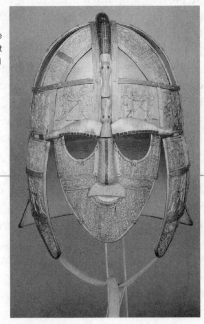

The elaborate helmet of a seventh-century Anglo-Saxon king, recovered from his ship burial at Sutton Hoo on the southeast coast of England, shows the wealth and culture of these rulers. The king was buried in a ship some 90 feet long with benches for 40 oarsmen. Although the body had totally disappeared over the centuries, the burial chamber held, in addition to this unique helmet with historiated die-struck bronze panels, a magnificent sword with gold and garnet cloissoné pommel, a set of spears, gold shoulder clasps, probably the remains of a magnificent roman-style leather armor, and many other objects of Eastern Mediterranean, Anglo-Saxon, Frankish, and Scandinavian origins.

During the century and a half following the Synod of Whitby, Anglo-Saxon Christian civilization blossomed. Contact with the Continent and especially with Rome increased. The monasteries of Monkwearmouth and Jarrow became centers of learning, culminating in the writings of Bede (673–735), the greatest scholar of his century. His history of the English church and people is the finest historical work of the early Middle Ages.

By the eighth century, England itself had begun to send Christian missionaries to the Continent to convert their still-pagan Germanic cousins. Until the late eighth and ninth centuries, when the Germanic Vikings began to attack Anglo-Saxon settlements, England furnished the Continent with many of its leading thinkers and scholars.

The Franks: An Enduring Legacy

In the fourth century, various small Germanic tribes along the Rhine coalesced into a loose confederation known as the Franks. A significant group of them, the Salians, made the mistake of attacking Roman garrisons and were totally defeated. The Romans resettled the Salians in a largely abandoned region of what is now Belgium and Holland. There, they formed a buffer to protect Roman colonists from other Germanic tribes and provided a ready supply of recruits for the Roman army. During the fourth and fifth centuries, these Salian Franks and their neighbors assumed an increasingly important role in the military defense of Gaul and began to spread out of their "reservation" into more settled parts of the province. Although many high-ranking Roman officers of the fourth century were Franks, most were neither conquerors nor members of the military elite. Rather, they were soldier-farmers who settled beside the local Roman peoples they protected.

In 486, Clovis, leader of the Salian Franks and commander of the barbarized Roman army, staged a successful coup (possibly with the approval of the Byzantine emperor), defeating and killing Syagrius, the last Roman commander in the West. Although Clovis ruled the Franks as king, he worked closely with the existing Gallo-Roman aristocracy as he consolidated his control over various Frankish factions and over portions of Gaul and Germany that were held by other barbarian kingdoms. Clovis's early conversion to orthodox Christianity helped to ensure the effectiveness of this Gallo-Roman cooperation. Clovis converted, hoping that God would give him victory over his enemies and that his new faith would win the support of the Roman aristocracy in Gaul. The king's baptism convinced many of his subjects to convert as well and paved the way for the assimilation of Franks and Romans into a new society. This Frankish society became the model for European social and political organization for over 1,000 years.

The mix of Frankish warriors and Roman aristocrats spread rapidly across western Europe. Clovis and his successors absorbed the Visigothic kingdom of

Toulouse, the Thuringians, and the kingdom of the Burgundians and expanded Frankish hegemony through modern Bavaria and south of the Alps into northern Italy. Unlike other barbarian kingdoms such as those of the Huns or Ostrogoths, which evaporated almost as soon as their great founders died, the Frankish synthesis was enduring. Although the dynasty established by Clovis, called the Merovingian after a legendary ancestor, lasted only until the mid-eighth century, the Frankish kingdom was the direct ancestor of both France and Germany.

After Clovis's death in 511, his kingdom was divided among his four sons. For the next 200 years, the heart of the Frankish kingdom, the region between the Rhine and Loire rivers, was often divided into the kingdoms of Neustria, Burgundy, and Austrasia, each ruled by a Merovingian king. The outlying regions of Aquitaine and Provence to the south and Alemania, Thuringia, and Bavaria to the east were governed by Frankish dukes appointed by the kings. Still, the Frankish world was never as divided as Anglo-Saxon England. In the early eighth century, a unified Frankish kingdom reemerged as the dominant force in Europe.

Living in the New Europe

The substitution of Germanic kings for imperial officials made few obvious differences in the lives of most inhabitants of Italy, Gaul, and Spain. The vast majority of Europeans were poor farmers whose lives centered on their villages and fields. Nevertheless, fundamental if imperceptible changes were transforming daily life at every level of society. The slaves and semifree peasants of Rome gradually began to form new kinds of social groups and to practice new forms of agriculture as they merged with the Germanic warrior-peasants. Elite Gallo-Roman landowners came to terms with their Frankish conquerors, and these two groups began to coalesce into a single unified aristocracy. In the same way that Germanic and Roman society began to merge, Germanic and Roman traditions of governance united between the sixth and eighth centuries to create a powerful new kind of medieval kingdom.

Creating the European Peasantry

Three fundamental changes transformed rural society during the early Middle Ages. First, Roman slavery virtually disappeared. Second, the household emerged as the primary unit of social and economic organization. Third, Christianity spread throughout the rural world. Economics, not ethics, destroyed Roman slavery. In the kind of slavery that was typical of the Roman world, large gangs of slaves were housed in dormitories and directed in large-scale operations by overseers. This form of slavery demanded a highly organized form of estate management and could be quite costly, since slaves had to be fed and housed year-round. Since slaves did not always reproduce at a rate sufficient to replace themselves, the supply had to be replenished from elsewhere. However, as the empire ceased to expand, the supply of fresh captives dwindled. As cities shrank, many markets for agricultural produce disappeared, making market-oriented large-scale agriculture less profitable. Furthermore, the Germanic societies that settled in the West had no tradition of gang slavery.

As a result, from the sixth through the ninth centuries, owners abandoned the practice of keeping gangs of slaves in favor of the less complicated practice of establishing slave families on individual plots of land. The slaves and their descendants cultivated these plots, made annual payments to their owners, and also cultivated the undivided portions of the estate, the fruits of which went directly to the owner. Thus slaves became something akin to sharecroppers. Gradually, they began to intermarry with hereditary tenant farmers and others who, though nominally free, found themselves in an economic situation much like that of slaves. By the ninth century, the distinction between slaves who had acquired traditional rights to their farms, or **manses**, and free peasants who held and worked manses belonging to others was blurred. By the tenth and eleventh centuries, peasant farmers throughout much of Europe were subject to the private justice of their landlords, no matter whether their ancestors had been slave or free. Although not slaves in the classical sense, the peasantry had fused into a homogeneous unfree population.

Rural Households

The division of estates into separate peasant holdings contributed to the second fundamental transformation of European peasant society: the formation of the household. Neither the Roman tradition of slave agriculture nor the Germanic tradition of clan organization had encouraged the household as the basic unit of society. Now individual slaves and their spouses were placed on manses, which they and their children were expected to cultivate. The household had become the basic unit of Western economy.

The household was more than an economic unit, however. It was also the first level of government. The head of the household, whether slave or free, male or female—women, particularly widows, were often heads of households—exercised authority over its other members. This authority made the householder a link in the chain of the social order, which stretched from the peasant hovel to the royal court.

Peasant life centered on the house, the village, and the field. Peasant houses often consisted simply of two or three rooms in which dwelt both the human and animal members of the household. The rhythm of peasant life was tied to the agricultural cycle, which had changed little since antiquity. Although women and men worked together on the harvest, peasants normally divided labor into male and female tasks. Husbands and sons worked in the fields. Wives and daughters tended chickens, prepared the dark bread that was the staple of their diet, spun, and wove.

Peasant culture, like peasant society, experienced a fundamental transformation during the early Middle Ages: the peasantry became Christian. The spread of Christianity throughout the rural world began in earnest in the sixth century, when bishops and monks began to replace the peasant's traditional agrarian cults with Christian feasts, rituals, and beliefs.

Christianity penetrated more deeply into rural society with the systematic establishment of parishes, or rural churches. By the ninth century, this parish system began to cover Europe. Bishops founded parish churches in the villages of large estates, and owners were obligated to set aside one-tenth of the produce of their estates for the maintenance of the parish church. The priests who staffed these churches came from the local peasantry and received a basic education in Latin and in Christian ritual from their predecessors and from their bishops. The continuing presence of priests in each village had a profound effect on the daily lives of Europe's peasants.

Creating the European Aristocracy

At the same time that a homogeneous peasantry was emerging from the blend of slaves and free farmers, a homogeneous aristocracy was evolving out of the mix of Germanic and Roman traditions. In Germanic society, the elite had owed its position to a combination of inherited status and wealth, perpetuated through military command. Families who produced great military commanders were thought to have a special war-luck granted by the gods. The war-luck bestowed on men and women of these families a near-sacred legitimacy. This legitimacy made the aristocrats largely independent of their kings. In times of war, kings might command, but otherwise, the extent to which they could be said to govern aristocrats was minimal.

The Roman aristocracy was also based on inheritance, but of land rather than leadership. During the third and fourth centuries, Roman aristocrats' control of land extended over the people who worked that land. At the same time, great landowners were able to free themselves from provincial government. Like their Germanic counterparts, Roman aristocrats acquired a sacred legitimacy, but within the Christian tradition. They monopolized the office of bishop and became identified with the sacred and political traditions associated with the Church.

In Spain and Italy, the religious differences separating Arians and orthodox Christians impeded the fusion of the Germanic and Roman aristocracies. In Gaul, the conversion of Clovis and his people facilitated the rapid blending of the two worlds. North of the Loire River, where the bulk of the Franks had settled, Roman aristocrats soon became Franks. By the mid-sixth century, the descendants of Bishop Remigius of Reims, who had baptized Clovis, had Frankish names and considered themselves Franks. Still, the Roman aristocratic tradition of great landholders became an integral part of the identity of the Frankish elite.

In the late sixth century, this northern Frankish aristocracy found its own religious identity and legitimacy in the Irish monasticism introduced by Saint Columbanus (543–615) and other wandering monks. Irish monks worked closely with the Frankish aristocrats, who encouraged them to build monasteries on their estates. Eventually, these monasteries amassed huge landholdings and became major economic and political centers headed by aristocrats who abandoned secular life for the cloister.

South of the Loire River, conditions were decidedly different. Here, Irish monasticism was less important than episcopal office. The few Frankish and Gothic families who had settled in the south were rapidly absorbed into the Gallo-Roman aristocracy, which drew its prestige from control of local religious and secular power. Latin speech and Roman culture distinguished these "Romans," regardless of their ancestry.

Aristocratic Lifestyle

Aristocratic life was similar whether north or south of the Loire, in Anglo-Saxon England, Visigothic Spain, or Lombard Italy. Aristocratic family structures were loosely knit clans that traced descent from important ancestors through either the male or the female line. Clans jealously guarded their autonomy against rival clans and from royal authority.

Feasting and Fighting. The aristocratic lifestyle focused on feasting, hospitality, and the male activities of hunting and warfare. In southern Europe, great nobles lived in spacious villas, often surrounded by solid stone fortifications, an inheritance of Roman traditions. In the north, Frankish and Anglo-Saxon nobles lived in great wooden halls, richly decorated but lacking fortifications. During the fall and winter, aristocratic men spent much of their time hunting deer and wild boar in their forests. In March, as soon as the snows of winter had begun to melt and roads had become passable, aristocrats gathered their retainers, who had enjoyed their winter hospitality, and marched to war. The enemy varied. It might be rival families with whom feuds were nursed for generations. It might be raiding parties from a neighboring region. Or the warriors might join a royal expedition led by the king and directed against a rival kingdom. Whoever the enemy was, warfare brought the promise of booty and glory.

Women in Aristocratic Society. Within this aristocratic society, women played a wider and more active role than had been the case in either Roman or barbarian antiquity. In part, women's new role was due to the influence of Christianity, which recognized the distinct—though always inferior—rights of women, fought against the barbarian tradition of allowing chieftains numerous wives, and acknowledged women's right to lead a cloistered religious life. In addition, the combination of Germanic and Roman familial traditions permitted women to participate in court proceedings, to inherit and dispose of property, and, if widowed, to serve as tutors and guardians for their minor children. Finally, the long absence of men at the hunt, at the royal court, or on military expeditions left wives in charge of the domestic scene for months or years at a time. The religious life in particular opened to aristocratic women possibilities of autonomy and authority that had previously been unknown in the West.

Governing Europe

The combination in the early Middle Ages of the extremes of centralized Roman power and fragmented barbarian organization produced a wide variety of governmental systems. At one end of the spectrum were the politically fragmented Celtic and Slavic societies. At the other end were the Frankish kingdoms, in which descendants of Clovis, drawing on the twin heritages of Roman institutions and Frankish tradition, attempted not simply to reign but to rule.

Kings and Aristocrats. Rulers and aristocrats both needed and feared each other. Kings had emerged out of the Germanic aristocracy and could rule only in cooperation with aristocrats. Aristocrats were concerned primarily with maintaining and expanding their own spheres of control and independence. They perceived royal authority as a threat. Still, they needed kings. Strong kings brought victory against external foes and thus maintained the flow of booty to the aristocracy. Aristocrats in turn redistributed the spoils of war among their followers to preserve the bonds of warrior society. Thus, under capable kings, aristocrats were ready to cooperate, not as subjects but as partners.

As the successors of Germanic war leaders and late Roman generals, kings were primarily military commanders. During campaigns and at the annual **Marchfield**, when the free warriors assembled, the king was all-powerful. At those times he could cut down his enemies with impunity. At other times the king's role was strictly limited. His direct authority extended only over the members of his household and his personal warrior band.

Royal Justice. The king's role in administering justice was similarly ambivalent. He was not the source of law, which was held to be simply the customs of the past, nor was he responsible for enforcing this customary law. Enforcement was the duty of individuals and families. Only if they wanted did they bring their grievances to the king or his agents for arbitration or judgment. However, even though they could not formally legislate, kings effectively molded law and legal procedure by collecting, selecting, clarifying, and publishing customary laws.

As heirs of Roman governmental tradition, kings sought to incorporate these traditions into their roles. By absorbing the remains of local administration and taxation, kings acquired nascent governmental systems. Through the use of written documents, Roman scribes expanded royal authority beyond the king's household and personal following. Tax collectors continued to fill royal coffers with duties collected in markets and ports.

Finally, by assuming the role of protector of the Church, kings acquired the support of educated and experienced ecclesiastical advisers and the right to intervene in disputes involving clergy and laity. Further, as defenders of the Church, kings could claim a responsibility for the preservation of peace and the administration of justice—two fundamental Christian (but also Roman) tasks.

Royal Administration. Early medieval kings had no fixed capitals from which they governed. Instead, they were constantly on the move, supervising their kingdoms and consuming the produce of their estates. Since kings could not be everywhere at once, they were represented locally by aristocrats who enjoyed royal favor. In the Frankish world these favorites were called *counts,* and their districts were called *counties.* In England, royal representatives were termed *ealdormen,* and their regions were known as *shires.* Whether counts or ealdormen, these representatives were military commanders and judicial officers drawn from aristocratic families close to the king. Under competent and effective kings, partnership with these aristocratic families worked well. Under less competent rulers and during the reigns of minors, these families often managed to turn their districts into hereditary, almost autonomous regions.

The Carolingian Achievement

The Merovingian dynasty initiated by Clovis presided over the synthesis of Roman and Germanic society. It was left to the Carolingians who followed to forge a new Europe. In the seventh century, members of the new aristocracy were able to take advantage of royal minorities and dynastic rivalries to make themselves into virtual rulers of their small territories. By the end of the century, the kings had become little more than symbolic figures in the Frankish kingdoms. The real power was held by regional strongmen called *dukes.* The most successful of these aristocratic factions was that led by Charles Martel (ca. 688–741) and his heirs, known as the Carolingians.

Charles Martel. This family had risen to prominence in the seventh century by controlling the office of mayor of the palace in Austrasia, the highest court official who advised the king as spokesman for the aristocracy. The Carolingians increased their influence by marrying their sons to daughters of other aristocratic families. In the late seventh century, they extended their control to include Neustria and Burgundy as well as Austrasia. By the second quarter of the eighth century, Charles Martel, while not king, was the acknowledged ruler of the Frankish kingdom.

Charles Martel was ruthless, ambitious, and successful. He crushed rivals in his own family, subdued competing dukes, and united the Frankish realm. He was successful in part because he molded the Frankish cavalry into the most effective military force of the time. His mounted, heavily armored warriors were extremely effective but very costly. He financed them with property confiscated from his enemies. In return for oaths of absolute fidelity, he gave his followers, or **vassals**, estates, which they held as long as they served him faithfully. With this new army he practiced a scorched-earth policy against his opponents that left vast areas of Provence and Aquitaine desolate for decades.

Charles Martel looked beyond military power to the control of religious and cultural institutions. He supported Anglo-Saxon missionaries such as Boniface (ca. 680–755), who were trying to introduce on the Continent the Roman form of Christianity they knew in England. This hierarchical style of Christianity served Carolingian interests in centralization, especially since Charles appointed his loyal supporters as bishops and abbots. Missionaries and Frankish armies worked hand in hand to consolidate Carolingian rule.

The ecclesiastical policy that proved most crucial to later Carolingians was Charles's support of the Roman papacy. Charles caught the attention of Pope Gregory III (731–741) in 732, after a battle near Tours in which Charles defeated a Muslim force that was attempting to continue the northward expansion of Islam. A few years later, when the pope needed protection from the Lombards to maintain his central Italian territories, he sought and obtained help from the Frankish leader.

Pippin III. The alliance with the papacy solidified during the lifetime of Charles's son Pippin (ca. 714–768). Pippin inherited his father's power, but since he was not of the royal Merovingian family, he had no right to the title of king. No Frankish tradition provided a precedent by which a rival family might displace the Merovingians. Pippin turned instead to the pope, seeking legitimacy in religious authority. In a carefully orchestrated exchange between Pippin and Pope Zacharias (741–752), the latter declared that the individual who exercised the power of king ought also to have the title. Following this declaration the last Merovingian was deposed, and in 751 a representative of the pope anointed Pippin king of the Franks.

The alliance between the new dynasty and the papacy marked the first union of royal legitimacy and ecclesiastical sanction in European history. The new Frankish kingship led Europe into the first political, social, and cultural restructuring of the West since the end of the Roman Empire.

Charlemagne and the Renewal of the West

Pippin's son Charlemagne was the heir of the political, religious, and social revolutions begun by his grandfather and father. As the leader of a powerful, united

This bronze equestrian statue of a king dates from the ninth century. The rider wears the typical Frankish attire of hose, tunic, and long riding cloak. The subject is often identified as Charlemagne or his grandson Charles the Bold. The Carolingians admired Roman bronze equestrian statues. The most famous was the statue of Marcus Aurelius, mistaken for a statue of Constantine the Great, which stood outside of the pope's Lateran palace (now in the museum on the Capitoline Hill). Charlemagne was particularly impressed with an equestrian statue of Theoderic which stood in Ravenna and brought it to his palace complex in Aachen. This now lost bronze may well be the model for the much smaller Carolingian statue.

Frankish kingdom for over 40 years, Charlemagne changed the West more profoundly than anyone since Augustus.

Almost every spring, Charlemagne assembled his Frankish armies and led them against internal or external enemies. In wars of aggression his armies were invincible. Not only were they better armed and mounted, but their ability to transport men and matériel great distances was unmatched.

War booty fueled Charlemagne's renewal of European culture. As a Christian king, he considered it his duty to reform the spiritual life of his kingdom and to bring it into line with his concept of the divinely willed order. To achieve this goal, he needed a dedicated and educated clergy. Most of the native clergy were poorly educated and indifferent in their observance of the rules of religious life. Charlemagne set about creating a reformed, educated clergy.

The Carolingian Renaissance

Charlemagne recruited leading intellectuals from England, Spain, Ireland, and Italy to the royal court to lead a thorough educational program. The architect of his cultural reform, Alcuin of York (ca. 732–804), directed a school for young lay and ecclesiastical aristocrats in the king's palace and encouraged the king to finance a wide variety of educational programs. Charlemagne supported schools in great monasteries such as Fulda and St. Gall for the training of young clerics and laymen. These schools needed books. Charlemagne's educational reformers

MAP DISCOVERY

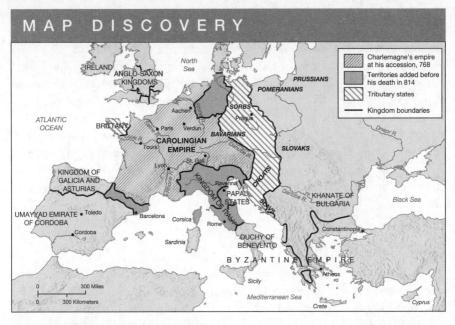

Charlemagne's empire at his accession, 768

Territories added before his death in 814

Tributary states

Kingdom boundaries

CHARLEMAGNE'S EMPIRE, 814

Compare the empire of Charlemagne with that of Hadrian (p. 119). How similar are they? How does Charlemagne's Frankish Empire compare geographically with the Byzantine Empire in 814 (p. 159)? What new barbarian peoples now appear on the peripheries of the empire?

---

scoured Italy for fading copies of works by Virgil, Horace, and Tacitus with the same determination with which his builders hunted antique marbles and columns for his chapel. Alcuin and others corrected and copied classical texts that had been corrupted by generations of haphazard transmission. Caroline **minuscule**, the new style of handwriting that was developed to preserve these texts, was so clear and readable that during the Renaissance, humanists adopted it as their standard script.

The reformers of this era laid the necessary foundation for what has been called the **Carolingian Renaissance**. Their successors in the ninth century built on this foundation to make creative contributions in theology, philosophy, and historiography and to some extent in literature. The pursuit of learning was not a purely clerical affair. In the later ninth century, great aristocrats were highly literate and collected their own personal libraries. Count Everard of Friuli, who died in 866, left an estate that included over 50 books, among them works by Augustine, histories, saints' lives, and seven law books. Elite women participated fully in the Carolingian Renaissance. One example is the noblewoman Dhuoda, who composed a manual of instruction for her son.

Educational reform went hand in hand with reform of ecclesiastical institutions. Charlemagne and his son Louis the Pious (814–840) worked to establish the Benedictine rule as the norm for monastic life and to reform the parish clergy. The goal was a purified and organized clergy performing its essential role of celebrating Christian ritual and praying for the Frankish king. At the same time, the monasteries were to provide competent clerics to serve the royal administration at every level. These reforms were expensive. The fiscal reorganization of ecclesiastical institutions was as far-reaching as their cultural reform. For the first time, Frankish synods or councils made *tithing* mandatory, specifying that one-tenth of all agricultural harvests was to go to the maintenance of church buildings, support of the clergy, and care of the poor. Monasteries flourished.

Carolingian Government

Charlemagne recognized that conquest alone could not unify his enormous kingdom with its vast differences in languages, laws, customs, and peoples. The glue that held it together was loyalty to him and to the Roman Church. He appointed as counts throughout Europe members of the great Frankish families who had been loyal to his family for generations. In addition to supervising the royal estates in their counties, each spring these counts led the local military contingent, which included all the free men of the county. Counts also presided over local courts, which exercised jurisdiction over the free persons of the county. The king maintained his control over the counts by sending teams of emissaries, or **missi dominici**, composed of bishops and counts, to examine the state of each county.

Charlemagne recognized that while his representatives might be drawn from Frankish families, he could not impose Frankish legal and cultural traditions on all his subjects. The only universal system that might unify the kingdom was Roman Christianity. Unity of religious practices, directed by the reformed and educated clergy, would provide spiritual unity. Furthermore, since the clergy could also participate in the administration of the kingdom, they could guarantee administrative unity as well. Carolingian monarchs did not intend the enriched and reformed Church to be independent of royal authority; rather, it was to be an integral part of the Carolingian system of government. However, at least some of the educated clerics and lay aristocrats who participated in the system formed a clear political ideology based on Augustinian concepts of Christian government. They attempted to educate Charlemagne and his successors to the duties of a king: maintaining peace and providing justice.

Carolingian government was no modern bureaucracy or state system. It was a mobile palace that included the royal household and ecclesiastical and secular aristocrats. The laymen and clerics who served the king were tied to him by personal oaths of loyalty rather than by any sense of dedication to a state or nation.

Still, the attempts at governmental organization were far more sophisticated than anything that the West had seen for four centuries or would see again for another four.

The size of Charlemagne's empire approached that of the old Roman Empire in the West. Only Britain, southern Italy, and parts of Spain remained outside Frankish control. With the reunification of most of the West and the creative adaptation of Roman traditions of culture and government, it is not surprising that Charlemagne's advisers began to compare his empire to that of Constantine. This comparison was accentuated by Charlemagne's conquest of Lombard Italy and his protection of Pope Leo III—a role traditionally played by the Byzantine emperors. By the end of the eighth century, the throne in Constantinople was held by a woman. Irene (752–802) was powerful and capable, but Western male leaders considered her unfit by reason of her sex for such an office. All these factors finally converged in one of the most momentous events in Western political history: Charlemagne's imperial coronation on Christmas Day in the year 800.

Historians debate the precise meaning of this event, particularly since Charlemagne was said to have remarked afterward that he would never have entered St. Peter's Basilica in Rome had he known what was going to happen. Presumably, he meant that he wanted to be proclaimed emperor by his Frankish people rather than by the pope, since this is how he had his son Louis the Pious acclaimed emperor in 813. Nevertheless, the imperial coronation of 800 subsequently took on great significance. Louis attempted to make his imperial title the sole basis for his rule, and for the next thousand years, Germanic kings traveled to Rome to receive the imperial diadem and title from the pope. In so doing, they inadvertently strengthened papal claims to enthrone—and at times to dethrone—emperors.

Carolingian Art

The same creative adaptation of the classical heritage that gave birth to a new Western empire produced a new Western art. The artistic traditions of the barbarian world consisted almost entirely of the decoration of small, portable objects such as weapons, jewelry, and, after conversion, manuscripts. Barbarian art was essentially nonrepresentational and consisted primarily of elaborate interlaced geometric forms of great sophistication.

For Charlemagne and his reformers, such abstract art was doubly inappropriate. Not only was it too distant from the Roman heritage that they were trying to emulate, but it could not be used for instruction or propaganda. Therefore, Charlemagne invited Italian and Byzantine artists and artisans to his kingdom to teach a form of representational art that would decorate as well as educate. However, these southern traditions were no more slavishly followed by northern artists than were Roman political traditions wholly taken over by Charlemagne's

An example of the animal style common in the Celtic-Germanic art of the early Middle Ages, this wooden dragon head is the terminal of a post from a seventh-century Scandinavian ship. Dragon heads decorated not only the prows of ships but house gables, sleds, wagons, and even bedposts. The intricate interlaced geometric patterns on the head appear also in stone carvings and in complex manuscript illuminations, a tradition particularly developed in Ireland and the British Isles.

government. The synthesis of Mediterranean and northern artistic traditions produced a dynamic plastic style of representation in which figures seem intensely alive and active. These figures, which appear in manuscript illuminations, ivories, and bas-reliefs, are often arranged in narrative cycles that engage the mind as well as the eye.

THE CAROLINGIANS AND THE PAPACY

ca. 680–755	Boniface, Anglo-Saxon missionary to the Continent; supported by Charles Martel
ca. 688–741	Charles Martel, acknowledged ruler of the Frankish kingdom
731–741	Papacy of Gregory III; began alliance between papacy and the Carolingians
732	Battle of Tours
ca. 714–768	Pippin III; strengthens Carolingian alliance with the papacy
751	Representative of the papacy anoints Pippin king of the Franks
768–814	Reign of Charlemagne; establishes Carolingian Empire; patron of the Carolingian Renaissance
800	Charlemagne crowned emperor by Pope Leo III
814–840	Reign of Charlemagne's son, Louis the Pious
843	Lothair, Louis the German, and Charles the Bald divide the kingdom

After the Carolingians: From Empire to Lordships

Alien, dynamic, and potentially threatening neighbors surrounded the Carolingian kingdom. To the west was Anglo-Saxon England; to the east were the Slavic and Byzantine worlds. Scandinavia lay to the north, and Al-Andalus threatened to the south. In the later ninth and tenth centuries, the Frankish kingdom collapsed, owing in part to the actions of these neighbors but primarily to the kingdom's own internal weaknesses.

Charlemagne, despite his imperial title, had remained dependent on his traditional power base, the Frankish aristocracy. For them, learned concepts of imperial renovation meant little. They wanted wealth and power. Under Charlemagne, the empire's prosperity and relative internal peace had resulted largely from continued successful expansion at the expense of neighbors. Its economy had been based on plunder and the redistribution of war booty among the aristocracy and wealthy churches. As wars of conquest under Charlemagne gave place to defensive actions against Magyars, Vikings, and Saracens, the supply of wealth dried up. Aristocratic supporters were rewarded with estates within the empire and thus became enormously wealthy and powerful.

Disintegration of the Empire

Competition among Charlemagne's descendants as well as grants to the aristocracy weakened central authority. Charlemagne had bequeathed a united empire to his son Louis the Pious (814–840). Louis's three sons, in contrast, fought one another over their inheritance, and in 843 they divided the empire among them. The eldest son, Lothair (840–855), who inherited his father's imperial title, received an unwieldy middle portion that stretched from the Rhine south through Italy. Louis the German (840–876) received the eastern portions of the empire. The youngest son, Charles the Bald (840–877), was allotted the western portions. In time, the western kingdom became France, and the eastern kingdom became the core of Germany. The middle kingdom, which included modern Holland, Belgium, Luxembourg, Lorraine (or Lotharingia, from "Lothair"), Switzerland, and northern Italy, remained a disputed region into the twentieth century.

The disintegration of the empire meant much more than its division among Charlemagne's heirs. In no region were his successors able to provide the degree of peace and public control that he had established. The Frankish armies, designed for wars of aggression, were too clumsy and slow to deal with the lightning raids of Northmen, Magyars, and Saracens. The constant need to please aristocratic supporters made it impossible for kings to prevent aristocrats from absorbing free peasants and churches into their economic and political spheres. Increasingly, these magnates were able to transform the offices of count and bishop into inherited familial positions. They also determined who would reign in their kingdoms and sought kings who posed no threat to themselves.

THE DIVISION OF CHARLEMAGNE'S EMPIRE

Consider how Charlemagne's grandsons divided his empire. What major symbolic locations remained in the kingdom of Emperor Lothair? Do the kingdoms of Kings Charles and Louis appear more culturally and ethnically homogeneous than that of their brother? Into what states would their two kingdoms eventually develop?

Most aristocrats saw this greater autonomy as their just due. Only dukes, counts, and other local lords could organize resistance to internal and external foes at the local level. They needed both economic means and political authority to provide protection and maintain peace. These resources could be acquired only at the expense of royal power. Therefore, during the late ninth and tenth centuries, much of Europe found its equilibrium at the local level as public powers, judicial courts, and military authority became the private possession of wealthy families.

Emergence of France and Germany

Ultimately, new royal families emerged from among these local leaders. The family of the counts of Paris, for example, gained enormous prestige from the fact that they had led the successful defense of the city against the Vikings from 885 to 886. For a time they alternated with Carolingians as kings of the West Franks. After the ascension of Hugh Capet in 987, they entirely replaced the Carolingians.

In a similar manner, the eastern German kingdom, which was divided into five great duchies, began to elect non-Carolingians as kings. In 919, the dukes of this region elected as their king Duke Henry of Saxony (919–936), who had proven his abilities fighting the Danes and Magyars. Henry's son, Otto the Great (936–973), proved to be a strong ruler who subdued the other dukes and definitively crushed the Magyars. In 962, Otto was crowned emperor by Pope John XII (955–964), thus reviving the empire of Charlemagne, though only in its eastern half. However, the dukes of this eastern kingdom chafed constantly at the strong control the Ottonians attempted to exercise at their expense. Although the empire Otto reestablished endured until 1806, he and his successors never matched the political or cultural achievements of the Carolingians.

By the tenth century, the early medieval kingdoms, based on inherited Roman notions of universal states and barbarian traditions of charismatic military leadership, had all ended in failure. After the demise of the Carolingian Empire, the West began to find stability at a more local but also more permanent level. However, the local nature of Western society did not mean that the Roman and Carolingian traditions were forgotten. Carolingian religious reform, classical learning, and political ideology were preserved in the following centuries.

Cluny

Church reform took on a new life in 909 with the foundation of the monastery of Cluny in eastern France. Cluniac monks, drawn from the lesser aristocracy, were God's shock troops, fighting evil with their prayers with the same vigor that their secular cousins fought the enemy with their swords. Cluny, inspired by the monastic program of Louis the Pious and granted immunity from secular interference, became the center of an extraordinary expansion of Benedictine monasticism throughout the West.

The revival of classical learning that was begun in Carolingian schools, although hampered by the new wave of invasions that began in the latter ninth century, continued in centers such as St. Gall, Auxerre, and Corvey. During the late ninth and tenth centuries, Western Christian civilization spread to the north and east. By the year 1000, Scandinavia, Poland, Bohemia, and even Hungary had become Christian kingdoms with national churches whose bishops were approved by the pope. Among the aristocracy, just as all restraints on this warrior elite seemed to have been thrown off, a gradual process of transformation of their material and mental world began. Encouraged by Cluniac monasticism and by episcopal exhortations, nobles began to consider limiting their violence against one another and placing it instead in the service of Christendom.

SUMMARY

The Making of the Barbarian Kingdoms, 500–750   The independent power of barbarian kingdoms undercut the illusion of imperial unity in the West. The destruction of Italy by war and disease paved the way for the Lombards to overthrow the Ostrogoths. The Visigoths of Gaul and Spain sought to unify the indigenous population of their kingdom through law and religion. The Anglo-Saxons established a number of small kingdoms in Britain. Conversion to Christianity in Britain came from the outside. Clovis, leader of the Salian Franks, worked closely with the Gallo-Roman aristocracy to establish his control over parts of Gaul and Germany. In the early eighth century, a unified Frankish kingdom reemerged as the dominant force in Europe.

Living in the New Europe   Three fundamental changes transformed rural society during the early Middle Ages. First, Roman slavery virtually disappeared. Second, the household emerged as the primary unit of social and economic organization. Third, Christianity spread throughout the rural world. At the same time that a homogeneous peasantry was emerging from the blend of slaves and free farmers, a homogeneous aristocracy was evolving out of the mix of Germanic and Roman traditions. The combination in the early Middle Ages of the extremes of centralized Roman power and fragmented barbarian organization produced a wide variety of governmental systems.

The Carolingian Achievement   Charles Martel laid the foundations of Carolingian power and initiated a crucial alliance between the Carolingians and the Roman papacy. This alliance was solidified during the reign of Charles's son, Pippin III. Pippin's son Charlemagne ruled over a united Frankish kingdom for over 40 years, introducing profound change in the West. His power was fueled by unceasing conquest. The fruits of conquest funded his renewal of European culture, a renewal that came to be known as the Carolingian Renaissance. Charlemagne used loyalty to himself and to the Roman Church to unify his domain. Charlemagne's imperial coronation by the pope set an important precedent. The same creative adaptation of the classical heritage that gave birth to a new Western empire produced a new Western art.

After the Carolingians: From Empire to Lordships   As wars of conquest under Charlemagne gave place to defensive actions against Magyars, Vikings, and Saracens, aristocrats demanded independent wealth and power in exchange for loyalty. Three of Charlemagne's grandsons divided his empire in 843. In all three regions, centralized control declined. The rise of local leaders led to the emergence of new regional powers in France and Germany. Cluniac monks played an important role in shaping the cultural development of the European aristocracy.

QUESTIONS FOR REVIEW

1. What social and political forces encouraged division within the various Gothic, Anglo-Saxon, and Frankish kingdoms?
2. How did the household and the parish provide new units for organizing European society?
3. How did the aristocracy evolve out of Germanic and Roman traditions, and how was the aristocracy both a support and a threat to the kingdoms of the early Middle Ages?
4. What were Charlemagne's achievements?
5. Why did Charlemagne's empire not outlive him for long?

The High Middle Ages, 900–1300

The Countryside

Between the years 1000 and 1300, Europe's population almost doubled, from approximately 38 million to 74 million. Various reasons have been proposed for this growth: less warfare and raiding, the decline of slavery, gradually improving agricultural techniques and equipment, and possibly a slowly improving climate.

During the tenth century, the great forests that had covered most of Europe began to be cut back as population spread out from the islands of cultivation.

The Peasantry: Serfs and Freemen

The peasants who engaged in the opening of this internal frontier were the descendants of the slaves, unfree farmers, and petty free persons of the early Middle Ages. Across much of northwestern Europe, in particular in France in the eleventh century, the various gradations in status disappeared, and the peasantry formed a homogeneous social category loosely described as **serfs**. Although they were not slaves in a legal sense, their degraded status, their limited or nonexistent access to public courts of law, and their enormous dependency on their lords left them in a situation similar to that of the Carolingian slaves settled on individual farmsteads in the ninth century. Each year, peasants paid their lords certain fixed portions of their meager harvests. In addition, they had to work a certain number of days on the **demesne**, or reserve of the lord, the produce of which went directly to him for his use or sale. Finally, they were required to make ritual payments symbolizing their subordination.

Most peasants led lives of constant insecurity. They were poorly housed, clothed, and fed; subject to the constant scrutiny of their lords; and defenseless against natural or human-made disasters.

Peasants' houses were clustered in villages on manors or large estates. In some parts of Europe, this was the result of their lord's desire to keep a close eye on his labor supply. Beginning in the tenth century in central Italy and elsewhere, lords forced peasants to abandon isolated farmsteads and traditional villages and to move into small, fortified settlements. In these new villages, peasants were obligated to have disputes settled in the lord's court, to grind their grain in the lord's mill, and to bake their bread in the lord's oven—all primary sources of revenue for the lord.

Each morning men went out to their fields, which surrounded the village. In some villages, each peasant householder held thin strips of widely scattered land, while pasturage and woodland were exploited in common. Such an open-field system allotted all peasant households a portion of all the different sorts of land. In other villages, each household tended a unified parcel of land. Such closed fields generally corresponded with greater divergences in wealth within the village and encouraged more independence.

Agricultural Innovation. Agricultural technology gradually changed the ways that peasants worked their land and the amount of food they could produce. Instead of a light plowshare that simply cut a furrow, a heavier plow with a moldboard—a curved iron plate attached above the plowshare to lift and turn the soil, depositing it to one side of the furrow—spread across Europe. It increased production in the heavy-soil areas north of the Alps and in bottom lands.

With the introduction of new technology for plowing came new systems of crop rotation. Traditionally, farmers divided their land into two parts, one planted, the other plowed (usually twice) but allowed to remain fallow. Around the eighth century, some peasants began to introduce a **three-field system**: One-third of the land was planted in autumn with wheat or rye, one-third remained fallow, and one-third was planted in spring with barley, rye, or a leguminous crop such as beans or peas that added nutrients to the soil. As this innovation became standard after the year 1000, the result was a greatly increased yield, a minimal increase in labor, and an improved diet.

While the men worked the fields, women took charge of the domestic tasks. These included carding wool, spinning, weaving, caring for the family's vegetable garden, bearing and raising children, and brewing the thick, souplike beer that was a primary source of carbohydrates in the peasant diet. During harvest, women worked in the fields alongside the men.

Beer, black bread, beans, cabbage, onions, and cheese made up the typical peasant diet. Meat was a rarity and usually came from pigs. Inadequate agricultural methods and inefficient storage systems left the peasantry in constant threat of famine.

Negotiating Freedom. The expansion of arable land offered new hope and opportunities to peasants. Population growth, as rapid as it was between the tenth and twelfth centuries, did not keep up with the increasing demand for laborers in newly settled areas of Europe. Lords were often willing to make special arrangements with groups of peasants to encourage them to bring new land under cultivation. From the beginning of the twelfth century, peasant villages acquired from their lord the privilege to deal with him and his representatives collectively rather than individually. Villages purchased the right to control petty courts and to limit fines imposed by the lord's representative. Peasants acquired protection from arbitrary demands for labor and extraordinary taxes.

These good times did not last forever. Gradually, during the late twelfth and thirteenth centuries, the labor market stagnated. As a result, lay and ecclesiastical lords found that they could profit more by hiring cheap laborers than by demanding customary services and payments from their serfs. They also found that their serfs were willing to pay for increasing privileges.

In purchasing a wide variety of privileges, peasants were, in effect, purchasing their freedom. This free peasantry benefited the emerging states of western Europe, since kings and towns could extend their legal and fiscal jurisdictions over these persons and their lands at the expense of the nobility. By the fourteenth century, serfs were a rarity in many parts of western Europe.

Even as western serfs were acquiring a fragile freedom, the free peasants in much of eastern Europe and Spain were losing it. In much of the Slavic world, through the eleventh century, peasants lived in large, roughly territorial communes of free families. Gradually, however, princes, churches, and aristocrats began to build great landed estates. By the thirteenth century—under the influences of Western and Byzantine models and of the Mongols, who dominated much of the Slavic world from 1240—lords began to acquire political and economic control over the peasantry. In all of these regions the decline of the free peasantry accompanied the decline of public authority to the benefit of independent nobles. The aristocracy rose on the backs of the peasantry.

The Aristocracy: Warriors and Heiresses

Beginning in the late tenth century, writers of legal documents began to use an old term in a novel manner to designate certain powerful free persons who belonged neither to the old aristocracy nor to the peasantry. The term was *miles*, which in classical Latin meant "soldier." As it was used in the Middle Ages, we would translate it as "knight." The knightly function gradually came to entail a certain status and lifestyle.

The center of the knightly lifestyle was northern France. From there the ideals of knighthood, or **chivalry**, spread out across Europe, influencing aristocrats as far east as Byzantium. The essence of this lifestyle was fighting. Through warfare this aristocracy had maintained or acquired its freedom, and through warfare it justified its privileges.

The origins of this small elite (probably nowhere more than 2 percent of the population) were diverse. Many of its members were descended from the old aristocracy of the Carolingian age. Such noble families, proud of their independence and ancestry, maintained their position through complex kin networks, mutual defense pacts with other nobles, and control of castles, from which they could dominate the surrounding countryside.

Aristocratic Education. For the sons of such nobles, preparation for a life of warfare began early, often in the entourage of a maternal uncle or a powerful lord. Boys learned to ride, to handle heavy swords and shields, to manage a lance on horseback, and to swing an ax with deadly accuracy. They also learned lessons about honor, pride, and family tradition. The culmination of this education for English and French nobles came in a ceremony of knighting. An adolescent of age 16 to 18 received a sword from an older, experienced warrior. No longer a "boy," he now became a "youth," ready to enter the world of fighting for which he had trained.

A youth was a noble who had been knighted but who had not married or acquired land either through inheritance or as a reward from a lord for service and thus had not yet established his own "house." He led the life of a warrior. This was an extraordinarily dangerous lifestyle, and many youths did not survive to the next stage in a knight's life, that of acquiring land, wife, honor, and his own following of youths.

The period between childhood and maturity was as dangerous for noblewomen as for men. Marriage was the primary form of alliance between noble houses, and the production of children was essential to the continued prosperity of the family. Therefore, the daughters of the nobility were generally brought up for marriage and procreation. They were usually married at around age 16 and then were expected to produce as many children as possible. Many noblewomen died in childbirth, often literally exhausted by frequent successive births.

In this martial society, the official political and economic status of women declined considerably. Because they were considered unable to participate in warfare, in northern Europe women were also frequently excluded from inheritance, estate management, courts, and public deliberations.

Still, the most powerful women were widows who had borne sons and who could play a major part in raising them. Such women, experienced in management by years of directing the households of their husbands, well connected by

A knight receives a token from a lady in this image from a manuscript from ca. 1300 that contains the works of more than 100 German courtly love poets. The ideals of chivalry and courtly love glorified women in literature and song, but in real life the subordinate status of women reflected the values of a martial society.

kinship, and experienced in court intrigue from years of attending assemblies in the company of their husbands and sons, could often hold their own with their male counterparts. Their support and alliances were actively sought by aristocrats, kings, and churches.

Land and Loyalty. The noble lifestyle required wealth, and wealth meant land. The nobility was essentially a society of heirs who had inherited not only land but also the serfs who worked their manors. Lesser nobles acquired additional property from great nobles and from ecclesiastical institutions in return for binding contracts of mutual assistance. This tradition was at least as old as the Carolingians, who granted their followers land in return for military service. In later centuries, counts and lesser lords continued this tradition, exchanging land for support. Individual knights became **vassals** of lay or ecclesiastical magnates, swearing fealty or loyalty to the lord and promising to defend and aid him. In return, the lord swore to protect his vassal and granted him a means of support by which the vassal could maintain himself while serving his lord. Usually, this grant, termed a **fief**, was a parcel of productive land and the serfs and privileges attached to it, which the vassal and his heirs could hold as long as they provided the designated service to the lord.

Individual lords often had considerable numbers of vassals, who might also be the vassals of other lay and secular lords. The networks formed vital social and political structures. Individuals often held fiefs from, and owed service to, more than one lord, and not all of the individuals in a given county or duchy owed their primary obligation to the count or duke. Likewise, often most of a noble's land was owned outright rather than held in fief, thus making the feudal bond less central to his status. As a result, these bonds—anachronistically called **feudalism** by French lawyers of the sixteenth and seventeenth centuries—constituted just one more element of a social system tied together by kinship, regional alliances, personal bonds of fealty, and the surviving elements of Carolingian administration inherited by counts and dukes. In much of Europe, the society of the eleventh and twelfth centuries was one of intensely local autonomous powers in which public order and political authority were spread as widely as ever in European history.

The Church: Saints and Monks

Most medieval people, whether peasants or lords, lived in a world of face-to-face encounters, a world in which abstract creeds counted for little. In this world, religion meant primarily action, and the essential religious actions were the liturgical celebrations performed by the clergy. Although many of the parish priests had received only rudimentary instruction from their predecessors and had minimal knowledge of Latin and theology, such intellectual shortcomings were not important. Ordinary lay people just wanted priests who would not extort them by selling the sacraments, would not seduce their wives and daughters, and would remain in the village to perform the rituals necessary to keep the supernatural powers well disposed toward the community.

The most important of these supernatural powers was not some distant divinity but the saints—local, personal, even idiosyncratic persons. During their lives, saintly men and women had shown that they enjoyed God's special favor. After their deaths they continued to be the link between the divine and earthly spheres. Through their bodies, preserved as relics in the monasteries of Europe, they continued to live among mortals even while participating in the heavenly court. Thus they could be approached and won over through offerings, bribes, oaths, and rituals of supplication and submission. Some saints attracted national or even international pilgrimages. As the recipients of gifts to the saints, monastic communities became wealthy and powerful.

Monastic Culture. In addition to orchestrating the cult of saints, monasteries also took responsibility for the cult of the ordinary dead. In particular, monastic communities commemorated and prayed for members of noble families who, through donations of land, had become especially associated with the monastic community. Across Europe, noble families founded monasteries on their own lands or invited famous abbots to reorganize existing monasteries.

Monasteries were communities that specialized in prayer and therein found their social justification. They were also enormously rich and powerful. The monastery of Cluny, in saving souls through prayer, became the first international organization of monastic centers, with abbeys and dependent communities, called priories, throughout Europe. The abbots of Cluny were among the most powerful and influential people of the eleventh and twelfth centuries, considered to be the equals of kings, popes, and emperors. To remain in form for the strenuous liturgical commemoration of living and dead patrons, Cluniac monks largely abandoned the tradition of manual work, leaving such mundane activities to their thousands of serfs and lay agents.

Monastic Reform. The Cluniac monks' comparative luxury and concentration on liturgy to the neglect of other spiritual activities led some monastic reformers to call for a return to simplicity, separation from the rest of society, and a deeper internal spirituality. Chief among these groups were the Cistercians, who, under the dynamic leadership of Bernard of Clairvaux (1090–1153), spread their rigorous ascetic form of monasticism from England to the Vienna woods. The Cistercians built monasteries in the wilderness and discouraged the kinds of close ties with secular society that the Cluniacs had established.

The rural Church not only served the lay population but worked to transform it. Although monks and bishops were spiritual warriors, most abhorred bloodshed among Christians and sought to limit the violence of aristocratic life. This attitude combined altruistic and selfish motives, since Church property was often the focus of aristocratic greed. The decline of public power and the rise of aristocratic autonomy and violence were particularly marked in southern France. There, beginning in the tenth century, churchmen organized the Peace of God and the Truce of God, movements that attempted to protect peasants, merchants, and clerics from aristocratic violence and to limit the times when warfare was allowed. During the eleventh century, the goals of warfare were shifted from attacks against other Christians to the defense of Christian society. This redirection produced the **Crusades**, religious wars of conquest authorized by popes and directed against Europe's non-Christian neighbors.

Crusaders: Soldiers of God

The Crusades left a complex and troubling legacy in world civilization. Between 1096 and 1272, waves of zealous and adventuresome European Christians set out to do battle with the Muslims. The First Crusade originated in 1095, when Pope Urban II (1088–1099), hoping to direct noble violence away from Christendom, urged Western knights to use their arms to free the Holy Land from Muslim occupation. In return, he promised to absolve them from all of the punishment due for their sins in this life or the next. After terrible hardships, the crusaders succeeded in taking Jerusalem in 1099 and established a Latin Kingdom in Palestine. For over two centuries, bands of Western warriors went on armed pilgrimages to defend this precarious kingdom. The Second Crusade (1145–1149) ended in defeat and disaster at the hands of Seljuk Turks in Asia Minor. In 1187, the Muslim commander Saladin recaptured Jerusalem, causing Emperor Frederick Barbarossa and the kings

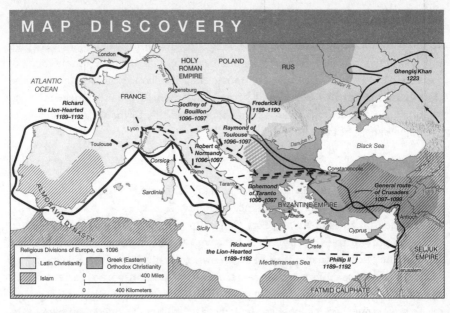

MAP DISCOVERY

THE CRUSADES

Examine the religious divisions of Europe and the major crusade routes. What different geographical and political obstacles did crusaders face depending on whether they traveled by land or by water? How did the divisions of Christianity and Islam affect the course of the Crusades?

---

of France and England, Philip II Augustus and Richard the Lion-Hearted, to embark on the Third Crusade (1187–1192). This crusade also failed, but Richard signed a peace treaty with Saladin. Five subsequent crusades accomplished little.

The Idea of the Crusades

Although military failures, the Crusades appealed particularly to younger sons and knights who hoped to acquire in the East the status that constricting lineages denied them in the West. Other such holy wars were directed against the Muslims in Spain, the Slavs in eastern Europe, and even heretics and political opponents in France and Italy.

The Crusades were brutal and vicious, but crusaders themselves were motivated by a combination of religious conviction—most knew that they would probably not survive these wars—and the hope of material gain. Doubts about the spiritual significance of such wars contributed to their decline. So, too, did the rise of centralized monarchies, whose rulers usually viewed the Crusades as wasteful and futile. The age of the Crusades passed with the age of the independent warrior aristocracy.

Medieval Towns

To the traditional rural mind, towns seemed somehow immoral. Nobles disdained urban society for its lack of respect for aristocracy and its disinterest in their cult of violence. Still, as rude warriors were transformed into courtly nobles, these nobles were drawn to urban luxuries and became indebted to urban moneylenders to maintain their "gracious" lifestyles. For many peasants, towns were refuges from the hopelessness of their normal lives.

Italian Cities

Urban life had never ceased in Italy, which had maintained its urban traditions and ties with the Mediterranean world since antiquity.

The coastal cities of Amalfi, Bari, Genoa, and especially Venice had continued to play important roles in commerce both with the Byzantines and with the new Muslim societies. With nothing of their own to trade but perhaps salt and, in Venice, glass, these cities acted as go-betweens for the transport of eastern spices, silks, and ivories, which they exchanged for Western iron, slaves, timber, grain, and oil. To protect their merchant ships, Italian coastal cities developed their own fleets, and by the eleventh century they were major military forces in the Mediterranean.

Merchants and Capitalists. As the merchants of the Italian towns penetrated the markets at the western end of the great overland spice routes connecting China, India, and central Asia with the Mediterranean, they established permanent merchant colonies in the East. When expedient, they did not hesitate to use military force to win concessions.

By the thirteenth century, Italian merchants had spread far beyond the Mediterranean. The great merchant banking houses of Venice, Florence, and Genoa had established offices around the Mediterranean and Black seas; south along the Atlantic coast of Morocco; east into Armenia and Persia; west to London, Bruges, and Ghent; and north to Scandinavia. Some individual merchants, the Venetian Marco Polo (1254–1324), for example, traded as far east as China and even entered the service of the Great Khan.

These international commercial operations required more sophisticated systems of commercial law and credit. Italian merchants responded by developing double-entry bookkeeping, limited-liability partnership, commercial insurance, and international letters of exchange. Complex commercial affairs also required a system of credit and interest-bearing loans, an idea that was abhorrent to traditional rural societies. Churchmen condemned borrowing and lending at credit, but bankers found ways of hiding interest payments in contracts, thus allowing lender and seller to participate in the growing world of credit-based transactions.

Underlying the expanding commercial developments was a basic change: a new mentality that considered commerce an honorable occupation. By the twelfth century, wealthy citizens, whether descended from successful merchants or from landed aristocrats, were indifferently termed magnates. The rest of the town's population were called *populars*. The difference between the two was essentially economic.

Communal Government. In the eleventh and early twelfth centuries, many Italian towns bought off or expelled their traditional lords such as counts and bishops, thus allowing the magnates and populars of these cities to create their own governing institutions or communes. Within many towns the magnates formed their own corporation—the society of knights—to protect their privileged position. Families of nobles and magnates, whose cultural values were similar to those of the rural aristocracy, competed with each other for honor and power. Feuds fought out between noble families and their vassals in city streets were frequent events in Italian towns.

Opposing the magnates were popular corporations—the society of the people—which sought to rein in the violent and independent-minded nobles. Each of these popular organizations, dominated by the prominent leaders of craft and trade associations, had its own elected officers and its own military, headed by a "captain of the people," who might command as many as 1,000 troops against the magnates.

To maintain civic life in spite of these conflicts, cities established complex systems of government in which officers were selected by series of elections and lotteries designed to prevent any one faction from seizing control. Sovereignty lay with the *arengo*, or assembly, which included all adult male citizens. Except in very small communes this body was too large to function efficiently, so most communes selected a series of working councils. Generally, executive authority was vested in consuls, whose numbers varied widely and who were chosen from various factions and classes. When these consuls proved unable to overcome the partisan politics of the factions, many towns turned to hiring *podestas*, nonpolitical professional city managers from outside the community. These were normally magnates from other communes who had received legal educations and who served for relatively short periods.

Northern Towns

Merchant and manufacturing towns also developed along the Baltic and North seas and the English Channel. Scandinavian fish and timber, Baltic grain, English wool, and Flemish cloth circulated by sea around Scandinavia, Lithuania, northern Germany, Flanders, and England, linking them in a common economic network.

In the eleventh century, Flanders, lacking the land for large-scale sheep grazing and facing a growing population, began to specialize in the production of high-quality cloth made from English wool. At the same time, England, which experienced an economic and population decline following the Norman Conquest, began to export the greater part of its wool to Flanders to be worked. By the late eleventh century, the production of wool cloth began to develop from a cottage

MAP DISCOVERY

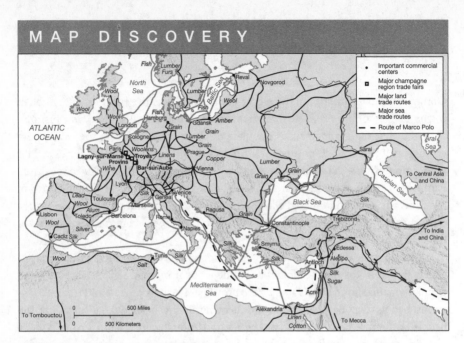

MEDIEVAL TRADE NETWORKS

Examine the major trade routes of the High Middle Ages. What commodities and products were plentiful in Europe but scarce in the eastern Mediterranean? What regions were the major wool producers? The major cloth producers? How might silks from the East have arrived in London?

occupation into Europe's first major industry. Now manufacture was concentrated in towns, and men replaced women at the looms. Furthermore, production was closely regulated and controlled by a small group of extremely wealthy merchant-drapiers (cloth makers).

Concentration of capital, specialization of labor, and increase of urban population created vibrant, exciting cities that were essentially composed of three social orders. At the top were wealthy patricians, the merchant-drapiers. Through their control of raw materials, equipment, capital, and distribution the merchant-drapiers controlled the cloth trade and thus the economic and political life of the Flemish wool towns. Through their closed associations, or **guilds**, they controlled production and set standards, prices, and wages. They also controlled communal government by monopolizing urban councils.

At the bottom of urban society were the unskilled and semiskilled artisans. These poorly paid workers led an existence that was more precarious than that of most peasants.

Between the patricians and the workers stood the masters, the skilled craftsmen who controlled the day-to-day production of cloth and lesser crafts. They organized

The complex process of spinning, weaving, dying, and marketing woolen cloth gave rise to complex social and economic structures while bringing great wealth to Flemish cities. In this fifteenth-century manuscript illumination, an elite master dyer supervises the work of his laborers. The rise of the woolen industry created new urban elites as well as the first European proletarians.

into guilds to protect themselves from competition. The masters often leased their looms or other equipment from the merchant-drapiers and received from them raw materials and wages to be distributed to their workers.

The Fairs of Champagne

Tying together the northern and southern commercial worlds were the great fairs of Champagne. Six times during the year, the towns of Champagne hosted trade fairs, allowing merchants from north and south to meet, bargain, and trade under the protection of the local counts.

Northern merchants offered cloth. From Italy came merchants of great Italian trading companies to purchase northern cloth for resale throughout the Mediterranean. Southern merchants brought silks, sugar, salt, alum (a chemical that was essential in cloth manufacture), and, most important, spices to trade at the fairs.

These great international exchanges connected the financial and marketing centers of the south with the manufacturing and trading communities of the north, tying the northern world to the south more effectively than had any system since the political institutions of the Roman Empire.

Scholasticism and Urban Intellectual Life

The urban world of the twelfth and thirteenth centuries created forms of religious and cultural expression particularly suited to it. The cathedral schools shifted away from monastic education to an education aimed more at participation in the affairs of the world. Young men were taught the essential urban skills of writing, computation, and law.

The Medieval University. In the late eleventh and early twelfth centuries, the pace of urban intellectual life quickened. The combination of population growth, improved agricultural productivity, political stability, and educational interest culminated in what has been called the renaissance of the twelfth century. Bologna and Paris became the undisputed centers of the new educational movements. Bologna specialized in the study of law, while Paris became the leader in the study of liberal arts and theology. Students at Bologna organized a **universitas**, or guild of students, the first true university.

In the early twelfth century, students from across Europe flocked to Paris to study with the greatest and most original intellect of the century, Peter Abelard (1079–1142). Abelard's intellectual method combined the tools of legal analysis perfected in Bologna with Aristotelian logic and laid the foundation of what has been called the **Scholastic method**. Logical reasoning, Abelard believed, could be applied to all problems, even those concerning the mysteries of faith.

This illustration from a fourteenth-century manuscript shows Henry of Germany delivering a lecture to university students in Bologna.

The intellectual ferment Abelard began in Paris continued long after him. By 1200, education had become so important in the city that the universitas, or corporation of professors, was granted a charter by King Philip Augustus, who guaranteed its rights and immunities from the control of the city.

Students at the University of Paris began their studies at around age 14 or 15 in the faculty of arts. After approximately six years, they received a bachelor of arts degree, which was a prerequisite to enter the higher faculties of theology, medicine, or law. After additional years of reading and commenting on specific texts under the supervision of a master, they received the title of master of arts, which gave them the license to teach anywhere within Christian Europe.

The intellectual life of the universities through the thirteenth and fourteenth centuries was dominated by Aristotelian thought. The introduction of the works of Aristotle into the West between 1150 and 1250 created an intellectual crisis every bit as profound as that of the Newtonian revolution of the seventeenth century or the Einsteinian revolution of the twentieth. For centuries, Western thinkers had depended on the Christianized Neoplatonic philosophy of Origen and Augustine. Aristotle was known in the West only through his basic logical treatises, which in the twelfth century, thanks in large part to the work of Peter Abelard, had become the foundation of intellectual work. Logic, or dialectic, was seen as the universal key to knowledge, and the university system was based on its rigorous application to traditional texts of law, philosophy, and Scripture.

The Aristotelian Challenge. Beginning in the late twelfth century, Christian and Jewish scholars began translating Aristotle's treatises on natural philosophy, ethics, and metaphysics into Latin. Suddenly, Christian intellectuals who had already accepted the Aristotelian method were brought face to face with Aristotle's conclusions: a world without an active, conscious God, a world in which everything from the functioning of the mind to the nature of matter could be understood without reference to a divine creator.

As the full impact of Aristotelian philosophy began to reach churchmen and scholars, reactions varied from condemnation to whole-hearted acceptance. To many, it appeared that there were two irreconcilable kinds of truth, one knowable through divine revelation and the other through human reason.

One Parisian scholar who refused to accept the dichotomy of faith and reason was Thomas Aquinas (1225–1274), a professor of theology and the most brilliant intellect of the High Middle Ages. Aquinas refused to accept the possibility that human reason, which was a gift from God, led necessarily to contradictions with divine revelation. Properly applied, the principles of Aristotelian philosophy could not lead to error, Aquinas argued. However, human reason unaided by revelation could not always lead to certain conclusions. Questions about such matters as the nature of God, creation, and the human soul could not be resolved by reason alone. In developing his thesis, Aquinas recast Christian doctrine and philosophy, replacing their Neoplatonic foundation with an Aristotelian base. Although not universally accepted in the thirteenth century, Aquinas's synthesis came to dominate Christian intellectual life for centuries.

Preaching and Poverty. Aquinas was a member of a new religious order, the Dominicans, who along with the Franciscans appeared in response to the social and cultural needs of the new urbanized, monetized European culture. Lay persons and clerics alike were concerned with the growing wealth of ecclesiastical institutions, and across southern Europe especially, individual reformers attacked the wealthy lifestyles of monks and secular clergy as un-Christian.

Torn between their own involvement in a commercial world and an inherited Christian-Roman tradition that looked on commerce and capital as degrading, reformers called for a return to what they imagined to have been the life of the primitive Church, one that emphasized both individual and collective poverty. Although many reformers were condemned as heretics and were sporadically persecuted, the reform movement continued to grow and threatened to destroy the unity of Western Christendom.

The people who preserved the Church's unity aimed at reforming the Church from within. Francis of Assisi (1182–1226), the son of a prosperous Italian merchant, rejected his luxurious life in favor of one of radical poverty and service to others. Convinced of the importance of obedience, Francis asked Pope Innocent III to approve the way of life he had chosen for himself and his followers. The pope granted his wish, and the Order of Friars Minor, or Franciscans, grew by thousands, drawing members from as far away as England and Hungary.

An altarpiece by Bonaventura Berlinghieri depicting Saint Francis of Assisi painted less than a decade after the saint's death in 1226. The frontal position of the main figure, the way that his feet seem to float rather than to stand firmly on the ground, and the gold-leaf background all point to the Byzantine tradition of icon painting still important in Italy in the thirteenth century. Francis is shown with the stigmata—symbolic marks that represent the wounds Christ received on the cross. He is flanked by two angels, and around him are six scenes from his life. The image of Francis with the signs of Christ's passion in his hands and feet became essential elements in the depiction of this new type of saint who urged imitation of the life of Jesus, both in his poverty and in his suffering.

Francis insisted that his followers observe strict poverty, both individually and collectively. The order could not own property, nor could its members even touch money. They were expected to beg for their food as they traveled from town to town, preaching, performing manual labor, and serving the poor. Francis did not approve of women followers leading such a life but insisted that they pursue radical poverty within cloistered convents that were often within the walls of towns.

The order of friars founded by Dominic (1170–1221) also adopted a rule of strict poverty, but their primary focus was on preaching. This order emphasized intellectual activity and higher education and spoke out against heresies. Thus the Dominicans too gravitated toward the cities of western Europe and especially toward its great universities.

The Invention of the State

The disintegration of the Carolingian Empire in the tenth century left political power fragmented among a wide variety of political entities. In general, these were of two types. The first, the papacy and the empire, were elective traditional structures that claimed universal sovereignty over the Christian world, based on a sacred view of political power. The second, largely hereditary and less extravagant in their religious and political pretensions, were the limited kingdoms that arose within the old Carolingian world or on its borders.

The Universal States: Empire and Papacy

The Frankish world east of the Rhine River had been less affected than the kingdom of the West Franks by the onslaught of Vikings, Magyars, and Saracens. The eastern Frankish kingdom, a loose confederacy of five duchies—Saxony, Lorraine, Franconia, Swabia, and Bavaria—had preserved much of the Carolingian religious, cultural, and institutional traditions. In 919, Duke Henry I of Saxony (919–936) was elected king, and his son Otto I (936–973) laid the foundation for the revival of the empire. Otto inflicted a devastating defeat on the Magyars in 955. In 951, Otto invaded and conquered Lombardy. Eleven years later, he entered Rome, where he was crowned emperor by the pope.

The Medieval Empire. Otto, known to history as "the Great," established the main outlines of German imperial policy for the next 300 years. This policy included conflict with the German aristocracy, reliance on bishops and abbots as imperial agents, and preoccupation with Italy. His successors, both in his own Saxon dynasty (919–1024) and in the succeeding dynasties, the Salians (1024–1125) and the Staufens (1138–1254), continued this tradition. Magnates elected the German kings, who were then consecrated as emperors by the pope. Royal fathers were generally able to bring about the election of their sons, but magnates continued to exercise real power in royal elections. The magnates' ability to expand their own power and autonomy at the expense of their Slavic neighbors to the east also contributed to the weakness of the German monarchy.

To counter such aristocratic power, emperors looked to the Church both for the development of the religious cult of the emperor as "the Anointed of the Lord" and as a source of military and political support. Like the Carolingians, the Saxon and Salian emperors needed a purified, reformed Church that was free of local aristocratic control to serve the interests of the emperor. This imperial church was the cornerstone of the empire.

The laymen on whom the emperor could rely, particularly from the eleventh century, were trusted household serfs whom the emperors used as their agents. Despised by the freeborn nobility, they tended at first to be loyal supporters of the emperor. In the twelfth century, they adopted the chivalric ideals of their aristocratic neighbors and took advantage of conflicts between emperor and pope to acquire autonomy. As old noble families died out, ministerial families replaced them as a new hereditary aristocracy.

Otto the Great had entered Italy to secure his southern flank. His successors became embroiled in Italian affairs until, in the thirteenth century, they abandoned Germany altogether. As the emperors were drawn further into papal and Italian politics, frequently with disastrous results, Germany became merely a source of men and matériel with which to fight the Lombard towns and the pope. From the eleventh through the thirteenth centuries, emperors granted German princes autonomy in return for their support.

The Papacy. The early successes of this imperial program created the seeds of its own destruction. Imperial efforts to reform the Church resulted in a second, competing claimant to universal authority: the papacy. In the later tenth and early eleventh centuries, emperors had intervened in papal elections, deposed and replaced corrupt popes, and worked to ensure that bishops and abbots would be educated, competent churchmen. The most impressive reformer was Leo IX (1049–1054). Leo condemned simony, the practice of buying Church offices, and fostered monastic reforms such as that of Cluny. He also encouraged the efforts of a group of young reformers drawn from across Europe.

Investiture and Reform. In the next decades these new, more radical reformers began to advocate a widespread renewal of the Christian world, led not by emperors but by popes. These reformers pursued an ambitious set of goals. They sought to reform the morals of the clergy and in particular to eliminate married priests. They tried to free churches and monasteries from lay control both by forbidding lay men and women from owning churches and monasteries and by eliminating simony. They particularly condemned **lay investiture**, the practice by which kings and emperors appointed bishops and invested them with the

THE EMPIRE OF OTTO THE GREAT, CA. 963. The Ottonian Empire included not only Germany, but also Slavic lands to the east and disputed regions such as Lorraine to the west.

symbols of their office. Finally, they insisted that the pope, not the emperor, was the supreme representative of God on earth and as such had the right to exercise a universal sovereignty.

Every aspect of the reform movement met with strong opposition throughout Europe. Emperor Henry IV (1056–1106) clashed head-on with Pope Gregory VII (1073–1085) over the emperor's right to appoint and to install or invest bishops in their offices.

In the end, the conflict weakened both the empire and the papacy. In 1075, the emperor Henry IV, supported by many German bishops, attempted to depose Gregory. In return, Gregory excommunicated and deposed Henry, freed the German nobility from their obligations to him, and encouraged them to rebel. As anti-imperial strength grew, Henry took a desperate gamble. Crossing the Alps in the dead of winter in 1077, he arrived before the castle of Canossa in northern Italy, where Gregory was staying. Dressed as a humble penitent, Henry stood in the snow, asking the pope for forgiveness and reconciliation. As a priest, the pope could not refuse, and he lifted the excommunication. Once more in power, Henry resumed appointing bishops. In 1080, Gregory again excommunicated and deposed Henry, but this time the majority of the German nobles and bishops remained loyal to the emperor, and Henry marched on Rome. Deserted by most of his clergy, Gregory fled to southern Italy and died in Salerno in 1085.

Henry did not long enjoy his victory. Gregory's successors rekindled the opposition to Henry and even convinced Henry's own son to join in the revolt. The conflict ended only in 1122, when Emperor Henry V (1106–1125) and Pope Calixtus II (1119–1124) reached an agreement known as the Concordat of Worms, which differentiated between the royal and spiritual spheres of authority and allowed the emperors a limited role in episcopal election and investiture. This compromise changed the nature of royal rule in the empire, weakening the emperors and contributing to the long-term decline of royal government in Germany.

The decline that began with the investiture controversy continued as emperors abandoned political power north of the Alps to pursue their ambitions in Italy. Frederick I Barbarossa (1152–1190) gained the support of the German princes for his largely futile efforts in northern Italy by granting them extraordinary privileges. His successors continued his policy of focusing on Italy with no better success. In 1230, Frederick II (1215–1250) conceded to each German prince sovereign rights in his own territory. From the thirteenth to the nineteenth centuries, these princes ruled their territories as independent states, leaving the office of emperor a hollow title.

The investiture controversy ultimately compromised the authority of the pope as well as that of the emperor. First, the series of compromises beginning with the Concordat of Worms established the potent Western idea of separate spheres of authority for secular and religious government. Second, although in the short run popes were able to exercise enormous political influence, from the thirteenth century they were increasingly unable to make good their claims to absolute authority.

The Pinnacle of Papal Power. During the pontificate of Innocent III (1198–1216), the papacy reached the height of its power. Innocent made and deposed emperors, excommunicated kings, summoned a crusade against heretics in the south of France, and placed whole countries such as England and France under interdict, that is, the suspension of all religious services, when rulers dared to contradict him. Still, he found time to support Francis of Assisi and Dominic and, in 1215, to call the Fourth Lateran Council, which culminated the reforms of the past century.

During the thirteenth century, the papacy continued to perfect its legal system and its control over clergy throughout Europe. However, politically the popes were unable to assert their claims to universal supremacy. This was true both in Italy, where the communes in the north and the kingdom of Naples in the south resisted direct papal control, and in the emerging kingdoms north of the Alps, where monarchs successfully intervened in Church affairs. The old claims of papal authority rang increasingly hollow.

Chronology

PROMINENT POPES AND RELIGIOUS FIGURES OF THE HIGH MIDDLE AGES

1049–1054*	Pope Leo IX
1073–1085	Pope Gregory VII
1088–1099	Pope Urban II
1098–1179	Hildegard of Bingen
1119–1124	Pope Calixtus II
1170–1221	Saint Dominic
1182–1226	Saint Francis of Assisi
1198–1216	Pope Innocent III
1225–1274	Saint Thomas Aquinas
1294–1303	Pope Boniface VIII

*Dates for popes are dates of reign.

The Nation-States: France and England

The claims of kings were much more modest than those of emperors or popes. Kings laid claim to a limited territory; they were only one of many representatives of God on earth; and finally, they were far from absolute rulers. During the tenth and eleventh centuries, the powers of justice, coinage, taxation, and military command, once considered public, had been usurped by aristocrats and nobles. Kings needed the support of these magnates, and often—as in the case of France—these dukes and counts were wealthier and more powerful than the kings. Still, between the tenth and fourteenth centuries, some monarchies, especially those of France and England, developed into powerful, centralized, and vigorous kingdoms. In the process they gave birth to what has become the modern state.

France: Biology, Bureaucracy, and Sanctity. In 987, when Hugh Capet was elected king of the West Franks, no one suspected that his successors would become the most powerful rulers of Europe. The dukes of Normandy, descendants of Vikings whose settlement had been recognized by Frankish kings, ruled their duchy with an authority of which the kings could only dream. Less than a century later, Duke William of Normandy expanded his power even more by conquering England. In the twelfth century, the English kings ruled the Angevin Empire, a vast collection of hereditary lands on both sides of the English Channel. Other nobles, such as the counts of Flanders and the counts of Poitou, also seemed more impressive than the house of Hugh Capet. Nevertheless, under Hugh's successors, the kingdom of France became the most powerful monarchy in Europe and the center of European learning, architecture, and art.

The medieval French monarchy owed its creation in large part to biology and bureaucracy. Between 987 and 1314, every royal descendant of Hugh Capet (after whom the dynasty was called the Capetian) left a male heir—an extraordinary record for a medieval family. By simply outlasting the families of their great barons, the Capetian kings were able to absorb lands when other families became extinct.

The Capetians' long run of biological luck, combined with the practice of having a son crowned during his father's lifetime and thus being firmly established before his father's death, was only part of the explanation for the Capetian success. The Capetians also wisely used their position as consecrated sovereigns to build a power base in the Ile de France (the region around Paris) and among the bishops and abbots of the kingdom and then to insist on their feudal rights as the lords of the great dukes and counts of France. It was this foundation that Louis VII's son Philip II (1180–1223) used to create the French monarchy.

Philip II was known to posterity as Augustus, or the aggrandizer, because through his ruthless political intrigue and brilliant organizational sense he more than doubled the territory he controlled and more than quadrupled the revenue of the French crown. Philip's greatest coup, however, was the confiscation of all the continental possessions of the English King John (1199–1216), the son of Henry II of England and Eleanor of Aquitaine. Although John was sovereign in England, as lord of Normandy, Anjou, Maine, and Touraine, he was technically a vassal of King Philip. When John married the fiancée of one of his continental vassals, the outraged vassal appealed to Philip in his capacity as John's lord. Philip summoned

John to appear before the royal court, and when he refused to do so, Philip ordered him to surrender all of his continental fiefs. This meant war, and one by one, John's continental possessions fell to the French king.

To govern these vast regions, Philip needed an effective administrative system. Using members of families from the old royal demesne, he set up administrative officials called *baillis* and *seneschals*, nonfeudal salaried agents who collected his revenues and represented his interests. The baillis in particular, who were drawn from commoner families and often had received their education at the University of Paris, were the foundation of the French bureaucracy, which grew in strength and importance through the thirteenth century. By governing the regions of France according to local traditions but always with an eye to the king's interest, these bureaucrats did more than anyone else to create a stable, enduring political system.

Philip's grandson Louis IX (1226–1270) fine-tuned this administrative machine and, through his own piety, endowed it with the aura of sanctity. Generous, brave, and capable, Louis took seriously his obligation to provide justice for the poor and protection for the weak. The goodwill and devotion that Louis won from his subjects were a precious heritage that benefited his successors for centuries.

The growth of royal power transformed the traditional role of the aristocracy. As the power and wealth of the French kings increased, the ability of the nobles to maintain their independence decreased. Royal judges undermined lords' control over the peasantry. Royal revenues enabled kings to hire warriors rather than relying on traditional feudal levies. At the same time, the increasing expenses of the noble lifestyle forced all but the wealthiest aristocrats to look for sources of income beyond their traditional estates. Increasingly, they found this in royal service. Thus, in the thirteenth century the nobility began to lose some of its independence to the state.

England: Conquest, Accounting, and Cooperation. A very different path brought the English monarchy to a level of power similar to that of the French by the end of the thirteenth century. While France was made by a family and its bureaucracy, the kingdom that was originally forged by Alfred and his descendants was transformed by the successors of William the Conqueror.

When King Edward the Confessor (1042–1066) died, three claimants disputed the succession. Anglo-Saxon sources insist that Edward and his nobles had chosen Earl Harold Godwinson (ca. 1022–1066) over Duke William of Normandy and the Norwegian king Harold III (1045–1066). Harold of Norway and William sailed for England. Harold Godwinson defeated the Norwegian's army and killed the king, but he met his end shortly afterward on the bloody field of Hastings, and William the Conqueror secured the throne.

William's England was a small, insular kingdom that had been united by Viking raids little more than a century before. Hostile Celtic societies bordered it to the north and west. Still, it had important strengths. First, the king of the English was not simply a feudal lord, a first among equals—he was a sovereign. Second, Anglo-Saxon government had been participatory, with the freemen of each shire taking part in court sessions and sharing the responsibilities of government. Finally, the king had agents, or *reeves*, in each shire (shire reeves, or sheriffs) who were responsible for representing the king's interests, presiding over the local court, and collecting royal taxes and incomes.

This ability to raise money was the most important aspect of the English kingship for William the Conqueror and his immediate successors. England was seen primarily as a source of revenue. To tap this wealth, the Norman kings transformed rather than abolished Anglo-Saxon governmental traditions, adding Norman feudal bonds and administrative control to Anglo-Saxon kingship.

William preserved English government while replacing Anglo-Saxon officers with his continental vassals, chiefly Normans and Flemings. He rewarded his supporters with land confiscated from the defeated Anglo-Saxons, but he was careful to give out land only in fief. In contrast to continental practice, in which many lords owned vast estates outright, in England all land was held directly or indirectly by the king. Because he wanted to know the extent of his new kingdom and its wealth, William ordered a comprehensive survey of all royal rights. The recorded account, known as the Domesday Book, was the most extensive investigation of economic rights since the Merovingians abandoned the late Roman tax rolls.

William and his successors needed an efficient system of controlling England when they were away. To that end, they developed the royal court, an institution inherited from their Anglo-Saxon predecessors, into an efficient system of fiscal and administrative supervision. The most important innovation was the use of a large checkerboard, or exchequer, which functioned like a primitive computer to audit the returns of their sheriffs. Annual payments were recorded on long rolls of parchment called pipe rolls, the first continuous accounting system in Europe. These improved accounting methods produced the most efficient and prosperous royal administration in Europe.

In the first half of the twelfth century, almost two decades of warfare over the succession greatly weakened royal authority, but Henry II (1154–1189) reestablished central power by reasserting his authority over the nobility and through his legal reforms. Using his continental wealth and armies, he brought the English barons into line, destroyed private castles, and reasserted his rights to traditional royal incomes. He strengthened royal courts by expanding royal jurisdiction at the expense of Church tribunals and of the courts of feudal lords.

Henry's efforts to control the clergy led to one of the epic clashes of the investiture struggle. The archbishop of Canterbury, Thomas à Becket (ca. 1118–1170), although a personal friend of Henry, refused to accept the king's claim to jurisdiction over clergy. For six years, Becket lived in exile on the Continent and infuriated Henry by his stubborn adherence to the letter of Church law. He was allowed to return to England in 1170, but that same year he was struck down in his own cathedral by four knights eager for royal favor. The king did penance but, unlike the German emperors, ultimately preserved royal authority over the English Church.

Henry's program to assert royal courts over local and feudal ones was even more successful, laying the foundation for a system of uniform judicial procedures throughout the kingdom: the common law. Henry's legal system simplified and cut through the complex tangle of local and feudal jurisdictions concerning land law.

Henry's son John may have made the greatest contribution to the development of the English state by losing Normandy and most of his other continental lands. Loss of these territories forced English kings to concentrate on ruling England, not on their continental territories. Moreover, John's financial difficulties, brought about by his unsuccessful wars to recover his continental holdings, led him to such extremes of fiscal extortion that his barons, prelates, and the townspeople of London revolted. In June 1215, he was forced to accept the "great charter of liberties," or **Magna Carta**, a conservative feudal document demanding that he respect the rights of his vassals and of the burghers of London. The great significance of the document was its acknowledgment that the king was not above the law.

John and his weak, ineffective son Henry III (1216–1272), although ably served by royal judges, were forced by their failures to cede considerable influence to the great barons of the realm. Henry's son Edward I (1272–1307), a strong and effective king who conquered Wales, defended the remaining continental possessions against France, and expanded the common law, found that he could turn baronial involvement in government to his own advantage. By summoning his barons, bishops, and representatives of the towns and shires to participate in a "parley," or "parliament," he could raise more funds for his wars. Like similar Spanish, Hungarian, and German assemblies of the thirteenth century, these assemblies were occasions to consult, to present royal programs, and to extract extraordinary taxes for specific projects. They were also opportunities for those who were summoned to petition the king for redress of grievances. However, since the growing wealth of the towns and countryside made their financial support essential, these groups came to anticipate that they had a right to be consulted and to consent to taxation.

Through a system of royal courts and justices employing local juries and a tradition of representative parliaments, this forced self-government, coupled with an exacting system of accounting, increased the power of the English monarchy. By 1300, France, with its powerful royal bureaucracy, and England, with its courts and accountants, were the most powerful states in the West.

SUMMARY

The Countryside   Between 1000 and 1300, Europe's population almost doubled. Across much of northwestern Europe in the eleventh century, the peasantry formed a homogeneous social category loosely described as serfs. Agricultural technology gradually changed the ways that peasants worked their land and the amount of food they could produce. Changing conditions in western Europe led to a transition from serfdom to free labor. At the same time, free peasants in eastern Europe and Spain lost their freedom. The essence of the aristocratic lifestyle was fighting. In this martial society, the official political and economic status of women declined considerably. Vassals pledged loyalty to lords in exchange for land. Clergy met the religious needs of both commoners and elites. Monasteries often served the interests of aristocrats. Monastic reformers called for a more stringent separation of the clergy from secular society. The church both served the lay population and worked to transform it. The Crusades were a military failure.

Medieval Towns   Italian towns served as commercial links between East and West. Italian merchants developed sophisticated systems of commercial law and credit. In the eleventh and early twelfth centuries, many Italian towns created their own governing institutions or communes. Merchant and manufacturing towns also developed along the Baltic and North seas and the English Channel. The textile industry linked England and Flanders. Tying together the northern and southern commercial worlds were the great fairs of Champagne. The towns and cities of the twelfth and thirteenth centuries gave rise to new forms of religious and cultural expression, including the medieval university. The introduction of the works of Aristotle into the West between 1150 and 1250 created an intellectual crisis. The Franciscans and Dominicans responded to the needs of a changing Europe.

The Invention of the State   Otto I laid the foundation of the Holy Roman Empire. The policies of Otto and his successors were characterized by conflict with the German aristocracy, reliance on clergy as imperial agents, and preoccupation with Italy. The pope emerged as a challenger to the emperor for the claim of universal authority. Church reformers stressed the authority of the clergy over secular rulers. The investiture controversy pitted the papacy against the empire. The papacy reached the pinnacle of its power during the pontificate of Innocent III. Biology and bureaucracy helped the Capetians build the medieval French monarchy. The growth of royal power transformed the traditional role of the French aristocracy. The Norman kings of England transformed rather than abolished Anglo-Saxon governmental traditions. Henry II increased central power by asserting his authority over the nobility and through his legal reforms. Under Henry's son John, England lost most of its continental territories and John was forced to accept the Magna Carta. The reign of Edward I saw the emergence of the English parliament.

QUESTIONS FOR REVIEW

1. How did the different social roles of peasants, knights, and clergymen interact and complement each other?
2. In what ways did life in the urban world pose a threat to the values and priorities of aristocrats and churchmen?
3. How were the pope and the Holy Roman Emperor both dependent on each other and in conflict?
4. Why would Europe's medieval kings ultimately be more successful than the Holy Roman Emperor or the papacy in establishing strong, centralized states?

CHAPTER

The Later Middle Ages, 1300–1500

Politics as a Family Affair

In the fourteenth and fifteenth centuries, politics centered on the ambitions of great families. Everywhere, family politics threatened the fragile institutional developments of the thirteenth century. Aristocrats competed for personal power and used public office, military command, and taxing power for private ends. What mattered was neither territorial boundaries nor political divisions but marriage alliances, kinship, and dynastic ambitions.

The Struggle for Central Europe

Five ambitious families competed for dominance in the empire: the Luxembourgs, the Wittelsbachs, the Habsburgs, the Premysls, and the house of Anjou. The protracted wars and maneuvers that these families conducted for dominance in the empire resembled nothing so much as the competition that had taken place three centuries earlier for dominance in feudal France.

Eastern Expansion. For over a century, not only great princes but also monks, adventurers, and simple peasants streamed into the kingdoms and principalities of eastern Europe. Since the early thirteenth century, the Teutonic orders had used the sword to spread Christianity along the Baltic coast. The pagan inhabitants of these regions had to choose between conversion and expulsion. When they fled, their fields were turned over to land-hungry German peasants.

By the fifteenth century, religious and secular German lords had established a new agrarian economy, modeled on western European estates, in regions that were previously unoccupied or sparsely settled by the indigenous Slavic peoples. This economy specialized in the cultivation of grain for export to the west.

Central European Kingdoms. Farther south, the Christian kingdoms of Poland, Bohemia, and Hungary beckoned different sorts of westerners. Newly opened silver and copper mines in Bohemia, Silesia, southern Poland, and Hungarian Transylvania needed skilled miners, smelters, and artisans. Many were recruited from the overpopulated regions of western Germany.

The wealth of eastern Europe, its abundant land, and its relative freedom attracted both peasants and merchants. The promise of profitable marriages with eastern royalty drew ambitious aristocrats. Continually menaced by one another and by the aggressive German aristocracy to the west, the royal families of Poland, Hungary, and Bohemia were eager to make marriage alliances with powerful aristocratic families from farther afield. Nobles of the eastern European kingdoms were pleased to confirm the election of such outsiders. The elections prevented powerful German nobles from claiming succession to the Bohemian, Hungarian, and Polish thrones. At the same time, the families of the western European aristocracy did not have sufficiently strong local power bases to challenge the autonomy of the eastern nobility.

Charles IV (1347–1378) was typical of these restless dynasts. His grandfather, Emperor Henry VII (1308–1313), had arranged for his son John of Luxembourg to marry Elizabeth (d. 1330), the Premysl heiress of Bohemia, and thus acquire the Bohemian crown in 1310. By mastering the intricate politics of the decaying Holy Roman Empire, John arranged the deposition of the Wittelsbach emperor Louis IV (1314–1347) and secured the election of Charles as king of the Romans, that is, heir of the empire, in 1346. The following year the Bohemian crown passed to Charles.

As king of Bohemia, Charles worked to make Prague a cultural center by combining French and Czech traditions. He imported artisans, architects, and artists to transform and beautify his capital. In 1348, he founded a university in Prague, the first in the empire, modeled on the University of Paris. Keenly interested in history, Charles provided court historians with the sources necessary to write their histories of the Bohemian kingdom.

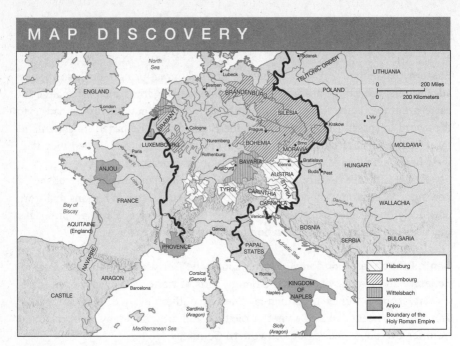

CENTRAL AND EASTERN EUROPE, CA. 1378

Examine this complex map of rival dynasties in fourteenth-century Europe. How do you explain the discontinuous territorial holdings of these great competing families? To what extent could the regions of the Holy Roman Empire be considered a state in 1378? Based on the text discussion, where might the Habsburgs be expected to extend and consolidate their power in the east?

The effects of Charles's cultural policies were far-reaching—but in directions he never anticipated. His interests in Czech culture and religious reform bore unexpected fruit during the reign of his son Sigismund, king of Germany (1410–1437), Bohemia (1419–1437), and Hungary (1387–1437) and Holy Roman Emperor (1433–1437). During Sigismund's reign, Czech religious and political reformers came into open conflict with the powerful German-speaking minority at the University of Prague. Led by the theologian Jan Hus (ca. 1372–1415), this reform movement ultimately challenged the authority of the Roman Church and became the direct predecessor of the great Reformation of the sixteenth century.

Even while building up his beloved city of Prague, Charles was dismantling the Holy Roman Empire. In 1356, he issued the **Golden Bull**, an edict that officially recognized what had long been the reality, namely, that the various German princes and kings were autonomous rulers. The bull also established the procedure by which future emperors would be elected. Thereafter, the emperor was chosen by seven great princes of the empire without the consultation or interference of

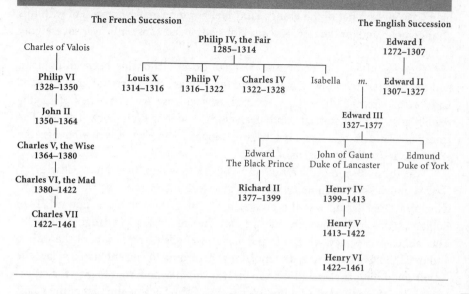

The French Succession

The English Succession

Charles of Valois

Philip IV, the Fair
1285–1314

Edward I
1272–1307

Philip VI
1328–1350

Louis X
1314–1316

Philip V
1316–1322

Charles IV
1322–1328

Isabella   *m.*   Edward II
1307–1327

John II
1350–1364

Edward III
1327–1377

Charles V, the Wise
1364–1380

Edward
The Black Prince

John of Gaunt
Duke of Lancaster

Edmund
Duke of York

Charles VI, the Mad
1380–1422

Richard II
1377–1399

Henry IV
1399–1413

Charles VII
1422–1461

Henry V
1413–1422

Henry VI
1422–1461

POLITICS AS A FAMILY AFFAIR

the pope. The procedure made disputed elections less likely, but it acknowledged that the office itself was less significant.

The same process that sapped the power of the emperor also reduced the significance of the princes. The empire fragmented into a number of large kingdoms, duchies, free towns, and sovereign bishoprics in the west. The inhabitants of these territories, often ruled by foreigners who had inherited sovereign powers through marriage, organized themselves into estates—political units of knights, burghers, and clergy—to present a united front in dealing with their prince. The princes, in turn, did not enjoy any universally recognized right to rule and were forced to negotiate with their estates for any powers they actually enjoyed.

A Hundred Years of War

The political map of western Europe was no less a patchwork quilt of family holdings than was the empire. In the Iberian Peninsula, power struggles and futile wars engaged the three Christian monarchies of Castile, Aragon, and Portugal. Only with the marriage of Ferdinand of Aragon and Isabella of Castile in 1469 did something like a unified Spain begin to emerge from this world of family rivalries.

Similar struggles threatened to overwhelm the feudal monarchies of France and England in the fourteenth and fifteenth centuries. In both kingdoms, weakening economic climates and demographic catastrophe exacerbated dynastic crises and fierce competition.

Three long-simmering disputes triggered the series of campaigns collectively termed the **Hundred Years' War**. The first issue was conflicting rights in Gascony in southern France. Since the mid-thirteenth century, the kings of England had held Gascony as a fief of the French king. Neither monarchy was content with this arrangement, and for the next 75 years, kings quarreled constantly over sovereignty in the region.

The second point of contention was the close relationship between England and the Flemish cloth towns, which were the primary customers for English wool. Early in the fourteenth century, Flemish artisans rose up in a series of bloody revolts against the aristocratic cloth dealers who had long monopolized power. The count of Flanders and the French king supported the wealthy merchants; the English sided with the artisans.

The third dispute concerned the royal succession in France. Charles IV (1322–1328), the son of Philip IV, the Fair, died without an heir. The closest descendant of a French king was the grandson of Philip the Fair, King Edward III of England (1327–1377). However, Edward was the son of Philip's daughter Isabella. The French aristocracy, which did not want an English king to inherit the throne and unite the two kingdoms, pretended that according to ancient Frankish law, the crown could not pass through a woman. Instead, they preferred to give the crown to a cousin of the late king, Philip VI (1328–1350), who became the first of the Valois kings of France. At first, the English voiced no objection to Philip's accession, but in 1337, when the dispute over Gascony again flared up and Philip attempted to confiscate the region from his English "vassal" Edward III, the English king declared war on Philip. Edward's stated goal was not only to recover Gascony but also to claim the crown of his maternal grandfather.

Chivalry and Warfare. Though territorial and dynastic rivalries were the triggers that set off the war, its deeper cause was chivalry. The elites of Europe were both inspired by and trapped in a code of conduct that required them not only to maintain their honor by violence but also to cultivate violence to increase that honor. For a ruler like Edward, obsessed with knightly glory, war with France was the ideal way to win honor and fame.

In spite of his chivalric ideals, Edward was practical when it came to organizing and financing his campaigns. Philip shared Edward's ideals but lacked his rival's practicality and self-assurance. Philip surrounded himself with aristocratic advisers who formed the most brilliant court of Europe, dispensing the royal treasure to his favorites, and dreaming of leading a great crusade to free the Holy Land. However, as the first French king in centuries who was elected rather than born into the right of succession, he treated the magnates from whose ranks he had come with excessive deference. He hesitated to press them for funds and deferred to them on matters of policy even while missing opportunities to raise other revenue from towns and merchants. Finally, although a competent warrior, Philip was no match in strategy or tactics for his English cousin.

Still, the sheer size and wealth of France should have made it the favorite in any war with England. Its population of roughly 16 million made it by far the largest and most densely populated kingdom in Europe. It was a major producer of cereal, wines, and cloth. The Flemish cloth towns, subdued by Philip in 1328, were the most industrialized area of Europe. England, by contrast, was a small, sparsely populated kingdom of under 5 million, and its economy was much less tied into international trade.

At the start of the war, Philip could rely on an income roughly three to five times greater than that of Edward. His greater income was matched by greater expenses, however, and he had no easy way to raise extraordinary funds for war. In contrast, the English king could use Parliament as an efficient source of war subsidies. Edward could also extract great sums from taxes on England's wool exports.

War was expensive. In spite of chivalrous ideals, nobles no longer fought as vassals of the king but as highly paid mercenaries. The nature of this service differed greatly on the two sides of the Channel. In France, the tactics and personnel had changed little since the twelfth century. The core of any army was the body of heavily armored nobles who rode into battle with their lords, supported by lightly armored knights. Behind them marched infantrymen recruited from towns and armed with pikes. Although the French also hired mercenary Italian crossbowmen, the nobles despised them and never used them effectively.

In contrast, centuries of fighting against Welsh and Scottish enemies had sharpened the English armies and their tactics. The great nobles continued to serve as heavily armored horsemen, but professional companies of foot soldiers raised by individual knights made up the bulk of the army. These professional companies consisted largely of pikemen and, most important, longbowmen. Although it was not as accurate as the crossbow, the English longbow had a greater range. Moreover, when massed archers fired volleys of arrows into enemy ranks, they proved extremely effective against enemy pikemen and even lightly armored cavalry.

English Successes. The first real test of the two armies came at the Battle of Crécy in 1346. When an overwhelmingly superior French force advanced against the English army, the English massed their archers on a hill and rained arrows down on the French cavalry, which attacked in a glorious but suicidal manner. The English victory was total. Strangely enough, the French learned nothing from the debacle. In 1356, Philip's successor John II (1350–1364) rashly attacked an English army at Poitiers and was captured. In 1415, the French blundered in a different way at Agincourt. This time, most of the heavily armored French knights dismounted and attempted to charge the elevated English position across a muddy field. Barely able to walk and unable to rise if they fell, all were captured. Out of fear that his numerically inferior army would be overwhelmed if the French recovered their breath, the English king ordered over 1,500 French nobles and 3,000 ordinary soldiers killed. English losses were fewer than 100.

Pitched battles were not the worst defeats for the French. More devastating were the constant raiding and systematic destruction of the French countryside by the English companies.

Raiding and pillaging continued for decades, even during long truces between the French and English kings. The French kings were powerless to prevent such destruction, just as they were unable to defeat the enemy in open battle. Since the kings were incapable of protecting their subjects or winning in battle, the "silken thread binding together the kingdom of France," as one observer put it, began to unravel, and the kingdom that had been so painstakingly constructed by the Capetian monarchs began to fall apart. Not only did the English make significant territorial conquests, but the French nobles began behaving much like those in the Holy Roman Empire, carving out autonomous lordships. Whole regions of the kingdom slipped entirely from royal authority. Duke Philip the Good of Burgundy (1396–1467) allied himself with England against France and profited from the war to form a far-flung lordship that included Flanders, Brabant, Luxembourg, and Hainaut. By the time of his death, he was the most powerful ruler in Europe. Much of the so-called Hundred Years' War was actually a French civil war.

During this century of war, the French economy suffered even more than the French state. Trade routes were broken, and commerce declined as credit disappeared. Politically and economically, France seemed doomed.

The battle of Agincourt (1415) was one of the great battles of the Hundred Years' War. The heavily armored French cavalry met defeat at the hands of a much smaller force of disciplined English pikemen and longbowmen.

Joan of Arc and the Salvation of France. Salvation came at the hands of a simple peasant girl from the county of Champagne. By 1429, the English and their Burgundian allies held virtually all of northern France, including Paris. Now they were besieging Orléans, the key to the south. The heir to the French throne, the dauphin, was the weak-willed and uncrowned Charles VII (1422–1461). To him came Joan of Arc (1412–1431), an illiterate but deeply religious girl who bore an incredible message of hope. She claimed to have heard the voices of saints ordering her to save Orléans and have the dauphin crowned according to tradition at Reims.

Eventually convinced of her sincerity, if not of her ability, Charles allowed her to accompany a relief force to Orléans. The French army, its spirit buoyed by the belief that Joan's simple faith was the work of God, defeated the English and ended the siege. This victory led to others, and on 16 July 1429, Charles was crowned king at Reims.

After the coronation, Joan's luck began to fade. She failed to take Paris, and in 1431 she was captured by the Burgundians, who sold her to the English. Eager to get rid of the troublesome girl, the English had her tried as a heretic. Charles made no move to save her, even though she had saved his kingdom. She was burned at the stake in Rouen on 30 May 1431.

Despite Joan's inglorious end, the tide had turned. The French pushed the English back toward the coast. In the final major battle of the war, fought at Formigny in 1450, the French used a new and telling weapon to defeat the English: gunpowder. Rather than charging the English directly, as they had done so often before, they mounted cannon and pounded the English to bits. Gunpowder completed the destruction of the chivalric traditions of warfare begun by archers and pikemen. By 1452, English continental holdings had been reduced to the town of Calais. The continental warfare of more than a century was over.

The English Wars of the Roses. Though war on the Continent had ended, warfare in England was just beginning. In some ways, the English monarchy had suffered even more from the Hundred Years' War than had the French. At the outset, English royal administration had been more advanced than that of the French. The system of royal agents, courts, and parliaments had created the expectation that the king could preserve peace and provide justice at home while waging successful and profitable wars abroad. As the decades dragged on without a decisive victory, the king came to rely on the aristocracy, enlisting its financial assistance by granting these magnates greater power at home.

War created powerful and autonomous aristocratic families with their own armies. Under a series of weak kings these families fought among themselves. Ultimately, they took sides in a civil war to determine the royal succession. For 30 years, from 1455 to 1485, supporters of the house of York, whose badge was the white rose, fought the rival house of Lancaster, whose symbol was the red rose. The English Wars of the Roses, as the conflict came to be called, finally ended in 1485, when Henry Tudor of the Lancastrian faction defeated his opponents. He inaugurated a new era as Henry VII (1485–1509), the first king of the Tudor dynasty.

Life and Death in the Later Middle Ages

By the end of the thirteenth century, population growth in the West had strained available resources to the breaking point. All arable land was under cultivation, and even marginal moorland, rocky mountainsides, and plains were being pressed into service to feed a growing population. At the same time, kings and nobles demanded ever-higher taxes and rents to finance their wars and extravagant lifestyles. The result was a precarious balance in which a late frost, a bad harvest, or hungry mercenaries could mean disaster. Population began to decline slowly around 1300, and the downturn became catastrophic within 50 years. Between 1300 and 1450, Europe's population fell by more than 30 percent. It did not recover until the seventeenth century.

Dancing with Death

Between 1315 and 1317, the first great famine of the fourteenth century, triggered by crop failures and war, struck Europe. People died by the thousands. Urban workers, because they were chronically undernourished, were particularly hard hit. Although this was the greatest famine in medieval memory, it was not the last. Disease accompanied famine. Crowded and filthy towns, opposing armies with their massed troops, and overpopulated countrysides provided fertile ground for the spread of infectious disease. Moreover, the greatly expanded trade routes of the thirteenth and fourteenth centuries, which carried goods and grain between East and West, also provided highways for deadly microbes.

Between 1347 and 1352, from one-third to one-half of Europe's population died from a virulent combination of bubonic, septicemic, and pneumonic plagues, known to history as the **Black Death**. The disease, carried by the fleas of infected rats, traveled the caravan routes from central Asia. It arrived in Messina, Sicily, aboard a merchant vessel in October 1347. From there the Black Death spread up the boot of Italy and then into southern France, England, and Spain. By 1349, it had reached northern Germany, Portugal, and Ireland. The following year the Low Countries, Scotland, Scandinavia, and Russia fell victim.

Plague was all the more terrifying because its cause, its manner of transmission, and its cure were totally unknown until the end of the nineteenth century. Preachers saw the plague as divine punishment for sin. Ordinary people frequently accused Jews of causing it by poisoning drinking water. The medical faculty of Paris announced that it was the result of the conjunction of the planets Saturn, Jupiter, and Mars, which caused a corruption of the surrounding air.

Responses to the plague were equally varied. In many German towns, terrified Christian citizens looked for outside scapegoats and slaughtered the Jewish community. Cities, aware of the risk of infection although ignorant of its process, closed their gates and turned away outsiders. Individuals with means fled to country houses or locked themselves in their homes to avoid contact with others. Nothing worked. As devastating as the first outbreak of the plague was, its aftershocks were even more catastrophic. Once established in Europe, the disease continued to return roughly once each generation. The last outbreak of the plague in Europe was the 1771 epidemic in Moscow that killed 60,000.

Although no solid statistics exist from the fourteenth century, the plague certainly killed more people than all of the wars and famines of the century. It was the greatest disaster ever to befall Europe. The Black Death touched every aspect of life, hastening a process of social, economic, and cultural transformation that was already under way. The initial outbreak shattered social and economic structures. Fields were abandoned, workplaces stood idle, international trade was suspended. Traditional bonds of kinship, village, and even religion were broken by the horrors of death, flight, and failed expectations.

MAP DISCOVERY

Spread of the Black Death

1346
1347
1348
1349
1350
1351 and later

General route of the Black Death

Revolts

SPREAD OF THE BLACK DEATH AND PEASANT REVOLTS

How closely did the spread of the Black Death follow the medieval trade networks shown in the map on p. 210? What was the general direction and average annual speed of the disease's spread? Was the Black Death only a disaster to western Europe? Note the locations of peasant revolts. Based on the chapter discussion, what similarities and differences existed among the groups that revolted in the later Middle Ages? Was there a relationship between the devastation of the plague and the outbreak of revolts?

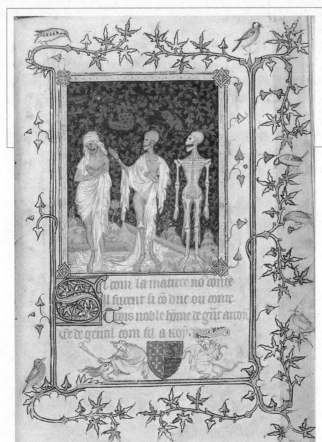

A page from the fourteenth-century psalter and prayer book of Bonne of Luxembourg, duchess of Normandy. The three figures of the dead shown here contrast with three living figures on the facing page of the psalter to illustrate a moral fable.

Across Europe, moralists reported a general lapse in traditional ethics, a breakdown in the moral codes. The most troubling aspect of this breakdown was what one defender of the old order termed "the plague of insurrection" that spread across Europe. This plague was brought on by the dimming of the hopes held by the survivors of the Black Death.

The Plague of Insurrection

Initially, even this darkest cloud had a silver lining. Lucky survivors of the plague soon found other reasons to rejoice. Property owners, when they finished burying their dead, discovered that they were far richer in land and goods. At the other end of the social spectrum, the plague had eliminated the labor surplus. Peasants were suddenly in great demand. For a time, at least, they were able to negotiate substantially higher wages and an improved relationship with landlords.

These hopes were short lived. The rise in expectations produced by the redistribution of wealth and the labor shortage created new tensions. Landlords sought laws forcing peasants to accept pre-plague wages and tightened their control over serfs to prevent them from fleeing to cities or other lords. At the same time, governments attempted to benefit from laborers' greater prosperity by imposing new taxes. In cities, where the plague had been particularly devastating, the demographic decline sharply lowered demand for goods and thus lowered the need for manufacturing and production of all kinds. Like rural landowners, master craftsmen sought legislation to protect their incomes. New laws reduced production by restricting access to trades and increased masters' control over the surviving urban laborers. Social mobility, once a characteristic of urban life, slowed to a halt. Membership in guilds became hereditary, and young apprentices and journeymen had little hope of ever rising to the level of independent master craftsmen.

These new tensions led to violence when kings added their demands for new war taxes to the landlords' and masters' attempts to erase the peasants' and workers' recent gains. The first revolts took place in France, where peasants and townspeople, disgusted with the incompetence of the nobility in their conduct of the war against England, feared that their new wealth would be stolen from them by corrupt and incompetent aristocrats.

The Jacquerie. In 1358, to ransom King John II from the English, the French government attempted to increase taxes on the peasantry. At the same time, local nobles increased their rents and demands. Peasants in the area of Beauvais, north of Paris, fearing that they would lose their modest gains of the previous ten years, rebelled against their landlords. The revolt—known as the **Jacquerie** for the archetypical French peasant, Jacques Bonnehomme—was a spontaneous outburst directed against the nobility, whom the peasants saw as responsible for all their ills. Without real leadership or program, peasants attacked as many nobles as they could find, killing men, women, and children and burning their homes and castles. Because the Church largely supported the power structure, the uprising was also strongly anticlerical. Churches were burned, and priests were killed. Success bred further attacks, and the disorganized army of peasants began to march south toward Paris, killing, looting, and burning everything associated with the despised nobility.

In the midst of this peasant revolt, Etienne Marcel (ca. 1316–1358), a wealthy Parisian cloth merchant, led an uprising of Parisian merchants, which sought to take control of royal finances and force fiscal reforms on the dauphin, the future Charles V. Although initially the rebels were primarily members of the merchant and guild elite, Marcel soon enlisted the support of the radical townspeople against the aristocracy. He even made overtures to the leaders of the Jacquerie to join forces. For a brief time it appeared that the aristocratic order in France might succumb. However, in the end, peasant and merchant rebels were no match for professional armies. The Jacquerie met its end at Meaux, outside Paris, where an aristocratic force cut the peasants to pieces. Survivors were systematically hunted down and hanged or burned alive. The Parisian revolt met a similar fate. Aristocratic armies surrounded the city and cut off its food supply. Marcel was assassinated, and the dauphin Charles regained the city.

The English Peasants' Revolt and Urban Uprisings. The French revolts set the pattern for similar uprisings across Europe. Rebels were usually relatively prosperous peasants or townspeople whose economic situations were threatened by aristocratic attempts to turn back the clock to the period before the Black Death. For example, in 1381, English peasants, reacting to new and hated taxes, rose in a less violent but more coordinated revolt known as the Great Rebellion. These outbursts indicated not necessarily the desperation of Europe's peasantry, but the new belief that they could change their lives for the better through united action.

Urban artisans imitated the example of their rural cousins. The town rebels were generally independent artisans and small tradesmen who wanted to break the control of the powerful guilds. In spite of the brutal suppression and ultimate failure of popular revolts, they became permanent if intermittent features on the European social landscape.

Living and Dying in Medieval Towns

Population decline, war, and class conflict in France and the Low Countries fatally weakened the vitality of the commercial and manufacturing system of northwestern Europe. These same events reduced the market for Italian goods and undermined the economic strength of the great Italian cities. Events outside of Europe also led to the decline of Italian economic power. In the course of the fourteenth and fifteenth centuries, the Mongol Khanates gradually lost power or were absorbed into local traditions. The disintegration of the Mongol Empire and the rise of new, aggressive kingdoms caused disruptions of the Silk Route and Italian trade with China and India. Soon, Europeans would begin to look for alternative routes to the east.

Economic Shifts. The setbacks of the Italians worked to the advantage of German towns in the disintegrating empire. Along the Baltic Sea, in Scandinavia, and in northern Germany, towns such as Lübeck, Lüneburg, Visby, Bremen, and Cologne formed a commercial and political alliance to control northern trade. During the second half of the fourteenth century this **Hanseatic League**—the word *hansa* means "company"—monopolized the northern grain trade and forced Denmark to grant its members exclusive rights to export Scandinavian fish throughout Europe. Hanseatic merchants established colonies from Novgorod to London to Bruges and even Venice. They carried dried and salted fish to Prague and supplied grain from Riga to England and France.

English towns also profited from the decline of Flanders and France. The population decline of the fourteenth century led many English landowners to switch from traditional farming to sheep raising, since pasturing sheep required few workers and promised cash profits. While surviving peasants were driven off the land and forced to beg for a living, lords produced more wool than ever before. However, instead of exporting the wool to Flanders to be made into cloth, the English began to make cloth themselves. Protected by high tariffs on imports and low duties on exports, England had become a major exporter of finished cloth by the middle of the fifteenth century.

Addressing Poverty and Crime. The combination of economic depression, plague, and rural crisis deepened the misery of the growing population of urban poor. Medieval towns responded by developing new means of public assistance and social control.

Traditionally, charity, whether by individuals or organizations, had been a religious act that focused more on the soul of the giver than on the life of the recipient. Hospitals, for example, were all-purpose religious institutions providing lodging for pilgrims, the elderly, and the ill. By the fourteenth century, such pious institutions had become inadequate to deal with the increasing numbers of poor and ill. Towns began to assume control over a centralized system of public assistance. Although men and women who had taken religious vows staffed these institutions, city governments contributed to their budgets and oversaw their finances. Cities also attempted to rationalize the distribution of charity according to need and merit. Antwerp, for example, established a centralized relief service, which distributed badges to those deemed worthy of public assistance. Only people who wore the badges could receive food.

Breaking on the wheel was a particularly gruesome punishment inflicted on condemned criminals during the later Middle Ages. The criminal's broken limbs are threaded through the spokes of the wheel and tied with ropes. The mocking executioner holding leftover rope stands at the right. To the left are three seemingly sympathetic spectators.

One consequence of poverty was increased crime, which led to repressive measures and harsh punishments. During the later Middle Ages, gruesome forms of mutilation and execution became common for a long list of offenses. Petty larceny was punished with whipping, cutting off ears or thumbs, branding, or expulsion. In some towns, robbery of an amount over three pence was punished with death. Death by hanging might be replaced by more savage punishments. Drowning, boiling, burning, and burial alive, a particularly common punishment for women, were frequently used methods of execution. The frequency of such punishments increased with their severity.

The Spirit of the Later Middle Ages

In spite of the constant presence of death, Europeans of the later Middle Ages celebrated life with vigor, creativity, and a growing sense of individuality and independence. During the fourteenth century, the Church failed to provide unified leadership. The institutional division of the Church was paralleled by divisions over how to lead the proper Christian life. Many devout Christians developed independent lifestyles that were intended to bring them closer to God without reliance on the Church hierarchy. Some elaborated beliefs that the church branded as heresy. Others called into question the philosophical bases of theological speculation that had developed since the time of Abelard and Aquinas. Finally, the increasing pluralism of European culture gave rise to new literary traditions that both celebrated and criticized the medieval legacy of Christianity, chivalry, and social order.

The Crisis of the Papacy

In 1305, the College of Cardinals elected as pope the bishop of Bordeaux. The new pope, who took the name Clement V (1305–1314), was close to Philip IV of France. Clement took up residence not in Rome but in the papal city of Avignon on the east bank of the Rhone River. Technically, Avignon was a papal estate within the Holy Roman Empire. Actually, with France just across the river, the pope at Avignon was under French control.

The Avignon Papacy. For the next 70 years, French popes and French cardinals ruled the Church. The traditional enemies of France as well as religious reformers who expected leadership from the papacy looked on this situation with disgust.

The popes of Avignon were more successful in achieving their financial goals than in winning political power. Although they attempted to follow an independent course in international affairs, their French orientation eroded their influence in European politics, especially in the Holy Roman Empire.

Frustrated politically, the Avignon popes concentrated on perfecting the legal and fiscal system of the Church and were enormously successful in concentrating the vast financial and legal power of the Church in the papal office. From the papal court, or *curia*, they created a vast and efficient central bureaucracy whose primary role was to increase papal revenues.

Revenues came from two main sources. The less lucrative but ultimately more critical source was the sale of **indulgences**. The Church claimed that the purchase of a papal indulgence could reduce the buyer's time in purgatory or be used to assist the souls of family members already in purgatory. Papal "pardoners" working on commission used high-pressure sales pitches to sell indulgences across Europe.

The second and major source of papal income was the sale of Church offices, or *benefices*. Popes claimed the right to appoint bishops and abbots to all benefices and to collect a hefty tax for the appointment. Papal appointees often acquired numerous offices and viewed them merely as sources of income, leaving pastoral duties, when they were performed at all, to hired local clergy.

The Great Schism. In 1377, Pope Gregory XI (1370–1378) returned from Avignon to Rome but died almost immediately on arrival. Thousands of Italians, afraid that the cardinals would elect another Frenchman, surrounded the church where they were meeting and demanded an Italian pope. The terrified cardinals elected an Italian, who took the name Urban VI (1378–1389). Once elected, Urban attempted to reform the curia, but he did so in a most undiplomatic way, insulting the cardinals and threatening to appoint enough non-French bishops to their number to end French control of the curia. The cardinals soon left Rome and announced that because the election had been made under duress, it was invalid and Urban should resign. When he refused, they held a second election and chose a Frenchman, Clement VII (1378–1394), who took up residence in Avignon. The Church now had two heads, both with reasonable claims to the office.

The chaos created by this so-called **Great Schism** divided Western Christendom. In every diocese, when a bishop died, his successor had to be appointed by the pope. But by which pope? To whom did taxes go? Who received the income from the sale of indulgences or benefices? Did appeals in the Church courts go to Rome or to Avignon? More significantly, since each pope excommunicated the supporters of his opponent, everyone in the West was under a sentence of excommunication. Could anyone be saved?

Nothing in Church law or tradition offered a solution to this crisis. Nor did unilateral efforts to settle the crisis succeed. France twice invaded Italy in an attempt to eliminate Urban but failed both times. When Urban and Clement died, cardinals on both sides elected successors. By the end of the fourteenth century, France and the empire were exasperated with their popes, and even the cardinals were determined to end the stalemate.

Conciliarism. Church lawyers argued that only a general council could end the schism. Both popes opposed **conciliarism** because it suggested that an assembly of the Church rather than the pope held supreme authority. However, in 1408, cardinals from both sides summoned a council in the Italian city of Pisa. The council deposed both rivals and elected a new pope. But this solution only made matters worse, since neither pope accepted the council's decision. Europe now had to contend with not two but three popes, each claiming to be the true successor of Saint Peter.

Six years later, the Council of Constance managed a final solution. There, under the patronage of the emperor-elect Sigismund (1410–1437), cardinals, bishops, abbots, and theologians from across Europe met to resolve the crisis. Their goal was not only to settle the schism but also to reform the Church to prevent a recurrence of such a scandal. The participants at Constance hoped to restructure the Church as a limited monarchy in which the powers of the pope would be controlled through frequent councils. The Pisan and Avignon popes were deposed. The Roman pope, abandoned by all of his supporters, abdicated. Before doing so, however, he formally convoked the council to preserve the tradition that a general council had to be called by the pope. Finally, the council elected as pope an Italian cardinal who was not aligned with any of the claimants. The election of the cardinal, who took the name of Martin V (1417–1431), ended the schism.

The relief at the end of the Great Schism could not hide the very real problems left by over a century of papal weakness. The prestige of the papacy had been permanently compromised. Everywhere, the Church had become more national in character. The conciliarist demand for control of the Church, which had ended the schism, lessened the power of the pope. Moreover, during the century between Boniface VIII and Martin V, new religious movements had taken root across Europe, movements that the political creatures who had occupied the papal office could neither understand nor control. The disintegration of the Church loomed ever closer as pious individuals turned away from the organized Church and sought divine help in personal piety, mysticism, or even magic.

Discerning the Spirit of God

When Joan of Arc first appeared before the dauphin in 1429, he feared that she was a witch. Only a physical examination by matrons, which determined that she was a virgin, persuaded him otherwise—witches were believed to have had intercourse with the devil. Everyone in the late Middle Ages was familiar with witches, saints, and heretics. Distinguishing among them was often a matter of perspective.

Witchcraft. Accusations of witchcraft were relatively rare in the Middle Ages. The age of witch hunts occurred later, in the sixteenth and seventeenth centuries. During the Middle Ages, magic was believed to exist in a wide variety of forms, but its definition was fluid, and its practitioners were not always considered evil. Only at the end of the fifteenth century, with the publication of the *Witches' Hammer,* a handbook for inquisitors, did the European witch craze begin in earnest. Earlier, authorities feared more those people who sought their own pacts not with the devil but with God.

Lay Piety. Even as Europeans were losing respect for the institutional Church, people everywhere were seeking closer and more intimate relationships with God.

Distrusting the formal institutions of the Church, lay persons and clerics turned to private devotions and to mysticism to achieve union with the divine.

In the fourteenth and fifteenth centuries, a great many pious lay men and women chose to live together to strive for spiritual perfection without entering established religious orders. The Brethren of the Common Life in the Rhineland and Low Countries dedicated themselves to preaching, charity, and a pious life.

Christians of the later Middle Ages sought to imitate Christ and venerated the Eucharist, or communion wafer, which the Church taught was the actual body of Jesus. Male mystics focused on imitating Jesus in his poverty, his suffering, and his humility. Women developed their own form of piety, which focused not on wealth and power but on spiritual nourishment, particularly as provided by the Eucharist. For women mystics, radical fasting became preparation for the reception of the Eucharist, which was often described in highly emotional and erotic terms.

Heresy and Revolt

Only a thin line separated the saint's heroic search for union with God from the heretic's identification with God. Members of the sect were hunted down, and many were burned as heretics. The specter of the Inquisition, the ecclesiastical court system that was charged with ferreting out heretics, hung over all such communities.

John Wycliffe. When unorthodox Christians were protected by secular lords, the ecclesiastical courts were powerless. This was the case with John Wycliffe (ca. 1330–1384), an Oxford theologian who attacked the doctrinal and political bases of the Church. He taught that the value of the sacraments depended on the worthiness of the priest administering them, that Jesus was present in the Eucharist only in spirit, that indulgences were useless, and that salvation depended on divine predestination rather than individual merit. Normally, these teachings would have led him to the stake. But he had also attacked the Church's right to wealth and luxury, an idea whose political implications pleased the English monarchy and nobility. Only under Henry V (1413–1422) were Wycliffe's followers, known as Lollards, vigorously suppressed by the state. Before this condemnation took place, however, Wycliffe's teachings reached the kingdom of Bohemia through the marriage of Charles IV's daughter Anne of Bohemia to the English king Richard II. Anne took with her to England a number of Bohemian clerics, some of whom studied at Oxford and absorbed Wycliffe's political and religious teachings, which they then took back to Bohemia.

Jan Hus. In Prague, some of Wycliffe's less radical teachings took root among the theology faculty of the new university, where the leading proponent of Wycliffe's teachings was Jan Hus (1373–1415), an immensely popular young master and preacher. Although Hus rejected Wycliffe's ideas about the priesthood and the sacraments, he and other Czech preachers attacked indulgences and demanded a reform of Church liturgy and morals. They grafted these religious demands onto an attack on German dominance of the Bohemian kingdom. These attacks outraged both the Pisan pope John XXIII (1410–1415) and the Bohemian king Wenceslas IV (1378–1419), who favored the German faction. The pope excommunicated Hus, and the king expelled the Czech faculty from the university. Hus was convinced that he was no heretic and that a fair hearing would clear him. He therefore agreed to travel to the Council of Constance under promise of safe conduct from the emperor-elect Sigismund to defend his position. There, he was tried on a charge of heresy, convicted, and burned at the stake.

News of Hus's execution touched off a revolt in Bohemia. Unlike the peasant revolts of the past, however, this revolt had broad popular support throughout all levels of Czech society. Peasants, nobles, and townspeople saw the attack on Hus and his followers as an attack on Czech independence and national interest by a Church and an empire controlled by Germans. Soon a radical faction known as the Taborites was demanding the abolition of private property and the institution of a communal state. Although moderate **Hussites** and Bohemian Catholics combined to defeat the radicals in 1434, most of Bohemia remained Hussite through the fifteenth century. The sixteenth-century reformer Martin Luther declared himself a follower of Jan Hus.

Religious Persecution in Spain

Through the thirteenth century, even as kings of England and France expelled Jews from their kingdoms and as they were subjected to sporadic pogroms and massacres in Germany, Jews and Muslims were tolerated on the Iberian Penninsula. This fragile existence was shattered in the fourteenth and fifteenth centuries. The causes were complex: a declining economy, political unrest, Christian triumphalism as the reconquest moved into its last stages, and nascent nationalism all increased intercultural tensions. In 1391, mendicant friars inflamed Aragon with preaching against Jews and caused widespread violent attacks. Thereafter, in towns across Spain Christians rose up in arms against their Jewish neighbors in riots animated both by a hatred of Jews and a protest against the king. Thousands died and thousands more were forced to convert.

The Muslim population fared no better. In the fifteenth century, Muslims faced conversion or expulsion, first to Granada and, after that last Muslim principality fell in 1492, to North Africa. Those who resisted were hunted down, their villages destroyed, and their populations dispersed.

William of Ockham and the Spirit of Truth

As in other areas of life in the later Middle Ages, intellectuals questioned the basic suppositions of their predecessors, directing intellectual activity away from general speculations and toward particular, observable reality.

The person primarily responsible for this new intellectual climate was the English Franciscan William of Ockham (ca. 1300–1349). Excommunicated for his defense of radical poverty, Ockham joined the imperialist cause at the court of Emperor

Louis IV. Imperial power, he argued, derived not from the pope but from the people. He believed that people should be free to determine their own form of government and to elect rulers. They should be able to make their choice directly, as in the election of the emperor by electors who represent the people, or implicitly, through continuing forms of government. In either case, Ockham believed, government should be entirely secular and neither popes nor bishops nor priests should have any role. Ockham went still further. He denied the absolute authority of the pope, even in spiritual matters. Rather, Ockham argued, parishes, religious orders, and monasteries should send representatives to regional synods, which in turn would elect representatives to general councils. Ockham's ideas on Church governance offered the one hope for a solution to the Great Schism that erupted shortly after his death. The Council of Constance, which ended the schism, was the fruit of Ockham's political theory.

As radical as Ockham's political ideas were, his philosophical outlook was even more extreme and exerted a more direct and lasting influence. The Christian Aristotelianism that developed in the thirteenth century had depended on the validity of general concepts called universals, which could be analyzed through the use of logic. Aquinas and others who studied the eternity of the world, the existence of God, the nature of the soul, and other philosophical questions believed that people could reach general truths by abstracting universals from particular, individual cases. Ockham argued that universals were merely names, no more than convenient tags for discussing individual things. He stated that universals had no connection with reality and could not be used to reason from particular observations to general truths. This radical **nominalism** (from the Latin *nomen*, "name") thus denied that human reason could aspire to certain truth. For Ockham and his followers, philosophical speculation was essentially a logical, linguistic exercise, not a way to certain knowledge.

Just as Ockham's political theory dominated the later fourteenth century, his nominalist philosophy won over the philosophical faculties of Europe. Since he had discredited the value of Aristotelian logic to increase knowledge, the result was, on the one hand, a decline in abstract speculation and, on the other, a greater interest in scientific observation of individual phenomena. In the next generation, Parisian professors, trained in the tradition of Ockham, laid the foundation for scientific studies of motion and the universe that led to the scientific discoveries of the sixteenth and seventeenth centuries.

Vernacular Literature and the Individual

Just as the religious and philosophical concerns of the later Middle Ages developed within national frameworks and criticized accepted authority from the perspective of individual experience, so too did the vernacular (as opposed to Latin) literatures of the age begin to explore the place of the individual within an increasingly complex society. Across Europe, authors reviewed the traditional values of society with a critical eye, reworking and transforming traditional literary genres into statements both personal and profound.

Italy. In Italy, a trio of Tuscan poets, Dante Alighieri (1265–1321), Petrarch (1304–1374), and Boccaccio (1313–1375), not only made Italian a literary language but composed in it some of the greatest literature of all time. Dante, the first and greatest of the three, wrote the *Divine Comedy* during the last years of his life.

The *Divine Comedy* is a view of the whole Christian universe, populated with people from antiquity and from Dante's own day. The poem is both a sophisticated summary of philosophical and theological thought at the beginning of the fourteenth century and an astute political commentary on his times. The poet sets this vision within a three-part poetic journey through hell (*Inferno*), purgatory (*Purgatorio*), and heaven (*Paradiso*). The *Divine Comedy* is Dante's personal summary of all that is good and bad in medieval culture and politics.

England. Dante had set his great poem within a vision of the other world. Emerging English literature was more firmly rooted in contemporary society. William Langland (ca. 1330–1395) and Geoffrey Chaucer (ca. 1343–1400) both presented images of their social milieu. In *Piers Plowman*, Langland presents society from the perspective of the peasantry. Chaucer's work, *The Canterbury Tales*, is much more sophisticated and wide-ranging, weaving together the whole spectrum of late medieval literature and life.

Chaucer placed his tales in the mouths of a group of 30 pilgrims traveling to the tomb of Thomas à Becket at Canterbury. The tales that they tell are drawn from folklore, Italian literature, the lives of the saints, courtly romance, and religious sermons. However, Chaucer played with the tales and their genres in the retelling. In his mastery of the whole heritage of medieval culture and his independent use of this heritage, Chaucer proved himself the greatest English writer before Shakespeare.

Chronology

THE LATER MIDDLE AGES, 1300–1500

1305–1377	Babylonian Captivity (Avignon papacy)
1337–1452	Hundred Years' War
1347–1352	Black Death spreads throughout Europe
1358	Jacquerie revolt of French peasants; Etienne Marcel leads revolt of Parisian merchants
1378–1417	Great Schism divides Christianity
1381	Great Rebellion of English peasants
1409–1410	Council of Pisa
1414–1417	Council of Constance ends Great Schism
1415	Jan Hus executed
1431	Death of Joan of Arc
1455–1485	English Wars of the Roses

France. Much of Italian and English literature drew material and inspiration from French, which continued into the fifteenth century to be the language of courtly romance, projecting an unreal world of allegory and nostalgia for a glorious if imaginary past. Popular literature, which developed largely in the towns, often dealt with courtly themes but with a critical and more realistic eye.

In this literary world an extraordinary woman, who was widowed at 25, was able to earn a living for herself and her family with her pen. As a successful woman of letters, Christine de Pisan (1364–ca. 1430) fought the stereotypical medieval image of women as weak, sexually aggressive temptresses. With wit and reason, she argued that women could be virtuous and showed the fallacies of traditional antifeminist preaching, poetry, and belief. Christine's life and writing epitomized the new possibilities and new interests of the fifteenth century. They included an acute sense of individuality, a willingness to look for truth not in the clichés of the past but in actual experience, and a readiness to defend one's views with tenacity. Although an heir of the medieval world, Christine, like her contemporaries, already embodied the attitudes of a new age.

That new age was reflected in a second tradition in fifteenth-century France, that of realist poetry. Around 1453, just as the English troops were enduring a final battering from the French artillery, Duke Charles of Orléans (1394–1465) organized a poetry contest. Each contestant was to write a ballad that began with the contradictory line "I die of thirst beside the fountain." The duke, himself an outstanding poet, wrote an entry that embodied the traditional courtly themes of love and fortune.

An unexpected and very different entry came from the duke's prison. The prisoner-poet, François Villon (1432–ca. 1464), was a child of the Paris streets, an impoverished student, a barroom brawler, a killer, and a thief. He was also the greatest realist poet of the Middle Ages, and his poetry won him release from prison. His entry read:

> I die of thirst beside the fountain,
> Hot as fire, my teeth clattering,
> At home I am in an alien land;
> I shudder beside a glowing brazier,
> Naked as a worm, gloriously dressed,
> I laugh and cry and wait without hope,
> I take comfort and sad despair,
> I rejoice and have no joy,
> Powerful, I have no force and no strength,
> Well received, I am expelled by all.

The duke focused on the sufferings of love, the thief on the physical sufferings of the downtrodden. The two poets represent the contradictory tendencies of literature in the later Middle Ages. The themes and ideas that were expressed ranged from the polished, traditional values of the aristocracy trying to maintain the ideals of chivalry in a new and changed world to the views of ordinary people, by turns reverent or sarcastic, joyful or despondent.

SUMMARY

Politics as a Family Affair   In the fourteenth and fifteenth centuries, politics centered on the ambitions of great families. This was particularly the case in central Europe, where five families competed for control of the Holy Roman Empire. Emperor Charles IV helped spark cultural renewal in central Europe. His Golden Bull contributed to political disintegration of the empire. Dynastic issues played a central role in the Hundred Years' War. Early English successes gave way to eventual French victory. The monarchies of both France and England were damaged by the war. Civil war in England followed defeat in France, with the Tudor family emerging triumphant.

Life and Death in the Later Middle Ages   Famine and disease decimated the population of Europe. Between 1347 and 1352, the Black Death killed between one-third and one-half of Europe's population. Responses to the plague varied widely. Social disruption followed demographic collapse. Peasants and townspeople fought to hold onto gains made in the aftermath of the plague. Events in Europe and abroad contributed to a decline in Italian economic power. The Hanseatic League dominated the Baltic trade. Towns employed new measures to address poverty and crime.

The Spirit of the Later Middle Ages   The papacy declined in the fourteenth century. During the Avignon papacy, French popes concentrated the financial and legal power of the Church in the papal office. The Great Schism resulted in a divided Christendom and weakened the papacy. Belief in witchcraft was widespread in the Middle Ages, but witchcraft trials were rare. Disgust with the formal institutions of the Church stimulated a turn to private devotion, mysticism, and sometimes heresy. John Wycliffe and Jan Hus led important challenges to the Church. The persecution of Jews and Muslims in Spain grew out of religious and political anxieties. William of Ockham challenged the Aristotelian foundations of medieval scholarship. The vernacular literatures of the later Middle Ages explored the place of the individual within a complex society.

QUESTIONS FOR REVIEW

1. What social and political forces prevented both the Holy Roman Emperors and the French kings from uniting the lands they ruled?
2. How did disease transform social relations in fourteenth-century Europe?
3. Why did a division in the papacy mean both political chaos and spiritual fear for Europeans?
4. How did the vernacular literature of Dante, Chaucer, and Christine de Pisan represent a departure from previous literary traditions?

The Italian Renaissance

Renaissance Society

What was the Renaissance? A French word for an Italian phenomenon, *renaissance* literally means "rebirth." The word captures both the emphasis on humanity that characterized Renaissance thinking and the renewed fascination with the classical world. But the Renaissance was an age rather than an event. There is no moment at which the Middle Ages ended. Late medieval society was artistically creative, socially well developed, and economically diverse. Yet eventually, the pace of change accelerated, and it is best to think of the Renaissance as an era of rapid transitions. Encompassing the two centuries between 1350 and 1550, it passed through three distinct phases. The first, from 1350 to 1400, was characterized by a declining population, the uncovering of classical texts, and experimentation in a variety of art forms. The second phase, from 1400 to 1500, was distinguished by the creation of a set of cultural values and artistic and literary achievements that defined Renaissance style. The large Italian city-states developed stable and coherent forms of government and the warfare between them gradually ended. In the final period, from 1500 to 1550, invasions from France and Spain transformed Italian political life, and the ideas and techniques of Italian writers and artists radiated to all points of the Continent.

Cities and Countryside

The Italian peninsula differed sharply from other areas of Europe in the extent to which it was urban. By the late Middle Ages, nearly one in four Italians lived in a town, in contrast to one in ten elsewhere. Not even the plague did much to change this ratio. By 1500, seven of the ten largest cities in the West were in Italy. Naples, Venice, and Milan, each with a population of more than 100,000, led the rest. But it was the numerous smaller towns, with populations nearer to 1,000, that gave the Italian peninsula its urban character. Cities dominated their regions economically, politically, and culturally and served as convenient centers of judicial and ecclesiastical power. The diversified activities of their inhabitants created vast concentrations of wealth, and Italy was the banking capital of the world.

Although cities may have dominated Renaissance Italy, by present standards they were small in both area and population. A person could walk across fifteenth-century Florence in less than half an hour. In 1427, its population was 37,000, only half its pre-plague size.

Urban populations were organized far differently than rural ones. On the farms the central distinctions involved ownership of land. Some farmers owned their estates outright and left them intact to their heirs. Others were involved in a sharecropping system by which absentee owners of land supplied working capital in return for half of the farm's produce. A great gulf in wealth separated owners from sharecroppers. Those who owned their land normally lived with surplus; those who sharecropped always lived on the margin of subsistence.

In the city, however, distinctions were based first on occupation, which largely corresponded to social position and wealth. Cities began as markets, and the privilege to participate in the market defined citizens. City governments provided protection for consumers and producers by creating monopolies through which standards for craftsmanship were maintained and profits for craftsmen were guaranteed. These monopolies were called guilds or companies. Each large city had its own hierarchy of guilds. At the top were the important manufacturing groups—clothiers, metalworkers, and the like. Just below them were bankers, merchants, and the administrators of civic and Church holdings. At the bottom were grocers, masons, and other skilled workers. Roughly speaking, all of those within the guild structure, from bottom to top, lived comfortably. Yet the majority of urban inhabitants were not members of guilds. Many managed to eke out a living as wage laborers; many more were simply destitute. As a group, these poor people constituted as much as half of the entire population. Most depended on civic and private charity for their very survival.

MAP DISCOVERY

LARGEST CITIES IN WESTERN EUROPE, CA. 1500

Examine the locations of western Europe's largest cities at the beginning of the sixteenth century. Where were these cities concentrated? What was the least urbanized part of Europe? Based on this information, why do you suppose the Mediterranean Sea was considered the center of Europe? What was distinctive about the Holy Roman Empire?

The disparities between rich and poor were overwhelming. The concentration of wealth in the hands of an ever-narrowing group of families and favored guilds characterized every large city. In Florence, for example, 10 percent of the families controlled 90 percent of the wealth, with an even more extreme concentration at the top.

Production and Consumption

The concentration of wealth and the way in which it was used defined the Renaissance economy. Economic life is bound up in the relationship between supply and demand. The late medieval economy, despite the development of international banking and long-distance trade, was still an economy of primary producers: Between 70 and 90 percent of Europe's population was involved in subsistence agriculture. Even in Italy, which contained the greatest concentration of urban areas in the world, agriculture predominated. The manufacture of clothing was the only other significant economic activity. Most of what was produced was for local consumption rather than for the marketplace. Even in good times, more than 80 percent of the population lived at subsistence level with food, clothing, and shelter their only expenses. Therefore, when we discuss the market economy of the Renaissance, we are discussing the circumstances of the few rather than the many.

The defining characteristic of the early Renaissance economy was population change. Recurring waves of plague kept population levels low for more than a century. This dramatic reduction in population depressed economic growth. The general economy did not revive until the sustained population increase toward the end of the fifteenth century. Until then, in both agriculture and manufacturing, supply outstripped demand.

On the farms, surviving farmers occupied the best land and enlarged their holdings. In the shops, finished products outnumbered the consumers who survived the epidemics. Overproduction meant lower prices for basic commodities, and the decline in population meant higher wages for labor. At the lowest levels of society, survivors found it easier to earn their living and even to create a surplus than had their parents. For a time the lot of the masses improved.

But for investors, such economic conditions meant that neither agriculture nor cloth making was particularly attractive. In such circumstances, consumption was more attractive than investment, but it was not merely the perceived shortage of profitable investment opportunities that brought on the increase in conspicuous consumption during the fifteenth century. In the psychological atmosphere created by unpredictable, swift, and deadly epidemics, luxurious living seemed an appropriate response. Moreover, although tax rates increased, houses and personal property normally remained exempt, making luxury goods attractive investments. For these reasons the production and consumption of luxuries soared.

The Experience of Life

Luxury helped to improve a life that for rich and poor alike was short and uncertain. Renaissance children who survived infancy found their lives governed by parentage and by gender. In parentage, the great divide was between those who lived with surplus and those who lived at subsistence. The first category encompassed the wealthiest bankers and merchants down to those who owned their own farms or engaged in small urban crafts. The vast majority of urban and rural dwellers were members of the second category. About the children of the poor we know very little, other than that their survival was unlikely. Eldest sons were favored; younger daughters were disadvantaged. In poor families, however, this favoritism meant little more than early apprenticeship to day labor in the city or farm labor in the countryside. Girls were frequently sent out as domestic servants far from the family home.

Childhood. Children of the wealthy had better chances for survival than did children of the poor. For the better off, childhood might begin with "milk parents," in the home of the family of a wet nurse who would breast-feed the baby through infancy.

Only the very wealthy could afford a live-in wet nurse, which would increase the child's chances of survival. Again, daughters were more likely to be sent far from home and least likely to have their nursing supervised.

During the period between weaning and apprenticeship, Renaissance children lived with their families. Sons could expect to be apprenticed to a trade, probably between the ages of 10 and 13. Most, of course, learned the crafts of their fathers, but not necessarily in their father's shop. Sons inherited the family business and its most important possessions—tools of the trade or beasts of labor for the farm.

Marriage and the Family. Expectations for daughters centered on their chances of marriage. For a girl, dowry was everything. If a girl's father could provide a handsome one, her future was secure; if not, the alternatives were a convent, which would take a small bequest, or a match lower down the social scale, where the quality of life deteriorated rapidly. Daughters of poor families entered domestic service in order to have a dowry provided by their masters. The dowry was taken to the household of the husband. There, the couple resided until they established their own separate family. If the husband died, it was to his parental household that the widow returned.

Women married in late adolescence, usually around the age of 20. Among the wealthy, marriages were perceived as familial alliances and business transactions rather than love matches. The dowry was an investment on which fathers expected a return, and while the bride might have some choice, it was severely limited. Compatibility was not a central feature in matchmaking. Husbands were, on the average, ten years older than their wives and likely to leave them widows.

Men married later—near the age of 25 on the farms, nearer 30 in the cities because of the cost of setting up in trade or on the land. Late marriage meant long supervision under the watchful eye of father or master, an extended period between adolescence and adulthood. Many men, even with families, never succeeded in setting up separately from their fathers or older brothers.

Men came of age at 30 but were thought to be old by 50. Thus for men, marriage and parenthood took place in middle age rather than in youth. Valued all their lives more highly than their sisters, male heads of households were the source of all power in their domiciles, in their shops, and in the state. They were responsible for overseeing every aspect of the upbringing of their children. But their wives were essential partners who governed domestic life. Women labored not only at the hearth, but in the fields and shops as well. Their economic contribution to the well-being of the family was critical, both in the dowry they brought at marriage and in the labor they contributed to the household. If their wives died, men with young children remarried quickly.

In most cases, death came suddenly. Epidemic diseases, of which plague was the most virulent, struck with fearful regularity. They struck harder at the young—children and adolescents, who were the majority of the population—and hardest in the summer months, when other viruses and bacteria weakened the population.

Starvation was rare, less because of food shortage than because the seriously under-nourished were more likely to succumb to disease than to famine. In urban areas, the government would intervene to provide grain from public storehouses at times of extreme shortage; in the countryside, large landholders commonly exercised the same function.

The Quality of Life

Although life may have been difficult during the Renaissance, it was not unfulfilling. Despite constant toil and frequent hardship, people of the Renaissance had reason to believe that their lives were better than those of their ancestors and that their children's lives would be better still. On the most basic level, health improved and, for those who survived plague, life expectancy increased owing to the relative surplus of grain throughout the fifteenth century and the wider variety of foods consumed. This diversification of diet resulted from improvements in transportation and communication, which brought more goods and services to a growing number of towns in the chain that linked the regional centers to the rural countryside.

The towns and cities also introduced a new sense of social and political cohesiveness. The city was something to which people belonged. In urban areas, they could join social groups of their own choosing and develop networks of support that were not possible in rural environments. Blood relations remained the primary social group. Kin were the most likely source of aid in times of need, and charity began at home. Kin groups extended well beyond the immediate family, with both cousins and in-laws laying claim to the privileges of blood. The urban family could also depend on the connections of neighborhood. In some Italian cities, wealth or occupation determined housing patterns. In others, like Florence, rich and poor lived side by side and identified themselves with their small administrative unit and with their local church. Thus they could participate in relationships with others both above and below them in social scale. From their superiors they gained connections that helped their families; from their inferiors they gained devoted clients.

As in the Middle Ages, the Church remained the spatial, spiritual, and social center of people's lives. Though Renaissance society became more worldly in outlook, this worldliness took place within the context of an absorbing devotional life. The Church provided explanations for both the mysterious and the mundane. The clergy performed the rituals of baptism, marriage, and burial that measured the passage of life. Religious symbols also adorned the flags of militia troops, the emblems of guilds, and the regalia of the city itself. The Church preserved holy relics that were venerated for their power to protect the city or to endow it with particular skills and resources. Through its holy days, as much as through its rituals, the Church helped to channel leisure activities into community celebrations.

A growing sense of civic pride and individual accomplishment were underlying characteristics of the Italian Renaissance, enhanced by the development of social cohesion and community solidarity that both Church and city-state fostered. The Renaissance was not an event whose causes were the result of the efforts of the few or whose consequences were limited to the privileged. In fact, the Renaissance was not an event at all. Family values that permitted early apprenticeships in surrogate households and emphasized the continuity of crafts from one generation to the next made possible the skilled artists of the Renaissance cities. The stress on the production of luxury goods placed higher value on individual skills and therefore on excellence in workmanship. Church and state sought to express social values through representational art. One of the chief purposes of wall murals was to instruct the unlettered in religion, to help them visualize the central episodes in Christian history. The grandiose architecture and statuary that adorned central places were designed to enhance civic pride and communicate the protective power of public institutions.

Renaissance Art

In every age, artistic achievement represents a combination of individual talent and predominant social ideals. Artists may be at the leading edge of the society in which they live, but it is the spirit of that society that they capture in word or song or image. Artistic disciplines also have their own technical development. Individually, Renaissance artists were attempting to solve problems about perspective and three-dimensionality that had defeated their predecessors. But the particular techniques or experiments that interested them owed as much to the social context as they did to the artistic one. For example, the urban character of Italian government led to the need for civic architecture, public buildings on a grand scale. The celebration of individual achievement led to the explosive growth of portraiture. Not surprisingly, major technological breakthroughs were achieved in both areas.

This relationship between artist and social context was especially important in the Renaissance, when artists were closely tied to the crafts and trades of urban society and to the demands of clients who commissioned their work. Although it was the elite who patronized art, it was skilled tradespeople who produced it. Artists normally followed the pattern of any craftsman: An apprenticeship begun as a teenager and a long period of training and work in a master's shop. This form of education gave the aspiring artist a practical bent and a keen appreciation for the business side of art. Studios were identified with particular styles and competed for commissions from clients, especially the Church. Wealthy individuals commissioned art as investments, as marks of personal distinction, and as displays of public piety.

The survival of so many Renaissance masterpieces allows us to reconstruct the stages by which the remarkable artistic achievements of this era took place. Although advances were made in a variety of fields during the Renaissance, the three outstanding areas were architecture, sculpture, and painting. Few Renaissance artists confined themselves to one area of artistic expression, and many created works of enduring beauty in more than one medium.

An Architect, a Sculptor, and a Painter

The century that culminated in Michelangelo's extraordinary achievements began with the work of three Florentine masters who deeply influenced one another's development: Brunelleschi (1377–1446), Donatello (1386–1466), and Masaccio (1401–1428). In the Renaissance, the dominant artistic discipline was architecture. Buildings were the most expensive investment patrons could make, and the technical knowledge necessary for their successful construction was immense. By 1400, the Gothic style of building had dominated western Europe for over two centuries. Its characteristic pointed arches, vaulted ceilings, and slender spires had simplified building by removing the heavy walls that were formerly thought necessary to support great structures. Gothic construction permitted greater height, a characteristic that was especially desirable in cathedrals, which stretched toward the heavens.

It was Brunelleschi who decisively challenged the principles of Gothic architecture by recombining its basic elements with those of classical structures. Basing his designs on geometric principles, Brunelleschi reintroduced planes and spheres as dominant motifs. His greatest work was the dome on the cathedral in Florence, begun in 1420. Brunelleschi is generally credited with having been the first Renaissance artist to have understood and made use of perspective, though it was immediately put to more dramatic effect in sculpture and painting.

In sculpture, the survival of Roman and Hellenistic pieces, mostly bold and muscular torsos, conveyed the direct influence of classical art. Donatello translated these classical styles into more naturalistic forms. Donatello revived the free-standing statue, which demanded greater attention to human anatomy because it was viewed from many angles. He also led the revival of the equestrian statue, sculpting the Venetian captain-general Gattamelata for a public square in Padua. This enormous bronze horse and rider (1445–1450) relied on the standpoint of the viewer to achieve its overpowering effect. This use of **linear perspective** is also seen in Donatello's breathtaking altar scenes of the miracles of Saint Anthony in Padua, which resemble nothing so much as a canvas cast in bronze.

These altar scenes evince the unmistakable influence of the paintings of Masaccio. His frescoes in the Brancacci Chapel in Florence were studied and sketched by all of the great artists of the next generation, who unreservedly praised his naturalism. What most claim the attention of the modern viewer are Masaccio's shading of light and shadow and his brilliant use of linear perspective to create the illusion that a flat surface has three dimensions.

Renaissance Style

By the middle of the fifteenth century, a recognizable Renaissance style had triumphed. The outstanding architect of this period was Leon Battista Alberti (1404–1472), whose treatise *On Building* (1452) remained the most influential work on the subject until the eighteenth century. Alberti consecrated the geometric principles laid down by Brunelleschi and infused them with a humanist spirit. He

Donatello's bronze statue *Judith Slaying Holofernes* symbolized the Florentines' love of liberty and hatred of tyranny.

revived the classical dictum that a building, like a body, should have an even number of supports and, like a head, an odd number of openings. This furthered precise geometric calculations in scale and design.

No sculptor challenged the preeminence of Donatello for another 50 years, but in painting there were many contenders for the garlands worn by Masaccio. The first was Piero della Francesca (ca. 1420–1492), who broke new ground in his concern for the visual unity of his paintings. Another challenger was Sandro Botticelli (1445–1510), whose classical themes, sensitive portraits, and bright colors set him apart from the line of Florentine painters with whom he studied.

This concern with beauty and personality is also seen in the paintings of Leonardo da Vinci (1452–1519), whose creative genius embodied the Renaissance ideal of the "universal man." Leonardo's achievements in scientific, technical, and artistic endeavors read like a list of all of the subjects known during the Renaissance. His detailed anatomical drawings and the method he devised for rendering them, his botanical observations, and his engineering inventions (including models for a tank and an airplane) testify to his unrestrained curiosity. His paintings reveal a continuation of the scientific application of mathematics to matters of proportion and perspective.

From Brunelleschi to Alberti, from Masaccio to Leonardo da Vinci, Renaissance artists placed a unique stamp upon visual culture. By reviving classical themes, geometric principles, and a spirit of human vitality, they broke decisively from the dominant medieval traditions. Art became a source of individual and collective pride, produced by masters, but consumed by all. Cities and wealthy patrons commissioned great works of art for public display. New buildings rose everywhere, adorned with the statues and murals that still stand as a testimony to generations of artists.

Michelangelo

The artistic achievements of the Renaissance culminated in the creative outpourings of Michelangelo Buonarroti (1475–1564). Uncharacteristically, he came from a family of standing in Florentine society. At the age of 14, over the opposition of his father, he was apprenticed to a leading painter and spent his spare time in Florentine churches, copying the works of Masaccio, among others.

In 1490, Michelangelo gained a place in the household of Lorenzo de Medici. He claimed to have taught himself sculpturing during this two-year period, a remarkable feat considering the skills required. In the Medici household he came into contact with leading Neoplatonists, who taught that humankind was on an ascending journey of perfectibility toward God. These ideas can be seen as one source of the heroic concept of humanity that Michelangelo brought to his work.

In 1496, Michelangelo moved to Rome, where his abilities as a sculptor brought him to the attention of Jacopo Galli, a banker. Galli commissioned a classical work for himself and procured another for a French cardinal, which became the *Pietà*. The *Pietà* created a sensation in Rome, and by the time Michelangelo returned to Florence in 1501, at the age of 26, he was already acknowledged as one of the great sculptors of his day. He was immediately commissioned to work on an enormous block of marble that had been quarried nearly a half-century before and had defeated the talents of a series of carvers. He worked continuously for three years on his *David* (1501–1504), a piece that completed the union between classical and Renaissance styles.

Though Michelangelo always believed himself to be primarily a sculptor, his next outstanding work was in the field of painting. In 1508, Pope Julius II summoned Michelangelo to Rome and commissioned him to decorate the ceiling of the small ceremonial chapel that had been built next to the new papal residence. Michelangelo's plan was to portray, in an extended narrative, human creation and those Old Testament events that foreshadowed the birth of the Savior. His representations were simple and compelling: The fingers of God and Adam nearly touching, Eve with one leg still emerging from Adam's side, and the half-human snake in the temptation are all majestically evocative.

The *Pietà*, the *David*, and the paintings of the Sistine Chapel were the work of youth. Michelangelo's crowning achievement, the building of Saint Peter's basilica in Rome, was the work of age. The base work of Saint Peter's had already been laid, and drawings for its completion had been made 30 years earlier by Donato Bramante. Michelangelo altered these plans in an effort to bring more light into the church and to provide a more majestic facade outside. His main contribution, however, was the design of the great dome, which centered the interior of the church on Saint Peter's grave. More than the height, it is the harmony of Michelangelo's design that creates the sense of the building thrusting upward like a Gothic cathedral of old. Michelangelo did not live to see the dome of Saint Peter's completed.

Renaissance art served Renaissance society, reflecting both its concrete achievements and its visionary ideals. This art was a synthesis of old and new, building on classical models, particularly in sculpture and architecture, but adding newly discovered techniques and skills. But Renaissance artists did more than construct and adorn buildings or celebrate and beautify spiritual life. Inevitably, their work expressed the ideals and aspirations of the society in which they lived—the new emphasis on learning and knowledge, on the here and now rather than the hereafter, and, most important, on humanity and its capacity for growth and perfection.

Renaissance Ideals

Renaissance thought went hand in glove with Renaissance art. Scholars and philosophers searched the works of the ancients to find the principles on which to build a better life. They scoured monastic libraries for forgotten manuscripts, discovering, among other things, Greek poetry, history, the works of Homer and Plato, and Aristotle's *Poetics*. Their rigorous application of scholarly procedures for the collection and collation of these texts was one of the most important contributions of the Renaissance intellectuals who came to be known as **humanists.** Although humanism was by no means antireligious, it was thoroughly secular in outlook.

Humanists celebrated worldly achievements. Pico della Mirandola's *Oration on the Dignity of Man* (1486) is the best known of a multitude of Renaissance writings influenced by the discovery of the works of Plato. Pico believed that people could perfect their existence on earth because God had endowed humans with the capacity to determine their own fate. This emphasis on human potential found expression in the celebration of human achievement.

Thus humanists studied and taught the humanities, the skills of disciplines such as **philology**, the art of language, and **rhetoric**, the art of expression. Though they were mostly lay people, humanists applied their learning to both religious and secular studies. Their interest in human achievement and human potential must be set beside their religious beliefs. As Petrarch stated quite succinctly, "Christ is my God; Cicero is the prince of the language I use."

Humanists and the Liberal Arts

The most important achievements of humanist scholars centered on ancient texts. It was the humanists' goal to discover as much as had survived from the ancient world and to provide texts of classical authors that were as full and accurate as possible.

The creation of Adam and Eve, a detail from Michelangelo's frescoes on the ceiling of the Sistine Chapel. The Sistine frescoes had become obscured by dirt and layers of varnish and glue applied at various times over the years. In the 1980s, they were cleaned to reveal their original colors.

Studying the Classical World. Although much was already known of the Latin classics, few of the central works of ancient Greece had been recovered. Humanists preserved this heritage by reviving the study of the Greek language and by translating Greek authors into Latin. After the fall of Constantinople in 1453, Italy became the center for Greek studies as Byzantine scholars fled the Ottoman conquerors. Humanists also introduced historical methods in studying texts, establishing principles for determining which of many manuscript copies of an ancient text was the oldest, the most accurate, and the least corrupted by their copyists. The humanist emphasis on the humanistic disciplines fostered new educational ideals. Along with the study of theology, logic, and natural philosophy, which had dominated the medieval university, humanist scholars stressed the importance of grammar, rhetoric, moral philosophy, and history. They believed that the study of these "liberal arts" should be undertaken for its own sake. This gave a powerful boost to the ideal of the perfectibility of the individual that appeared in so many other aspects of Renaissance culture.

Humanists furthered the secularization of Renaissance society through their emphasis on the study of the classical world. The rediscovery of Latin texts during the late Middle Ages spurred interest in all things ancient.

Philology and Lorenzo Valla. The study of the origins of words, their meaning, and their proper grammatical usage may seem an unusual foundation for one of the most vital of all European intellectual movements. But philology was, in fact, the humanists' chief concern. This can best be illustrated by the work of Lorenzo Valla (1407–1457). Valla entered the service of Alfonso I, king of Naples, and applied his humanistic training to affairs of state. The kingdom of Naples bordered on the Papal States, and its kings were in continual conflict with the papacy. The pope asserted the right to withhold recognition of the king, a right that was based on the jurisdictional authority supposedly ceded to the papacy by the Emperor Constantine in the fourth century—the so-called Donation of Constantine. Applying historical and philological critiques to the text of the Donation, Valla proved beyond doubt that the Donation was a forgery and papal claims based on it were without merit.

Civic Humanism. Valla's career demonstrates the impact of humanist values on practical affairs. Although humanists were scholars, they made no distinction between an active and a contemplative life. A life of scholarship was a life of public service. This **civic humanism** is best expressed in the writings of Leon Battista Alberti (1404–1472), whose treatise *On the Family* (1443) is a classic study of the new urban values, especially prudence and thrift. Alberti extolled the virtues of "the fatherland, the public good, and the benefit of all citizens."

Alberti's own life might have served as a model for the most influential of all Renaissance tracts, Castiglione's *The Courtier* (1528). Baldesar Castiglione (1478–1529) directed his lessons to the public life of the aspiring elite. It was his purpose to prescribe the characteristics that would make the ideal courtier, who was as much made as born. Castiglione's perfect courtier was an amalgam of all that the elite of Renaissance society held dear. He was to be educated as a scholar, he was to be occupied as a soldier, and he was to serve his state as an adviser.

Renaissance Science

As the spirit of the Renaissance looked back to the classical world and ahead to the achievements that would come from the adaptation of ancient wisdom, so Renaissance scientific inquiry was focused in two directions. The first was text-based knowledge derived from recovered works mainly from classical Greece; the second was experiment-based knowledge achieved through observation.

The biological sciences were given new life by the recovery of the writings of Hippocrates and Galen. Medicine became a subject for learned inquiry and the medical school at Padua was considered the greatest in Europe. The work of Hippocrates concerned diagnosing common diseases and attempting to find treatments. Galen's studies of the human body, rediscovered, formed the basis for a new interest in anatomy and led to experiments in human dissection. Such experimentation improved knowledge of anatomy, which led to advances in setting broken bones and treating injuries.

While the life sciences were advanced through attention to ancient texts, engineering developed through the experiences of Renaissance craftsmen and artists who were attempting to solve practical problems of proportion, stability, and height in the buildings, bridges, and ultimately domes that they built. Most of the important advances in engineering were actually made in the service of military ventures. Leonardo da Vinci attempted to apply a theory of mechanics to Renaissance warfare, and he made drawings for the creation of war machines such as tanks and flying machines such as airplanes. But he was expert in building working models of machines, in advising princes on their fortifications, and suggesting improvements in the art of gunnery. All his contributions were made by experimentation rather than through text-based learning. Wherever he went, Leonardo built workshops to construct models and kept careful notebooks of the results of his trials. This spirit of experimentation would ultimately lead to the birth of a recognizably scientific method in the next century.

Machiavelli and Politics

At the same time that Castiglione was drafting a blueprint for the idealized courtier, Niccolò Machiavelli (1469–1527) was laying the foundation for the realistic sixteenth-century ruler. No Renaissance work has been more important or more controversial than Machiavelli's The Prince (1513). With Machiavelli, for better or worse, begins the science of politics.

The Prince is a handbook for a ruler who would establish a lasting government. It attempts to set down principles culled from historical examples and contemporary events to aid the prince in attaining and maintaining power. By study of these precepts and by their swift and forceful application, Machiavelli believed, the prince might even control fortune itself. What made The Prince so remarkable in its day, and what continues to enliven debate over it, is that Machiavelli was able to separate all ethical considerations from his analysis. Whether this resulted from cynicism or from his own expressed desire for realism, Machiavelli uncompromisingly instructed the would-be ruler to be half human and half beast— to conquer neighbors, to murder enemies, and to deceive friends. Steeped in the humanist ideals of fame and virtù—a combination of virtue and virtuosity, of valor, character, and ability—he sought to reestablish Italian rule and place government on a stable scientific basis that would end the perpetual conflict among the Italian city-states.

The Politics of the Italian City-States

The absence of a unifying central authority in Italy, resulting from the collapse of the Holy Roman Empire and the papal schism, allowed ancient guilds and confraternities to transform themselves into self-governing societies. By the beginning of the fifteenth century, the Italian **city-states** were the center of power, wealth, and culture in the Christian world.

This dominion rested on several conditions. First, their geographical position favored the exchange of resources and goods between East and West. A great circular trade encompassed the Byzantine Empire, the North African coastal states, and the Mediterranean nations of western Europe. The Italian peninsula dominated the circumference of that circle. Its port cities, Genoa and Venice especially, became great maritime powers through their trade in spices and minerals. Moreover, just beyond the peninsula to the north lay the vast and populous territories of the Holy Roman Empire. Their continuous need for manufactured goods, especially cloth and metals, was filled by long caravans that traveled from Italy through the Alps. Finally, the city-states and their surrounding areas were agriculturally self-sufficient.

The Five Powers

Although there were dozens of Italian city-states, by the early fifteenth century five had emerged to dominate the politics of the peninsula. In the south was the kingdom of Naples, the only city-state governed by a hereditary monarchy. Its politics were mired in conflicts over its succession.

Bordering Naples were the Papal States, whose capital was Rome but whose territories stretched far to the north and lay on both sides of the spiny Apennine mountain chain that extends down the center of the peninsula. Throughout the fourteenth and early fifteenth centuries the territories under the nominal control of the Church were largely independent and included such thriving city-states as Bologna, Ferrara, and Urbino. Even in Rome the weakened papacy had to contend with noble families for control of the city.

The three remaining dominant city-states—Florence, Milan, and Venice—were bunched together in the north. Florence, center of Renaissance culture, was one of the wealthiest cities of Europe before the devastations of the plague and the sustained economic downturn of the late fourteenth century. Nominally, Florence was a republic, but during the fifteenth century it was ruled in effect by its principal banking family, the Medici.

To the north of Florence was the duchy of Milan, the major city in Lombardy. Milan's economic life was oriented northward to the Swiss and German towns beyond the Alps, and its major concern was preventing foreign invasions. The most warlike of the Italian cities, Milan was a despotism, ruled for nearly two centuries by the Visconti family.

The last of the five powers was the republic of Venice, which became the leading maritime power of the age. Until the fifteenth century, Venice was less interested in

MAP DISCOVERY

ITALY, 1494

Notice how Italy was organized into city-states at the end of the fifteenth century. Which were the largest city-states? Which city-states seem most susceptible to foreign invasion? Which states had the best positioning for trade? When the wars of Italy began in 1494 (discussed later in this chapter), France sided with Milan against Naples, Florence, and the Papal States. Based on the positions of the combatants, what do you think would have been the likeliest route for the French invasion? Which city-states could the French avoid fighting?

securing a landed empire than in dominating a seaborne one. The republic was ruled by a hereditary elite, headed by an elected **doge**, who was the chief magistrate of Venice, and a variety of small elected councils.

The political history of the Italian peninsula during the late fourteenth and early fifteenth centuries is one of unrelieved turmoil. Wherever we look, the governments of the city-states were threatened by foreign invaders, internal conspiracies, or popular revolts. In the 1370s, the Genoese and Venetians fought their fourth war in little more than a century, this one so bitter that the Genoese risked much of their fleet in an unsuccessful effort to conquer Venice itself. Florence and Milan were constantly at war with each other. Nor were foreign threats the only dangers. In Milan, three Visconti brothers inherited power. Two murdered the third, and then the son of one murdered the other to reunite the inheritance. The Venetians executed one of their military leaders, who was plotting treachery. One or another Florentine family usually faced exile when governments there changed hands. Popular revolts channeled social and economic discontent against the ruling elites in Rome, Milan, and Florence. The revolt of the "Ciompi" (the wooden shoes) in Florence in 1378 was an attempt by poorly paid wool workers to reform the city's exclusive guild system and give guild protection to the wage laborers lower down the social scale.

By the middle of the fifteenth century, however, two trends were apparent amid this political chaos. The first was the consolidation of strong centralized governments within the large city-states. These took different forms but yielded a similar result: internal political stability. The return of the popes to Rome after the Great Schism restored the pope to the head of his temporal estates and began a long period of papal dominance over Rome and its satellite territories. In Milan, one of the great military leaders of the day, Francesco Sforza (1401–1466), seized the reins of power after the failure of the Visconti line. The succession of King Alfonso I in Naples ended a half century of civil war. In both Florence and Venice, the grip of the political elite over high offices was tightened by placing greater power in small advisory councils and, in Florence, by the ascent to power of the Medici family. In sum, this process is known as the rise of signorial rule.

The rise of the signories made possible the second development of this period: the establishment of a balance of power within the peninsula. Sforza's consolidation of power in Milan initially led to warfare, but ultimately it formed the basis of the Peace of Lodi (1454). This established two balanced alliances, one between Florence and Milan and the other between Venice and Naples. These states, along with the papacy, pledged mutual nonaggression, a policy that lasted for nearly 40 years.

The Peace of Lodi did not bring peace. It only halted the long period in which the major city-states struggled against one another. Under cover of the peace, the large states continued the process of swallowing up their smaller neighbors and creating quasi-empires. Civilian populations were overrun, local leaders were exiled or exterminated, tribute money was taken, and taxes were levied. Each of the five states either increased its mainland territories or strengthened its hold on them. Venice and Florence especially prospered.

Venice: A Seaborne Empire

Venice owed its prosperity to trade rather than conquest. Its position at the head of the Adriatic permitted access to the raw materials of both East and West. The rich Alpine timberland behind the city provided the hardwoods necessary for ship-building. The inhabitants of the hinterland were steady consumers of grain, cloth, and the new manufactured goods—glass, silk, jewelry, and cottons—that came pouring onto the market in the late Middle Ages.

But the heart of Venetian success lay in the way in which it organized its trade and its government. The key to Venetian trade was its privileged position with the Byzantine Empire. Venice had exchanged with the Byzantines military support for tax concessions that gave Venetian traders a competitive edge in the spice trade with the East. The spice trade was so lucrative that special ships were built to accommodate it. These galleys were constructed at public expense and doubled as the Venetian navy in times of war. By controlling these ships, the government strictly regulated the spice trade. Rather than allow the wealthiest merchants to dominate it, as they did in other cities, Venice specified the number of annual voyages and sold shares in them at auction based on a fixed price. This practice allowed big and small merchants to gain from the trade and encouraged all merchants to find other trading outlets.

Like its trade, Venetian government was also designed to disperse power. Although it was known as the Most Serene Republic, Venice was not a republic in the sense that we use the word; it was rather an oligarchy—a government by a restricted group. Political power was vested in a Great Council whose membership had been fixed at the end of the thirteenth century. From the body of the Great Council, which numbered about 2,500 at the end of the fifteenth century, was chosen the Senate, a council about one-tenth the size, whose members served a one-year term. It was from the Senate that the true officers of government were selected: the doge, who was chosen for life, and members of a number of small councils, who administered affairs and advised the doge. Members of these councils were chosen by secret ballot in an elaborate process by which nominators were selected at random. Terms of office on the councils were extremely short in order to limit factionalism and to prevent any individual from gaining too much power.

With its mercantile families firmly in control of government and trade, Venice created a vast overseas empire in the East during the thirteenth and fourteenth centuries. Naval supremacy allowed the Venetians to offer protection to strategic outposts in return for either privileges or tribute. But in the fifteenth century, Venice turned westward. In a dramatic reversal of its centuries-old policy, it began a process of conquest in Italy itself. There were several reasons for this new policy. First, the Venetian navy was no longer the unsurpassed power that it once had been. Wars with Genoa had drained resources, and the revival of the Ottoman Turks in the East posed a growing threat that ultimately resulted in the fall of Constantinople (1453) and the end of Venetian trading privileges. Outposts in Dalmatia and the Aegean came under assault from both the Turks and the king of Hungary, cutting heavily into the complicated system by which goods were circulated by Venetian merchants. It was not long before Portuguese competition affected the most lucrative of all the commodities traded by the Venetians: pepper. Perhaps more important, mainland expansion offered new opportunities for Venice. Not all Venetians were traders, and the new industries that were being developed in the city could readily benefit from control of mainland markets. Most decisive of all, opportunity was knocking. In Milan, Visconti rule was weakening, and the Milanese territories were ripe for picking.

Venice reaped a rich harvest. From the beginning of the fifteenth century to the Peace of Lodi, the Most Serene Republic engaged in unremitting warfare. Its successes were remarkable. It pushed out to the north to occupy all the lands between the city and the Habsburg territories; it pushed to the east until it straddled the entire head of the Adriatic; and it pushed to the west almost as far as Milan itself. The western conquests, in particular, brought large populations under Venetian control, which, along with their potential as a market, provided a ready source of taxation. By the end of the fifteenth century, the mainland dominions of Venice were contributing nearly 40 percent of the city's revenue at a cost far smaller than that of the naval empire a century earlier.

Florence: Spinning Cloth into Gold

Florentine prosperity was built on banking and wool. Beginning in the thirteenth century, Florentine bankers were among the wealthiest and most powerful in the world. Florentine financiers established banks in all the capitals of Europe and the East. In the Middle Ages, bankers served more functions than simply handling and exchanging money. Most were also tied to mercantile adventures and underwrote industrial activity. So it was in Florence that international bankers purchased high-quality wool to be manufactured into the world's finest woven cloth.

The activities of both commerce and cloth manufacture depended on external conditions, and so the wealth of Florence was potentially unstable. In the mid-fourteenth century, instability came with the plague that devastated the city. Nearly 40 percent of the entire population was lost in the single year 1348, and recurring outbreaks continued to ravage the survivors. Loss of workers and markets seriously disrupted manufacturing. By 1380, cloth production had fallen to less than a quarter of pre-plague levels. On the heels of plague came wars. The costs of warfare created a massive public debt. Every Florentine of means owned shares in this debt, and the republic was continually devising new methods for borrowing and staving off crises of repayment.

As befitted a city whose prosperity was based on manufacturing, Florence had a strong guild tradition. The most important guilds were associated with banking and cloth manufacture, but they included the crafts and food processing trades as well. Only guild members could participate in government, electing the nine *Signoria* who administered laws, set tax rates, and directed foreign and domestic policy. Like that of Venice, Florentine government was a republican oligarchy, and like Venice, it depended on rotated short periods in office and selections by lot to avoid factionalism. But Florence had a history of factionalism that was longer than its history of republican government. Its formal structures were occasionally altered so that powerful families could gain control of the real centers of political power, the small councils and emergency assemblies through which the Signoria governed. Conservative leadership drawn from the upper ranks of Florentine society guided the city through the wars of the early fourteenth century. But soon afterward, the leaders of its greatest families—the Albizzi, the Pazzi, and the Medici—again divided Florentine politics into factions.

The ability of the Medici to secure a century-long dynasty in a government that did not have a head of state is just one of the mysteries surrounding the history of this remarkable family. Cosimo de Medici (1389–1464) was one of the richest men in Christendom when he returned to the city in 1434 after a brief exile. His leading position in government rested on supporters who were able to gain a controlling influence on the Signoria. Cosimo built his party carefully, banishing his Albizzi enemies, recruiting followers among the craftsmen he employed, and even paying delinquent taxes to maintain his voters' eligibility. Most important, emergency powers were invoked to reduce the number of citizens qualified to vote for the Signoria until the majority were Medici backers.

Cosimo's grandson, Lorenzo (1449–1492), held strong humanist values instilled in him by his mother, Lucrezia Tornabuoni, who organized his education. He brought Michelangelo and other leading artists to his garden; he brought Pico della Mirandola and other leading humanists to his table. Lorenzo's power was based on his personality and reputation. His diplomatic abilities were the key to his survival. Almost immediately after Lorenzo came to power, Naples and the papacy began a war with Florence, a war that was costly to the Florentines in both taxation and lost territory. In 1479, Lorenzo traveled to Naples and personally convinced the

A view of Florence in 1490.

Neapolitan king to sign a separate treaty. This restored the Italian balance of power and ensured continued Medici rule in Florence.

There is some doubt whether Lorenzo should be remembered by the title "the Magnificent" that was bestowed on him. His absorption in politics came at the expense of the family's commercial enterprises, which were nearly ruined during his lifetime. Moreover, the emergency powers that Lorenzo invoked to restrict participation in government changed forever the character of Florentine republicanism, irredeemably corrupting it. There is no reason to accept his enemies' judgment that Lorenzo was a tyrant, but the negative consequences of his rule cannot be ignored. In 1494, two years after Lorenzo's death, the peninsula was plunged into the wars that turned it from the center of European civilization into a satellite region.

The End of Italian Hegemony, 1450–1527

In the course of the Renaissance, western Europe was Italianized. For a century, the city-states dominated the trade routes that connected East and West. Italian manufactures, such as Milanese artillery, Florentine silk, and Venetian glass, were prized above all others. The ducat and the florin, two Italian coins, were universally accepted in an age when every petty prince minted his own. The peninsula exported culture in the same way that it exported goods. Humanism quickly spread across the Alps, aided by the recent invention of printing (which the Venetians soon dominated), and Renaissance standards of artistic achievement were known worldwide and everywhere imitated. The city-states shared their technology as well. The compass and the navigational chart, projection maps, double-entry bookkeeping, eyeglasses, the telescope—all profoundly influenced what could be undertaken.

Political and Military Unrest. But it was not in Italy that the rewards of such achievement were enjoyed. There, the seeds of political turmoil and military imperialism, combined with the rise of the Ottoman Turks, were to reap a not unexpected harvest. Under the cover of the Peace of Lodi, the major city-states had scrambled to enlarge their mainland empires. By the end of the fifteenth century, they eyed one another warily. Each expected the others to begin a peninsulawide war for hegemony and took the steps that ultimately ensured the contest. Each shared the dream of recapturing the glory that was Rome. Long years of siege and occupation had militarized the Italian city-states.

The Italian Decline. The disunited Italians were not able to meet the challenge of the most remarkable military leader of the age, the Ottoman prince Mehmed II (1451–1481), who conquered Constantinople and Athens and threatened Rome itself.

Venice was most directly affected by the Ottoman advance. Not only was its favored position in eastern trade threatened, but during a prolonged war at the end of the fifteenth century the Venetians lost many of their most important commercial outposts. Ottoman power closed off the markets of eastern Europe, and by 1480, Venetian naval supremacy was a thing of the past.

Successive popes pleaded in vain for holy wars to halt the advance of the Ottoman Turks. The fall of Constantinople in 1453 was an event of epochal proportions for Europeans; many believed that it foreshadowed the end of the world. Yet it was Italians rather than Ottomans who plunged the peninsula into the wars from which it never recovered.

The Wars of Italy (1494–1529) began when Naples, Florence, and the Papal States united against Milan. At first this alliance seemed little more than another shift in the balance of power. But rather than call on Venice to redress the situation, the Milanese leader, Ludovico Sforza, sought help from the French. An army of French cavalry and Swiss mercenaries, led by Charles VIII of France (1483–1498), invaded the peninsula in 1494. With Milanese support, the French swept all before them. Florence was forced to surrender Pisa, a humiliation that led to the overthrow of the Medici and the establishment of French sovereignty. The Papal States were next to be occupied, and within a year Charles had conquered Naples without engaging the Italians in a single significant battle. Unfortunately, the Milanese were not the only ones who could play at the game of foreign alliances. The Venetians and the pope united and called on the services of King Ferdinand of Aragon and the Holy Roman Emperor. Italy was now a battleground in what became a total European war for dynastic supremacy. The city-states used their foreign allies to settle old scores and to extend their own mainland empires. At the turn of the century, Naples was dismembered. In 1509, the pope conspired to organize the most powerful combination of forces yet known against Venice. All of the mainland possessions of the Most Serene Republic were lost, but by a combination of good fortune and skilled diplomacy, Venice itself survived. Florence was less fortunate, becoming a pawn first of the French and then of the Spanish. The final blow to Italian hegemony was the sack of Rome in 1527 by German mercenaries.

Chronology

ITALIAN POLITICS

1378	Ciompi revolt in Florence
1389–1464	Cosimo de Medici; leads rise of Medici to domination of Florence
1400–1450	Ottomans establish domination of the Balkans
1443	Naples and Sicily reunited under Alfonso I of Aragon
1449–1492	Lorenzo de Medici; plays important role as patron of the arts
1453	Fall of Constantinople
1454	Peace of Lodi
1494–1529	Wars of Italy
1494	Charles VII of France invades Italy
1509	Pope organizes successful coalition aimed at Venice
1527	German mercenaries sack Rome

SUMMARY

Renaissance Society Italy was far more urban than other parts of Europe. Urban populations were organized by occupation, which largely corresponded to social position and wealth. City governments reflected the centrality of commerce and trade to city life. Economic conditions promoted the production and consumption of luxury items. Renaissance children who survived infancy found their lives governed by parentage and by gender. Most city dwellers lived at subsistence. For many people, life improved in the aftermath of the plague. Towns and cities introduced a new sense of social and political cohesiveness. The Church remained the spatial, spiritual, and social center of people's lives.

Renaissance Art The social, economic, and political context of Renaissance Italy shaped the era's remarkable artistic achievements. In painting, sculpture, and architecture, Renaissance artists challenged old models, developed new techniques, and created a new style. By reviving classical themes, geometric principles, and a spirit of human vitality, artists broke decisively from the dominant medieval traditions. The artistic achievements of the Renaissance culminated in the creative outpourings of Michelangelo Buonarroti.

Renaissance Ideals It was the humanists' goal to discover as much as had survived from the ancient world and to provide texts of classical authors that were as full and accurate as possible. The humanist emphasis on the humanistic disciplines fostered new educational ideals. Humanists furthered the secularization of Renaissance society through their emphasis on the study of the classical world. Although humanists were scholars, they made no distinction between an active and a contemplative life. Castiglione tried to define the perfect Renaissance courtier. Renaissance scientific inquiry focused on analysis of classical works and experiment-based knowledge. Machiavelli's *The Prince* set down rules for attaining and maintaining power.

The Politics of the Italian City-States At the beginning of the fifteenth century the Italian city-states were the center of power, wealth, and culture in the Christian world. Five city-states dominated Italy: Naples, Venice, Florence, Milan, and the Papal States. Venice's wealth and power were initially based on seaborne trade with the East. Venetian government was designed to disperse power. In the fifteenth century, Venice turned West and engaged in wars of conquest. Florentine prosperity was built on banking and cloth manufacture. The Medici came to dominate Florence. The Peace of Lodi did not end competition between the Italian city-states. Invasion by France and Spain marked the beginning of Italian decline.

QUESTIONS FOR REVIEW

1. What social and cultural conditions were peculiar to the Italian peninsula, and how might those conditions have contributed to the Renaissance?
2. What were the principal characteristics of the Renaissance style in the visual arts?
3. What is humanism, and why was the study of languages so important to the humanists?
4. In what ways did the ideas of Niccolò Machiavelli reflect the reality of politics in the city-states of Renaissance Italy?

The European Empires

European Encounters

The sixteenth century was an age of exploration. Knowledge bequeathed from the past created curiosity about the present. Technological change made long sea voyages possible, and the demands of commerce provided incentives. Ottoman expansion on the southern and eastern frontiers of the Continent threatened access to the goods of the East on which Europeans had come to rely.

To pay for eastern goods, especially spices, Western gold and silver flowed steadily eastward. As supplies of precious metals dwindled, economic growth in Europe slowed. Throughout the fifteenth century, ever-larger amounts of Western specie were necessary to purchase ever-smaller amounts of Eastern commodities. Europe faced a severe shortage of gold and silver, a shortage that threatened its standard of living and its prospects for economic growth. The search was on for new sources of gold.

Africa and a Passage to India

It was the Portuguese who made the first dramatic breakthroughs in exploration and colonization. The Portuguese had long sailed the Atlantic, where they had established bases in the Azores and Madeira islands. Their small ships, known as **caravels**, were ideal for ocean travel, and their navigators were among the most skillful in the world. Yet they were unable to participate in the lucrative Mediterranean trade in bullion and spices until the expanding power of the Ottomans threatened the traditional eastern sea routes.

Prince Henry the Navigator. In the early fifteenth century, the Portuguese gained a foothold in northern Africa and used it to stage voyages along the continent's unexplored western coast. Like most explorers, the Portuguese were motivated by a mixture of faith and greed. Establishing southern bases would enable them to surround their Muslim enemies while also giving them access to the African bullion trade. Under the energetic leadership of Prince Henry the Navigator (1394–1460), the Portuguese pushed steadily southward.

Prince Henry's systematic program paid off in the next generation. By the 1480s, Portuguese outposts had reached almost to the equator, and in 1487, Bartolomeu Dias (ca. 1450–1500) rounded the tip of Africa and opened the eastern African shores to Portuguese traders. The aim of these enterprises was access to Asia rather than Africa. A decade later, Vasco da Gama (ca. 1460–1524) rounded the Cape of Good Hope and crossed into the Indian Ocean. When he returned to Lisbon in 1499, laden with the most valuable spices of the East, Portuguese ambitions were achieved. Larger expeditions followed, one of which, blown off course, touched the South American coast of Brazil, which was soon subsumed within the Portuguese dominions.

The Beginnings of the Slave Trade. The exploration of the African coast also brought the Portuguese into contact with Muslim traders who had developed connections between North Africa and the middle of the continent. They bartered for gold, ivory, and exotic spices, and slaves. Slavery was a common feature of the cultures that interacted in Africa. Europeans had used slaves in ancient times and had developed a theory that justified slavery by capture. Muslims were dependent upon them for their armies and bought many slaves from European sources. Africans enslaved those who were captured in tribal wars and sold them out of Africa, first to Muslim traders and then to the Portuguese. By the 1470s it was estimated that over a thousand African slaves a year were being imported into Portugal and that a significant percentage of those were sold to Spanish masters who also saw their value in farming.

In these early decades, slaves were viewed as just another trading commodity and valued only in regard to their profit. Ships were still small, voyages still risky, and capital still scarce. The agricultural use of African slaves was limited by the small amount of commercial agriculture undertaken by Europeans. The Portuguese held a monopoly on transporting slaves from Africa, but the trade soon centered in

Seville where Italians dominated it. This was a significant, if unplanned development. Seville would soon become the center of the Spanish overseas empire, and the Spanish colonies in America would soon become the destination for most of the African slaves bought by Europeans.

MAP DISCOVERY

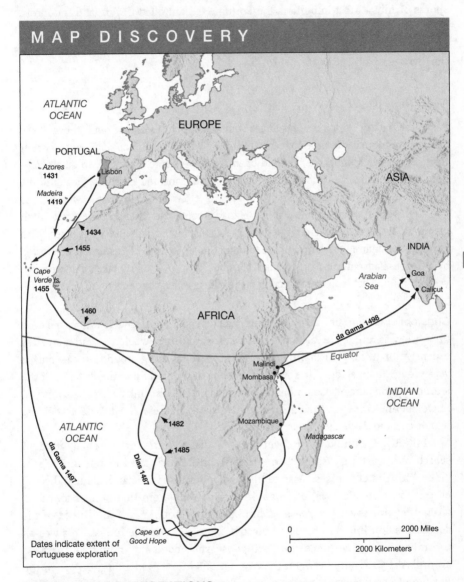

Dates indicate extent of Portuguese exploration

PORTUGUESE EXPLORATIONS

Examine the routes of the Portuguese explorers. What was their strategy of exploration? How long did it take for explorers to round the tip of Africa? What was the ultimate goal of Portuguese seafarers?

The Asian Trade. Building on their experience in West Africa, the Portuguese came to the East as traders rather than as conquerors. They developed a policy of establishing military outposts to protect their investments and subduing native populations only when necessary. By the beginning of the sixteenth century, the Portuguese Empire spanned both the eastern and western coasts of Africa and the western shores of India. Most important, the Portuguese controlled Ceylon and Indonesia, the precious Spice Islands from which came cloves, cinnamon, and pepper. Almost overnight, Lisbon became one of the trading capitals of the world, tripling in population between 1500 and 1550.

Mundus Novus

While the bulk of Portuguese resources were devoted to the Asian trade, those of the Spanish kingdom came to be concentrated in the New World. Though larger and richer than its western neighbor, Spain had been segmented into a number of small kingdoms and principalities and divided between Christians and Muslims. Not until the end of the fifteenth century, when the crowns of Aragon and Castile were united and the Muslims were expelled from Granada, could the Spanish concentrate their resources. By then they were far behind in establishing commercial enterprises. With Portugal dominating the African route to India, Queen Isabella of Castile was persuaded by a Genoese adventurer, Christopher Columbus (ca. 1446–1506), to take an interest in a western route. That interest resulted in one of the greatest accidents of history.

Christopher Columbus. Like all well-informed people of his day, Columbus believed the world was round. He calculated that a westward course would be shorter and less expensive than the path that the Portuguese were breaking around Africa—but he was wrong. He misjudged the size of the globe by a quarter and the distance of the journey by 400 percent. Columbus sailed westward into the unknown in 1492, and on 12 October he landed in the Bahamas, on an island that he named San Salvador. He had discovered a *Mundus Novus*, a New World.

Initially, Columbus's discovery was a disappointment. He had gone in search of a western passage to the Indies and he had failed to return to Spain laden with Eastern spices. Despite his own belief that the islands he had discovered lay just off the coast of Japan, it was soon apparent that he had found an altogether unknown landmass. Columbus's own explorations and those of his successors continued to focus on discovering a route to the Indies. This was all the more imperative once the Portuguese succeeded in finding the passage around Africa. Rivalry between the two nations intensified after 1500, when the Portuguese began exploring the coast of Brazil. In 1494, the **Treaty of Tordesillas** had confined Portugal's right to the eastern route to the Indies as well as to any undiscovered lands east of an imaginary line fixed west of the Cape Verde Islands. This entitled Portugal to Brazil. The Spanish received whatever lay west of the line.

This sixteenth-century map of Java and the Moluccas shows European traders bartering for spices. At the upper left, a ship laden with the rich cargo sails for markets in Europe.

Spanish-backed explorations soon proved the value of the newly discovered lands. In 1513, Vasco Núñez de Balboa (1475–1517) crossed the Isthmus of Panama and became the first European to view the Pacific Ocean. The discovery of this ocean refueled Spanish ambitions to find a western passage to the Indies.

Ferdinand Magellan. In 1519, Ferdinand Magellan (ca. 1480–1521), a Portuguese mariner in the service of Spain, set sail in pursuit of Columbus's goal of reaching the Spice Islands by sailing westward. His voyage, which he did not live to complete, remains the most astounding of the age. It was left to his navigator, Sebastian Elcano (ca. 1476–1526), to complete the first circumnavigation of the globe. In 1522, three years and one month after setting out, Elcano returned to Spain with a single ship and 18 survivors of the crew of 280. But in his hold were spices of greater value than the cost of the expedition. His return provided practical proof that the world was round, but it also demonstrated that the vastness of the Pacific Ocean made a western passage to the Indies uneconomical. The circumnavigation of Magellan and Elcano brought to an end the first stage of the Spanish exploration of the New World.

The Spanish Conquests

The exploits of Hernando Cortés (1485–1547) opened the next stage of Spanish discovery. The Spanish colonized the New World along the model of their reconquest of Spain. Individuals were given control over land and the people on it in return for military service. The interests of the crown were threefold: to convert the natives to

Christianity, to extend sovereignty over new dominions, and to gain profit from the venture. The colonial entrepreneurs had a singular interest: to grow rich. Most of the colonizers came from the lower orders of Spanish society.

Many of the protective measures taken by the crown to ensure orderly colonization and fair treatment of the natives were ineffective in practice. During the first decades of the sixteenth century, Spanish captains and their followers subdued the Indian populations of the Caribbean Islands and put them to work on the agricultural haciendas they had carved out for themselves.

Life on the hacienda, however, did not always satisfy the ambitions of the Spanish colonizers. Hernando Cortés was one such conquistador. Having participated in the conquest of Cuba, Cortés sought an independent command to lead an expedition into the hinterland of Central America, where a fabulous empire was rumored to exist. Having gathered a force of 600 men, Cortés sailed across the Gulf of Mexico in 1519 and established a fort at Vera Cruz, where he garrisoned 200 men. With 400 soldiers, he marched 250 miles through steamy jungles and over rugged mountains before glimpsing the first signs of the great Aztec civilization. The Aztec Empire was a loose confederation of native tribes that the Aztec had conquered during the previous century. It was ruled by the emperor Montezuma II (1502–1520) from his capital at Tenochtitlán. Invited to an audience with the Aztec emperor, Cortés and his men saw vast stores of gold and silver.

The conquest of the Aztecs took nearly a year and remains an overwhelming feat of arms. Nearly 100,000 natives from the tribes that the Aztecs had conquered supported the Spanish assault.

By 1522, Cortés was master of an area larger than all of Spain. But the cost in native lives was staggering. In 30 years, a population of approximately 25 million had been reduced to fewer than 2 million. Most of the loss was due to exposure to European diseases such as smallpox, typhoid, and measles, against which the indigenous peoples had no immunity. Their labor-intensive system of agriculture could not survive the rapid decrease in population, and famine followed pestilence.

This tragic sequence was repeated everywhere the Europeans appeared. In 1531, Francisco Pizarro (ca. 1475–1541) conquered the Peruvian Empire of the Incas, vastly extending the territory under Spanish control. A huge silver mine was discovered in 1545 at Potosí in what is now southern Bolivia, and the gold and silver that poured into Spain in the next quarter century helped to support Spanish dynastic ambitions in Europe. During the course of the sixteenth century, over 200,000 Spaniards migrated across the ocean. Perhaps one in ten were women, who married and set up families. Succeeding generations created huge haciendas built with the forced labor of black African slaves.

The Legacy of the Encounters

By the seventeenth century, long-distance trade had begun to integrate the regions of the world into a single marketplace. Slaves bought in Africa mined silver in South America. The bullion was shipped to Spain, where it was distributed across Europe.

Most went to Amsterdam to settle Spanish debts, Dutch bankers having replaced the Italians as the paymasters of Europe. From Holland, some of the silver traveled east to the Baltic Sea, the Dutch lifeline, where vital stores of grain and timber were purchased for home consumption. Even more of this silver was carried to Asia to buy spices in the Spice Islands, cottons in India, or silk in China. Millions of ounces flowed from America to Asia via the European trading routes. On the return voyage, Indian cottons were traded in Africa to purchase slaves for the South American silver mines.

Gold, God, and Glory. Gold, God, and glory neatly summarized the motives of the European explorers. Yet many technological problems had to be overcome before these goals could be achieved. Advances in navigational skills, especially in dead reckoning and later in calculating latitude from the position of the sun, were essential preconditions for covering the distances that were to be traveled. Ship designs became more sophisticated. The magnetic compass and the astrolabe were indispensable tools. Better maps and charts fueled both ambitions and abilities.

Nor was it happenstance that European forces conquered the peoples they encountered in both the east and west. Generations of warfare against Muslims had honed the skills of Christian warriors. European ships were sturdily built and armed with cannons that could be used on land or at sea. Soldiers were well-equipped and battle-tested. Military leaders were trained and experienced in the arts of siege and the tactics of divide and conquer.

The Columbian Exchange. The encounters between Europeans and native Americans were a cultural and intellectual event of the first magnitude. But it was also an ecological and biological event with enormous consequences—a transfer of microbes, animals, and plants known as the **Columbian Exchange.**

The mixing of populations that had historically remained separate had effects that no one could have foreseen. First and foremost were issues of public health. When the Spanish explorers arrived in the Caribbean islands, they carried agents of common diseases such as measles, smallpox, and influenza that raged in European population centers and killed many thousands each year but to which survivors carried a lifetime immunity. The native populations of the Americas endured their first exposure to these diseases all at once and millions succumbed in the first half-century of contact.

Disease was not the only unanticipated exchange that resulted from the encounters. On their ships the Spanish explorers brought horses, pigs, cows, and other domesticated animals unknown in the Americas. Not only did these new animals change patterns of work among the native populations, but they also changed dietary customs. Pork and beef gradually entered the diet of those who traded with the colonists and ultimately that of the general population.

Nor was the exchange one-sided. Beginning in the 1550s, European naturalists catalogued thousands of unknown species, a small number of which were suited to the different climates and soils of Europe. Among the most important of these

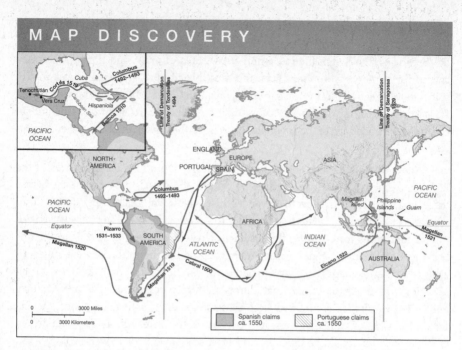

MAP DISCOVERY

CLAIMS OF SPAIN AND PORTUGUAL TO OVERSEAS EMPIRES

Examine the voyages of discovery and the claims to overseas empires. How did Portuguese and Spanish exploration differ? What was the effect of the Treaty of Tordesillas on their travel and claims? Why was it believed at the time that Portugal was the more powerful empire?

species were a number of foodstuffs that ultimately had a transforming effect on the European diet. They included tomatoes, potatoes, chili peppers, and chocolate.

European Reflections. Riches and converts, power and glory, all came in the wake of exploration. But in the process of discovering new lands and new cultures, Europe also learned something of its own aspirations. Early Portuguese voyagers went in quest of the mythical Prester John, a saintly figure who was said to rule a heaven on earth in the middle of Africa. The first children born on Madeira were named Adam and Eve, though this slave plantation of sugar and wine was an unlikely Garden of Eden. The optimism of those who searched for the fountain of youth in the Florida swamps was not only that they would find it there, but that a long life was worth living. Contact with the cultures of the New World also forced a different kind of thinking about life in the old one. The supposed customs of strange lands provided the setting for one of the great works of English social criticism, Sir Thomas More's *Utopia* (1516).

Europe also discovered and revealed a darker side of itself in the age of exploration. Accompanying the boundless optimism and assertive self-confidence that made so much possible was a tragic arrogance and callous disregard toward native

Contact with cultures of the New World forced Europeans into a different way of thinking about the old world. In this detail from *The Cognoscenti*, a seventeenth-century Flemish painting, English scholars and navigators examine European encounters with new lands and new cultures.

peoples. Though they encountered heritages that were in some ways richer than their own, few westerners harbored any appreciation of them. European expansion revealed the rapaciousness, greed, and cruelty of many European conquerors. These were the impulses of the Crusades rather than of the Renaissance.

Chronology

EUROPEAN ENCOUNTERS

1394–1460	Henry the Navigator; leads Portuguese effort to increase sea power
1487	Bartolomeu Dias rounds tip of Africa
1492	Columbus arrives in New World
1497–1499	Vasco da Gama leads expedition to India
1498	Castilian women begin arriving in the New World
1500–1550	Population of Lisbon triples
1516	Publication of Thomas More's *Utopia*
1519–1522	Ferdinand Magellan leads expedition that circumnavigates globe
1522	Hernando Cortés completes conquest of Aztecs
1531	Francisco Pizarro conquers Incas

The Formation of States

In the middle of the fifteenth century there were many factors working against the formation of large states in Europe. The most obvious involved simple things such as transportation and communication. The distance that could be covered quickly was very small. In wet and cold seasons, travel was nearly impossible. Large areas were difficult to control and to defend. Communication was not only subject to the hazards of travel. Distinct languages or dialects, a principal feature of small states, contributed to separate cultures. Customary practices, common ancestry, and shared experiences helped to define a sense of community through which small states defined themselves.

To these natural forces that acted to maintain the existence of small units of government were added invented ones. To succeed, a prince had to establish supremacy over a number of rivals. For the most part, states were inherited. Short lives meant prolonged disputes about inheritance. Rulers had to defend their thrones from rivals with strong claims to legitimacy.

Rulers also had to defend themselves from the ambitions of their mightiest subjects. The constant warfare of the European nobility was one of the central features of the later Middle Ages. To avoid resort to arms, princes and peers entered into all manner of alliances, using their children as pawns and the marriage bed as the chessboard. Rulers also faced independent institutions within their states, powerful organizations that had to be won over or crushed. By the end of the fifteenth century, the long process of taming the Church was about to enter a new stage. Fortified towns presented a different problem. They possessed both the labor and the wealth necessary to raise and maintain armies. They also jealously guarded their privileges. Rulers who could not tax their towns could not rule their state. Finally, most kingdoms had assemblies representing the propertied classes, especially in matters of taxation. Some, like the English Parliament and the Spanish Cortes, were strong; others, like the Imperial Diet and the French Estates-General, were weak. But everywhere, they posed an obstacle to the extension of the power of princes.

In combination, these factors slowed and shaped the process of state formation. But neither separately nor together were they powerful enough to overcome it. The fragmentation of Europe into so many small units of government made some consolidation inevitable; and as the first large states took shape, the position of smaller neighbors grew ever more precarious.

This was especially true by the end of the fifteenth century because of the increase in the destructive power of warfare. Technological advances in cannonry and in the skills of gunners and engineers made medieval fortifications untenable. Gunpowder decisively changed battlefield tactics. It made heavy armor obsolete and allowed for the development of a different type of warfare. Infantry armed with long pikes or small muskets became the crucial components of armies that were growing ever larger. Systems of supply were better, sources of small arms were more available, and the rewards of conquest were more tangible. What could not be inherited or married could be conquered.

Eastern Configurations

The interplay of factors that encouraged and inhibited the formation of states is most easily observed in the eastern parts of Europe. There the different paths taken by Muscovy and Poland-Lithuania stand in contrast. At the beginning of the sixteenth century, the principality of Muscovy was the largest European political unit. Muscovy's growth was phenomenal. Under Ivan III, "the Great" (1462–1505), Muscovy expanded to the north and west. During a long series of wars it annexed Novgorod and large parts of Livonia and Lithuania. Between 1460 and 1530, Muscovy increased its territory by 1.5 million square miles.

A number of factors led to the rise of Muscovy. First, external threats had diminished. The deterioration of the Mongol Empire, which had dominated south-central Russia, allowed Ivan to escape the yoke of Mongol rule that the Russian princes had worn for centuries. Second, the fall of Constantinople made Muscovy the heir to eastern Christendom, successor to the Roman and Byzantine empires. Third, Ivan the Great was fortunate in having no competitors for his throne. He was able to use other social groups to help administer the new Muscovite territories without fear of setting up a rival to power.

Ivan extended the privileges of his nobility and organized a military class, the members of which received land as a reward for their fidelity. He also developed a new theory of sovereignty that rested on divine rather than temporal power. Traditionally, Russian princes ruled their lands by patrimony. They owned both estates and occupants. Ivan the Great extended this principle to cover all lands to which there was an ancient Russian claim and combined it with the religious authority of the Orthodox Church. Both he and his successors ruled with the aid of able Church leaders, who were normally part of the prince's council.

Ivan the Terrible. What made the expansion of Muscovy so impressive is that land once gained was never lost. The military and political achievements of Ivan the Great were furthered by his son Vasili and his more famous grandson Ivan IV, "the Terrible" (1533–1584). Ivan IV defeated the Mongols on his southeastern border and incorporated the entire Volga basin into Muscovy. But his greatest ambition was to gain a port on the Baltic Sea and establish a northern outlet for commerce. His objective was to conquer Livonia, but in nearly three decades of warfare between Muscovy and Poland-Lithuania, with whom Livonia had allied itself, Muscovy's territorial victories fell short of the real prize. Furthermore, Ivan's northern campaigns seriously weakened the defense of the south. In 1571, the Crimean Tatars advanced from their territories on Muscovy's southwestern border and inflicted a powerful psychological blow when they burned the city of Moscow. Although the Tatars were eventually driven off Muscovite soil, expansion in both north and south was at an end for the next 75 years.

By the reign of Ivan IV, Muscovite society was divided roughly into three groups: the hereditary nobility, known as the boyars; the military service class; and the peasantry, who were bound to the land. There was no large mercantile presence in Muscovy, and its urban component remained small. The boyars, who were powerful landlords of great estates, owed little to the tsar. They inherited their lands and did not necessarily benefit from expansion and conquest. Members of the military service class, on the other hand, were bound to the success of the crown. Their military service was a requirement for the possession of their estates, which were granted out of lands gained through territorial expansion. Gradually, the new military service class grew in power and prestige, largely at the expense of the older boyars. Ivan IV used members of the military service class as legislative advisers and elevated them in his parliamentary council (the Zemsky Sobor), which also contained representatives of the nobility, clergy, and towns.

Unlike his grandfather, Ivan IV had an abiding mistrust of the boyars and it was his treatment of them that earned him the nickname "the Terrible." During his brutal suppression of supposed conspiracies, several thousand families were massacred by Ivan's own orders and thousands more by the violent excesses of his agents. He also forcibly relocated boyar families. This practice made the boyars' situation similar to that of the military service class, whose members owed their fortunes to the tsar. For the first time the boyars were required to perform military service to the tsar.

All of these measures contributed to the breakdown of local networks of influence and power and to a disruption of local governance. But they also made possible a system of central administration, one of Ivan IV's most important achievements. Ivan IV promoted the interests of the military service class over those of the boyars, but he did not destroy the nobility. New boyars were created, especially in conquered territories, and these new families owed their positions and loyalty to the prince. Both boyars and the military benefited from Ivan's policy of binding the great mass of people to the land. Serfdom made possible the prolonged absence of military leaders from their estates and contributed to the creation of the military service class. In the long term, however, serfdom retarded economic development by removing the incentive for large landholders to make investments in commerce or to improve agricultural production.

Poland-Lithuania. The growth of an enlarged and centralized Muscovy stands in contrast to the experiences of Poland-Lithuania during the same period. At the end of the fifteenth century, Casimir IV (1447–1492) ruled the kingdom of Poland and the grand duchy of Lithuania. His son Wladislaw II ruled Bohemia (1471–1516) and Hungary (1490–1516).

While the Polish-Lithuanian monarchs enjoyed longevity similar to that of the Muscovites, those who ruled Hungary and Bohemia were not so fortunate. By the sixteenth century, a number of claimants to both crowns existed, and the competition was handled by diplomacy rather than war. The formal union of the Polish and

Lithuanian crowns in 1569 also involved the decentralization of power and the strengthening of the rights of the nobility in both countries. In the end, the states split apart. The Russians took much of Lithuania; the Ottomans took much of Hungary. Bohemia, which in the fifteenth century had been ruled more by its nobles than by its king, was absorbed into the Habsburg territories after 1526.

There were many reasons why a unified state failed to develop in east-central Europe. First, wars with the Ottomans and the Russians absorbed resources. Second, the princes faced rivals to their crowns. These contests for power necessitated concessions to leading citizens, which decreased the princes' ability to centralize their kingdoms or to effect real unification among them. The nobility of Hungary, Bohemia, and Poland-Lithuania all developed strong local interests that increased over time. War, rivalries for power, and a strong nobility prevented any one prince from dominating this area as the princes of Muscovy dominated theirs.

The Western Powers

As in the east, there was no single pattern to the consolidation of the large western European states. They, too, were internally fragmented and externally imperiled. While England had to overcome the ruin of decades of civil war, France and Spain faced the challenges of invasion and occupation. Each nation formed its state differently: England by administrative centralization, France by good fortune, and Spain by dynastic marriage.

The Taming of England. Alone among European states, England suffered no threat of foreign invasion during the fifteenth century. This island fortress might easily have become the first consolidated European state were it not for the ambitions of the nobility and the weakness of the crown. For 30 years, the English aristocracy fought over the spoils of a helpless monarch. The Wars of the Roses (1455–1485) were as much a free-for-all among the English peerage as they were a contest for the throne between the houses of Lancaster and York.

Three decades of intermittent warfare had predictable results. The houses of Lancaster and York were both destroyed. Edward IV (1461–1483) succeeded in gaining the crown for the house of York, but he was never able to wear it securely. When he died, his children, including his heir, Edward V (1483), were placed in the protection of their uncle Richard III (1483–1485). Richard's usurpation led to civil war, and he was killed by the forces of Henry Tudor at the battle of Bosworth Field in 1485. By the end of the Wars of the Roses, the monarchy had lost both revenue and prestige.

It was left to Henry Tudor to deal with the power of the nobility and the poverty of the monarchy. No English monarch had held secure title to the throne for over a century. Henry Tudor, as Henry VII (1485–1509), put an end to this dynastic instability at once. He married Elizabeth of York, in whose heirs would rest the legitimate claim to the throne. He also began the long process of taming his overmighty subjects.

Traitors were hanged and turncoats were rewarded. He and his son Henry VIII (1509–1547) adroitly created a new peerage, which soon was as numerous as the old feudal aristocracy. These new nobles owed their titles and loyalty to the Tudors.

The financial problems of the English monarchy were not so easily overcome. The English landed classes had established the principle that only on extraordinary occasions were they to be required to contribute to the maintenance of government. This principle was defended through their representative institution, the Parliament. When the kings of England wanted to tax their subjects, they had first to gain the assent of Parliament. Though Parliaments did grant requests for extraordinary revenue, especially for national defense, they did so grudgingly. The English landed elites were not exempt from taxation, but they were able to control the amount of taxes they paid.

Since the king was, therefore, dependent on the efficient management of his own estates, English state building required the growth of centralized institutions that could oversee royal lands and collect royal customs. Gradually, medieval institutions such as the Exchequer were supplanted by newer organs that were better able to adjust to modern methods of accounting, record keeping, and enforcement.

Not until the middle of the next reign was the English monarchy again solvent. As a result of his dispute with the papacy, Henry VIII confiscated the enormous wealth of the Catholic church and, with one stroke, solved the Crown's monetary problems (see Chapter 13). But the real contribution that Henry and his chief minister, Thomas Cromwell (ca. 1485–1540), made to forming an English state was the way in which this windfall was administered. Cromwell accelerated the process of centralizing government that had begun under Edward IV. He divided administration according to its functions by creating separate departments of state, modeled on courts. These new departments were responsible for record keeping, revenue collection, and law enforcement. Each had a distinct jurisdiction and a permanent trained staff. Cromwell coordinated the work of these distinct departments by expanding the power of the Privy Council, which included the heads of these administrative bodies. Through a long evolution, the Privy Council came to serve as the king's executive body. Cromwell also saw the importance of Parliament as a legislative body. Through Parliament, royal policy could be turned into statutes that had the assent of the political nation. If Parliament was well managed, issues that were potentially controversial could be defused. Laws passed by Parliament were more easily enforced locally than were proclamations issued by the king.

The Unification of France. The forces working against the consolidation of a French state were formidable. France was surrounded by aggressive and powerful neighbors with whom it was frequently at war. Its greatest nobles were semi-independent princes who were constant rivals for the throne. French people were primarily loyal to their province and viewed the pretensions of the monarchy with deep suspicion. France was also splintered by profound regional differences. The north and south were divided by culture and by language (the *langue d'oc* in the south and the *langue d'oil* in the north).

The first obstacles to unification that were overcome were the external threats to French security. For over a century the throne of France had been contested by the kings of England. The so-called Hundred Years' War, which was fought intermittently between 1337 and 1453, originated in a dispute over the inheritance of the French crown and English possessions in Gascony in southern France (see Chapter 10).

The struggle between the kings of England and the kings of France allowed French princes and dukes, who were nominally vassals of the king, to enhance their autonomy by making their own alliances with the highest bidder. When the English were finally driven out of France in the middle of the fifteenth century, the kings of France came into a weakened and divided inheritance.

Nor was England the only threat to the security of the French monarchy. On France's eastern border, in a long arching semicircle, were the estates of the dukes of Burgundy. While England and France were locked in deadly embrace, Burgundy systematically grew, absorbing territory from both the Holy Roman Empire and France. The conquest of Lorraine finally connected the ducal estates in one long, unbroken string. The power of Burgundy threatened its neighbors in all directions. Both France and the empire were too weak to resist its expansion, but the confederation of Swiss towns to the southwest of Burgundy was not. In a series of stunning military victories, Swiss forces repelled the Burgundians from their lands and demolished their armies. Charles the Bold, the last Valois duke of Burgundy, fell at the Battle of Nancy in 1477. His estates were quickly dismembered. France recovered its ancestral territories, including Burgundy itself, and through no effort of its own was now secure on its eastern border.

The king who was most associated with the consolidation of France was Louis XI (1461–1483). He inherited an estate that had been exhausted by warfare and civil strife. More by chance than by plan, he vastly extended the territories under the dominion of the French crown and, more important, subdued the nobility. But during the course of his reign, Louis XI gradually won back what he had been forced to give away. Years of fighting both the English and each other left the ranks of the French aristocracy depleted. As blood spilled on the battlefields, the stocks of fathers and sons ran low. Estates to which no male heirs existed fell forfeit to the king. In this manner, the crown absorbed Anjou and Maine in the northwest and Provence in the south. More important, Louis XI ultimately obtained control of the two greatest independent fiefs, Brittany and Orléans, by marrying his son Charles to the heiress of Brittany and his daughter Jeanne to the heir of Orléans. When, in 1527, the lands of the duke of Bourbon fell to the crown, the French monarch ruled a unified state.

Long years of war established the principle of royal taxation, which was essential to the process of state building in France. This enabled the monarchy to raise money for defense and for consolidation. Because of the strength of the nobles, most taxation fell only on the commoners, the so-called third estate. Although there was much complaint about taxes, the French monarchy established a broad base for taxation and a high degree of compliance long before any other European nation.

Along with money went soldiers, needed to repel the English and to defend the crown against rebels and traitors. Again the French monarchy was the first to establish the principle of a national army, raised and directed from the center but quartered and equipped regionally. From the nobility were recruited the cavalry, from the towns and countryside the massive infantry. Fortified towns received privileges in return for military service to the king. Towns supplied small arms, pikes, and swords and later pistols and muskets. By the beginning of the sixteenth century, the French monarch could raise and equip an army of his own.

The Marriages of Spain. Before the sixteenth century there was little prospect of a single nation emerging on the Iberian peninsula. North African Muslims, called Moors, occupied the province of Granada in the south; the stable kingdom of Portugal dominated the western coast. The Spanish peoples were divided among a number of separate states. The two most important were Castile, the largest and wealthiest kingdom, and Aragon, which was composed of a number of quasi-independent regions, each of which maintained its own laws and institutions. Three religions and four languages (not including dialects) widened these political divisions. And the different states had different outlooks. Castile was, above all, determined to rid itself of the Moors in Granada and to convert to Christianity its large Jewish population. Aragon played in the high-stakes game for power in the Mediterranean. It claimed sovereignty over Sicily and Naples and exercised it whenever it could.

When Ferdinand of Aragon and Isabella of Castile secretly exchanged wedding vows in 1469, both their homelands were rent by civil war. In Castile, Isabella's brother Henry IV (1454–1474) struggled unsuccessfully against the powerful Castilian nobility. In Aragon, Ferdinand's father, John II (1458–1479), faced a revolt by the rich province of Catalonia on one side and the territorial ambitions of Louis XI of France on the other. Joining the heirs together increased the resources of both kingdoms.

Ferdinand and Isabella (1479–1516) took the first steps toward forging a Spanish state. Their most notable achievement was the final recovery of the lands that had been conquered by the Moors. For centuries the Spanish kingdoms had fought against the North African Muslims who had conquered large areas of the southern peninsula. The *reconquista* was characterized by short bursts of warfare followed by long periods of wary coexistence. By the middle of the fifteenth century, the Moorish territory had been reduced to the province of Granada. The final stage of the reconquista began in 1482 and lasted for a decade. It was waged as a holy war and was financed in part by grants from the pope and the Christian princes of Europe. In 1492, Granada finally fell, and the province was absorbed into Castile.

The reconquista played an important part in creating a national identity for the Christian peoples of Spain. To raise men and money for the war effort, Ferdinand and Isabella mobilized their nobility and town governments and created a central organization to oversee the invasion. The conquered territories were used to reward the men who had aided the effort, though the crown maintained control and jurisdiction over most of the province. But the idea of the holy war also had a darker side and an unanticipated consequence. The Jewish population that had lived peacefully in Castile and Aragon became another object of hostility. Many Jews had risen to prominence in government and in skilled professions. Others, who had accepted conversion to Christianity and were known as *conversos*, had become powerful figures in church and state.

Both groups were now attacked. The conversos fell prey to a special church tribunal created to examine their sincere devotion to Catholicism. This was the **Spanish Inquisition**, which, though it used traditional judicial practices—torture to gain confessions, public humiliation to show contrition, and burnings at the stake to maintain purity—used them on a scale never before seen. Thousands of conversos were killed, and many more families had their wealth confiscated to be used for the reconquista. In 1492, the Jews were expelled from Spain. Though the reconquista and the expulsion of the Jews inflicted great suffering on victims and incalculable loss to the Castilian economy, both events enhanced the prestige of the Catholic monarchs.

The joint presence of Ferdinand and Isabella in the provinces of Spain was symbolic of the unity they strove to achieve. Ferdinand made Castilian the official language of government in Aragon and even appointed Castilians to Aragonese posts. He and Isabella actively encouraged the intermarriage of the two aristocracies and the expansion of the number of wealthy nobles who held land in both kingdoms. Nevertheless, these measures did not unify Spain or erase the centuries-long tradition of hostility among the diverse Iberian peoples.

It was left to the heirs of Ferdinand and Isabella to forge together the Spanish kingdoms, and the process was a painful one. The hostility to a foreign monarch that both the Castilian nobility and the Aragonese towns had shown to Ferdinand and Isabella increased dramatically at the accession of their grandson Charles V (1516–1556), who had been born and raised in the Low Countries, where he ruled over Burgundy and the Netherlands. Through a series of dynastic accidents, Charles was heir to the Spanish crown with its possessions in the New World and to the vast Habsburg estates that included Austria. Charles established his rule in Spain gradually. For a time he was forced to share power in Castile and to suppress a disorganized aristocratic rebellion.

Because of his foreign obligations, Charles was frequently absent from Spain. During those periods he governed through regents and royal councils that did much to centralize administration. Though Castile and Aragon had separate councils, they were organized similarly and had greater contact than before. Charles V realized the importance of Spain, especially of Castile, in his empire. He established a permanent bureaucratic court, modeled on that of Burgundy, and placed able Spaniards at the head of its departments.

Flemish tapestry showing Isabella and Ferdinand attended by courtiers and ladies-in-waiting.

The most important factor in uniting the Spanish kingdoms, however, was the fact that Charles V brought Spain to the forefront of European affairs in the sixteenth century. Spanish prowess, whether in arms or in culture, became a source of national pride that helped to erode regional identity. Gold and silver from the New World helped to finance Charles's great empire, and he achieved nearly all of the ancient territorial ambitions of the Spanish kingdoms. In Italy, he prosecuted Aragonese claims to Sicily and Naples. In the north, he held on firmly to the kingdom of Navarre, which had been annexed by Ferdinand, and secured Spain's border with France. In the south, he blocked off Ottoman and Muslim expansion. The reign of Charles V ushered in the dawn of Spain's golden age.

The Dynastic Struggles

The formation of large states throughout Europe led inevitably to conflicts among them. Long chains of marriages among the families of the European princes meant that sooner or later the larger powers would lay claim to the same inheritances and test the matter by force. Thus the sixteenth century was a period of almost unrelieved general warfare in Europe.

Power and Glory

Wars were fought to further the interests of princes rather than the interests of national sovereignty or international Christianity. They were certainly not fought in the interests of their subjects. States were an extension of a prince's heritage. The wars of the sixteenth century were dynastic wars.

The New Monarchs waged war and defended their territories in new ways. Internal security depended on locally raised forces or hired mercenaries. Both required money, which was becoming available in unprecedented quantities as a result of the increasing prosperity of the early sixteenth century and the windfall of gold and silver from the New World. Developments in transport and supply enabled campaigns to take place far from the center of a state. Finally, communications were improving. The need for knowledge about potential rivals or allies had the effect of expanding the European system of diplomacy. Resident agents were established in all the European capitals, and they had a decisive impact on war and peace. Their dispatches formed the most reliable source of information about the strengths of armies or the weaknesses of governments, about the births of heirs or the deaths of princes.

The Italian Wars

The struggle for supremacy in Europe in the sixteenth century pitted the French house of Valois against the far-flung estates of the Habsburg Empire. Yet the wars took place in Italy. The rivalries among the larger Italian city-states proved to be fertile ground for the newly consolidated European monarchies. Both French and Spanish monarchs had remote but legitimate claims to the kingdom of Naples in southern Italy. In 1494, the French king, Charles VIII, took up an invitation from the ruler of Milan to intervene in Italian affairs. His campaign was an unqualified, if fleeting, success. He marched the length of the peninsula, overthrew the Medici in Florence, forced the pope to open the gates of Rome, and finally seized the crown of Naples. But the French appetite for Italian territory was not sated. Soon a deal was struck with Ferdinand of Aragon to divide the kingdom of Naples in two. All went according to plan until these thieves fell out among themselves. In the end, Spain wound up with all of Naples and France was left with nothing but debts and grievances.

Therefore, when Francis I came to the French throne and Charles V came to the Spanish, Naples was just one of several potential sources of friction. Not only had Ferdinand betrayed the French in Naples, he had also broken a long-standing peace on the Franco-Spanish border by conquering the independent but French-speaking kingdom of Navarre. Francis could be expected to avenge both slights. Charles, on the other hand, was the direct heir of the dukes of Burgundy. From his childhood he longed for the restoration of his ancestral lands, including Burgundy itself, which had been gobbled up by Louis XI after the death of Charles the Bold. Competition between Francis and Charles became all the more ferocious when Charles's grandfather, the Holy Roman Emperor Maximilian I (1486–1519), died in 1519. Both monarchs launched a vigorous campaign for the honor of succeeding him.

Charles V, who now inherited the Habsburg lands in Austria and Germany, succeeded to this eminent but empty dignity. His election as Holy Roman Emperor not only aggravated the personal animosity among the monarchs, but added another source of conflict in Italy. When Louis XII (1498–1515) had succeeded to the throne of France, he had laid claim to the duchy of Milan through an interest of his wife's, though he was unable to enforce it. Francis I proved more capable. In 1515, he stunned all of Europe by crushing the vaunted Swiss mercenaries at the battle of Marignano. But the duchy of Milan was a territory under the protection of the Holy Roman Emperor, and it soon appealed for imperial troops to help repel the French invaders. Milan was strategically important to Charles V because it was the vital link between his Austrian and Burgundian possessions. Almost as soon as he took up the imperial mantle, Charles V was determined to challenge Francis I in Italy.

The key to such a challenge was the construction of alliances among the various Italian city-states and most especially with England, whose aid both Charles and Francis sought to enlist in the early 1520s. Henry VII had found foreign alliances a ready source of cash, and he was always eager to enter into them as long as they did not involve raising armies and fighting wars. Henry VIII was made of sterner stuff. He longed to reconquer France and to cut a figure on the European scene. Charles V made two separate trips to London, and Henry crossed the Channel in 1520 to meet Francis I.

The result of these diplomatic intrigues was an alliance between England and the Holy Roman Empire. English and Burgundian forces would stage an invasion of northern France, while Spanish and German troops would again attempt to dislodge the French from Italy. The strategy worked better than anyone could have imagined. In 1523, Charles's forces gained a foothold in Milan by taking the heavily fortified town of Pavia. Two years later, Francis was ready to strike back. At the head of his own royal guards, he massed Swiss mercenaries and French infantry outside Pavia and made ready for a swift assault. Instead, a large imperial army arrived to relieve the town, and in the subsequent battle, the French suffered a shattering defeat. Francis I was captured.

The victory at Pavia, which occurred on Charles V's twenty-fifth birthday, seemingly made him master of all of Europe. His ally Henry VIII urged an immediate invasion and dismemberment of France and began raising an army to spearhead the attack. But Charles's position was much less secure than it appeared. The Ottomans threatened his Hungarian territories, and the Protestants threatened his German lands. He could not afford a war of conquest in France. His hope now was to reach an agreement with Francis I for a lasting European peace, and for this purpose the French king was brought in captivity to Madrid. Charles's terms, however, led not to peace but to 30 years of warfare.

Jean Clouet, *Portrait of Francis I* (sixteenth century). Rivalry between Francis and Charles V plunged Europe into decades of war.

Charles demanded that Burgundy be returned to him. Though Francis was hardly in a position to bargain, he held out on this issue for as long as possible and secretly prepared a disavowal of the final agreement before it was made. By the Treaty of Madrid in 1526, Francis I yielded Burgundy and recognized the Spanish conquest of Navarre and Spanish rule in Naples. The agreement was sealed by the marriage of Francis to Charles's sister, Eleanor of Portugal. But marriage was not sufficient security for such a complete capitulation. To secure his release from Spain, Francis was required to leave behind as hostages his seven- and eight-year-old sons until the treaty was fulfilled. For three years the children languished in Spanish captivity.

No sooner had he set foot on French soil than Francis I renounced the Treaty of Madrid. Despite the threat that this posed to his children, Francis argued that the terms had been extracted against his will, and he even gained the sanction of the pope for violating his oath. Setting France on a war footing, he began seeking new allies. Henry VIII, disappointed with the meager spoils of his last venture, switched sides. So, too, did a number of Italian city-states, including Rome. Most important, Francis I entered into an alliance with the Ottoman sultan, Suleiman the Magnificent (1520–1566), whose armies were pressing against the southeastern borders of the Holy Roman Empire. In the year following Pavia, the Ottomans secured an equally decisive triumph at Mohacs, which cut Hungary in two and threatened Vienna, the eastern capital of the Habsburg lands. Almost overnight, Charles V had been turned from hunter into hunted. The Ottoman threat demanded immediate attention in Germany, the French and English were preparing to strike in the Low Countries, and the Italian wars continued. In 1527, Charles's unpaid German mercenaries stormed through Rome, sacked the papal capital, and captured the pope. Christian Europe was mortified.

The struggle for European mastery ground on for decades. The Treaty of Cateau-Cambrésis in 1559 brought to a close 60 years of conflict. In the end, the French were no more capable of dislodging the Habsburgs from Italy than were the Habsburgs of forcing the Ottomans out of Hungary. The great stores of silver that poured into Castile from the New World were consumed in the fires of continental warfare. In 1557, both France and Spain declared bankruptcy to avoid foreclosures by their creditors. For the French, the Italian wars were disastrous. They seriously undermined the state's financial base, eroded confidence in the monarchy, and thinned the ranks of the ruling nobility. The adventure begun by Charles VIII in search of glory brought France nearly to ruin. It ended with fitting irony. After the death of Francis I, his son Henry II (1547–1559) continued the struggle. Henry never forgave his father for abandoning him in Spain, and he sought revenge on Charles V, who had been his jailer. He regarded the Treaty of Cateau-Cambrésis as a victory and celebrated it with great pomp and pageantry. Among the feasts and festivities were athletic competitions for the king's courtiers and attendants. Henry II entered the jousting tournament and there was killed.

SUMMARY

European Encounters   The need to establish secure trade routes with the East fueled early European expansion. Portugal, under the leadership of Prince Henry the Navigator, explored the coast of Africa. Portuguese exploration resulted in a commercial empire in the East and the acceleration of the slave trade. The voyages of Columbus initiated the process of Spanish conquest in the Americas. Profit, the spread of Christianity, and glory drove European expansion.

The Formation of States   Although the obstacles to large state formation were formidable in the fifteenth century, they were not powerful enough to stop the process from moving forward. The rulers of Muscovy took advantage of favorable circumstances to create a vast state. In the aftermath of the Wars of the Roses, Henry VII helped transform England's poor and weak monarchy into a stable and efficient institution. Luck played an important role in the consolidation of royal authority in France under Louis XI. The marriage of Ferdinand of Aragon and Isabella of Castile started the process of national unification in Spain.

The Dynastic Struggles   The sixteenth century was a period of almost constant dynastic warfare. The New Monarchs waged war and defended their territories in new ways. The struggle for supremacy in Europe in the sixteenth century pitted the

French house of Valois against the far-flung estates of the Habsburg Empire. Most of the actual fighting took place in Italy. Emperor Charles V secured the support of Henry VIII of England in his battle with France for supremacy in Italy. French defeat and the capture of Francis I allowed Charles V to force the French king to accept the harsh terms of the Treaty of Madrid. The situation soon reversed itself with a number of Charles's allies, including Henry VIII, switching sides and supporting the French. The struggle for European mastery ground on for decades, with the Treaty of Cateau-Cambrésis in 1559 finally bringing the conflict to a close.

QUESTIONS FOR REVIEW

1. What impulses in European society were revealed by the global exploration and conquests of the Portuguese and the Spanish?
2. What qualities characterized the New Monarchies and what are some of the best examples of such princely states?
3. How and why did the experience of political and territorial unification differ in England, France, and Spain?
4. How did war between the great European monarchies contribute to unity within each?

CHAPTER

The Reform of Religion

The Intellectual Reformation

In the early sixteenth century, reformers throughout western Europe preached new ideas about religious doctrine and religious practice. At first these ideas took the form of a sustained critique of the Roman Catholic Church, but they soon developed a momentum of their own. Some reformers remained within traditional Catholicism; others moved outside and founded new Protestant churches. Wherever this movement for religious reform, whether Catholic or Protestant, appeared, it was fed by new ideas. And the rapid communication of new ideas was made possible by the development of printing, which appeared in Germany in the late fifteenth century and spread across Europe in the succeeding decades. Yet printing was as much a result as a cause of the spread of ideas. The humanist call for a return to the study of the classics and for the creation of accurate texts, first heard in Italy, aroused scholars and leaders in all of the European states. Their appetite for manuscripts exhausted the abilities of the scribes and booksellers who reproduced texts. Printing responded to that demand.

The Print Revolution

Printing, one of the true technological revolutions in western history, was not invented. It developed as a result of progress made in allied industries, especially papermaking and goldsmithing. A number of German craftsmen experimented with using movable metal type to make exact reproductions of manuscripts on paper. In the 1450s in Mainz, Johannes Gutenberg (ca. 1400–1468) and his partners succeeded and published their famous Bibles.

Once it was begun, printing spread like wildfire. Most of the early printed works were either religious or classical. Bibles, church service books, and the commentaries of the Church Fathers were most common. Cicero topped the list of classical authors.

An early German print shop. The man at the left operates the screw press while an apprentice (right) stacks the printed sheets. The man in the back is setting type for the next impression.

Printing rapidly came to be a basic part of life. In the first 40 years after the presses were first set up, perhaps as many as 20 million books were produced and distributed. Printing changed the habits of teachers and students, the way in which the state conducted its business, and the methods of legal training and legal proceedings. Compilations of laws could now be widely distributed and more uniformly enforced. Printing had a similar effect on the development of scientific study. The printing press popularized the discoveries of the New World and contributed to the reproduction of more accurate charts and maps, which in turn facilitated further discovery. Printing also helped to standardize language by frequent repetition of preferred usage and spelling. Perhaps most important, printing created an international intellectual community whose ideas could be dispersed the length and breadth of the Continent. The printing press enhanced the value of ideas and of thinking. Nothing could be more central to the reform of religion.

Christian Humanism

Many of the ideas that spread across Europe as the result of the printing revolution originated in Italian humanism (see Chapter 11). The revival of classical literature, with its concern for purity in language and eloquence in style, was one of the most admired achievements of the Renaissance. By the beginning of the sixteenth century, the force of humanism was felt strongly in northern and western Europe, where it was grafted onto the traditional theological teaching. The combination was a new and powerful intellectual movement known as **Christian humanism**.

The humanism of the north differed from that of the Italian city-states. Although the Italian humanists were certainly Christian, they were interested in secular subjects, especially in mastering classical languages and translating classical texts. Italian humanists had established techniques for the recovery of accurate texts and had developed principles for compiling the scholarly editions that now poured forth from the printing presses. Christian humanists applied these techniques to the study of the authorities and texts of the Church. Most of the new humanists had been trained in Italy, where they devoted themselves to the mastery of Greek and Latin. They had imbibed the idea that scholars, using their own critical faculties, could establish the authority of texts and the meaning of words. Building on the patient work of their predecessors and the advantages offered by printing, this new generation of humanists brought learning to educated men and women throughout Europe.

Christian humanism was a program of reform rather than a philosophy. It aimed to make better Christians through better education. Humanists were especially interested in the education of women. Thomas More (1478–1535) raised his daughters to be among the educated elite of England. Renowned women scholars held places at Italian universities. Humanist educational principles posed an implicit challenge to Roman Catholicism. Schools had once been the monopoly of the

Church, which used them to train clergymen. Literacy itself had been preserved over the centuries so that the gospel could be propagated.

By the sixteenth century these purposes had been transformed. Schools now trained many people who were not destined for careers in the Church, and literacy served the needs of the state, the aristocracy, and the merchant classes. More important, as the humanists perfected their techniques of scholarship, the Church continued to rely on traditional methods of training and traditional texts. Rote memorization of the opinions of others was more highly valued than critical thinking. The Vulgate Bible was used throughout western Christendom. It was now a thousand years old.

The Humanist Movement

Many humanist criticisms of Church teaching focused on its failure to inspire individuals to live a Christian life. Humanist writers were especially scathing about popular practices that bordered on superstition, such as pilgrimages to holy places or the worship of relics from the early history of the Church. Christian humanists wanted to inspire Christians.

Christian humanism was an international movement. The humanists formed the elite of the intellectual world of the sixteenth century, and their services were sought by princes and peers as well as by the most distinguished universities. In fact, the New Monarchs supported the humanists and protected them from their critics.

The centerpiece of humanist reforms was the translation of Christian texts. Skilled in Greek and Latin, informed by scholars of Hebrew and Aramaic, humanist writers prepared new editions of the books of the Bible and of the writings of the early Church Fathers.

The Wit of Erasmus

Orphaned at an early age, Desiderius Erasmus of Rotterdam (ca. 1466–1536) was educated by the Brothers of the Common Life, a lay brotherhood that specialized in schooling children and preparing them for a monastic life. Marked out early by his extraordinary intellectual gifts, Erasmus entered a monastery and was then allowed to travel to pursue his studies, first in France and then in England.

Erasmus devoted his life to restoring the direct connection between the individual Christian and the textual basis of Christian doctrine. Although he is called the father of biblical criticism, Erasmus was not a theologian. He was more interested in the practical impact of ideas than in the ideas themselves. His scathing attacks on the Scholastics, popular superstition, and the pretensions of the traditionalists in the Church and the universities all had the same goal: to restore the experiences of Christ to the center of Christianity.

Though his patrons were the rich and his language was Latin, Erasmus also hoped to reach men and women lower down the social order, those whom he believed the Church had failed to educate. "The doctrine of Christ casts aside no age, no sex, no fortune or position in life. It keeps no one at a distance."

The Lutheran Reformation

On the surface, the Roman Catholic Church appeared to be as strong as ever at the beginning of the sixteenth century. Yet everywhere in Europe, the cry was for reform. Wherever one turned, one saw abuses. Parish livings were sold to the highest bidder to raise money. This was simony. Rich appointments were given to the kinsmen of powerful Church leaders rather than to those who were most qualified. This was nepotism. Individual clergymen accumulated numerous positions whose responsibilities they could not fulfill. This was pluralism. Some priests who took the vow of chastity lived openly with their concubines. Some mendicants who took the vow of poverty dressed in silk and ate from golden plates.

The Spark of Reform

Europe was becoming more religious. The signs of religious fervor were everywhere. Cities hired preachers to expound the gospel. Pilgrims to the shrines of saints clogged the roadways every spring and summer. Endowments of masses for the dead increased. Henry VII of England provided money for 10,000 masses to be said for his soul. Even city merchants might bequeath funds for several hundred masses. In the chantries, where such services were performed, there were neither enough priests nor enough altars to supply the demand.

People wanted more from the Church than the Church could possibly give them. Humanists condemned visits to the shrines as superstitious; pilgrims demanded that the relics be made more accessible. Reformers complained of pluralism; the clergy complained that they could not live on the salary of a single office. Civic authorities demanded that the established Church take greater responsibility for good works; the pope demanded that civic authorities help to pay for them.

Contradiction and paradox dominated the movements for reform. Though the most vocal critics of the Church complained that its discipline was too lax, for many ordinary people its demands were too rigorous. The obligations of penance and confession weighed heavily on them. Church doctrine held that sins had to be washed away before the souls of the dead could enter heaven. Until then, they suffered in purgatory. Sins were cleansed through penance, the performance of acts of contrition assigned after confession. But the ordeal of confession kept many people away. It is hardly surprising that the sale of **indulgences** became a popular substitute for penance and confession.

The Sale of Indulgences

An indulgence was a portion of the treasury of good works performed by righteous Christians throughout the ages. Indulgences could be granted to people who wanted to atone for their sins. Strictly speaking, an indulgence supplemented penance rather than substituted for it. It was effective only for the contrite—for sinners who repented of their sins. But as the practice of granting indulgences spread, this subtle distinction largely disappeared. The living bought indulgences to cleanse the sins of the dead, and some even bought indulgences in anticipation of sins they had not yet committed.

By the sixteenth century, to limit abuses by local church authorities, only the pope, through his agents, could grant indulgences. Popes used special occasions to offer an indulgence for pilgrimages to Rome or for contributions to special papal projects. Other indulgences were licensed locally, usually at the shrines of saints or at churches that contained relics.

The indulgence controversy was a symptom rather than a cause of the explosion of feelings that erupted in the small German town of Wittenberg in 1517. In that year the pope was offering an indulgence to help finance the rebuilding of Saint Peter's Basilica in Rome. The pope chose Prince Albert of Brandenburg (1490–1545) to distribute the indulgence in Germany, and Albert hired the Dominican friar Johann Tetzel (ca. 1465–1519) to preach its benefits.

Martin Luther Challenges the Church

Enthusiasm for the indulgence spread to the neighboring state of Saxony, where the ruler, Frederick III, the Wise (1463–1525), banned its sale. Frederick's great collection of relics carried their own indulgences, and Tetzel offered unwelcome competition. But

An anonymous caricature of Johann Tetzel, whose sale of an indulgence inspired Martin Luther's Ninety-five Theses. Tetzel answered with 122 theses of his own but was rebuked and disowned by the Catholics.

Saxons flocked into Brandenburg to make their purchases, and by the end of October, Tetzel was not very far from Wittenberg Castle, where Frederick's relics were housed. On All Saints' Day the relics would be opened to view. On the night before, Martin Luther (1483–1546), a professor of theology at Wittenberg University, posted on the door of the castle church ninety-five theses attacking indulgences and their sale.

In so doing, Luther was following the Scholastic tradition of disputation, in which scholars presented propositions, or theses, for open debate with all comers. Luther's theses were controversial, but they were meant to be. Only circumstance moved Luther's theses from the academic to the public sphere. Already there was growing concern among clergy and theologians about Tetzel's blatant sale of indulgences.

Luther's theses focused this concern and finally communicated it beyond the walls of the Church and the university. The theses were quickly translated into German and spread throughout the Holy Roman Empire.

Martin Luther's Faith

In his youth Martin Luther had studied for a career in law, but against his father's wishes he entered an Augustinian monastery and was ordained a priest in 1507. He received his doctorate at the university in Wittenberg and was appointed to the theology faculty in 1512.

In all outward appearances, Luther was successful and contented, but beneath this tranquil exterior lay a soul in torment. Despite his devotion, he could not erase his sense of sin; he could not convince himself that he could achieve the righteousness God demanded of him.

Knowledge of his salvation came to Luther through study. His internal agonies led him to ponder over and over again the biblical passages that described the righteousness of God. In the intellectual tradition in which he had been trained, that righteousness was equated with law. The righteous person either followed God's law or was punished by God's wrath. It was this understanding that tormented him.

Even before he wrote his Ninety-five Theses, Luther had made the first breakthrough by a unique reading of the writings of Saint Paul. "I pondered night and day until I understood the connection between the righteousness of God and the sentence 'The just shall live by faith.' Then I grasped that the justice of God is the righteousness by which through grace and pure mercy, God justifies us through faith. Immediately I felt that I had been reborn and that I had passed through wide open doors into paradise!" Finally he came to believe that the righteousness of God was a gift freely given to the faithful and that to receive God's righteousness, one had only to believe in God's infinite mercy. It was this belief that fortified Luther during his years of struggle with both civil and Church powers.

Over the next several years, Luther refined his spiritual philosophy and drew out the implications of his newfound beliefs. His religion was shaped by three interconnected tenets. First came justification by faith alone—**sola fide**. An individual's everlasting salvation came from faith in God's goodness rather than from the performance of good works. Sin could not be washed away by penance, and it could not be forgiven by indulgence. Second, faith came only through the knowledge and contemplation of the Word of God—*sola scriptura*. All that was needed to understand the justice and mercy of God was contained in the Bible. Reading the Word, hearing the Word, expounding on and studying the Word—this was the path to faith and through faith to salvation. Third, all who believed in God's righteousness and had achieved their faith through the study of the Bible were equal in God's eyes. The priesthood included all believers. Each followed his or her own calling and found his or her own faith through Scripture. Ministers and preachers could help others to learn God's Word, but they could not confer faith.

From Luther to Lutheranism

The first to feel the seriousness of Luther's challenge to the established order was the reformer himself. The head of Luther's order, a papal legate, and finally the Emperor Charles V all called for Luther to recant his views on indulgences. Luther was excommunicated by Pope Leo X in 1521 and ordered by Charles V to appear before the diet, or assembly, in Worms, Germany, in April of that year. There he gave the same infuriating reply: If he could be shown the places in the Bible that contradicted his views, he would gladly change them. Charles V declared Luther an enemy of the empire. In both Church and state he was now an outlaw.

In fact, during the three years between the posting of his theses and his appearance before the emperor, Luther came to conclusions that were much more radical than his initial attack on indulgences. He came to believe that the papacy was a human rather than a divine invention. Therefore, he denounced both the papacy and the general councils of the Church. In his *Address to the Christian Nobility of the German Nation* (1520) he called on the princes to take the reform of religion into their own hands.

But Luther had attracted powerful supporters as well as powerful enemies. Prince Frederick III of Saxony consistently intervened on his behalf, and the delicate international situation forced Luther's chief antagonists to move more slowly than they might have wished. The pope hoped first to keep Charles V off the imperial throne and then to maintain a united front with the German princes against him. Charles V, already locked in his lifelong struggle with the French, needed German military support and peace in his German territories. These factors consistently played into Luther's hands.

While the pope and the emperor were otherwise occupied, Luther refined his ideas and won important converts. As time passed, Luther's reputation grew, not only in Germany, but all over Europe. Between 1517 and 1520, he published 30 works, all of which achieved massive sales. Luther's individual accomplishments were remarkable, but what turned his theology into a movement, which after 1529 came to be known as Protestantism, was the support he received among German princes and within German cities.

Princes and Cities. Individual princes turned to Luther's theology for several reasons. First and foremost was sincere religious conviction. Second were political and economic factors. As German princes worked to centralize their administrations, protect themselves from predatory neighbors, and increase their revenues, they felt the burden of papal exactions. Taxes and gifts flowed south to a papacy dominated by Italians. Luther's call for civil rulers to lead their own churches meant that civil rulers could keep their own revenues.

The Reformation spread particularly well in the German cities, especially those to which the emperor had granted the status of freedom from the rule of any prince. The cities had long struggled with the tension of the separate jurisdictions of state and Church. Much urban property was owned by the Church and so was exempt from taxation and law enforcement, and the clergy constituted a significant proportion of urban populations. Reformed religion stressed the equality of clergy and laity and thus the indisputable power of civil authorities. Paradoxically, it was because the cities contained large numbers of priests that Luther's ideas reached the cities quickly. Many of his earliest students served urban congregations and began to develop doctrines and practices that, though based on Luther's ideas, were adapted to the circumstances of city life. Moreover, the imperial free cities were also centers of the printing trade and home to many of the most noted humanists who were initially important in spreading Luther's ideas.

Luther's message held great appeal for the middle orders in the towns. These groups resented the privileges given to priests and members of religious orders who paid no taxes and were exempt from the obligations of citizenship. The level of anticlericalism, always high in Germany, was especially acute in cities that were suffering economic difficulties. Pressure from ordinary people and petty traders forced town leaders into action. The evangelism of reforming ministers created converts and an atmosphere of reform. Support from members of the ruling oligarchy both mobilized these pressures and capitalized on them. Town governments secured their own autonomy over the Church, tightening their grip on the institutions of social control and enhancing the social and economic authority of their members.

The Appeal for Women. Religious reform appealed to women as well as men, but it affected them differently. Noblewomen were among the most important defenders of Protestant reformers, especially in states in which the prince opposed it. Marguerite of Navarre (1492–1549), sister of Francis I, frequently intervened with her brother on behalf of individual Lutherans who fell afoul of Church authorities. Mary of Hungary (1505–1558) played a similar role in the Holy Roman Empire. Bona, wife of Sigismund I of Poland, was especially important in eastern reform. An Italian by birth, Bona (1493–1558) was a central figure in spreading both Renaissance art and humanist learning into Poland.

Luther's reforms also appealed to women who were not so highly placed in society. The doctrine of the equality of all believers put men and women on an equal spiritual footing even if it did nothing to break the male monopoly of the ministry. In the private sphere, family life became the center of faith when salvation was removed from the control of the Church.

By following humanist teaching on the importance of educating women of the upper orders and by encouraging literacy, the reformers did much that was uplifting. Girls' schools were founded in a number of German cities, and townswomen could use their newly acquired skills in their roles as shopkeepers, family accountants, and teachers of their children. But there were losses as well as gains. The attack on the worship of saints and especially of the Virgin Mary removed female images from religion. Protestantism was male-dominated in a way that Catholicism was not. Moreover, the emphasis on reading the Bible tended to reinforce the image of women as weak and inherently sinful. The dissolution of the convents took away the one institution that valued women's gender and allowed them to pursue a spiritual life outside marriage.

The Spread of Lutheranism

By the end of the 1520s, the empire was divided between cities and states that accepted reformed religion and those that adhered to Roman Catholicism. Large German communities across northern Europe, mostly founded as trading outposts, became focal points for the penetration of reformist ideas.

Merchants and students carried Luther's ideas into Scandinavia, but there the importance of political leaders was crucial. Christian III (1534–1559) of Denmark had been present at the Diet of Worms when Luther made his famous reply to Charles V. Christian was deeply impressed by the reformer, and after a ruinous civil war he confiscated Catholic Church property in Denmark and created a reformed religion under Luther's direct supervision.

Paradoxically, Lutheranism came to Sweden as part of an effort to throw off the yoke of Danish dominance. When Gustav I Vasa (1523–1560) led a successful uprising against the Danes and became king of Sweden, he encouraged the spread of Protestant ideas.

As important as Protestant ideas were in northern and central Europe, they proved most fertile in the Swiss towns of the empire. Here was planted the second generation of reformers, theologians who drew radical new conclusions from Luther's insights. In the east, Huldrych Zwingli (1484–1531) brought reformed religion to the town of Zurich. Educated at the University of Basel and deeply influenced by humanist thought early in his career, Zwingli was a preacher among the Swiss mercenary troops that fought for the empire. In 1516, he met Erasmus in Basel and, under his influence, began a study of the Greek writings of the Church Fathers and of the New Testament. Zwingli was also influenced by reports of Luther's defiance of the pope, for his own antipapal views were already developing.

MAP DISCOVERY

Intensity of gray represents the approximate strength of Lutheranism

THE SPREAD OF LUTHERANISM

Observe the extent of Lutheranism across Europe in the sixteenth century. Where was Lutheranism concentrated? Notice how Lutheranism swept through entire states. How was Europe divided between Protestants and Catholics?

Perhaps most decisively for his early development, Zwingli was stricken by plague in 1519. In his life-and-death struggle he came to a profoundly personal realization of the power of God's mercy.

These experiences became the basis for the reform theology that Zwingli preached in Zurich. He believed that the Church had to recover its earlier purity and to reject the innovations in practices that successive popes and general councils had brought in. He stressed the equality of believers, justification by faith alone, and the sufficiency of the gospel as authority for church practice. He attacked indulgences, penance, clerical celibacy, prayers to the Virgin, statues and images in churches, and a long list of other practices. He regarded the Mass as a commemorative event rather than one that involved the real presence of Christ. His arguments were so effective that the town council adopted them as the basis for a reform of religion.

The principles that Zwingli preached quickly spread to neighboring Swiss states. Practical as well as theological, Zwingli's reforms were carried out by the civil government with which he allied himself. This was not the same as the protection that princes had given to Lutherans. Rather, in the places that came under Zwingli's influence, there was an important integration of church and state. He stressed the divine origins of civil government and the importance of the magistrate as an agent of Christian reform.

This theocratic idea—that the leaders of the state and the leaders of the church were linked—became the basis for further social and political reform.

The Protestant Reformation

By the middle of the 1530s, Protestant reform had entered a new stage. Luther did not intend to form a new religion; his struggle had been with Rome. His religion was one of protest. The second generation of reformers faced a different task. The new reformers were the church builders who had to systematize doctrine for a generation that had already accepted religious reform. Their challenge was to draw out the logic of reformed ideas and to create enduring structures for reformed churches.

Geneva and Calvin

The Reformation came late to Geneva. In the sixteenth century, Geneva was under the dual government of the duchy of Savoy and the Catholic bishop of the town, who was frequently a Savoy client. The Genevans also had their own town council, which traditionally struggled for power against the bishop. By the 1530s the council had gained the upper hand. The council confiscated Church lands and institutions, secularized the Church's legal powers, and forced the bishop and most of his administrators to flee the city. War with Savoy inevitably followed, and Geneva would certainly have been crushed into submission except for its alliance with neighboring Bern, a potent military power among the Swiss towns.

Geneva was saved and was free to follow its own course in religious matters. In 1536, the adult male citizens of the city voted to become Protestant. But there was as yet no reformer in Geneva to establish a Protestant program and no clear definition of what that program might be.

John Calvin (1509–1564) was born in France, the son of a bishop's secretary. His education was based on humanist principles, and he learned Greek and Hebrew, studied theology, and received a legal degree from the University of Orléans.

This painting depicts a Calvinist service in Lyon, France, in 1564. The men and women are segregated, and the worshippers are seated according to rank. An hourglass times the preacher's sermon.

Around the age of 20 he converted to Lutheranism. Francis I was determined to root Protestants out of France, and Calvin fled Paris. Persecution of Protestants continued in France, and one of Calvin's close friends was burned for heresy. Ultimately, Calvin decided to settle in Strasbourg, where he could retire from public affairs and live out his days as a scholar.

War between France and the empire clogged the major highways to Strasbourg. Therefore Calvin and his companions detoured through Geneva, where Guillaume Farel (1489–1565), one of Geneva's leading Protestant reformers, persuaded Calvin to remain in Geneva and lead its reformation.

Calvin's greatest contributions to religious reform came in church structure and discipline. Like Luther and Zwingli, he believed that salvation came from God's grace. But more strongly than his predecessors, he believed that the gift of faith was granted only to some and that each individual's salvation or damnation was predestined before birth. The doctrine of **predestination** was a traditional one, but Calvin emphasized it differently and brought it to the center of the problem of faith. Those who were predestined to salvation were obliged to govern; those who were predestined to damnation were obliged to be governed.

Calvin structured the institution of the Genevan church in four parts: the pastors, who preached the Word to their congregations; the doctors, who studied and wrote; the deacons, who oversaw the institutions of social welfare, such as hospitals and schools, run by the church; and finally the elders of the church, who governed the church in all moral matters. They were the most controversial part of Calvin's establishment and the most fundamental. They had the power to discipline. Chosen from among the elite of the city, the 12 elders enforced the strict Calvinist moral code that extended into all aspects of private life.

The structure that Calvin gave to the Genevan church soon became the basis for reforms throughout the Continent. The Calvinist church was self-governing, independent of the state, and therefore capable of surviving and even flourishing in a hostile environment. Expanded over the course of several editions, Calvin's *The Institutes of the Christian Religion* became the most influential work of Protestant theology. Perhaps its greatest impact was in Britain, where the reformation took place not once but twice.

The English Reformation

The king of England wanted a divorce. Henry VIII had been married to Catherine of Aragon (1485–1536) as long as he had been king, and she had borne him no male heir to carry on his line. She had given birth to six children and endured several miscarriages, yet only one daughter, Mary, survived. Henry came to believe that this was God's punishment for his marriage. Catherine had been married first to Henry's older brother, who had died as a teenager, and there was at least one scriptural prohibition against marrying a brother's wife. A papal dispensation had been provided for the marriage; now Henry wanted a papal dispensation for an annulment. For three years his case ground its way through the papal courts. Catherine of Aragon was the aunt of the Emperor Charles V, and the emperor had taken her side in the controversy. With imperial power in Italy at its height, the pope was content to hear all of the complex legal and biblical precedents argued at leisure.

By 1533, Henry could wait no longer. He had already impregnated Anne Boleyn (ca. 1507–1536), one of the ladies-in-waiting at his court, and for the child—which Henry was certain would be a boy—to be legitimate, a marriage would have to take place at once. Legislation was prepared in Parliament to prevent papal interference in the decisions of England's courts, and Thomas Cranmer (1489–1556), archbishop of Canterbury, England's highest ecclesiastical officer, agreed to annul Henry's first marriage and celebrate his second. This was the first step in a complete break with Rome. Under the guidance of Thomas Cromwell (ca. 1485–1540), the English Parliament passed statute after statute that made Henry supreme head of the Church in England and owner of its vast wealth. Monasteries were dissolved, and a Lutheran service was introduced. On 7 September 1533, Anne Boleyn gave birth not to the expected son, but to a daughter, the future Queen Elizabeth I.

The Church of England. Henry's reformation was an act of state, but the English Reformation was not. There was an English tradition of dissent from the Roman Church that stretched back to the fourteenth century. Anticlericalism was especially virulent in the towns, where citizens refused to pay fees to priests for performing services such as burial. And humanist ideas flourished in England, where Thomas More, John Colet, and a host of others supported both the new learning and its efforts to reform spiritual life. Luther's attack on ritual and the Mass and his emphasis on Scripture and faith echoed the lost Lollard program and found many recruits in London and the northern port towns.

Protestantism grew slowly in England because it was vigorously repressed. Like Francis I and Charles V, Henry VIII viewed actual attacks on the established church as potential attacks on the established state. Henry had earned the title Defender of the Faith from the pope in 1521 for authoring an attack on Luther.

Henry's divorce unleashed a groundswell of support for religious change. The king's own religious beliefs remained a secret, but Anne Boleyn and Thomas Cromwell sponsored Lutheran reforms, and Thomas Cranmer put them into practice. Religion was legislated through Parliament, and the valuable estates of the Church were sold to the gentry. These practices found favor with both the legal profession and the landed elites and made Protestantism more palatable among these conservative groups. It was in the reign of Edward VI (1547–1553), Henry's son by his third wife, that the central doctrinal and devotional changes were made. Church service was now conducted in English, and the first two English prayer books were created. The Mass was reinterpreted along Zwinglian lines and became the Lord's Supper, the altar became the communion table, and the priest became the minister. Preaching became the center of the church service, and concern about the education of learned ministers resulted in commissions to examine and reform the clergy.

Beginning in the 1530s, state repression turned against Catholics. Those who would not swear the new oaths of allegiance or recognize the legality of Henry VIII's marriage suffered for their beliefs as the early Protestants had suffered for theirs. Thomas More and over 40 others paid with their lives for their opposition. An uprising in the north in 1536, known as the Pilgrimage of Grace, was suppressed, but Catholicism continued to flourish in England, surviving underground during the reigns of Henry and Edward and reemerging under Mary I (1553–1558).

The Successors of Henry VIII. Mary Tudor, the first woman to rule England, held to the Catholic beliefs in which her mother, Catherine of Aragon, had raised her, and she vowed to bring the nation back to her mother's church. She reestablished papal sovereignty, abolished Protestant worship, and introduced a crash program of education in the universities to train a new generation of priests. Catholic retribution for the blood of their martyrs was not long in coming. Cranmer and three other bishops were burned for heresy.

Nearly 800 Protestants fled the country rather than suffer a similar fate. These Marian exiles, as they came to be called, settled in a number of reformed communities, Zurich, Frankfurt, and Geneva among them. There they imbibed the second generation of Protestant ideas, especially Calvinism, and from there they began a propaganda campaign to keep reformed religion alive in England. It was the Marian exiles who were chiefly responsible for the second English reformation, which began in 1558 when Mary died and her half-sister, Elizabeth I (1558–1603), came to the throne.

Under Elizabeth, England returned to Protestantism, but not the Protestantism that had come before. Even the most advanced reforms during Edward's reign now seemed too moderate for the returning exiles. Against Elizabeth's wishes, the English church adopted the Calvinist doctrine of predestination and the simplification (but not wholesale reorganization) of the structure of the church. But it did not become a model of thoroughgoing reformation. The Thirty-nine Articles (1563) continued the English tradition of compromising points of disrupted doctrine and of maintaining traditional practices wherever possible.

The Reformation of the Radicals

Schism breeds schism. That was the stick with which Catholic Church and civil authorities beat Luther from the beginning. By attacking the authority of the established church and flouting the authority of the established state, he was fomenting social upheaval. But he insisted that his own ideas buttressed rather than subverted authority, especially civil authority under whose protection he had placed the Church. As early as 1525, peasants in Swabia appealed to Luther for support in their social rebellion. They based some of their most controversial demands, such as the abolition of tithes and labor service, on biblical authority. Luther instructed the rebels to lay down their arms and await their just rewards in heaven. But Luther's ideas had a life of their own. He clashed with Erasmus over free will and with Zwingli over the Mass. Toward the end of his life he felt that he was holding back the floodgates against the second generation of Protestant thinkers. Time and again, serious reformers wanted to take one or another of his doctrines further than he was willing to go himself.

The most dangerous threat to the establishment of an orthodox Protestantism came from groups who were described, not very precisely, as **Anabaptists**. Though this label—which means, literally, "baptism again"—identified people who practiced adult baptism, it was mainly used to tar religious opponents with the brush of extremism. Anabaptists appeared in a number of German and Swiss towns in the 1520s. Taking seriously the doctrine of justification by faith, Anabaptists argued that only believers could be members of the true church of God. Because baptism was the sacrament through which entry into the church took place, Anabaptists reasoned that it was a sacrament for adults rather than infants. But infant baptism was a core doctrine for both Catholics and Protestants. It symbolized the acceptance of Christ, and without it, eternal salvation was impossible. It was a practical doctrine. Unbaptized infants who died could not be accepted in heaven, and infant mortality was appallingly common.

Thus the doctrine of Anabaptism posed a psychological as well as a doctrinal threat to the reformers. But the practice of adult baptism paled in significance compared to many of the other conclusions that religious radicals derived from the principle of sola scriptura—by the Word alone. Some groups argued the case that since true Christians were only those who had faith, all others must be cast out of the church. These true Christians formed small separate sects. Many believed that their lives were guided by the Holy Spirit, who directed them from within. Some went further and denied the power of civil authority over true believers. Some argued for community of goods among believers and rejected private property. Others literally followed passages in the Old Testament that suggested polygamy and promiscuity.

Wherever they settled, these small bands of believers were persecuted to the brutal extent of the laws of heresy. Catholics burned them, Protestants drowned them, and they were stoned and clubbed out of their communities. There was enough substance in their ideas and enough sincerity in their patient sufferings that they continued to recruit followers as they were driven from town to town, from Germany into the Swiss cities, and from Switzerland into Bohemia and Hungary. There, on the eastern edges of the empire, the largest groups of Anabaptists finally settled.

The Catholic Reformation

Catholics felt the same impulses toward a more fulfilling religious life as Protestants and complained of the same abuses of clerical, state, and papal powers. But the Catholic response was to reform the church from within. A new personal piety was stressed, which led to the founding of additional spiritual orders. The ecclesiastical hierarchy became more concerned with pastoral care and initiated reforms of the clergy at the parish level. The challenge of converting other peoples, Asians and Amerindians especially, led to the formation of missionary orders and to a new emphasis on preaching and education. Protestantism itself revitalized Catholicism.

The Spiritual Revival

The quest for individual spiritual fulfillment dominated later medieval Roman Catholicism. Erasmus, Luther, and Zwingli were all influenced by a Catholic spiritual movement known as the **New Piety**. It was propagated in Germany by the Brethren of the Common Life, a lay organization that stressed the importance of personal meditation on the life of Christ. The Brethren taught that a Christian life should be lived according to Christ's dictates as expressed in the Sermon on the Mount. They instructed their pupils to lead a simple ascetic life with personal devotion at its core. These were the lessons that the young Erasmus found so liberating and the young Luther so stifling.

The New Piety, with its emphasis on a simple personal form of religious practice, was a central influence on Christian humanism. It is important to realize that humanism developed within the context of Catholic education and that many churchmen embraced the new learning and supported educational reform or patronized works of humanist scholarship. The leading Christian humanists remained within the Catholic Church even after many of their criticisms had formed the basis of Protestant reforms.

This combination of piety and humanism imbued the ecclesiastical reforms initiated by Church leaders. Cardinal Jiménez de Cisneros, who also served as inquisitor-general of the Spanish Inquisition, undertook a wide-ranging reorganization of Spanish religious life in the late fifteenth century. Though not every project was successful, Jiménez de Cisneros's program took much of the sting out of Protestant attacks on clerical abuse, and there was never a serious Protestant movement in Spain.

The most influential reforming bishop was Gian Matteo Giberti (1495–1543) of Verona. Using his own frugal life as an example, Giberti rigorously enforced vows, residency, and the pastoral duties of the clergy. He founded almshouses to aid the poor and orphanages to house the homeless. In Verona, Giberti established a printing press, which turned out editions of the central works of Roman Catholicism, especially the writings of Augustine.

The most important indication of the reforming spirit within the Roman Church was the foundation of new religious orders in the early sixteenth century. Devotion to a spiritual life of sacrifice was the chief characteristic of the lay and clerical orders that had flourished throughout the Middle Ages. In one French diocese, the number of clergy quadrupled in the last half of the fifteenth century. Although the number of entrants to the traditional orders of Franciscans and Dominicans did not rise as quickly, the growth of lay communities such as the Brethren of the Common Life attested to the continuing appeal of Catholic devotionalism. Devotionalism was particularly strong in Italy, where a number of new orders received papal charters.

In Spain, Saint Teresa of Ávila (1515–1582) led the reform of the Carmelites. She believed that women had to withdraw totally from the world around them to achieve true devotion. Against the wishes of the male superiors of her order, she founded a convent to put her beliefs into practice and began writing devotional tracts such as *The Way of Perfection* (1583). In 1535, Angela Merici (ca. 1474–1540) established the Ursulines, one of the most original of the new foundations, composed of young unmarried girls who remained with their families but lived chaste lives devoted to the instruction of other women.

Loyola's Pilgrimage

The thirteenth child of a Spanish noble family, Saint Ignatius Loyola (1491–1556) trained for a military life in the service of Castile. In 1521, he was one of the garrison defenders when the French besieged Pamplona. A cannonball shattered his leg, and he was carried home for a long enforced convalescence. There, he slowly and carefully read the only books in the castle: a life of Christ and a history of the saints. His reading inspired him. Before, he had sought glory and renown in battle. But when he compared the truly heroic deeds of the saints to his own vainglorious exploits, he decided to give his life over to spirituality.

Loyola was not a man to do things by halves. He resolved to model his life on the sufferings of the saints about whom he had read. He renounced his worldly goods and endured a year-long regimen of physical abstinence and spiritual nourishment in the town of Manresa. During this period, he began to have visions, which later culminated in a mystical experience in which Loyola believed Christ called him directly to His service.

Like Luther, Loyola was tormented by his perceived inability to achieve grace through penance, but unlike Luther he redoubled his efforts. He recorded the techniques he used during this vigil in *The Spiritual Exercises*, which became a handbook for Catholic devotion. In 1523, crippled and barefoot, he made a pilgrimage to Jerusalem. He returned to Spain intent on becoming a priest.

Rubens's (1577–1640) *The Miracles of Saint Ignatius Loyola*. Founder of the Society of Jesus, Loyola prepared his Jesuit recruits for an active, rather than a contemplative, life.

By this time, Loyola had adopted a distinctive garb that attracted both followers and suspicion. Twice, the Spanish ecclesiastical authorities summoned him to be examined for heresy. In 1528, he decided to complete his studies in France, where he and a small group of friends eventually decided to form a brotherhood after they became priests. They devoted themselves to the cure of souls and took personal vows of poverty, chastity, and obedience to the pope. On a pilgrimage to Rome, Loyola and his followers again attracted the attention of ecclesiastical authorities. Loyola explained his mission to them and in 1540 won the approval of Pope Paul III to establish a new holy order, the Society of Jesus.

Loyola's Society was founded at a time when the spiritual needs of the Church were being extended beyond the confines of Europe. Loyola volunteered his followers, who came to be known as Jesuits, to serve in the remotest parts of the world. One disciple, Francis Xavier (1506–1552), made converts to Catholicism in the Portuguese port cities in the East and then in India and Japan. Other Jesuits became missionaries to the New World, where they offered Christian consolation to the Amerindian communities. By 1556, the Society of Jesus had grown from 10 to 1,000, and Loyola had become a full-time administrator in Rome.

Loyola's most fundamental innovation in these years was the founding of schools to train recruits for his order. Jesuit training was rigorous. Since they were being prepared for an active rather than a contemplative life, Jesuits were not cloistered during their training. Jesuit schools were opened to the laity, and lay education became one of the Jesuits' most important functions.

Chronology

THE REFORMATION AND THE COUNTER-REFORMATION

1517	Luther writes his Ninety-five Theses
1521	Luther is excommunicated and declared an enemy of the empire; Henry VIII receives title Defender of the Faith
1523	Zwingli expounds his faith in formal disputation
1533	Henry VIII divorces Catherine of Aragon, marries Anne Boleyn, and breaks with the Church of Rome
1536	Calvin publishes *Institutes of the Christian Religion*
1540	Loyola receives papal approval for Society of Jesus
1545–1563	Council of Trent
1553	Mary I restores Catholicism in England
1563	Elizabeth I enacts the Thirty-nine Articles, which restores Protestantism to England

The Counter-Reformation

The Jesuits were both the culmination of one wave of Catholic reform and the advance guard of another. They combined the piety and devotion that stretched from medieval mysticism through humanism, diocesan reforms, and the foundations of new spiritual orders. But they also represented an aggressive Catholic response that was determined to meet Protestantism head on and repel it—the **Counter-Reformation**. This was the Church militant. Old instruments such as the Inquisition were revived, and new weapons such as the Index of Prohibited Books were forged. But the problems of fighting Protestantism were not only those of combating Protestant ideas. Like oil and water, politics and religion failed to combine. Emperor Charles V and the hierarchy of the German church demanded thoroughgoing reform of the Catholic Church; the pope and the hierarchy of the Italian church resisted the call. Brothers in Christ, pope and emperor were mortal enemies in everything else.

At the emperor's instigation, the first serious preparations for a general council of the Church were made in the 1530s. The papacy warded it off. The complexities of international diplomacy were one factor—the French king was even less anxious to bring peace to the empire than the pope was—and the complexities of papal politics were another. The powers of a general council in relation to the powers of the papacy had never been clarified. After the advent and spread of Protestantism, successive popes had little reason to believe that in this gravest crisis of all, a council would be mindful of papal prerogatives. In fact, Catholic reformers were as bitter in their denunciations of papal abuses as Protestants were. The second attempt to arrange a general council of the Church occurred in the early 1540s. Again the papacy warded it off.

These factors ensured that when a general council of the Church finally did meet, its task would not be an easy one. The northern churches, French and German alike, wanted reforms of the papacy; the papacy wanted a restatement of orthodox doctrine. Many princes whose states were divided among Catholics and Protestants wanted compromises that might accommodate both. Ferdinand I, king of Bohemia, saw the council as an opportunity to bring the Hussites back into the fold. Charles V and the German bishops wanted the leading Protestant church authorities to offer their own compromises on doctrine that might form a basis for reuniting the empire. The papacy wanted traditional church doctrine reasserted.

The general council of the Church that finally met in Trent from 1545 to 1563 thus had nearly unlimited potential for disaster, but it ended in total victory for the views of the papacy. For all of the papacy's seeming weaknesses, an Italian pope always held the upper hand at the council. Fewer than one-third of the delegates came from outside Italy. The French looked on the council suspiciously and played only a minor role, and the emperor forbade his bishops to attend after the council moved to Bologna.

Yet for all of these difficulties, the councillors at Trent made some real progress. They corrected a number of abuses, of which the sale of indulgences was the most substantive. They formulated rules for the better regulation of parish priests and stressed the obligation of priests and bishops to preach to their congregations. They ordered seminaries to be founded in all dioceses where there was not already a university so that priests could receive sufficient education to perform their duties. They prepared a new modern and uniform Catholic service and centralized and updated the Index of Prohibited Books to include Protestant writings from all over the Continent.

The Council of Trent made no concessions to Protestants, moderate or radical. The redefinition of traditional Roman Catholicism drew the doctrinal lines clearly and ended decades of confusion. But it also meant that the differences between Catholics and Protestants could now be settled only by the sword.

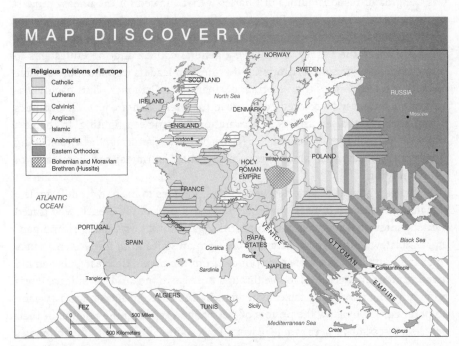

MAP DISCOVERY

THE RELIGIOUS DIVISIONS OF EUROPE, CA. 1555

Which was the largest religious denomination by the middle of the sixteenth century? Which states were most at risk of internal religious warfare? Notice the difference in the ways in which Lutheranism and Calvinism spread. Where did Catholicism remain untouched by the new religions?

The Empire Reacts

Warfare dominated the reform of religion almost from its beginning. The burnings, drownings, and executions by which both Catholics and Protestants attempted to maintain religious purity were but raindrops compared to the sea of blood that was shed in sieges and on battlefields beginning in the 1530s. The Catholic divisions were clear. The empire continued to be engaged in the west with its archenemy, France, and in the south with the ever-expanding Ottoman Empire. Charles V needed not only peace within his own German realms, but positive support for his offensive and defensive campaigns. He could never devote his full resources to suppressing Protestant dissent.

Yet there was never a united Protestant front to suppress. The north German towns and principalities that accepted Lutheranism in the 1520s had had a long history of warfare among themselves. Added to this was the division between Luther and Zwingli over doctrinal issues that effectively separated the German and Swiss components of the Reformation from each other.

Although both the Protestant and the Catholic sides were internally weak, it was the greater responsibilities of Charles V that allowed for the uneasy periods of peace. Each pause gave the Protestant reformers new life. Lutheranism continued to spread in the northern part of the empire, Zwinglian reform in the south. Charles V asked the papacy to convoke a general council and the Protestants to stop evangelizing in new territories. But Protestant leaders were no more capable of halting the spread of the Reformation than were Catholics. Thus each violation of each uneasy truce seemed to prove treachery. In 1546, just after Luther's death, both sides raised armies in preparation for renewed fighting. In the first stage of war, Charles V scored a decisive victory, capturing the two leading Protestant princes and conquering Saxony and Thuringia, the homeland of Lutheran reform.

Charles V's greatest victories were always preludes to his gravest defeats. The remaining Protestant princes were driven into the arms of the French, who placed dynastic interests above religious concerns. Again Europe was plunged into general conflict, with the French invading the German states from the west, the Turks from the south, and the Protestant princes from the north. Charles V, now an old and broken man, was forced to flee through the Alps in the dead of winter and was brought to the bargaining table soon after. By the Peace of Augsburg in 1555 the emperor agreed to allow the princes of Germany to establish the religion of their people. Protestant princes would govern Protestant states, and Catholic princes would govern Catholic states. The Peace of Augsburg ended 40 years of religious struggle in Germany.

SUMMARY

The Intellectual Reformation   Printing played a key role in the promotion and development of religious reform. Christian humanists applied the tools of Italian humanists to the Bible and the works of the Church fathers. Christian humanists emphasized education, especially of women. The life and work of Erasmus epitomized Christian humanism.

The Lutheran Reformation   Europe was becoming more religious in the late fifteenth and early sixteenth centuries. People wanted more from the Church than it could give, stimulating criticism as well as devotion. Martin Luther was tormented by the question of how salvation was attained. His eventual solution focused on three principles: a foundation built on the Word, justification by faith alone, and the priesthood of all believers. The political conflict between the pope and the emperor created both allies and enemies for Luther. By the end of the 1520s, the Holy Roman Empire was split between Catholics and adherents to the reformed religion. Lutheranism spread beyond Germany, its reception varying with local conditions.

The Protestant Reformation   In the 1530s Protestantism entered a new phase, with a second generation of reformers establishing new churches at the same time as they expanded on reformed ideas. John Calvin's theology emphasized predestination. Under his leadership, Geneva became a theocracy. Politics was the driving force behind Henry VIII's decision to break with the Catholic Church. Under his successors, England went back and forth between Protestantism and Catholicism, ending with a Protestant compromise under Elizabeth I. Throughout Europe, some Protestants pushed the reformed theology to radical conclusions.

The Catholic Reformation   A desire for spiritual fulfillment dominated later medieval Roman Catholicism. New religious orders were established to meet the needs of changing times. Saint Ignatius of Loyola founded the Jesuits, an order that played a key role in combating Protestantism and promoting Catholic education throughout the world. The Counter-Reformation saw the advent of new tools for imposing orthodoxy. Tensions between the pope and the emperor delayed the convening of a general council to forge the Catholic response to the Protestant challenge. The Council of Trent promulgated many reforms, but made no compromises with Protestantism. Warfare in the Holy Roman Empire culminated with the Peace of Augsburg (1555). Henceforth, the emperor would allow the princes of Germany to establish the religion of their people.

QUESTIONS FOR REVIEW

1. How did humanism prepare the way for the Reformation?
2. What motivated Martin Luther?
3. What were the differences between the reforming ideas of Luther, Zwingli, and Calvin?
4. How did the Catholic Church respond to the challenges posed by the Protestant Reformation?

Europe at War, 1555–1648

The Crises of the Western States

"Un roi, une foi, une loi"—"One king, one faith, one law." This was a prescription that members of all European states accepted without question in the sixteenth century. Society was an integrated whole, equally dependent on monarchical, ecclesiastical, and civil authority for its effective survival. A European state could no more tolerate the presence of two churches than it could the presence of two kings. But the Reformation had created two churches. The coexistence of Catholics and Protestants in a single realm posed a stark challenge to accepted theory and traditional practice.

The problem proved intractable because it admitted only one solution: total victory. There could be no compromise for several reasons. Religious beliefs were profoundly held. Religious controversy was more than a life-and-death struggle: It was a struggle between everlasting life and eternal damnation. Doomed, too, was the practical solution of toleration. To the modern mind, toleration seems so logical that it is difficult to understand why it took over a century of bloodshed before it came to be grudgingly accepted by the most bitterly divided countries. But toleration was not a practical solution in a society that admitted no principle of organization other than one king, one faith.

The French Wars of Religion

No wars are more terrible than civil wars. The loss of lives and property is staggering, but the loss of communal identity is greater still. Generations pass before societies recover from their civil wars. Such was the case with the **French wars of religion.**

The Spread of Calvinism and Religious Division. Protestantism came late to France. Not until after Calvin reformed the Church in Geneva and began to export his brand of Protestantism did French society begin to divide along religious lines. By 1560, there were over 2,000 Protestant congregations in France, and their membership totaled nearly 10 percent of the French population. Calvin and his successors achieved their greatest following among the middle ranks of urban society: merchants, traders, and artisans. They also found a receptive audience among aristocratic women, who eventually converted their husbands and children.

However, the wars of religion were brought on by more than the rapid spread of Calvinism. Equally important was the vacuum of power that had been created when Henry II (1547–1559) died in a jousting tournament. Surviving Henry were his extraordinary widow, Catherine de Médicis, three daughters, and four sons, the oldest of whom, Francis II (1559–1560), was only 15 years old. Under the influence of his beautiful young wife, Mary, Queen of Scots, Francis allowed Mary's relatives, the Guise family, to dominate the great offices of state and to exclude their rivals from power. The Guises controlled the two most powerful institutions of the state: the army and the Church.

The Guises were staunchly Catholic, and among their enemies were the Bourbons, princes of the blood with a direct claim to the French throne but also a family with powerful Protestant members. The revelation of a Protestant plot to remove the king

Catherine de Médicis (1519–1598), the wife of Henry II of France, was the real power behind the throne during the reigns of her sons Charles IX (1560–1574) and Henry III (1574–1589). Her overriding concern was to ensure her sons' succession and to preserve the power of the monarchy.

from Paris provided the Guises with an opportunity to eliminate their most potent rivals. The Bourbon duc de Condé, the leading Protestant peer of the realm, was sentenced to death. But five days before Condé's execution, Francis II died, and Guise power evaporated. The new king, Charles IX (1560–1574), was only 10 years old and firmly under the grip of his mother, Catherine de Médicis, who now declared herself regent of France.

Civil War. Condé's death sentence convinced him that the Guises would stop at nothing to gain their ambitions. Force would have to be met with force. Protestants and Catholics alike raised armies and, in 1562, civil war ensued. Once the wars began, the leading Protestant peers fled the court, but the position of the Guises was not altogether secure. Henry Bourbon, king of Navarre, was the next in line to the throne should Charles IX and his two brothers die without male heirs. Henry had been raised in the Protestant faith by his mother, Jeanne d'Albret, whose own mother, Marguerite of Navarre, was among the earliest protectors of the **Huguenots**, as the French Calvinists came to be called.

The inconclusive nature of the early battles might have allowed for the pragmatic solution by Catherine de Médicis had it not been for the assassination of the duc de Guise in 1563 by a Protestant fanatic. This act added a personal vendetta to the religious passions of the Catholic leaders. They encouraged the slaughter of Huguenot congregations and openly planned the murder of Huguenot leaders. Protestants gave as good as they got. In open defiance of Valois dynastic interests, the Guises courted support from Spain, while the Huguenots imported Swiss and German mercenaries to fight in France. Noble factions and irreconcilable religious differences were pulling the government apart.

The Saint Bartholomew's Day Massacre. By 1570, Catherine was ready to attempt another reconciliation. She announced her plans for a marriage between her daughter Margaret and Henry of Navarre, a marriage that would symbolize the spirit of conciliation between the crown and the Huguenots. The marriage was to take place in Paris during August 1572. The arrival of Huguenot leaders from all over France to attend the marriage ceremony presented an opportunity of a different kind to the Guises and their supporters. If leading Huguenots could be assassinated in Paris, the Protestant cause might collapse, and the truce that the wedding signified might be turned instead into a Catholic triumph.

Saint Bartholomew was the apostle whom Jesus described as a man without guile. Ironically, it was on his feast day that the Huguenots who had innocently come to celebrate Henry's marriage were led like lambs to the slaughter. On 24 August 1572 the streets of Paris ran red with Huguenot blood. Although frenzied, the slaughter was inefficient. Henry of Navarre and a number of other important Huguenots escaped the carnage and returned to their urban strongholds. In the following weeks, the violence spread from Paris to the countryside, and thousands of Protestants paid for their beliefs with their lives.

One King, Two Faiths

The Saint Bartholomew's Day Massacre was a transforming event in many ways. In the first place, it prolonged the wars. A whole new generation of Huguenots now had an attachment to the continuation of warfare: Their fathers and brothers had been mercilessly slaughtered. By itself, the event was shocking enough; in the atmosphere of anticipated reconciliation created by the wedding, it screamed out for revenge. And the target for retaliation was no longer limited to the Guises and their followers. By accepting the results of the massacre, the monarchy sanctioned it and spilled Huguenot blood on itself. For more than a decade, Catherine de Médicis had maintained a distance between the crown and the leaders of the Catholic movement. That distance no longer existed.

The Theory of Resistance. After Saint Bartholomew's Day, Huguenot theorists began to develop the idea that resistance to a monarch whose actions violated divine commandments or civil right was lawful. For the first time, Huguenot writers provided a justification for rebellion. Perhaps most importantly, a genuine revulsion against the massacres swept the nation. A number of Catholic peers now joined with the Huguenots to protest the excesses of the crown and the Guises. These Catholics came to be called the **politiques**, from their desire for a practical settlement of the wars. They were led by the duke of Anjou, who was next in line to the throne when Charles IX died in 1574 and Henry III (1574–1589) became king.

Painting of the Saint Bartholomew's Day Massacre. The massacre began in Paris on 24 August 1572, and the violence soon spread throughout France.

Against them, in Paris and a number of other towns, the Catholic League was formed, a society that pledged its first allegiance to religion. The League took up where the Saint Bartholomew's Day Massacre left off, and the slaughter of ordinary people who professed the wrong religion continued. Matters grew worse in 1584 when the duke of Anjou died. With each passing year it was becoming apparent that Henry III would produce no male heir. After the duke's death, the Huguenot Henry of Navarre was the next in line for the throne. Catholic Leaguers talked openly of altering the royal succession and began to develop theories of lawful resistance to monarchical power. By 1585, when the final civil war began—the war of the three Henrys, named for Henry III, Henry Guise, and Henry of Navarre—the crown was in the weakest possible position. Paris and the Catholic towns were controlled by the League, and the Protestant strongholds were controlled by Henry of Navarre. King Henry III could not abandon his capital or his religion, but neither could he gain control of the Catholic party. The extremism of the Leaguers kept the politiques away from court; without the politiques there could be no settlement.

In December 1588, Henry III summoned Henry Guise and Guise's brother to a meeting in the royal bedchamber. There, they were murdered by the king's order. The politiques were blamed for the murders—revenge was taken on a number of them—and Henry III was forced to flee his capital. He made a pact with Henry of Navarre, and together royalist and Huguenot forces besieged Paris. All supplies were cut off from the city, and only the arrival of a Spanish army prevented its fall. In 1589, Catherine de Médicis died, her ambition to reestablish the authority of the monarchy in shambles, and in the same year a fanatic priest gained revenge for the murder of the Guises by assassinating Henry III.

Henry IV. Now Henry of Navarre came into his inheritance. But after nearly 30 years of continuous civil war, it was certain that a Huguenot could never rule France. If Henry was to become king of all France, he would have to become a Catholic king. It is not clear when Henry made the decision to accept the Catholic faith—"Paris is worth a Mass," he reportedly declared—but he did not announce his decision at once. Rather, he strengthened his forces, tightened his bonds with the politiques, and urged his countrymen to expel the Spanish invaders. He finally made his conversion public and in 1594 was crowned Henry IV (1589–1610). A war-weary nation was willing to accept him.

In 1598, Henry proclaimed the **Edict of Nantes**, which granted limited toleration to the Huguenots. It was the culmination of decades of attempts to find a solution to the existence of two religions in one state. It was a compromise that satisfied no one, but it was a compromise that everyone could accept. "One king, two faiths" was as apt a description of Henry IV as it was of the settlement. Yet neither Henry's conversion nor the Edict of Nantes stilled the passions that had spawned and sustained the French wars of religion. Sporadic fighting between Catholics and Huguenots continued, and fanatics on both sides fanned the flames of religious hatred. Henry IV survived 18 attempts on his life before he was finally felled by an assassin's knife in 1610, but by then he had established the monarchy and brought a semblance of peace to France.

THE FRENCH WARS OF RELIGION

1559	Death of Henry II
1560	Protestant duc de Condé sentenced to death
1562	First battle of wars of religion
1563	Catholic duc de Guise assassinated; Edict of Amboise grants limited Protestant worship
1572	Saint Bartholomew's Day Massacre
1574	Accession of Henry III
1576	Formation of Catholic League
1584	Death of duc d'Anjou makes Henry of Navarre heir to throne
1585	War of the three Henrys
1588	Duc de Guise murdered by order of Henry III
1589	Catherine de Médicis dies; Henry III assassinated
1594	Henry IV crowned
1598	Edict of Nantes

The World of Philip II

While France was caught up in religious strife, Spain, by the middle of the sixteenth century, had achieved the status of the greatest power in Europe. The dominions of Philip II (1556–1598) of Spain stretched from the Atlantic to the Pacific; his continental territories included the Netherlands in the north and Milan and Naples in Italy. In 1580, Philip became king of Portugal, uniting all the states of the Iberian peninsula. With the addition of Portugal's Atlantic ports and its sizable fleet, Spanish maritime power was now unsurpassed. Philip saw himself as a Catholic monarch fending off the spread of heresy. He came to the throne at just the moment that Calvinism began its rapid growth in northern Europe and provided the impetus for the greatest crisis of his reign: the revolt of the Netherlands.

Though Philip's father, Charles V, amassed a great empire, he had begun only as the duke of Burgundy. Charles's Burgundian inheritance encompassed a diverse territory in the northwestern corner of Europe. The 17 separate provinces of this territory were called the Netherlands, or the Low Countries, because of the flooding that kept large portions of them under water. The Netherlands, one of the richest and most populous regions of Europe, was an international leader in manufacturing, banking, and commerce. In the southern provinces, French was the background and language of the inhabitants; in the northern ones, Germans had settled, and Dutch was spoken.

The Low Countries had accepted the Peace of Augsburg in a spirit of conciliation in which it was never intended. Here, Catholics, Lutherans, Anabaptists, and Calvinists peaceably coexisted. As in France, this situation changed dramatically with the spread of Calvinism. The heavy concentration of urban populations in the Low Countries provided the natural habitat for Calvinist preachers, who made converts across the entire social spectrum. As Holy Roman Emperor, Charles V may have made his peace with Protestants, but as king of Spain he had not. Charles V had maintained the purity of the Spanish Catholic Church through a careful combination of reform and repression.

Philip II intended to pursue a similar policy in the Low Countries. With papal approval, he initiated a scheme to reform the hierarchy of the Church by expanding the numbers of bishops, and he invited the Jesuits to establish schools for orthodox learning. Simultaneously, he strengthened the power of the Inquisition and ordered the enforcement of the decrees of the Council of Trent. The Protestants sought the protection of their local nobles, who, Catholic or Protestant, had their own reasons for opposing the strict enforcement of heresy laws. Provincial nobles and magistrates resented both the policies that were being pursued and the fact that they disregarded local autonomy. Town governors and noblemen refused to cooperate in implementing the new laws.

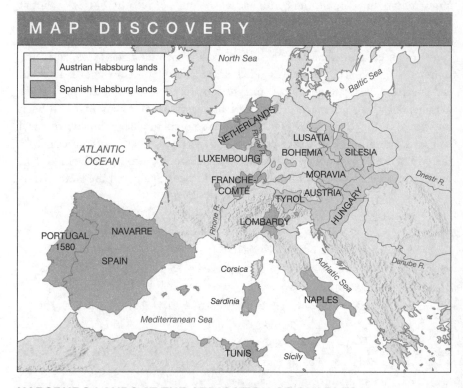

MAP DISCOVERY

HABSBURG LANDS AT THE ABDICATION OF CHARLES V

Notice how dispersed were the states controlled by Charles V when he abdicated the throne in 1556. Why did he divide his empire between son Philip II and brother Ferdinand I? What made it possible for the Netherlands to revolt from Spanish control?

The Revolt of the Netherlands

The passive resistance of nobles and magistrates was soon matched by the active resistance of the Calvinists. Unable to enforce Philip's policy, Margaret of Parma, his half-sister, whom Philip had made regent, agreed to a limited toleration. But in the summer of 1566, before this toleration could be put into effect, bands of Calvinists unleashed a storm of iconoclasm in the provinces, breaking stained glass windows and statues of the Virgin and the saints, which they claimed were idolatrous. Helpless in the face of determined Calvinists and apathetic Catholics, local authorities could not protect Church property. Iconoclasm gave way to open revolt. Fearing social rebellion, even the leading Protestant noblemen took part in suppressing these riots.

Rebellion and War. In Spain, the events in the Netherlands were treated for what they were: open rebellion. Despite the fact that Margaret had already restored order, Philip II was determined to punish the rebels and enforce the heresy laws. A large military force under the command of the duke of Alba (1507–1582) was sent from Spain as an army of occupation. Alba lured leading Protestant noblemen to Brussels, where he publicly executed them in 1568. He also established a military court to punish participants in the rebellion, a court that came to be called the Council of Blood. The Council handed down over 9,000 convictions, 1,000 of which carried the death penalty. As many as 60,000 Protestants fled beyond Alba's jurisdiction. Alba next made an example of several small towns that had been implicated in the iconoclasm. He allowed his soldiers to pillage the towns at will before slaughtering their entire populations and razing them to the ground. By the end of 1568, royal policy had gained a sullen acceptance in the Netherlands, but for the next 80 years, with only occasional truces, Spain and the Netherlands were at war.

Chronology

REVOLT OF THE NETHERLANDS

1559	Margaret of Parma named regent of the Netherlands
1566	Calvinist iconoclasm begins revolt
1567	Duke of Alba arrives in Netherlands and establishes Council of Blood
1568	Protestant Count Egmont executed
1572	Protestants capture Holland and Zeeland
1573	Alba relieved of his command
1576	Sack of Antwerp; Pacification of Ghent
1581	Catholic and Protestant provinces split
1585	Spanish forces take Brussels and Antwerp
1609	Twelve Years' Truce

The Protestants Rebel. Alba's policies had driven Protestants into rebellion, and this forced the Spanish government to maintain its army by raising taxes from the provinces that had remained loyal. Soon the loyal provinces were also in revolt, not over religion but over taxation and local autonomy. Tax resistance and fear of an invasion from France left Alba unprepared for the series of successful assaults Protestants launched in the northern provinces during 1572. The Protestant generals established a permanent base in the northwestern provinces of Holland and Zeeland. By 1575, they had gained a stronghold that they would never relinquish. Prince William of Orange (1533–1584) assumed the leadership of the two provinces, which were now united against the tyranny of Philip's rule.

Spanish government was collapsing all over the Netherlands. William ruled in the north, and the States-General, a parliamentary body composed of representatives from the separate provinces, ruled in the south. Margaret of Parma had resigned in disgust at Alba's tactics, and Alba had been relieved of his command when his tactics failed. No one was in control of the Spanish army. The soldiers, who had gone years with only partial pay, now roamed the southern provinces looking for plunder. Brussels and Ghent had both been targets, and in 1576 the worst atrocities of all occurred when mutinous Spanish troops sacked Antwerp. Over 7,000 people were slaughtered, and nearly one-third of the city burned to the ground.

The "Spanish fury" in Antwerp effectively ended Philip's rule over his Burgundian inheritance. The Protestants had established a permanent home in the north. The States-General had established its ability to rule in the south, and Spanish policy had been totally discredited. To achieve a settlement, the Pacification of Ghent of 1576, the Spanish government conceded local autonomy in taxation, the central role of the States-General in legislation, and the immediate withdrawal of all Spanish troops from the Low Countries. This rift among the provinces was soon followed by a permanent split. In 1581, one group of provinces voted to depose Philip II while a second group decided to remain loyal to him. Philip II refused to accept the dismemberment of his inheritance or to recognize the independent Dutch state that now existed in Holland.

Meanwhile, Protestant England under Elizabeth I (1558–1603) had sided with the Dutch Protestants opposing Philip II. During Elizabeth's reign, England and Spain entered a long period of hostility. English pirates raided Spanish treasure ships returning to Europe, and Elizabeth covertly aided both French and Dutch Protestants. Finally, in 1588, Philip decided to invade England. A great fleet set sail from the Portuguese coast to the Netherlands, where a large Spanish army was waiting to be conveyed to England.

The **Spanish Armada** comprised over 130 ships, many of them the pride of the Spanish and Portuguese navies. They were bigger and stronger than anything possessed by the English, whose forces were largely merchant vessels hastily converted for battle. But the English ships were faster and more easily maneuverable in the unpredictable winds of the English Channel. They also carried guns that could easily be reloaded for multiple firings, whereas the Spanish guns were designed to discharge only one broadside before hand-to-hand combat ensued. With these advantages, the

The defeat of the immense armada that Philip II sent to invade England in 1588 dealt a serious blow to Spain's standing in Europe.

English were able to prevent the Armada from reaching port in the Netherlands and to destroy many individual ships as they were blown off course.

Throughout the 1580s and 1590s, Spanish military expeditions attempted to reunite the southern provinces and to conquer the northern ones. But Spanish successes in the south were outweighed by the long-term failure of their objectives in the north. In 1609, Spain and the Netherlands concluded the Twelve Years' Truce, which tacitly recognized the existence of the state of Holland. By the beginning of the seventeenth century, Holland was not only an independent state; it was one of the greatest rivals of Spain and Portugal.

The Struggles in Eastern Europe

In eastern Europe, dynastic struggles outweighed the problems created by religious reform. Muscovy remained the bulwark of Eastern Orthodox Christianity, immune from the struggles over the Roman faith. Protestantism did spread into Poland-Lithuania, but its presence was tolerated by the Polish state. The spread of dissent was checked not by repression, but by a vigorous Catholic reformation led by the Jesuits. The domestic crises in the East were crises of state rather than of the Church. In Muscovy, the disputed succession that followed the death of Ivan the Terrible plunged the state into anarchy and civil war. Centuries of conflict between Poland-Lithuania and Muscovy came to a head with the Poles' desperate gamble to seize control of their massive eastern neighbor. War between Poland-Lithuania and Muscovy inevitably dominated the politics of the entire region. The Baltic states, most notably Sweden, soon joined the fray.

Kings and Diets in Poland

Until the end of the sixteenth century, Poland-Lithuania was the dominant power in the eastern part of Europe. It was economically healthy and militarily strong. Through its Baltic ports, especially Gdansk, Poland played a central role in international commerce and a dominant role in the northern grain trade. The vast size of the Polish state made defense difficult, and during the course of the sixteenth century it had lost lands to Muscovy in the east and to the Crimean Tatars in the south. But the permanent union with Lithuania in 1569 and the gradual absorption of the Baltic region of Livonia more than compensated for these losses. Matters of war and peace, of taxation, and of reform were placed under the strict supervision of the Polish Diet, a parliamentary body that represented the Polish landed elite. The diet also carefully controlled religious policy. Roman Catholicism was the principal religion in Poland, but the state tolerated numerous Protestant and Eastern creeds. In the Warsaw Confederation of 1573, the Polish gentry vowed "that we who differ in matters of religion will keep the peace among ourselves."

The biological failure of the Jagiellon monarchy in Poland ended that nation's most successful line of kings. Without a natural heir, the Polish nobility and gentry, who officially elected the monarch, had to peddle their throne among the princes of Europe. When Sigismund III (1587–1632) was elected to the Polish throne in 1587, he was also heir to the crown of Sweden. Sigismund accepted the prohibitions against religious repression outlined in the Warsaw Confederation, but he actively encouraged the establishment of Jesuit schools, the expansion of monastic orders, and the strengthening of the Roman Catholic Church.

All of these policies enjoyed the approval of the Polish ruling classes. But the diet would not support Sigismund's efforts to gain control of the Swedish crown, which he inherited in 1592 but from which he was deposed three years later. If Sigismund triumphed in Sweden, all Poland would get was a part-time monarch. The Polish Diet consistently refused to give the king the funds necessary to invade Sweden successfully. Nevertheless, Sigismund mounted several unsuccessful campaigns against the Swedes that sapped Polish money and manpower.

Muscovy's Time of Troubles

The wars of Ivan the Great and Ivan the Terrible in the fifteenth and sixteenth centuries were waged to secure agricultural territory in the west and a Baltic port in the north. Both objectives came at the expense of Poland-Lithuania. But after the death of Ivan the Terrible in 1584, the Muscovite state began to disintegrate. For years it had been held together only by conquest and fear. Ivan's conflicts with the boyars, the hereditary nobility, created an aristocracy that was unwilling and unable to come to the aid of Ivan's successors. By 1601, the crown was plunged into a crisis of legitimacy known as the **Time of Troubles**. Ivan had murdered his heir in a fit of anger and left his half-witted son to inherit the throne. This led to a vacuum of power at the center as well as a struggle for the spoils of government. Private armies ruled great swaths of the state, and pretenders to the crown—all claiming

EASTERN EUROPE, CA. 1550 after the consolidation of Russia and the growth of Poland. The eastern part of Europe was still sparsely populated and economically underdeveloped.

to be Dimitri, the lost brother of the last legitimate tsar—appeared everywhere. Ambitious groups of boyars backed their own claimants to the throne. So, too, did ambitious foreigners who eagerly sought to carve up Muscovite possessions.

Muscovy's Time of Troubles was Poland's moment of opportunity. While Muscovy floundered in anarchy and civil war, Poland looked to regain the territory that it had lost to Muscovy over the previous century. Sigismund abandoned war with Sweden to intervene in the struggle for the Russian crown. Polish forces crossed into Muscovy, and Sigismund's generals backed one of the strongest of the false Dimitris, but their plan to put him on the throne failed when he was assassinated. Sigismund used the death of the last false Dimitri as a pretext to assert his own claim to the Muscovite crown. More Polish forces poured across the frontier. In 1610, they took Moscow, and Sigismund proclaimed himself tsar, intending to unite the two massive states.

The Russian boyars, so long divided, now rose against the Polish enemy. The Polish garrison in Moscow was starved into submission, and a native Russian, Michael Romanov (1613–1645), was chosen tsar by an assembly of landholders, the Zemsky Sobor. He made a humiliating peace with the Swedes—who had also taken advantage of the Time of Troubles to invade Muscovy's Baltic provinces—in return for Swedish assistance against the Poles. Intermittent fighting continued for another 20 years. In the end, Poland agreed to peace and a separate Muscovite state but only in exchange for large territorial concessions.

The Rise of Sweden

Sweden's rise to power during the seventeenth century was as startling as it was swift. Until the Reformation, Sweden had been part of the Scandinavian confederation ruled by the Danes. Although the Swedes had a measure of autonomy, they were very much a junior partner in Baltic affairs. Denmark controlled the narrow sound that linked the Baltic Sea with the North Sea, and its prosperity derived from the tolls it collected on imports and exports. When, in 1523, Gustav I Vasa led the uprising of the Swedish aristocracy that ended Danish domination, he won the right to rule over a poor, sparsely populated state with few towns or developed seaports. The Vasas ruled Sweden in conjunction with the aristocracy. Although the throne was hereditary, the part played by the nobility in elevating Gustav I Vasa (1523–1560) gave the nobles a powerful voice in Swedish affairs. Through the council of state, known as the Rad, the Swedish nobility exerted a strong check on the monarch.

Sweden's aggressive foreign policy began accidentally. When in the 1550s the Teutonic Knights found themselves no longer capable of ruling in Livonia, the Baltic seaports that had been under their dominion scrambled for new alliances. Muscovy and Poland-Lithuania were the logical choices, but the town of Reval, an important outlet for Russian trade near the mouth of the Gulf of Finland, asked Sweden for protection. After some hesitation, since the occupation of territory on the southern shores of the Baltic would involve great expense, Sweden fortified Reval in 1560. A decade later, Swedish forces captured Narva, farther to the east, and consolidated Sweden's hold on the Livonian coast. By occupying the most important ports on the Gulf of Finland, Sweden could control a sizable portion of the Muscovite trade. As the Swedes secured the northern Livonian ports, more of the Muscovy trade moved to the south and passed through Riga, which would have to be captured or blockaded if the Swedes were to control commerce in the eastern Baltic.

Sigismund's aggressive alliance with the Polish Jesuits had persuaded the Swedish nobility that he would undermine their Lutheran church, and Sigismund was deposed in favor of his uncle Charles IX (1604—1611). War between Sweden and Poland resulted from Sigismund's efforts to regain the Swedish crown, and the Swedes used the opportunity to blockade Riga and to occupy more Livonian territory. The Swedish navy was far superior to any force that the Poles could assemble, but on land, Polish forces were masters. The Swedish invasion force suffered a crushing defeat and had to retreat to its coastal enclaves. The Poles now had an opportunity to retake all of Livonia, but, as always, the Polish Diet was reluctant to finance Sigismund's wars. Furthermore, Sigismund had his eyes on a bigger prize. Rather than follow up its Swedish victory, Poland invaded Muscovy.

Meanwhile, the blockade of Riga and the assembly of a large Swedish fleet in the Baltic threatened Denmark. The Danes continued to claim sovereignty over Sweden and took the opportunity of the Polish-Swedish conflict to reassert it. In 1611, under the energetic leadership of the Danish king Christian IV (1588–1648), Denmark invaded Sweden from both the east and the west. The Danes captured the towns of Kalmar and Alvsborg and threatened to take Stockholm. To end the Danish war, Sweden accepted humiliating terms in 1613, renouncing all claims to the northern coasts and recognizing Danish control of the Arctic trading route.

Paradoxically, these setbacks became the springboard for Swedish success. Fear of the Danes led both the English and the Dutch into alliances with Sweden. These countries all shared Protestant interests, and the English were heavily committed to the Muscovy trade, which was still an important part of Swedish commerce. Fear of the Poles had a similar effect on Muscovy. In 1609, the Swedes agreed to send 5,000 troops to Muscovy to help repel the Polish invasion. In return, Muscovy agreed to cede to Sweden its Baltic possessions. This was accomplished in 1617 and gave Sweden complete control of the Gulf of Finland.

In 1611, during the middle of the Danish war, Charles IX died and was succeeded by his son Gustavus Adolphus (1611–1632), one of the leading Protestant princes of his day. Gustavus's greatest skills were military, and he inherited an ample navy and an effective army. Unlike nearly every other European state, Sweden raised its forces from its own citizens. Gustavus introduced new weapons such as

THE RISE OF SWEDEN. For the only time in its history, Sweden acquired territories on the European mainland.

the light mobile gun and reshaped his army into standard-size squadrons and regiments, which were easier to administer and deploy.

The calamitous wars that Gustavus inherited from his father occupied him during the early years of his reign. He was forced to conclude the humiliating peace with the Danes in 1613 and to go to war with the Russians in 1614 to secure the Baltic coastal estates that had been promised in 1609. Gustavus's first military initiative was to resume war with Poland to force Sigismund to renounce his claim to the Swedish throne. In 1621, Gustavus landed in Livonia and in two weeks captured Riga, the capstone of Sweden's Baltic ambitions. Occupation of Riga increased Swedish control of the Muscovy trade and deprived Denmark of a significant portion of its customs duties. Gustavus now claimed Riga as a Swedish port and successfully demanded that ships sailing from there pay tolls to Sweden rather than Denmark. By the mid-seventeenth century, Sweden ranked among the leading Protestant powers.

The Thirty Years' War, 1618–1648

In time, the isolated conflicts that dotted the corners of Europe were joined together. In 1609, Spain and the Dutch Republic had signed a truce that was to last until 1621. In over 40 years of nearly continuous fighting, the Dutch had carved out a state in the northern Netherlands. They used the truce to consolidate their position and increase their prosperity. Spain had reluctantly accepted Dutch independence, but Philip III (1598–1621), like his father before him, never abandoned the objective of recovering his Burgundian inheritance. By the beginning of the seventeenth century, Philip had good reasons for hope. Beginning in the 1580s, Spanish forces had reconquered the southern provinces of the Netherlands. The prosperous towns of Brussels, Antwerp, and Ghent were again under Spanish control, and they provided a springboard for another invasion.

The Twelve Years' Truce gave Spain time to prepare for the final assault. During this time, Philip III attempted to resolve all of Spain's other European conflicts so that he could then give full attention to a resumption of the Dutch war. Circumstance smiled on his efforts. In 1603, the pacific James I (1603–1625) came to the English throne. Secure in his island state, James I desired peace among all Christian princes. He quickly concluded the war with Spain that had begun with the attempted invasion of the Spanish Armada, and he entered into negotiations to marry his heir to a Spanish princess. In 1610, the bellicose Henry IV of France was felled by an assassin's knife. French plans to renew war with Spain were abandoned with the accession of the eight-year-old Louis XIII (1610–1643). The **Thirty Years' War** was about to begin.

Bohemia Revolts

The Peace of Augsburg had served the German states well. The principle that the religion of the ruler was the religion of the state complicated the political life of the Holy Roman Empire, but it also pacified it. Though rulers had the right to enforce uniformity on their subjects, in practice many of the larger states tolerated more than one religion. By the beginning of the seventeenth century, Catholicism and Protestantism had achieved a rough equality within the German states, symbolized by the fact that of the seven electors who chose the Holy Roman Emperor, three were Catholic, three were Protestant, and the seventh was the emperor himself, acting as king of Bohemia. This situation was not unwelcome to the leaders of the Austrian Habsburg family who succeeded Emperor Charles V. By necessity, the eastern Habsburgs were more tolerant than their Spanish kinfolk. The head of their house was elected king of Bohemia and king of Hungary, both states with large Protestant populations.

A Fatal Election. In 1617, Mathias, the childless Holy Roman Emperor, began making plans for his cousin, Ferdinand Habsburg, to succeed him. Ferdinand was a very devout and very committed Catholic. To ensure a Catholic majority among the electors, the emperor relinquished his Bohemian title and pressed for Ferdinand's election as the new king of Bohemia. The Protestant nobles of Bohemia forced the new king to accept the strictest limitations on his political and religious powers, but once elected, Ferdinand had not the slightest intention of honoring the provisions that had been thrust on him. His opponents were equally strong willed. When Ferdinand violated Protestant religious liberties, a group of noblemen marched to the royal palace in Prague in May 1618, found two of the king's chief advisers, and hurled them out of an upper-story window.

The Defenestration of Prague, as this incident came to be known, initiated a Protestant counteroffensive throughout the Habsburg lands. Fear of Ferdinand's policies led to Protestant uprisings in Hungary as well as Bohemia. The men who seized control of the government declared Ferdinand deposed and the throne vacant. But they had no candidate to accept their crown. Whatever their religion, princes were always uneasy about the overthrow of a lawful ruler. Whoever came to be called king of Bohemia in place of Ferdinand would have to face the combined might of the Habsburgs. When Emperor Mathias died in 1619, Ferdinand succeeded to the imperial title as Ferdinand II (1619–1637), and Frederick V, one of the Protestant electors, accepted the Bohemian crown.

Frederick V, the "Winter King." Frederick was a sincere but weak Calvinist whose credentials were much stronger than his abilities. His mother was a daughter of Prince William of Orange and his wife, Elizabeth, was a daughter of James I of England. It was widely believed that Elizabeth's resolution that she would "rather eat sauerkraut with a king than roast meat with an elector" decided the issue. No decision could have been more disastrous for the fate of Europe. Frederick ruled a geographically divided German state known as the Palatinate. One hundred miles separated the two segments of his lands, but both were strategically important. The Lower Palatinate bordered on the Catholic Spanish Netherlands and the Upper Palatinate on Catholic Bavaria.

Once Frederick accepted the Bohemian crown, he was faced with a war on three fronts. Ferdinand II had no difficulty enlisting allies to recover the Bohemian crown, since he could pay them with the spoils of Frederick's lands. Spanish troops from the Netherlands occupied the Lower Palatinate, and Bavarian troops occupied the Upper Palatinate. Frederick, by contrast, met rejection wherever he turned. Neither the Dutch nor the English would send more than token aid; both had advised him against breaking the imperial peace. The Lutheran princes of Germany would not enter into a war between Calvinists and Catholics, especially after Ferdinand II promised to protect the Bohemian Lutherans.

At the Battle of the White Mountain in 1620, Ferdinand's Catholic forces annihilated Frederick's army. Frederick and Elizabeth fled to Denmark, and Bohemia was left to face the wrath of Ferdinand, the victorious king and emperor. The retribution was horrible. Mercenaries who had fought for Ferdinand II were allowed to sack Prague for a week. Elective monarchy was abolished, and Bohemia became part of the hereditary Habsburg lands. Free peasants were enserfed and subjected to imperial law. Nobles who had supported Frederick lost their lands and their privileges. Calvinism was repressed and thoroughly rooted out, consolidating forever the Catholic character of Bohemia. Frederick's estates were carved up, and his rights as elector were transferred to the Catholic duke of Bavaria. The Battle of the White Mountain was a turning point in the history of central Europe, for it forced all Protestant nations to arm for war.

The War Widens

For the Habsburgs, religious and dynastic interests were inseparable. Ferdinand II and Philip III of Spain fought for their beliefs and for their patrimony. Their victory gave them more than they could have expected. Ferdinand swallowed up Bohemia and strengthened his position in the empire. Philip gained possession of a vital link in his supply route between Italy and the Netherlands. Spanish expansion threatened France. The occupation of the Lower Palatinate placed a ring of Spanish armies around France from the Pyrenees to the Low Countries. The French too searched for allies. But French opinion remained divided over which was the greater evil: Spain or Protestantism.

Chronology

THE THIRTY YEARS' WAR

1618	Defenestration of Prague
1619	Ferdinand Habsburg elected Holy Roman Emperor; Frederick of the Palatinate accepts the crown of Bohemia
1620	Catholic victory at Battle of the White Mountain
1621	End of Twelve Years' Truce; war between Spain and Netherlands
1626	Danes form Protestant alliance under Christian IV
1627	Spain declares bankruptcy
1630	Gustavus Adolphus leads Swedish forces into Germany
1631	Sack of Magdeburg; Protestant victory at Breitenfeld
1632	Protestant victory at Lützen; death of Gustavus Adolphus
1635	France declares war on Spain
1640	Portugal secedes from Spain
1643	Battle of Rocroi; French forces repel Spaniards
1648	Peace of Westphalia

The Danes Respond. Frederick, now in Holland, refused to accept the judgment of battle. He lobbied for a grand alliance to repel the Spaniards from the Lower Palatinate and to restore the religious balance in the empire. Though his personal cause met with little sympathy, his political logic was impeccable, especially after Spain again declared war on the Dutch. A grand Protestant alliance—secretly supported by the French—brought together England, Holland, a number of German states, and Denmark. It was the Danes who led this potentially powerful coalition. In 1626, a large Danish army under the command of King Christian IV engaged imperial forces on German soil. But Danish forces could not match the superior numbers and the superior leadership of the Catholic mercenary forces under the command of the ruthless and brilliant Count Albrecht von Wallenstein (1583–1634). In 1629, the Danes withdrew from the empire and sued for peace.

If the Catholic victory at the White Mountain in 1620 threatened the well-being of German Protestantism, the Catholic triumph over the Danes threatened its survival. More powerful than ever, Ferdinand II was determined to turn the religious clock back to the state of affairs that had existed when the Peace of Augsburg was concluded in 1555. He demanded that all lands that had then been Catholic but had since become Protestant must now be returned to the Catholic fold. He also proclaimed that because the Peace of Augsburg made no provision for the toleration of Calvinists, they would no longer be tolerated in the empire. These policies together constituted a virtual revolution in the religious affairs of the German states, and they proved impossible to impose. Ferdinand succeeded in only one thing: He united Lutherans and Calvinists against him. Moreover, the costs of the war were heavy even for the victors. Wallenstein, who had over 130,000 men in arms, would no longer take orders from anyone, and Ferdinand II was forced to dismiss him from service.

Protestant Gains. In 1630, King Gustavus Adolphus of Sweden decided to enter the German conflict to protect Swedish interests. While Gustavus Adolphus struggled to construct his alliance, imperial forces continued their triumphant progress. In 1631, they besieged, captured, and put to the torch the town of Magdeburg. Perhaps three-fourths of the 40,000 inhabitants of the town were brutally slaughtered. The sack of Magdeburg marked a turning point in Protestant fortunes. It gave the international Protestant community a unifying symbol that enhanced Gustavus's military efforts. Brandenburg and Saxony joined Gustavus Adolphus, allowing him to open a second front in Bohemia. In the autumn of 1631, this combination overwhelmed the imperial armies. Gustavus won a decisive triumph at Breitenfeld, while the Saxons occupied Prague.

Gustavus Adolphus lost no time in pressing his advantage. While Ferdinand II pleaded with Wallenstein to again lead the imperial forces, the Swedes marched west to the Rhine, easily conquering the richest of the Catholic cities and retaking the Lower Palatinate. In early 1632, Protestant forces plundered Bavaria, but Wallenstein resumed his command and chose to chase the Saxons from Bohemia rather than the Swedes from Bavaria. Not until the winter of 1632 did the armies of Gustavus and Wallenstein finally meet. At the Battle of Lützen, the Swedes won the field but lost their beloved king. Wounded in the leg, the back, and the head, Gustavus Adolphus died. In less than two years he had decisively transformed the course of the war and the course of Europe's future. Protestant forces now occupied most of central and northern Germany.

The Long Quest for Peace

The final stages of the war involved the resumption of the century-old struggle between France and Spain. When the Twelve Years' Truce expired in 1621, Spain again declared war on the Dutch. Dutch naval power was considerable, and the Dutch took the war to the far reaches of the globe, attacking Portuguese settlements in Brazil and in the East and harassing Spanish shipping on the high seas. In 1628, the Dutch captured the entire Spanish treasure fleet as it sailed from the New World. Spain had declared bankruptcy in 1627, and the loss of the whole of the next year's treasure from America exacerbated an already catastrophic situation.

These reversals, combined with the continued successes of Habsburg forces in central Europe, convinced Louis XIII and his chief minister, Cardinal Richelieu, that the time for active involvement in European affairs was now at hand. Throughout the early stages of the war, France had secretly aided anti-Habsburg forces. Gustavus Adolphus's unexpected success dramatically altered French calculations. Now it was evident that the Habsburgs could no longer combine their might, and Spanish energies would be drained off in the Netherlands and central Europe. The time had come to take an open stand. In 1635, France declared war on Spain.

Gustavus Adolphus of Sweden, shown at the battle of Breitenfeld in 1631. The battle was the first important Protestant victory of the Thirty Years' War. Gustavus died on the battlefield at Lützen in the following year.

France took the offensive first, invading the Spanish Netherlands. In 1636, a Spanish army struck back, pushing to within 25 miles of Paris before it was repelled. Both sides soon began to search for a settlement, but pride prevented them from laying down their arms. Spain toppled first. Its economy in shambles and its citizens in revolt over high prices and higher taxes, it could no longer maintain its many-fronted war. The Swedes again defeated imperial forces in Germany. The Dutch destroyed much of Spain's Atlantic fleet in 1639, and the Portuguese rose up against the union of crowns that had brought them nothing but expense and the loss of crucial portions of their empire. In 1640, the Portuguese regained their independence. In 1643, Spain gambled once more on a knockout blow against the French. But at the Battle of Rocroi, exhausted French troops held out, and the Spanish invasion failed.

By now, the desire for peace was universal. Most of the main combatants had long since perished: Philip III, ever optimistic, in 1621; Frederick V, an exile to the end, in 1632; Gustavus Adolphus, killed at Lützen in the same year; Wallenstein, murdered by order of Ferdinand II in 1634; Ferdinand himself in 1637; and Louis XIII in 1643, five days before the French triumph at Rocroi. Those who succeeded them did not have the same passions, and after so many decades the longing for peace was the strongest emotion on the Continent.

In 1648, a series of agreements, collectively known as the Peace of Westphalia, established the outlines of the political geography of Europe for the next century. Its focus was on the Holy Roman Empire, and it reflected Protestant successes in the final two decades of war. Sweden gained further territories on the Baltic, making it master of the north German ports. France, too, gained in territory and prestige. It kept the vital towns in the Lower Palatinate through which Spanish men and matériel had moved, and though it did not agree to come to terms with Spain immediately, France's fear of encirclement was at an end. The Dutch gained statehood through official recognition by Spain and through the power they had displayed in building and maintaining an overseas empire.

Territorial boundaries were reestablished as they had existed in 1624, giving the Habsburgs control of both Bohemia and Hungary. The independence of the Swiss cantons was now officially recognized as were the rights of Calvinists to the protection of the Peace of Augsburg, which again was to govern the religious affairs of the empire. Two of the larger German states were strengthened as a counterweight to the emperor's power. Bavaria was allowed to retain the Upper Palatinate, and Brandenburg, which ceded some of its coastal territory to Sweden, gained extensive territories in the east. The emperor's political control over the German states was also weakened. German rulers were given independent authority over their states and the imperial diet, rather than the emperor, was empowered to settle disputes. Thus weakened, future emperors ruled in the Habsburg territorial lands with little ability to control, or influence, or even arbitrate German affairs. The judgment that the Holy Roman Empire was neither holy, nor Roman, nor an empire was now irrevocably true.

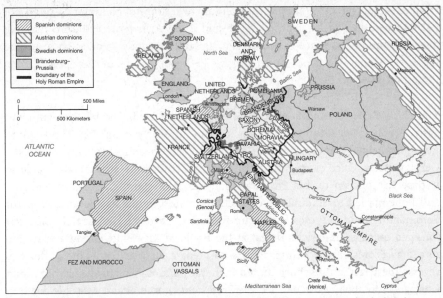

The Peace of Westphalia, 1648, recognized the new boundaries of European states that included an independent Portugal and the United Netherlands. It also recognized the growth of the Ottoman Empire into the Balkans.

SUMMARY

The Crises of the Western States   The Reformation created two churches, setting off a series of political conflicts that could only be resolved by war. Calvinism found a receptive audience in France among the middle ranks of urban society and aristocratic women. The French Wars of Religion were brought about by the spread of Calvinism and the political vacuum created when Henry II died unexpectedly. Civil war broke out in France in 1562. The assassination of the duc de Guise in 1563 pushed the violence to new levels. The Saint Bartholomew's Day Massacre in 1572 prolonged the war and prompted Protestants to develop theories of resistance to unjust monarchs. Henry IV brought the wars to an end and proclaimed the Edict of Nantes. Philip II of Spain took the lead in fighting for Catholic dominance in Europe. His efforts to restore Catholicism to England failed. His religious policies in the Low Countries led to rebellion and war.

The Struggles in Eastern Europe   Dynastic issues, rather than religious conflict, led to political upheaval in eastern Europe. Conflict between Sigismund III and the Polish Diet over war with Sweden weakened the state. Following the death of Ivan the Terrible, Muscovy descended into a Time of Troubles. Poland and Sweden took advantage of Muscovy's problems. Michael Romanov became tsar. Fighting continued for 20 years, ending with territorial concessions to Poland. Sweden made a rapid rise to power in the seventeenth century. War broke out between Sweden and Poland when the Swedes deposed Sigismund III. Sweden was saved from crushing defeat by the recalcitrance of the Polish Diet and Sigismund's decision to invade Muscovy. Under Gustavus, Sweden rose to become one of Europe's leading Protestant powers.

The Thirty Years' War, 1618–1648 The isolated conflicts of the late sixteenth and early seventeenth centuries joined together in the Thirty Years' War. The Peace of Augsburg helped Protestants and Catholics to achieve rough equality within the German states. Once elected king of Bohemia, Ferdinand Habsburg attempted to impose Catholicism on his Protestant subjects. Protestant uprisings in Hungary and Bohemia led to Ferdinand's deposition. In 1619, Ferdinand became Emperor Ferdinand II and the Protestant elector Frederick V became king of Bohemia. War followed quickly. Frederick's defeat at the Battle of the White Mountain in 1620 forced all Protestants in central Europe to prepare for war. Ferdinand's efforts to reverse the Peace of Augsburg united Lutherans and Calvinists against him. King Gustavus Adolphus of Sweden led the Protestant counterattack. After his death in 1632, the war entered a new phase focused on the struggle between France and Spain. Peace was finally achieved in 1648 with the Treaty of Westphalia.

QUESTIONS FOR REVIEW

1. How was Henry IV able to bring peace to France after decades of civil war?
2. What were the political and religious connections between the armada launched against England by Philip II and the revolt of the Netherlands?
3. How did Sweden rise to become one of Europe's great powers in the first half of the seventeenth century?
4. How did religion help spark and spread the Thirty Years' War?
5. What were the effects of the Peace of Westphalia on political arrangements in the heart of Europe?

CHAPTER 15

The Experiences of Life in Early Modern Europe, 1500–1650

Economic Life

There was no typical sixteenth-century European. Language, custom, geography, and material conditions separated people in one place from those in another. Contrasts between social groups were more striking still.

Nonetheless, one distinctive sixteenth-century experience that all groups shared, though they could only dimly perceive it, was change. In general, one generation improved on the situation of the last. Agriculture increased; more land was cleared, more crops were grown, and better tools were crafted. On the negative side, irreplaceable resources were lost as more trees were felled, more soil was eroded, and more fresh water was polluted. These changes and dynamic transformations in economic and social conditions affected everyday life in the sixteenth century.

Rural Life

In the sixteenth century, as much as 90 percent of the European population lived on farms or in small towns in which farming was the principal occupation. Villages were small and relatively isolated. These villages, large or small, prosperous or poor, were the bedrock of the sixteenth-century state. The manor, the parish, and the rural administrative district were the institutional infrastructures of Europe. Each organized the peasantry for its own purposes. Manorial rents supported the lifestyle of the nobility; parish tithes supported the works of the Church; local taxes supported the power of the state. Rents, tithes, and taxes easily absorbed more than half of the wealth produced by the land.

To survive on what remained, the village community had to be self-sufficient. In good times, there was enough to eat and some to save for the future. Hard times meant hunger and starvation. One in every three harvests was bad; one in every five was disastrous.

The Sixteenth-Century Household. Hunger and cold were the constant companions of the average European. Everywhere in Europe, homes were inadequate shelter against the cold and damp. Most were built of wood and roofed in thatch. The typical house was one long room with a stone hearth at the end.

People had relatively few household possessions. The essential piece of furniture was the wooden chest, which was used for storage. A typical family could keep all of its belongings in the chest, which could then be buried or carried away in time of danger. The chest had other uses as well. Its flat top served as a table or bench or a raised surface on which food could be placed. Tables and stools were becoming more common during the sixteenth century, though chairs were still a great luxury.

The scale of life was small, and its pace was controlled by nature: up at dawn, asleep at dusk, long working hours in summer, short ones in winter. For most people, the world was bounded by the distance that could be traveled on foot. Those who stayed all their lives in their rural villages may never have seen more than a hundred other people at once. Their wisdom, handed down through generations, was of the practical experience that was necessary to survive the struggle with nature.

Reliance on Agriculture. Peasant life centered on agriculture. Technology and technique varied little across the Continent, but there were significant differences depending on climate and soil. Across the great plain, the breadbasket that stretched from the Low Countries to Poland-Lithuania, the most common form of crop growing was still the three-field rotation system. In this method, winter crops such as wheat or rye were planted in one field; spring crops such as barley, peas, or beans were planted in another; and the third field was left fallow. More than 80 percent of what was grown on the farm was consumed on the farm. Rye and barley were the staples for peasants. Most was baked into the coarse black bread that was the mainstay of the peasant diet. In one form or another, grain provided over 75 percent of the calories in a typical diet.

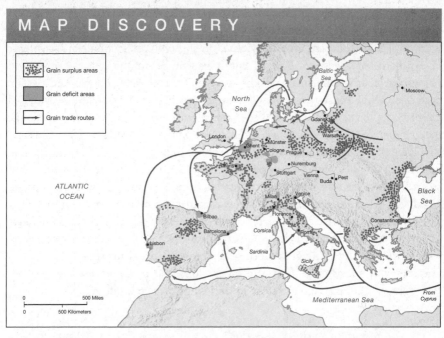

Grain surplus areas

Grain deficit areas

Grain trade routes

Baltic
Sea

Moscow

North
Sea

Gdansk

Warsaw

London

Ghent Münster
Cologne Prague

Paris Nuremburg
Stuttgart Vienna
Buda Pest

ATLANTIC
OCEAN

Black
Sea

Milan Venice
Genoa
Florence

Constantinople

Bilbao

Barcelona Corsica Rome

Lisbon

Sardinia

Sicily

0   500 Miles

0   500 Kilometers

Mediterranean Sea

From
Cyprus

GRAIN SUPPLY AND TRADE IN SIXTEENTH-CENTURY EUROPE

Where were the breadbaskets of Europe located? What was the relationship between
urban areas and grain supply? How did grain move from suppliers to consumers?

The warm climate and dry weather of Mediterranean Europe favored a
two-crop rotation system. With less water and stronger sunlight, half the land had
to be left fallow each year to restore its nutrients. Here, fruit, especially grapes and
olives, was an essential supplement to the diet. With smaller cereal crops, wine replaced beer as a beverage.

Animal husbandry was the main occupation in the third agricultural area of
Europe, the mountainous and hilly regions. Sheep, the most common animal, provided the raw material for almost all clothing. In western Europe, their wool was the
main export of both England and Spain. Pigs were prevalent in woodland settlements.
They foraged for food and were kept, like poultry, for slaughter. Oxen were essential as
draft animals. In the dairying areas of Europe, cattle produced milk, cheese, and but-
ter; in Hungary and Bohemia, the great breeding center of the Continent, they were
raised for export; almost everywhere else, they were used as beasts of burden.

Most agricultural land was owned not by those who worked it, but by lords who
let it out in various ways. The land was still divided into manors, and the manor
lord, or **seigneur**, was still responsible for maintaining order, administering justice,
and arbitrating disputes. Lords were not necessarily individual members of the nobility; in fact, the lords were more commonly the Church or the state. In western
Europe, peasants generally owned between one-third and one-half of the land they
worked; eastern European peasants owned little if any land. But by the sixteenth

century, almost all peasants enjoyed security of tenure on the land they worked. In return for various forms of rents, they used the land as they saw fit and could hand it down to their children. Labor service was being replaced by monetary payments in northern and western Europe, but it continued in the east. German and Hungarian peasants normally owed two or three days' labor on the lord's estate each week, while Polish peasants might owe as much as four days. Labor service tied the peasants to the land they worked. Eastern European peasants were less mobile than peasants in the west, and as a result, towns were fewer and smaller in the east.

Though the land in each village was set out in large fields so that crops could be rotated, families owned their own pieces within the field, usually in scattered strips. There were also large common fields used as pasture, as well as common woodlands where animals foraged, fuel was gathered, and game was hunted.

Farm work was ceaseless toil. Six or seven times a year, farmers tilled the fields to spread animal manure below the surface of the soil. Calamities lurked everywhere, from rain and drought to locusts and crows. Most farms could support only one family at subsistence level, and excess sons and daughters had to fend for themselves, either through marriage in the village or by migration to a town.

Town Life

In the country, people worked to the natural rhythm of the day and season. In the town, the bell tolled every hour. In the summer, the laborers gathered at the town gates at four in the morning, in the winter at seven. The bell signaled the time for morning and afternoon meals as well as the hour to lay down tools and return home. Wages were paid for hours worked—seven in winter, as many as sixteen in midsummer.

The Heart of Commerce. In all towns, an official guild structure organized and regulated labor. Rules laid down the requirements for training, the standards for quality, and the conditions for exchange. Only those who were officially sanctioned could work in trades, and each trade could perform only specified tasks.

While the life of the peasant community turned on self-sufficiency, that of the town turned on interdependence. The town was one large marketplace in which the circulation of goods dictated the residents' survival. Men and women in towns worked as hard as people on farms, but town dwellers generally received a more varied and more comfortable life in return. This is not to suggest that hunger and hardship were unknown in towns. Urban poverty was endemic and grew worse as the century wore on. In most towns, as much as one-quarter of the entire population might be destitute, living on casual day labor, charity, or crime. But the institutional network of support for the poor and homeless was stronger. The urban poor fell victim more often to disease than to starvation.

Towns were distinguished by the variety of occupations that existed within them. The preparation and exchange of food dominated small market towns. In these small towns, men divided their time between traditional agricultural pursuits—there were always garden plots and even substantial fields attached to towns—and manufacturing.

Almost every town made and distributed to the surrounding area some special product that drew to the town the wealth of the countryside.

The Workforce. In larger towns, the specialization of labor was more intense, and wage earning was more essential. Large traders dominated the major occupations such as baking, brewing, and cloth manufacture, leaving distribution in the hands of the family economy, where there might still be a significant element of bartering. Piecework handicrafts became the staple for less prosperous town families, who prepared raw materials for the large manufacturers or finished products before their sale.

In large towns there were also specialized trades that women performed. There were 55 midwives in Nuremberg in the middle of the sixteenth century, and a board of women chosen from among the leading families of the town supervised their work. Nursing the sick also seems to have been an exclusively female occupation. So, too, was prostitution, which was officially sanctioned in most large towns in the early sixteenth century.

Most town dwellers, however, lived by unskilled labor. The most lucrative occupations were strictly controlled, so people who flocked to towns in search of employment usually hired themselves out as day laborers, hauling and lifting goods onto carts or boats or delivering water and food. After the first decades of the century, the supply of laborers exceeded the demand, and town authorities were constantly attempting to expel the throngs of casual workers. The most fortunate of such workers might succeed in becoming servants.

Domestic service was a critical source of household labor. Even families who were on the margins of subsistence employed servants to undertake innumerable household tasks, which allowed parents to pursue their primary occupations.

Just as towns grew by the influx of surplus rural population, they sustained themselves by the import of surplus agricultural production. Most towns owned vast tracts of land, which they leased to peasants or farmed by hired labor. All towns had municipal storehouses of grain to preserve their inhabitants from famine during harvest failures.

Economic Change

Over the course of the sixteenth century, the European population increased by about one-third, much of the growth taking place in the first 50 years. Rough estimates suggest the rise to have been from about 80 million to 105 million. Europe had finally recovered from the devastation of the Black Death, and by 1600 its population was greater than it had ever been. Demographic growth was even more dramatic in the cities. In 1500, only four cities had populations greater than 100,000; in 1600, there were eight. Fifteen large cities more than doubled their populations.

The rise in population dramatically affected the lives of ordinary Europeans. In the early part of the century, the first phase of growth brought prosperity. Because there was uncultivated land that could be plowed and enough commons and woodlands to be shared, population increase was a welcome development. Even when rural communities began to reach their natural limits, opportunity still existed in the burgeoning towns and cities. At first the cycle was beneficial. Surplus on the farms led to economic growth in the towns. Growth in the towns meant more opportunities for people on the farms. The first waves of migrants to the towns found opportunity everywhere. Apprenticeships were easy to find, and the shortage of casual labor kept wages at a decent rate.

This window of opportunity could not remain open forever. With more mouths to feed, more crops had to be planted, and new fields were carved from less fertile areas. In England and the Low Countries, large drainage projects were undertaken to reclaim land for crops. In the east, so-called forest colonies sprang up, clearing space in the midst of woodlands for new farms.

By midcentury, the window of opportunity shut more firmly on people who were attempting to enter the urban economy. New restrictions were put in place that meant that newly arrived immigrants could enter only the less profitable small crafts.

As workers continued to flood into the towns, real wages began to fall, not only among the unskilled but throughout the workforce. The fall in real wages took place against a backdrop of inflation that has come to be called the **Price Revolution**. Over the course of the century, cereal prices increased between fivefold and sixfold, and prices of manufactured goods increased between twofold and threefold. Most of the rapid increase came in the second half of the century, a result of both population growth and the import of precious metals from the New World. The Price Revolution was felt throughout the Continent and played havoc with government finances, international trade, and the lives of ordinary people.

Ever-increasing prices created profound social dislocation and threw into turmoil all groups and sections of the European economy. Some people became destitute; others became rich beyond their dreams. The towns were particularly hard hit, for they exchanged manufactured goods for food and so suffered when grain prices rose faster than those of other commodities. Landholders who derived their income from rents were squeezed; those who received payment in kind reaped a windfall of more valuable agricultural goods. As long as ordinary peasants consumed what they raised, the nominal value of commodities did not matter. But if some part of their subsistence was obtained by labor, they were in grave peril.

There was now an enormous incentive to produce a surplus for market and to begin to specialize in particular grains that were in high demand. Every small scrap of land that individual peasant families could bring under cultivation would now yield foodstuffs that could be exchanged for manufactured goods that had been unimaginable luxuries a generation earlier. The tendency for all peasants to hold roughly equivalent amounts of land abruptly ceased. The fortunate could now become prosperous by selling their surplus. The unfortunate found ready purchasers for their strips and common rights.

The beneficial cycle now turned vicious. Those who had sold out and left the land looking for prosperity in the towns were forced to return to the land as agrarian laborers. In western Europe, they became the landless poor, seasonal migrants without the safety net of rooted communal life. In eastern Europe, labor service enriched

People per square mile
- Over 60
- 30 to 60
- 10 to 30
- Under 10

POPULATION DENSITY IN EUROPE, CA. 1600

Which parts of Europe were most populated in the early seventeenth century? Which were least populated? What was the relationship between population and water route access?

the landed nobility, who were able to sell vast stores of grain in the export market. Poland-Lithuania became a major supplier of cereals to northern Europe. But agricultural surplus from the east could not make up for the great shortfall in the west. By the end of the sixteenth century, the western European states faced a crisis of subsistence.

SOCIAL LIFE

The basic assumption of sixteenth-century European society was inequality. The group, rather than the individual, was the predominant unit in society. The first level of the social order was the family and the household, then came the village or town community, and finally the gradations of ranks and orders of society at large. Each group had its own place in the social order, and each performed its own essential function. Society was the sum of its parts. This traditional social organization was severely tested over the course of the sixteenth century.

Social Constructs

Hierarchy was the dominant principle of social organization in the sixteenth century. The hierarchy of masters, journeymen, and apprentices dominated trades; trades themselves existed in a hierarchy. Civic government was a hierarchy of officials led by the elite of councillors and mayors. Among the peasants was the hierarchy of free-holder, laborer, and leaseholder, as well as the more flexible social hierarchy among the ancient and prosperous families and the newer and struggling ones. The family itself was hierarchically organized, with the wife subordinate to her husband, the children to their parents, and the apprentices and servants to their master and mistress. Hierarchy was a principle of orderliness that helped to govern social relations.

Status rather than wealth determined the social hierarchy of the sixteenth century. It conferred privileges and exacted responsibilities according to rank. Status was everywhere apparent. It was confirmed in social conventions such as bowing and hat doffing. In towns and cities, the clothing people were allowed to wear, even the foods they were allowed to eat, reflected status. Status was signified by titles, not just in the ranks of the nobility, but even in ordinary communities of masters and mistresses, goodmen and goodwives. The acceptance of status was an everyday, unreflective act. Inequality was an unquestioned fact of life.

Images that people used to describe both the natural world and their social world reinforced the functional nature of hierarchy. The most elaborate image was that of the **Great Chain of Being**, a description of the universe in which everything had a place, from God at the top to inanimate objects such as rocks and stones at the bottom. For ordinary people, the Great Chain of Being expressed the belief that all life was interconnected, that every link was a part of a divinely ordered universe and was as necessary as every other.

The second metaphor that was used to describe society stressed this notion of interdependency even more strongly. This was the image of the Body Politic, in which the head ruled, the arms protected, the stomach nourished, and the feet labored. In the state, the king was the head, the church was the soul, the nobles were the arms, the artisans were the hands, and the peasants were the feet. Like the Chain of Being, the Body Politic was a profoundly conservative concept of social organization that precluded the idea of social mobility.

Social Structure

The Great Chain of Being and the Body Politic were static concepts of social organization. But in the sixteenth century, European society was in a state of dynamic change. Fundamentally, all European societies were divided between nobles and commoners, though relationships between the two orders differed from place to place.

The Nobles. Nobility was a legal status that conferred certain privileges on its holders and passed by inheritance from one generation to the next. Though various systems of title were in use across the Continent, the hierarchy of prince, duke, earl, count, and baron was roughly standard.

Because rulers conferred these titles on individuals, elevating some to higher ranks and others from commoner to noble, the nobility was a political order as well as a social one. Political privileges were among the nobility's most important attributes. In many countries, the highest offices of the state and the military were reserved for members of the nobility. Noblemen were also granted rights of political participation in the deliberative bodies of the state.

Finally, members of the nobility held economic privileges, a result both of their rank and of their role as lords on the lands they owned. In almost every state, the nobility was exempt from most kinds of taxation. The interests of the nobles conflicted directly with those of the ruler, and the larger the number of tax exemptions for the nobility, the stronger was its power in relation to the monarch.

Privileges implied obligations. Initially, the nobility was the warrior caste of the state, and its primary obligations were to raise, equip, and lead troops into battle. By the sixteenth century, the military needs of the state had far surpassed the military power of its nobility. Warfare had become a national enterprise that required central coordination. Nobles became administrators as much as warriors, though it is fair to say that many did both. The French nobility came to be divided into the nobility of the sword and the nobility of the robe—that is, warriors and officeholders.

Nobles also had the obligation of governing at both the national and the local level. At the discretion of the ruler, they could be called to engage in any necessary occupation, no matter how disruptive to their economic or family affairs. They administered their estates and settled the disputes of their tenants. In times of want, they were expected to provide for the needy. The obligation of good lordship was implicitly understood, if not always explicitly carried out, between lord and peasant.

Town Elite and Gentry. The principal distinction in sixteenth-century society was between lord and commoners, but it was not the only one. A new social group was emerging in the towns—a group that had neither the legal nor the social privileges of nobility but performed many of the same functions. The towns remained a separate unit of social organization in most states, enjoying many of the same political and economic privileges as the nobility. Representatives of the towns met with the nobles and the king and were the most important part of the national deliberative assemblies, like the English Parliament or the French estates. Towns were granted legal rights to govern their own citizens, to engage in trade, and to defend themselves by raising and storing arms. Though they paid a large share of most taxes, towns also received large tax concessions.

Georges de La Tour, *The Fortune Teller*. In the painting, which serves as a warning to the naive about the wicked ways of the world, a fashionably dressed young innocent is drawn into the snare of the wily fortune teller.

As individuals, members of the town elite held no special status in society at large. Some were among the richest people in the state, but they had to devise their own systems of honor and prestige. In Venice, the *Book of Gold* distinguished the local elite from the ranks of ordinary citizens. In France and Spain, some of the highest officers of leading towns were granted noble status. In England, wealthy guild members could become knights, a rank just below noble status.

In rural society, the transformation of agricultural holdings in many places also created a group that fit uncomfortably between lords and commoners. The accumulation of larger and larger estates, by purchase from the nobility, the state, or the church, made lords—in the sense of landowners with tenants—of many who were not lords in rank. They received rents and dues from their tenants, administered their estates, and preserved the so-called moral economy that sustained the peasants during hard times. In England, this group came to be known as the gentry, and there were parallel groups in Spain, France, and the Holy Roman Empire. The gentry aspired to the privileges of the nobility.

Social stratification also marked rural communities. In many German villages, a principal distinction was made between those who held land in the ancient part of the settlement—the Esch—and those who held land in those areas into which the village had expanded. The Esch was normally the best land. But interestingly, the holders of the Esch were tied to the lord of the estate, while holders of the less desirable lands were free peasants. Here, freedom to move from place to place was less valued than was the right to live in the heart of the village.

Just the opposite set of values prevailed in English villages, where freeholders were in the most enviable position. They led the movements to break up the common fields for planting and were able to initiate legal actions against their lord. Whenever village land was converted to freehold, unfree tenants would go into debt to buy it.

In towns, the order of rank below the elite pertained as much to the kind of work that one performed as it did to the level at which the work was undertaken. The critical division in town life was between those who had the freedom of the city—citizens—and those who did not. Citizenship was restricted to membership in certain occupations and was closely regulated. It could be purchased, but most citizenship was earned by becoming a master in one of the guilds. Only males could be citizens.

Social Change

In the sixteenth century, social commentators believed that change was transforming the world in which they lived.

The New Rich. Many factors promoted social change during the course of the sixteenth century. First, population increase necessitated an expansion of the ruling orders. With more people to govern, there had to be more governors who could perform the military, political, and social functions of the state. Second, opportunities to accumulate wealth expanded dramatically with the Price Revolution. Traditionally, wealth was calculated in land and tenants rather than in

Feeding the Hungry, by Cornelius Buys, 1504. A maidservant is doling out small loaves to the poor and the lame at the door of a wealthy person's home. The poor who flocked to the towns were often forced to rely on charity to survive.

the possession of liquid assets such as gold and silver. But with the increase in commodity prices, surplus producers could rapidly improve their economic position. Moreover, state service became a source of unlimited riches. The profits to be made from tax collecting, officeholding, or the law could easily surpass those to be made from landholding. And the newly rich clamored for privileges.

The New Poor. Social change was equally apparent at the bottom of the social scale, but here it could not be so easily absorbed. The continuous growth of population created a group of landless poor who squatted in villages and clogged the streets of towns and cities. Rough estimates suggest that as many as one-quarter of all Europeans were destitute.

Traditionally, local communities cared for their poor. Widows, orphans, and the handicapped, who would normally constitute over half of the poor in a village or town, were viewed as the "deserving poor," worthy of the care of the community through the Church or private almsgiving. Catholic communities such as Venice created a system of private charity that paralleled the institutions of the Church. Though Protestant communities took charity out of the control of the Church, they were no less concerned about the plight of the deserving poor. In England, a special tax, the poor rate, supported the poor.

Charity was an obligation of the community, but as the sixteenth century wore on, the number of destitute people grew beyond the ability of the local community to care for them. Many of those who now begged for alms fell outside the traditional categories of the deserving poor. They were men and women who were capable of working but incapable of finding more than occasional labor. They left their native communities in search of employment and thus forfeited their claims on local charity. Most wound up in the towns and cities, where as strangers they had no claim on local charity.

The problem of crime complicated the problems of poverty and vagrancy. Increasing population and increasing wealth equaled increasing crime; the addition of the poor to the equation aggravated the situation. The poor, outsiders to the community without visible means of support, were the easiest targets of official retribution. Throughout the century, numerous European states passed vagrancy laws. Sexual offenses were criminalized, especially bastardy, since the birth of illegitimate children placed an immediate burden on the community. Prostitutes, who had long been tolerated and regulated in towns, were now persecuted. Rape increased. Capital punishment was reserved for the worst crimes—murder, incest, and grand larceny being most common—but, not surprisingly, executions were carried out mostly on outsiders to the community.

Peasant Revolts

The economic and social changes of the sixteenth century had serious consequences. Most telling was the upswing of violent confrontations between peasants and their lords. Across Europe and with alarming regularity, peasants took up arms to defend themselves from what they saw as violations of traditional rights and obligations. Most revolts chose leaders, drew up petitions of grievances, and organized the rank and file into a semblance of military order. Leaders were literate—drawn more commonly from among the lower clergy or minor gentry than from the peasantry—political demands were moderate, and tactics were sophisticated. But peasant revolts so profoundly threatened the social order that they were met with the severest repression.

Agrarian Changes. It is essential to realize that while peasants revolted against their lords, at bottom their anger and frustration were caused by agrarian changes that could be neither controlled nor understood. As population increased and market production expanded, many of the traditional rights and obligations of lords and peasants became oppressive.

For example, conflict arose over enclosing crop fields. An **enclosure** was a device—normally a fence or hedge that surrounded an area—to keep a parcel of land separate from the planted strips of land owned by the villagers. It could be used for grazing animals or raising a specialty crop for the market. But an enclosure destroyed the traditional form of village agriculture whereby decisions on which crops to plant were made communally. It became one of the chief grievances of the English peasants. But while enclosures broke up the old field system in many villages, they were a logical response to the transformation of land ownership that had already taken place. As more and more land was accumulated by fewer and fewer families, it made less and less sense for them to work widely scattered strips all over the village. If a family could consolidate its holdings by swaps and sales, it could gain an estate that was large enough to be used for both crops and grazing. An enclosed estate allowed wealthy farmers to grow more luxury crops for market or to raise only sheep on a field that had once been used for grain.

Enclosure was a process that both lord and rich peasant undertook, but it drove the smallholders from the land and was thus a source of bitter resentment for the poorer peasants. It was easy to protest the greed of the lords who, owning the most land, were the most successful enclosers. But enclosures resulted more from the process whereby villages came to be characterized by a very small elite of large landholders and a very large mass of smallholders and landless poor. It was an effect rather than a cause.

Uprising in Germany. The complexity of these problems is perhaps best revealed in the series of uprisings that are known collectively as the German Peasants' War. It involved tens of thousands of peasants, and it combined a whole series of agrarian grievances with an awareness of the new religious spirit preached by Martin Luther. Luther condemned both lords and peasants—the lords for their rapaciousness, the peasants for their rebelliousness. Though he had a large following among the peasants, his advice that earthly oppressions be passively accepted was not followed. The Peasants' War was directed against secular and ecclesiastical lords, and the rebels attacked both economic and religious abuses. The combination of demands, such as the community's right to select its own minister and the community's right to cut wood freely, attracted a wide following in the villages and small towns of southern and central Germany. The printed demands of the peasantry, the most famous of which was the Twelve Articles of the Peasants of Swabia (1525), helped to spread the movement far beyond its original bounds. The peasants organized themselves into large armies led by experienced soldiers, but ultimately, movements that refused compromise were ruthlessly crushed.

At base, the demands of the peasantry addressed the agrarian changes that were transforming German villages. Population growth was creating more poor villagers who could only hire out as laborers but who demanded a share of common grazing and woodlands. Because the presence of these poor people increased the taxable wealth of the village, they were advantageous to the lord. But the strain they placed on resources was felt by both the subsistence and surplus farmers. Tensions within the village were all the greater in that the landless members were the kin of the landed. If they were to be settled properly on the land, then the lord would have to let the village expand. If they were to be kept on the margins of subsistence, then the more prosperous villagers would have to be able to control their numbers and their conduct. In either case, the peasants needed more direct responsibility for governing the village than existed in their traditional relationship with their lord. Therefore, the peasants of Swabia demanded release of the village peasantry from the status of serfs. They wanted to be allowed to move off the land, to marry out of the village without penalty, and to be free of the death taxes that further impoverished their children. They also wanted stable rents fixed at fair rates, a limit placed on labor service, and a return to the ancient customs that governed relations between lords and peasants. All of these proposals were backed by an appeal to Christian principles of love and charity. They were profoundly conservative.

The demands of the German peasants reflected a traditional order that no longer existed. In many places, the rents and tithes that the peasants wanted to control no longer belonged to the lords of the estates. They had been sold to town corporations or wealthy individuals who purchased them as an investment and expected to realize a fair return. Most tenants did enjoy stable and fixed rents, but only on their traditional lands. As they increased their holdings, perhaps to keep another son in the village or to expand production for the market, they were faced with the fact that rents were higher and land was more expensive than it had been before. Marriage fines, death duties, and labor service were oppressive, but they balanced the fact that traditional rents were very low. In many east German villages, peasants willingly increased their labor service for a reduction in their money rents. It was hardly likely that they could have both. If the peasants were being squeezed, and there can be little doubt that they were, it was not only the lords who were doing the squeezing. The Church took its tenth, the state increased its exactions, and the competition for survival and prosperity among the peasants themselves was ferocious. Peasants were caught between the jaws of an expanding state and a changing economy. When they rebelled, the jaws snapped shut.

Chronology

SOCIAL AND ECONOMIC CHANGE

1450–1550	Population of France doubles
1500–1600	Population of Europe increases by about one-third
1500–1600	Population of England doubles; population of London quadruples
1500–1600	Price revolution leads to declines in real wages
1514	Revolt of Hungarian peasants
1524–1525	German Peasants' War
1600	Europe reaches new population high of about 105 million

Private and Community Life

The great events of the sixteenth century—discovery of the New World, consolidation of states, increasing incidence and ferocity of war, and reform of religion—all had a profound impact on the lives of ordinary people. However slowly and intermittently these developments penetrated to isolated village communities, they were inextricably bound up with the experiences and world view of all Europeans.

The Family

Sixteenth-century life centered on the family, the primary kinship group. European families were predominantly nuclear, composed of a married couple and their children. Yet, however families were composed, kinship had a wider orbit than just parents and children. In-laws, step relations, and cousins were considered part of the kin group and could be called on for support in a variety of contexts from charity to employment and business partnerships. In towns, such family connections created large and powerful clans.

In a different sense, family was lineage, the connections between preceding and succeeding generations. This was an important concept among the upper ranks of society, in which ancient lineage, genuine or fabricated, was a valued component of nobility. Even in peasant communities, however, lineage existed in the form of the strips in the field that were passed from generation to generation and named for the family that owned them.

The family was also an economic unit. It was the basic unit for the production, accumulation, and transmission of wealth. Occupation determined the organization of the economic family. Every member of the household had his or her own functions that were essential to the survival of the unit. Tasks were divided by gender and by age, but there was far more intermixture than is traditionally assumed.

Finally, the family was the primary unit of social organization. It was in the family that children were educated and the social values of hierarchy and discipline were taught. Authority in the family was strictly organized in a set of three overlapping categories. At the top was the husband, head of the household, who ruled over his wife, children, and servants. All members of the family owed obedience to the head. Children owed obedience to their parents, male or female. Similarly, servants owed obedience to both master and mistress. Male apprentices were under the authority of the wife, mother, and mistress of the household. The importance of the family as a social unit was underscored by the fact that people who were not attached to families attracted suspicion in sixteenth-century society. Single men were often viewed as potential criminals, single women as potential prostitutes.

Though the population of Europe was increasing in the sixteenth century, families were not large. Throughout northern and western Europe, the size of the typical family was two adults and three or four children. Women married around age 25, men slightly later. Most women could expect about 15 fertile years and seven or eight pregnancies if neither they nor their husbands died in the interim. Only three or four children were likely to survive beyond the age of 10. In her fertile years, a woman was constantly occupied with infants. Constant pregnancy and child care may help explain some of the gender roles that men and women assumed in the sixteenth century. Biblical injunctions and traditional stereotypes help explain others. Whether a woman was pregnant or not, her labor was a vital part of the domestic economy, especially until the first surviving children were strong enough to assume their share. The woman's sphere was the household. On the farm, she was in charge of the preparation of food, the care of domestic animals, the care and education of children, and the manufacture and cleaning of the family's clothing. In towns, women supervised the shop that was part of the household. They sold goods, kept accounts, and directed the work of domestics or apprentices.

Jan Vermeer's, *The Milkmaid* (1658–1660) shows a domestic servant absorbed in her household tasks. Homes were sparsely furnished, though this family was rich enough to possess a table, an earthenware bowl and jug, and a footstove that held hot coals (seen on the floor behind the maid).

The man's sphere was the public one: the fields in rural areas, the streets in towns. Men plowed, planted, and did the heavy reaping work of farming. They made and maintained essential farm equipment and had charge of the large farm animals. They marketed surplus produce and made the few purchases of equipment or luxury goods. Men performed the labor service that was normally due the lord of the estate, attended the local courts in various capacities, and organized the affairs of the village. In towns, men engaged in heavy labor, procured materials for craft work, and marketed their product if it was not sold in the household shop. Only men could be citizens of the towns or full members of most craft guilds, and only men were involved in civic government.

While male roles were constant throughout the life cycle, as men trained for and performed the same occupations from childhood to death, female roles varied greatly depending on the situation. While under the care of fathers, masters, or husbands, women worked in the domestic sphere; once widowed, they assumed the public functions of head of household. Many women inherited shops or farmland; most became responsible for the placement and training of their children. But because of the division of labor on which the family depended and because of the inherent social and economic prejudices that segregated public and domestic roles, widows were particularly disadvantaged.

Communities

The family was part of a wider community. On the farm, this community was the rural village; in the town, it was the ward, quarter, or parish in which the family lived.

Community life must not be romanticized. Interpersonal violence, lawsuits, and feuds were common in both rural and urban communities. Like every other aspect of society, the community was socially and economically stratified, gender roles were segregated, and resources were inequitably divided. But the community was also the place where people found their social identity. It provided marriage partners for its families, charity for its poor, and a local culture for all of its inhabitants.

Identities and Customs. The two basic forces that tied the rural community together were the lord and the priest. The lord set conditions for work and property ownership that necessitated common decision making on the part of the village farmers. Use of the common lands, the rotation of labor service, and the form in which rents in kind were paid were all decisions that had to be made collectively. Communal agreement was also expressed in communal resistance to violations of custom or threats to the moral economy. All these forms of negotiation fused individual families into a community. So, too, in a different way did the presence of the parish priest or minister, who attended all the pivotal events of life—birth, marriage, and death. The church was the only common building of the community; it was the only space that was not owned outright by the lord or an individual family. The scene of village meetings and ceremonies, it was the center of both spiritual and social life. The parish priest served as a conduit for all the news of the community and the focal point for the village's festive life.

Weddings and Festivals. The most common ceremony was the wedding, a public event that combined a religious rite and a community procession with feasting and festivity. It took different forms in different parts of Europe and in different social groups. Many couples were engaged long before they were married, and in many places it was the engagement that was most important to the individuals and the wedding that was most important to the community. Traditional weddings involved the formal transfer of property, an important event in rural communities where the ownership of strips of land or common rights concerned everyone. The public procession, "the marriage in the streets," as it was sometimes called in towns, proclaimed the union throughout the community.

Other ceremonies were equally important in creating a shared sense of identity within the community. In both town and countryside, the year was divided by a number of festivals that defined the rhythm of toil and rest. They coincided with both the seasonal divisions of agricultural life and the central events of the Christian calendar. Christmas and Easter were probably the most widely observed Christian holidays, but **Carnival**, which preceded Lent, was a frenzied round of feasts and parties that resulted in a disproportionate number of births nine months later.

In addition to feasting, dancing, and play, festivals often included sports, such as soccer or wrestling, which served to channel aggressions. At such times, village elders would also arbitrate disputes, and marriage alliances or property transactions would be arranged.

Festivals further cemented the political cohesion of the community. Seating arrangements signaled the hierarchy of the community, and public punishment of offenders reinforced deference and social and sexual mores. Youth groups or the village women might band together to shame a promiscuous woman or to place horns on the head of a cuckolded husband. These forms of community ritual worked not only to punish offenders but also to reinforce the social and sexual values of the village as a whole.

Popular Beliefs and the Persecution of Witches

Ceremony and festival are reminders that sixteenth-century Europe was still a pre-literate society. Despite the introduction of printing and the millions of books that were produced during the period, the vast majority of Europeans conducted their affairs without the benefit of literacy. Outside a small circle of intellectuals, there was little effective knowledge about either human or celestial bodies. But this does not mean that ordinary people lived in a constant state of terror and anxiety. They used the knowledge they did have to form a view of the universe that conformed to their experiences and responded to their hopes.

Magical Practices. These beliefs blended Christian teaching and folk wisdom with a strong strain of magic. Popular belief in magic could be found everywhere in Europe, and it operated in much the same way as science does today. Only skilled practitioners could perform magic. It was a technical subject that combined expertise in the properties of plants and animals with theories about the composition of human and heavenly bodies. It had its own language, a mixture of ancient words and sounds with significant numbers and catch phrases. Magicians specialized. Alchemists worked with rocks and minerals, astrologers with the movement of the stars. Witches were thought to understand the properties of animals especially well.

Magical practices appealed to people at all levels of society. The wealthy favored astrology and paid handsomely to discover which days and months were the most auspicious for marriages and investments. The poorest villagers sought the aid of herbalists to help control the constant aches and pains of daily life. Sorcerers and wizards were called on in more extreme circumstances, such as a threatened harvest or matters of life and death. These magicians competed with the remedies offered by the Church. Special prayers and visits to the shrines of particular saints were believed to have similar curative value. Magical and Christian beliefs were often practiced simultaneously. It was not until the end of the century, when Protestant and Catholic leaders condemned magical practices and began a campaign to root them out, that magic and religion came into conflict.

Magical practices served a variety of purposes. Healing was the most common, and many "magical" brews were effective remedies for the minor ailments for which they were prescribed. Most village magicians were women because it was believed that women had unique knowledge and understanding of the body.

Magic was also used for predictive purposes. Certain charms and rituals were believed to have the power to affect the weather, the crops, and even human events. As always, affairs of the heart were as important as those of the stomach. Magicians advised the lovesick on potions and spells that would gain them the object of their desires. Finally, it was believed that magic had the power to alter the course of nature and could be used for both good and evil purposes.

The Witch Craze. Magic for evil was black magic, or witchcraft. Witches were believed to possess special powers that put them into contact with the devil and the forces of evil, which they could then use for their own purposes. Belief in the prevalence of good and evil spirits was Christian as well as magical. But the Church had gradually consigned the operation of the devil to the afterlife and removed his direct agency from earthly affairs. Beginning in the late fifteenth century, Church authorities began to prosecute large numbers of suspected witches. By the end of the sixteenth century, there was a continentwide witch craze. Confessions were obtained under torture, as were further accusations.

Witches were usually women, most often unmarried or widowed. In a sample of more than 7,000 cases of witchcraft prosecuted in early modern Europe, over 80 percent of the defendants were women. There is no clear explanation for why women fulfilled this important and powerful role. Belief in women's special powers over the body through their singular ability to give birth is certainly one part of the explanation, for many stories about the origins of witches suggest that they were children fathered by the devil and left to be raised by women. This sexual element of union with the devil and the common belief that older women were sexually aggressive combined to threaten male sexual dominance. Witches were also believed to have peculiar physical characteristics. Accused witches were strip-searched to find the devil's mark, which might be any bodily blemish. Another strand of explanation lies in the fact that single women existed on the fringes of society, isolated and exploited by the community at large. Their occult abilities thus became a protective mechanism that gave them a function within the community while they remained outside it.

It is difficult to know how important black magical beliefs were in ordinary communities. Most of the daily magic that was practiced was a mixture of charms, potions, and prayers that mingled magical, medical, and Christian beliefs. Misfortunes that befell particular families or social groups were blamed on the activities of witches. The campaign of the established churches to root out magic was directed largely against witches. The churches transposed witches' supposed abilities to communicate with the devil into the charge that they worshiped the devil. Because there was such widespread belief in the presence of diabolical spirits and in the capabilities of witches to control them, Protestant and Catholic church courts could easily find witnesses to testify in support of the charges against individual witches. Over 100,000—perhaps several times that many—condemned witches in Europe were burned, strangled, drowned, or beheaded. Yet wherever sufficient evidence exists to understand the circumstances of witchcraft prosecutions, it is clear that the community itself was under some form of social or economic stress rather than that there was any increase in the presence or use of witches.

SUMMARY

Economic Life Roughly 90 percent of Europe's population lived on farms or in small farming towns. Most Europeans faced the constant threat of famine, cold, and disease. Peasant life centered on agriculture. In towns, life revolved around commerce. Most town dwellers were unskilled laborers. Europe's population grew rapidly in the sixteenth century. Population growth led to inflation. The Price Revolution had dramatic consequences for all Europeans.

Social Life A belief in hierarchy and a static society underlay European social thought. The belief in hierarchy was expressed through the metaphors of the Great Chain of Being and the Body Politic. Europeans were divided between nobles and commoners. Nobility conferred privileges and responsibilities. Town elites and gentry occupied a social space between lord and commoners. Social change transformed European society at both the top and bottom. Economic and social change created tensions that were expressed in peasant revolts such as the German Peasants' War.

Private and Community Life Sixteenth-century life centered on the family. European families were predominantly nuclear. Within the family, tasks were organized by gender and by age. The family mirrored the hierarchy of the larger society. The woman's sphere was the home. The man's sphere was the public world. Families were part of wider communities. The lord and the priest helped tie communities together. Ceremonies and festivals served to reinforce community identity. There was widespread belief in magic and witchcraft. The sixteenth century saw a dramatic increase in the number of prosecutions of suspected witches.

QUESTIONS FOR REVIEW

1. What physical forces and social customs shaped the everyday life of Europe's rural population?
2. What was the nature of demographic change in the sixteenth century, and what was its impact on the European economy?
3. How are the terms "stratification," "hierarchy," and "status" useful for understanding social relations in early modern Europe?
4. How were the different roles of men and women within the family reflected in the different lives of men and women in the wider community?

The Royal State in the Seventeenth Century

The Rise of the Royal State

The wars that dominated the early part of the seventeenth century had a profound impact on the western European states. Not only did they cause terrible suffering and deprivation, but they also demanded efficient and better-centralized states to conduct them. War was both a product of the European state system and a cause of its continued development. As armies grew in size, their matériel needs grew in volume. As the battlefield spread from state to state, defense became government's most important function. More and more power was absorbed by the monarch and his chief advisers; more and more of the traditional privileges of aristocracy and of towns were eroded. At the center of these rising states, particularly in western Europe, were the king and his court. In the provinces were tax collectors and military recruiters.

Divine Kings

In the early sixteenth century, monarchs treated their states and subjects as personal property. Correspondingly, rulers were praised in personal terms, for their virtue, wisdom, or strength. By the early seventeenth century, the monarchy had been transformed into an office of state. Now rulers embodied their nation, and, no matter what their personal characteristics, they were held in awe because they were monarchs.

Thus, as rulers lost direct personal control over their territory, they gained indirect symbolic control over their nation. This symbolic power was manifested everywhere. By the beginning of the seventeenth century, monarchs had permanent seats of government attended by vast courts of officials, place seekers, and servants. The idea of the capital city emerged, with Madrid, London, and Paris as models. Here, the grandiose style of the ruler stood proxy for the wealth and glory of the nation.

Portraits of rulers conveyed the central message. Elizabeth I was depicted astride a map of England or clutching a rainbow and wearing a gown woven of eyes and ears to signify her power to see and hear her subjects. Peter Paul Rubens (1577–1640) represented 21 separate episodes in the life of Marie de Médicis, queen regent of France.

Monarchy was also glorified in literature. National history, particularly of recent events, enjoyed wide popularity. Its avowed purpose was to draw the connection between the past and the present glories of the state.

Shakespeare and Kingship. Many of the plays of William Shakespeare (1564–1616) dealt with monarchy. He set many of his plays at the courts of princes, and even comedies such as *Measure for Measure* (1604) and *The Tempest* (1611) centered on the power of the ruler to dispense justice and to bring peace to his subjects. Shakespeare's history plays focused entirely on the character of kings. In Shakespeare's tragedies, a

Queen Elizabeth I of England. This portrait was commissioned by Sir Henry Lee to commemorate the queen's visit to his estate at Ditchley. Here the queen is the very image of Gloriana—ageless and indomitable.

flaw in the ruler's personality brought harm to the world around him. Shakespeare's concentration on the affairs of rulers helped to reinforce their dominating importance in the lives of all of their subjects.

Monarchy and Law. The political theory of the **divine right of kings** further enhanced the importance of monarchs. This theory held that the institution of monarchy had been created by God and the monarch functioned as God's representative on earth.

The idea of divine origin of monarchy was uncontroversial, and it was espoused not only by kings. In 1614, the French Estates-General agreed that "the king is sovereign in France and holds his crown from God only." This sentiment echoed the commonplace view of French political theorists. The greatest writer on the subject, Jean Bodin (1530–1596), called the king "God's image on earth."

Kings were nevertheless bound by the law of nature and the law of nations. They could not deprive their subjects of their lives, their liberties, or their property without due cause established by law.

The Court and the Courtiers

In reality, the day-to-day affairs of government had grown beyond the capacity of any monarch to handle them. The expansion in the powers of the western states absorbed more officials than ever. At the beginning of the sixteenth century, the French court of Francis I employed 622 officers; at the beginning of the seventeenth century, the court of Henry IV employed over 1,500. Yet the difference was not only in size. Members of the seventeenth-century court were becoming servants of the state as well as of the monarch.

Expanding the court was one of the ways in which monarchs co-opted potential rivals within the aristocracy. In return, those who were favored received royal grants of titles, lands, and income. As the court expanded, so did the political power of courtiers. Royal councils—a small group of leading officeholders who advised the monarch on state business—grew in significance. The council assumed management of the government and soon began to advocate policies for the monarch to adopt.

Yet the court still revolved around the monarch. The monarch appointed, promoted, and dismissed officeholders at will. As befitted this type of personal government, most monarchs chose a single individual to act as a funnel for private and public business. This was the "favorite," whose role combined varying proportions of best friend, right-hand man, and hired gun. Favorites lasted only as long as they retained their influence with the monarch.

The Drive to Centralize Government

Europe's divine monarchs shared a common goal: to extend the authority of the monarch over his state and to centralize his control over the machinery of governance. One of the chief means by which kings and councilors attempted to expand the authority of the state was through the legal system.

Administering justice was one of the sacred duties of the monarchy. The complexities of ecclesiastical, civil, and customary law gave trained lawyers an essential role in government. As the need for legal services increased, royal law courts multiplied and expanded. In France, the Parlement of Paris, the main law court of the state, became a powerful institution that contested with courtiers for the right to advise the monarch.

In Spain, the *letrados*—university-trained lawyers who were normally members of the nobility—were the backbone of royal government. Formal legal training was a requirement for many of the administrative posts in the state. In Castile, members of all social classes frequently used the royal courts to settle personal disputes. The expansion of a centralized system of justice thus joined the interests of subjects and the monarchy.

In England, central courts situated in the royal palace of Westminster grew, and the lawyers and judges who practiced in them became a powerful profession. They were especially active in the House of Commons of the English Parliament, which, along with the House of Lords, had extensive advisory and legislative powers. More important than the rise of the central courts, however, was the rise of the local ones. The English crown extended royal justice to the counties by granting legal authority to members of the local social elite. These justices of the peace, whose position can be traced to medieval times, became agents of the crown in their own localities. Justices were given power to hear and settle minor cases and to imprison people who had committed serious offenses until the assizes, the semiannual sessions of the county court.

Assizes combined the ceremony of rule with its process. Royal authority was displayed in a great procession to the courthouse that was led by the judge and the county justices, followed by the grand and petty juries of local citizens who would hear the cases, and finally by the carts carrying the prisoners to trial. Along with the legal business that was performed, assizes were occasions for edifying sermons, typically on the theme of obedience.

Efforts to integrate center and locality extended to more than the exercise of justice. The monarch also needed officials who could enforce royal policy in localities where the special privileges of groups and individuals remained strong. By the beginning of the seventeenth century, the French monarchy had begun to rely on new central officials known as **intendants** to perform many of the tasks of the provincial governors. During the reign of Louis XIII, Cardinal Richelieu (1585–1642) expanded the use of the intendants, and by the middle of the century they had become a vital part of royal government.

The Lords Lieutenant were a parallel institution created in England. Unlike every other European state, England had no national army. Every English county was required to raise, equip, and train its own militia. Lords Lieutenant were in charge of these trained bands. The lieutenants were chosen from the greatest nobles of the realm, but they delegated their work to members of the local gentry, large landholders who took on their tasks as a matter of prestige rather than profit.

Efforts to centralize the Spanish monarchy could not proceed so easily. The separate regions over which the king ruled maintained their own laws and privileges.

Attempts to apply Castilian rules or implant Castilian officials always drew opposition from other regions. In 1625, Count-Duke Olivares (1587–1645), favorite of King Philip IV (1621–1665), proposed a plan to help unify Spain and solve the dual problems of military manpower and military finance. After 1621, Spain was fighting in the Netherlands and Germany. Olivares called for a Union of Arms to which all the separate regions of the empire, including Mexico, Peru, Italy, and the dominions in Iberia, would contribute. Olivares was able to establish at least the principle of unified cooperation, but not all of the Iberian provinces were persuaded to contribute. Catalonia stood on its ancient privileges and refused to grant either troops or funds.

The Taxing Demands of War

More than anything else, the consolidation of the state was propelled by war, which required increased governmental powers of taxation. Perhaps half of all revenue of the western states went to finance war. To maintain its military forces, the state had to squeeze every penny from its subjects. Old taxes had to be collected more efficiently, and new taxes had to be introduced and enforced. Such unprecedented demands for money on the part of the state were always resisted. The privileged challenged the legality of levying taxes; the unprivileged tried to avoid paying them.

The economic hardships caused by the ceaseless military activity touched everyone. Those in the direct path of battle had little left to feed themselves, let alone to provide to the state. The disruption of the delicate cycle of planting and harvesting devastated local communities. Armies plundered ripened grain and trampled seedlings as they moved through fields. The conscription of village men and boys removed vital skills and labor from the community. Peasants were squeezed by the armies for crops, by the lords for rents, and by the state for taxes.

In fact, the inability of the lower orders of European society to finance a century of warfare was clear from the beginning. In Spain and France, much wealth was beyond the reach of traditional royal taxation. The nobility and many of the most important towns had long enjoyed exemption from basic taxes on consumption and wealth. European taxation was regressive, falling most heavily on those who were least able to pay. Rulers and subjects alike recognized the inequities of the system, and regime after regime considered overhauling the national tax system but ultimately settled for new emergency levies. Nevertheless, the fiscal crisis that the European wars provoked did result in an expansion of state taxation.

Still, no matter how much new revenue was provided for war finance, more was needed. New taxes and increased rates of traditional taxation created suffering and a sense of grievance throughout the western European states. Opposition to taxation was not based on greed. The state's right to tax was not yet an established principle. Monarchs received certain forms of revenue in return for grants of immunities and privileges to powerful groups in their state. The state's efforts to go beyond these restricted grants was viewed as theft of private property.

Throughout the seventeenth century, monarchy was consolidating its position as a form of government. The king's authority came from God, but his power came from his people. By administering justice, assembling armies, and extracting resources through taxation, the monarch ruled as well as governed. The richer and more powerful the king, the more potent was his state. His subjects began to identify themselves as citizens of a nation and to see themselves in distinction to other nations.

The Crises of the Royal State

The expansion of the functions, duties, and powers of the state in the early seventeenth century was not universally welcomed in European societies. The growth of central government came at the expense of local rights and privileges held by organized bodies such as the Church and the towns or by individuals such as provincial officials and aristocrats. The state proved to be a powerful competitor for the meager surplus produced on the land. As rents and prices stabilized in the early seventeenth century, after a long period of inflation, taxation increased, especially with the gathering momentum of the Thirty Years' War.

It was not only taxation that aroused opposition. Social and economic regulation meant more laws, more lawyers, and more agents of enforcement. State regulation was disruptive and expensive at a time when the fragile European economy was in decline. The early seventeenth century was a time of hunger in most of western Europe. Subtle changes in climate reduced the length of growing seasons and the size of crops. Bad harvests in the 1620s and 1640s left disease and starvation in their wake. And the wars ground on.

By the middle of the seventeenth century, a Europe-wide crisis was taking shape. Bread riots and tax revolts had become increasingly common in the early seventeenth century. As the focus of discontent moved from local institutions to the state, the forms of revolt and the participants also changed. Members of the political elite began to formulate their own grievances against the expansion of state power. A theory of resistance, first developed in the French wars of religion, came to be applied to political tyranny and posed a direct challenge to the idea of the divine right of kings. By the 1640s, all of these forces converged, and rebellion exploded across the Continent.

The Need to Resist

Europeans lived more precariously in the seventeenth century than in any period since the Black Death. One benchmark of crisis was population decline. In the Mediterranean, the Spanish population fell from 8.5 million to 7 million, and the Italian population from 13 million to 11 million. The ravages of the Thirty Years' War were most clearly felt in central Europe. Germany lost nearly one-third of its people; Bohemia lost nearly half. England, the Netherlands, and France were hardest hit in the first half of the century and only gradually recovered by 1700. Population decline had many causes, and direct casualties from warfare were only a very small component.

The indirect effects of war—the disruption of agriculture and the spread of disease—were far more devastating.

All sectors of the European economy from agriculture to trade stagnated or declined in the early seventeenth century, but peasants were hardest hit. The surplus from good harvests did not remain in rural communities to act as a buffer for bad ones. Tens of thousands died during the two great subsistence crises in the late 1620s and the late 1640s.

Acute economic crisis led to rural revolt. As the French peasants reeled from visitations of plague, frost, and floods, the French state was raising the taille, the tax on basic commodities that fell most heavily on the lower orders. A series of French rural revolts in the late 1630s protested tax increases. The *Nu-Pieds* ("barefooted") rose against changes in the salt tax; other peasants rose against new levies on wine. These revolts typically began with the murder of a local tax official, the organization of a peasant militia, and the recruitment of local clergy and notables. The rebels forced temporary concessions from local authorities but never achieved lasting reforms. Each revolt ended with the reimposition of order by the state.

The most spectacular popular uprisings occurred in Spanish-occupied Italy. In the spring of 1647, in the Sicilian city of Palermo, violence broke out in the wake of a disastrous harvest, rising food prices, and relentless taxation. As grain prices rose, the city government subsidized the price of bread, running up huge debts in the process. When the town governors could no longer afford the subsidies, they decided to reduce the size of the loaf rather than increase its price. The women of the city rioted when the first undersized loaves were placed on sale, and soon the entire city was in revolt. Commoners who were not part of the urban power structure led the revolt, and for a time they achieved the abolition of Spanish taxes on basic foodstuffs. Their success provided the model for a similar uprising in Naples, the largest city in Europe. The revolt began in 1647 after the Spanish placed a tax on fruit. A crowd gathered in protest, burned the customs house, and murdered several local officials. The rebels again achieved the temporary suspension of Spanish taxation. But neither of the Italian urban revolts could attract support from the local governors or the nobility. Both uprisings were eventually crushed.

EUROPEAN POPULATION DATA (IN MILLIONS)							
Year	1550	1575	1600	1625	1650	1675	1700
England	3.0	—	4.0	4.5	—	5.8	5.8
France	—	20.0	—	—	—	—	19.3
Italy	11.0	13.0	13.0	13.0	12.0	11.5	12.5
Russia	9.0	—	11.0	8.0	9.5	13.0	16.0
Spain	6.3	—	7.6	—	5.2	—	7.0
All Europe	85.0	95.0	100.0	100.0	80.0	90.0	100.0

The Right to Resist

Rural and urban revolts by members of the lower orders of European society were doomed to failure. Not only did the state control vast military resources, but it could count on the loyalty of the governing classes to suppress local disorder. Only when disgruntled local elites joined the angry peasants did the state face a genuine crisis. Traditionally, aristocratic rebellion was sparked by rival claimants to the throne. By the early seventeenth century, however, hereditary monarchy was too firmly entrenched to be threatened by aristocratic rebellions. The principles of hereditary monarchy and the divine right of kings laid an unshakable foundation for royal legitimacy. But if the monarch's right to rule could no longer be challenged, was the method of rule equally unassailable? Were subjects bound to their sovereign in all cases whatsoever?

Resistance Theory. Luther and Calvin had preached a doctrine of passive obedience. Magistrates ruled by divine will and must be obeyed in all things, they argued. Both left a tiny crack in the door of absolute submission, however, by recognizing the right of lesser magistrates to resist their superiors if divine law was violated. During the French civil wars, a broader theory of resistance began to develop. In attempting to defend themselves from accusations that they were rebels, a number of Huguenot writers responded with an argument that accepted the divine right of kings but maintained that kings were placed on earth by God to uphold piety and justice. When they failed to do so, lesser magistrates were obliged to resist them. Because God would not institute tyranny, oppressive monarchs could not be acting by divine right. Therefore, the king who violated divine law could be punished. In the most influential of these writings, *A Defense of Liberty Against Tyrants* (1579), Philippe Duplessis-Mornay (1549–1623) took the critical next step and argued that the king who violated the law of the land could also be resisted.

In the writings of both the French Huguenots and the Dutch Protestants there remained strict limits to this right to resist. These authors accepted divine right theory and restricted resistance to other divinely ordained magistrates.

Logic soon drove the argument further. If it was the duty of lesser magistrates to resist monarchical tyranny, why was it not the duty of all citizens to do so? This question was posed by the Jesuit professor Juan de Mariana (1536–1624) in *The King and the Education of the King* (1598). Since magistrates were first established by the people and then legitimated by God, magistrates were nothing other than the people's representatives. If it was the duty of magistrates to resist the tyranny of monarchs, Mariana reasoned, then it must also be the duty of every individual citizen.

In defense of the English Revolution, the great English poet John Milton (1608–1674) built on traditional resistance theory. In *The Tenure of Kings and Magistrates* (1649), Milton expanded on the conventional idea that society was formed by a covenant, or contract, between ruler and ruled. The king, in his coronation oath, promised to uphold the laws of the land and to rule for the benefit of his subjects. The subjects promised to obey. Either side's failure to meet obligations broke the contract.

Resistance and Rebellion. By the middle of the seventeenth century, resistance theory provided the intellectual justification for a number of attacks on monarchical authority. In 1640, simultaneous rebellions in the ancient kingdoms of Portugal and Catalonia threatened the Spanish monarchy. The Portuguese successfully dissolved the rather artificial bonds that had been created by Philip II and resumed their separate national identity. Catalonia, the easternmost province of Spain, which Ferdinand of Aragon had brought to the union of crowns in the fifteenth century, presented a more serious challenge. Throughout the 1620s, Catalonia, with its rich Mediterranean city of Barcelona, had consistently rebuffed Olivares's attempts to consolidate the Spanish provinces. The Catalan Cortes—the representative institution of the towns—refused to make even small contributions to the Union of Arms or to successive appeals for emergency tax increases. Catalonian leaders feared that these demands were only an entering wedge. They did not want their province to go the way of Castile, where taxation was as much an epidemic as was plague.

Catalonia resisted demands for contributions to the Spanish military effort, but soon the province was embroiled in the French war, and Olivares was forced to bring troops into Catalonia. The presence of the soldiers and their conduct inflamed the local population. In the spring of 1640, an unconnected series of peasant uprisings took place. Soldiers and royal officials were slain, and the Spanish viceroy of the province was murdered. But the violence was not directed only against outsiders. Attacks on wealthy citizens raised the specter of social revolt.

It was at this point that a peasant uprising broadened into a provincial rebellion. The political leaders of Barcelona sanctioned the rebellion and decided to lead it. They declared that Philip IV had violated the fundamental laws of Catalonia and that in consequence their allegiance to the crown of Spain was dissolved. They turned to Louis XIII of France, offering him sovereignty if he would preserve their liberties. In fact, the Catalonians simply exchanged a devil they knew for one they did not. The French happily sent troops into Barcelona to repel a Spanish attempt to crush the rebellion. Now two armies occupied Catalonia. The Catalan rebellion lasted for 12 years. When the Spanish finally took Barcelona in 1652, both rebels and ruler were exhausted from the struggle.

The revolt of the Catalans posed a greater external threat to the Spanish monarchy than it did an internal one. In contrast, the French **Fronde**, an aristocratic rebellion that began in 1648, was more directly a challenge to the underlying authority of the state. It too began in response to fiscal crises brought on by war. Throughout the 1640s, the French state, tottering on the edge of bankruptcy, had used every means of creative financing that its ministers could devise. Still, it was necessary to raise traditional taxes and to institute new ones. The first tactic revived peasant revolts, especially in the early years of the decade; the second led to the Fronde.

The Fronde was a rebellion against the regency government of Louis XIV (1643–1715), who was only four years old when he inherited the French throne. His mother, Anne of Austria (1601–1666), ruled as regent with the help of her Italian adviser, Cardinal Mazarin (1602–1661). In the circumstances of war, agricultural crisis, and financial stringency, no regency government was going to be popular, but Anne and Mazarin made the worst of a bad situation. They initiated new taxes on office-holders, Parisian landowners, and the nobility. Soon all three groups united against them, led by the Parlement of Paris, the highest court in the land, in which new decrees of taxation had to be registered. When the Parlement refused to register a number of the new taxes proposed by the government and soon insisted on the right to control the crown's financial policy, Anne and Mazarin struck back by having a number of Parlement members arrested. But in 1648, barricades went up in Paris, and the court, along with the nine-year-old king, fled the capital. Quickly, the Fronde—which took its name from the slingshots that children used to hurl stones at carriages—became an aristocratic revolt aimed not at the king but at his advisers. Demands for Mazarin's resignation, the removal of the new taxes, and greater participation in government by nobles and Parlement were coupled with profuse statements of loyalty to the king.

The duc de Condé, leader of the Parisian insurgents, courted Spanish aid against Mazarin's forces, and the cardinal was forced to make concessions to prevent a Spanish invasion of France. The leaders of the Fronde agreed that the crown must overhaul its finances and recognize the rights of the administrative nobility to participate in formulating royal policy. But they had no concrete proposals to accomplish either aim. Nor could they control the deteriorating political situation in Paris and a number of provincial capitals, where urban and rural riots followed the upper-class attack on the state. The catastrophic winter of 1652, with its combination of harvest failure, intense cold, and epidemic disease, brought the crisis to a head. Louis XIV was declared old enough to rule, and his forces recaptured Paris, where he was welcomed as a savior. The Fronde accomplished little other than to demonstrate that the French aristocracy remained an independent force in politics. Like the Catalonian revolt, it revealed the fragility of the absolute state on the one hand, yet its underlying stability on the other.

The English Civil War

The most profound challenge to monarchical authority in the seventeenth century took place in England. In 1603, James I succeeded his cousin Elizabeth I without challenge. He was not a lovable monarch, but he was capable, astute, and generous. Though he relied on Elizabeth's most trusted ministers to guide state business, James was soon plunged into financial and political difficulties. He never escaped either.

Charles I. James's financial problems resulted directly from the fact that the tax base of the English monarchy was undervalued. For decades the monarchy had staved off a crisis by selling lands that had been confiscated from the Church in the mid-sixteenth century. But this solution reduced the Crown's long-term revenues and made it dependent on extraordinary grants of taxation from Parliament. Royal demands for money were met by parliamentary demands for political reform. The most significant, in 1628, during the reign of Charles I, led to the formulation of the Petition of Right, which restated the traditional English freedoms from arbitrary arrest and imprisonment (habeas corpus), from nonparliamentary taxation, and from the confiscation of property by martial law.

Religious problems mounted on top of economic and political difficulties. **Puritans** were demanding thoroughgoing church reforms. One of the most contentious issues raised by some Puritans was the survival in the Anglican Church of the Catholic hierarchy of archbishops and bishops. These Puritans demanded the abolition of this episcopal form of government and its replacement with a presbyterial system similar to that in Scotland, in which congregations nominated their own representatives to a national assembly. Neither James I nor his son, Charles I, opposed religious reform, but to achieve their reforms, they strengthened episcopal power. In the 1620s, Archbishop William Laud (1573–1645) rose to power in the English church by espousing a Calvinism so moderate that many denied it was Calvinism at all. One of Laud's first projects after he was appointed archbishop of Canterbury was to establish a consistent divine service in England and Scotland by creating new prayer books.

It fell to the unfortunate dean of St. Giles Cathedral in Edinburgh to introduce the new Scottish prayer book in 1637. The reaction was immediate: Someone threw a stool at his head, and dozens of women screamed that "popery" was being brought to Scotland. Citizens rioted, and the clergy and the nobility resisted the use of the new prayer book. To Charles I the opposition was rebellion, and he began to raise forces to suppress it. But the Scots fought back, and by the end of 1640 an army of Charles's Scottish subjects had successfully invaded England.

Now the fiscal and political problems of the Stuart monarchs came into play. For 11 years, Charles I had managed to live from his own revenues. He had accomplished this by a combination of economy and the revival of ancient feudal rights that struck hard at the governing classes. He levied fines for unheard-of offenses, expanded traditional taxes, and added a brutal efficiency to the collection of

Charles I by Daniel Myrtens. The antagonism between Charles and Parliament sparked a civil war in England.

revenue. While these expedients sufficed during peacetime, they could not support an army and war. Charles I was again dependent on grants from Parliament, which he reluctantly summoned in 1640.

The Long Parliament. The **Long Parliament**, which met in November 1640 and sat for 13 years, saw little urgency in levying taxes to repel the Scots. Parliament proposed a number of constitutional reforms that Charles I reluctantly accepted. The Long Parliament would not be dismissed without its own consent. In the future, Parliaments

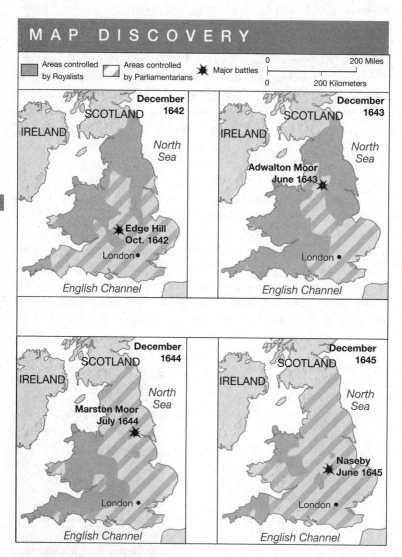

MAP DISCOVERY

ENGLISH CIVIL WAR

How would you describe the geographical divisions at the beginning of the war in 1642? Who appears to have been winning the war by December 1643? How did the war progress between 1644 and 1645?

would be summoned once in every three years. Due process in common law would be observed, and the ancient taxes that the Crown had revived would be abolished.

At first, Charles I could do nothing but bide his time and accept these assaults on his power and authority. Once he had crushed the Scots, he would be able to bargain from a position of strength. But as the months passed, it became clear that Parliament had no intention of providing him with money or forces. By the end of 1641, Charles's patience had worn thin. In the summer of 1642, he left the capital and headed north where he raised the royal standard and declared the leaders of Parliament rebels and traitors. England was plunged into civil war.

After nearly three years of inconclusive fighting, Parliament won a decisive victory at Naseby in June 1645 and brought the war to an end the following summer. The king was in captivity, bishops had been abolished, a Presbyterian church had been established, and limitations were placed on royal power. All that was necessary to end three years of civil war was the king's agreement to abide by the judgment of battle.

But Charles I had no intention of surrendering either his religion or his authority. Despite the rebels' successes, they could not rule without him, and he would concede nothing as long as opportunities to maneuver remained. In 1647 there were opportunities galore. The war had proved ruinously expensive to Parliament. It owed enormous sums to the Scots, to its own soldiers, and to the governors of London. Each of these elements had its own objectives in a final settlement of the war, and they were not altogether compatible. London feared the parliamentary army, unpaid and camped dangerously close to the capital. The Scots and the English Presbyterians in Parliament feared that the religious settlement that had already been made would be sacrificed by those known as Independents, who desired a more decentralized church. The Independents feared that they would be persecuted just as harshly by the Presbyterians as they had been by the king. In fact, the war had settled nothing.

The English Revolutions

Charles I happily played both ends against the middle until the army decisively ended the game. In June 1647, parliamentary soldiers kidnapped the king and demanded that Parliament pay their arrears, protect them from legal retribution, and recognize their service to the nation. Those in Parliament who opposed the army's intervention were impeached, and when London Presbyterians rose up against the army's show of force, troops moved in to occupy the city. The civil war, which had come so close to resolution in 1647, had now become a military revolution. Religious and political radicals flocked to the army and encouraged the soldiers to support their programs and to resist disbandment. New fighting broke out in 1648, as Charles encouraged his supporters to resume the war. But forces under the command of Sir Thomas Fairfax (1612–1671) and Oliver Cromwell (1599–1658) easily crushed the royalist uprisings in England and Scotland. The army now demanded that Charles I be brought to justice for his treacherous conduct both before and during the war. When the majority in Parliament refused, still hoping to reach an accommodation with the king, the soldiers again acted decisively. In December 1648, army regiments were sent to London to purge the two houses of Parliament of those who opposed the army's demands. The remaining members, contemptuously called the Rump Parliament, voted to bring the king to trial for his crimes against the liberties of his subjects. On 30 January 1649, Charles I was executed, and England was declared to be a commonwealth. The monarchy and the House of Lords were abolished, and the nation was to be governed by what was left of the membership of the House of Commons.

Oliver Cromwell. For four years, the members of the Rump Parliament struggled with proposals for a new constitution, achieving little. In 1653, Oliver Cromwell, with the support of the army's senior officers, forcibly dissolved the Rump and became the leader of the revolutionary government. When Cromwell's Parliament proved no more capable of governing than had the Rump, a written constitution, The Instrument of Government (1653), established a new polity. Cromwell was given the title Lord Protector, and he was to rule along with a freely elected Parliament and an administrative body known as the council of state.

Cromwell was able to smooth over conflicts and hold the revolutionary cause together through the force of his own personality. Though many urged him to accept the crown of England and begin a new monarchy, Cromwell steadfastly held out for a government in which fundamental authority resided in Parliament. Until his death he defended the achievements of the revolution.

But a sense that only a single person could effectively rule a state remained strong. When Cromwell died in 1658, his oldest son Richard was proposed as the new lord protector, but Richard had very little experience in either military or civil affairs. Without an individual to hold the movement together, the revolution fell apart. In 1659, the army again intervened in civil affairs, dismissing the recently elected Parliament and calling for the restoration of the monarchy. After a period of negotiation in which the king agreed to a general amnesty with only a few exceptions, the Stuarts were restored when Charles II (1649–1685) took the throne in 1660.

Twenty years of civil war and revolution had their effect. Absolute monarchy had become constitutional monarchy with the threat of revolution behind the power of Parliament and the threat of anarchy behind the power of the Crown.

The Glorious Revolution. The threats of revolution and of anarchy proved potent in 1685 when James II (1685–1688) came to the throne. A declared Catholic, James attempted to use his power of appointment to foil the constraints that Parliament imposed on him. He elevated Catholics to leading posts in the military and in the central government and began a campaign to pack a new Parliament with his supporters. This proved to be too much for the governing classes, which entered into negotiations with William, prince of Orange, who was the husband of Mary Stuart, James's eldest daughter. In 1688, William landed in England with a small force. Without support, James II fled to France, the English throne was declared vacant, and William and Mary were proclaimed king and queen of England. There was little bloodshed and little threat of social disorder, and the event soon came to be called the **Glorious Revolution**. Its achievements were set down in the Declaration of Rights (1689), which was presented to William and Mary before they took the

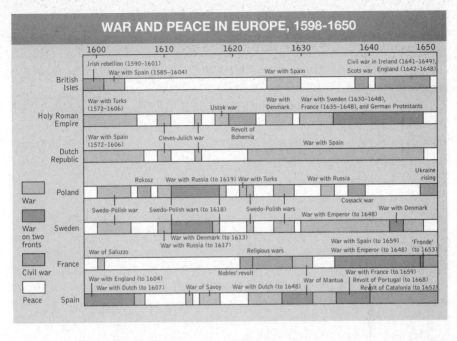

WAR AND PEACE IN EUROPE, 1598–1650

throne. The declaration reasserted the fundamental principles of constitutional monarchy as they had developed over the previous half-century. Security of property and the regularity of Parliaments were guaranteed. The Toleration Act (1689) granted religious freedom to nearly all groups of Protestants. The liberties of the subject and the rights of the sovereign were to be in balance.

The events of 1688 in England reversed a trend toward increasing power on the part of the Stuarts. This second episode of resistance resulted in the development of a unique form of government, which, a century later, spawned dozens of imitators. John Locke (1632–1704) was the theorist of the Revolution of 1688. He was heir to the century-old debate on resistance, and he carried the doctrine to a new plateau. In *Two Treatises on Government* (1689), Locke developed the contract theory of government. Political society was a compact that individuals entered into freely for their own well-being. It was designed to maintain each person's natural rights: life, liberty, and property. Natural rights were inherent in individuals; they could not be given away. The contract between rulers and subjects was an agreement for the protection of natural rights. When rulers acted arbitrarily, they were to be deposed by their subjects, preferably in the relatively peaceful manner in which James II had been replaced by William III.

The Zenith of the Royal State

The midcentury crises tested the mettle of the royal states. Over the long term, the seventeenth-century crises had two different consequences. First, they provided a check to the exercise of royal power. Fear of recurring rebellions had a chilling effect on policy, especially taxation. Reforms of financial administration, long overdue, were one of the themes of the later seventeenth century. Even as royal government strengthened itself, it remained concerned about the impact of its policies. The memory of rebellion also served to control the ambitions of factious noblemen and town oligarchies.

If nothing else, these episodes of opposition to the rising royal states made clear the universal desire for stable government, which was seen as the responsibility of both subjects and rulers. The natural advantages of monarchy had to be merged with the interests of the citizens of the state and their desires for wealth, safety, and honor. After so much chaos and instability the monarchy had to be elevated above the fray of day-to-day politics to become a symbol of the nation's power and glory.

In England, Holland, and Sweden a form of constitutional monarchy developed in which rulers shared power, in varying degrees, with other institutions of state. In England it was Parliament; in Holland, the town oligarchies; in Sweden, the nobility. But in most other states in Europe there developed a pure form of royal government known as **absolutism**. Absolute monarchy revived the divine right theories of kingship and added to them a cult of the personality of the ruler.

The Nature of Absolute Monarchy

Locke's theory of contract provided one solution to the central problem of seventeenth-century government: how to balance the monarch's right to command and the subjects' duty to obey.

The English solution was most suited to a state that was largely immune from invasion and land war. Constitutional government required a higher level of political participation of citizens than did absolute monarchy. Greater participation meant greater freedom of expression, greater toleration of religious minorities, and greater openness in the institutions of government. All were dangerous. The price that England paid was a half-century of governmental instability.

The alternative to constitutional monarchy was absolute monarchy. It, too, found its leading theorist in England. Thomas Hobbes (1588–1679), in his greatest work, *Leviathan* (1651), argued that people came together to form a government for the most basic of all purposes: self-preservation. Without government they were condemned to a life that was "solitary, poor, nasty, brutish, and short." To escape, individuals pooled their power and granted it to a ruler. The terms of the Hobbesian contract were simple: Rulers agreed to rule; subjects agreed to obey.

The main features of absolute monarchy were all designed to extend royal control. As in the early seventeenth century, the person of the monarch was revered. Courts grew larger and more lavish in an effort to enhance the glory of the monarchy and thereby of the state. "*L'état, c'est moi*" ("I am the state"), Louis XIV was supposed to have said. As the king grew in stature, his competitors for power all shrank. Large numbers of nobles were herded together at court under the watchful eye of monarchs who now ruled rather than reigned. The king shed the cloak of his favorites and rolled up his own sleeves to manage state affairs. Representative institutions were weakened or cast aside. Monarchs needed standing armies trained in the increasingly sophisticated arts of war, so the military was expanded and made an integral part of the machinery of government.

Yet the absolute state was never as powerful in practice as it was in theory. Nor did it ever exist in its ideal shape. Absolutism was always in the making, never quite made. Its success depended on a strong monarch who knew his own will and could enforce it. It depended on unity within the state, on the absence or ruthless suppression of religious or political minorities. The absolute ruler needed to control information and ideas to limit criticism of state policy. Ultimately, the absolute state rested on the will of its citizens to support it.

Absolutism in the East

Frederick William, the Great Elector of Brandenburg-Prussia (1640–1688), made highly effective use of the techniques of absolutism. In 1640, he inherited a scattered and ungovernable collection of territories. The nobility, known as *die Junker*, enjoyed immunity from almost all forms of direct taxation, and the towns had no obligation to furnish men or supplies for military operations beyond their walls.

When Frederick William attempted to introduce an excise—the commodity tax on consumption that had so successfully financed the Dutch Revolt and the English Revolution—he was initially rebuffed. But military emergency overcame legal precedents. By the 1650s, Frederick William had established the excise in the towns, though not in the countryside.

With the excise as a steady source of revenue, the Great Elector set about forming one of the most capable and best disciplined standing armies of the age. He organized one of the first departments of war to oversee all of the details of the creation of his army, from housing and supplies to the training of young officer candidates. This department was also responsible for the collection of taxes. By integrating military and civilian government, Frederick William established an efficient state bureaucracy that was particularly responsive in times of crisis. The creation of the Prussian army was the force that led to the creation of the Prussian state.

The same materials that forged the Prussian state led to the transformation of Russia. Soon after the young Tsar Peter I, known later as "the Great" (1682–1725), came to the throne, he realized that he could compete with the western states only by learning to play their game.

Like Frederick William, Peter concentrated on military reform. He understood that if Russia was to flourish in a world dominated by war and commerce, it would have to reestablish its hold on the Baltic ports. This meant dislodging the Swedes from the Russian mainland and creating a fleet to protect Russian trade. Neither goal seemed likely. The Swedes were one of the great powers of the age, constant innovators in battlefield tactics and military organization. Peter studied their every campaign. His first wars against the Swedes ended in humiliating defeats, but with each failure came a sharper sense of what was needed to succeed.

First Peter introduced a system of conscription and created a standing army. He unified the military command at the top and stratified it in the field. He established promotion based on merit and established military schools to train cadets for the next generation of officers.

Finally, in 1709, Peter realized his ambitions. At the battle of Poltava, the Russian army routed the Swedes, wounding King Charles XII, annihilating his infantry, and capturing dozens of his leading officers. After the battle of Poltava, Russia gradually replaced Sweden as the dominant power in the Baltic.

As an absolute ruler, Peter the Great's power was unlimited, but it was not uncontested. He secularized the Russian Orthodox church, subjecting it to state control and confiscating much of its wealth. He broke the old military service class, which attempted a coup d'état when he was abroad in the 1690s. By the end of his reign, the Russian monarchy was among the strongest in Europe.

The Origins of French Absolutism

Nowhere was absolutism as successfully implanted as in France. Louis XIII (1610–1643) was only eight years old when he came to the throne, and he grew slowly into his role under the tutelage of Cardinal Richelieu. It was Richelieu's vision that stabilized French government. As chief minister, Richelieu saw clearly that France's survival and prosperity depended on strengthening royal power. He preached a doctrine of *raison d'état* ("reason of state"), in which he placed the needs of the nation above the privileges of its most important groups. Richelieu saw three threats to stable royal government: the Huguenots, the nobles, and the most powerful provincial governors.

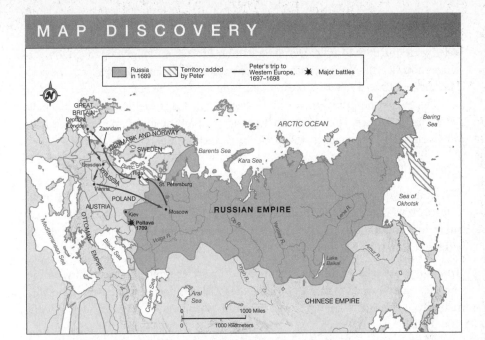

EXPANSION OF RUSSIA UNDER PETER THE GREAT

Notice the extent of the Russian Empire in 1689 and territory added by Peter the Great. What was important about the new territory? What was the role of the battle of Poltava in expanding the empire? The route of Peter's trip to western Europe is marked here. Why did he travel where he did? Based on the chapter discussion, what impact did his trip have on the way he ruled his empire?

Richelieu took measures to control all three. The power of the nobles was the most difficult to attack. The nobles' long tradition of independence from the crown had been enhanced by the wars of religion. The ancient aristocracy, the nobility of the sword, felt themselves to be in a particularly vulnerable position. Their world was changing, and their traditional roles were becoming obsolete. Professional soldiers replaced them at war, professional administrators at government. Mercantile wealth threatened their economic superiority, and the growth of the nobility of the robe—lawyers and state officials—threatened their social standing. They were hardly likely to take orders from a royal minister such as Richelieu.

To limit the power of local officials, Richelieu used intendants to examine their conduct and reform their administration. He made careful appointments of local governors and brought more regions under direct royal control. Against the Calvinists, who were called Huguenots in France, Richelieu's policy was more subtle. He was less interested in challenging their religion than their autonomy. In 1627, when the English sent a force to aid the Huguenots against the government, Richelieu and Louis XIII abolished the Huguenots' privileges. They were allowed to maintain their religion but not their special status. Finally, in 1685, Louis XIV revoked the Edict of

Nantes, which had guaranteed civil and religious rights to the Huguenots. All forms of Protestant worship were outlawed, and the ministers who were not hunted down and killed were forced into exile. Despite a ban on Protestant emigration, over 200,000 Huguenots fled the country, many of them carrying irreplaceable skills with them to Holland and England in the west and to Brandenburg in the east.

Richelieu's program was a vital prelude to the development of absolute monarchy in France. The cardinal did not act without the full support of Louis XIII, but there can be no doubt that Richelieu was the power behind the throne.

Louis le Grand

Not quite five years old when Louis XIII died, Louis XIV was tutored by Cardinal Jules Mazarin (1602–1661), Richelieu's successor as chief minister. Mazarin was more ruthless and less popular than his predecessor, but like Richelieu, he was an excellent administrator.

The King and His Ministers. In order to pacify the rebellious nobility of the Fronde, who opposed Mazarin's power, Louis XIV was declared to have reached his majority at the age of 13. But it was not until Mazarin died 10 years later, in 1661, that the king began to rule.

Louis was blessed with able and energetic ministers. The two central props of his state—money and might—were in the hands of dynamic men, Jean-Baptiste Colbert (1619–1683) and the Marquis de Louvois (1639–1691). Colbert was Louis's chief minister for finance. Colbert's fiscal reforms were so successful that in less than six years a debt of 22 million French pounds had become a surplus of 29 million. Colbert achieved this astonishing feat not by raising taxes but by increasing the efficiency of their collection. Until Louis embarked on his wars, the French state was solvent.

To Louvois, Louis's minister of war, fell the task of reforming the French army. During the Fronde, royal troops were barely capable of defeating the makeshift forces of the nobility. By the end of the reign, the army had grown to 400,000, and its organization had been thoroughly reformed.

Louis XIV furthered the practice of relying on professional administrators to supervise the main departments of state and to offer advice on matters of policy. He built on the institution of the intendant that Richelieu had developed with so much success. Intendants were now a permanent part of government, and their duties expanded from their early responsibilities as coordinators and mediators into areas of policing and tax collection. It was through the intendants that the wishes of central government were made known in the provinces.

The Court of Versailles. Though Louis XIV was well served, it was the king himself who set the tone for French absolutism. The acting of majesty was central to Louis's rule. His residence at Versailles was the most glittering court of Europe. When the court and king moved there permanently in 1682, Versailles became the envy of the Continent. But behind the imposing facade of Versailles stood a well-thought-out plan for domestic and international rule.

This Hyacinthe Rigaud portrait of Louis XIV in his coronation robes shows the splendor of *Le Roi Soleil* (the Sun King), who believed himself to be the center of France as the sun is the center of the solar system.

Louis XIV attempted to tame the French nobles by requiring their attendance at his court. Louis established a system of court etiquette so complex that constant study was necessary to prevent humiliation. While the nobility studied decorum, they could not plot rebellion.

During Louis's reign, France replaced Spain as the greatest nation in Europe. Massive royal patronage of art, science, and thought brought French culture to new heights. The French language replaced Latin as the universal European tongue. France was the richest and most populous European state, and Louis's absolute rule finally harnessed these resources to a single purpose. France became a commercial power rivaling the Netherlands, a naval power rivaling England, and a military power without peer. It was not only for effect that Louis took the image of the sun as his own. In court, in the nation, and throughout Europe, everything revolved around him.

Louis XIV made his share of mistakes. His aggressive foreign policy ultimately bankrupted the crown. But without doubt, his greatest error was to persecute the Huguenots. As an absolute ruler, Louis regarded the Huguenots, with their separate communities and distinct forms of worship, as an affront to his authority. Supporters of the monarchy celebrated the revocation of the Edict of Nantes in 1685 as an act of piety. But the persecution of the Huguenots was a social and political disaster for France. The Huguenots who fled to other Protestant states spread stories of atrocities that stiffened European resolve against Louis. Those who remained became an embittered minority who pulled at the fabric of the state at every chance. Nor did the official abolition of Protestantism have much effect on its existence. Against these policies the Huguenots held firmly to their beliefs. There were well over one million French Protestants, undoubtedly the largest religious minority in any state. Huguenots simply went underground, practicing their religion secretly and gradually replacing their numbers. No absolutism, however powerful, could succeed in eradicating religious beliefs.

SUMMARY

The Rise of the Royal State   Monarchs became the symbolic center of the state. Their power was based on the theory of the divine right of kings. As the scope of affairs of government grew, so too did the number and importance of royal officials. Europe's monarchs sought to extend their authority and centralize their states. The consolidation of the state was driven by the demands of war. War required ever-increasing state revenues.

The Crises of the Royal State   The expansion of royal power met stiff resistance. The ravages of war, famine, and disease pushed Europeans toward rebellion. Europeans developed new political theories to justify resistance to tyrannical monarchs. Major rebellions shook Spain and France. In England, the policies of the Stuart kings led to civil war and the execution of Charles I. Oliver Cromwell ruled England as Lord Protector until his death in 1658. The Stuarts were restored in 1660 when Charles II took the throne. The policies of James II led to the Glorious Revolution in 1688. He was replaced by William and Mary, who accepted the provisions of the Declaration of Rights.

The Zenith of the Royal State   England became a constitutional monarchy. Most other European states moved in the direction of absolutism. Absolute monarchs revived the theory of the divine right of kings and added a cult of personality of the ruler. The main features of absolute monarchy were designed to extend royal control. Absolute monarchies were never as powerful in practice as in theory. Frederick William of Prussia and Peter the Great of Russia used reform of the military to strengthen their states and consolidate central control. Cardinal Richelieu laid the foundations of French absolutism. Louis XIV benefited from active and able ministers. He used compulsory attendance at his court at Versailles to limit the independence of the nobility. His aggressive foreign policy ultimately bankrupted the crown. His greatest mistake was his persecution of the Huguenots.

QUESTIONS FOR REVIEW

1. How did war in the seventeenth century contribute to the creation of more powerful monarchical states?
2. What religious and political ideas were developed to justify resistance to monarchical authority?
3. What political and religious problems combined to bring England to civil war, and what results did the conflict produce in English government?
4. How did rulers such as Frederick William of Brandenburg, Peter the Great, or Louis XIV, and theorists such as Hobbes, justify absolute monarchical power?

absolutism   Government in which power was consolidated in the hands of a divinely ordained monarch; typified by reverence for the monarch, weakening of representative institutions, and expansion of military.

agricultural revolution   Changes in the traditional agricultural system during the eighteenth century that included enclosure, introduction of fodder crops, intensified animal husbandry, and commercial market orientation.

alchemy   Study of metals in an effort to find their essence through purification. Medieval alchemists attempted to find precious metals such as silver and gold as the essence of base metals such as lead and iron.

Allies   In World War I, the United States, Great Britain, France, and Russia—the alliance that opposed and defeated the Central Powers of Germany and Austria-Hungary and their allies.

Anabaptists   Part of the radical Reformation, Protestant groups that varied in belief but agreed on the principle of adult baptism.

anarchism   A political movement based on rejection of extant political systems; most prominent in less-industrialized Western nations.

anti-Semitism   Hostility toward and discrimination against Jews.

appeasement   British policy of making concessions to Germany in the 1930s in order to avoid war. It allowed Hitler to militarize the Sudetenland and eventually take all of Czechoslovakia.

April Theses   Lenin's promise to the Russian people and challenge to the Provisional Government to provide peace, land, and bread. These three issues became the rallying cries for the second Russian revolution and for the withdrawal of Soviet Russia from World War I.

Arians   During the early Christological controversies, followers of the Alexandrine theologian, Arius, who believed that Jesus was not equal to God the Father.

Axis Powers   In World War II, the alliance of Germany, Italy, and later Japan.

balance of power   Distribution of power among nations in alliances so that any one nation is prevented from dominating the others.

Balfour Declaration   The commitment by the British government issued in 1917 to support a Jewish homeland in Palestine.

Berlin Wall   Barrier built by East Germany in 1961 to halt an exodus of skilled professionals to the West; opened in 1989 as a prelude to the reunification of East and West Germany.

Big Three   The British, Soviet, and U.S. leaders who coordinated defeat of Germany and Japan in World War II and negotiated postwar settlements. Referred to Churchill, Stalin, and Roosevelt until 1945; Attlee, Stalin, and Truman by summer 1945.

Black Death   The virulent combination of bubonic, septicemic, and pneumonic plagues that destroyed between one third and one half of the population of Europe between 1347 and 1352.

blitzkrieg   "Lightning war"; the rapid advance accompanied by armored vehicles that typified the German military during World War II.

Bolsheviks   Radical faction of Marxist Social Democrats following a political theory based on necessity of violent revolution. The Bolsheviks came to power with Lenin in November 1917.

bourgeoisie   A French term referring to the commercial classes of Europe after the seventeenth century; primarily an urban class.

Brezhnev Doctrine Policy of Soviet leader Leonid Brezhnev that approved the use of military intervention in the internal affairs of Soviet allies to prevent counterrevolution.

cahiers de doléances Lists of grievances sent with representatives to the French Estates-General in 1789; demonstrated the existence of a widespread public political culture in France.

caliph The successors of Muhammad who served as political and religious leaders of the Islamic world (see Umma).

capitularies The written instructions for the implementation of royal directives at the local level produced by the clerics of the Carolingian court.

caravels Small Portuguese ships developed in the fifteenth century that were ideal for ocean travel.

Carnival One of the traditional sixteenth-century festivals, the feasts and carousing of which preceded the onset of Lent.

Carolingian Renaissance The cultural revival of classical learning sponsored by the emperor Charlemagne. New schools and the copying of manuscripts were among its important achievements.

cartels Combinations of firms in a given industry to fix prices and establish production quotas.

Cartesianism Philosophy of René Descartes that rested on the dual existence of mind and matter, a principle that enabled the use of skepticism to create certainty.

Central Powers Germany and Austria-Hungary during World War I.

chartism An English working-class reform movement that flourished in the 1830s and 1840s and that demanded universal male suffrage (right to vote), payment for parliamentary service, equal electoral districts, and secret ballots.

chivalry The ideals of knighthood, most notably fighting, that spread from northern France across Europe in the High Middle Ages.

Christian humanism The application of the principles of humanistic education, particularly philology, to the documents of Christianity. It resulted in a program of reform through better education.

Christological controversies The debate about the Christian Trinity (Father, Son, and Holy Spirit) and the relationship between humanity and divinity within it. It caused great division and conflict in the Church and society from the third to the fifth centuries.

city-states Self-governing political units centered upon an urban area. During the fifteenth and sixteenth centuries, city-states took on various forms of government, including republics such as Venice and oligarchies such as Milan.

civic humanism The use of humanistic training and education in the service of the state. Many humanists became advisers to princes or republican governments, holding high office and helping to establish policy.

Cold War The diplomatic and ideological confrontation between the Soviet Union and the United States that began in the aftermath of World War II, dividing the world into two armed camps.

collectivization Soviet plan under Stalin to create large communal state farms to replace private farms owned by peasants.

coloni Tenant farmers who worked on the estates of wealthy landowners in the Roman Empire.

colonization Process by which colonies, or new settlements with links to a parent state, are established.

Columbian Exchange The transfer of microbes, animals, and plants in the encounters between Europeans and Native Americans during the age of exploration.

Comecon The Council for Mutual Economic Assistance established in 1949 with bilateral agreements between the Soviet Union and eastern European states. Comecon was Stalin's response to the U.S. Marshall Plan in western Europe, but rather than providing aid it sought to integrate and control the economies of eastern Europe for Soviet gain.

The Communist Manifesto A call to arms written in 1848 by Karl Marx and Frederich Engels in which they defined in general terms the class struggle in industrializing Europe.

conciliarism The movement proposed by church lawyers in which only a general council of bishops could end the Great Schism.

condottiere A mercenary military leader who sold his services and that of his private army to the highest bidder; used in the wars between the Italian city-states.

Congress of Vienna A meeting of European powers after the Napoleonic wars in 1815; established a balance of power to preserve the status quo in post-revolutionary Europe.

conscription Compulsory service of citizens in the army. France was the first modern state to enforce conscription. The ability to draft all able-bodied men was a key component in the Revolutionary and Napoleonic wars.

conservatism Nineteenth-century ideology that favored tradition and stability and only gradual, or "organic," growth and change.

containment Cold War policy of resisting the spread of Soviet communism.

Continental System The economic boycott of England by Napoleon during the wars beginning in 1803.

Counter-Reformation Catholic response to repel Protestantism.

Crusades Religious wars of conquest directed against non-Christians and heretics in the eleventh through the thirteenth centuries.

Crystal Palace Exhibition This international exhibition, held in London in 1851 in a specially built see-through exhibition hall, featured the greatest technological advances of the day and served as a spur for further industrialization.

culture Those shared beliefs, values, customs, and practices that humans transmit from generation to generation through learning.

cuneiform A form of writing from Mesopotamia characterized by wedge-shaped symbols pressed into wet clay tablets to record words.

Cynics Followers of a Hellenistic Greek philosophy that rejected the world as the source of evil and unhappiness and advocated the reduction of possessions, connections, and pleasures to the absolute minimum.

Declaratory Act A statute enacted in England in 1766 that stated that Parliament held sovereign jurisdiction over the North American colonies.

decolonization Withdrawal of Western nations from colonies in Africa and Asia after World War II.

decurions Members of the city councils in the Roman Empire. Initially, they were the backbone of the provincial elite but by the third and fourth centuries were crippled by their personal responsibility for provincial taxes.

deists Those who believed that God created the universe but then did not intervene in its operation.

Delian League League of Greek cities formed to drive out the Persian invaders. Its leader, Athens, turned it into its own empire.

demesne Land kept by a medieval lord for his direct profit and worked a specified number of days each week by his peasants.

democracy Form of government in which the citizens choose their leaders; began in Athens, Greece, in the fifth century B.C.E.

de-Stalinization Process initiated by Nikita Khrushchev beginning in 1956 that reversed many of Stalin's repressive policies in the Soviet Union.

détente From the French word meaning a relaxation in tension, cooperation between the two superpowers, the Soviet Union and the United States. This policy was characterized by improved U.S.-Soviet diplomatic relationships in the 1970s to lessen the possibility of nuclear war.

dictator   In the Roman Republic, an official who was granted unlimited power to rule the state for a period up to six months in a time of emergency. Sulla and Caesar both used the dictatorship for political ends.

diplomas   The records of royal grants and decisions produced by clerics in medieval courts.

divine rights of kings   Political theory that held that the institution of monarchy had divine origin and that the monarch functioned as God's representative on earth.

doge   Chief magistrate of the Venetian Republic who served for life.

Eastern Question   The question posed by the Great Powers about the future of the Ottoman territories.

Edict of Nantes   The proclamation by Henry IV of France granting limited toleration to Huguenots.

ekklesia   The assembly of all free male Athenian citizens.

emirs   Local military commanders who took control of provincial administration in the Islamic world at the expense of the caliphs by the tenth century.

empiricism   The philosophy propounded by Aristotle which rejected Plato's idea of abstract Forms in favor of practical observation and explanation, building general theories from particular data.

enclosure   In the eighteenth century, the closing off of common and public land within the open field system to foster private landholding.

Enlightenment   Philosophical and intellectual movement that began in Europe during the eighteenth century. The movement was characterized by a wave of new learning, especially in the sciences and mathematics, and the application of reason to solve society's problems.

entrepôt   A place where goods were brought for storage before being exchanged; a commercial concept originated by the Dutch.

Epicureans   Those who adhered to a Hellenistic Greek philosophy that the world was a random collection of atoms (atheistic and materialistic), and that one must pursue pleasure, but only in moderation as excess causes pain.

equestrians   In the early Roman Republic, the equestrians were one of the richest classes in the Roman army, those who could afford to maintain a horse. By the late republic, their role expanded into banking and commerce.

Estates-General   An official body assembled periodically by the medieval French state, consisting of representatives from three separate groups or "estates": those who prayed (the Church), those who fought (the aristocracy), and those who worked (commoners). Long in disuse by the monarch, it was convened by Louis XVI in 1789.

ethnic cleansing   Term introduced in the Balkan war of the 1990s to describe the systematic killing and forcible removal of one ethnic group by another.

ethnos   Large rural territorial units in the Dark Age and Archaic Greece focused around a central religious sanctuary and dominated by a local oligarchy, such as in Aetolia.

Etruscans   Peoples native to Italy who influenced the formation of the Roman state.

eunomia   The good order and obedience to the law which was the ideal of Sparta's militaristic society.

euro   Common currency of the European Union; accepted as common currency by all members of the European Union except the United Kingdom.

European Economic Community (EEC)   Formed in 1957 by Belgium, the Netherlands, Luxembourg, Italy, France, and West Germany to provide a single, integrated European market. Also known as the Common Market.

European Union (EU)   Formed in 1992 to succeed the European Community in terms of economic integration; members share defensive, social, and economic policies as well.

extraterritoriality   Exempted all foreigners in China from Chinese legal jurisdiction; practiced within foreign "spheres of influence" in China.

Factory Act (1833)   British Parliamentary legislation that prohibited factory work by children under age nine, provided two hours of daily education for factory children, and limited labor for adults to twelve hours each day.

fascism   Rooted in mass politics of the late-nineteenth century, a totalitarian political system that glorifies the state and subordinates the individual to the state's needs. First emerging in Italy after World War I, fascism appeared in virtually all European countries, but particularly Germany.

feudalism   Anachronistic term used by early modern lawyers to describe medieval relations of vassalage.

fief   A parcel of productive land along with the serfs and privileges attached to it granted by a lord to a knightly follower (vassal) in return for loyalty and military service.

Final Solution   The term used by the Third Reich to refer to the extermination of all people deemed unfit; resulted in the execution of 11 million men, women, and children, 6 million of them Jews.

First Triumvirate   Political alliance among Pompey, Crassus, and Caesar to share power in the Roman Republic.

fodder crops   Crops that were grown not for human consumption but to improve the nutrients in the soil. Some, such as turnips, were also used as animal feed.

Forms   In Plato's philosophy, the perfect ideal that underlies all worldly objects. In recollecting them from one's previous existence one communes with all that is good, true, and beautiful.

Fourteen Points   U.S. President Woodrow Wilson's idealistic set of guidelines drawn up as part of the peace process whose goal was to create a lasting peace after World War I.

French wars of religion   Violent clashes between French Catholics and Calvinists (Huguenots) from 1562–1598.

Fronde   An aristocratic revolution in France beginning in 1648 during the minority of Louis XIV, which was initiated by the tax policies of the minority government under Cardinal Mazarin.

futurists   Artists and intellectuals of the late nineteenth and early twentieth century who wanted to create a new culture free from traditional Western civilization. Futurists lionized technology, the masses, violence, and upheaval.

generation gap   The baby boom following World War II resulted in a generation that came of age in the 1960s. The gap refers to the divergence in values between a large cohort of adolescents and young adults and their parents that resulted in more liberal values and socio-cultural mores.

geopolitics   Politics of geography; based on recognition that certain areas of the world are valuable for political reasons.

Girondins   French revolutionary faction that was more moderate than the Jacobins.

glasnost   A Russian term meaning openness; one of the programs of reform initiated by Mikhail Gorbachev in the 1980s.

Glorious Revolution   Change of government in England in 1688–1689 when the Catholic monarch James II was replaced by the Dutch ruler William of Orange. Called "glorious" because it supposedly was accomplished without bloodshed.

Gnostics   An early Christian group that interpreted scripture as gnosis, or secret wisdom, and believed that Jesus had no human element. They were opposed by many bishops.

Golden Bull   The edict of emperor Charles IV in 1356 recognizing that German princes and kings were autonomous rulers.

Great Chain of Being   A hierarchic model of social organization common in the fifteenth and sixteenth centuries in which all parts of creation held a specific place in a divinely ordered universe.

Great Depression   Devastation of the global economy that began in 1929 with the U.S. stock market crash and lasted through the 1930s.

Great Purge   A series of executions between 1934 and 1938 in the Soviet Union that removed Joseph Stalin's political enemies.

Great Reform Bill of 1832   An extension of the right to vote in England to men of the middle class that resulted in a 50 percent increase in those eligible to vote.

Great Schism   The conflict (1378–1415) between two sets of rival popes based in Rome and Avignon that divided the loyalties of states and individuals across Europe.

guilds   Professional associations of merchants or artisans that offered protection of members and regulation of a particular trade or craft.

hadith   The written form of the Sunnah, practices established by the prophet Muhammad that guide the interpretation of the Qur'an.

Hanseatic League   A commercial and political alliance of northern German towns established in the late fourteenth century to monopolize the grain and fish trade of the Baltic Sea.

Hijra   In early Islam, the journey undertaken by Muhammad from Mecca to Medina in 622 in order to govern Medina and calm its internal political dissension.

Holocaust   During World War II, mass extermination of Jews by the Nazis under Adolph Hitler.

Holy Alliance   Prussia, Austria, and Russia, under the leadership of Tsar Alexander I, agreed to protect the peace and the Christian religion following the Congress of Vienna.

honestiores   The privileged classes of the later Roman Empire: senators, municipal gentry, and the military.

hoplites   In Archaic Greece, armed infantry soldiers.

Huguenots   French Calvinists led by Henry of Navarre. Huguenots were victims of the St. Bartholomew's Day Massacre, a slaughter of numerous Protestants in Paris in 1572 during the French wars of religion.

humanists   Scholars who studied and taught the humanities, the skills of disciplines such as philology—the art of language—and rhetoric—the art of expression; concentrated on ancient texts.

humiliores   The lower classes of the later Roman Empire whose status declined from the period of the *Pax Romana* and who suffered disproportionately from the tax increases of the period.

Hundred Years' War   A series of military engagements between England and France (1337–1452) over territorial and dynastic rivalries.

Hussites   Followers of Jan Hus who attacked the sale of indulgences and German political dominance in the kingdom of Bohemia. After his execution, they led a partially successful revolt.

iconoclasts   Breakers of icons; opponents of the mediating use of icons (religious images) in worship. Most emperors supported this faction in eighth- and early ninth-century Byzantium.

iconodules   Venerators of icons; the ecclesiastical faction that resisted the iconoclasts. Most of the people and lesser clergy were iconodules.

icons   Sacred images.

imperium   The powers conferred on magistrates by the Roman people: the supreme power to command, to execute the law, and to impose the death penalty.

indulgences   Remission of temporal punishment in Purgatory due to one's sins. Originally granted for performing pious acts, but later acquired through a grant to the church treasury. In the sixteenth century, indulgences were sold to raise money for the papacy; a critical issue in the Lutheran reform.

industrialization   Process by which production becomes mechanized.

Industrial Revolution   Sustained period of economic growth and change brought on by technological innovations in the process of manufacturing; began in Britain in the mid-eighteenth century.

intendants Officials appointed by the central government in France to oversee the local administration of the regional aristocracy; a critical component of the centralization of the French state.

iron curtain The term coined by former British Prime Minister Winston Churchill to describe the ideological divide between western and eastern Europe after World War II.

Jacobins One of the political factions of the French National Convention that seized the initiative provided by the sans-culottes to take control of the radical revolution in the late eighteenth century; led by Maximilien Robespierre.

Jacquerie The revolt of French peasants against the aristocracy and crown in 1358. It was part of the struggle for rights caused by the labor shortage after the Black Death.

jihads Holy wars waged by Muslims against their religious enemies.

jingoism Use of public opinion to stir support for one's own nation and hatred for another nation; used extensively by political leaders to justify imperial expansion.

joint-stock companies Business enterprises that raise capital by selling shares to individuals who receive dividends on their investments.

kouros Nude statues of young men that were a common subject in Archaic art. The stiff posture demonstrates the influence of Egyptian sculpture.

Kristallnacht "Crystal night" in German; refers to the night of 9 November 1938 when mobs directed by the Nazis destroyed the homes, businesses, and synagogues of German Jews.

laissez-faire An economic theory that required government to cease interference with private economic activity; Adam Smith and the physiocrats were its leading proponents.

lay investiture The practice by which kings and emperors appointed bishops and invested them with the symbols of their office. It led to conflict between the papacy and the emperors in the eleventh century.

Lebensraum "Living room"; one of Hitler's foreign policy objectives to extend the borders of Germany in eastern and central Europe.

liberalism A political philosophy based on freedom of the individual and the corruptibility of authority; associated with constitutional reform in the first half of the nineteenth century.

Linear B A syllabic form of writing from the late Greek Bronze Age which preserves the earliest known form of Greek. It was used by Mycenaean elites almost entirely for record keeping.

linear perspective A technique developed in painting to give a flat surface the appearance of depth and dimension.

Long Parliament An English Parliament that officially met from 1640 to 1653. It forced reforms under Charles I, defeated the royal armies during the English Civil War, and tried and executed the king.

maat In Egyptian thought, the ideal state of the universe and of society which the pharaoh was supposed to uphold.

Magna Carta The "great charter" limiting royal power that King John was forced to sign in 1215.

manses Farms worked by slaves, serfs, and freemen in the Middle Ages.

Marchfield The assembly of all free warriors in the early Germanic kingdoms in which the king's authority was all-powerful.

Marshall Plan The U.S. economic aid program for European countries after World War II; intended to establish U.S. economic influence in European markets.

mercantilism A popular state economy of the seventeenth century; involved bullionism, protective tariffs, and monopolies.

metics The non-Athenian residents of Athens who comprised about half of the free population of the city. They were active in commerce and banking.

Minoan civilization The culture of Crete in the Middle Bronze Age (2000–1550 B.C.E.) in which elites based at great palaces, such as Knossos, dominated the island politically, economically, and religiously.

minuscule New style of handwriting developed in the Carolingian Renaissance to preserve texts; later adopted as standard script.

Mishnah In Jewish law, the oral interpretation of the Torah (scripture) that was developed by the Pharisees and later developed into an extensive written body of legal interpretation.

missi dominici Teams of counts and bishops that examined the state of each county in the Carolingian Empire on behalf of the king.

monasticism The life of monks devoted to God, from the fourth century onward, either as part of communal organization or in solitary life. Monasticism began in Egypt as a rejection of the worldliness of civilization.

monopoly Exclusive control of a market or industry; a form of economic regulation in which special privileges are granted in return for financial considerations and an agreement to abide by the rules set out by the state.

Mycenaean Late Greek Bronze Age civilization that arose ca. 1600 B.C.E. at Mycenae and that encompassed the Greek mainland and parts of Asia Minor. Myceneans developed the Linear B script.

mystery cults Religions that promised immediate, personal contact with a deity that would bring immortality.

Napoleonic Code The recodification of French law carried out during Napoleon's reign.

nationalities problem The existence of numerous ethnic minorities within the borders of the Soviet Union leading to demands for self-determination and political independence.

natural selection A theory advanced by Charles Darwin that accounted for evolution of species; a realist scientific approach.

Navigation Acts English economic legislation providing that colonial goods could only be shipped in English ships.

Nazism National Socialism; German variant of fascism.

Neolithic era The New Stone Age (8000–6500 B.C.E.) in which modern man developed agriculture and the first villages.

New Economic Policy (NEP) A state-planned economic policy in the Soviet Union between 1921 and 1928; based on agricultural productivity, it required set payments from peasants; surpluses could be sold on the free market.

new imperialism Imperialism practiced by European countries after 1870 that was, in essence, the domination by industrial powers over the nonindustrial world. Distinguished from the earlier acquisition of territory, new imperialism took a variety of forms including territorial occupations, colonization, exploitation of labor and raw materials, and development of economic spheres of influence.

New Monarchies The more centralized European governments of western Europe created in the fifteenth and sixteenth centuries.

New Piety An aspect of the Roman Catholic reform movement; originated among the Brethren of the Common Life with an emphasis on simplicity and more personalized religious practice.

nominalism The doctrine of William of Ockham that argued that abstract terms or universals do not represent real existing things and that thus human reason could not aspire to certain truth.

North Atlantic Treaty Organization (NATO) An organization founded in 1949 the members of which signed a defense pact to protect those countries bordering the North Atlantic.

nuclear club The group of nations in possession of atomic weapons, originally consisting of the United States and the Soviet Union. By 1974, the nuclear club included Great Britain, France, the People's Republic of China, and India.

Old Regime The old order; political and social system of France in the eighteenth century before the French Revolution.

oligarchy Government by an elite few.

optimates The traditionalist Roman political faction that succeeded the Gracchi and sought to preserve the senatorial oligarchy against the populares.

Orthodox Christianity The official "right-teaching" faith of Constantinople as opposed to the heterodox peoples on the margins of the Byzantine Empire.

ostracism A practice in Athenian democracy by which anyone deemed to threaten the constitution could, by popular vote, be exiled for ten years without the loss of property.

Paleolithic era The Old Stone Age (600,000–10,000 B.C.E.) in which advanced primates developed into Neanderthals and also modern man. They hunted food or collected it by gathering.

Paris Commune Created in 1871 in the aftermath of the Franco-Prussian War; crushed by the national army after a brief struggle; symbol of revolution for radical politicians, including Marxists.

parties A form of political organization in which members of the British parliament divided into groups with identifiable interests. Whigs and Tories were the first political parties.

Patent of Toleration An edict of Joseph II of Austria in 1781 that granted freedom of worship to Protestants and members of the Greek Orthodox Church, in addition to Roman Catholics.

paterfamilias The male head of household in the Roman family. His power was absolute, including the power of life and death.

patricians Leaders of the gentes, or clans, in early Roman society.

Pax Romana The two centuries of peace and stability in the early Roman Empire inaugurated by the emperor Augustus.

perestroika A Russian term meaning restructuring; part of Mikhail Gorbachev's attempts to reform the Soviet government and economy in the 1980s.

Peterloo Massacre In August 1819, the English army troops policing a political crowd gathered near Manchester, England, lost control resulting in the deaths of 11 and the injury of hundreds of others.

phalanx A tightly ordered and well-disciplined body of elite Greek warriors in heavy armor that attacked in close formation with long spears.

philology The art of language; one of the most important aspects of humanist studies, based on models of ancient texts.

philosophes A French term for the intellectuals of the eighteenth-century Enlightenment. Voltaire, Diderot, and Condorcet were leading philosophes.

physiocrats A group of French thinkers who subscribed to the view that land was wealth and thus argued that improvements in agricultural activity should take first priority in state reforms.

pictograms The earliest form of writing in Mesopotamia, ca. 3500 B.C.E., in which pictures represented particular objects, such as animals.

Pietà A painting or sculpture of Mary mourning the dead Jesus. The most famous was carved by Michelangelo and is in St. Peter's Basilica.

plebs Families not organized into gentes, or clans, in early Roman society. The lower classes.

pogroms State-organized massacres of Jews.

polis The city-state of Archaic and Classical Greece, particularly found on the shores of the Aegean. A city formed the center of government (tyranny, oligarchy, or democracy) and of religious life with temples on its citadel (acropolis).

politiques During the sixteenth-century French wars of religion, a group of Catholics who joined with Huguenots to demand a practical settlement of the wars.

populares The Roman political faction that succeeded the Gracchi whose leaders appealed to the masses as a source of power.

Popular Front Socialist governments established in both France and Spain in the 1930s; the French version failed to solve the Great Depression and was voted out of office; the creation of a socialist republic in Spain initiated a civil war.

Pragmatic Sanction The document that attempted to secure the recognition of Maria Theresa as heiress to the Habsburg possessions of Charles VI.

Prague Spring Popular uprising and reform movement in 1968 Czechoslovakia, ended by Soviet invasion in August 1968.

predestination A fundamental principle of Calvin's theology: the belief that all Christians are predestined to either heaven or hell from the act of creation.

presbyters The priests of the early Christian tradition who were subordinated to bishops as hierarchy developed in the Church.

Price Revolution The dramatic price inflation of the fifteenth and sixteenth centuries; caused by monetary debasement and the influx of bullion from the New World.

princeps "First citizen"; the title assumed by the emperor Augustus to reassure public opinion by preserving the traditional constitutional forms.

Proclamation of the German Empire The creation in 1871 of the nation-state of Germany by uniting the 38 German states into a single national entity.

proletariat The industrial working class.

pronatalism State programs implemented after the Second World War to encourage women to have larger families.

Puritans English Protestants who sought to purify the Church of England of all traces of Catholicism.

putting-out system Mobilization of the rural labor force for commercial production of large quantities of manufactured goods; raw materials put out to homes of workers where manufacture took place.

Quadruple Alliance Pact signed in 1815 by the four powers who defeated Napoleon—Great Britain, Austria, Russia, and Prussia—for the purpose of protecting Europe against future French aggression.

Quintuple Alliance The Quadruple Alliance plus France, which joined the pact in 1818.

quinine An important nineteenth-century medical advance derived from cinchona that was an effective treatment for malaria; it permitted large numbers of Europeans to travel without risking death and disease.

realism An artistic and literary style that criticized industrialized society and rejected bourgeois concepts of morality.

realpolitik Pragmatic political theory advanced by Otto von Bismarck; ruthless pursuit by any means, including illegal and violent ones, in the interests of the state.

reconquista The Christian reconquest of the Iberian peninsula from the Spanish Muslims or Moors; completed in 1492 under Ferdinand and Isabella.

Reformation A movement to reform and purify the Catholic Church that resulted in the creation of new religious denominations in Europe collectively known as Protestants.

Reichstag The national legislative body of the German Empire; elected by universal male suffrage.

Reign of Terror The period from 1793 to 1794 when Maximilien Robespierre assumed leadership of the Committee of Public Safety and oversaw the revolutionary tribunals that sentenced about 40,000 people to execution.

Renaissance A "rebirth" of classical learning and emphasis on humanity that characterized the period between 1350 and 1550.

rhetoric The art of expression and persuasion.

Risorgimento The nineteenth-century movement to reunite Italy.

romanticism An artistic and literary tradition based on emotions rather than the intellect; rejection of classical traditions in favor of "nature"; often associated with nationalism.

salons Informal social gatherings during the Enlightenment, frequently organized by women, in which topics of intellectual interest were discussed.

sans-culottes Literally "those without knee-breeches"; working-class revolutionaries who initiated the radical stage of the French revolution in 1792.

Schlieffen Plan The strategy of the German high command at the outset of World War I, predicated on knocking France out of the war.

Scholastic method The combination of legal analysis from the new university at Bologna with Aristotelian logic established by Peter Abelard in the twelfth century to create the primary method of study in medieval universities.

scientific revolution In the sixteenth and seventeenth centuries, a period of new scientific inquiry, experimentation, and discovery that resulted in a new understanding of the universe based on mathematical principles and led to the creation of the modern sciences, particularly astronomy and physics.

scramble for Africa The colonization of Africa as part of the new imperialism. This domination of Africa by Germany, Britain, and France ended with the crisis at Fashoda.

Second Triumvirate Alliance of Octavian, Mark Anthony, and Lepidus following the assassination of Julius Caesar to defeat the assassins and control the Roman Empire.

seigneur Manor lord responsible for maintaining order, administering justice, and arbitrating disputes among tenants.

serfs Peasants of degraded status and very limited legal rights who were dependent on the lords in the High Middle Ages. They formed the great bulk of the population.

Shi'ites Muslims who follow the tradition that legitimate leadership of Islam can only come through the descendants of 'Ali, whom they regard as the last orthodox caliph.

sola fide A fundamental principle of Luther's theology: justification of Christians by faith alone.

sola scriptura By the Word alone; emphasis on scriptural authority in preference to the canons of the Church, a fundamental element of Luther's theology.

Solidarity A non-communist Polish labor organization founded by Lech Walesa in the Gdansk shipbuilding yards; legalized in 1989 as a political movement, it won a victory in the first Polish democratic elections.

sophists Professional teachers in fifth-century Greece who traveled from city to city instructing students, for a fee, in rhetoric, the art of persuasion.

soviets Councils of workers in Russia formed after 1905 that became one center of power after the overthrow of the tsar; source of power for Lenin and the Bolsheviks.

Spanish Armada The Spanish fleet sent in 1588 to transport troops from the Low Countries for an invasion of England; defeated by the English fleets of Elizabeth I.

Spanish Inquisition An ecclesiastical tribunal utilized to combat heresy and non-Christians; used by Ferdinand and Isabella against the conversos, or converted Jews of Spain.

spheres of influence Diplomatic term used to connote territorial influence or control of weaker nations not necessarily occupied by the more powerful ones. The term was first used to explain one kind of control of western European powers in the 1800s during African imperialism, and was later used to describe European and Japanese territorial control and influence over markets in China at the end of the nineteenth century.

Stoics Followers of the Hellenistic Greek philosophy propounded by Zeno, which teaches that orderliness is proper to the universe and that happiness derives from embracing one's divinely ordained role and unhappiness from rejecting it.

strategoi   Generals, the military commanders of themes in the Byzantine Empire. They were responsible for civil and military administration.

sunnah   In Islamic theology, the practices established by the prophet Muhammad. They were initially preserved by oral tradition.

Sunnis   The majority tradition of Islam that accepts that political succession should be based on consensus, the existing political order, and a leader's merits.

synod   A meeting of bishops called to debate Church policy, such as that at Whitby in 664, which established the customs of the Roman Church among Angles and Saxons.

Table of Ranks   Official state hierarchy in Russia under Peter the Great that established the social position or rank of individuals according to categories of military service, civil service, and ownership of landed estates.

tetrarchy   Rule by four; Diocletian's attempt to regulate the suggestion of the Roman Empire by dividing the empire into eastern and western parts, with both an augustus and a junior emperor, or caesar, ruling each part.

Thermidorian Reaction   Revolt beginning in July 1794 (the month of Thermidor) against the radicalism of the French Revolution, leading to the downfall and execution of Robespierre and the end of the Reign of Terror.

Third Estate   Branch of the French Estates-General consisting of the bourgeoisie and the working classes; separated from the other estates to form the National Assembly in 1789.

Third Reich   "The Third Empire"; Hitler's government, established after 1933.

third world   The former colonies of European and Asian imperialism; sought to separate themselves from European economic control after independence; operated in the United Nations as a nonaligned bloc.

Thirty Years' War   War lasting from 1618–1648.

three-field system   An efficient agricultural system in which one-third of the land was planted in autumn with wheat or rye, one-third remained fallow, and one-third was planted in spring with a crop that added nutrients to the soil.

Time of Troubles   The period of disruption within Russia following the death of Ivan the Terrible; only ended with the Polish invasion of Russia.

Torah   The body of law in Hebrew scripture.

Tories   Members of a political party in England that in the seventeenth century defended the principle of hereditary succession to the crown; in opposition to the Whigs. The Tories sought to preserve the traditional political structure and supported the authority of the Anglican church.

total war   War that requires mobilization of the civilian population in addition to the military; typified by centralized governments with limits on economy and civil rights.

Treaty of Brest-Litovsk   The Treaty between Russia and Germany signed in March 1918 whereby Soviet Russia withdrew from World War I.

Treaty of Tordesillas   A 1494 agreement that recognized Portugal's claims to Brazil, but gave all of the remainder of the New World to Spain.

Treaty of Versailles   Peace settlement with Germany at the end of World War I; included the War Guilt Clause fixing blame on Germany for the war and requiring massive reparations.

triangular trade   A three-way trade system during the seventeenth century involving the shipment, for example, of calicoes to Africa for slaves who were transported to the East Indies in exchange for sugar, which was shipped to Europe.

Triple Alliance   An alliance founded in 1882 between Germany, Austria-Hungary, and Italy at Germany's instigation for the purpose of securing mutual support on the European continent.

Triple Entente   Alliance founded in 1907 between France, Britain, and Russia. With the defection of Russia from the Three Emperors' League, it hemmed in Germany on both eastern and western borders.

tyrants Rulers who had seized power illegally. Tyrannies replaced oligarchies in many *poleis* in Archaic Greece, such as at Corinth and Athens. The term did not have the negative connotations it does today, as many tyrants were popular leaders welcomed by their subjects.

Umma The community of all believers in the Islamic faith. Initially, it was both a political and religious supertribe of Arabs.

universitas The guilds of students that formed the first true universities from the twelfth century onward.

utilitarianism Jeremy Bentham's philosophical plan to ensure social harmony through measurement of pleasure and pain or the greatest happiness of the greatest number; a liberal philosophy.

vassals Knights sworn to fealty or loyalty to a lord; in return the lord granted the vassal a means of support, or fief.

Villanovans Peoples of the first Iron Age culture in Italy (1000–800 B.C.E.), which was based in the north. They made iron tools and weapons and placed the ashes of their dead in large urns.

Warsaw Pact Defensive alliance organization formed in 1955 by Albania, Bulgaria, Romania, Czechoslovakia, Hungary, Poland, East Germany, and the Soviet Union. The alliance served as a strategic buffer zone against NATO forces.

Weimar Republic German government founded at the end of the First World War; used by German general staff as scapegoat for German defeat and harsh peace terms; overthrown in 1933.

welfare state The tendency of post–World War II states to establish safety nets for citizens in areas of birth, sickness, old age, and unemployment.

wergeld In Germanic society, the payment in reparation for crimes in place of blood vengeance. Tribal leaders used it to reduce internal hostilities.

Whigs Members of a political party in England that in the seventeenth century supported the Protestant succession and a broad-based Protestantism and advocated a constitutional monarchy that limited royal power; in opposition to the Tories. The Whigs were later identified with social and parliamentary reform.

zemstvos Local elected assemblies in Russia during the reign of Alexander II; representatives elected by landowners, townspeople, and peasants.

ziggurat Babylonian tiered towers (or step-pyramids) from ca. 2000 B.C.E. that were dedicated to gods and stood near temples. They were among the most important buildings of Babylonian cities.

Zionism A program initiated by Theodor Herzl to establish an independent Jewish state in Palestine.

Zollverein A unified trading zone created by Prussia in which member states adopted the liberal Prussian customs regulations; an attempt to overcome the fragmented nature of the German economy.

CHAPTER 1

General Reading

Cambridge Ancient History, vol. 1 (Cambridge: Cambridge University Press, 1990). Contains essays on every aspect of ancient civilizations.

Barry Cunliffe, *Europe Between the Oceans 9000 BC–1000* (New Haven: Yale University Press, 2008). A broad survey of western Eurasia by an archaeologist.

Brian Fagan, 2007. *World Prehistory: A Brief Introduction*, 7th ed. (New York: Prentice-Hall, 2007). Excellent introduction to prehistory.

Barbara S. Lesko, ed. *Women's Earliest Records from Ancient Egypt and Western Asia: Proceedings of the Conference on Women in the Ancient Near East* (Atlanta: Scholars Press, 1989). Important collection of essays on all aspects of women in ancient societies.

Before Civilization

Barry Cunliffe, *Prehistoric Europe: An Illustrated History* (Oxford: Oxford University Press, 1997). An engaging introduction to early Europe.

Brian M. Fagan, *People of the Earth: An Introduction to World Prehistory*, 7th ed. (New York: Prentice Hall, 2007). Excellent introduction to the prehistory of Europe and Asia.

Daniel Lord Smail, *On Deep History and the Brain* (Berkeley: University of California Press, 2008). An historian's challenging argument on the importance of the Paleolithic.

Colin Renfrew, *Prehistory: The Making of the Human Mind* (New York: Modern Library 2008). A classic introduction to prehistory.

Mesopotamia: Between the Two Rivers

Guillermo Algaze, *Ancient Mesopotamia at the Dawn of Civilization: The Evolution of an Urban Landscape* (Chicago: University of Chicago Press, 2008). The relationship between ecology and civilization between the Tigris and Euphrates rivers.

Jean Bottero, *Everyday Life in Ancient Mesopotamia* (Baltimore: Johns Hopkins University Press, 2001). Social history of Mespotamia by a leading expert.

Gwendolyn Leick, *The Babylonians, An Introduction* (New York: Routledge, 2003). General introduction to Babylonian history.

Marc Van de Mieroop, *A history of the ancient Near East, ca. 3000–323 BC*, 2nd ed. (Malden, Mass.: Blackwell Pub., 2007). An excellent survey on Near Eastern history.

The Gift of the Nile

Cyril Aldred, *The Egyptians*, 3rd rev. ed. (New York: Thames & Hudson, 1998). Readable general history of ancient Egypt focusing on culture.

Barbara Mertz, *Red Land, Black Land: Daily Life in Ancient Egypt*, 2nd ed. (New York: William Morrow, 2008). A readable account of daily life.

Ian Shaw, ed. *The Oxford History of Ancient Egypt* (Oxford: Oxford University Press, 2000). Comprehensive collaborative survey of ancient Egypt.

Between Two Worlds

John Curtis, *Ancient Persia* (Cambridge, MA: Harvard University Press, 1990). Brief overview of ancient Iran.

Lester L. Grabbe, *Ancient Israel: What Do We Know and How Do We Know It?* (London; New York: T & T Clark, 2007). Reliable introduction to the history and archaeology of ancient Israel.

Henry Jackson Flanders, Robert Wilson Crapps, and David Anthony Smith, *People of the Covenant: An Introduction to the Hebrew Bible*, 4th ed. (New York: Oxford University Press, 1996). A balanced introduction to Hebrew and Jewish history that draws on both Jewish and Christian scholarship.

A. T. Olmstead, *History of Assyria* (Chicago: University of Chicago Press, 1975). The fundamental survey of the Assyrian Empire.

CHAPTER 2

General Reading

S. B. Pomeroy, et. al. *Ancient Greece: A Political, Social, and Cultural History* (Oxford: Oxford University Press, 1998). An important introduction to Greek society and culture.

Greece in the Bronze Age to 700 B.C.E.

M. I. Finley, *Early Greece: The Bronze and Archaic Ages*, 2d ed. (New York: W. W. Norton, 1982). A very readable overview by a leading Greek historian.

Eliezer D. Oren, ed. *The Sea Peoples and Their World: A Reassessment* (Philadelphia, Pa.: University Museum, University of Pennsylvania, 2000). Essays on the debates concerning the Sea Peoples..

Cynthia W. Shelmerdine, ed. *The Cambridge Companion to the Aegean Bronze Age* (Cambridge; New York: Cambridge University Press, 2008). Up to date survey of early Aegean civilizations.

William Taylour, *The Mycenaeans* (London: Thames & Hudson, 1990). General overview of Mycenaean civilization and daily life based on archaeology.

Archaic Greece, 700–500 B.C.E.

John Boardman, *The Greeks Overseas* (New York: Thames & Hudson, 1982). A description of varieties of Greek involvement abroad and their effects on Greece by a distinguished archaeologist.

———, *Greek Sculpture: Archaic Period* (New York: Thames & Hudson, 1985). A well-illustrated survey of early Greek sculpture.

Anne L. Klinck, *Women's Songs in Ancient Greece* (McGill-Queen's University Press: Montreal and Kingston, 2008). An anthology of texts presenting women's performance in Greek poetry.

Catherine Morgan, *Early Greek States beyond the Polis* (New York: Routledge, 2003). A reevaluation of the relationship between ethne and polis in the Archaic period.

H. A. Shapiro, ed. *The Cambridge companion to archaic Greece* (Cambridge; New York: Cambridge University Press, 2007). Comprehensive survey of the archaic period.

Anthony Snodgrass, *Archaic Greece: The Age of Experiment* (Totowa, NJ: Biblio Distribution Center, 1980). An excellent survey of the creative achievements of the Archaic period.

Mark Stansbury-O'Donnell, *Vase Painting, Gender, and Social Identity in Archaic Athens* (New York, NY: Cambridge University Press, 2006). A study of how images on archaic vases can inform concerning social order, gender, ritual and myth.

Christopher Tadgell, *Hellenic Classicism: The Ordering of Form in the Ancient Greek World.* (New York: Whitney Library of Design, 1998). A survey of Greek art and architecture to the construction of Athens' Acropolis.

A Tale of Three Cities

Paul Cartledge, *Sparta and Lakonia: A Regional History 1300–362 B.C.* 2nd ed. (New York: Routledge, Chapman & Hall, 2002). The best survey of Spartan history.

J. B. Salmon, *Wealthy Corinth: A History of the City to 338 B.C.* (New York: Oxford University Press, 1984). A comprehensive history of early Corinth.

David Whitehead, *The Demes of Attica (ca. 508–250 B.C.)* (Princeton, NJ: Princeton University Press, 1986). An excellent study of Athenian politics and society.

CHAPTER 3
General Reading

Cambridge Ancient History, 2d ed., vols. 5 (1989) and 7 (1984). Contains essays on most aspects of Greek history.

Pierre Vidal-Naquet, *The Black Hunter: Forms of Thought and Forms of Society in the Greek World* (Baltimore: The Johns Hopkins University Press, 1998). A brilliant exploration of Greek society and politics approached through its margins, its contradictions, and its oppositions.

War and Politics in the Fifth Century B.C.E.

Lindsay Allen, *The Persian Empire* (Chicago: University of Chicago Press, 2005). Up to date comprehensive survey of ancient Persia.

Sue Blundell, *Women in Ancient Greece* (Cambridge, MA: Harvard University Press, 1995). A good place to start for an understanding of women in classical Greece.

Charles W. Fornara and Loren J. Samons II, *Athens from Cleisthenes to Pericles* (Berkeley: University of California Press, 1991). Detailed survey of the development of Athenian democracy and empire.

Yvon Garlan, *Slavery in Ancient Greece* (Ithaca, NY: Cornell University Press, 1988). A basic study of Greek slavery.

Victor Davis Hanson, *A War Like No Other. How the Athenians and Spartans Fought the Peloponnesian War* (New York: Random House, 2005). An account of the war that emphasizes its novelty and carnage..

Nigel M. Kennell, *The Gymnasium of Virtue: Education and Culture in Ancient Sparta* (Chapel Hill: University of North Carolina Press, 1995). An investigation of Spartan culture.

Helen King, *Hippocrates' Woman: Reading the Female Body in Ancient Greece* (New York: Routledge, 1998). A study of Greek medical theory concerning women and women's bodies.

Josiah Ober, *Mass and Elite in Democratic Athens: Rhetoric, Ideology, and the Power of the People* (Princeton, N.J.: Princeton University Press, 1989). An important investigation into the working of Athenian democracy.

P. J. Rhodes, *Ancient Democracy and Modern Ideology* (London: Duckworth Academic, 2003). An essay from a prominient Greek historian exploring the modern uses of Athenian democracy.

Athenian Culture in the Hellenic Age

J. Boardman, *Greek Art,* 3d ed. (New York: Thames & Hudson, 1985). A handbook introduction by period.

W. Burkert, *Greek Religion* (Cambridge, MA: Harvard University Press, 1985). General survey of the topic.

Mark Golden, *Greek Sport and Social Status* (Austin: University of Texas Press, 2008). A study of the intersection of Greek sport and culture and society.

Simon Goldhill, *Reading Greek Tragedy* (New York: Cambridge University Press, 1986). A general introduction to Athenian tragedy.

David Roochnik, *Retrieving the Ancients: an Introduction to Greek Philosophy* (Malden, MA: Blackwell Pub., 2004). A fresh introduction to Greek philosophers.

C. J. Rowe, *Plato* (New York: St. Martin's, 1984). A good survey of the philosopher's thought.

From City-States to Macedonian Empire, 404–323 B.C.E.

A. B. Bosworth, *Conquest and Empire* (New York: Cambridge University Press, 1988). A scholarly but readable account of Alexander the Great.

Waldemar Heckel and Lawrence A. Tritle, eds. *Alexander the Great: A New History* (Chichester, U.K.; Malden, MA: Wiley-Blackwell, 2009). A fresh collective history of Alexander by international experts.

The Hellenistic World

J. Barnes et al., *Science and Speculation* (New York: Cambridge University Press, 1982). A collection of papers on Hellenistic science.

Peter Green, *Alexander to Actium: The Historical Evolution of the Hellenistic Age* (Berkeley: University of California Press, 1990). A broad examination of the Hellenistic period.

Peter Green, ed., *Hellenistic History and Culture* (Berkeley: University of California Press, 1993). A stimulating series of articles and debates on Hellenistic civilization.

Sarah B. Pomeroy, *Families in Classical and Hellenistic Greece: Representations and Realities* (Oxford: Clarendon Press; New York: Oxford University Press, 1998). Greek society, gender, and sexuality based on written, archaeological, and iconographic sources.

CHAPTER 4
Primary Sources

Many of the works of Polybius, Livy, Cato, Caesar, Cicero, and other Roman authors are available in English translation from Penguin Books. The first volume—*Roman Civilization, Selected Readings, Vol. I: The Republic* (1951), by Naphtali Lewis and Meyer Reinhold—contains a wide selection of documents with useful introductions. An excellent selection of Roman historical writing can be found in Ronald Mellor, *The Roman Historians* (New York: Routledge, 1999).

The Western Mediterranean to 509 B.C.E.

Graeme Barker and Tom Rasmussen, *The Etruscans* (Oxford: Blackwell Publishers, 2000). An introduction to Etruscan studies and history.

Serge Lancel, *Carthage: A History* (Oxford: Blackwell Publishers, 1997). A basic introduction.

From City to Empire, 509–146 B.C.E.

Nigel Bagnall, *The Punic Wars* (London: Hutchinson, 1990). Survey of the wars between Rome and Carthage.

Mary Beard and Michael Crawford, *Rome in the Late Republic* (Ithaca, NY: Cornell University Press, 1985). A short interpretive essay on the crisis of the late republic.

John Boardman, Jasper Griffin, and Oswyn Murray, *The Oxford History of the Roman World* (New York: Oxford University Press, 2001). A balanced collection of essays on all aspects of Roman history and civilization.

K. R. Bradley, *Slavery and Society at Rome* (New York: Cambridge University Press, 1994). The place of slavery in the Roman world.

Klaus Bringmann, *A History of the Roman Republic* (Cambridge, UK; Malden, MA: Polity, 2007). A clear narrative of the Republic by a distinguished European scholar.

Tim Cornell, *The Beginnings of Rome, 1000–264 B.C.* (New York: Routledge, 1995). A new look at the origins of Rome.

Gary Forsythe, *A Critical History of Early Rome: from Prehistory to the First Punic War* (Berkeley: University of California Press, 2005). A fresh reappraisal of the early history of Rome.

Republican Civilization

Geza Alfoldy, *The Social History of Rome* (Berlin: Walter de Gruyter, 1988). A survey of Rome that emphasizes the relationship between social structure and politics.

Erich S. Gruen, *Culture and National Identity in Republican Rome* (Ithaca, NY: Cornell University Press, 1992). Important lectures by a major figure in the field.

Erich S. Gruen, *The Hellenistic World and the Coming of Rome*, 2 vols. (Berkeley: University of California Press, 1984). A detailed history of the Hellenistic world, presenting Rome's gradual and unintended rise to dominance in it.

Sarah B. Pomeroy, ed., *Women's History and Ancient History* (Chapel Hill: University of North Carolina Press, 1991). The place to begin for the history of women in antiquity.

The Crisis of Roman Virtue

Alan E. Astin, *Cato the Censor* (New York: Oxford University Press, 1978). An excellent biography of Cato that also analyzes his writings.

Pat Southern, *Pompey the Great* (Stroud, England: Tempus Publishing Ltd., 2002). The most recent biography of the triumvir.

CHAPTER 5

Primary Sources

Major selections of the works of Caesar, Cicero, Tacitus, Plutarch, Suetonius, and Marcus Aurelius are available in English translation from Penguin Books. The second volume by Naphtali Lewis and Meyer Reinhold, *Roman Civilization Selected Readings, Vol. II: The Empire* (1951), contains a wide selection of documents with useful introductions.

The Price of Empire

E. Badian, *Roman Imperialism in the Late Republic* (Ithaca, NY: Cornell University Press, 1968). A study of the contradictory forces leading to the development of the empire.

Mary Beard and Michael Crawford, *Rome in the Late Republic* (Ithaca, NY: Cornell University Press, 1985). An analysis of the political processes of the late republic as part of the development of Roman society, not simply the decay of the republic.

Henrik Mouritsen, *Plebs and Politics in the Late Roman Republic* (Cambridge: Cambridge University Press, 2001). A study of the political role of the masses in the last years of the republic.

The End of the Republic

Robert Gurval, *Actium and Augustus: the Politics and Emotions of Civil War* (Ann Arbor: University of Michigan Press, 1998). Important study of the end of the republic.

A. J. Langguth, *A Noise of War: Caesar, Pompey, Octavian, and the Struggle for Rome* (New York: Simon & Schuster, 1994). The era of the civil wars and the end of the republic.

Elizabeth Rawson, *Cicero: A Portrait* (Ithaca, N.Y. Cornell University Press, 1983). A sensitive biography of the great orator.

Ronald Syme, *The Roman Revolution* (Oxford, U.K.; New York: Oxford University Press, 2002). A classic study of the fall of the republic and the rise of Augustus.

The Augustan Age and the *Pax Romana*

J. B. Campbell, *The Emperor and the Roman Army* (New York: Oxford University Press, 1984). Essential for understanding the military's role in the Roman Empire.

Eve D'Ambra, *Roman Women* (Cambridge; New York: Cambridge University Press, 2007). An analysis of the daily lives of Roman women examined through material and written sources.

Albrecht Dihle, *Greek and Latin Literature of the Roman Empire: From Augustus to Justinian* (New York: Routledge, 1994). A survey of classical literature.

Catharine Edwards and Greg Woolf, ed., *Rome the Cosmopolis* (New York: Cambridge University Press, 2003). An innovative collection of essays examining the relationship between Rome and its empire.

Karl Galinsky, *Augustan Culture* (Princeton, NJ: Princeton University Press, 1998). An important study of the cultural world of Augustus.

J. E. Lendon, *Empire of Honour: The Art of Government in the Roman World* (Oxford: Oxford University Press, 2001). A provocative study of Roman despotism and the support it enjoyed from the ruling classes of the provinces.

Fergus Millar, *The Emperor in the Roman World* (Ithaca, NY: Cornell University Press, 1992). A study of emperors, stressing their essential passivity by responding to initiatives from below.

D. A. West and A. J. Woodman, *Poetry and Politics in the Age of Augustus* (New York: Cambridge University Press, 1984). The cultural program of Augustus.

Religions from the East

Clifford Ando, *The Matter of the Gods: Religion and the Roman Empire* (Berkeley: University of California Press, 2008). A fresh examination of the role of reason and tradition in Roman religion.

Schuyler Brown, *The Origins of Christianity: A Historical Introduction of the New Testament*, rev. ed. (Oxford: Oxford University Press, 1993). A balanced and comprehensive introduction to early Christianity.

Ekkehard W. Stegemann and Wolfgang Stegemann, *The Jesus Movement: A Social History of Its First Century* (Minneapolis: Fortress Press, 1999). A new survey of the first century of Christianity.

The Culture of Antonine Rome

Jane F. Gardner, *Women in Roman Law and Society* (Bloomington: Indiana University Press, 1986). A study of the extent of freedom and power over property enjoyed by Roman women.

Peter Garnsey and Richard Saller, *The Roman Empire: Economy, Society, and Culture* (Berkeley: University of California Press, 1987). A topical study of imperial administration, economy, religion, and society, arguing the coercive and exploitative nature of Roman civilization in relation to the agricultural societies of the Mediterranean world.

Fergus Millar, *Rome, the Greek World, and the East: The Roman Republic and the Augustan Revolution* (Chapel Hill: University of North Carolina Press, 2000). A collection of essays by a leading historian surveying Rome's rise to empire.

Paul Veyne, *The Roman Empire* (Cambridge, Mass.: Belknap Press of Harvard University Press, 1997). A compelling account of private life in imperial Rome.

CHAPTER 6

The Crisis of the Third Century

G. W. Bowersock, Peter Brown, and Oleg Grabar, eds, *Late Antiquity: a Guide to the Postclassical World* (Cambridge, Mass.: Belknap Press of Harvard University Press, 1999). A comprehensive introduction to Late Antiquity.

Peter Brown, *The World of Late Antiquity, A.D. 150–750* (New York: Harcourt Brace Jovanovich, 1971). A brilliant essay on the cultural transformation of the ancient world.

Averil Cameron, *The Later Roman Empire, A.D. 284–430* (Cambridge, MA: Harvard University Press, 1993). An important survey by an authority.

Hans-Werner Goetz, Jorg Jarnut and Walter Pohl, eds., *Regna and Gentes: The Relationship between Late Antique and Early Medieval Peoples and Kingdoms in the Transformation of the Roman World* (Leiden, The Netherlands: Brill, 2003). A series of essays on the transformation of the Classical world.

Malcolm Todd, *The Early Germans* (Oxford: Blackwell Publishers, 1992). A general introduction to pre-Roman Germanic society.

The Empire Restored

T. D. Barnes, *The New Empire of Diocletian and Constantine* (Cambridge, MA: Harvard University Press, 1982). A current examination of the transformations brought about under the two great emperors.

Ramsay MacMullen, *Paganism in the Roman Empire* (New Haven, CT: Yale University Press, 1981). A sensible introduction to the varieties of Roman religion in the imperial period.

Imperial Christianity

G. W. Bowersock, *Martyrdom and Rome* (New York: Cambridge University Press, 1995). A new look at Christian martyrdom in antiquity.

Peter Brown, *Authority and the Sacred: Aspects of the Christianisation of the Roman* (Cambridge: Cambridge University Press, 1995). A highly readable account of the emergence of Christianity in the Roman world by the leading historian of late antiquity.

W. H. C. Fend, *The Rise of Christianity* (London: Darton, Longman and Todd, 1984). A panoramic survey of Christianity from its origins to the seventh century.

Ramsay MacMullen, *Christianizing the Roman Empire (100–400)* (New Haven, CT: Yale University Press, 1984). A view of Christianity's spread from the perspective of Roman history.

A Parting of the Ways

Peter Brown, *The Rise of Western Christendom* (Cambridge, MA: Blackwell, 2003). A survey of late antiquity by a master scholar and stylist.

Patrick J. Geary, *The Myth of Nations: The Medieval Origins of Europe* (Princeton, NJ: Princeton University Press, 2001). An essay examining the relationship between modern nationalism and ethnic groups in late antiquity.

Judith Herrin, *The Formation of Christendom* (Princeton, NJ: Princeton University Press, 1987). A history of the transformed Mediterranean world, east and west, to 800 from the perspective of a noted Byzantinist.

Brian Ward-Perkins, *The Fall of Rome and the End of Civilization* (Oxford: Oxford University Press, 2005). An archaeologist's argument against seeing the end of Antiquity as a period of peaceful transition. An account of the decline in material culture at the end of Antiquity.

Herwig Wolfram, *The Roman Empire and Its Germanic Peoples* (Berkeley: University of California Press, 1997). Important general survey of the place of the barbarians in the Roman world.

CHAPTER 7

The Byzantines

Jonathan Harris, *Byzantium and the Crusades* (London and New York: Hambledon and London, 2003). A new treatment of relations between Byzantium and Western Europe.

Judith Herrin, *Byzantium: The Surprising Life of a Medieval Empire* (London Penguin, 2008). Brief and lively new synthesis by a leading Byzantinist.

Alexander P. Kazhdan, ed., *The Oxford Dictionary of Byzantium* (New York: Oxford University Press, 1991). Standard reference for Byzantine history and culture.

Michael Maas, ed. *The Cambridge companion to the Age of Justinian* (Cambridge; New York: Cambridge University Press, 2005). Collaborative guide to the sixth century Empire.

Cyril Mango, *Byzantium: The Empire of New Rome* (New York: Scribner's, 1980). An imaginative and provocative reevaluation of the Byzantine world.

John Moorhead, *Justinian* (New York: Macmillan, 1994). A readable biography of the great emperor.

Dimitri Obolensky, *Byzantium and the Slavs* (Crestwood, NY: St. Vladimir's Seminary Press, 1994). A survey of the Byzantine Empire's relations with eastern Europe.

The Rise of Islam

Aziz Al-Azmeh, *Arabic Thought and Islamic Societies* (London: Routledge, Chapman & Hall, 1986). A demanding but valuable introduction to Islamic intellectual history.

Albert Hourani, *A History of the Arab Peoples* (New York: Warner Books, 1992). A clear, thoughtful survey of Arab history for nonspecialists.

Robert G. Hoyland, *Arabia and the Arabs: From the Bronze Age to the Coming of Islam* (New York: Routledge, 2001). A comprehensive survey of the early history of Arabia.

Hugh Kennedy, *The Prophet and the Age of the Caliphates* (White Plains, NY: Longman, 1986). A valuable summary of the early political history of Islam.

Nasser D. Khalili, *Islamic art and culture: a Visual History* (Woodstock; New York: Overlook Press, 2006). A broad introduction to Islamic art through the centuries.

Bernard Lewis, *Islam in History: Ideas, People, and Events in the Middle East* (Chicago: Open Court, 1993). Broad synthesis of Islam.

Bernard Lewis, *The Muslim Discovery of Europe* (New York: W. W. Norton, 1985). Views of the West by Muslim travelers.

Fatima Mernissi, *Women and Islam: An Historical and Theological Enquiry* (Oxford: Basil Blackwell, 1991). Sympathetic study of women in Islam.

Roy P. Mottahedeh, *The Mantle of the Prophet: Religion and Politics in Iran* (New York: Simon and Schuster, 1985). An important introduction to the social values and structures of western Iran and southern Iraq in the tenth and eleventh centuries.

Seyyed Hossein Nasr, *Islam: Religion, History, and Civilization* (San Francisco: HarperSanFrancisco, 2003). A brief and balanced introduction to Islam in historical perspective.

The Byzantine Apogee and Decline, 1000–1453

Michael Angold, *The Byzantine Empire, 1025–1204* (White Plains, NY: Longman, 1997). A solid survey of the Byzantine Empire prior to the capture of Constantinople by the Latins.

P. M. Holt, *The Age of the Crusades: The Near East from the Eleventh Century to 1517* (White Plains, NY: Longman, 1986). An excellent survey of the political history of the Near East in the later Middle Ages.

CHAPTER 8
The Making of the Barbarian Kingdoms, 500–750

Paul M. Barford, *The Early Slavs: Culture and Society in Early Medieval Eastern Europe* (Ithaca, NY: Cornell University Press, 2001). An introduction to eastern Europe in the early Middle Ages.

James Campbell, ed., *The Anglo-Saxons* (Oxford: Phaidon, 1982). A collection of essays on Anglo-Saxon England by an outstanding group of archaeologists and historians.

Roger Collins, *Visigothic Spain, 409–711* (Malden, MA: Blackwell Pub., 2004). A survey of early medieval Spain to the Islamic conquest.

Florin Curta, *The Making of the Slavs: History and Archaeology of the Lower Danube Region, Ca. 500–700* (Cambridge [England]; New York: Cambridge University Press, 2001). A challenging account of Slavic ethnogenesis based on texts and archaeology.

F. Donald Logan, *The Vikings in History* (New York: HarperCollins, 1991). General introduction to the Vikings.

Rosamond McKitterick, ed. *The Early Middle Ages: Europe 400–1000* (New York: Oxford University Press, 2001). A collective introduction to early medieval history.

Walter Pohl, ed., with Helmut Reimitz, *Strategies of Distinction: The Construction of Ethnic Communities, 300–800* (Leiden, The Netherlands: Brill, 1998). An important collection devoted to early medieval ethnicity.

Chris Wickham, *The Inheritance of Rome: A History of Europe from 400 to 1000* (London: Allen Lane; New York: Penguin Group, 2009). A dense but rewarding synthesis by one of the leading specialists of our time.

Ian Wood, *The Merovingian Kingdoms 450–751* (London: Longman, 1994). Excellent survey of early Frankish history with an emphasis on government.

Living in the New Europe

Lisa M. Bitel, *Women in Early Medieval Europe, 400–1100* (Cambridge: Cambridge University Press, 2002). A valuable survey of women in the early Middle Ages.

Bonnie Effros, *Creating Community with Food and Drink in Merovingian Gaul* (New York: Palgrave Macmillan, 2002). An examination of an early medieval society through their social practices.

Yitzhak Hen, *Roman Barbarians: The Royal Court and Culture in the Early Medieval West* (Basingstoke; New York: Palgrave Macmillan, 2007). A comprehensive survey of cultural production at the barbarian courts..

The Carolingian Achievement

Paul Fouracre, *The Age of Charles Martel* (New York: Longman, 2000). An exploration of the Frankish world in the early eighth century.

Valerie L. Garver, *Women and Aristocratic Culture in the Carolingian World* (Ithaca: Cornell University Press, 2009). An examination of elite women in the Frankish world.

Rosamond McKitterick, *The Frankish Kingdoms Under the Carolingians, 751–987* (New York: Longman, 1983). A very detailed study of Carolingian history with an emphasis on intellectual developments.

Rosamond McKitterick, ed., *The New Cambridge Medieval History, c. 700–c. 900, vol. II* (Cambridge: Cambridge University Press, 1995). An excellent collective history of all aspects of Europe in the eighth and ninth centuries.

Janet L. Nelson, *The Frankish World, 750–900* (London: Hambledon Press, 1996). An excellent and balanced survey.

After the Carolingians: From Empire to Lordships

Georges Duby, *The Early Growth of the European Economy: Warriors and Peasants from the Seventh to the Twelfth Century* (Ithaca, NY: Cornell University Press, 1974). An imaginative survey of the economic and social forces forming in Europe in the early Middle Ages.

Heinrich Fichtenau, *Living in the Tenth Century: Studies in Mentalities and Social Orders* (Chicago: University of Chicago Press, 1990). A brilliant evocation of the quest for order on the Continent following the dissolution of the Carolingian Empire.

Timothy Reuter, *Germany in the Early Middle Ages, 800–1056* (New York: Longman, 1991). A readable, original survey of early German history by a British scholar thoroughly knowledgeable about current German scholarship.

CHAPTER 9

The Countryside

Robert Bartlett, *The Making of Europe: Conquest, Colonization, and Cultural Change, 950–1350* (Princeton, NJ: Princeton University Press, 1993). A challenging study of European expansion.

Frederic Cheyette, *Ermengard of Narbonne* (Ithaca, NY: Cornell University Press, 2001). An evocative account of Provençal society in the eleventh and twelfth centuries.

Georges Duby, *The Chivalrous Society* (Berkeley: University of California Press, 1978). Essays on the French aristocracy by the leading medieval historian.

Georges Duby, *The Knight, the Lady, and the Priest: The Making of Modern Marriage in Medieval France* (New York: Pantheon Books, 1984). A short study of the conflict between lay and religious social values in medieval France.

John France, *Western Warfare in the Age of the Crusades, 1000–1300* (Ithaca, NY: Cornell University Press, 1999). Warfare in the High Middle Ages.

Richard W. Kauper, *Chivalry and Violence in Medieval Europe* (Oxford: Oxford University Press, 2001). A comprehensive look at the relationship between chivalry and medieval violence.

Jonathan Riley-Smith, *The Crusades, Christianity, and Islam* (New York: Columbia University Press, 2008). A brief summation by one of the great authorities on the meanings and motivations of the crusades.

Medieval Towns

Hilde De Ridder-Symoens, ed., *A History of the University in Europe, Vol. 1: Universities in the Middle Ages* (Cambridge: Cambridge University Press, 1991). A multi-authored comprehensive history of medieval universities to 1500.

P. J. Jones, *The Italian City-State: From Commune to Signoria* (Oxford, NY: Clarendon Press, 1997). Major survey of Italian urban history.

Robert S. Lopez, *The Commercial Revolution of the Middle Ages, 950–1350* (New York: Cambridge University Press, 1971). An excellent survey of medieval commercial history.

Joseph H. Lynch, *The Medieval Church: A Brief History* (London and New York: Longman, 1992). A short introduction to medieval Church history.

David Nicholas, *The Growth of the Medieval City* (New York: Addison-Wesley Longman, 1997). A survey of the diversity of medieval urban development from late antiquity to the 1330s.

Norman Pounds, *The medieval City* (Westport, Conn.: Greenwood Press, 2005). A modern introduction to medieval urban history.

The Invention of the State

Robert Bartlett, *England under the Norman and Angevin Kings, 1075–1225* (Oxford: Oxford University Press, 2000). A survey of England from the eleventh to thirteenth centuries.

Thomas N. Bisson, *The Crisis of the Twelfth Century: Power, Lordship, and the Origins of European Government* (Princeton, N.J.: Princeton University Press, 2009). An important argument for the rise of centralized government.

Jean Dunbabin, *France in the Making, 843–1180* (New York: Oxford University Press, 1985). Good overview of the formation of France.

Horst Fuhrmann, *Germany in the High Middle Ages, c. 1050–1200* (New York: Cambridge University Press, 1986). A fresh synthesis of German history by a leading German historian.

William Chester Jordan, *Europe in the High Middle Ages* (New York: Viking, 2003). A comprehensive survey.

Bernard F. Reilly, *The Medieval Spains* (Cambridge: Cambridge University Press, 1993). Comprehensive survey of the social, political, and cultural history of the medieval Iberian peninsula.

Teofilo F. Ruiz, *From Heaven to Earth: The Reordering of Castilian Society, 1150–1350* (Princeton, NJ: Princeton University Press, 2004). An intelligent examination of the relationship between language and social and political change in Spain.

Joseph R. Strayer, *On the Medieval Origins of the Modern State* (Princeton, NJ: Princeton University Press, 1970). A very brief but imaginative account of medieval statecraft by a leading historian of French institutions.

CHAPTER 10

General Reading

Johan Huizinga, *The Autumn of the Middle Ages,* trans. Rodney J. Payton and Ulrich Mammitzsch (Chicago: University of Chicago Press, 1996). An important translation of the classic interpretation of culture and society in the Burgundian court in the Later Middle Ages.

Daniel Waley, *Later Medieval Europe: From Saint Louis to Luther* (London: Longman, 1985). A brief introduction with a focus on Italy.

Politics as a Family Affair

Richard W. Kaeuper, *Chivalry and Violence in Medieval Europe* (Oxford: Oxford University Press, 1999). A fine analysis of the complex relationship between chivalric ethos and the violence of aristocratic society in the Middle Ages.

Joachim Leuschner, *Germany in the Late Middle Ages* (Amsterdam: Elsevier, 1980). An introduction to late medieval German history.

Jean W. Sedlar, *East Central Europe in the Middle Ages, 1000–1500* (Seattle: University of Washington Press, 1994). A thematic introduction to the medieval history of the region that today comprises Poland, the Czech Republic, Slovakia, Hungary, Romania, Bulgaria, Albania, and the former Yugoslavia.

Life and Death in the Later Middle Ages

Bronislaw Geremek, *The Margins of Society in Late Medieval Paris*, trans. Jean Birrell (Cambridge: Cambridge University Press, 1987). A landmark study of the urban poor in the Later Middle Ages.

John Kelly, *The Great Mortality: An Intimate History of the Black Death* (London: Fourth Estate, 2005). A popular, well-written account of the great fourteenth-century plague.

James M. Murray, *Bruges, Cradle of Capitalism, 1280–1390* (Cambridge; New York: Cambridge University Press, 2005). A history of the most important commercial city in northern Europe.

David Nicholas, *The Growth of the Medieval City: From Late Antiquity to the Early Fourteenth Century* (London, New York: Longman, 1997). A comprehensive survey of medieval towns.

Teofilo F. Ruiz, *Spanish Society 1400–1600* (Harlow: Longman, 2001). A sensitive and original survey of Spanish society at the end of the Middle Ages.

Daniel Waley, *Later Medieval Europe, 1250–1520*, 3rd ed. rev. by Peter Denley. (New York: Longman, 2001). A brief, revised introduction focusing on western Europe.

The Spirit of the Later Middle Ages

Renate Blumenfeld-Kosinski, ed., trans. Kevin Brownlee, *The Selected Writings of Christine De Pizan: New Translations, Criticism* (New York: Norton, 1997). A selection of de Pizan's works and of scholarship on her. The place to start for learning about her.

Caroline Walker Bynum, *Holy Feast and Holy Fast: The Religious Significance of Food to Medieval Women* (Berkeley: University of California Press, 1987). An imaginative and scholarly examination of the role of food in the spirituality of medieval women.

Eamon Duffy, *The Stripping of the Altars: Traditional Religion in England, 1400–1580* (New Haven: Yale University Press, 1992). A revisionist study of local religion at the end of the Middle Ages.

David A. Fein, *François Villon Reconsidered* (New York: Macmillan, 1997). Villon's poetry and his life examined by an authority.

Malcolm Lambert, *Medieval Heresy: Popular Movements from the Gregorian Reform to the Reformation*, 2nd ed. (Oxford: Blackwell, 1992). A comprehensive survey of heretical movements from the eleventh to the sixteenth centuries.

Scott L. Waugh and Peter D. Diehl, eds., *Christendom and Its Discontents: Exclusion, Persecution, and Rebellion, 1000–1500* (New York: Cambridge University Press, 1995). Important collection of essays on heresy and dissent in western Europe.

CHAPTER 11

General Reading

P. Burke, *Culture and Society in Renaissance Italy* (Princeton, NJ: Princeton University Press, 1999). A good introduction to social and intellectual developments.

Paul Grendler, ed., *Encyclopedia of the Renaissance* (New York: Scribners, 1999). A valuable reference work for all aspects of the Renaissance.

Denys Hay, *The Italian Renaissance* (Cambridge, England: Cambridge University Press, 1977). The best first book to read, an elegant interpretive essay.

John Jeffries Martin, *The Renaissance World* (London, Routledge, 2007). An accessible and wide ranging survey of the entire period labeled the Renaissance.

Renaissance Society

Carlo Cipolla, *Before the Industrial Revolution: European Society and Economy, 1000–1700*, 3rd ed. (New York: W. W. Norton, 1994). A sweeping survey of social and economic developments across the centuries.

Richard Goldthwaite, *The Economy of Renaissance Florence* (Baltimore, MD: Johns Hopkins University Press, 2009). The leading economic historian of the period examines the complex workings of the Florentine economy from banking, trade, and the commercialization of art.

J. R. Hale, *Renaissance Europe: The Individual and Society* (Berkeley: University of California Press, 1978). A lively study that places the great figures of the Renaissance in their social context.

D. Herlihy and C. Klapisch-Zuber, *Tuscans and Their Families* (New Haven, CT: Yale University Press, 1985). A difficult but rewarding study of the social and demographic history of Florence and its environs.

Margaret L. King, *Women of the Renaissance* (Chicago: University of Chicago Press, 1991). A study by a leading women's historian.

Renaissance Art

Michael Baxandall, *Painting and Experience in Fifteenth-Century Italy* (Oxford, England: Oxford University Press, 1972). A study of the relationship between painters and their patrons and of how and why art was produced.

Samuel Edgerton, *The mirror, the window, and the telescope: how Renaissance linear perspective changed our vision of the universe* (Ithaca, NY: Cornell University Press, 2009). An arresting study that amalgamates art and science through the study of masters of perspective like Brunelleschi and Massacio.

Anthony Grafton, *Leon Battista Alberti: Master Builder of the Italian Renaissance* (New York: Hill and Wang, 2000). A lucid biographical study of a truly renaissance man.

Frederick Hartt, *History of Italian Renaissance Art* (Englewood Cliffs, NJ: Prentice-Hall, 1974). The most comprehensive survey, with hundreds of plates.

Howard Hibbard, *Michelangelo* (New York: Harper & Row, 1974). A compelling biography of an obsessed genius.

Lisa Jardine and Jerry Brotton, *Global Interests: Renaissance Art Between East and West* (Ithaca, NY: Cornell University Press, 2000). A bold argument about Renaissance art and its relation to Ottoman culture.

Michael Levey, *Early Renaissance* (London: Penguin, 1967). A concise survey of art, clearly written and authoritative.

Linda Murray, *High Renaissance and Mannerism* (London: Thames & Hudson, 1985). The best introduction to late Renaissance art.

Renaissance Ideals

Hans Baron, *The Crisis of the Early Italian Renaissance* (Princeton, NJ: Princeton University Press, 1966). One of the most influential intellectual histories of the period.

James Hankins, *Renaissance civic humanism: reappraisals and reflections* (New York: Cambridge University Press, 2000). Leading scholars reflect on the nature of civic humanism, the obligations of the citizen, and the Platonic ideal of the philosopher king.

George Holmes, *The Florentine Enlightenment*, 2nd ed. (Oxford: Clarendon Press, 1992). A new edition of the best study of intellectual developments in Florence.

Quentin Skinner, *Machiavelli* (Oxford: Oxford University Press, 1981). A brief but brilliant biography.

The Politics of the Italian City-States

Gene Brucker, *Florence, The Golden Age 1138–1737* (Berkeley: University of California Press, 1998). The best single-volume introduction to Florentine history with excellent illustrations.

J. R. Hale, *Florence and the Medici* (London: Thames & Hudson, 1977). A compelling account of the relationship between a city and its most powerful citizens.

F. W. Kent, *Lorenzo de' Medici and the art of magnificence* (Baltimore, MD: Johns Hopkins University Press, 2004). A reevaluation of the role Lorenzo the Magnificent played in Florentine politics and art.

Frederic C. Lane, *Venice: A Maritime Republic* (Baltimore, MD: Johns Hopkins University Press, 1973). A complete history of Venice that stresses its naval and mercantile developments.

Lauro Martines, *Power and Imagination: City-States in Renaissance Italy* (New York: Alfred A. Knopf, 1979). An important interpretation of the politics of the Italian powers.

Eugene F. Rice, Jr., *The Foundations of Early Modern Europe, 1460–1559*, 2nd ed. (New York: W. W. Norton, 1994). The best short synthetic work.

Charles Stinger, *The Renaissance in Rome* (Bloomington, IN: University of Indiana Press, 1998). A thorough account of one of the great ages in the history of Rome.

CHAPTER 12

General Reading

David Nicholas, *The Transformation of Europe 1300–1600* (New York: Oxford University Press, 1999). A comprehensive survey that emphasizes continuities between the sixteenth century and the preceding period.

Eugene Rice, *The Foundations of Early Modern Europe, 1460–1559*, 2nd ed. (New York: Norton, 1994). An outstanding synthesis.

Merry Wiesner-Hanks, *Early Modern Europe, 1450–1789* (New York: Cambridge University Press, 2006). An outstanding synthesis of the early modern world.

European Encounters

C. R. Boxer, *The Portuguese Seaborne Empire, 1415–1825* (London: Hutchinson, 1968). The best history of the first of the explorer nations.

J. H. Elliott, *The Old World and the New, 1492–1650* (Cambridge: Cambridge University Press, 1970). A brilliant look at the reception of knowledge about the New World by Europeans.

John H. Elliott, *Spain, Europe and the Wider World 1500–1800* (New Haven, CT: Yale University Press, 2009). The leading historian of early modern Spain rethinks its imperial age.

Felipe Fernandez-Armesto, *Columbus* (Oxford: Oxford University Press, 1991). The best of the recent studies. Reliable, stimulating, and up-to-date.

Anthony Pagden, *Lords of All the World: Ideologies of Empire in Spain, Britain and France, c. 1500–c. 1800* (New Haven, CT: Yale University Press, 1995). A fresh look at the ideas behind the European encounter with the New World.

Martin W. Sandler and Dennis Reinhartz, *Atlantic Ocean: The Illustrated History of the Ocean That Changed the World* (New York: Sterling, 2008). The experience of sailors and sailing in the first great age of discovery.

Hugh Thomas, *Rivers of Gold: The Rise of the Spanish Empire* (London: Widenfeld & Nicholson, 2004). A breathtaking retelling of Spain's New World Empire.

The Formation of States

S. B. Chrimes, *Henry VII* (Berkeley: University of California Press, 1972). A traditional biography of the first Tudor.

James Collins, *The State in Early Modern France* (New York: Cambridge University Press, 1995). A study of the unification of France and development of its political institutions.

Robert O. Crummey, *The Formation of Muscovy, 1304–1613* (London: Longman, 1987). The best one-volume history.

Sean Cunningham, *Henry VII* (London: Routledge, 2007). The most recent biography of England's state builder.

Norman Davies, *God's Playground: A History of Poland, Vol. 1, The Origins to 1795* (New York: Columbia University Press, 1982). The best treatment in English of a complex history.

Bernard Guenée, *States and Rulers in Later Medieval Europe* (London: Basil Blackwell, 1985). An engaging argument about the forces that helped shape the state system in Europe.

Henry Kamen, *The Spanish Inquisition: A Historical Revision* (New Haven, CT: Yale University Press, 1998). The best recent assessment of the power and activities of the Inquisition.

Paul M. Kendall, *Louis XI: The Universal Spider* (New York: Norton, 1971). A highly entertaining account of an unusual monarch.

John Lynch, *Spain, 1516–1598: From Nation State to World Empire* (Cambridge, MA: Blackwell, 1994). A valuable and expert survey.

Jaroslav Miller, *Urban societies in East-Central Europe: 1500–1700* (London, Ashgate, 2008). Urbanization in the forgotten states of Europe.

Helen Rawlings, *The Spanish Inquisition* (London: Wiley-Blackwell, 2006). An attempt to view the Inquisition in a broad social context.

J. H. Shennan, *The Origins of the Modern European State, 1450–1725* (London: Hutchinson, 1974). An analytic account of the rise of the state.

The Dynastic Struggles

Jeremy Black, *European warfare, 1494–1660* (London: Routledge, 2002). A valuable account of an age of unrelenting warfare.

J. R. Hale, *War and Society in Renaissance Europe* (Stroud, England: Sutton, 1998). Assesses the impact of war on the political and social history of early modern Europe.

William Maltby, *The Reign of Charles V* (New York: Palgrave, 2002). The most recent study of one of Europe's great emperors.

David Potter, *A History of France, 1460–1560* (London: Macmillan, 1995). A reliable survey that connects medieval and early modern developments.

Julius R. Ruff, *Violence in Early Modern Europe 1500–1800* (New York: Cambridge University Press, 2001). A social contextualization of European warfare.

J. J. Scarisbrick, *Henry VIII* (New Haven: Yale University Press, 1997). The definitive biography.

CHAPTER 13
General Reading

Owen Chadwick, *The Reformation* (London: Penguin Books, 1972). An elegant and disarmingly simple history of religious change.

Patrick Collinson, *The Reformation: a history* (New York: Random House, 2004). A brief account by England's leading historian of religion.

Diarmaid MacCulloch, *The Reformation* (London: Viking, 2003). A vastly impressive survey of the Reformation from a leading scholar.

Steven Ozment, *The Age of Reform, 1250–1550* (New Haven, CT: Yale University Press, 1980). An important interpretation of an epoch of religious change.

Ulinka Rublack, *Reformation Europe* (New York: Cambridge University Press, 2005). A cultural history of religious change.

Hubert J. Smith, *God's Hundred Years: A Brief History of the Reformation* (Cambridge, Lutterworth Press, 2007). An accessible study of the origins and development of Protestantism.

James D. Tracy, *Europe's Reformations, 1450–1650: Doctrine, Politics, And Community* (London, Rowman & Littlefield, 2nd ed., 2006). The long reformation that dominated European politics for two centuries.

The Intellectual Reformation

E. Eisenstein, *The Printing Revolution in Early Modern Europe* (Cambridge: Cambridge University Press, 1983). An abridged edition of a larger work that examines the impact of printing upon European society.

Jean François Gilmont and Karin Maag (eds.), *The Reformation and the Book* (London, Ashgate, 1998). The significance of printing and the book trade in speading ideas of Protestantism.

Adrian Johns, *The Nature of the Book: Print and Knowledge in the Making* (Chicago: University of Chicago Press, 1998). A major synthesis with an unusual interpretation.

Andrew Pettegree, *The French Book and the European Book* World (New York: Brill, 2007). The explosion of printing in Paris and the role of booksellers in the sixteenth century.

R. W. Scribner, *For the Sake of Simple Folk* (Cambridge: Cambridge University Press, 1994). A study of the impact of the Reformation on common people. Especially good on the iconography of reform.

James Tracy, *Erasmus of the Low Countries* (Berkeley, CA:, 1996). A brief biography of the great Dutch humanist.

The Lutheran Reformation

Roland H. Bainton, *Here I Stand: A Life of Martin Luther* (Peabody, MA: Hendrickson, 2009 Publishers). The single most compelling biography of Luther.

Robert Kolb, *Martin Luther: Confessor of the Faith* (New York: Oxford University Press, 2009). Luther's thought set within the context of German politics.

Bernd Moeller, *Imperial Cities and the Reformation* (Durham, NC: Labyrinth Press, 1982). A central work that defines the connection between Protestantism and urban reform.

Heiko Oberman, *Luther: Man Between God and the Devil* (New York: Doubleday, 1992). English translation of one of the best German biographies of Luther. Sets Luther within the context of late medieval spirituality.

G. R. Potter, *Huldrych Zwingli* (New York: St. Martin's Press, 1984). A difficult but important study of the great Swiss reformer.

Lyndal Roper, *The Holy Household: Women and Morals in Reformation Augsburg* (Oxford: Oxford University Press, 1991). The best work to show the impact of the Reformation on family life and women.

R. W. Scribner, *The German Reformation* (Atlantic Highlands, NJ: Humanities Press, 1986). An excellent introduction, especially to the social history of the Reformation.

The Protestant Reformation

William Bousma, *John Calvin* (Oxford: Oxford University Press, 1988). A study that places Calvin within the context of the social and intellectual movements of the sixteenth century.

Claus-Peter Clasen, *Anabaptism, A Social History, 1525–1618* (Ithaca, NY: Cornell University Press, 1972). An important study of the Anabaptist movement.

A. G. Dickens, *The English Reformation*, 2nd ed. (London: Batsford, 1989). The classic study of reform in England.

R. Po-chia Hsia, *The world of Catholic renewal, 1540–1770* (New York: Cambridge University Press, 2nd. ed., 2005). Catholicism resurgent in the early modern world.

Heiko Augustinus Oberman and Donald Weinstein, *The two Reformations: the journey from the last days to the new world* (New Haven, CT: Yale University Press, 2003). Reflections on the age of religious transformation by one of the most important historians of the Reformation.

J. J. Scarisbrick, *Henry VIII* (Berkeley: University of California Press, 1968). The classic biography of the larger-than-life monarch.

Kirsi Stjerna, *Women and the Reformation* (London, Blackwell Pub, 2008). The role of women in spreading new religious ideas.

The Catholic Reformation

Jean Delumeau, *Catholicism Between Luther and Voltaire* (Philadelphia: Westminster Press, 1977). An important reinterpretation of the Counter-Reformation.

Carlos Eire, *From Madrid to Purgatory* (Cambridge: Cambridge University Press, 1995). A brilliant study of the Spanish culture of death during the Counter-Reformation.

W. W. Meissner, *Ignatius of Loyola: The Psychology of a Saint* (New Haven, CT: Yale University Press, 1994). A searching study of the founding spirit of the Counter-Reformation.

John W. O'Malley, *Trent and All That: Renaming Catholicism in the Early Modern Era* (Cambridge, MA: Harvard University Press, 2000). A re-examination of Catholicism in the century surrounding the Council of Trent.

A. D. Wright, *The Counter-Reformation* (New York: St. Martin's Press, 1984). A comprehensive survey.

CHAPTER 14

General Reading

M. S. Anderson, *The Origins of the Modern European State System, 1494–1618* (London: Longman, 1998). A survey of developments stressing war and diplomacy across all of Europe.

Jan de Vries, *The European Economy in an Age of Crisis* (Cambridge: Cambridge University Press, 1976). A comprehensive study of economic development, including long-distance trade and commercial change.

J. H. Elliott, *Europe Divided, 1559–1598* (New York: Harper & Row, 1968). An outstanding synthesis of European politics in the second half of the sixteenth century.

Mark W. Konnert, *Early Modern Europe: The Age of Religious War, 1559–1715* (Orchard Park, NY: Broadview Press, 2006). The most recent survey.

Geoffrey Parker, *Europe in Crisis, 1598–1648* (London: William Collins and Sons, 1979). Compelling study of European states in the early seventeenth century.

The Crises of the Western States

Susan Brigden, *New Worlds, Lost Worlds: The Rule of the Tudors, 1485–1603* (New York: Viking, 2001). The latest volume in the Penguin History of Britain series.

Graham Darby, *The origins and development of the Dutch revolt* (London, Routledge, 2001). A recent collection of essays by leading historians presents the latest findings from a variety of perspectives.

Barbara Diefendorf, *The St. Bartholomew's Day Massacre* (New York: Bedford/ St. Martins, 2008). A valuable introduction with a selection of primary documents.

Michael A. R. Graves, *Henry VIII: a study in kingship* (London: Pearson Longman, 2003). An accessible biography of one of England's most powerful monarchs.

J. A. Guy, *Tudor England* (Oxford: Oxford University Press, 1988). A magisterial survey by the leading scholar of Tudor England.

Mack P. Holt, *The French wars of religion, 1562–1629* (New York: Cambridge University Press, 2nd ed., 2005). The best account of civil war, assassination, and ultimate stability.

Henry Kamen, *The Duke of Alba* (New Haven CT: Yale University Press, 2004). A biography of one of the great military figures of the age.

Henry Kamen, *Spain, 1469–1714* (London: Longman, 1983). A thorough survey with valuable interpretations.

Robert Kingdon, *Myths about the St. Bartholomew's Day Massacres, 1572–76* (Cambridge, MA: Harvard University Press, 1988). A study of the impact of a central event in the history of France.

R. J. Knecht, *The French Civil Wars, 1562–1598* (New York: Pearson Education, 2000). A compact survey of the religious, social, and political dimensions of the conflicts that raged in France through the second half of the sixteenth century.

D. M. Loades, *Elizabeth I* (London: Continuum International, 2003.) A compelling biography of the last of the Tudors.

John Lynch, *Spain, 1516–1598: From Nation State to World Empire* (Cambridge, MA: Blackwell, 1994). An expert survey.

Garrett Mattingly, *The Armada* (Boston: Houghton Mifflin, 1959). Still the classic account, despite recent reinterpretations.

Geoffrey Parker, *The Dutch Revolt* (London: Penguin Books, 1977). An outstanding account of the tangle of events that comprised the revolts of the Netherlands.

Geoffrey Parker, *Philip II* (Boston: Little, Brown, 1978). The best introduction.

Richard Rex, *The Tudors* (London: Tempus, 2005). A brief introduction to England's golden age.

Michael Roberts, *Gustavus Adolphus and the Rise of Sweden* (London: English Universities Press, 1973). A highly readable account of Sweden's rise to power.

Robert Tittler and Norman Jones (eds.), *A companion to Tudor Britain* (London: Wiley-Blackwell, 2004). Essays by leading scholars on every aspect of the Tudor world.

C. V. Wedgwood, *William the Silent, William of Nassau, Prince of Orange, 1533–1584* (New York: Norton, 1968). A stylish biography.

Alison Weir, *Elizabeth the Queen* (London: J. Cape, 1998). A lively biography of the great queen.

The Struggles in Eastern Europe

David Kirby, *Northern Europe in the Early Modern Period: The Baltic World, 1492–1772* (London: Longman, 1990). The best single volume on Baltic politics.

S. F. Platonov, *The Time of Troubles* (Lawrence: University Press of Kansas, 1970). A good narrative of the disintegration of the Muscovite state.

Michael Roberts, *The Swedish Imperial Experience* (Cambridge: Cambridge University Press, 1979). Reflections on Swedish history by the preeminent historian of early modern Sweden.

The Thirty Years' War

Ronald G. Asch, *The Thirty Years War: The Holy Roman Empire and Europe, 1618–1648* (New York: Macmillan, 1997). A rich account of the destruction the war caused in the Empire.

Graham Darby, *The Thirty Years' War* (London, 2001). A brief introduction and narrative of a complex war.

J. H. Elliott, *Richelieu and Olivares* (Cambridge: Cambridge University Press, 1984). A comparison of statesmen and statesmanship in the early seventeenth century.

Peter Limm, *The Thirty Years' War* (London: Longman, 1984). An excellent brief survey with documents.

Geoffrey Parker, ed., *The Thirty Years' War*, 2nd ed. (London: Routledge, 1997). A revised edition of the standard survey of the conflict.

Boris F. Porshnev, *Muscovy and Sweden in the Thirty Years' War, 1630–1635* (New York: Cambridge University Press, 1995). The great Russian historian's account of the Thirty Year's War in the east.

CHAPTER 15

General Reading

Peter Burke, *Popular Culture in Early Modern Europe* (New York: Harper & Row, 1978). A lively survey of cultural activities among the European populace.

Henry Kamen, *European Society, 1500–1700* (London: Hutchinson, 2000). A general survey of European social history.

Peter Laslett, *The World We Have Lost: Further Explored* (New York: Scribners, 1984). One of the pioneering works on the family and population history of England.

Economic Life

Judith Bennett, *Ale, Beer, and Brewsters: Women's Work in a Changing World* (Oxford: Oxford University Press, 1996). An important study of the role of women in one of the most traditional trades.

Fernand Braudel, *Civilization and Capitalism: The Structures of Everyday Life* (New York: Harper & Row, 1981). Part of a larger work filled with fascinating detail about the social behavior of humankind during the early modern period.

Emmanuel Le Roy Ladurie, *The French Peasantry, 1450–1660* (London: Scholar Press, 1987). A complex study of the lives of the French peasantry.

Peter Musgrave, *The Early Modern European Economy* (New York: St. Martin's Press, 1999). A multidimensional survey of economic life.

Patrick O'Brien and Derek Keene (eds), *Urban achievement in early modern Europe: golden ages in Antwerp, Amsterdam, and London* (New York: Cambridge University Press, 2001). Essays by leading economic historians from a comparative perspective.

Social Life

Yves-Marie Bercé, *Revolt and Revolution in Early Modern Europe* (New York: St. Martin's Press, 1987). A study of the structure of uprisings throughout Europe by a leading French historian.

Edward Bever, *The Realities of Witchcraft and Popular Magic in Early Modern Europe: Culture, Cognition and Everyday Life* (London: Palgrave Macmillan, 2008). A brief introduction to the relationship between magic and culture.

Jonathan Dewald, *The European Nobility 1400–1800* (Cambridge: Cambridge University Press, 1996). An outstanding survey based on a wide range of sources.

Cissie C. Fairchilds, *Women in early modern Europe, 1500–1700* (London: Pearson/ Longman, 2007). An argument for female agency in a patriarchal world.

Kaspar von Geyretz, *Religion and Culture in Early Modern Europe, 1500–1800* (Oxford: Oxford University Press, 2008). How ideas influenced social practices.

Barbara J. Harris, *English aristocratic women, 1450–1550: marriage and family, property and careers* (Oxford: Oxford University Press, 2002). A study of elite women and their role in lineage.

Roger B. Manning, *Hunters and Poachers: A Social and Cultural History of Unlawful Hunting in England, 1485–1640* (Oxford: Oxford University Press, 1993). Crime, cultural conflict, and social disorder intersect in the history of poaching.

Edward Muir, *Ritual in Early Modern Europe* (Cambridge: Cambridge University Press, 1997). A fascinating account of the transformations in concepts of time and the body in early modern Europe.

Barry Reay, *Popular Cultures in England, 1550–1750* (New York: Addison Wesley Longman, 1998). A sound and insightful thematic survey.

E. M. W. Tillyard, *The Elizabethan World Picture* (New York: Harper & Row, 1960). The classic account of the social constructs of English society.

Natalie Zemon Davis, *Women on the Margins: Three Seventeenth-Century Lives* (Cambridge, MA: Harvard University Press, 1995). Three short and stimulating biographies of early modern European women by a leading historian of popular culture.

Private and Community Life

Richard Adair, *Courtship, illegitimacy, and marriage in early modern England* (Manchester: Manchester University Press, 1996). A study of the dynamics of love both inside and outside of wedlock.

Helen Berry and Elizabeth A. Foyster (eds.), *The Family in Early Modern England* (New York: Cambridge University Press, 2007). A collection of essays by the leading historians of family life in England.

Roger Chartier, ed., *A History of Private Life, Vol. 3, Passions of the Renaissance* (Cambridge, MA: Harvard University Press, 1989). A lavishly illustrated study of the habits, mores, and structures of private life from the fifteenth to the eighteenth centuries.

Stuart Clark, *Thinking with Demons: The Idea of Witchcraft in Early Modern Europe* (Oxford: Oxford University Press, 1997). A sensitive reading of the sources for the study of witchcraft.

Beatrice Gottlieb, *The Family in the Western World from the Black Death to the Industrial Age* (Oxford: Oxford University Press, 1994). An outstanding introduction to the transformations in the lives of families.

R. A. Houston, *Literacy in Early Modern Europe* (London: Longman, 1988). How literacy and education became part of popular culture from 1500 to 1800.

Brian Levack, *The Witch-Hunt in Early Modern Europe* (London: Longman, 1987). A study of the causes and meaning of the persecution of European witches in the sixteenth and seventeenth centuries.

R. Muchembled, *Popular Culture and Elite Culture in France, 1400–1750* (Baton Rouge: Louisiana State University Press, 1985). A detailed treatment of the practices of two conflicting cultures.

Steven Ozment, *Ancestors: The Loving Family in Old Europe* (Cambridge, MA: Harvard University Press, 2001). A brief and accessible survey by a leading historian, making a spirited defense of early modern family life against historians who have portrayed the premodern family in grim terms.

D. Underdown, *Revel, Riot, and Rebellion* (Oxford: Oxford University Press, 1985). An engaging study of popular culture and its relationship to social and economic structures in England.

Merry E. Wiesner, *Women and Gender in Early Modern Europe* (Cambridge: Cambridge University Press, 1993). The best introduction to European women's history.

CHAPTER 16

General Reading

Perry Anderson, *Lineages of the Absolutist State* (London: NLB Books, 1974). A sociological study of the role of absolutism in the development of the Western world.

Euan Cameron, ed., *Early Modern Europe: An Oxford History* (Oxford, New York: Oxford University Press, 1999). Valuable essays by leading historians with well-chosen topics and illustrations.

Thomas Munck, *Seventeenth-Century Europe, 1598–1700* (New York: St. Martin's Press, 2005). A comprehensive survey.

David Sturdy, *Fractured Europe 1600–1721* (Oxford: Blackwell, 2002). A thorough survey of the complex military and political events of the long seventeenth century.

The Rise of the Royal State

Yves-Marie Bercé, *The Birth of Absolutism* (London: Macmillan, 1996). A history of France from the reign of Louis XIV to the eve of the Revolution by a leading historian of France.

Philip Edwards, *The Making of the Modern English State, 1460–1660* (London: Palgrave, 2001). A survey of how the medieval monarchy became modern.

J. H. Elliott, *Richelieu and Olivares* (Cambridge: Cambridge University Press, 1984). A brilliant dual portrait.

J. H. Elliott and Jonathan Brown, *A Palace for a King* (New Haven, CT: Yale University Press, 1980). An outstanding work on the building and decorating of a Spanish palace.

Alan James, *The origins of French absolutism, 1598–1661* (London: Pearson Longman, 2006). A study of kingship and the expansion of the bureaucracy.

Graham Parry, *The Golden Age Restor'd* (New York: St. Martin's Press, 1981). A study of English court culture in the reigns of James I and Charles I.

The Crises of the Royal State

Jacqueline Broad and Karen Green, *A history of women's political thought in Europe, 1400–1700* (Cambridge: Cambridge University Press, 2009). Includes chapters on women's writings about the Fronde and the Revolution of 1688.

Barbara Donagan, *War in England 1642–1649* (Oxford: Oxford University Press, 2008). A study of the nature of early modern warfare.

Tim Harris, *Revolution: The Great Crisis of the British Monarchy, 1685–1720* (London: Allen Lane, 2006). The Revolution of 1688 told from the perspective of the British archipelago.

Jonathan Israel, ed., *The Anglo-Dutch Moment* (Cambridge: Cambridge University Press, 1991). Essays by an international team of scholars on the European dimensions of the Revolution of 1688.

M. A. Kishlansky, *A Monarchy Transformed* (London: Penguin Books, 1996). A narrative survey of a remarkable era.

G. Parker and L. Smith, eds., *The General Crisis of the Seventeenth Century* (London: Routledge & Kegan Paul, 1978). A collection of essays on the problem of the general crisis.

Quentin Skinner, *The Foundations of Modern Political Thought*, 2 vols. (Cambridge: Cambridge University Press, 1978). A seminal work on the history of ideas from Machiavelli to Calvin.

W. A. Speck, *The Revolution of 1688* (Oxford: Oxford University Press, 1988). The best single volume on the event that transformed England into a global power.

Lawrence Stone, *The Causes of the English Revolution* (New York: Harper & Row, 1972). A vigorously argued explanation of why England experienced a revolution in the mid-seventeenth century.

The Zenith of the Royal State

Joseph Bergin, *The Rise of Richelieu* (New Haven, CT: Yale University Press, 1991). A fascinating portrait of a consummate politician.

Peter Burke, *The Fabrication of Louis XIV* (New Haven, CT: Yale University Press, 1992). A compelling account of a man and a myth.

Paul Dukes, *The Making of Russian Absolutism* (London: Longman, 1982). A thorough survey of Russian history in the seventeenth and eighteenth centuries.

Nicholas Henshall, *The Myth of Absolutism: Change and Continuity in Early Modern European Monarchy* (London: Longman, 1992). A searching examination of the problem of absolutism in the western European states.

Vasili Klyuchevsky, *Peter the Great* (London: Random House, 1958). A classic work, still the best study of Peter.

H. W. Koch, *A History of Prussia* (London: Longman, 1978). A comprehensive study of Prussian history, with an excellent chapter on the Great Elector.

Geoffrey Parker, *The Military Revolution* (Cambridge: Cambridge University Press, 1988). A lucid discussion of how power was organized and deployed in the early modern state.

John Wolf, *Louis XIV* (New York: Norton, 1968). An outstanding biography of the Sun King.

CHAPTER 1

You can obtain more information about the first civilizations at the Websites listed below. See also the Companion Website that accompanies this text, *www.pearsonhighered.com/kishlansky*, which contains an online study guide and additional resources.

Before Civilization

Origins of Humankind
www.pbs.org/wgbh/evolution/humans/humankind/
Educational information on prehistory of humanity.

Rock Art Links—Petroglyphs and Pictographs
www.electronics-ee.com/Art/Art_History/Rock_Art.htm
Online database of links to prehistoric rock art throughout the world.

Prehistoric Cultures
www.d.umn.edu/cla/faculty/troufs/anth1602/
A course Website at the University of Minnesota–Duluth that links to materials on prehistoric cultures around the world.

Mesopotamia

ABZU: Guide to Resources for the Study of the Ancient Near East Available on the Internet
www.etana.org/abzu/
A major site for all aspects of Ancient Mesopotamia and Egypt maintained by the Oriental Institute of the University of Chicago.

Egypt

NM's Creative Impulse: Egypt
http://eawc.evansville.edu/egpage.htm
Award-winning site for Egyptian history.

Survey of Ancient Egypt
www.cofc.edu/~piccione/hist270/index.html
Excellent class Web page on Ancient Egypt.

Egyptian Kings
touregypt.net/kings.htm
A site that provides information on all of the pharaohs.

Giza Plateau Computer Model
www.oi.uchicago.edu/OI/DEPT/COMP/GIZ/MODEL/Giza_Model.html
A site devoted to Giza with a computer model of its pyramids and other monuments.

Israel

The Hebrews: A Learning Module
www.wsu.edu/~dee/HEBREWS/HEBREWS.HTM
An excellent course site devoted entirely to the ancient Hebrews.

The Israel Museum, Jerusalem: Archaeology
http://www.english.imjnet.org.il/htmls/article_15.aspx?co=13013&bsp=12940
Site on early Israel archaeology.

Nineveh and Babylon

Babylon
http://www.livius.org/ba-bd/babylon.html
A brief history of Babylon with further links.

CHAPTER 2

You can obtain more information about early Greece at the Websites listed below. See also the Companion Website that accompanies this text, *www.pearsonhighered. com/kishlansky*, which contains an online study guide and additional resources.

General Websites

The Perseus Digital Project
www.perseus.tufts.edu/
A digital library dedicated to all aspects of ancient Greek civilization.

Thomas R. Martin, An Overview of Classical Greek History
www.perseus.tufts.edu/cgi-bin/ptext?doc=1999.04.0009
This page of The Perseus Digital Project includes an extremely detailed outline of Greek history up to the death of Alexander, with wonderful links to other sources.

Greece in the Bronze Age

Palace of Knossos in Minoan Crete
www.dilos.com/region/crete/kn_01.html
A site devoted to the city of Knossos.

Bureaucrats and Barbarians
www.wsu.edu/~dee/MINOA/CONTENTS.HTM
A site devoted to Minoan and Mycenean civilizations.

Archaic Greece

The British Museum Compass
www.thebritishmuseum.ac.uk/compass/
Search the British Museum Collection, which includes Greek antiquities.

Educated Women in Ancient Society
www.domz.org/Society/People/Women/History/Ancient
A site devoted to elite women in Greece and their education.

Classical Myth: The Ancient Sources
http://web.uvic.ca/grs/department_files/classical_myth/index.html
A site devoted to classical mythology with iconography of Greek mythical figures.

A Tale of Three Cities

Everything Spartan, Lakonian, and Messenian
www.geocities.com/Athens/Aegean/7849
A site dedicated to Sparta.

The Coming of Persia

Internet Ancient History Sourcebook: Persia
www.fordham.edu/halsall/ancient/asbook05.html
A site devoted to sources of ancient Persian history.

CHAPTER 3

You can obtain more information about classical and Hellenistic Greece at the Websites listed below. See also the Companion Website that accompanies this text: *www.pearsonhighered.com/kishlansky*, which contains an online study guide and additional resources.

War and Politics in the Fifth Century B.C.E.

Articles on Ancient Persia
www.livius.org/persia.html
Links to articles on many aspects of ancient Persian history.

The Greeks: Crucible of Civilization
www.pbs.org/empires/thegreeks/
A Public Broadcasting System site devoted to ancient Greece.

The Peloponnesian War
www.multimania.com/sdelille/gdpa.html
A site developed by Sven Delille on the Peloponnesian War.

Diotima: Women and Gender in the Ancient World
www.stoa.org/diotima/
A site devoted to women and gender in antiquity.

Alexander the Great
history.boisestate.edu/westciv/alexander/
Dr. Ellis L. Knox's page devoted to Alexander the Great.

The Hellenistic World

A Brief History of Clocks: From Thales to Ptolemy
www.perseus.tufts.edu/GreekScience/Students/Jesse/CLOCK1A.html
A history of clocks in the Hellenistic world.

Archimedes
www.mcs.drexel.edu/~crorres/Archimedes/contents.html
A site devoted to Archimedes and Hellenistic science.

CHAPTER 4

You can obtain more information about early Rome at the Websites listed below. See also the Companion Website that accompanies this text, *www.pearsonhighered. com/kishlansky*, which contains an online study guide and additional resources.

General Websites

Carthage (Tunsinia)
www.archaelogy.about.com/od/cterms/g/carthage.htm
A site with links to information on Carthage archaeology.

From City to Empire

Frank E. Smitha's World History: The Rise of Ancient Rome
fsmitha.com/h1/ch15.htm
An outline by Frank Smitha of early Roman history beginning with the legendary accounts of Rome's foundation.

The Forum Romanum: History and Religion
http://intranet.grundel.nl/thinkquest/homehis.html
A Thinkquest site on Roman history and religion including links to Roman archaeology.

Republican Civilization

Women's Life in Greece and Rome
www.stoa.org/diotima/anthology/wlgr/
A site devoted to women in Rome and Greece.

Republican Roman Government
www.utexas.edu/depts/classics/faculty/Riggsby/RepGov.html
A detailed explanation of the republican constitution of Rome.

CHAPTER 5

You can obtain more information about imperial Rome at the Websites listed below. See also the Companion Website that accompanies this text, *www.pearsonhighered. com/kishlansky*, which contains an online study guide and additional resources.

General Websites

Ancient/Classical History with N. S. Gill: The Gracchi
ancienthistory.about.com/od/gracchi/
An introduction to the Gracchi with links to other sites.

Pompeii Forum Project
www.iath.virginia.edu/pompeii/page-1.html
A great site devoted to the Roman city of Pompeii, which was destroyed by Mount Vesuvius in 79 C.E.

The End of the Republic

History & Literature of the Roman Revolution
johara.web.wesleyan.edu/CCIV274links.html
Dr. Jim O'Hara's Web page devoted to the end of the Roman Republic.

The Cicero Home Page
www.utexas.edu/depts/classics/documents/Cic.html
A site dedicated to Cicero, including texts of his orations and a bibliography.

The Vergil Project
Vergil.classics.upenn.edu/
A site dedicated to providing resources and teaching materials on Virgil.

The Augustan Age and the *Pax Romana*

Augustus and the Foundation of the Empire
www.carthage.edu/outis/augustus.html
A Web page devoted to the Emperor Augustus with links to archaeology and art of the Augustan age.

Reborn Rome
www.romereborn.virginia.edu
A site that provides a virtual tour of the Roman Forum.

The Corinth Computer Project
http://corinth.sas.upenn.edu/
A computer reconstruction of Roman Corinth.

The Dinur Center for Research in Jewish History: Second Temple and Talmudic Era
http://jewishhistory.huji.ac.il/Internetresources/historyresources/second_temple_and_talmudic_era.htm/
A site at The Hebrew University of Jerusalem with links to many other sites concerning Judaism and early Christianity.

CHAPTER 6

You can obtain more information about the transforming Roman world at the Websites listed below. See also the Companion Website that accompanies this text, *www.pearsonhighered.com/kishlansky*, which contains an online study guide and additional resources.

General Websites

ORB Online Encyclopedia: Late Antiquity in the Mediterranean
www.nipissingu.ca/department/history/MUHLBERGER/ORB/LT-ATEST.HTM
A guide to late antiquity in the Mediterranean.

The Crisis of the Third Century

Worlds of Late Antiquity
www.georgetown.edu/faculty/jod/wola.html
A comprehensive site dedicated to late antiquity created by Professor James O'Donnell.

The Empire Restored

Diocletian's Palace
www.st.carnet.hr/split/diokl.html
A site devoted to Emperor Diocletian's palace in modern Split.

Imperial Christianity

Resources for Constantine the Great
shsu.edu/~eng_wpf/con-hist.html
Links connecting to sites concerning Constantine.

A Parting of the Ways

A Visual Tour Through Late Antiquity
www.nipissingu.ca/department/history/muhlberger/4505/show.htm
Images of people and places of late antiquity.

CHAPTER 7

You can obtain more information about the classical legacy in the East at the Websites listed below. See also the Companion Website that accompanies this text, *www.pearson-highered.com/kishlansky*, which contains an online study guide and additional resources.

The Byzantines

Byzantium: Byzantine Studies on the Internet
www.fordham.edu/halsall/Byzantium/
A major site with links to every aspect of Byzantine civilization maintained by Paul Halsall.

Medieval Sourcebook: The Institutes of Justinian, 535 C.E.
www.fordham.edu/halsall/basis/535institutes.html
www.fordham.edu/halsall/source/corpus1.html
Extensive selections from the *Institutes*, a digest of laws and legal opinions designed for law students. The *Institutes*, the *Codex Justinianus*, and the *Digest* were part of the *Corpus Iurus Civilis* (Body of Civil Law) issued under Justinian. This codification of Roman law stands as a great monument of Western jurisprudence.

The Rise of Islam

IslamiCity.com—Education
www.islamicity.com/education/islamiceducation
A site for Islamic history maintained by IslamiCity, dedicated to advancing Islamic information, fostering community, and educating people about Islam.

Internet Islamic History Sourcebook
www.fordham.edu/halsall/islam/islamsbook.html
Paul Halsall's site dedicated to sources on Islamic history and culture.

About Islam and Muslims
www.ummah.org.uk/what-is-islam/index.html
A site devoted to explaining Islam maintained by the UNN Islamic Society.

Welcome to Isfahan!
www.isfahan.org.uk/
A site devoted to eleventh-century Isfahan, capital of medieval Persia.

The Metropolitan Museum of Art: Islamic Art
metmuseum.org/collections/department.asp?dep=14
A guide to New York's Metropolitan Museum Islamic collection.

The Byzantine Apogee and Decline

The Glory of Byzantium
metmuseum.org/explore/Byzantium/byzhome.html
A site dedicated to Byzantine art and history at the Metropolitan Museum of Art.

Church History with a Focus on Orthodoxy
aggreen.net/church_history/c_histry.html
A site dedicated to Orthodox Christianity with links to Byzantine history and culture.

CHAPTER 8

You can obtain more information about the West in the early Middle Ages at the Websites listed below. See also the Companion Website that accompanies this text, *www.pearsonhighered.com/kishlansky*, which contains an online study guide and additional resources.

General Websites

The Labyrinth: Resources for Medieval Studies
www.georgetown.edu/labyrinth/labyrinth-home.html
Labyrinth is the central Website for all medieval studies.

The Making of the Barbarian Kingdoms

Medieval Art at the Metropolitan Museum
metmuseum.org/collections/view50.asp?dep=17
A look at some of the Metropolitan Museum's collection of medieval art, including migration-period jewelry.

Living in the New Europe

Wharram Percy: The Lost Medieval Village
loki.stockton.edu/~ken/wharram/wharram.htm
A site devoted to exploring a lost medieval village from Roman times to the High Middle Ages.

The Carolingian Achievement

St. Gall Monastary Plan
stgallplan.org
A site devoted to Carolingian material and textual culture.

After the Carolingians

Viking Archaeology
bubl.ac.uk/link/v/vikingarchaeology.htm
A site devoted to Viking society and archaeology.

CHAPTER 9

You can obtain more information about the High Middle Ages at the Websites listed below. See also the Companion Website that accompanies this text, *www.pearsonhighered.com/kishlansky*, which contains an online study guide and additional resources.

General Websites

Medieval Women
http://labyrinth.georgetown.edu
Links to resources on medieval women.

Byzantine and Medieval Studies Links
www.fordham.edu/halsall/medweb/
Professor Paul Halsall's links to the medieval world.

The Countryside

Castles on the Web
www.castlesontheweb.com/
An entire Website dedicated to castles, abbeys, and medieval churches.

Medieval Towns

Durham Cathedral and Castle
www.dur.ac.uk/~dlaowww/c_tour/tour.html
A virtual tour of Durham's cathedral.

Paris at the Time of Philippe Auguste
www.philippe-auguste.com/uk/index.html
Medieval Paris at the end of the twelfth century.

Medieval Toledo
geocities.com/Athens/Academy/8636/Toledo.html
A site devoted to the city of Toledo in the Middle Ages with an emphasis on its Jewish history links to other related Spanish sites.

The Invention of the State

Les Capetiens-Les Croisades (Capetians to the Crusades)
philae.sas.upenn.edu/French/caroly.html
A hypertext site devoted to Capetian France (in French).

Medieval England
http://labyrinth.georgetown.edu/
The Labyrinth site with links to every aspect of medieval England.

Magna Carta
www.medieval sources.co.uk/portal_magna.htm
A site devoted to the Magna Carta, with links to images of the manuscripts.

Ebstorf World Map
http://weblab.uni-lueneburg.de/kulturinformatik/projekte/ebskart/content/start.html
An interactive reproduction of a thirteenth century world map.

CHAPTER 10

You can obtain more information about the Later Middle Ages at the Websites listed below. See also the Companion Website that accompanies this text, *www.pearsonhighered. com/kishlansky*, which contains an online study guide and additional resources.

Politics as a Family Affair

Web Gallery of Art: Bohemian School
www.wga.hu/index.html
Overview of art and architecture in Bohemia under the patronage of Charles IV.

Life and Death in the Later Middle Ages

Internet Resources on the Black Death
www.historyguide.org/ancient/death.html
An annotated list of Web links to sites about the Great Plague of the fourteenth century.

CHAPTER 11

You can obtain more information about the Italian Renaissance at the Websites listed below. See also the Companion Website that accompanies this text, *www.pearsonhighered.com/kishlansky*, which contains an online study guide and additional resources.

Renaissance Society

NM's Creative Impulse: Renaissance
www.history.evansville.net/renaissa.html#Resources
A site of links to a wide array of subjects relating to the era of the Renaissance. A good starting point.

The Florentine Republic

www.mega.it/eng/egui/epo/secrepu.htm
The history of the Florentine Republic with links to major tourist attractions and buildings. Brief biographies of important Florentine citizens can also be found.

Renaissance Art

Renaissance Art
www.anu.edu.au/ArtHistory/renart/pics.art/index_1.html
A pictorial guide to the major artists of the Italian Renaissance and their works. Thumbnail representations lead to links on specific pieces.

Leon Battista Alberti—Great Buildings Online
www.greatbuildings.com/architects/Leon_Battista_Alberti.html
A page devoted to Alberti's architecture with a brief biography and links to pictures.

Michelangelo Buonarroti
www.mega.it/eng/egui/pers/micbuon.htm
A Website devoted to Michelangelo with a variety of links to text and images of Renaissance Florence.

WebMuseum: The Italian Renaissance (1420–1600)
www.ibiblio.org/wm/paint/tl/it-ren/
Reproductions of Renaissance art, with accompanying text.

CHAPTER 12

You can obtain more information about the European empires at the Websites listed below. See also the Companion Website that accompanies this text, *www.pearsonhighered.com/kishlansky*, which contains an online study guide and additional resources.

European Encounters

Discoverers Web
www.win.tue.nl/cs/fm/engels/discovery/
A site devoted to all ages of discovery with maps, short biographies, and time lines. There are links to the writings of Columbus, Cortés, and others of the early voyagers.

The Columbus Navigation Homepage
www.minn.net/~keithp/
Everything you ever wanted to know about Christopher Columbus.

1492: An Ongoing Voyage
www.loc.gov/exhibits/1492
A Library of Congress online exhibit on the causes and consequences of European exploration and expansion.

Christopher Columbus—A Culinary History
www.castellobanfi.com/features/story_3.html
A site devoted to the food and drink associated with a long ocean voyage in the fifteenth century.

Medieval Sourcebook: Exploration and Expansion
www.fordham.edu/halsall/sbook1z.html
Dozens of primary sources relating to the voyages of discovery.

The Formation of States

Henry VIII: Intrigue in the Tudor Court
www.archsoc.com/games/Henry.html
A board game that teaches both history and strategy.

CHAPTER 13

You can obtain more information about the reform of religion at the Websites listed below. See also the Companion Website that accompanies this text, *www.pearsonhighered.com/kishlansky*, which contains an online study guide and additional resources.

The Lutheran Reformation

Lutherstadt Wittenberg, Martin Luther
www.wittenberg.de/e/seiten/personen/luther.html
A site devoted to Martin Luther and the city of Wittenberg. Texts of the famous Ninety-five Theses and other of Luther's writings as well as pictures of locations associated with the Lutheran reformation.

The Protestant Reformation

The Reformation Guide
www.educ.msu.edu/homepages/laurence/reformation/index.htm
The Reformation guide is the best starting place for information about all aspects of the Protestant Reformation. Dozens of links to follow.

Discovery and Reformation
www.wsu.edu/~dee/REFORM/REFORM.HTM
A primarily text-based site created by Washington State University, with profiles of key individuals and explanations of the issues at stake.

Project Wittenberg
www.iclnet.org/pub/resources/text/wittenberg/wittenberg-home.html
The home page of Project Wittenberg, containing a large number of texts (including hymns) by Luther and other reformers.

Tudor History
tudorhistory.org/
A site with links to a variety of subjects relating to England under the Tudors. Biographies of the kings and queens, bibliographies, maps, and documents.

Reformation Picture Gallery
www.mun.ca/rels/hrollmann/reform/pics/pics.html
Contemporary pictures of leading reformers and the places associated with the Protestant Reformation. Excellent reproductions, especially from woodcuts.

Internet Modern History Sourcebook: Reformation Europe
www.fordham.edu/halsall/mod/modsbook02.html
Sources for both the Reformation and Counter-Reformation with links to other valuable sites.

CHAPTER 14

You can obtain more information about Europe at war at the Websites listed below. See also the Companion Website that accompanies this text, *www.pearsonhighered.com/kishlansky*, which contains an online study guide and additional resources.

The Crises of the Western States

Internet Modern History Sourcebook: Early Modern West
www.fordham.edu/halsall/mod/modsbook1.html#Conflict
Links to documents on the French wars of religion, the invasion of the Spanish Armada, and the Thirty Years' War.

WebMuseum: The Northern Renaissance (1500–1615)
www.ibiblio.org/wm/paint/tl/north-ren/
Links to pictures and portraits from the late sixteenth and early seventeenth centuries.

Pieter Brueghel the Elder: *The Triumph of Death*
www.ibiblio.org/wm/paint/auth/bruegel/death.jpg
A Web page depicting Peter Brueghel's *Triumph of Death*, one of the most evocative paintings of the destruction wrought by warfare in early modern Europe.

The Thirty Years' War, 1618–1648

The Avalon Project: Treaty of Westphalia
www.yale.edu/lawweb/avalon/westphal.htm
The full text of the Treaty of Westphalia that ended the Thirty Years' War.

CHAPTER 15

You can obtain more information about life in early modern Europe at the Websites listed below. See also the Companion Website that accompanies this text, *www.pearsonhighered.com/kishlansky*, which contains an online study guide and additional resources.

Social Life

Internet Modern History Sourcebook: Everyday Life in Premodern Europe
www.fordham.edu/halsall/mod/modsbook04.html
A site with links to sources, pictures, and accounts of everyday life in early modern Europe. A good place to start.

Modern History Sourcebook: Social Conditions in 17th Century France
www.fordham.edu/halsall/mod/17france-soc.html
Documents illustrating social conditions in early modern France.

Private Life

Witchcraft
www.kenyon.edu/projects/margin/witch.htm
A site with links to sources concerning European witchcraft. Also includes suggestions for further reading and a brief overview of the subject.

Witches and Witchcraft
Womenshistory.about.com/cs/witches
This site offers historical information about witches and witchcraft in Europe and America and includes links to related sites.

Life in Tudor England
englishhistory.net/tudor/tudorlife.html
Part of a comprehensive site on Tudor England, this section on life in Tudor England offers information on topics including food and drink, pastimes and entertainment, and mental illness.

CHAPTER 16

You can obtain more information about the royal state in the seventeenth century at the Websites listed below. See also the Companion Website that accompanies this text, *www.pearsonhighered.com/kishlansky*, which contains an online study guide and additional resources.

The Crises of the Royal State

Internet Modern History Sourcebook: Constitutional States
www.fordham.edu/halsall/mod/modsbook06.html
Links to sources relating to the reign of Charles I and the revolution against him.

The Execution of Charles I
www.baylor.edu/BIC/WCIII/Essays/charles.1.html
Excerpts from primary sources describing the execution of Charles I.

The Zenith of the Royal State

Baroque Living History Society: L'Age d'Or & Kirke's Lambs
www.kipar.org/

A site on the Golden Age of France in the seventeenth century but with extensive links to English and Dutch materials on a variety of subjects.

Chateau de Versailles
www.chateauversailles.fr/en
The Website of Versailles, with views of the gardens and rooms inside the palace. (Version of site in English.)

Creating French Culture
www.loc.gov/exhibits/bnf/bnf0005.html
The Library of Congress's exhibition on the Age of Absolutism shows manuscripts, medals, and portraits of leading figures at the French court.

Chapter 1: 7 Artist/Pacific Press Service **12** © The Trustees of the British Museum. Eileen Tweedy/Picture Desk, Inc./Kobal Collection **20** Egyptian. Sculpture-Busts. Thebes. Osiride Head of Hatshepsut, originally from a statue, Dynasty 18, c. 1503–1482 B.C. Provenance: Thebes, Deir el Bahri. Limestone, painted. H. 64 cm. H. with crown 124.5 cm. The Metropolitan Museum of Art, Rogers Fund, 1931. (31.3.157) Photograph © 1983. The Metropolitan Museum of Art / Art Resource. **24** Jehu, King of Israel, prostrating himself before King Shalmaneser III of Assyria. Basalt bas-relief on the black stele of Shalmaneser III. Assyrian, 9th BCE. British Museum, London, Great Britain. Erich Lessing/Art Resource, NY **Chapter 2: 35** "The Serpent Goddess of Knossos". Archaeological Museum, Heraklion, Crete, Greece. Copyright Nimatallah/Art Resource, NY **37** Funeral mask from the royal tombs at Mycenae, c. 1500 BC. Beaten gold, height 12 in. National Archaeological Museum, Athens, Greece. Art Resource, NY. **40** Scala/Art Resource, N.Y. **44** "Moschophoros (calf bearer), marble, c. 570 BC Archaic Greek (with dedication by Rhonbos; sculptor probably called Phaidimos) © Acropolis Museum Athens". Picture Desk, Inc. / Kobal Collection. **52** Lee Boltin Picture Library **Chapter 3: 62** Art Resource/Reunion des Musees Nationaux **68** Scala/Art Resource, N.Y. **73** Alinari/Art Resource, N.Y. **78** Bridgeman-Giraudon/Art Resource, N.Y. **Chapter 4: 87** Hirmer Fotoarchiv, Munich, Germany **97** Bridgeman-Giraudon/Art Resource, N.Y. **102** Scala/Art Resource, N.Y. **Chapter 5: 106** Landesmuseum Mainz **117** Erich Lessing/Art Resource, N.Y. **124** Caticomb of Priscilla/ Benedettine di Priscilla/Pontificia Commissione di Archeologia Sacra, for Catacombe di Priscilla. © foto Pontificia Commissione di Archeologia Sacra **127** © Biblioteca Apostolica Vaticana (Vatican) (Vat. lat. 2057 fol. 147, recto. Math 11a NS.10). Pontificia Commissione di Archeologia Sacra **Chapter 6: 132** Bibliotheque Nationale. Paris, France. Erich Lessing/Art Resource, NY **140** St. Peter's, Vatican, Rome, Italy/The Bridgeman Art Library **146** Public Domain **Chapter 7: 154** Court of Emperor Justinian. Ca. 547 CE. Early Christian mosaic, 264 x 365 cm. S. Vitale, Ravenna, Italy. Scala/Art Resource, NY **159** © British Library Board. All Rights Reserved (Add MS 19352, fol. 27v) **168** Istanbul University Library **Chapter 8: 177** Fototeca Unione, American Academy, Rome/ The Bridgeman Art Library International **181** British Museum/Eileen Tweedy/ Picture Desk, Inc./Kobal Collection **190** Bridgeman-Giraudon/Art Resource, N.Y. **194** Eirik Irgens Johnsen. © Museum of Cultural History–University of Oslo, Norway **Chapter 9: 204** © British Library Board. All Rights Reserved. 1022251.501 MS Harl. 4431. fol. 376 **211** © British Library Board. All Rights Reserved. 1022251.491 MS ROY 15 E III, fol.269r **212** Art Resource/Bildarchiv Preussischer Kulturbesitz **214** Scala/Art Resource, N.Y. **Chapter 10: 232** His Grace the Archbishop of Canterbury and the Trustees of Lambeth Palace Library **236** The Metropolitan Museum of Art, The Cloisters Collection. 1969 (69.86). Image © The Metropolitan Museum of Art / Art Resource, NY. **239** Stadt Soest, Stadtarchiv **Chapter 11: 257** Scala/Art Resource, N.Y. **260** Scala/Art Resource, N.Y. **268** Scala/Art Resource, N.Y. **Chapter 12: 277** Bridgeman-Giraudon/Art Resource, N.Y. **281** © National Gallery, London/Art Resource, NY **290** Instituto Amatller de Arte Hispanico, Barcelona, Spain **293** Musee du Louvre, Paris/Bridgeman Art Library, London/SuperStock, Inc. **Chapter 13: 297** Private collection/The Bridgeman Art Library International **301** Kunstsammlungen Der Vest Coburg **308** BGE, Centre d'iconographie genevoise **314** Rubens, Peter Paul (1577–1640). The Miracle of Saint Ignatius Loyola. Oil sketch. 105.5 x 74 cm. Kunsthistorisches Museum, Vienna, Austria. Photo Credit: Erich Lessing / Art Resource, NY **Chapter 14: 322** Art Resource, N.Y. **324** Francois Dubois, "Le Massacre de la Saint Barthelemy", 1572–1584. Oil on canvas, 94 cm x 154 cm. Musee Cantonal des Beaux-Arts de Lausanne. Photo J.-C. Ducret, Musee Cantonal des Beaux-Arts de Lausanne. **330** Erich Lessing/Art Resource, N.Y. **339** Musee des Beaux-Arts de Strasbourg. Photo Musees de la Ville de Strasbourg. **Chapter 15: 351** Georges de La Tour, (1593–1652). The Fortune Teller. Probably 1630's. 40 1/8 x 48 5/8" (101.9 x 123.5 cm). Rogers Fund, 1960 (60.30). The

in, 8; first civilizations in, 8–15, 29;
gods, divinities and mortals in, 11–13;
Hammurabi, old Babylonian empire
and, 14–15; Hebrew society's origins
in, 23; ramparts of Uruk and, 8–10;
Sargon's expansion of, 13–14; The
Standard of Ur, 12; tools, technology
and writing in, 10–11.

Messenia, 35, 47, 48, 49

Messiah, 123. *See also* Jesus of Nazareth

Metals, 11. *See also* Copper; Gold; Silver

Metalworkers, 11

Metics (foreigners), 61, 80

Metoikoi. *See* Metics (foreigners)

Michelangelo Buonarroti, 256, 258–259,
260, 268

Middle Ages, early (500-900):
Carolingian achievement and,
188–194; empire to lordships and,
195–198; living in new Europe
during, 183–188; making of Barbarian
kingdoms in, 176–183; west in,
176–199

Middle Ages, high (900-1300), 224–225;
aristocracy, warriors and heiresses in,
202–205; Aristotelian challenge in,
213–214; church, saints and monks
in, 205–206; countryside in, 200–207;
crusaders, soldier of God and,
206–207; invention of state and,
215–223; medieval towns in, 208–215;
medieval university in, 212–213;
peasantry, serfs and freemen in,
200–202; preaching and poverty
in, 214–215; prominent popes and
religious figures of, 219

Middle Ages, later (1300-1500), 248;
chronology, 246; dancing with
death in, 234–236; discerning spirit
of God in, 242–243; famine in, 234;
heresy and revolt in, 243–244; hundred
years of war in, 229–233; life and
death in, 234–240; living and dying
in medieval towns during, 238–240;
papacy's crisis in, 240–242; plague
of insurrection in, 236–238; politics as
family affair in, 226–233; religious
persecution in Spain and, 244; spirit

of, 240–247; struggle for central
Europe in, 226–229; vernacular
literature and individual in, 245–247;
William of Ockham, spirit of truth
and, 244–245

Middle Kingdom (Egypt), 19, 23, 29

Middle Stone Age. *See* Mesolithic era
(Middle Stone Age)

Midwives, 347

Milan, 250, 263, 292

Miles (soldier or knight), 202–203

Miletus, 54

Military: centuries, 89; Egyptian tactics,
20; Etruscan Rome and, 89; Imperial
Rome and, 106; rise of Roman
government and, 131–132; service
class of Muscovites, 284; Tiglath-
pileser's, 27. *See also* Sparta;
War(s)

"Milk parents," 252

Milkmaid, The (Vermeer), 358

Miltiades, 58

Milton, John, 370

Miniscule, 191

Minoan Crete. *See* Crete, Minoan

Minos (king), 32

Minverva (goddess), 89

Miracles of Saint Ignatius Loyola, The
(Rubens), 314

Mishnah (second law), 26

Missi dominici (emissaries), 192

Missionaries: Anglo-Saxon, 189; Irish,
181; pagan conquerors and Christian,
180–182

Mithras, 122

Mithridates VI (king), 110

Monarchy, 48; divine right of kings
and, 365; "favorites" in service of, 365;
glorified in literature, 364; law and,
365; royal state and nature of absolute, 379. *See also* Kings

Monasteries, 182, 190; Cluny, 197–198,
205–206, 216; monastic culture and,
205–206; monastic reform and, 206;
wealth and power associated with,
205–206. *See also* Monks

Monasticism: Byzantine, 159–160;
Christianity and, 144–145

R

Ra (god), 16

Radicals, 311–312

Ramses II (king), 15, 22

Razi Al-, 169

Reason: Archaic Greece's myths and, 43; dichotomy of faith and, 213–214

Rebellions: aristocratic, 370, 371–372; French Fronde, 372, 382; Great, 238; peasant, 311; resistance and, 371–372; Scottish prayer-book, 374; Spartacus, 10. *See also* Revolts; Revolutions

Recared (king), 179

Recluses: Christianity, hermits, monks and, 143–144; women, 145–146

Reconquista, 288–299

Red Sea, 20

Reeves (king's agents), 222

Reformation: Catholic, 312–318; counter, 315–316; Geneva, Calvin and, 307–308; intellectual, 296–299; Lutheran, 300–307; Protestant, 307–312; of religion, 296–319; two churches created by, 320; war and, 317–318

Reforms: Athens and Cleisthenes', 52–53; Athens and Solon's, 50–51, 52; Catholic, 312–318; Classical Rome and fiscal, 137–138; Diocletian and fiscal, 137–138; English, 309–310; Lutheran, 300–307; monastic, 206; printing and intellectual, 297–298; Protestant, 307–312; radicals and, 311–312; religion and, 296–319; Roman Catholic Church and, 197–198, 205–206, 216, 312–318; Sparta and Lycurgus', 47–48, 51; states, investiture and, 216, 218–219. *See also* the Reformation

Relics, 301

Religio (binding power), 100

Religion(s): Akhenaten consolidation of royal power and, 21; Catholic reformation and, 312–318; eastern, 121–126; first civilizations and, 6–7; French wars of, 321–323; intellectual reformation and, 296–299; legislated by Parliament, 310; Lutheran reformation and, 300–307; Minoan Cretan society and, 33–34; mystery cults and, 122; Protestant reformation and, 307–312; Puritanism, 373; reform of, 296–319; reformation of radicals and, 311–312; Roman, 100, 117–118; tolerance for, 178; women and, 7, 100. *See also* Arianism; Christianity; Islam; Judaism

Religious orders: Carmelites, 313; Dominicans, 214–215; Franciscans, 214–215; Jesuits, 314, 315, 326, 333, 370; Ursulines, 313

Religious persecution: Anabaptists and, 311–312; Protestants and, 307, 310, 322–323, 382; Spain's, 244, 289

Remigius of Reims (bishop), 185

Remus, 87

Renaissance (rebirth) 168; art, 255–259; ideals, 259–261; Italian, 249–272

Resistance: need for, 368–369; rebellion and, 371–372; right to, 370–372; theory, 370–371

Revolts: Black Death and peasant, 235; Bohemia, 335–336; Ciompi, 265; Dutch, 380; early modern Europe and peasant, 354–356; English peasant, 238; German peasant, 355–356; heresy and, 243–244; Islam, division and, 167; Jacquerie and peasant, 237–238; of Netherlands, 326–329; *nu-pieds*, 369; Palermo, 369; Protestant, 336; slave, 107, 133; Swabia peasant, 311

Revolutions: English, 378–380; Germanic society and, 135; intellectual reformation and printing, 297–298; Islam and 'Abbasid, 166–167; wages and price, 348

Revolutions, English: chronology, 380; Cromwell and, 376; glorious, 376–377; royal state and, 375–377

Rhetoric, 259

Rhodes, 84

Richard II (king), 243

Richard III (king), 285

Richard the Lion-Hearted (king), 207

Richelieu (cardinal), 339, 366, 381–382

Riguad, Hyacinthe, 383

Rituals, Mesopotamian, 12–13

Rock of Gilbraltar, 166

Tutankhamen (king), 21, 22
Twelve Articles of the Peasants of
Swabia, 355
Twelve Years' Truce, 329, 335, 338
Two Treatises on Government (Locke), 377
Typhoid, 278
Tyranny, 50, 54; of Athenians Peisistratus
and Hippias, 51–52; of Corinth's
Cypselus and Periander, 46, 47;
hereditary, 41
Tyrants: Archaic Greek colonists and,
40–41; Gelon of Syracuse, 84–85;
thirty, 71
Tyrrhenian Sea, 86

U

'Ubayd Allah the Fatimid, 167
Ufu, 11
Ukraine, 36
'Umar (caliph), 164
Umayyads, 165, 174–175; 'Abbasid
caliphates and, 166–167
Umma, 162, 163, 164, 165
Unconquered Sun cult, 138
Underworld, symbols, 35
"Universal man," 257
Universitas (guild of students), 212
University: medieval, 212–213; Orléans,
307; Paris, 213, 227; Prague, 228
Uprisings: Parisian merchant, 237. *See
also* Revolts
Ur, 8, 14; The Standard of, 12; at war, 13
Urban IV (pope), 241
Urbino, 263
Ursulines, 313
Uruk, 28; *ensi* and *lugal* in, 10;
Gilgamesh, king of, 10, 12–13;
Mesopotamia and archeological
ramparts of, 8–10; population growth
in, 8; urban life and slaves in, 10; at
war, 13; women's status in, 10
'Uthman (caliph), 165
Ut-napishtim (fictional character), 13
Utopia (More), 280

V

Valens (emperor), 147, 149
Valerian, 132

Valla, Lorenzo, 261
Vandals, 147–148, 155, 176, 178
Vasili, 283
Vassals (followers), 189, 204, 209
Venetians, 170, 172
Venice, 208, 250, 263, 264; Great Council
and, 266; as seaborne empire, 266–267
Venus (goddess), 100. *See also* Aphrodite
Vera Cruz, 278
Vermeer, Jan, 358
Vernacular literature: England and, 246;
France and, 247; individual and,
245–247; Italy and, 246
Versailles, 383–384
Vespasian, 119
Vienna, 293
Vikings, 182, 194, 195, 197, 215
Villanovans, 83
Villon, François, 247
Virgil, 118, 191
Virgin Mary, 305, 306
Virtue, crisis of Roman, 101–103
Visconti family, 263
Visigoths, 148, 155; Alaric II of, 147, 177;
Spain and, 179–180, 186. *See also* the
Goths
Volscians, 91

W

Wages, Price Revolution and, 348
Wales, 180
Walid, Khalid ibn al-(general), 164
Wallenstein, Albrecht von (count), 338,
339, 340
War(s): Archidamian, 64, 66; Carthage
and Rome at, 92, 93, 95; Carthage and
Syracuse at, 84–85; English civil,
372–375; Europe and Thirty Years',
334–341, 368; Europe at, 320–342;
European empires and Italian,
291–294; France and religion, 321–323;
German peasants', 355–356; god of, 87;
Hellenistic Greece's fifth-century
politics and, 57–66; holy, 163, 270, 288;
Hundred Years', 229–233, 287; Imperial
Rome's winners and losers in, 105–107;
Italian city-states at, 265; of Italy, 270;
jihads, 163; Jugurtha and Imperial

9; marketplace, 76–80; Rome and crisis of classical, 130–135; Rome's transformation and classical, 130–152; silver and gold in new, 290; spirit, 7; symbols of under, 35. *See also Mundus novus*

Writers: Dhuoda, 191; Hellenistic, 78; Herodotus, 68; Thucydides, 69. *See also* Playwrights; Poets

Writing: Caroline miniscule and, 191; cuneiform and, 11; disappearance of, 36; Linear A, 32; Mesopotamia's technology and, 10–11; Phoenician technology of, 39–40; pictograms and, 11, 19

Wycliffe, John, 243

X

Xavier, Francis, 315

Xerxes (king), 58, 59, 60, 85

Y

Yahweh (god), 24, 26, 140

"Year of the Four Emperors," 119, 121

Yemen, 160

Youth, state terrorism by Sparta's, 48

Z

Zacharias (pope), 189

Zagros Mountains, 14, 22

Zealots, 122

Zemsky Sobor, 332

Zeno (emperor), 79, 148, 153

Zeus (god), 42, 100

Ziggurats, 12

Zoroastrians, 165

Zwingli, Huldrych, 308, 311, 318; doctrinal issues between Luther and, 317; mass and, 306, 312

Additional Titles of Interest

Note to Instructors: These selected titles can be packaged with this book at a significant discount. Contact your local Pearson sales representative for details on how to create a Penguin Value Package.

Anonymous, *The Epic of Gilgamesh*
Homer, *The Iliad*
Homer, *The Odyssey*
Herodotus, *The Histories*
Plato, *The Republic*
St. Augustine, *The Confession of St. Augustine*
Procopius, *The Secret History*
Einhard, *Two Lives of Charlemagne*
Anonymous, *The Song of Roland*
Abelard, *The Letters of Abelard & Heloise*
Alighieri, *The Divine Comedy*
De Pizan, *Treasure of the City of Ladies*
Machiavelli, *The Prince*
More, *Utopia*
De Cervantes, *Don Quixote*
Rousseau, *The Social Contract*
Shelly, *Frankenstein*
Mill, *On Liberty*
Von Clausewitz, *On War*
Marx, *The Communist Manifesto*
Orwell, *1984*
Solzhenitsyn, *One Day in the Life of Ivan Denisovich*

For a complete list of titles, go to: *http://www.pearsonhighered.com/historyvaluepacks/*